THE COMPARATIVE HERMENEUTICS OF RABBINIC JUDAISM

VOLUME TWO

SEDER MOED

THE COMPARATIVE HERMENEUTICS OF RABBINIC JUDAISM

VOLUME TWO

SEDER MOED

JACOB NEUSNER

Academic Studies in the History of Judaism
Global Publications, Binghamton University
2000

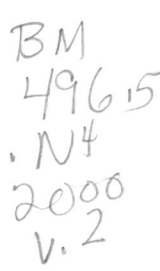

Copyright © 2000 by Jacob Neusner

All rights reserved. No portion of this publication may be duplicated in any way without the expressed written consent of the publisher, except in the form of brief excerpts of quotations for the purposes of review.

Library of Congress Cataloging-in-Publication Data

Jacob Neusner, *The Comparative Hermeneutics of Rabbinic. Volume II. Seder Moed*

1. Hermeneutics   2. Judaic Studies   3. Religious Studies
4. Yebamot   5. Ketubot   6. Sotah

ISBN 1-586840-11-8

Published by Academic Studies in the History of Judaism
Distributed by Global Publications, ICGS
Binghamton University, State University of New York
Binghamton, New York, USA 13902-6000
Phone: (607) 777-4495. Fax: 777-6132
E-mail: pmorewed@binghamton.edu
http://ssips.binghamton.edu

ACADEMIC STUDIES IN
THE HISTORY OF JUDAISM

Editor-in-Chief

Jacob Neusner
Bard College

Editorial Committee

Alan J. Avery-Peck, *College of the Holy Cross*

Bruce D. Chilton, *Bard College*

William Scott Green, *University of Rochester*

James Strange, *University of South Florida*

TABLE OF CONTENTS

PREFACE ix

1. TRACTATE YEBAMOT 1

   I. The Definition of the Category-Formation 1
   II. The Foundations of the Halakhic Category-Formations 6
   III. The Exposition of the Components of the Given Category-Formation by the Mishnah-Tosefta-Yerushalmi-Bavli 8
   IV. Documentary Traits 79
       A. The Mishnah and the Tosefta 79
       B. The Yerushalmi and the Bavli 80
   V. The Hermeneutics of Yebamot 81
       A. What Fuses the Halakhic Data into a Category-Formation? 83
       B. The Activity of the Category-Formation 87
       C. The Consistency of the Category-Formation 92
       D. The Generativity of the Category-Formation 92

2. TRACTATE KETUBOT 95
   I. The Definition of the Category-Formation 95
   II. The Foundations of the Halakhic Category-Formations 99
   III. The Exposition of the Components of the Given Category-Formation by the Mishnah-Tosefta-Yerushalmi-Bavli 101
   IV. Documentary Traits 146
       A. The Mishnah and the Tosefta 146
       B. The Yerushalmi and the Bavli 146
       C. The Aggadah: The Liturgical Context of Ketubot 146
   V. The Hermeneutics of Ketubot 148
       A. What Fuses the Halakhic Data into a Category-Formation? 151
       B. The Activity of the Category-Formation 158
       C. The Consistency of the Category-Formation 161
       D. The Generativity of the Category-Formation 161

3. TRACTATE NEDARIM 163
   I. The Definition of the Category-Formation 163
   II. The Foundations of the Halakhic Category-Formations 170
   III. The Exposition of the Components of the Given Category-Formation by the Mishnah-Tosefta-Yerushalmi-Bavli 172
   IV. Documentary Traits 201
       A. The Mishnah and the Tosefta 201
       B. The Yerushalmi and the Bavli 202
       C. The Aggadah and the Halakhah in the Bavli 202
   V. The Hermeneutics of Nedarim 204

		A.	What Fuses the Halakhic Data into a Category-Formation?	205
		B.	The Activity of the Category-Formation	207
		C.	The Consistency of the Category-Formation	209
		D.	The Generativity of the Category-Formation	210

4. TRACTATE NAZIRITE 215

	I.		The Definition of the Category-Formation	215
	II.		The Foundations of the Halakhic Category-Formations	222
	III.		The Exposition of the Components of the Given Category-Formation by the Mishnah-Tosefta-Yerushalmi-Bavli	224
	IV.		Documentary Traits	253
		A.	The Mishnah and the Tosefta	253
		B.	The Yerushalmi and the Bavli	253
		C.	The Aggadah and the Halakhah in the Bavli	253
	V.		The Hermeneutics of Nazir	256
		A.	What Fuses the Halakhic Data into a Category-Formation?	256
		B.	The Activity of the Category-Formation	259
		C.	The Consistency of the Category-Formation	263
		D.	The Generativity of the Category-Formation	263

5. TRACTATE SOTAH 265

	I.		The Definition of the Category-Formation	265
	II.		The Foundations of the Halakhic Category-Formations	271
	III.		The Exposition of the Components of the Given Category-Formation by the Mishnah-Tosefta-Yerushalmi-Bavli	274
	IV.		Documentary Traits	300
		A.	The Mishnah and the Tosefta	300
		B.	The Yerushalmi and the Bavli	300
		C.	The Aggadah and the Halakhah in the Bavli	301
	V.		The Hermeneutics of Sotah	304
		A.	What Fuses the Halakhic Data into a Category-Formation?	304
		B.	The Activity of the Category-Formation	320
		C.	The Consistency of the Category-Formation	321
		D.	The Generativity of the Category-Formation	321

6. TRACTATE GITTIN 323

	I.		The Definition of the Category-Formation	323
	II.		The Foundations of the Halakhic Category-Formations	329
	III.		The Exposition of the Components of the Given Category-Formation by the Mishnah-Tosefta-Yerushalmi-Bavli	329
	IV.		Documentary Traits	362
		A.	The Mishnah and the Tosefta	362

		B.	The Yerushalmi and the Bavli	362
	V.	The Hermeneutics of Gittin		362
		A.	What Fuses the Halakhic Data into a Category-Formation?	362
		B.	The Activity of the Category-Formation	368
		C.	The Consistency of the Category-Formation	371
		D.	The Generativity of the Category-Formation	372

7. TRACTATE QIDDUSHIN   375

	I.	The Definition of the Category-Formation		375
	II.	The Foundations of the Halakhic Category-Formations		382
	III.	The Exposition of the Components of the Given Category-Formation by the Mishnah-Tosefta-Yerushalmi-Bavli		382
	IV.	Documentary Traits		402
		A.	The Mishnah and the Tosefta	402
		B.	The Yerushalmi and the Bavli	402
		C.	The Aggadah of incarnate sanctification	402
	V.	The Hermeneutics of Qiddushin		406
		A.	What Fuses the Halakhic Data into a Category-Formation?	406
		B.	The Activity of the Category-Formation	408
		C.	The Consistency of the Category-Formation	410
		D.	The Generativity of the Category-Formation	411

PREFACE

Hermeneutics, conventionally defined as "theory of interpretation," in Rabbinic Judaism finds its data in the modes of analytical thought that produce useful knowledge out of the facts deriving from three sources. These sources are [1] the Torah, Scripture and tradition, [2] nature, and [3] the social order constituted by holy Israel, the latter two as contemplated and classified to begin with by the Torah. These data require structure, proportion, order, balance, rationalization. What theory of interpretation identifies among those data points of likeness and contrast that define category-formations of cogency and proportion? That is the question I systematically answer, following the sequence of the Halakhic category-formations of the Mishnah-Tosefta-Yerushalmi-Bavli. Hermeneutics then articulates the results of a distinctive mode of thought, and, in the Halakhah, it is the analogical-contrastive kind. That is to say, analytical thought defining the category-formations that are subject to hermeneutical reflection proceeds in accord with the rules of analogical-contrastive thinking.

These rules are simply stated. Things are alike and fall into the same classification, all arrayed in conformity with that classification's governing rule, its cogent data, and its range of consequent exegetical problems.[1] Or they are unlike and fall into contrasting, opposite classifications, with contrary governing rules. Each of these generative rules applies the logic of the hermeneutical principle to the cogent data that are selected for interpretation by the governing hermeneutics. And each within that same overriding logic produces its urgent exegetical problems. Then the issue of hermeneutics — again, defined conventionally and publicly as "theory of interpretation" — is, [1] what modes of analytical thought have generated a given category-formation, [2] with what result, and [3] to what end? What is at stake here is to explain how the Rabbinic sages have created, time and again, category-formations that transform and transcend the data that are interpreted. For the hermeneutics of Judaism produces a single result time and again, and that is, the formation of wholes that add up to more than the sums of the parts. In the language used here, category-formations yielded by the theory of interpretation impart to the se-

---

[1] That exegesis is the effect of hermeneutics, its program defined thereby, forms a rule well-established by the history of the exegesis of any classical document. On analogical-contrastive thought, see especially G. E. R. Lloyd, *Polarity and Analogy. Two Types of Argumentation in Early Greek Thought.* Cambridge, 1966: Cambridge University Press.

lected data meaning and consequence that vastly transcend the qualities of the data viewed out of categorical context.

Part of my lifelong inquiry into the definition of Judaism in its classical documents, this project addresses the hermeneutics of the Halakhic documents, within the very particular framework defined by the native category-formations of the Halakhah. Those category-formations embody the results of a theory of interpretation of the normative rules of the Pentateuch and associated laws of tradition, of nature and of Israel's social order. Each component of the work contributes to our knowledge of that theory: the way the Rabbinic sages read the diverse texts of the law, their rules for the formation of molecules out of atoms, active knowledge out of raw data. Here, therefore, I analyze the topical framework within which the Halakhic compilations conduct their discourse, the entire Halakhah being organized by subject-matter and within a logic comprised by two components:

First, the organizing logic imputes coherence to the requirements of topical exposition.

Second, the logic insists, within the concrete case, abstract principles are to be encapsulated. The case embodies the rule.

Specifically, in this protracted exercise I identify the theory of how a given topic is defined out of the data of the Torah, nature and society and is to be interpreted. That requires, specifically, moving backward from exegesis of cases to hermeneutics of topics, that is, from the evidence of the (consequent) exegesis that gives actuality to that theory backward to the (causative) theory of interpretation itself. What modes of analogical-contrastive thinking are in play in the hermeneutics of interpreting data in one way, rather than in some other. What I mean, concretely, is, organizing data within one category-formation, rather than some other.

The category-formations of Rabbinic Judaism in its normative, Halakhic component form the building blocks of that Judaism, its organizing and rationalizing constructions. And we everywhere encounter their definitive status: they dictate the character of the tractates of the Halakhah, Mishnah-Tosefta-Yerushalmi-Bavli. That is to say, Rabbinic Judaism in its normative corpus of Halakhah comes to us in four documents, the Mishnah, the Tosefta, the Yerushalmi (Talmud of the Land of Israel), and the Bavli (Talmud of Babylonia). All appeal to the same category-formations, that is definitions of data deemed to cohere. So a huge testimony to the hermeneutics of Rabbinic Judaism comes to us in the definitive documents. It follows that, in a routine way, documentary hermeneutics also enters in. Therefore I further compare and contrast the theory of presenting a given topic that dictated the character of the one document with the theory that governed in another of the cognate writings of Judaism. The results of that comparison are mostly, but not entirely nega-

The Comparative Hermeneutics of Rabbinic Judaism II

tive. Having completed my preliminary account of the hermeneutics of the Aggadah, at certain points here I further take up the task to come: the comparison of the Halakhic and the Aggadic hermeneutics of Rabbinic Judaism.

With these principles in mind, readers will follow as I parse the title of the project as a whole, which allows a simple definition of the project.

HERMENEUTICS: First comes the key-word, "hermeneutics." What issue falls into the category of hermeneutics, within the conventional and accepted definition, "the theory of interpretation of a received document"? The hermeneutics of a religion of a textual community such as is represented by the Halakhic documents governs how a given topic is going to be defined ("category-formation") and expounded by the cognate texts of that community. To begin with, the hermeneutics determines the category-formations of that textual community, by which I mean, how random data fall into common classifications and thereby form coherent compositions. Hermeneutics in guiding the formation of organizing categories thereby defines the rules of coherence - how one and one equal two - and the conclusions to be drawn for further cases from that fact - how one apple and one apple equal two apples. It guides reading the facts received from holy Scriptures and (in the case of Rabbinic Judaism, with its tri-partite sources of a single truth) the organizing of the data set forth by nature and by society as well. The hermeneutics brought to bear upon the data of Scripture, society, and nature dictates questions that will be raised and those that will not be raised. It further predetermines the entire exegetical program, so allowing a system to extend and amplify itself to the outer boundaries of imagination. Hermeneutics here, in the context of Rabbinic Judaism, forms the theory that guides the formulation and transmission of tradition from generation to generation. To use the language of the present project, hermeneutics guides the identification of systemic categories and their agglutination in category-formations; hermeneutics states the theory that produces paradigms and identifies problems of detailed exegesis thereof - whether in the raw data of Scripture, the social and historical order, or nature.

HERMENEUTICS AND EXEGESIS: How do I conceive hermeneutics to relate to the detailed work of exegesis (in which, in this context, I am not engaged)? Common usage suffices: hermeneutics forms the governing process of interpreting data, mediating chaos into order, and exegesis takes up the consequent, episodic challenges to harmonious reason, coherence, cogency. First therefore in logic comes the theory of interpretation, then follows its application to specific problems. Hermeneutics then predetermines the program of exegesis, the rules for not only solving, but to begin with identifying, ad hoc problems. Accordingly, hermeneutics defines the exegetical task, that is, the work of dealing with detail in a consistent, rational manner. That is because hermeneutics identifies what, within a received piece of writing, requires attention, framing problems for exegetical inquiry in a particular setting. Defining rationality, hermeneutics explains the coherence of the bits and pieces of the writing.

COMPARATIVE HERMENEUTICS: as briefly indicated at the outset, to identify the governing rationality I progress from detail to generalization, from the results of a process of exegetics to what I conceive to form the generative hermeneutics, from the manner of the exegesis of details to the guiding hermeneutics of the whole. This I do in an encompassing framework, reading first the documents - the Mishnah, Tosefta, Yerushalmi, and Bavli - in sequence, then the entire corpus of authoritative writings viewed whole. In due course, comparative hermeneutics of Rabbinic Judaism extends from the Halakhah to the Aggadah, from norms of behavior to norms of belief. And that brings us to the second key word of the title: what of the "comparative" exercise? Here, if "hermeneutics" derives from the theory of exposition of a given topic by their category-formations, "comparative hermeneutics" concerns itself with the logical next step. That is, the comparison and contrast of the respective theories of the exposition of a single program of topics in cognate documents, for the Halakhah, and ultimately for the cognate genres of writing, the Halakhah and the Aggadah, as well. How a given topic is expounded, the issues people deem to inhere therein and to require exposition - description, analysis, and interpretation - these rules of interpretation in particular terms embody the general theory of how to make sense of a received, determinate tradition, that is, the Torah or "Judaism." In this part of the larger project, I deal with the comparative hermeneutics of the Halakhic category-formations, producing a negative result (so I anticipate). In the next part, I return to the comparison of the hermeneutics of the Halakhah and the Aggadah, which I have already defined in more than a preliminary way.

But how productive is the comparison of the Halakhic hermeneutics of the four Halakhic documents? Alas, readers will quickly note that comparing the several documents' reading of a common topic or problem repeatedly yields a severely limited range of results. These are two. First, the two Talmuds take up secondary and derivative problems. Second, the Tosefta sometimes clarifies the Mishnah and sometimes makes a statement of its own. So the upshot of the comparison of the hermeneutics of the Halakhic documents in dealing with a common range of data is negative. I do not discern among the successor-documents even significant variations in the Mishnah's Halakhic hermeneutics. That negative result is important, to be sure, but reaching it induces a certain tedium. As the project unfolds, beyond Chapter One of this unit, Pesahim, I shall comment only when I note in a successor-document a fundamentally new theory of interpreting Halakhic data. But, compensating for that disappointment, at specific points we find that the Aggadah contributes its distinctive perspective, and the comparison of the hermeneutics of the Halakhah of a given topic and the hermeneutics of the Aggadah of that same topic, as set forth by the Bavli in particular, yields more than routine results.

RABBINIC JUDAISM: What of "Rabbinic Judaism"? That language refers to the Judaic religious system - way of life, world view, realized by a determinate "Israel" - portrayed, for the present purpose, solely by the Rabbinic documents of the classical age, the first six centuries of the Common Era: the Mishnah, Tosefta, Yerushalmi, Bavli, and Midrash-compilations produced by authorities of the Rabbinic tradition in particular. Now, as a matter of fact, these documents not only come to us with a vast exegetical literature. They themselves constitute an exercise of exegesis as well: they systematically mediate between a corpus of information, deriving from various sources but encompassing Scripture in particular, and the formulation of law in expository, not exegetical, form by the Mishnah and the Tosefta. So far as the history of religions is the exegesis of exegesis, this is a project at the very heart of the history of religions as that discipline takes up the Judaic problematic in its larger enterprise.

PRACTICING COMPARISON: I present a systematic comparison of Mishnah-Tosefta-Yerushalmi-Bavli on how each document determines what it wants to know, and say, about a shared agendum of specified subjects. What may we expect the Mishnah to do with its topic? What then does the Tosefta want to accomplish in the presentation of the same topic, whether in dialogue with the Mishnah or not (that is an autonomous question)? When the Yerushalmi takes up the same topic, what interests its framers? Finally, how does the Bavli recapitulate the subject, and what are the traits of its mind in addressing a common heritage? I do not know a systematic account of these matters, and that is what I am trying to achieve. For the mighty labor may produce modest results, but very solid ones: we know how Rabbinic Judaism in the Halakhah worked out its theory of interpreting the topical program, the corpus of native category-formations, that encompass and impose rationality upon the vast corpus of details that all together comprise the norms of that Judaism: the hermeneutics of the Halakhic sector.

WHAT IS AT STAKE IN THIS PROJECT? A distinguished historian of religion once said, "The history of religions is the exegesis of exegesis." In a profound sense, that judgment animates an entire field of learning, and here, within my approach to matters, always from the bottom, the raw data, upward, hermeneutics is the exegesis of exegesis. In this project in the history of religions, I undertake an inductive account, through systematic inquiry into data, of the hermeneutics of the principal documents of Rabbinic Judaism. At issue is the theory of interpretation that guides the sages in their exposition of the topics that they define and expound. That theory is realized in the category-formations, of Rabbinic Judaism in the documents that expound those formations. These documents fall into two classes, Halakhic, normative for behavior, and Aggadic, normative - if in a different way - for belief. I have dealt with the latter and here continue my study of the former. I aim at an account of how the two classes of writing fuse, the Halakhic and the Aggadic, and for that purpose require a systematic account of the native category-formations that govern in each class - hence the present project. I use the word "hermeneutics" to refer to the process of interpretation - embodied in the results in systematization, rationalization, configuration and representation - that guides thought the data of the Halakhah, their configuration and their articulation.[2] I undertake the comparison and contrast of the rules of interpretation realized in the respective documents (so far as these vary, as they do occasionally). That is what I mean, in the present context, by the comparative hermeneutics of the Rabbinic Judaism: the rules for interpreting the topics that all together comprise the Halakhah, the norms of actuality, of that Judaism.

The goal of this study is to define the main lines of that process, the hermeneutics of the Halakhah, as that hermeneutics governs the formation and articulation of native category-formations out of a mass of data, some deriving from Scripture, some from natural reason, and further guides the interpretation and articulation of each of those native category-formations. A subsidiary goal is comparative, namely, an effort to identify evidence of variation within the hermeneutics of the native category-formations as these categories are set forth in the successive documents of the Halakhah, from the Mishnah, ca. 200, which is primary, to the Tosefta, ca. 300, Yerushalmi, ca. 400, and Bavli, ca. 600.

RECAPITULATING THE INTRODUCTION: The Introduction to the entire project, in Volume II, provides a systematic account of the theoretical framework. But readers will want to have in hand a brief picture of the procedures that, in the shank of the book, I follow to elicit the information that I seek. Here are the issues and how I investigate the data pertinent to them.

[1] THE DEFINITION OF A CATEGORY-FORMATION: what topics are covered within an established category-formation, corresponding to a tractate of Mishnah-Tosefta-Yerushalmi-Bavli? How is the encompassing formation defined, and what principles of selection govern the selection of data that are encompassed? Here the character of Rabbinic Judaism, defined by its dialogue with Scripture and (in some measure) the dialectics of its relationship

---

[2] That in various philosophical settings, for other purposes altogether, the word has been defined very differently need not prevent us from using it in its conventional sense. I do not enter into the philosophers' debate of "hermeneutics versus epistemology" or pretend even to follow it.

therewith, defines the logically-consequent question: the hermeneutical stimulus, Scripture or some logic perceived internal to the native-category itself. And that leads to the second issue.

[2] THE FOUNDATIONS OF THE HALAKHIC CATEGORY-FORMATIONS: Two sources for category-formations present themselves: Scripture and some kind of autonomous logic, e.g., the organization of data through the identification of species of a common genus. In the former case these questions emerge: Does a category-formation correspond to one of Scripture, e.g., a passage of Scripture that systematically expounds a topic? An example of an affirmative case is the category-formation Negaim, which corresponds to Leviticus 13-14. An instance of a negative case is the category-formation Berakhot, which occasionally utilizes data supplied by the Written Torah but entirely on its own identifies a large category of activity and defines, divides, and organizes the pertinent data. In the later case - the working of autonomous logic - can we specify the workings of that logic? An instance of an affirmative answer comes to us from Berakhot, which organizes around the classification of data within the genus, the individual's obligations to Heaven, a variety of species, carefully limited to those that share common traits dictated by the genus.

[3] THE EXPOSITION OF THE COMPONENTS OF A GIVEN CATEGORY-FORMATION BY THE MISHNAH-TOSEFTA-YERUSHALMI-BAVLI: This brings us to the heart of the matter. That is, the hermeneutical core of the category-formation. Here I systematically ask, how is the topic expounded in the successive documents, and what traits of mind, what theory of consequence and significance, in those documents dictate the course of exposition? Here I have to present the Halakhah, in abbreviated form, but in a comprehensive manner. I undertake to describe what each document contributes to the exposition of the Halakhic category-formation. That is where I find the data that tell me what hermeneutical principles are in play, how successive sets of sages represented by the four documents of the Halakhah mediate the category-formation in their literary labor.

I did exactly that - a presentation of the successive documentary treatments of one and the same topic - for a different purpose in my *The Halakhah. An Encyclopaedia of the Law of Judaism.* There I constructed a précis of the Halakhah. articulated in detail in the four successive documents of the halakhah. These are signaled in the following type-faces: **the Mishnah**, the Tosefta, *the Talmud of the Land of Israel,* and THE TALMUD OF BABYLONIA. Here I draw upon, but have revised, that presentation

I cite, from the Tosefta, Yerushalmi, and Bavli, those passages that represent fresh initiatives, but not those that merely take up and amplify what has already been said. This requires a labor of selection, sorting through the types of Halakhic expositions in the Tosefta, Yerushalmi, and Bavli, with special interest in the approach to Halakhic presentation, analysis, and reconstruction particular to the successive documents in sequence. The outcome is to specify a documentary hermeneutics, e.g., the Bavli's characteristic way of analyzing a problem, the Yerushalmi's typical manner of disposing not of a passage of the Mishnah (which does not concern us here) but of a native-category received from the Mishnah.

In my repertoire for the Tosefta, Yerushalmi, and Bavli, therefore, I omit glosses and clarifications of the Mishnah's initial presentation of the Halakhah. I stipulate in advance that the successor-documents have made integral to their hermeneutics a theory of tradition that encompasses a labor of clarification. I find no need to give a great many demonstrations of that established fact. So I make no reference to what merely recapitulates the received formulation of the Halakhah in the Mishnah. I lay stress, rather, upon what is not only characteristic of the successor-compilations in sequence but original to each of them, again in sequence. Here I do not elaborately cite what the documents say, but rather describe their contribution in a few words, based on an abstract of the text.

It follows that, since the successor-documents undertake to amplify the received statement of the Halakhah that the Mishnah sets forth, my portrayal of matters omits reference to that fact. Where the Tosefta pursues its own program, where the Yerushalmi and the Bavli raise fresh questions of Halakhic description, analysis, and interpretation, there I cite, in as brief a form as possible, what is said. In general, therefore, I cite just so much of the texts as is absolutely necessary in order to make the point at hand. So while I start with already-completed work, the articulation of the project requires a very different presentation of the Halakhah from the one that served in the *Religious Commentary*.

[4] DOCUMENTARY TRAITS: For each category-formation I conclude with some remarks upon the traits of the respective documents' expositions, seeking to generalize out of the particularities we shall have examined. That is the point at which results pertinent to the purpose of this project will emerge. I aim at laying a very, very solid foundation in data for the generalizations that I shall systematically set forth in the category-formations and then recapitulate at the end. These summary-remarks will prove fairly succinct, but well-founded. My initial experiment told me that I should work in pairs of documents, each set bearing its own distinctive task: the Mishnah and the Tosefta, then the two Talmuds.

[5] HERMENEUTICS OF A GIVEN CATEGORY-FORMATION: The hermeneutics of each category-formation is identified in the answers to the basic question that altogether account for the character and function of a cate-

gory-formation: what forms the center of interest, fusing the halakhic data into a well-delineated and lucidly articulated classification (genus, species)? Once I raise the issue of a category-formation, I invoke the three criteria that I identified for the study of the Aggadic counterpart in *my Native Category-Formation of the Aggadah*. These are the traits of [1] activity, meaning, a category-formation has the capacity to accommodate data in diverse settings, pertinent to a variety of issues, to form a whole that transcends the sum of the parts; [2] generativity, meaning, a category-formation has the power to extend its boundaries to new territory, to generate new problems and to solve them; and [3] consistency, meaning, a category-formation exhibits uniform results, its principles of interpreting data repeatedly producing a coherent and cogent outcome.

These then represent the five rubrics that serve to describe the hermeneutics of the Halakhic component of Rabbinic Judaism. I can think of no others. Future inquiry will surely lead to refinements, but I am confident that here I lay solid foundations for further description, analysis, and interpretation of the Halakhic construction, its structure and its system, and how that construction joins with its Aggadic counterpart, where and when it does.

ANALYTICAL VOCABULARY: I make use of the established, technical vocabulary of the field in which I work, that of history of religion, which may not be entirely familiar to readers not in that field. That analytical vocabulary, standard in history of religion in North America and in no way my invention, contains within itself the issues I pursue and the methods that I follow in addressing them. It is not idiosyncratic (though I may conduct the research in a way other historians of religion will find unfamiliar, with my focus on the distinctive documents at hand and my sustained interest in large-scale constructions of religious thought into systemic formations, e.g., theology). It is an established approach, and the purpose and goals of this project will elude readers who have not reflected for a moment on that well-established approach. Let me then briefly refer to the more frequently-used language.

CATEGORY, CATEGORY-FORMATION: By category I mean, that part of a proposition that allows the meanings of other words to be determined by virtue of its presence. In linguistics such terms are called collectively "the head noun." In descriptive theology these categories govern classification of data concerning what God has said and done, now recorded in the Torah. The single word of a statement that determines the meaning and properties of the whole, out of linguistics, here corresponds to those categories that govern — dictate what fits with what, and how things hold together — everywhere. In that context, a category gives way to a category-formation, that is, a large construction that functions in expository contexts the way a category functions in the smallest whole sense-unit.

A CATEGORY-FORMATION forms a principal building block of a theory of the social- or world-order. It is a main component of the structure and a principal part of the operating system, of that coherent account of the social order put forth by a set of cogent ideas in a corpus of authoritative writings that I have called "a system." From "category" we proceed to category-formation, the analogy to which in grammar is syntax. The rules of correct syntax — sentence-construction, in familiar terms — are to vocabulary as the rules of making connections and building constructions are to the native categories of a theological structure and system. Each dictates how the smallest whole units join to form clusters of meaning. The coherent phrases and even cogent sentences of a language correspond to the conceptual composites, the building blocks and even propositions of a theological system. Certain words in a language, as certain native categories in the documents of the Oral Torah, properly join together, forming intelligible clusters of meaning and even complete thoughts. Other words or native categories, when joined, jar. They yield gibberish. When we know which words may join with which others, and which not, formulating the theological counterpart to the rules of syntax of a language, we know the inner logic of the system: how to set forth statements that make sense. We may even explain why in context they make sense. Native categories such as "God," "Israel," "Sinai," "Torah," for example, combine and recombine. While meanings may well shift in context, within a prescribed range of possibilities, "God," ""gentiles," "idolatry" and "love," rarely join, and when "Sinai," "Torah, and "gentiles do, the negative (e.g., "why did the gentiles *not* accept...?") must make its appearance early and prominently. The distinction between category and category-formation is fully spelled out in my *Native Category-Formations of the Oral Torah*.[3]

What tells us that we deal with a category-formation of a system? As explained in the Introduction to this project, Volume One, I discern three indicative traits: those of a generative, active, coherence-imparting paradigm, to wit:

A PARADIGM GENERATIVE OF LOGIC OR RATIONALITY OF COHERENCE AND PROPORTION: A category-formation is defined, out of the vast range of data that comprise the system, by an active paradigm or pattern, one that may pertain to an event, person, idea, symbol or image that typifies

---

[3] *The Native Category-Formations of the Aggadah. I. The Later Midrash-Compilations.* Atlanta, 1999: Scholars Press for South Florida Studies in the History of Judaism, and *The Native Category-Formations of the Aggadah. II. The Earlier Midrash-Compilations.* Atlanta, 1999: Scholars Press for South Florida Studies in the History of Judaism.

and rationalizes events, persons, ideas, symbols (visual or verbal) or images (narrative or static).

ACTIVITY: Such a formation is one that plays an active role in holding together and organizing, rationalizing the discrete details of thought.

CONSISTENCY: And, most important, it is one that does so in a consistent manner, with predictable and regular, orderly results. I cannot overstate this point, which is the centerpiece of the entire composition.

In this context, then, I invoke the criteria of generativity, activity, and consistency. A category-formation in the Halakhah imposes a coherent logic upon the data that it draws together and forms of the whole a clear picture, an orderly statement. The category-formation can accommodate new problems and generate new propositions, dealing with time and with change. The source of the data that requires the categorical rationalization — Scripture, tradition, logic — makes no difference. The category-formation encompasses all and forms the whole into a cogent construction. Let me briefly point to concrete examples to instantiate this abstract definition of what a category-formation is and does.

DEFINING SOME SPECIALIZED VOCABULARY, E.G., LOCATIVE, UTOPIAN, ENLANDISED: Since Rabbinic Judaism recapitulates the Scriptural theology of the possession of the Land of Israel as a critical component of Israel's covenant with God and of the Temple and its cult as central medium for the divine service and relationship, I invoke three words in fixed, particular meanings. These are the binary opposites, utopian and locative, meaning, everywhere in general as against here in particular, and enlandised, a subset of locative, meaning the particularization of place by its identification with a distinctive geographical construction (fabrication, really), in the case of Rabbinic Judaism in the heritage of Scripture, the Land of Israel, Jerusalem, the Temple, and the like.

HIERARCHICAL CLASSIFICATION, ANALOGICAL-CONTRASTIVE REASONING: A fair part of the analytical vocabulary also derives from my *Judaism as Philosophy. The Method and Message of the Mishnah*[4] and the corpus of research that is summarized there, e.g., issues of hierarchical classification, analogical-contrastive reasoning, and the like. The analytical vocabulary is meant to turn cases into rules, rules into generalizations, generalizations into knowledge useful for analysis of other cases of religion altogether — the equivalent of mathematics for the physical sciences, I suppose.

MODES OF THOUGHT: Analogical-contrastive reasoning at the service of hierarchical classification represents a species of the genus, modes of

---

[4] Columbia, 1991: University of South Carolina Press. Paperback edition: Baltimore, 1999: The Johns Hopkins University Press.

thought. Let me conclude by briefly explaining the more general considerations that engage my interest. The documents of the Oral Torah appeal to a system of thought that everywhere defines matters and appeals to a self-evident logic of order, proportion, and balance that we can readily comprehend Its inner logic is always presupposed. Its modes of thought and even specific propositions dictate the identification of data that await analysis, the character of problems that require explanation, and the implications that define what is to be anticipated. Semantics is to grammar as models of analysis, explanation, and anticipation are to theology. The one identifies what is implicit in intelligible discourse and therefore intuitive or presupposed, the other, what is implicit in the particulars of religious discourse and therefore definitive of the a priori theological system — one that makes possible an immediate understanding of a range of statements that have never been made before but once made make sense. The specifics of cogent discourse turn out to derive from a generative structure, encompassing both modes of thought and massive conceptions of a concrete order. These modes we uncover by noting regularities of analytical procedure and repeated appeals to a finite corpus of explanations of a very particular character. It is at the point of anticipation that the specificities of the generative system come to the surface — but these turn out fully to embody the givens of the intellectual disciplines that govern: find the counterpart, establish the balance, take the measure of appropriate proportion.

This work stands at the beginning of inquiry. Enough has been said, however, in explaining the utilization of an analytical vocabulary in the service of research to indicate that, so far as I know, a new inquiry commences. This project has no antecedents in prior research on the history of Rabbinic Judaism in its formative centuries and documents. Every document, every detail we consider has been studied for many centuries and under diverse auspices. But apart from topical studies of severely limited use and even relevance, e.g., collections and arrangements of sayings on this and that, I could find no bibliography of any weight or substance to attach to this project and its companions. Only a few others, represented by the name of Max Kadushin, have ever pursued the inquiries followed here, and my systematic, already-published critique of prior works on "Judaism," whether theological or historical in intent, explains why I find no bibliography of any interest that pertains to this exercise.

It remains to acknowledge the support, for my research, of the University of South Florida, where I had the honor of holding a Distinguished Research Professorship in Religious Studies. Further support comes from Bard College, where, in the first semester of the academic year, I additionally held the position of Professor of Religion. Both at USF through the year and at Bard during fall semesters, I enjoy the friendship and collegiality in learning of many, with whom I undertake common projects in teaching and in writing.

These truly professional and accomplished people define the norm for scholarship in the American academy.

JACOB NEUSNER
BARD COLLEGE
neusner@bard.edu

1.
TRACTATE YEBAMOT

I. THE DEFINITION OF THE CATEGORY-FORMATION

SANCTIFYING THE HOUSEHOLD'S TABLE AND BED: The Israelite household defines one of the two loci of sanctification, the other being the Temple in Jerusalem. In both loci life is maintained and sustained. In both places time and space intersect, the advent of a particular occasion in the lunar calendar, adjusted by the solar seasons, imposing its special rules upon activities conducted in each. In both places considerations of sanctification come to concrete realization in the media for the sustenance of life: food rules for the table, rules governing procreation for the bed. And the same sources of uncleanness that renders food unacceptable on the altar make food unsuitable for the domestic table. And that observation brings us to the task of explaining how for the bed the Halakhah defines sanctification and, consequently, determines the processes of desacralization as well. In this initial category-formation and the longest of the lot, we deal with marriage under the aspect of Heaven, counterpart to marriage subject to man's intentionality, in both cases, establishing and severing the marital bond that sanctifies a woman to a particular man for purposes of procreation.

First, what exactly defines the status and substance of sanctification? In the Torah, to be holy is to be like God, to act like God. In Scripture God is explicit on that point at Lev. 19:2: "You shall be holy, for I the Lord your God am holy." Then to sanctify means, to do a deed such as God does. And in sages' view what God does above all else, which man and woman emulate, is create and sustain life now and restore the dead to life at the end of days. How God creates and sustains life defines the model by which man and woman do the same. The Torah through its law consecrates life in its critical aspects: propagation and sustenance. Accordingly, God created all life, with man and woman the climax of creation. Man and woman, like God, create life. In so doing, they are, they act, like God. It is no wonder, then, that God engages with man and woman at the critical foci of the life-processes, the bed for the propagation of life, the table for its maintenance.

But in this world the bed and the table may lose the status of sanctification, the one through the dissolution of the marriage, the other through the process and sources of pollution that Scripture itself describes at Leviticus Chapters Eleven through Fifteen. When, therefore, we turn to the ways in which the bed and the table, having been sanctified, are desacralized (for the bed) or fall from the status of sanctification into that of uncleanness (for the table), we find ourselves at the critical turning of the entire system of the Torah. And when we deal with the conjugal bond and its dissolution through divorce or death, what we find is where and how God engages with, ratifies, the processes of deconsecration, as much as he confirms those of sanctification. That engagement with deconsecration takes place, as Scripture makes explicit, in the Temple. It also comes to localization, as the Oral Torah insists, in the Israelite household, the other, and corresponding, locus of sanctification.

NASHIM IN CATEGORICAL CONTEXT: Let us begin with the first half of the Halakhah viewed whole, Zeraim, Moed, and Nashim, the complex that deals with nature, time, and family, respectively. The first of the Halakhah's six principal category-formations, Zera'im deals with the world of nature, agriculture and production of crops; the second, Moed, with time; the third, Nashim, with procreation, that is, marriage and the family. All three involve natural processes — those of nature, of the firmament above, and of man and woman together. The whole corresponds to the condition of creation in Eden in its three components: [1] the heavens and [2] earth and [3] man, all together. All three in common bring to their topics a distinctive, uniform set of questions, and ultimately we shall find it possible to identify the questions that characterize the Halakhic structure and system as a whole. It suffices here to note that, when the constitutive categories address the natural world of planting, harvesting and sharing, the results thereof, the rhythms of time in the lunar-solar calendar and seasons and the marking of time, and procreation and the family and the conformity with the commandment to be fruitful and multiply, a strikingly distinctive set of considerations repeatedly shapes the exegetical program throughout. But, beyond generalities, we stand a fair distance from the detailed and systematic definition of those pervasive considerations. We continue to pursue a preparatory inquiry: the hermeneutics that yields the category-formations and the message thereof.

NASHIM VIEWED WHOLE: There is no reading of any category-formation of Nashim without attention to its counterparts and opposites, all in comprehensive context. That is because a massive category-formation, comprised by Yebamot (Levirate marriages), Ketubot (marriage-agreements), Qiddushin (betrothals) and Gittin (writs of divorce), encompasses the entire matter of the marital bond, beginning and end, that is, establishing and severing it. No component or sub-component of that category-formation can be fully, comprehensively understood on its own. The hermeneutics of the whole — the proportions, balances, matching opposites, and governing logic — pervades the parts.

What theory of interpretation governs the selection and organization of data? At the outset, it suffices to say: the generative logic of analogical-contrastive reason does its work throughout: like is subject to the same rule, unlike to the opposite. As to the starting point already indicated in Moed — [1] differentiating the like versus [2] establishing the commonalities of the unlike — the organization of the whole leaves no doubt. We work with like categories and differentiate between them. Throughout we begin with the shared trait — bonding the sexes for the purpose of marriage and procreation or severing the marital bond one way or another — and then differentiate, moving from like to unlike. Then we want to differentiate diverse media for establishing the marital bond (e.g., at Qiddushin) or, in the present case, diverse media for severing it (Gittin, through a document, Yebamot, through heavenly intervention). Each of the principal category-formations, furthermore, presents its own subdivisions, and one task for the analysis of the governing hermeneutics is to explain how the parts are supposed to fit together, the principles of interpretation that have identified the pertinent data and organized them. Here we concentrate on only the first of the complex of category-formations covering marital bonds.

YEBAMOT IN PARTICULAR: The complex category-formation, Yebamot (Levirate marriages), encompasses three distinct classes of data: [1] the Levirate connection, [2] marriages that violate the restrictions of the Torah, [3] marriages the validity of which is subject to doubt. The status may be subject to doubt by reason of the status of the parties thereto, e.g., those in interstitial categories (neither minor nor adult). Or the doubt may be as to whether the husband has died, leaving the widow free to remarry. How these three distinct categories of the marital bond join together defines the problematics of the category-formation before us. The trait common to all three classes of marital bonds then is clear: relationships that depend upon Heaven's intervention (the Levirate connection) or that in Heaven's perspective are otherwise unconventional, e.g., interstitial or subject to doubt by reason of categorical unclarity (age, condition of the parties to the relationship).

Here, then, we address a component of a larger, encompassing, category-formation, the marital bond, in two parts, the formation of the marital bond and the severing of the same. The first — forming the marital bond — is to be divided into two components: the conventional or normal, covered at Qiddushin (betrothals, acts of sanctification) and Ketubot (marriage-contracts, acts of consummation); and the unconventional, dealt with at Yebamot. The second — severance of the marital bond — follows suit: death (yielding Yebamot) and a writ of divorce (Gittin). Having gone that far, we may divide the entire corpus of Halakhah into two large components: marital bonds subject to documentary or other tangible confirmation (Qiddushin, Ketubot, on the one side, Gittin on the other) and marital bonds effected in an intangible way, not by documents but by Heavenly intervention (Yebamot, on the one side, death on the other).

What is the theory of interpretation of the data at hand, that is, the special circumstances affecting the validity of a marriage? These are basically two: [1] a marital bond that survives the death of the husband and [2] a marital bond that is imperfect, subject to doubt by reason of interstitiality or unclarity as to the facts of the matter. To answer our question, we must ask, what characterizes all of the special circumstances under study here? And as soon as we ask the question, the answer — the principle of selection that the hermeneutics defines — presents itself: all involve Heaven's will, none man's. The death of a man without issue, leaving his wife to wed a surviving brother or obtain release from him, the condition of the minor or deaf-mute dealt with in marital bonds of an interstitial character, and the doubt as to whether the husband is alive or dead — all three classes of marriage-bond dealt with here come about not through the active intervention of man. He has not effected the betrothal of this woman to her Levir, the circumstance of the death without children of the brother has. Man has not defined the condition of the minor or of the deaf-mute. Man has not brought about the situation of doubt affecting the missing husband. So the entire category-formation before us joins together data that pertain to the marital bond effected or disrupted by Heaven's rules or Heaven's own intervention. The conventional severing of a marriage-bond, by a document executed by man, the ordinary establishment of a marriage-bond, by a document or other act, also executed by man (woman participating in both transactions, — these matters, dealt with in Gittin and Qiddushin, respectively, here find their counterparts: this is where Heaven, not man, acts, where, then, man's intentionality plays no important role (or none at all), but Heaven's program decides.

Accordingly, the profound reflections of the Halakhah of Moed (and, as other studies have shown, of Zeraim) upon the interplay between intentionality and action move onward, in the Halakhah of Yebamot, to take account of Heaven's will in particular, that is to say, the force of Heaven-determined circumstance. For the illustrative case, let us focus on the matter of the Levirate connection and its testimony as to the matter of intentionality. To do so, we contrast affect upon a marriage of death as against the affect of the writ of divorce, both of them affecting the initial act of intentionality that led to the sanctification of this woman to this man. A writ of divorce, abrogating the intentionality realized in the marital union, does not present the only way in which the Halakhah nullifies the initial act of consecration of a woman to a man. Death also serves to deconsecrate the conjugal bed, to bring to a conclusion the initial act of intentionality, of sanctification. But that is for a different reason. Now the governing intentionality — the man's intentionality in sanctifying this woman — has accomplished its purpose, which is, self-evidently, procreation. That is to say, if the husband dies having produced offspring, the wife automatically proceeds to the next marriage if she wishes. The act of consecration by that man of that woman has completely fulfilled its goal. The wife was consecrated for the purpose of procreation of that man in his household, that purpose has been realized by the man who has sanctified her for his purpose, and therefore the intentionality that has brought about the relationship has been fully realized in action: the transaction is sealed.

But what happens if the husband's goal in consecrating the woman — engendering children in his name ("name" standing for household, extended family) — has not come to fruition? Then, Scripture maintains, the original act of consecration has not accomplished its goal. Then desacralization of the original intention, confirmed by action, of sanctification, does not take place. The woman therefore remains consecrated for the as-yet-unrealized purpose embodied in the intention of betrothal and the action of consummation of the union. Then, so far as is possible, the widow bears the obligation to accomplish the intention that effected the original act of consecration. Here circumstance intervenes. Since at issue is the household, the Torah holds, if brothers survive the deceased, then a surviving brother of the childless deceased may take his place as husband of the widow. The law of Levirate marriage — marriage of the widow to a brother of the childless deceased husband for purpose of procreation — aims at bringing about the realization of that original act of consecration.

Scripture, along with the Halakhah, deems the widow's role in realizing the initial intentionality, to which she has acceded, to be active; she is the one who demands the realization of the original transaction. The surviving brother forms a mere instrumentality in the fulfillment of the deceased husband's and now widowed wife's agreement. The surviving brother(s) may then prevent the transaction, in which case the woman is freed of her status of sanctification, *removing the shoe* or the rite of removing the shoe then forming the counterpart to the presentation of a writ of divorce. But there is this obvious difference: now the unwilling brother takes the passive role, the outraged widow, the active one. It is that the embodiment and fulfillment of that sanctification that she has willingly accepted for herself that the surviving brother has refused to assist. She bears as heavy a stake in the transaction as the now-deceased husband; her brother-in-law has failed in his Heavenly task. So much for the primary constituent of the category-formation, Yebamot. In due course we shall consider how the secondary constituents fit in to this primary hermeneutical principle: the disposition of marital bonds when man's intentionality is set aside.

II. THE FOUNDATIONS OF THE HALAKHIC CATEGORY - FORMATIONS

The Written Torah frames matters in terms of maintaining the deceased's "name" in Israel. That means, the deceased's widow is to produce a child with a surviving brother, so carrying forward the purpose of the original union, if not as originally contemplated. The pertinent verse of Scripture is as follows:

> If brothers dwell together and one of them die and have no son, the widow of the dead man shall not be married to a stranger outside the family; her husband's brother shall go in to her and take her as his wife and perform the duty of a husband's brother to her. And it shall be that the firstborn son which she bears will succeed to the name of his dead brother, that his name may not be blotted out of Israel. But if the man does not want to take his brother's wife, then let his brother's wife go up to the gate to the elders and say, 'My husband's brother refuses to raise up a name to his brother in Israel; he will not perform the duty of my husband's brother.' Then the elders of his city shall call him and speak to him. But if he stands firm and says, 'I do not want to take her,' then his brother's wife shall come to him in the presence of the elders, remove his sandal from his foot, spit in his presence, and answer and say, 'So shall it be done to the man who will not build up his brother's house.' And his name shall be called in Israel, 'The house of him who had his sandal removed.'
>
> Deuteronomy 25:5-10

The match of the penalty — the deceased's brother is called a name — to the failure — not preserving the deceased's name — rests on the premise that the original act of consecration of this woman to this man meant to bring a new generation into being. To this should be added the explicit statement of Lev. 18:16:

> You shall not uncover the nakedness of your brother's wife; it is the nakedness of your brother.
>
> Leviticus 18:16

That would seem to prohibit the Levirate connection altogether. The opening unit of the Halakhah resolves that problem. It requires explanation, since it presupposes a conflict of rules in the Torah and the resolution of that conflict. To explain: when Heaven intervenes in a consecrated relationship and severs it, no writ of divorce is required to free the woman from the marriage.

In the Levirate connection, Heaven may also have arranged matters so that a union of a surviving brother with the widow contravenes other laws of the Torah. So Heaven bears responsibility for a complication of the Levirate connection comes about when the deceased childless man's widow is related to the surviving brother in a relationship prohibited by the Torah, e.g., if she is the sister of the surviving brother's wife. The potential conflict between the prohibition of consanguinity (and incest) and the requirement of Levirate marriage is worked out in the following passage of the Yerushalmi, which best serves to explain why on Heaven's part, the Levirate connection may prove null; then no rite of removing the shoe is carried out, just as, at the death of a husband who has produced offspring, no writ of divorce is necessary to sever the marital bond:

YERUSHALMI YEBAMOT 1:1 I:2

[A] It is written, "You shall not uncover the nakedness of your brother's wife; she is your brother's nakedness" (Lev. 18:16). The implication of this statement is that the prohibition applies, whether it is the wife of his brother from the same father [but not the same mother], or the wife of his brother from the same mother but not the same father], the wife of his brother who was alive at the same time and the wife of his brother who was not alive at the same time [but died before he was born, whether the brother was yet alive or whether the brother had already died, whether the brother had had children or whether the brother did not have children.

[B] [Is it then possible to suppose that] any woman in any of these categories] then has been removed from this categorical prohibition on account of Levirate marriage?

[C] [For brothers from the same mother only:] Here it is written, "If brothers dwell together, and one of them dies and has no son ..." (Deut. 25:5). And elsewhere it is written, "We are twelve brothers, sons of our father" (Gen. 42:32).

[D] Just as "brothers" used in this latter context refers to brothers from the same father [but from different mothers], so "brothers" stated here [with respect to the Levirate connection] means that they are brothers from the same father.

[E] [For contemporaries only:] "Together" indicates that we exclude reference to the wife of his brother who was not a contemporary.

[F] "And one of them dies" — that is, if the brother was yet alive, so that even if the brother divorced a wife and then died, this one [whom he had divorced] is exempt [from having to enter into Levirate marriage. She had to be married to the deceased at the moment of death].

[G] "And has no son" — lo, if he should have an offspring, she is exempt.

Then the Levirate requirement is set aside. But what is the status of the same woman's co-wives? May they enter into relationship with the surviving brother, even though the woman cannot? The answer is negative. If one of a group of co-wives cannot marry one of the surviving brothers, then the entire transaction is null. That fact carries us to the articulation of the Halakhah as set forth by the Oral Torah, since it is the point of the opening unit of the Halakhah as set forth in the Mishnah. The basic rule is set forth, in line with the foregoing exegesis, at M. 2:3: A general rule did they lay down in regard to the Levirate woman [widow of a deceased childless brother]: Any [sister-in-law] who is prohibited as one of the forbidden removes [of Leviticus Chapter Eighteen] neither executes the rite of removing the shoe nor is taken in Levirate marriage.

III. THE EXPOSITION OF THE COMPONENTS OF THE GIVEN CATEGORY-FORMATION BY THE MISHNAH-TOSEFTA-YERUSHALMI-BAVLI

As always, I set forth the main points of **the Mishnah (in bold face type)**, then at the appropriate place add the Tosefta's own presentation not merely the clarification or amplification of the Mishnah's Halakhah) (in ordinary type), thereafter *the Yerushalmi's (in italics),* and finally, THE BAVLI'S (IN BOLD FACE LOWER CASE TYPE). These are paraphrased and epitomized, they are not cited in full. I insert my observations on the points of special interest at the conclusion of each topical sub-unit. The units and sub-units derive from my own outline of the Mishnah-tractate, encompassing also the Tosefta-tractate; then the outline of the Yerushalmi, finally that of the Bavli.[1] Readers who compare the selections given here with the complete text will note that I omit disputed and schismatic opinion and discuss only the normative law.

I. WHEN THE LEVIRATE CONNECTION DOES NOT PERTAIN

   A. *WOMEN WHO ARE NEAR OF KIN TO THEIR DECEASED, CHILDLESS HUSBAND'S BROTHER BUT CANNOT ENTER INTO LEVIRATE MARRIAGE WITH THE DECEASED CHILDLESS HUSBAND'S BROTHER*
      M. 1:1 Fifteen women [who are near of kin to their deceased, childless husband's brother] [because they cannot enter

---

[1] These are cited with bibliographical data in the Introduction, Volume I.

into Levirate marriage with the deceased childless husband's brother also] exempt their co-wives, and the co-wives, from the rite of removing the shoe and from Levirate marriage, without limit. And these are they: (1) His daughter, and (2) the daughter of his daughter, and (3) the daughter of his son; (4) the daughter [by a former marriage] of his wife, and (5) the daughter of her son [by a former marriage], and (6) the daughter of her daughter [by a former marriage]; (7) his mother-in-law, and (8) the mother of his mother-in-law, and (9) the mother of his father-in-law [married to his brother by the same father]; (10) his sister by the same mother, and (11) the sister of his mother, and (12) the sister of his wife; (13) and the wife of his brother by the same mother, and (14) the wife of his brother who was not [alive] at the same time as he [but who died before he was born, in which case the surviving brother has no claim]; and (15) his [former] daughter-in-law [who then married his brother] — lo, these exempt their co-wives and the co-wives of their co-wives, from rite of removing the shoe and from Levirate marriage, without limit. And in the case of all of them, if they died [before the husband], or exercised the right of refusal, or were divorced [by the childless husband], or turned out to be barren — their co-wives are permitted [to enter into Levirate marriage, since they are not now deemed co-wives of a forbidden party]. But you cannot rule in the case of his mother-in-law and in the case of the mother of his mother-in-law, or in the case of the mother of his father-in-law [E], who turned out to be barren, or who exercised the right of refusal.

T. 1:1 Under what circumstances did they rule: If they died or were divorced, their co-wives are permitted [to enter into Levirate marriage] [M. Yeb. 1:1 J-K]? [If this happened] during the lifetime of the husband. But [if] after the death of the husband [they died or were divorced], their co-wives are prohibited [from entering into Levirate marriage]. [If] they exercised the right of refusal [M. Yeb. 1:1J] during the lifetime of the husband, their co-wives are permitted. [If they did so] after the death of the husband, their co-wives perform the rite of removing the shoe but do not enter into Levirate marriage [cf. M. Yeb. 1:2J].

T. 1:2 And any of them who turned out to be barren [M. Yeb. 1:1J], or who was [legally] married to someone else — whether this is in the lifetime of the husband or after the death of the husband — their co-wives are permitted. Any [young girl] who can exercise the right of refusal and has not exercised the right of refusal and [the husband of whom] dies [childless] — her co-wife performs the rite of removing the shoe and does not enter in Levirate marriage [M. Yeb. 1:2J].

T. 1:3 How [do we define a case in which] if their co-wives died. They are permitted [M. Yeb. 1:2G, M. 1:1J]? [If] his daughter or any one of all those forbidden degrees was married to his brother, and he [the brother] had another wife, and his daughter died, and afterward his brother died — her co-wife is permitted. [If] his brother died, and afterward his daughter died, her co-wife is prohibited.

T. 1:5 You turn out to rule: So long as the brothers are many, the co-wives are many. [If] the brothers are few, the co-wives are few. Just as, if they died or exercised the right of refusal or were divorced or turned out to be barren or were married to others, their co-wives are permitted [M. Yeb. 1:1J-K], so the co-wife of their co-wives who died or exercised the right of refusal or were divorced or turned out to be barren or married others — their co-wives are permitted.

T. 1:6 Just as they exempt [the co-wives] from marriage, so they exempt [them] from betrothal. Under what circumstances? In the case of a woman in which he has no right of consecration. But in the case of a woman in whom he has the right of consecration, their co-wives perform the rite of removing the shoe and do not enter into Levirate marriage.

M. 1:2 How do they exempt their co-wives [from the requirement of rite of removing the shoe and from Levirate marriage]? [If] his daughter or any one of all those forbidden degrees was married to his brother, and he [the brother] had another wife, and he [the brother] died [without children], just as his daughter is exempt [from Levirate marriage or rite of removing the shoe], so her co-wife is exempt. [If] the co-wife of the daughter went and married another of his brothers ["his second brother"], and he [the other brother] had another co-wife, and he [the other brother] died, just as the co-wife of his daughter [C] is exempt, so the co-wife of her co-wife is exempt, even if they are a hundred. How [do we define a case in which] if their co-wives died, they are permitted? [If] his daughter or any one of all those forbidden degrees was married to his brother, and he [the brother] had another wife, and his daughter died or was divorced, and afterward his brother died [without children] — her co-wife [now no longer a co-wife of his daughter] is permitted [to enter Levirate marriage with him]. And any [young girl] who can exercise the right of refusal and has not exercised the right of refusal — her co-wife performs the rite of removing the shoe and does not enter into Levirate marriage.

T 1:4 [If] the co-wife of his daughter went and married another of his brothers, and he [the other brother] had another wife [M. Yeb. 1:2D], [if] the co-wife died, and afterward his brother died, even though his daughter is alive, the co-wife of her co-wife is permitted.

[If] his brother died and afterward the co-wife died, even though his daughter is exempt [better: deceased] the co-wife of her co-wife is prohibited, even if they are a hundred [M. Yeb. 1:2A-F].

M. 1:3 Six forbidden degrees are subject to a more strict rule than these [the fifteen women referred to in M. 1:1], for they are [validly] married [only] to outsiders, [not to one's paternal brother], [and so] their co-wives are permitted: (1) his mother, and (2) the wife of his father, and (3) the sister of his father, and (4) his sister from the same father, and (5) the wife of his father's brother, and (6) the wife of his brother from the same father.

T. 1:7 Six forbidden degrees are subject to a more strict rule than these [the fifteen women referred to in M. Yeb. 1:1]. For they are married [only] to outsiders, [and their co-wives are permitted [M. Yeb. 1:3AB]: For the law of the co-wife applies only [to widows of] the brother. [If] they married brothers not as a transgression [but legally], their co-wives are exempt [from removing the shoe or Levirate marriage].

M. 1:4 The co-wives forbidden [to enter into Levirate marriage with] the other brothers. [If] they have performed the rite of removing the shoe, they are valid [for marriage with] the priesthood. [If] they have entered into Levirate marriage, they are invalid [for marriage with the priesthood].

T. 1:8 [If] these co-wives went and got married, they are valid, and the offspring is valid.

T. 1:9 [If] they entered into Levirate marriage. they are invalid, and the offspring is a Mamzer [M. Yeb. 1:4F-H].

M. 2:1 How [is it so that] the wife of his brother who was not a contemporary [exempts her co-wife from the requirement of Levirate marriage or rite of removing the shoe (M. 1:1)]? Two brothers — and one of them died, and a [further] brother was born to them, and afterward the second [brother] entered into Levirate marriage with the wife of his [deceased childless first] brother, and [then] he [the second brother too] died — the first [wife, who already had one time entered into Levirate marriage to the third, surviving brother does not enter into Levirate marriage with the new-born brother but rather] goes forth on the count of being the wife of his brother who was not a contemporary. And the second [wife, the one married to the second brother goes forth without Levirate marriage to the third, surviving brother or rite of removing the shoe] on the count of being her [the first brother's wife's] co-wife. [If] he [the second brother] had bespoken her [= had made a statement of intention, i.e., he did not enter into Levirate marriage with the sister-in-law but betrothed her by money or deed, which is not a total completion of Levirate marriage], and then he [the second brother] died, the second executes the rite of removing the shoe but does not enter into Levirate marriage.

T. 2:1 How is it so that the wife of his brother who was not a contemporary exempts her co-wife from the requirement of Levirate marriage or removing the shoe [M. Yeb. 1:1] [M . Yeb. 2:1 A]? Two brothers [living] at the same time, and one of them died without offspring, and the second survived, but did not complete bespeaking his Levirate wife before a brother was born to them [the first two brothers], and then he [the second brother] died — the first [brother's wife, that is, the sister-in-law of the second brother] goes forth on the grounds of being the wife of his brother who was not a contemporary. The second [brother's wife] either undertakes a rite of removing the shoe or enters into Levirate marriage. [If the second brother, before he died, did complete] bespeaking [the sister-in-law], but he did not complete effecting the marriage before a brother was born to them, and [then] he [the second brother] died, or a brother was born to them and afterward he did complete bespeaking [the sister-in-law] but did not complete effecting the marriage before the first brother died, [the second brother's] second wife [=his first brother's widow] goes forth [without removing the shoe let alone Levirate marriage] on the grounds of being the wife of his brother who was not a contemporary, and the [second brother's] first wife undertakes the rite of removing the shoe but does not enter into Levirate marriage [M. Yeb. 2:11]. What is "bespeaking"? [If the Levirate husband says,] "lo, thou art sanctified to me by money" or "by something worth money" or "by a writ." What is the language to be used in a writ? "I, So-and-so, the son of So-and so, take upon myself responsibility for Miss So-and so, my deceased childless brother's wife, to care for her and to supply maintenance for her in an appropriate way. This is with the proviso that the payment of her marriage-contract is the obligation of the estate of her [deceased] first husband." Just as the act of sanctification effects acquisition in the case of a woman only when both of them are agreed, so a statement of bespeaking effects acquisition of a sister-in-law only when both of them are agreed. What is the difference between an act of sanctification betrothal and bespeaking? The act of sanctification completes the transaction. The bespeaking does not complete the transaction.

M. 2:2 **Two brothers — and one of them died, and the second entered into Levirate marriage with the wife of his brother, and afterward a brother was born to them, and he [the second brother, who entered into Levirate marriage with the widow of the deceased first brother] died — the first [brother's wife] goes forth on the count of being the wife of his brother who was not a contemporary, and the second on the count of being her co-wife. [If] he [the second brother] had bespoken her and then died, the sec-**

ond executes the rite of removing the shoe but does not enter into Levirate marriage.

Y. 2:2 I.4 *In the case of any sister-in-law in which the whole of that woman does not lie within the range of a permitted relationship to the Levir, that aspect of the woman that is deemed [not] to fall within the possession of the Levir is held to constitute a consanguineous side to that woman. [If she is not wholly permitted to the Levir, then any part of her relationship to the Levir in which she is not permitted is treated as decisive, so that, as in general, so here], if there is a consanguineous relationship in one of the co-wives, that co-wife exempts her other co-wife [from marriage with the Levir].*

M. 2:3 A general rule did they lay down in regard to the Levirate woman [widow of a deceased childless brother]: (1) Any [sister-in-law] who is prohibited as one of the forbidden removes [of Leviticus Chapter Eighteen] neither executes the rite of removing the shoe nor is taken in Levirate marriage. (2) [If] she is prohibited [to her brother-in-law] by reason of a prohibition on account of a commandment or a prohibition on account of sanctity [e.g., the Levir may not marry a woman of her caste], she executes the rite of removing the shoe but is not taken in Levirate marriage. (3) [If] her sister is [also] her sister-in-law [widow of her childless brother-in-law], she either executes the rite of removing the shoe or is taken into Levirate marriage.

T. 2:2 The women of forbidden degrees of whom they spoke are not equivalent to his wife in any respect. They have no right to a marriage-contract, to disposition of the return on their property, to sustenance, or to indemnity [the provision of the replacement of clothing]. And he [the husband] does not retain the right to possess things which she finds or the fruit of her labor, or to annul vows which she may make. He does not inherit her estate. Nor is he permitted to make himself unclean in burying her [should he be a priest otherwise forbidden to have contact with the dead]. He has no power of sanctification over her. And she does not require a writ of divorce from him. She is invalid, and the offspring is a Mamzer.

M. 2:4 A prohibition on account of a commandment is a secondary grade [of forbidden removes] on account of the rulings of scribes. A prohibition on account of sanctity [of the Levir] is, for instance, the case of (1) a widow [married] to a high priest (Lev. 21:14), (2) a divorcée, or (3) a woman who has executed the rite of removing the shoe to an ordinary priest (Lev. 21:7), (4) a Mamzeret [daughter of parents never legally permitted to marry], (5) a [of the cast of Temple servants] to an Israelite, a daughter of an Israelite (6) to a Netin [male of the caste of Temple servants], or (7) to a Mamzer.

T. 2:3 A. A widow [married to] a high priest, a divorcee or a woman who has undergone the rite of removing the shoe to an ordinary priest [M. Yeb. 2:4B1-3] — lo, these are deemed as his legal wife in every respect. They have a right to a marriage-contract, to the disposition of the return on their property, to nourishment, and to indemnity [the provision of replacement of clothing which is worn out]. And he [the husband] does retain right to possess things which she finds and the fruit of her labor, and to annul vows which she may make. He does inherit her estate. But he does not make himself unclean in burying her. He does have the power of sanctification over her. and she does require a writ of divorce from him [to annul the marriage]. But she is invalid, and the offspring [of such a marriage] is invalid.

T. 2:4 A secondary grade [of forbidden degrees] on account of the rulings of scribes [M. 2:4A] — [such women] are not deemed as his legal wife in every respect. They have no right to a marriage contract, to disposition of the return of their property, to sustenance, or to indemnity [provision of the replacement of worn-out clothing]. But he [the husband] does not retain the right to possess things which she finds or the fruit of her labor or to annul vows which she may make. [Nonetheless] he does inherit her estate and he makes himself unclean for her in burying her [if he is a priest and otherwise prohibited from doing so]. He does have power of sanctification over her. And she does require a writ of divorce from him. She is valid, and the offspring [of such a union] is valid. [Nonetheless] they force him to divorce her. A secondary grade of forbidden degrees [listed at Leviticus Chapter Eighteen] on account of the rulings of scribes constitutes a prohibition on account of sanctity" [vs. M. Yeb. 2:4].

T. 2:5 There are women who [1] either effect the rite of removing the shoe or undergo Levirate marriage, [2] undergo Levirate marriage but do not effect the rite of removing the shoe, [3] effect the rite of removing the shoe but do not undergo Levirate marriage, [4] neither effect the rite of removing the shoe nor undergo Levirate marriage. [1] The forbidden degrees of whom we have spoken [at M. 1:1, 3: the women prohibited at Leviticus Chapter Eighteen] neither enter into Levirate marriage nor effect the rite of removing the shoe. In addition to them, the wife of a man who is a eunuch by nature, the wife of a man who bears sexual traits of both sexes, the wife of a brother from the same mother, the wife of a proselyte, the wife of a freed slave, and a barren woman, do not effect the rite of removing the shoe and do not enter into Levirate marriage [A4]. The deaf-mute and the idiot enter into Levirate marriage but do not effect a rite of removing the shoe [A2]. A woman prohibited by reason of a commandment and one prohibited by reason of sanctity [M. Yeb. 2:3C, 2:4] effect removing the shoe and do not enter into Levirate marriage [A3]. A woman who cannot bear children and one past menopause and all other women either effect a rite of removing the shoe or enter into Levirate marriage [A1].

T. 2:6 There are men who [1] either undergo a rite of removing the shoe or enter into Levirate marriage, [2] enter into Levirate marriage but do not undergo a rite of removing the shoe, [3] undergo a rite of removing the shoe but do not enter into Levirate marriage, [4] neither enter into Levirate marriage nor undergo a rite of removing the shoe. With the forbidden degrees of whom we have spoken [at M. Yeb. 1:1 3] men do not undergo the rite of removing the shoe nor do they enter into Levirate marriage [A4]. In addition to them, a eunuch by nature, a man who bears sexual traits of both sexes, a brother from the same mother, a proselyte, and a freed slave neither undergo the rite of removing the shoe nor enter into Levirate marriage. The deaf-mute and the idiot enter into Levirate marriage but do not undergo a rite of removing the shoe [A2]. Those who are subject to doubt undergo a rite of removing the shoe but do not enter into Levirate marriage [A3]. A man with crushed testicles and one whose penis is cut off, a eunuch by human action, [and] an old man either undergo a rite of removing the shoe or enter into Levirate marriage [A/l].

T. 3:1 The secondary grade of forbidden degrees on account of rulings of scribes [M. Yeb. 2:4A] [includes the following]: [1] The mother of his mother, [2] the mother of his father, [3] the wife of his father's father, [4] the wife of his father's mother, [5] the wife of his mother's brother by the same father, [6] the wife of his father's brother by the same mother, [7] the wife of the son of his son, and [8] the wife of the son of his daughter. A man is permitted to marry the wife of his father-in-law and the wife of his step-son, but is prohibited to marry the daughter of his step-son. And his step-son is permitted to marry his wife and his daughter. This woman [the wife of the step-son] says, "I am permitted to you, but my daughter is prohibited to you." His sister who also is his deceased childless brother's wife — [as to her sister, coming to him from a different brother] either effects a rite of removing the shoe or enters into Levirate marriage [M. Yeb. 2:3D]. How so? His daughter by a woman whom he has raped, married to his brother, and she has a sister from the same mother but by a different father, married to his other brother, and he [the brother] dies without children — she either performs the rite of removing the shoe or enters into Levirate marriage. [If] the daughter of his daughter is married to his brother, and the daughter of his wife is married to another of his brothers, and the daughter of the daughter of his wife is married to another of his brothers, and she has a sister by the same father and a different mother, married to another of his brothers, and he dies without children — she either performs the rite of removing the shoe or enters into Levirate marriage. The daughter of his son who is married to his brother, and the daughter of the son of his wife who is married to his brother, and she has a sister by the same mother but by a different father, married to his other brother, and he dies without children — she either performs a rite of removing the shoe or enters into Levirate marriage. His mother-in-law and the mother of his mother-in-law and the mother of his father-in-law married to his brother, and she has a sister, whether of the same father or of the same mother, married to his other brother, and he dies without children — she either performs a rite of removing the shoe or enters into Levirate marriage. His sister by the same mother, the sister of his mother by the same mother, the sister of his wife by the same mother, married to his brother, and she has a sister by the same father but by a different mother, married to his other brother, and he dies without children — either performs the rite of removing the shoe or enters into Levirate marriage. The sister of his mother on her father's side, and the sister of his wife on her father's side, married to his brother, and she has another sister from her mother but with a different father, married to the same brother, and he dies without children — she either performs the rite of removing the shoe or enters into Levirate marriage. The wife of his brother on his mother's side, and the wife of his brother who was not a contemporary, and his daughter-in-law, married to his brother [after the death of his son], and she has a sister, whether from on her father's side or on her mother's side, married to his other brother, and he dies without children — she either performs the rite of removing the shoe or enters into Levirate marriage.

God cannot contradict himself, so the laws of the Torah, as noted earlier, harmonize. Hence if circumstances create a conflict, then the demise of the childless husband under the circumstances outlined at M. 1:1 in no way imposes the Levirate bond, which never takes effect in any way, shape, or form (M. 1:4); if all of the surviving brother are not available for Levirate marriage, none is eligible; the bond does not take effect to begin with. The Tosefta serves as an amplification of, and commentary to, the Mishnah's statements. M. 1:3 is beautifully explained by T. 1:7: "for the law of the co-wife applies only to widows of the brother," excluding the stated relationships. The secondary amplifications, M. 2:1/T. 2:1 ff., do not change the picture. The clarity of M. 2:3 (with its footnote at M. 2:4) cannot be improved upon. The Halakhic presentation of the category-formation then focuses to begin with upon a derivative and subordinate issue, that is, the conflict of status: Levirate widow forbidden to marry a Levir; no primary issues implicit in the category-formation require attention.

B. *SURVIVING BROTHERS ELIGIBLE FOR LEVIRATE MARRIAGE: WHEN THE LEVIRATE CONNECTION IS NULL. CASES OF CONFUSION*

M. 2:5 He who has a brother of any sort — [that brother] imposes upon the wife of his [deceased, childless] brother the obligation of Levirate marriage. And [he is] his brother in every regard — except for him who has [a brother] from a female slave or from a gentile. He who has a son of any sort — he [the son] exempts the wife of his father from the obligation of Levirate marriage. And he [the son] is liable for hitting him [the father] or for cursing him. And [he is] his son in every regard — except for him who has a son from a female slave or from a gentile.

M. 2:6 He who betrothed one of two sisters and does not know which of them he betrothed gives a writ of divorce to this one and a writ of divorce to that one. [If] he died, and he had one brother, he [the brother] effects a rite of removing the shoe with both of them. [If] he [who died childless] had two [brothers], one of them effects a rite of removing the shoe and one of them enters into Levirate marriage. [If] they went ahead and married [the two women], they [the court] do not remove [the women] from their possession.

M. 2:7 Two [unrelated men] who betrothed two sisters — this one does not know which of them he betrothed, and that one does not know which of them he betrothed — this one gives two writs of divorce, and that one gives two writs of divorce. [If] they died, [if] this one has a brother and that one has a brother, this one effects the rite of removing the shoe with both of them, and that one effects the rite of removing the shoe with both of them. [If] this one had one [brother] and that one had two, the one [the sole brother of one of the deceased] effects a rite of removing the shoe with both of them. And [as to] the two [brothers of the other deceased] — one effects a rite of rite of removing the shoe with one of them, and [then] one enters into Levirate marriage with one of them. If they went ahead and married [the two widows out of betrothal], they do not remove them from their possession. [If] this one had two and that one had two [brothers], a brother of this one effects a rite of removing the shoe with one of them, and a brother of that one effects a rite of removing the shoe with one of them, A brother of this one enters into Levirate marriage with the woman with whom the other party's brother had effected a rite of removing the shoe, and a brother of that one enters into Levirate marriage with the woman with whom the other party's brother has effected a rite of removing the shoe. [If] the two went ahead and performed a rite of removing the shoe, then the [other] two should not enter into Levirate marriage. But one of them performs the rite of removing the shoe and one of them enters into Levirate marriage. **If they went ahead and married them, they do not remove them from their possession.**

T. 4:1 Two unrelated men who betrothed two sisters, this one does not know which one of them is betrothed, and that one does not know which one of them is betrothed — this one gives two writs of divorce, and that one gives two writs of divorce [M. Yeb. 2:7A-C]. [If] one of them died, the second man is prohibited [to marry] either one of the women. [If] one of the women died, both of the men are prohibited [to enter into Levirate marriage with the] second, [surviving sister]. [If both] men died, and one of them had one brother, he effects a rite of removing the shoe with both of them. [If there survived] two brothers, they effect a rite of removing the shoe with both women. If they went ahead and married [the two sisters], they must put them out.

T. 4:2 He who betrothed one of two unrelated women, and does not know which of them he betrothed, marries both of them. [If] he died and left behind one brother, he marries both of them. [If he left] two brothers, they marry the two women.

T. 4:3. Two brothers who betrothed two sisters, this one does not know which one of them he betrothed, and that one does nor know which one of them he betrothed, this one gives two writs of divorce, and that one gives two writs of divorce [M. Yeb. 2:7A-C]. [If] one of them died, the second one is prohibited [from entering into Levirate marriage] with either one of them. [If] one of them died, both of the brothers are prohibited [to enter into marriage] with the second sister. [If] they died and left yet one more brother, he performs a rite of removing the shoe with both sisters. [If they left] two brothers, they perform a rite of removing the shoe with both sisters. If they went ahead and married the two women, they must put them away. Two unrelated men who betrothed two unrelated women this one does not know which one of them he betrothed, and that one does not know which one of them he betrothed — this one gives two writs of divorce, and that one gives two writs of divorce. [If] one of them died, the second is permitted [to enter into ordinary marriage] with either one of the women. [If] one of the women died, either one of the two men is permitted [to enter into marriage with] the second woman. What should they then do [to make this possible (M)]? One of them gives a writ of divorce, and one of them marries her. [If] they died — this one has a brother, and that one has a brother — this one performs a rite of removing the shoe with this woman, and the other enters into Levirate marriage with that woman, and this one performs a rite of removing the shoe with that woman, and the other enters into Levirate marriage with that woman. If they went ahead [without following the stated procedure] and married them, they must put them away. It is a religious duty for the oldest [surviving brother to enter into Levirate marriage [with the deceased, childless brother's widow] [M. Yeb. 2:8A], but not for the oldest [widow] to be taken into Levirate marriage. But [the Levir] effects Levirate marriage with whichever widow [of his deceased, childless brother] he wishes.

M. 2:8 It is a religious duty for the oldest [surviving brother] to enter into Levirate marriage [with the deceased, childless brother's widow]. But if the youngest went ahead [and married her], he has acquired [the sister-in-law]. [Other cases in which an impropriety is or is not penalized:] He who is suspected [of having intercourse] with a slave woman who is subsequently set free, or with a gentile woman who subsequently converts, lo, this one should not marry [her]. But if he married her, they do not remove her from his possession. He who is suspected [of having intercourse] with a married woman, and they [the court] dissolved the marriage with her husband, even though he [the suspect] married [the woman], he must put her out.

T. 4:4 A well which is nearer to the water-course is to be filled first. If the second [person, whose well is farther away] went ahead and filled his, lo, this one is prompt and rewarded on that account. [If] this one went ahead and moved the water-course over to the well of his fellow, lo this one is prompt and rewarded on that account. A creditor and an heir, one of whom went ahead and took over movable goods — lo, this one is prompt and rewarded on that account. He who says to his fellow, "Go and betroth for me Miss Such-and-so," [and] he went and betrothed her for himself, "Go and buy me such and such an object," [and] he went and bought it for himself, what he has done is done. But he has behaved deceitfully. He who redeems a woman taken into captivity is permitted to marry her. He who testifies concerning a captive woman [that she has not been raped], lo, this one may not marry her. But if he married her, he does not have to put her away.

M. 2:9 He who delivers a writ of divorce from overseas and stated, "In my presence was it written and in my presence was it sealed" [and who thereby validates the writ] may not [then] marry his [the man's] wife [to whom he brought the writ of divorce]. [If he testified,] "He [the husband] has died," "I killed him," "They killed him," he may not then marry his [the deceased's] wife.

T. 4:5 He who delivers a writ of divorce from overseas and testified, "In my presence was it written and in my presence was it sealed may not then marry his [the man's] wife to whom he brought the writ of divorcee." [If he testified, "He [the husband] has died," "We killed him," "I killed him," he may not marry his wife. He who is suspected [of having intercourse] with a married woman who then was divorced by the other [after being divorced by her first husband, she remarried, and then was divorced again] — lo, this one [even now] may not marry her. But if he did marry her, he does not have to put her away. He who is suspected [of having intercourse] with a woman may not marry her mother, her daughter, or her sister. But if he did marry one of these, he need not put her away.

M. 2:10 A sage who forbade a woman to her husband by reason of [her] vow, lo, this [sage] may not marry her. [If] she exercised the right of refusal or performed the rite of removing the shoe in his presence, he may marry her, because [in these latter instances,] that is an unstipulated regularity of the court. And in the case of all of them [M. 2:9A-D, 2:10A-C] who had wives (and) [the wives of] whom [thereafter] died — the [other] women may be married to them [who secured the right to remarry]. And in the case of all of them who were married to other men and were divorced or widowed, they [then] are permitted to be married to them. And all of them are permitted to [marry] their sons or their brothers [of the aforementioned messengers, witnesses, or sages].

T. 4:6 A gentile or a slave who had sexual relations with an Israelite woman, even though the gentile went and converted, or the slave was freed, lo, such a one may not marry the woman. But if he married her, he need not put her away [cf. M. Yeb. 2:8C-E]. An Israelite who had sexual relations with a slave girl or with a gentile woman, even though the slave was freed, or the gentile woman converted, lo, this one may not marry her. But if he married her, he need not put her away. A sage who forbade a woman to her husband by reason of [her] vow against her husband, lo, this one may not marry her [M. Yeb. 2:10A]. And in the case of all of them who were married to other men who died, [M. Yeb. 2:10E], they [such widows] are permitted to be married to them [the sages of F]. And in the case of all of them [the judges, agents] who were married and [whose wives] died, they are permitted to be married to them [M. Yeb. 2:10E].

T. 4:8 There is he who is prompt and rewarded on that account, who is prompt and loses out on that account, who is restrained [in the exercise of what is permitted] and is rewarded on that account, and who is restrained and loses out on that account: He exercises restraint on the eve of the Sabbath, on the Sabbath, and after the Sabbath, on the eve of the seventh year, in the seventh year, in the year after the seventh year, during the intervening days of a festival, and all who are anxious about transgression, lo, such a one exercises restraint and is rewarded on that account.

We turn, now, from the special case of the Levirate widow who cannot enter into a marital relationship with a surviving brother to the more routine case in which the Levir is eligible for the Levirate marriage, but the Levirate connection is null for some extrinsic reason, having nothing to do with the existing marital relationships. We commence with a generalization, M. 2:5, then turn to how we sort out confusion. Here we impose the rite of removing the shoe as the means for severing the marital bond, equivalent to a writ of divorce. Because of the confusion, we cannot allow the Levirate marriage. M. 2:7 builds secondary instances of the same sort of problem. And the Tosefta's amplifications follow suit. M. 2:8/T. 4:4 (and note the construction of T. 4:8, along these same lines) is noteworthy because of Tosefta's following its familiar way of setting forth a principle: it gives illustrations of the rule that are not limited to the case at hand. That approach, followed systematically, would have yielded a quite other kind of category-formation; the selection and interpretation of the data would have taken another course altogether, and the Halakhah would have followed a different hermeneutical theory.

II. THE INTERSTITIAL CASE: THE FLAWED LEVIRATE CONNECTION AND THE RITE OF REMOVING THE SHOE

A. BROTHERS MARRIED TO SISTERS

M. 3:1 Four brothers — two of them married to two sisters — and those who are married to the sisters died — lo, these [surviving, childless widows] perform a rite of removing the shoe and do not enter into Levirate marriage [with the other two brothers]. And if they [the other two brothers] went ahead and married [the two sisters], they must put them away.

T. 5:1. Four brothers — two of them married to two sisters — and those who are married to the sisters died — lo, these [surviving, childless widows] perform a rite of removing the shoe but do not enter into Levirate marriage [with the other two brothers]. And if they went ahead and married [the two widows], they must put them away.

M. 3:2 [If] one of them [the sisters] was prohibited to one of the men by reason of being a forbidden degree [M. 2:3-4], he is prohibited to marry her. But he is permitted [to enter into Levirate marriage] with her sister. And the second [brother] is prohibited [to enter into Levirate marriage] with either of them. [If one of them was prohibited] by reason of being prohibited as a commandment or prohibited by reason of sanctity [M. 2:3-4], [the sister] performs the rite of removing the shoe but does not enter into Levirate marriage.

T. 5:2 [If] one of the women was the mother-in-law of one of the men, he is prohibited [to marry] her but permitted to marry her sister. And the second [brother] is prohibited from marrying either one of them. It turns out that the one who is prohibited is permitted, and the one who is permitted is prohibited. [If] one of the women was the mother-in-law of this one, and the second was the mother-in-law of that one — this one is prohibited to marry the mother-in-law of his own, but permitted to marry the mother-in-law of his brother. and that one is prohibited to marry the mother-in-law of his own, but permitted to marry the mother-in-law of his brother. This is the sort of case concerning which they have stated: The one who is prohibited to this one is permitted to that one, and the one who is prohibited to that one is permitted to this one.

Y. 3:2 I:1 [Illustrating the case of M. 3:2A:] If one raped a woman, who produced a daughter, and [the daughter] went and married his brother [on his father's side] and [this same daughter] has a sister on her mother's side, born of a different father, who is married to [the rapist's] other brother, [and this brother] died without children — lo this man [the rapist] is [of course] forbidden to marry his daughter, but he is permitted to marry her sister. Here is a case [in line with M. 2:3] in which there is a man's daughter and her sister, with the latter his Levirate sister-in-law, and with whom he may enter into Levirate marriage [= M. 3:2A].

M. 3:3 [If] one [of the sisters] was prohibited to one of the brothers by reason of being a forbidden degree, and the second was prohibited to another [of the brothers] by reason of being a forbidden degree, the one who is prohibited to this one is permitted to the other, and the one who is prohibited to the other one is permitted to this one. This is a case in which they have stated [M. 2:3]: [In a case in which] her sister also is her sister-in-law awaiting Levirate marriage, she either performs the rite of removing the shoe or enters into Levirate marriage [there being no prohibition in such a case by reason of a woman's being the sister of one who is subject to Levirate marriage with the surviving brother].

T. 5:3 [If] one of them was the mother-in-law of both of them, this one is prohibited to marry her, but permitted to marry her sister, and that one is prohibited to marry her but permitted to marry her sister. [If] two of the women were the mother-in-law of one of them, the second is permitted [Better: prohibited] to marry both of them. This is the general principle: So long as they are suitable for him, they are prohibited from marrying him by reason of not taking a woman in marriage with her sister [Lev. 18:18]. But if they were prohibited to him by reason of a forbidden degree of some other sort, he is prohibited from marrying her and permitted to marry her sister [M. Yeb. 3:3C].

Y. 3:3 I:3 If the first sister had a co-wife, if the Levir performed the rite of removing the shoe with her, her co-wife is freed. If the second sister had a co-wife, the Levir may marry the co-wife and preserve his marriage with his wife, but [of course] he is prohibited from marrying the second sister. [The co-wife is not forbidden, since she comes from a different family. He cannot marry the sister; the co-wife of the sister frees the sister from the Levirate connection anyhow.]

M. 3:4 Three brothers — two of them married to two sisters — or to a woman and her daughter — or to a woman and the daughter of her daughter — lo, these women perform the rite of removing the shoe and do not enter into Levirate marriage. [If] one of them was prohibited to him by reason of being a forbidden degree, he is prohibited to that one but permitted to [marry] her sister. [If the prohibition was] a prohibition deriving from a commandment or a prohibition of sanctity, the sisters perform the rite of removing the shoe but do not enter into Levirate marriage.

T. 5:4 Three brothers — two of them married to two sisters — or to a woman and her daughter, or to a woman and the daughter of her son — lo, these women perform the rite of removing the shoe and do not enter into Levirate marriage [M. Yeb. 3:4A-F]. Three brothers — two of them married to two sisters — and one of them is unmarried — one of the husbands of the sisters died, and the one who was unmarried went and married her [the childless widow of his brother], and afterward his second brother died — his wife [remains] with him, and this one [the widow of the just-now-perished brother] goes forth [without removing the shoe or Levirate marriage] on the grounds of being the sister of his wire [M. Yeb. 3:5A — F]. Three brothers — two of them married to two sisters, and one of them is unmarried — one of the husbands of the sisters died — this one who was unmarried [M. Yeb. 3:5] went and did not suffice to bespeak his Levirate sister-in-law before the wife of the surviving brother died, and afterward he [the unmarried one] died — [or] he bespoke her but did not suffice to marry her until the wife of the surviving brother died, and afterward he died — [or] he married her, and the wife of the surviving brother died, and afterward he died — lo, this one [the surviving sister] is exempt from removing the shoe and from Levirate marriage.

M. 3:5 Three brothers — two of them married to two sisters — and one [the third] of them is unmarried — one of the husbands of the sisters died, and this one who was unmarried bespoke her [the surviving sister] — and afterward his other brother died — he divorces his wife with a writ of divorce and with the rite of removing the shoe, and the wife of his brother with a rite of removing the shoe. This is the sort of case concerning which they have stated, "Woe is he because of his wife, and woe is he because of the wife of his brother."

M. 3:6 Three brothers — two of them married to two sisters — and one of them [the third] married to an unrelated woman — one of the husbands of the sisters died, and the brother married to the unrelated woman married his [the deceased, childless brother's] widow, and [then] he [the brother who was married to the unrelated woman and also to the widow of his deceased, childless brother went and] died — the first woman goes forth [without rite of removing the shoe or Levirate marriage] as the sister of his wife, and the second on the grounds of being her co-wife [neither one therefore entering into Levirate marriage or requiring a rite of removing the shoe with the surviving brother]. [If] he bespoke her [D] and died, the unrelated woman performs the rite of removing the shoe but does not enter into Levirate marriage. Three brothers — two of them married to two sisters — and one of them married to an unrelated woman — the one married to the unrelated woman died — and one of the brothers married to the sisters married his wife, then he too died — the first woman goes forth on grounds of being the sister of his wife, and the second on grounds of being the co-wife, [If] he bespoke her and then died, the unrelated woman performs the rite of removing the shoe, and does not enter into Levirate marriage.

T. 5:5 Three brothers — two of them married to two sisters — and one of them married to an unrelated woman — one of the husbands of the sisters died [M. Yeb. 3:6A-C], and he did not suffice to bespeak his Levirate sister-in-law before he died — this unrelated woman either performs the rite of removing the shoe or enters into Levirate marriage. [If] he bespoke her but did not suffice to marry her before he died, this unrelated woman performs the rite of removing the shoe but does not enter into Levirate marriage. [If] he married her and afterward he died, this unrelated woman is exempt from the rite of removing the shoe and from Levirate marriage. [If] the one who was married to the unrelated woman died, [if] one of the husbands of the sisters went and did not suffice to bespeak his Levirate sister-in-law before he died, this unrelated woman either effects the rite of removing the shoe or is taken in Levirate marriage. [If] he bespoke her but did not suffice to marry her before he died, this unrelated woman performs the rite of removing the shoe and does not enter into Levirate marriage. [If] he married her and afterward died, this unrelated woman is exempt from the rite of removing the shoe and from the requirement of Levirate marriage.

T. 3:6 Three brothers — two of them married to two sisters, and one of them married to an unrelated woman — the husband of one of the sisters died [M. Yeb. 3:6A-D] — and the one married to the unrelated woman went but did not suffice to bespeak his Levirate sister-in-law before the wife of the surviving brother died — and afterward he died — this unrelated woman either performs the rite of removing the shoe or is taken in Levirate marriage. [If] he bespoke her, but did not suffice to marry her before the wife of the surviving brother died, and afterward he died — this unrelated woman performs the rite of removing the shoe but is not taken in Levirate marriage. [If] he married her, and the wife of the surviving brother died, and afterward he died, both of them are exempt from the rite of removing the shoe and from Levirate marriage. [If] the one married to the unrelated woman died, [and] one of the husbands of the sisters went and did not suffice to bespeak his Levirate sister-in-law before the wife of the surviving brother died, and afterward he died, both of the women perform the rite of removing the shoe or enter into Levirate marriage. [If] he bespoke her but did not suffice to marry her before the wife of the surviving brother died, and afterward he died, both of these women perform the rite of removing the shoe and do not enter into Levirate marriage. [If] he married her, and the wife of the surviving brother died, and afterward he died, the act of sexual relations or the rite of removing the shoe of one of the women exempts her co-wife [from the requirement of either].

M. 3:7 Three brothers — two of them married to two sisters — and one of them married to an unrelated woman — one of the husbands of the sisters died, and the one married to an unrelated woman married his widow — and then the wife of the second brother died, and afterward the brother married to the unrelated woman died — lo, this [surviving sister] is prohibited to him for all time, since she had been prohibited to him for one moment [when her husband died, she was forbidden to his brother then married to her sister, as his wife's sister]. Three brothers — two of them married to two sisters, and one of them married to an unrelated woman — one of the husbands of the sisters divorced his wife — and the brother married to the unrelated woman died — and the one who divorced his wife married her [the unrelated woman], and he too died — this is the sort of case concerning which they have stated, "And in the case of all of them who died or were divorced, their co-wives are permitted [M. 1:1], [for the unrelated woman taken in Levirate marriage never was the co-wife of the sister of the wife of the surviving brother. The sister had been divorced before the Levirate marriage to the unrelated man ever took place].

The rite of removing the shoe is used, we realize, in place of the Levirate bond when, in the case of the Levirate connection, an impediment to a fully-valid Levirate marriage intervenes. In that way the Levirate bond is severed, and an invalid union is not effected. So the interstitial situation — a flawed Levirate connection — is dealt with: it is neither ignored nor confirmed. The illustrations produced by T. and Y. confirm the basic approach to the data. The governing principle is neatly summarized at T. 5:3: This is the general principle: So long as they are suitable for him, they are prohibited from marrying him by reason of not taking a woman in marriage with her sister [Lev. 18:18]. But if they were prohibited to him by reason of a forbidden degree of some other sort, he is prohibited from marrying her and permitted to marry her sister.

    B.   WHEN THE LEVIRATE CONNECTION IS SUBJECT TO DOUBT: FLAWED BETROTHAL OR DIVORCE

M. 3:8 And in every case [of M. 1:1's fifteen relatives] in which the betrothal or divorce [of the deceased brother] is subject to doubt, lo, these, the co-wives perform the rite of removing the shoe but [of course] do not enter into Levirate marriage. What is a case of doubt concerning betrothal? [If] he threw her a token of betrothal — it is a matter of doubt whether it landed nearer to him or nearer to her — this is a case in which there is doubt concerning betrothal. And a case of doubt concerning a writ of divorce? [If] one wrote the writ of divorce in his own hand, but there are no witnesses to attest the document — [if] there are witnesses to attest the document, but it is not dated — [if] it is dated, but it [contains the attestation of] only a single witness — this is a case in which the divorce is subject to doubt.

T. 5:7 What is a case of doubt concerning betrothal [M. Yeb. 3:8]? [If] a man betrothed a woman with something which may or may not be worth a perutah. Three brothers married to three unrelated women — and one of the brothers died — and the second brother bespoke her [the widow of his deceased, childless brother], and then he too died — lo, these [women perform the rite of removing the shoe and do not enter into Levirate marriage [M. Yeb. 3:9A-E]. But this is on the condition that the act of intercourse comes before the rite of removing the shoe. [If] he married her and afterward died, the act of intercourse or the rite of removing the shoe of one of the women exempts her co-wife.

The same principle — use of the rite of removing the shoe in a case of uncertainty — governs here as well. The Mishnah's rule is amplified by the Tosefta's illustration.

    C.   WHEN A BROTHER BESPEAKS THE LEVIRATE WIDOW BUT DIES BEFORE CONSUMMATING THE RELATIONSHIP

M. 3:9 Three brothers married to three unrelated women — and one of the men died, and the second brother bespoke her [the widow of his brother] and then he too died — lo, these perform the rite of removing the shoe and do not enter into Levirate marriage, since it is said, "And one of them dies . . . her brother-in-law will come unto her" [Dt. 25:5] — [referring to] the one who is subject to the Levirate power of a single brother-in-law, and not the one who is subject to the Levirate power of two brothers-in-law. Two brothers married to two sisters — and one of them died — and afterward the wife of the second died — lo, this one [surviving sister] is prohibited to him for all time, since she was prohibited to him for a single moment [as his wife's sister].

T. 5:8 Two brothers married to two sisters — and one of the brothers died, and afterward the wife of the second died — lo, this one is prohibited to him for all time, since she was prohibited to him for a single moment [M. Yeb. 3:91-L].

T. 7:1 He who bespeaks his deceased childless brother's widow and dies — she performs the rite of removing the shoe and does not enter into Levirate marriage [M. Yeb. 3:9].

Circumstances may also produce an interstitial situation, in which the rite of removing the shoe simply replaces Levirate marriage.

D. WHEN THE BROTHERS ACT IN ERROR

M. 3:10 Two men who betrothed two women, and at the time of their entry into the marriage-canopy, the two women [inadvertently] were exchanged for one another — lo, these men are liable for (1) having sexual relations with a married woman [namely, the betrothed of the other]. [If in addition] they were brothers, they are liable (2) on the count of having sexual relations with the wife of the brother. And if the women [in addition] were sisters, they are liable for (3) having sexual relations with a woman and her sister And if [at the time of sexual relations] they [in addition] were in their menstrual period, the men are liable for (4) having sexual relations with a menstruating woman. And they set them apart for three months, lest they be pregnant. And if they were minors, not yet fit to give birth, they are forthwith restored [to their proper husbands]. And if they were daughters of priests, they are invalid for eating heave offering.

T. 5:9 Two men who betrothed two women, and at the time of their entry into the marriage-canopy, the two women inadvertently] were exchanged for one another [M. Yeb. 3:10A-B] — lo, these [four parties, in all] are liable for sixteen sin-offerings: on the count of being brothers, and [2] on the count of being sisters, and [3] on the count of having intercourse with menstruating women, and [4] on account of intercourse with a married woman. If they are not brothers, they are liable for twelve sin-offerings. If they are not sisters, they are liable for eight, If they are not menstruating, they are liable for four. [If] the men were adult and the girls were minor, they are liable for only two. [If] the women were adult and the males' minors, the women are liable for two. If their father married them off, they are liable for eight.

T. 5:10 If one of them was adult, and the other male was a minor, the one who is subject to sexual relations with the minor is liable, for she is the wife of the adult. But the one who has sexual relations with the adult is exempt, for she is the wife of the minor.

The confusion brought about by inadvertence is sorted out along now-familiar lines.

    E.   *WHEN THE LEVIRATE CONNECTION IS EFFECTED IN ERROR*

M. 4:1 He who undergoes the rite of removing the shoe with his deceased childless brother's widow, and it turns out that she is pregnant, and she gives birth — when the offspring is timely [and not premature], he is permitted to marry her relatives, and she is permitted to marry his relatives, and he has not invalidated her from marrying into the priesthood. [If] the offspring is not timely, he is prohibited from marrying her relatives, and she is prohibited from marrying his relatives, and he has invalidated her from marrying into the priesthood.

M. 4:2 He who marries [enters into Levirate marriage with] his deceased childless brother's widow, and it turns out that she is pregnant, and she gives birth — when the offspring is timely, he must put her away, and they [both man and woman] are liable for a sacrifice. [If] the offspring is not timely, he may confirm [the marriage]. [If] it is a matter of doubt whether the offspring is born at nine months, therefore assigned to the first husband, or born at seven months, therefore assigned to the second, he must put her away. But the offspring is valid. And both of them are liable for a suspensive guilt offering.

T. 6:1 He who bespeaks his deceased childless brother's wife and she turns out to be pregnant and gives birth — when the offspring is timely [viable and capable of surviving], his act of bespeaking is no bespeaking. [It therefore follows that] he is permitted to marry her relatives, and she is permitted to marry his relatives. And he has not invalidated her from marrying into the priesthood. [If] the offspring is not timely [and cannot have survived], his act of bespeaking is bespeaking. He is prohibited from marrying her relatives, and she is prohibited from marrying his relatives. And he has invalidated her from marrying into the priesthood.

T. 6:2 He who marries his deceased childless brother's widow, and it turns out that she is pregnant and gives birth — when the offspring is timely, he must put her away, and they are liable for a sacrifice. [If] the offspring is not timely, he may confirm [the marriage] [M. Yeb. 4:2A-G]. [If] it is a matter of doubt whether or not the offspring is timely, they assign to the case two stringent rules [that is, he cannot keep the marriage going, and he divorces the woman both with a writ of divorce and with a rite of removing the shoe] [If] it is a matter of doubt whether the offspring is born at nine months, therefore assigned to the first husband, or born at seven months, therefore assigned to the second [M. Yeb. 4:2H], the first [of two such offspring] is suitable to be made high priest, but the second is deemed a Mamzer by reason of doubt.

T. 6:3 He who bespeaks his deceased childless brother's wife and she turns out to be pregnant — lo, in such a case her co-wife should not be married until it is clear that it is a foetus capable of surviving. For the offspring does not exempt [the co-wife from Levirate connection] until it comes forth into the world's light. A woman awaiting Levirate marriage who died — [the Levir] is permitted to marry her mother. What is her status as to maintenance and support? So long as the husband is liable, the Levirate brothers are liable. [If] the husband is not liable, then the Levirate brothers are not liable. He who marries his deceased childless brother's widow acquires the estate of his brother.

Y. 4:2 II:2 *If the child subject to doubt [of M. 4:2H] comes to collect his share in the estate of his father, they say to him, "That one [the Levir] is your father." If the Levir comes to take a share in the estate of his brother, they say to him, "This is the son [who may or may not be the son of the deceased. You have no claim on this estate, which passes to the son.]" Then what do they do? They make a compromise among themselves and divide up the estate of the deceased. Consequently, peace among the brothers [a compromise between the Levir and the son who may be his deceased brother's son] is a loss to the brother [and the succeeding sons, who will inherit only one half of the estate]. If there is contention among the brothers, it is a benefit to the brothers [who will succeed later on].*

Y. 4:2 II:3 *If the father of the deceased childless brother died, and the Levir and the child whose status is subject to doubt come to share in the estate [with the latter claiming to be the heir of the deceased childless son of the deceased grandfather], then there are among the sons those who are certainly heirs [namely, the surviving brothers, sons of the deceased father] and the son whose status is subject to doubt, [and this latter one cannot collect, since he cannot show for sure that he is the son and heir of the deceased son, for he may be the son of the Levir]. If the child subject to doubt died, [and the heirs of the child on his father's side and those on his mother's side wish to participate in the division of his estate, since we do not know for sure which one is his father, the heirs on his mother's side wish to take the estate] — in this case, there is the claim of the son[s] of the brother of his father whose claim is one of certainty [inheriting either if he is son of the Levir, so he is their brother, or if he is son of the deceased, so he is the son of the brother of their father], while the heirs of the mother lay a claim which is subject to doubt. If one of the brothers died, lo, we have the claim of a brother, which is a status beyond doubt, and that of the son of a brother, which claim is subject to doubt. If the mother of the child subject to doubt died, lo, there is the claim of her son, which is beyond doubt, and her husband, which is subject to doubt, [since we do not know whether or not the Levir was legally her husband, while we know that the child was certainly hers, so he inherits her property]. If the child subject to doubt died, and afterward his mother died, lo, we have here the claim of the son of the brother of his mother, which is beyond doubt, and the claim of the husband, which is subject to doubt. [The mother's property is retained in her family, there being no conduit to the family of her husband, the Levir, since the Levir's son has died before she did.] If the Levir died, and the child subject to doubt came to claim his share in the estate of his father, if the first party to die [the original father, who may or may not have had this son as his own,] was poor, they say to him, "He was your father." If he was rich, they say to him, "All of us are brothers, sons of brothers. Come and let us inherit the share of our father and the share of the brother of our father."*

When the Levirate connection is effected in error, the action produces no effects whatsoever; it is as though it never took place.

III. THE CONSEQUENCE OF THE LEVIRATE MARRIAGE

A. *PROPERTY RELATIONSHIPS*

M. 4:3 A woman awaiting Levirate marriage who received property — she sells or gives away the property [which she has received], and the transaction is confirmed. [If] she died, what do they do with her marriage contract and with the property which comes in and goes out with her [plucking property, that is, the husband enjoys the usufruct but the principal remains under the title of the wife]? The property remains in the possession of those who have a presumptive claim to it: The marriage contract is subject to the presumptive claim of the heirs of the husband. The property which comes in and goes out with her is subject to the presumptive claim of the heirs of the father.

M. 4:4 [If] he married her, lo, she is deemed to be in the status of his wife for every purpose, but in this matter only: [the charge of] her marriage contract [falls] onto the property of her first husband.

We turn to the effects of the Levirate marriage on the widow. The issue is the disposition of her estate when she was designated for the Levirate marriage, tantamount to betrothal, but the marriage was not yet consummated. The property is assigned to the presumptive heirs, as spelled out.

    B.   *PERSONAL RELATIONSHIPS*

    M. 4:5 It is the duty of the oldest surviving brother to enter into Levirate marriage. [If] he did not want to do so, they pass in turn to all the other brothers. [If] they [all] did not want to do so, they go back to the oldest and say to him, "Yours is the duty! Either undergo the rite of removing the shoe or enter into Levirate marriage."

    M. Bekh. 1:8 The requirement of Levirate marriage takes precedence over the ceremony of the rite of removing the shoe. At first, when they would consummate the Levirate marriage for the sake of fulfilling a commandment. But now, that they do not consummate the Levirate marriage for the sake of fulfilling a commandment, they have ruled: The requirement of the rite of removing the shoe takes precedence over the requirement of Levirate marriage.

    M. 4:6 [If the Levir proposed to] suspend [his decision, waiting] for a youngster to grow up, or for an adult to come from overseas, or for a deaf-mute or an idiot [to recover sound or sense], they do not listen to him. But they say to him: "Yours is the duty. Either undergo the rite of removing the shoe or enter into Levirate marriage."

These rules articulate what is readily surmised. All the brothers are eligible, but the oldest comes first. The Levirate marriage takes precedence over the rite of removing the shoe. But the motive must be pure: to carry out one's religious duty. The woman's circumstance is taken into consideration, M. 4:6.

    C.   *INHERITANCE*

    M. 4:7 He who undergoes a rite of removing the shoe with his deceased childless brother's widow, lo, he is deemed as one with the brothers for inheritance [of the deceased brother's estate]. And if there is a father [of the deceased brother] there [to share in the inheritance], the property reverts to the father. He who marries his deceased childless brother's widow, however, acquires the estate of his brother.

Once the marriage is consummated, the Levirate husband takes on the status of the widow's husband, pure and simple.

D.   *FURTHER MARRIAGES*

M. 4:7 He who undergoes a rite of removing the shoe with his deceased childless brother's widow is prohibited from marrying her relatives, and she is prohibited from marrying his relatives. He is prohibited from marrying her mother, her mother's mother, her father's mother, her daughter, the daughter of her daughter, the daughter of her son, and her sister while she is yet alive. But [his] brothers are permitted [to marry any of the forenamed]. And she is prohibited from marrying his father, the father of his father, his son, the son of his son, his brother, and the son of his brother. A man is permitted to marry the kinswoman of the co-wife of a woman with whom he has performed the rite of removing the shoe but is prohibited from marrying the co-wife of the kinswoman of a woman with whom he has performed the rite of removing the shoe.

T. 6:4 Four [relatives of a man] are liable [to extirpation for marrying the sister-in-law with whom the man performed removing the shoe], on the authority of the Torah, and four are secondary to them: his father, and his son, his brother, and the son of his brother — lo, these are liable on her account. The father of his father, the father of his mother, the son of his son, and the son of his daughter — lo, these are secondary to them [M. Yeb. 4:7J]. A strict rule applies to a divorcee, which does not apply to a woman with whom he has performed the rite of removing the shoe, and to the woman, with whom he has performed the rite of removing the shoe, which does not apply to the divorcee. The divorcee is permitted to return to the one who has divorced her [if she does not in the meanwhile remarry]. Therefore he is liable for punishment for marrying her kinswomen. A woman with whom he has performed the rite of removing the shoe is prohibited from returning to the man with whom she has performed the rite of removing the shoe. Therefore he is exempt from punishment if he marries one of her kinswomen.

M. 4:8 He who undergoes a rite of removing the shoe with his deceased childless brother's widow, and his brother married her sister, and [this brother] died — she performs a rite of removing the shoe and is not taken in Levirate marriage. And so: He who divorces his wife and his brother married her sister, and [his brother] died — lo, this one is exempt from the rite of removing the shoe and from Levirate marriage.

M. 4:9 A woman awaiting marriage with a Levir, the brother of whom betrothed her sister — they instruct him: "Wait until your older brother does a deed." [If] his brother underwent a rite of removing the shoe with her [the woman awaiting Levirate marriage] or married her, he may [then] marry his wife. [If] the deceased childless brother's widow died, he may marry his wife.

[If] the Levir died, let him [of A] put away his [betrothed] wife with a writ of divorce and the wife of his brother with a rite of removing the shoe.

M. 4:10 A deceased childless brother's widow should not perform the rite of removing the shoe or enter into Levirate marriage until three months have gone by. And so in the case of all other women: they should not become betrothed or enter marriage until three months have gone by [after the conclusion of a former marriage]. All the same are virgins and women who have had sexual relations, all the same are women who have been divorced and widows, all the same are married women and betrothed women.

B. 4:10 I.2/41B A DECEASED CHILDLESS BROTHER'S WIDOW FOR THE FIRST THREE MONTHS AFTER THE DEATH OF THE HUSBAND IS SUPPORTED BY THE ESTATE OF THE HUSBAND. THEREFORE SHE IS SUPPORTED NEITHER FROM THE ESTATE OF THE HUSBAND NOR FROM THE ESTATE OF THE LEVIR. IF THE LEVIR WENT TO COURT BUT THEN RAN OFF, SHE IS SUPPORTED BY THE ESTATE OF THE LEVIR. IF SHE WAS SUBJECT TO THE LEVIRATE RELATIONSHIP WITH A MINOR, SHE GETS NOTHING FROM HIM.

B. 4:10 I.3/41B A DECEASED CHILDLESS BROTHER'S WIDOW, WITH WHOM ONE OF THE BROTHERS HAS ENTERED INTO THE RITE OF REMOVING THE SHOE WITHIN THREE MONTHS OF THE DEATH OF THE HUSBAND STILL HAS TO WAIT FOR THREE MONTHS. IF THE RITE OF REMOVING THE SHOE WAS DONE AFTER THREE MONTHS, SHE DOES NOT HAVE TO WAIT FOR THREE MONTHS BEYOND THE PERFORMANCE OF THE RITE. THE THREE MONTHS OF WHICH THEY SPOKE PERTAINS TO THE TIME OF THE HUSBAND'S DEATH, NOT TO THE TIME OF THE LEVIR'S PERFORMING THE RITE OF REMOVING THE SHOE.

M. 4:11 Four brothers married to four women, and they died — if the oldest [surviving] brother among them wants to enter into Levirate marriage with all of them [the surviving, childless widows], he has the right to do so. He who was married to two women and who died — the act of sexual relations [in Levirate marriage] or the rite of removing the shoe of one of them exempts her co-wife [from the requirement to do the same]. [If] one of them was valid and one of them was invalid [for marriage into the priesthood], if he then performs the rite of removing the shoe, let him perform the rite of removing the shoe with the one invalid [for marriage into the priesthood]. And if he was going to enter into Levirate marriage, let him enter into Levirate marriage with the one who is valid [for marriage into the priesthood].

T. 6:4 Four [relatives of a man] are liable [to extirpation for marrying the sister-in-law with whom the man performed removing the shoe], on the authority of the Torah, and four are secondary to them: His father, and his son, his brother, and the son of his brother — lo, these are liable on her account. The father of his father, the father of his mother, the son of his son, and the son of his daughter — lo, these are secondary to them [M. Yeb. 4:7J]. A strict rule applies to a divorcee which does not apply to a woman with whom he has performed the rite of removing the shoe, and to the woman with whom he has performed the rite of removing the shoe which does not apply to the divorcee. The divorcee is permitted to return to the one who has divorced her [if she does not in the meanwhile remarry]. Therefore he is liable for punishment for marrying her kinswomen. A woman with whom he has performed the rite of removing the shoe is prohibited from returning to the man with whom she has performed the rite of removing the shoe. Therefore he is exempt from punishment if he marries one of her kinswomen .

T. 6:6 He who was married to two women and who died — the act of sexual relation s [in Levirate marriage] or the rite of removing the shoe of one of them exempts her co-wife [from the requirement to do the same] [M. Yeb. 4:11C-D]. [If] one of them was prohibited to one of the brothers by reason of a prohibition of a forbidden degree, and he [nonetheless] performed a rite of removing the shoe with her, he has done nothing whatsoever. He has not exempted her co-wife. But either she or her co-wife enters into Levirate marriage with one of the other brothers. [If] she was prohibited by reason of a commandment [of scribes (M. 2:3-4)] or by reason of sanctity [of the priesthood (M. 2:4)], [if] he performed the rite of removing the shoe with her or had sexual relations with her [as Levir], her co-wife is exempt [from doing the same].

M. 4:12 He who remarries a woman whom he has divorced [after she had wed someone else and was divorced or widowed], he who marries a woman with whom he has performed the rite of removing the shoe, and he who marries the kinswoman of a woman with whom he has performed the rite of removing the shoe [M. 4:7G-H] In the case of one who marries the kinswoman of a woman whom he has divorced, that the offspring is a Mamzer.

M. 4:13 What is the definition of a "Mamzer"? [The offspring of] any [marriage] for which the participants are liable to extirpation by Heaven. (1) His wife who died — he is permitted to marry her sister. (2) [If] he divorced her and afterward she died, he is permitted to marry her sister (3) [If] she was married to someone else and died, he is permitted to marry her sister. (4) His deceased childless brother's widow who died — he is permitted to

> marry her sister. (5) [If] he performed the rite of removing the shoe with her and she died, he is permitted to marry her sister.
>
> T. 6:7 The deceased childless brother's widow with whom her Levir has performed the rite of removing the shoe in a period of three months [from the death of her husband] must wait [from that time] for three months. [If] this took place three months after [the death of the husband], she does not have to wait for three [more] months. The three months of which they have spoken are three months after the death of her husband, and not three months after the rite of removing the shoe with her Levir. He who deposits a writ of divorce for his wife and says, "Do not deliver it to her before three months have passed," as soon as the writ of divorce reaches her hand, she is permitted to remarry forthwith. And one does not take account of the possibility that it is a superannuated writ of divorce [after the issuance of which the couple has had sexual relations]. The daughter of a priest who was married to an Israelite and the husband of who has died eat heave-offering in the evening [of the same day]. And one does not take account of the possibility that she is pregnant [and therefore not permitted to do so]. The widow of a childless brother, for the first three months after his death, is supported from the estate of her husband. After three months she is not supported either from her husband's estate or from her Levir's property. If her Levir went to court and [then] fled, lo, she is supported from his property. The deceased childless brother's widow should not engage in the rite of removing the shoe nor enter into Levirate marriage until three months have passed from the death of her husband. And just as they do not say to him to enter into Levirate marriage, so they do not say to him to perform the rite of removing the shoe. As to a beautiful captive [Deut. 21:13]: The Torah gave her thirty days, but sages have ruled that she has to wait three months, for the welfare of a possible offspring.
>
> T 6:8 He who has sexual relations with his deceased childless brother's widow for the sake of her beauty [or] for the sake of her property — they regard him [for having acted with improper motive] as if he has entered into contact with a woman of prohibited degree. And the offspring of such a union is near unto being a Mamzer.

The one who undergoes the rite of removing the shoe is as though he divorced the woman, and the status pertaining thereto then applies. That equivalency is made explicit, e.g., at M. 4:8. Bavli, B. 4:10 to M. 4:10, just supplies secondary and derivative amplification of the established law. M. 4:11 makes clear that if four brothers were married to four unrelated women, the surviving Levir may take them all in marriage. The other cases are self-evident in line with the basic principles already established. M. 4:12-13 take up the consequences of an illegal union. If someone marries a woman whom he cannot legally marry, he produces tainted offspring.

E. SEQUENCES OF LEVIRATE TRANSACTIONS

M. 5:1 There is a writ of divorce [that is valid] after [another] writ of divorce, and there is bespeaking after bespeaking, but there is nothing [validly done] after coition or after a rite of removing the shoe.

T. 7:2 How is the duty of Levirate marriage [carried out]? They bespeak her and afterward marry. [If] one has married her before bespeaking her, he has acquired [her as his wife]. He who bespeaks his deceased childless brother's widow has acquired her for himself and invalidated her for marrying any of the other surviving brothers. [If] any of the other brothers had sexual relations with her, bespoke her, gave her a writ of divorce, or performed the rite of removing the shoe with her, he has spoiled her for him [the brother who had originally bespoken the widow].

T. 7:3 "He who bespeaks his deceased childless brother's widow — her co-wife is invalid. He who gives a writ of divorce to his deceased childless brother's widow — both she and her co-wife are invalid. [If] he performed a rite of removing the shoe with her [after a writ of divorce], her co-wife is exempt [from doing so]. There is a writ of divorce after a writ of divorce, and a bespeaking after a bespeaking" [M. Yeb. 5:1E-F].

T. 7:5 Even though they have said, "Nothing whatsoever is valid after sexual relations, nonetheless a rite of removing the shoe after an act of sexual relations still invalidates the widow for marriage into the priesthood [as a woman with whom a valid rite of removing the shoe has been performed]."

Y. 5:1 I:1 "Her husband's brother shall go in to her" (Deut. 25:5) — this refers to an act of sexual relations. "And he shall take her as his wife" (Deut. 25:5) — this refers to the act of bespeaking [declaring his intent to enter into Levirate marriage, with the appropriate token of betrothal]. Is it possible to suppose that just as the act of sexual relations completes [the act of acquiring her as the surviving brother's wife], so the bespeaking [should complete acquisition of the sister-in-law as the Levir's wife]? Scripture states, "And perform the duty of the husband's brother to her" (Deut. 25:5). The whole section has been proclaimed for the purpose of Levirate marriage: The act of sexual relations completes the acquisition of the sister-in-law as the wife of the Levir, and the act of bespeaking does not do so. If that is the case, then what use is the act of bespeaking? It serves to prohibit the sister-in-law to the other surviving brothers.

M. 5:2 How so? [If a Levir] bespoke his childless brother's widow and [then] gave her a writ of divorce, she [none-

theless] requires a rite of removing the shoe from him. [If] he bespoke her and then performed a rite of removing the shoe, she [nonetheless] requires a writ of divorce from him. [If] he bespoke her and then had sexual relations, lo, this has been done in accord with its requirement.

Y. 5:2 II:1 [As to M. 5:2D-E, bespeaking, followed by a rite of removing the shoe,] an invalid rite of removing the shoe [such as is referred to here, since it does not accomplish the complete cutting of the tie to the Levirate sister-in-law] nonetheless releases. For what purpose? So that if someone else should come along and betroth her co wife, the co-wife is deemed to be subject to the betrothal. [Once removing the shoe has taken place with the one wife, the other is no longer bound.

M. 5:3 [If] one gave a writ of divorce and [then] bespoke [the childless brother's widow], she requires a writ of divorce and a rite of removing the shoe. [If] he gave a writ of divorce and then had sexual relations, she requires a writ of divorce and a rite of removing the shoe. [If] he gave a writ of divorce and performed the rite of removing the shoe, nothing whatsoever follows the rite of removing the shoe.

Y. 5:3 I:1 [As to M. 5:3A, she requires] a writ of divorce on account of his bespeaking, and removing the shoe because of the Levirate connection to him to which she is subject. [As to M. 5:3B, sexual relations, followed by a writ of divorce and a rite of removing the shoe:] that is to say an invalid act of sexual relations does not release the woman [on which account she requires removing the shoe. He could not keep the marriage going once he had given a writ of divorce, hence the sexual relations were out of order].

M. 5:4 (1) [If] he performed the rite of removing the shoe and [then] bespoke [the childless brother's widow], [or] (2) gave a writ of divorce, or had sexual relations [with her], or [if] he (1) had sexual relations, [then] bespoke [the woman], [or] (2) gave a writ of divorce or performed the rite of removing the shoe, nothing whatsoever follows the rite of removing the shoe. All the same are the cases of a single childless brother's widow with a single Levir, and two childless brothers' widows with a single Levir.

M. 5:5 How so? [If] he bespoke this one and bespoke that one, [they require] two writs of divorce and [one] rite of removing the shoe. [If] he bespoke this one and [gave] a writ of divorce to that one, she [the bespoken widow] requires a writ of divorce and the rite of removing the shoe. [If] he bespoke this one and had sexual relations with that one, they require two writs of divorce and [one] rite of removing the shoe. [If] he bespoke this one and performed the rite of removing the shoe with that one, the first one requires a writ of divorce.

T. 7:4 [If the Levir] had sexual relations with this one and had sexual relations with that one, had sexual relations with this one and bespoke that one [M. Yeb. 5:3D-E], had sexual relations with this one and gave a writ of divorce to that one, had sexual relations with this one and performed the rite of removing the shoe with that one, nothing whatsoever is valid after the rite of removing the shoe. [If] he performed the rite of removing the shoe with this one and performed the rite of removing the shoe with that one, performed the rite of removing the shoe with this one and bespoke that one [M. Yeb. 5:5A-B], performed the rite of removing the shoe with this one and gave a writ of divorce to that one, performed the rite of removing the shoe with this one and had sexual relations with that one — nothing whatsoever is valid after sexual relations.

M. 5:6 [If he gave a] writ of divorce to this one and a writ of divorce to that one, they require from him a rite of removing the shoe. [If he gave] a writ of divorce to this one and had sexual relations with that one, [the latter] requires a writ of divorce and a rite of removing the shoe. [If he gave] a writ of divorce to this one and bespoke that one, [the latter] requires a writ of divorce and a rite of removing the shoe. [If he gave] a writ of divorce to this one and performed removing the shoe with that one, nothing whatsoever follows the rite of removing the shoe.

M. 5:7 [If] he performed the rite of removing the shoe [with this one] and performed the rite of removing the shoe [with that one], or if he performed the rite of removing the shoe with this one and bespoke that one, or if he gave a writ of divorce to this one and had sexual relations with that one, if he had sexual relations with this one and had sexual relations with that one, or if he had sexual relations with this one and bespoke that one, or if he gave a writ of divorce to this one and performed the rite of removing the shoe with that one, nothing whatsoever follows the rite of removing the shoe. [And this is the rule] whether in the case of a single Levir and two childless brother's widows, or two Levirs and a single childless brother's widow.

M. 5:8 [If] he performed a rite of removing the shoe with one and bespoke one, gave a writ of divorce to one and had sexual relations with one, or had sexual relations and bespoke, and gave a writ of divorce and performed removing the shoe, nothing whatsoever follows the rite of removing the shoe whether this comes at the outset, or in the middle, or at the end. As to sexual relations: when this is at the outset, nothing whatsoever follows it. If this comes in the middle or at the end, there is something that follows it.

T. 7:2 sets the stage for the problems of this unit. We have several candidates for Levir, hence the possibility of multiple acts of bespeaking, one not necessarily knowing what the other has done. Hence the rule. M. 5:1 then states the principle, which is logical: once the relationship is either consummated or severed, no further transactions are possible in that context. T. 7:3 proceeds to outline the results of the rule, and T. 7:5 cites and glosses the Mishnah's statement. Y. 5:1 I:1 provides the anticipated exegetical basis for the rule. The remainder elaborates on the principle set forth at the outset.

F. *SEXUAL RELATIONS IN THE LEVIRATE MARRIAGE*

M. 6:1 He who has sexual relations with his childless brother's widow — whether inadvertently or deliberately, whether under constraint or willingly, even if he does so inadvertently and she deliberately, he deliberately and she inadvertently, he under constraint and she not under constraint, she under constraint and he not under constraint, all the same being the one who merely partially opens [uncovers the vagina] and the one who completes [entry therein] — has acquired [his sister-in-law as his Levirate wife]. And there is no distinction between one sort of sexual act and some other.

M. 6:2 And so: he who has sexual relations with any one of all the forbidden degrees that are listed in the Torah, or with any of those invalid [for sexual relations with him] — [for example] a widow to a high priest, a divorcée or a woman who has performed the rite of removing the shoe with an ordinary priest, a Mamzeret or a Netinah with an Israelite, and Israelite woman with a Mamzer or a Netin — has rendered her invalid [to marry a priest or, if she is a priest's daughter, to eat heave-offering]. And there is no distinction between one sort of sexual act and some other.

T. 8:1 A nine-year-and-one-day-old boy of Ammonite, Moabite, Egyptian, Edomite, Samaritan origin, a Netin, or Mamzer [of that age or older] who had sexual relations with the daughter of a priest, with the daughter of a Levite, or with the daughter of an Israelite, has rendered her invalid for marrying into the priesthood.

M. 6:1 underscores the primacy of sexual union: however it takes places, if the parties stand in the Levirate relationship, the Levirate connection is consummated. M. 6:2 applies the same principle to the standing of the daughter or wife of a priest: the physical act is all that matters. Then what about the interstitial categories, e.g., the pre-pubescent boy? That act is classified as physically decisive. The whole then stands at the head of a sizable exposition of forbidden marriages and how they affect the right to consume priestly rations accorded to the wives and daughters of priests.

IV. MARRIAGES THAT VIOLATE THE RESTRICTIONS OF THE TORAH. THE CONSEQUENCES FOR THE PRIESTHOOD AS TO THE CONSUMPTION OF PRIESTLY RATIONS

A. *A WIDOW TO A HIGH PRIEST, A DIVORCEE TO AN ORDINARY PRIEST*

M. 6:3 [If it is a marriage between] a widow and a high priest, [between] a divorcée or a woman who has performed the rite of removing the shoe and an ordinary priest — from the time of the betrothal, they should not eat heave-offering. [If] they were widowed or divorced — [if this is a severance of] the marriage, they remain invalid [for the purpose of eating food in the status of heave-offering]. [If this is a severance of] betrothal, they are valid [once more to eat heave-offering or to marry a priest].

M. 6:4 A high priest should not marry a widow, whether this is a woman widowed out of betrothal or widowed out of marriage. And he should not marry an adolescent. He should not marry a girl who has lost her virginity by reason of a blow from a piece of wood. [If] he betrothed a widow and then was appointed high priest, he may consummate the marriage. A woman awaiting marriage with her Levirate brother-in-law who came [for that purpose] before an ordinary priest, and then he [the eligible brother-in-law] was appointed high priest — even though he has bespoken her, lo, this one should not consummate the marriage. A high priest whose brother died performs the rite of removing the shoe and does not enter into Levirate marriage [with the surviving sister-in-law].

T. 8:2 A Levite woman who is taken captive — her daughter is valid to marry into the priesthood. Levites, who became unfit from the priesthood by their mothers — sages did not scruple concerning them. A Levite who was taken captive and who was raped — they give her tithe [to eat]. The daughter of a Levite born from a Netin-mother or from a Mamzeret-mother — they do not give her tithe to eat.

T. 8:3. An ordinary priest who married a sterile woman — lo, this one feeds her heave-offering [M. Yeb. 6:5A]. A high priest may not marry a woman whom he has raped or seduced. . But he may marry a girl who has exercised the right of refusal. A high priest whose brother has died performs the rite of removing the shoe [M. Yeb. 6:4I]. If there are other brothers available for the task, he does not perform the rite of removing the shoe. On what account did they rule, A high priest who has bespoken his deceased childless brother's widow should not marry her [M. Yeb. 6:4G — H]? Because bespeaking does not effect a complete [and unambiguous] act of acquisition.

Y. 6:4 II:2 *As to a woman he has raped or seduced, he should not marry such a woman [thereafter], but if he did marry her, they do not remove her from his domain. As to the woman whom another man has raped or seduced, he should not marry that woman, and if he did marry her, they remove her from his domain. He may not marry a minor-girl, but he may marry a girl who has exercised the right of refusal [against a husband assigned to her as a minor by her mother or brothers].*

M. 6:5 An ordinary priest should not marry a sterile woman, unless he already has a wife and children.

M. 6:6 [If] a man married a woman and lived with her for ten years and she did not give birth, he had no right to desist from having sexual relations with her. [If] he divorced her, she is permitted to marry someone else. The second husband is allowed to live with her for ten years. And if she miscarried, she counts the ten years from the time that she miscarried. The man is required to be fruitful and multiply but not the woman.

T. 8:4 A man should not desist from having sexual relations unless he has children [M. Yeb. 6:6A]. Grandchildren are deemed [for the purposes of the present rule] to be equivalent to children. [If] one of them died or one of them was made into a eunuch, he then is not permitted to desist from sexual relations. A man has no right to live without a woman, and a woman has no right to live without a man. A man has no right to drink a contraceptive drink so that he should not impregnate a woman, and a woman has no right to drink a contraceptive drink so that she should not become pregnant. A man has no right to marry a barren woman, an old woman, a sterile woman, or a minor, or any who cannot bear children. A woman has no right to be married even to a eunuch [sterile but capable of sexual relations].

T. 8:5 [If] a man married a woman and lived with her ten years and she did not give birth, he has no right to desist [from sexual relations] [M. Yeb. 6:6E], but he should put her away and pay off her marriage contract, lest it was because he did not merit being reproduced through her. And even though there is no proof for that proposition, there is at least Scriptural indication for it, as it is said, "At the end of ten years of Abram's dwelling in the land of Canaan" (Gen. 16:3). As is our way, we learn that living abroad does not count.

T. 8:6 A woman whose husband was old or sick, or who herself was sick, or whose husband was imprisoned, or whose husband went abroad — [the years with such husbands] do not count for her. [If] he divorced her, she should go and remarry someone else, lest it was because she did not merit being reproduced through him. And to what extent is she permitted to remarry? Up to three husbands. Beyond that point she should marry only someone who already has a wife and children. lo, if she should marry someone who has no wife and children, she goes forth without the payment of her marriage contract, because her marriage is in error.

M. 7:1 A widow wed to a high priest, a divorcée or a woman who has performed the rite of removing the shoe wed to an ordinary priest — [if] she brought in to him [as part of her dowry] "plucking"-slaves and "iron-flock"-slaves — the "plucking"-slaves do not eat food in the status of priestly rations [since she is not validly wed to the priest, so slaves to which she retains effective ownership, which are her property, do not gain the rights of slaves of a priest, but slaves to which he gains effective ownership do]. The "iron-flock"-slaves eat. What are "plucking"-slaves? [If] they died, the loss is hers, and if they increase in value, the increase is hers. Even though he [the husband] is liable to maintain them, lo, these do not eat food in the status of priestly rations. And what are "iron-flock"-slaves? [If] they die, the loss is his, but if they increase in value, the increase is his. Since he is responsible to replace them if they are lost, lo, these eat food in the status of priestly rations.

M. 7:2 An Israelite girl who married a priest and brought him slaves [as part of her dowry], whether these are "plucking"-slaves or "iron-flock"-slaves — lo, [the marriage being entirely valid,] these eat food in the status of priestly rations. And a priest's daughter who married an Israelite and brought him [as part of her dowry], either "plucking"- slaves or "iron-flock"-slaves, lo, these do not eat food in the status of priestly rations.

T. 9:1 An Israelite girl who married a priest and brought him "iron-flock"-slaves and iron-flock-slaves — "iron-flock"-slaves eat by virtue of her rights. But iron-flock-slaves eat by virtue of his rights [M. Yeb. 7:2]. What are "iron-flock"-slaves? Loss or profits, lo, both accrue to her. And what are iron-flock slaves? Loss or profit, lo, either accrues to him [M. Yeb. 7:1F-K]. [If] they are brought at fixed value, they are taken out at fixed value. [If] they come in as boys, they are taken out as young men. [If] they are brought in as young men, they are taken out as old men. In the case of both of them, the fruit of their labor belongs to the husband. In the case of both of them, the husband is liable to maintain them. In the case of both of them, they [husband or wife separately] cannot sell them. The husband cannot sell them, because they are mortgaged to his wife. And the wife cannot sell them, because the husband enjoys the fruit of their labor. [If he, the husband] died and left her as she was [childless], the "iron-flock"-slaves do not eat [heave-offering, if the master is a priest], just as she does not [eat heave-offering any longer]. The iron-flock slaves do eat [heave-offering] because they are in the possession of the [husband's] heirs until they are returned to her. [If] he left her children, these and those [types of slaves] continue to eat [heave-offering]. [If] he left her pregnant, these and those [types of slaves] do not eat. [If] he left her with children and left her pregnant, the "iron-flock"-slaves eat [heave-offering] just as she eats heave-offering. But the iron-flock slaves do not eat heave-offering, on account of the share of the foetus in them [M. Yeb. 7:3B].

T. 9:2 A priestly girl who married an Israelite, and brought to him [in her dowry] "iron-flock"-slaves and iron-flock-slaves — he died and left her as she was [childless] — the "iron-flock"-slaves do [not] eat heave-offering, just as she does [not] eat heave-offering. The iron-flock-slaves do not eat heave-offering, because they are in the presumptive possession of the heirs until they are returned to her. A priest who was a deaf-mute, an idiot, or a minor who purchased slaves — they do not eat heave-offering. But [if] a court acted in their behalf, or [if] a court appointed guardians for their estates, or [even if] the slaves came to them in an inheritance from some other source [than the priestly father], lo, these slaves do eat heave-offering. A priest who bought a slave, and an Israelite who owns even one hundredth of him — [the slave] does not eat heave-offering. The wife of a priest who bought slaves, or her slaves who bought slaves — lo, these eat heave-offering. The slave of a priest who ran away, and the wife of a priest who rebelled against him — [even if they do not know whether or not the priest is still alive] lo, these eat heave-offering. The man guilty of manslaughter should not go outside of the borders of the city of his refuge, in the assumption that the high priest still is alive.

M. 7:4 The foetus, the Levir, betrothal, a deaf-mute, a boy nine years and one day old invalidate [a woman from eating food in the status of priestly rations] but do not validate [her to do so]. [That is the case even if] it is a matter of doubt whether or not the boy is nine years and one day old, [or if] it is a matter of doubt whether or not he has produced two pubic hairs. [if] a house collapsed on him and on the daughter of his brother [his wife] and it is not known which of them died first, her co-wife performs removing the shoe and does not enter into Levirate marriage.

T. 9:3 The foetus, the Levir, betrothal, a deaf-mute, a boy nine years and one day old invalidate a woman from eating heave-offering but do not validate her to do so [M. Yeb 7:4A-B]. [If] his daughter of sound senses is married to his brother who was a deaf-mute, her co-wife is exempt from removing the shoe and from Levirate marriage, on the strength of an argument a fortiori: Now if the marriage of her daughter is valid, the marriage of her co-wife should be valid. If the marriage of her daughter is not valid, then the marriage of her co-wife should not be valid. [If] his daughter who was a deaf-mute was married to his brother who was of sound senses, her co-wife should perform a rite of removing the shoe but not enter into Levirate marriage. A deaf-mute whose father married her off, lo, she is deemed equivalent to a woman of sound senses for all purposes.

M. 7:5 The rapist and the seducer and the idiot do not invalidate [women with whom they have sexual relations] from eating food in the status of priestly rations and do not validate [them for eating food in the status of priestly rations]. But if they are not suitable to enter [into the congregation of] Israel (Dt. 22:2-4), lo, they do invalidate her from eating food in the status of priestly rations. How so [A-B]? An Israelite who had sexual relations with a priest's daughter — she [continues to] eat food in the status of priestly rations. [If] she turned out to be pregnant, she does not eat food in the status of priestly rations. [If] the foetus was removed from her womb, she eats food in the status of priestly rations. A priest who had sexual relations with an Israelite girl — she does not eat food in the status of priestly rations. [If] she turned out to be pregnant, she [still] does not eat food in the status of priestly rations [M. 7:3C]. If she gave birth [to a viable offspring], she does eat food in the status of priestly rations. It turns out that the power of the child is greater than that of the father [since the child validates or invalidates the mother for eating food in the status of priestly rations, which his father could not accomplish]. A slave invalidates by reason of having sexual relations but not by reason of offspring. How so? An Israelite girl married to a priest, or a priestly girl married to an Israelite, and she gave birth to a son with him, and the son went and trifled with a slave girl, and she produced a son from him — lo, this boy is a slave. [If] the mother of his [the slave's] father was an Israelite girl married to a priest, [if the father and son die] she does not eat food in the status of priestly rations [by reason of the grandson]. [If] she was a priest's daughter married to an Israelite, [despite the grandson] she does eat food in the status of priestly rations. A Mamzer invalidates and validates for eating. How so? An Israelite girl married to a priest, a priestly girl married to an Israelite — and she produced a daughter with him, and the daughter went and married a slave or a gentile and produced a son from him — lo, this son is a Mamzer [If] the mother of his mother was an Israelite girl married to a priest, [because of the Mamzer grandson, the grandmother] eats food in the status of priestly rations. [If she was] the daughter of a priest married to an Israelite, [because of the grandson, the grandmother] should not eat food in the status of priestly rations.

M. 7:6 A high priest — sometimes he invalidates [a woman from eating food in the status of priestly rations]. How so?

> A priestly girl married to an Israelite, and she produced a daughter by him, and the daughter went and married a priest and produced a son by him — lo, this [son] is worthy to be high priest standing and serving at the altar, and he validates his mother for eating food in the status of priestly rations, and [if his mother died] he invalidates his mother's mother. This lady then says, "[Let there] not [be many] like my [grand]son, the high priest, who [because he is yet alive] invalidates me from eating food in the status of priestly rations."

Scripture requires a high priest to marry a virgin, excluding a widow, and an ordinary priest may not marry a divorcée. If the women in question were themselves daughters of priests, thus formerly accorded the right to eat priestly rations, through the marriage they lose that right, hence, M. 6:43: from the time of betrothal they are not to eat heave-offering. The act of sexual relations with the priest they were forbidden to marry leaves them invalid, but if no sexual relations had taken place, they revert to their former status — the whole then amplifying what has just gone before. But the topical composition before us has its own integrity, and knowing how it has been inserted does not tell us how it has been assembled or chosen for the larger composite of which it forms a sizable component. That question is one of the hermeneutics of the category-formation, Yebamot, not a problem of a redactional character. The Halakhah, overall, as represented by the Mishnah (and by the Tosefta) represents a series of logical choices of data that serve to illustrate a given proposition, answer a set of questions deemed urgent; as we have it, in the documents the hermeneutics of which occupy us, issues of redactional connection or exegetical stimulus are distinctly subordinate. The exposition of the principle of M. 6:3 draws us back to matters of Levirate marriage at M. 6:4. The Tosefta's contribution is to apply the rule to the Levites. M. 6:5-6 underscore that the purpose of marriage is procreation, and retrojects that rule back upon the priest's marriage too. M. 7:1ff. introduces the disposition of the property, e.g., the dowry, of a woman illegally married to a high priest or an ordinary priest; the consumption of priestly rations by the property (e.g., slaves) of such a woman, and the like. M. 7:4 then moves on to the interstitial classes of males and their affect upon the right of a priestly-caste woman to eat priestly rations. M. 7:5 qualifies matters: in the present context, the act of coitus is not determinative; other considerations enter in. But if pregnancy results, then the picture changes.

B. *OTHER CONSIDERATIONS INVOLVED IN CONSU-MING PRIESTLY RATIONS. UNCLEANNESS*

M. 8:1 The uncircumcised [priest] and all unclean [priests] do not eat food in the status of priestly rations [Lev. 22:4-6]. Their wives and slaves do eat food in the status of priestly rations. One with crushed testicles or whose penis is cut off (Dt. 23:2) — they and their slaves do eat food in the status of priestly rations. Their wives do not eat food in the status of priestly rations. And if he did not have intercourse with her from the time that his testicles were crushed or his penis was cut off, lo, these [women] do eat food in the status of priestly rations.

T. 9:4 An Israelite girl of sound senses who was married to a priest who was a deaf-mute does not eat heave-offering. [If] she became pregnant, she does not eat heave-offering. An Israelite girl who was a deaf-mute who was married to a priest of sound senses does not eat heave-offering. [If] she became pregnant, she does not eat heave-offering. [If] she gave birth [to a sound foetus], she then does eat heave-offering. A priestly girl of sound senses who married an Israelite idiot immerses out of the embrace of her husband and then eats heave-offering in the evening [when the purification is complete]. [If] she became pregnant, she no longer eats heave-offering. [If] she gave birth, she does not eat heave-offering. Anyone who has seed of a priest, whether male or female, even seed of his seed, lo, such a woman eats heave-offering. [If] her daughter from an Israelite was married to a priest, she [the daughter] does not eat heave-offering, until she has seed from a priest first.

T. 10:1 An Israelite girl of sound senses who was betrothed to a priest of sound senses, but he did not suffice to marry her before he was made a deaf-mute — she does not eat heave-offering. [If] he died and left her before his Levir, even though he [the Levir] was a deaf-mute, she eats heave-offering. Greater is the power of the Levir to permit her to eat heave-offering than the power of the husband to do so. An Israelite girl of sound senses who was betrothed to a priest of sound senses, but he did not suffice to marry her before she was made a deaf-mute — she does not eat heave-offering. [If] he died and left her before his Levir, even though he [the Levir] was a deaf-mute, she eats heave-offering. Greater is the power of the Levir to permit her to eat heave-offering than the power of the husband to do so. An Israelite girl of sound senses who was married to a priest who was a deaf-mute does not eat heave-offering. [If] he died and left her before a Levir, [if] he was of sound senses, she eats heave-offering. [If] he was a deaf-mute, she does not eat heave-offering. She does not eat heave-offering until she enters the marriage-canopy for the sake of consummation of the marriage and has sexual intercourse with her husband for the sake of the marital relation. An Israelite girl who was a deaf-mute who was married to a priest of sound senses does not eat heave-offering. [If] he died and left her before a Levir, even though he [the Levir] is of sound senses, she does not eat heave-offering.

T. 10:2 An Israelite girl of sound senses who was betrothed to a priest of sound senses, and who entered the marriage canopy for the sake of marriage, but he [the husband] did not suffice to have sexual relations with her before his testicles were crushed or his penis was cut off [M. Yeb. 8:1] — lo, this one eats heave-offering, since she had entered the category of one permitted to do so, even for a single moment [M. Yeb. 8:4E-G]. [If] she was still betrothed when his testicles became crushed or his penis was cut off, lo, this one does not eat heave-offering. A widow betrothed to a high priest, a divorcee or a woman who had performed the rite of removing the shoe with an ordinary priest, who entered the marriage-canopy for the purpose of marriage, and [the priestly husband] did not have time to complete the act of sexual relations before he died, is valid for marriage into the priesthood and valid for eating heave-offering. [If] he actually had sexual relations with her, he has rendered her invalid for marriage into the priesthood and invalid for eating heave-offering. A [priest] does not exhibit defined sexual traits does not eat heave-offering. His wife and slaves do eat it. One who has his prepuce drawn forward and one who is born circumcised — lo, these eat heave-offering. A [priest] who bears the sexual traits of both sexes eats heave-offering but not Holy Things [M. Yeb. 8:6B]. A [priest] who does not exhibit defined sexual traits does not eat heave-offering [=J] or Holy Things.

M. 8:2 Who is he who has crushed testicles? Any one whose testicles are crushed, and even one of them. And one whose penis is cut off? Any whose sexual organ is cut off. But if so much as a hair thread of the crown remained, he is valid [to eat food in the status of priestly rations]. Those whose testicles are crushed or whose penis is cut off are permitted to have sexual relations with a female convert and a freed slave girl. They are prohibited only from coming into the congregation, since it is written, "He whose testicles are crushed and whose penis is cut off shall not enter the congregation of the Lord" (Dt. 23:2).

T. 10:3 Who is he who has crushed testicles? Any one whose testicles are crushed [M. Yeb. 8:2-B] — which are punctured or perforated, or one of which is lacking.

T. 10:4 Who is one whose penis is cut of J? Any one whose sexual organ is cut off from the crown and below. But if so much as a hair-thread of the crown remained [M. Yeb. 8:2C-E] — near the head and going around the top, he is valid. [If] it is perforated at the bottom, he is invalid, because it [the semen] pours out. [If] the hole is closed up, he is valid, because he can impregnate. This is one who is invalid and who once more returns to his state of validity.

> T. 10:6 Who is a eunuch by nature? Any male who survived for twenty years without producing two pubic hairs. Even if he produced two pubic hairs thereafter, lo, he is deemed a eunuch for all purposes. What are the indications thereof? Any who has no beard and whose skin is smooth [and not hairy].
>
> T. 10:7 Who is a sterile woman? Any female who survived for twenty years without producing two pubic hairs. Even if she produced two pubic hairs thereafter, lo, she is deemed sterile for all purposes. What are the indications thereof? Any who has no breasts, and whose hair is abnormal, and who finds sexual relations painful.

The cultic condition of the priest — uncleanness, unfitness by reason of uncircumcision — does not affect his wives' and slaves' status as to priestly rations, which they may consume. But his physical condition, e.g., if he lacks viable sexual organs, does affect his wives' right to do so, but not that of his property. T. 9:4ff. contains its own amplification of the basic rule of M. 8:1. T. 10:3-4, 6, serve as glosses of M. 8:2, which itself amplifies the foregoing.

C. *PROHIBITED MARRIAGES*

M. 8:3 The male Ammonite and Moabite are prohibited [from entering the congregation of the Lord (Dt. 23:4)], and the prohibition concerning them is forever. But their women are permitted forthwith. The Egyptian and the Edomite are prohibited only for three generations, all the same being males and females. Mamzerim [children of marriages penalized by extirpation, who can never marry valid Israelites] and Netinim [=descendants of the Gibeonites who deceived Joshua (Josh. 9:3ff), assigned the task of cutting wood and carrying water for the congregation and the altar] are prohibited, and the prohibition concerning them is forever, all the same being males and females.

M. 8:5 A eunuch does not perform the rite of removing the shoe and does not enter into Levirate marriage. And so: a sterile woman does not perform the rite of removing the shoe and is not taken in Levirate marriage. The eunuch who performed the rite of removing the shoe with his deceased childless brother's widow has not rendered her invalid [for marriage into the priesthood]. [If] he had sexual relations with her, he has rendered her invalid [for marriage into the priesthood], for it is an act of sexual relations of the character of fornication. And so: a sterile woman with whom the brothers have performed the rite of removing the shoe — they have not rendered her invalid [for marriage into the priesthood]. [If] they had sexual relations with her, they have rendered her invalid [for marriage into the priesthood], for it is an act of sexual relations of the character of fornication.

M. 8:6 A priest who was a eunuch by nature who married an Israelite girl, confers on her the right to eat food in the status of priestly rations. A person bearing traits of both sexes marries but is not taken in marriage.

T. 11:1 A person lacking clearly defined sexual traits who effected an act of betrothal — his act of betrothal is valid. [If] he was betrothed, his act of being betrothed is valid. He performs the rite of removing the shoe and they perform the rite of removing the shoe with his wife. If there are brothers available, however, he does not perform the rite of removing the shoe or enter into Levirate marriage. But in any event they enter into Levirate marriage with his wife.

T. 11:2 A eunuch by nature, a person exhibiting the traits of both sexes, a brother born of the same mother, a proselyte, and a freed slave do not perform the rite of removing the shoe and do not enter into Levirate marriage. How so? [If any of these] died and left wives and had surviving brothers [and if] the surviving brothers went and bespoke the wife, gave her a writ of divorce, or performed a rite of removing the shoe, they have done nothing whatsoever. [If] they have had sexual relations with her, they have invalidated her [from marrying into the priesthood] and are liable for a sacrifice. [If] the brothers [of any of these] died and left childless widows, and they had brothers and [if] the surviving brothers went and bespoke the wife, gave her a writ of divorce and performed a rite of removing the shoe they have done nothing whatsoever. And if they had sexual relations, they have rendered her invalid [for marrying into the priesthood], and they are liable for a sacrifice. A man with crushed testicles or whose penis is cut off or a eunuch by act of man and an old man either perform the rite of removing the shoe or enter into Levirate marriage. How so? [If they died and left wives and had surviving brothers, [and if] the surviving brothers came and bespoke the widow, gave her a writ of divorce or performed the rite of removing the shoe, what they have done is valid. [If] they had sexual relations with the widow, they have acquired her and freed her co-wives [from the obligation of Levirate connection]. [If] the brothers died and left wives, and they had surviving brothers, [and if] they came and bespoke the widow, gave her a writ of divorce, or performed the rite of removing the shoe, what they have done is valid. And if they had sexual relations with the widow, they have acquired her and exempted the co-wives [from the obligation of Levirate connection]. But they are prohibited to confirm the marriage [if the woman may come into the congregation], since it is said, one with crushed testicles or a cut off penis shall not enter into the congregation of the Lord (Deut. 23:2).

Y. 8:6 II:2 *If a person exhibiting traits of both sexes [androgyne] should betroth a woman, they do not scruple as to his act of betrothal. If he is taken in betrothal, they do scruple about his* *being betrothed. If he had sexual relations [with an invalid person] as a woman, he has been invalidated from eating heave-offering as are women [A person bearing sexual, traits of both sexes who had sexual relations with another such person and was invalidated from eating heave-offering] bestows the right to eat heave-offering upon his wives, but does not bestow that right upon his slaves. [He bestows the right to eat heave-offering upon his wives,] on the strength of the part of him that is male. He does not bestow that right upon his slaves on the strength of this one and that one. [A female] priest who has had sexual relations with a person with whom he cannot legally do so and so been profaned from the priesthood may not feed food in the status of heave-offering to her slaves.] [For] the aspect of him that is female has been profaned.*

M. 9:1 There are women permitted to their husbands and prohibited to their Levirs, permitted to their Levirs and prohibited to their husbands, permitted to these and to those, and prohibited to these and to those. These are women permitted to their husbands and prohibited to their Levirs: (1) An ordinary priest who married a widow, and who has a brother who is high priest; (2) a man of impaired priestly stock who married a valid woman, and who has a brother who is valid [as a priest]; (3) an Israelite who married an Israelite girl and who has a brother who is a Mamzer; (4) a Mamzer who married a female Mamzer, and who has a brother who is a valid Israelite — [These] are permitted to their husbands and prohibited to their Levirs.

M. 9:2 And these are permitted to their Levirs and prohibited to their husbands: (1) A high priest who betrothed a widow, and who has a brother who is an ordinary priest; (2) a valid [priest] who married a woman of impaired priestly stock and who has a brother of impaired priestly stock; (3) an Israelite who married a female Mamzer and who has a brother who is a Mamzer [offspring of a union subject to the penalty of extirpation, unable ever legitimately to marry a valid Israelite]; (4) a Mamzer who married an Israelite girl and who has a brother who is a valid Israelite — they are permitted to their Levirs and prohibited to their husbands. Prohibited to these and to those: (1) A high priest married to a widow [who thus is impaired], who has a brother who is a high priest or [who is] an ordinary priest; (2) a valid [priest] who married a woman of impaired priestly stock, and who has a brother who is a valid priest; (3) an Israelite who married a female Mamzer, and who has a brother who is an Israelite; (4) a Mamzer who married an Israelite girl, and who has a brother who is a Mamzer — these are prohibited to these and to those. And all other women are permitted to their husbands and to their Levirs.

M. 9:3 In what concerns the secondary remove [of forbidden degrees (M. 2:4)] by reason of scribal rulings: a woman within a secondary remove of kinship to the husband and not in a secondary remove of kinship to the Levir is prohibited to her husband and permitted to her Levir. [If] she is in a secondary remove of kinship to the Levir and not in a secondary remove of kinship to the husband, she is prohibited to the Levir and permitted to the husband. [If] she is in a secondary remove of kinship to this one and to that one, she is prohibited to this one and to that one. She has no rights to a marriage contract, or to the usufruct [of her "plucking"-property], or to alimony, or to worn clothes [indemnity, for clothes which have completely worn out] [e.g., for loss on "plucking"-property]. But an offspring of such a marriage is valid [for the priesthood]. And they force him to put her away. In the case of a widow wed to a high priest, a divorcee or a woman who has performed the rite of removing the shoe to an ordinary priest, a female Mamzer or a female Netin [=descendant of the Gibeonites who deceived Joshua (Josh. 9:3ff), assigned the task of cutting wood and carrying water for the congregation and the altar] to an Israelite, or an Israelite girl to a Netin or a Mamzer, she has a right to her marriage-settlement.

M. 9:4 An Israelite girl betrothed to a priest, pregnant by a priest, awaiting Levirate marriage with a priest, and so too: a priestly girl married to an Israelite — does not eat food in the status of priestly rations [see M. 7:4]. An Israelite girl betrothed to a Levite, pregnant by a Levite, awaiting Levirate marriage with a Levite, and so too: a Levite girl married to an Israelite — do not eat tithe. A Levite girl betrothed to a priest, pregnant by a priest, awaiting Levirate marriage with a priest, and so too, a priestly girl married to a Levite, eat neither food in the status of priestly rations nor tithe.

M. 9:5 An Israelite girl who married a priest eats food in the status of priestly rations. [If] he died and she had a child from him, she eats food in the status of priestly rations. [If] she married a Levite, she eats tithe. [If] he died and she had a child from him, she eats tithe. [If] she married an Israelite, she eats neither food in the status of priestly rations nor tithe. [If] he died, and she had a child from him, she eats neither food in the status of priestly rations nor tithe. [If] her son by an Israelite died, she eats tithe. [If] her son by a Levite died, she eats food in the status of priestly rations. [If] her son by a priest died, she eats neither food in the status of priestly rations nor tithe.

M. 9:6 A priest's daughter who married an Israelite does not eat food in the status of priestly rations. [If] he died and she had a child from him, she does not eat food in the status of priestly rations. [If] she married a Levite, she eats tithe. [If] he died and she had a child from him, she eats tithe. [If] she married a priest, she eats food in the status of priestly rations. [If] he died and she had a child from him, she eats food in the status of priestly rations. [If] her child from the priest died, she does not eat food in the status of priestly rations, [If] her child from the Levite died, she does not eat tithe. [If] her child from the Israelite died, she goes back to her father's house. Concerning such a one is it said, "And she shall return to her father's house, as in her girlhood. The food of her father she will eat" (Lev. 22:13).

We turn from marriages prohibited to the priesthood to other classes of invalid marriages by reason of caste-status, now to Scripture's prohibitions of marriage to Ammonites and Moabites, Egyptians and Edomites, on the part of Israelite women, and unions of Mamzerim and Netinim with Israelites of either sex; and the eunuch. Another class, already familiar, involves marriages encouraged by reason of the Levirate connection but forbidden by reason of considerations of caste status, as specified at M. 9:1-3. The exegetical program then is a familiar one, with its focus on the utilization of priestly rations.

    D.   *CONSEQUENCES OF VIOLATING THE PROHIBITIONS AGAINST MARRIAGE*

M. 10:1 The woman whose husband went overseas, and whom they came and told, "Your husband has died," and who remarried, and whose husband afterward returned, (1) goes forth from this one [the second husband] and from that one [the first] — And (2) she requires a writ of divorce from this one and from that. And she has no claim of (3) [payment of her] marriage contract, (4) of usufruct, (5) of alimony, or (6) of indemnification, either on this one or on that. (7) If she had collected anything from this one or from that, she must return it. (8) And the offspring is deemed a Mamzer, whether born of the one marriage or the other. And (9) neither one of them [if he is a priest] becomes unclean for her [if she should die and require burial]. And neither one of them has the right either (10) to what she finds or (11) to the fruit of her labor, or (12) to annul her vows. [If] (13) she was an Israelite girl, she is rendered invalid for marriage into the priesthood; a Levite, from eating tithe; and a priest girl, from eating heave-offering. And the heirs of either one of the husbands do not inherit her marriage settlement. And if they died, a brother of this one and a brother of that perform the rite of removing the shoe but do not enter into Levirate marriage. But if she should remarry without permission, [since the remarriage was an inadvertent transgression and null], she is permitted to return to him.

M. 10:2 [If] she was remarried at the instruction of a court, she is to go forth, but she is exempt from the requirement of bringing an offering. [If] she did not remarry at the instruction of a court, she goes forth, and she is liable to the requirement of bringing an offering. The authority of the court is strong enough to exempt her from the requirement of bringing a sacrifice. [If] the court instructed her to remarry, and she went and entered an unsuitable union, she is liable for the requirement of bringing an offering. For the court permitted her only to marry [properly].

T. 11:4 A woman whose husband went overseas, and whom they came and told, "Your husband has died," and whom the court instructed to remarry — and who went and remarried [M. Yeb. 10:2G-I] as a widow to a high priest or a divorcee or one who has performed the rite of removing the shoe to an ordinary priest, is liable for a sacrifice

M. 10:3 The woman whose husband and son went overseas, and whom they came and told, "Your husband died, and then your son died," and who remarried, and whom they afterward told, "Matters were reversed" goes forth [from the second marriage]. And earlier and later offspring are in the status of a Mamzer. [If] they told her, "Your son died and afterward your husband died," and she entered into Levirate marriage, and afterward they told her, "Matters were reversed," she goes forth [from the Levirate marriage]. And the earlier and later offspring are in the status of a Mamzer. [If] they told her, "Your husband died," and she married, and afterward they told her, "He was alive, but then he died," she goes forth [from the second marriage]. And the earlier offspring [born prior to the actual death of the husband] is a Mamzer, but the later is not a Mamzer. [If] they told her, "Your husband died," and she became betrothed, and afterward her husband came home, she is permitted to return to him. Even though the second man gave her a writ of divorce, he has not rendered her invalid from marrying into the priesthood.

T. 11:6 The status of Mamzer is not applicable to the offspring of a Levirate marriage [which is invalid]. If they said lo her, "Your husband has died," and she remarried, and afterward they said to her, "Your husband was alive, but then he died" [M. Yeb. 10:3J] lo, this one goes forth with a writ of divorce. And all the offspring which she produced while her husband was yet alive, lo, they are Mamzers. Those produced after the death of her husband are valid [M. Yeb. 10:3L]. If they said to her, "Your husband has died," and she was betrothed [better: entered into Levirate marriage], and afterwards they said to her, "He was alive, but he has died," lo, this one puts her away with a writ of divorce and a rite of removing the shoe. All the offspring which she produced while her husband was yet alive are Mamzers. Those which she produced after the death of her husband are valid. If they said to her, "Your Levirate brother-in-law has died," and she went and got married, and afterward they told her, "He was alive, but he now has died" — since she was not appropriate for remarriage but for Levirate marriage — lo, this one goes forth with a writ of divorce. The status of Mamzer is not applicable to the offspring of a Levirate marriage.

M. 10:4 He whose wife went overseas, and whom they came and told, "Your wife has died," and who married her sister, and whose wife thereafter came back — she is permitted to come back to him. He is permitted to marry the kinswomen of the second, and the second woman is permitted to marry his kinsmen. And if the first died, he is permitted to marry the second woman. [If] they said to him, "Your wife has died," and he married her sister, and afterward they said to him, "She was alive, but then she died" — the former offspring is a Mamzer [born before the wife died], and the latter [born after she died] is not a Mamzer.

T. 11:7 He whose wife went overseas, and whom they came and told, "Your wife has died," and [who] married her sister, and whom they afterward told, "She was then alive, but now she has died," lo, this one remains wed to the sister. And the former offspring is a Mamzer, but the latter offspring is not a Mamzer. [If] they told him, "Your wife has died," and he married her sister, and she went overseas, and they told him, "Your wife has died," and he married her sister, and she went overseas, and they told him, "Your wife has died," and he married her sister, and she went overseas, and lo, all of them are coming along — the first is his wife, and she exempts her co-wives. And all of the rest of them are not his wives. And if he has sexual relations with the second for the purposes of marital coition after the death of the first, the second is his wife, [and] exempts her co-wife, and all the rest of them are not his wives.

M. 10:5 (1) [If] they said to him, "Your wife has died," (2) and he married her sister by the same father, (3) [and they reported that] she died and he married her sister from the same mother, (4) [and they reported that] she died and he married her sister from the same father, (5) [and they reported that] she died, and he married her sister from the same mother — and it turns out that all of them are alive — he is permitted [to continue in marriage] with the first, the third, and the fifth, and they exempt their co-wives. But he is prohibited [to continue in marriage] with the second and the fourth, and sexual relations [of the Levir] with one of them does not exempt her co-wife. And if he had

intercourse with the second after the [actual] death of the first, he is permitted [to remain married to] the second and the fourth, and they exempt their co-wives. And he is prohibited [to remain married to] the third and the fifth. And sexual relations with one of them does not exempt her co-wife.

T. 11:5 A woman who went overseas with her husband, and who came and reported, "My husband has died," [and] remarried on her own testimony, and again she went overseas and came and said, "My husband has died," [and] she remarried on her own testimony, and again went overseas and came and said, "My husband has died," and remarried on her own testimony, and lo, all of them in fact are coming back — she goes forth from all of them. But she is permitted to remain married to the first [M. Yeb. 10:5]. The act of sexual relations or of removing the shoe on the part of the brother of the first exempts her co-wives. Those of [the brother of the] second and third do not exempt her co-wives. If the second had sexual relations with her for the purpose of marriage after the death of the first, the act of sexual relations or of removing the shoe on the part of the brother of second exempts her co-wives. Those of the third and the fourth do not exempt her co-wives.

When a marriage takes place that the law prohibits as specified, consequences follow of a most severe order for both property and offspring. We differentiate between deliberate and inadvertent action, so M. 10:1ff. The woman has a very heavy stake in ascertaining the facts of the matter and bears responsibility for her own deliberate actions. She is not merely a victim of circumstances. But in reality, to protect herself she ought to have actually seen the dead body of her husband. Faced with the choice of acknowledging her difficult situation and according to her full responsibility for her own condition, the Halakhah has taken the second way. To accord her responsibility, the Halakhah also imposes upon her heavy penalties indeed for the consequences of her deed. Within that principle, the cases at hand — all of them violations of prohibitions against marriage of one kind or another — make sense. If the woman remarries on false information, the marriage is null, the children Mamzerim, etc. If a court advised her, then in one aspect the penalties are reduced: the offering is not required. On the one side, the woman thus is given the right to exercise free will; on the other, she bears weighty responsibilities in exercising that right.

V. MARRIAGES THAT ARE SUBJECT TO DOUBT BY REASON OF THE STATUS OF THE PARTIES THERETO

A. *THE MARITAL BOND OF A BOY NINE YEARS AND ONE DAY OLD*

M. 10:6 A boy nine years and one day old invalidates [his deceased childless brother's widow] for the other brothers, and the other brothers invalidate her for him, But [while] he invalidates her at the outset, the brothers invalidate her at the outset and at the end. How so? A boy nine years and one day old who had sexual relations with his deceased childless brother's widow has invalidated her for the [other] brothers. [If one of] the brothers had sexual relations with her, bespoke her, gave her a writ of divorce, or performed the rite of removing the shoe with her, they have invalidated her for him.

T. 11:9 A deaf-mute with whom the rite of removing the shoe, was performed, a deaf-mute who performed the rite of removing the shoe, she who performs the rite of removing the shoe with an idiot, so too: an idiot-girl who performed the rite of removing the shoe, and she who performed the rite of removing the shoe with a minor goes forth. The status of Mamzer is not applicable to the offspring of Levirate marriage.

T. 11:10 A boy nine years and one day old who had sexual relations with his deceased childless brother's widow and then died — she performs the rite of removing the shoe but does not enter into Levirate marriage, for the act of sexual relations by a boy nine years and one day old is equivalent to the act of bespeaking of an adult. A boy nine years and one day old spoils [the deceased childless brother's widow for the other brothers in one way, and the brothers spoil her for him [M. Yeb. 10:6A — C] in four ways: He spoils her for the brothers through an act of sexual relations. But they spoil her for him through an act of sexual relations, a writ of divorce, an act of bespeaking, and a rite of removing the shoe [all of which, done by them, is valid] [M. Yeb. 10:6G-I]. And just as he does not invalidate her for the brothers by means of an act of bespeaking, a writ of divorce, and removing the shoe, so brothers [nine years old] do not spoil her for one another through a writ of divorce, an act of bespeaking, or a rite of removing the shoe. How so? Two brothers nine years and one day old — this one went and bespoke her, and that one went and bespoke her — this one went and gave her a writ of divorce, and that one went and gave her a writ of divorce — this one went and performed the rite of removing the shoe, and that one went and performed the rite of removing the shoe — he has done nothing whatsoever. [If] she this one went and had sexual relations with her, and that one went and had sexual relations with her, she is invalid for marriage with either one of them [M. Yeb. I 0:7A — C].

M. 10:7 A boy nine years and one day old who had sexual relations with his deceased childless brother's widow, and afterward his brother, who was nine years and one day old, had sexual relations with her, he [the latter] has invalidated her for marriage with him [the former].

Y. 10:7 I:1 How is it so that he does not invalidate her at the end [M. 10:7D]? Invalidates her only at the outset alone] if he has bespoken the woman. But if it is after he has had sexual relations with her, he invalidates her even at the end but [the main point is that] he may invalidate her for the brothers in only one way, while they may invalidate her for him in four different ways. [That is, at the outset or the end he may invalidate the sister-in-law for marriage with the other brothers in only one way, that is, with sexual relations, but not by giving a writ of divorce, a rite of removing the shoe, or bespeaking. These he may do only at the outset, but not at the end, after the brothers have done something else with the sister-in-law].

M. 10:8 A boy nine years and one day old who had sexual relations with his deceased childless brother's widow, and afterward he had sexual relations with her co-wife, has invalidated her for himself. A boy nine years and one day old who had sexual relations with his deceased childless brother's widow and then died — she performs the rite of removing the shoe but does not enter into Levirate marriage [with a Levir]. [If] he married a woman and died, lo, this one is exempt [from the Levirate connection entirely].

M. 10:9 A boy nine years and one day old who had sexual relations with his deceased childless brother's widow, and when he grew up, married another wife, and then died — if he did not have sexual relations with the first from the time that he reached maturity, the first performs the rite of removing the shoe but does not enter into Levirate marriage. And the second either performs the rite of removing the shoe or enters into Levirate marriage All the same is a boy nine years and one day old and one who is twenty years old but has not produced two pubic hairs.

T. 11:11 A boy nine years and one day old who had sexual relations with his deceased childless brother's widow and went and had sexual relations with her co-wife spoils her for himself. Under what circumstances? In the case of an act of sexual relations of a boy nine years and one day old. But a deaf-mute, an idiot, and a minor who have had sexual relations have effected an act of acquisition. And they have freed the co-wives [from the obligation of Levirate marriage]. An idiot or a minor who married wives and who died — their wives are exempt from the requirement of performing the rite of removing the shoe. This is the general principle: Any act of sexual relations [performed by them] which requires articulated consciousness is not a valid act of sexual relations. But any which does not require articulated consciousness — lo, this is a valid act of sexual relations.

We turn from invalid marriages to marriages that are subject to doubt, as noted, by reason of the interstitial status of the parties involved. A boy nine years and one day old is not yet a man but no longer a child. His act of sexual relations has taxonomic consequences, if not physical ones. He cannot consummate a marriage, but he also does not leave the woman unaffected. That yields the situations covered at M. 10:6ff./T. 11:9ff.

    B.   *SPECIAL CASES: THE RAPIST, THE CONVERT*
M. 11:1 They marry the kinswomen of a woman whom one has raped or seduced. He who rapes or seduces the kinswoman of his wife, however, is liable. A man marries the woman raped by his father or seduced by his father, raped by his son or seduced by his son.
    M. 11:2 The convert whose sons converted with her — they [the sons] neither perform the rite of removing the shoe nor enter into Levirate marriage, even if the conception of the first was not in a state of sanctity and the birth was in a state of sanctity, and the second was conceived and born in a state of sanctity. And so is the law in the case of a slave girl whose sons converted with her.
    T. 12:2 The convert whose sons converted with her — they neither perform the rite of removing the shoe nor enter into Levirate marriage [M. Yeb. 11:2A]. [If] their conception was not in a state of sanctity and their birth was not in a state of sanctity, they neither perform the rite of removing the shoe nor enter into Levirate marriage. And they are not liable [to observe the prohibition against marrying] the wife of one's brother. [If] her conception was not in a state of sanctity but her giving birth was in a state of sanctity, then they neither perform the rite of removing the shoe nor enter into Levirate marriage. But they are liable on account of [the prohibition against marrying] the wife of one's brother. [If] her conceiving and giving birth were in a state of sanctity, lo, she is equivalent to an Israelite for all purposes.

The physical act of sexual relations on the part of a rapist or seducer does not affect the status of the woman. He may marry her kin, as though he never had sexual relations with her. The convert has no family ties, fore or aft. Hence her sons are not brothers in the sense of the Torah's law of Levirate marriage. Here, physical genealogy is null.

C. *THE CONFUSION OF OFFSPRING*

M. 11:3 Five women [each of whom already has a son and then produced another], whose [other] offspring became confused with one another — they grew up in this state of confusion — and married wives and died — four [of the surviving brothers, whose mothers are known] perform the rite of removing the shoe with one widow, and one of them [the fifth] enters Levirate marriage with her. He and three [of the brothers] enter into the rite of removing the shoe with another, and one [other] enters into Levirate marriage with her [and so on]. It turns out that there are four rites of removing the shoe and one Levirate marriage for each of the surviving widows.

T. 12:3 Five women whose offspring were confused with one another [M. Yeb. 11:3A] — some of them are brothers, and some of them are not brothers — those who are brothers perform the rite of removing the shoe, and those who are not brothers enter into Levirate marriage. Some of them are priests and some of them are not priests — the priests perform the rite of removing the shoe and those who are not priests enter into Levirate marriage. Some of them are brothers and some of them are priests — they perform the rite of removing the shoe and do not enter into Levirate marriage. [If] there is a doubt whether a woman is his mother or his daughter or his sister — they perform the rite of removing the shoe and do not enter into Levirate marriage. This is the general rule: In all cases of doubt having to do with the deceased childless brother's widow, they perform the rite of removing the shoe and do not enter into Levirate marriage.

T. 12:4 What is the sort of case in which a man performs the rite of removing the shoe with his mother by reason of doubt? His mother and another woman have two males — they went and had two male sons in hiding [and the offspring are confused by reason of lack of access to light] — the first two went and married the mother of one another — and they died without offspring — this one performs the rite of removing the shoe with both of the widows, and that one performs the rite of removing the shoe with both of them. It turns out that this one performs the rite of removing the shoe with his mother by reason of doubt. What is the sort of case in which a man performs the rite of removing the shoe with his sister by reason of doubt? His mother and another woman — and they have two male offspring — they went and produced two female offspring in hiding — and they [K] married two brothers from the same father but not from the same mother — and they [the brothers] died without offspring — this one performs the rite of removing the shoe with both of them, and that one performs the rite of removing the shoe with both of them. It turns out that a man performs the rite of removing the shoe with his sister by reason of doubt.

T. 12:5 A. What is the sort of case in which a man performs the rite of removing the shoe with his daughter by reason of doubt? His wife and another woman produced two female offspring in hiding — and the two were married to two brothers from the same father [delete: but a different mother] — and they died without offspring — he performs the rite of removing the shoe with both of them. It turns out that this man performs the rite of removing the shoe with his daughter by reason of doubt.

M. 11:4 The woman whose offspring was confused with the offspring of her daughter-in-law — they grew up in a state of confusion, and married wives and died — the sons of the daughter-in-law perform the rite of removing the shoe and do not enter into Levirate marriage, for it is a matter of doubt concerning whether it is the wife of his brother or the wife of the brother of his father. And the sons of the old lady either perform the rite of removing the shoe or enter into Levirate marriage, for it is a matter of doubt concerning whether it is the wife of his brother or the wife of the son of his brother. [If] the valid ones died, the sons who were confused perform the rite of removing the shoe and do not enter into Levirate marriage with the [widows of the childless] sons of the old lady, for it is a matter of doubt concerning whether it is the wife of his brother or his father. And the sons of the daughter-in-law — one of them performs the rite of removing the shoe and one enters into Levirate marriage [with the widow, etc.] .

M. 11:5 A priest girl whose offspring was confused with the offspring of her slave girl — (1) lo, these [men] eat heave-offering. (2) And they [take and] divide a single share at the threshing floor. (3) And they do not contract uncleanness by contact with corpses [of those whom priests are obligated to bury]. (4) And they do not marry wives, whether valid or invalid [for marriage into the priesthood]. [If] the confused children grew up and freed one another, (4) they marry wives suitable for marriage into the priesthood. (3) And they do not become unclean by contact with corpses. And if they become unclean, they do not incur forty stripes, (1) And they do not eat heave-offering. And if they ate it, they do not pay back principal and an added fifth. (2) And they do not take a portion at the threshing floor. But they sell heave-offering. And the proceeds are theirs. And they do not take a share in the Holy Things of the sanctuary. And they do not give them Holy Things, but they do not take [their Holy Things] back from them. And they are free from the obligation to give the shoulder, cheeks, and maw [to a priest]. And their firstling [animal] should be put out to pasture until it suffers a blemish. And they apply to them the strict rules of the priesthood and the strict rules pertaining to ordinary Israelites.

T. 12:6 A. A priest-girl whose offspring was confused with the offspring of her slave-girl [M. Yeb. 11:5A] — they do not eat that which is heaved out of Most Holy Things [for the use of the priesthood], for slaves of priests do not eat from it. But they eat from that which is heaved out of Lesser Holy Things. for slaves of priests eat it. Both of them go out to the threshing floor and take a single portion [M. 11:5C]. For they do not give [heave-offering] to a slave unless his master is with him. If the confused sons grew up and freed one another [M. Yeb. 11:5G], they do not eat of that which is heaved out of Lesser Holy Things. For non-priests do not eat it.

M. 11:6 She who did not delay three months after her husband [divorced her or died] and remarried [M. 4:10] and gave birth, and it is not known whether the offspring is nine months old, belonging to the former husband, or seven months old, belonging to the latter, [if] she had sons by the first and sons by the second — they perform the rite of removing the shoe [with his widow] and do not enter into Levirate marriage. And so, too, he [the son of B] performs the rite of removing the shoe but does not enter into Levirate marriage in relationship to them [children of the two marriages]. [If] he had brothers by the first marriage and brothers by the second, but not from the same mother — he performs the rite of removing the shoe or enters into Levirate marriage. But as to them, one of them [from one marriage] performs the rite of removing the shoe, and one of them [the other marriage] enters into Levirate marriage.

T. 12:7 She who did not delay three months after her husband [divorced her or died] and remarried and gave birth [M. Yeb. 11:6A] — and it is not known [whether the offspring is of the first husband or the second] — if it falls within the range of probability of the first husband [if the woman gave birth seven months after the death of the first husband and the pregnancy was recognized a month after the remarriage, it is in the range of probability of the first husband], lo, it is the son of the first husband. [If] it falls within the range of probability of the second husband [if the woman gave birth nine months after the death of the first husband and was not known to be pregnant four months after his death], lo, it is the son of the second husband. If it is a matter of doubt whether it is nine months old, belonging to the first, or seven months, belonging to the second [M. Yeb. 11:6B], [if] the son hit this [man] and then went and hit that one, [or] cursed this one and then went and cursed that one — he is exempt from punishment. [But] if he hit both of them simultaneously [or] cursed both of them simultaneously, he is liable to punishment. [If] she had children from the first husband and children from the second, they perform the rite of removing the shoe and do not enter into Levirate marriage. And so he too performs the rite of removing the shoe for them, but does not enter into the Levirate marriage [M. Yeb. 11:6C — E]. If he had brothers from the first marriage and brothers from the second, not from the same mother, he performs the rite of removing the shoe with them or enters into Levirate marriage, and they for him: these perform the rite of removing the shoe and those enter into Levirate marriage [M . Yeb. 11:6F-H].

M. 11:7 [If] one of them [the husbands of M. 11:6A-B] was an Israelite and one a priest, he [of M. 11:6B] marries a woman appropriate for marriage into the priesthood. He does not become unclean by contact with corpses. And if he was made unclean, he does not incur forty stripes. And he does not eat heave-offering, If he ate it, he does not pay back the principal and added fifth. And he does not take a share at the threshing floor. But he sells [his own] heave-offering, and the proceeds are his. He does not take a share in the Holy Things of the sanctuary. And they do not give him Holy Things. But they do not remove his [Holy Things] from his own possession. And he is exempt from the requirement to give the priest the shoulder, cheeks, and maw. And a firstling belonging to him should be put out to pasture until it is blemished. And they apply to him the strict rules applicable to the priesthood and the strict rules applicable to Israelites. If both of them [A] were priests, he performs the rites of mourning for them, and they perform the rites of mourning for him. He does not become unclean for them, and they do not become unclean for him. He does not inherit them, but they do inherit him. And he is exempt for the transgression of smiting or cursing this one or that one [M. 11:6A-B, 11:7A, O]. And he goes up to the Temple for the priestly watch of this one and of that one. But he does not take a share in the priestly dues of either watch. If both of them belonged to a single priestly watch, then he does take a single portion [in the share of that watch].

T. 12:8 A woman concerning whom a bad name goes around — the offspring are valid, for children are in the presumptive paternity of [her] husband.

Another source of impediments to marriage involves unclarity as to genealogy. If we do not know for certain who is related to whom, we take account of the possibility of a Levirate connection, but we do not allow for Levirate marriage.

VI.   THE RITE OF REMOVING THE SHOE

M. 12:1 The proper way to carry out the rite of removing the shoe is before three judges, and even though the three of them are laymen [it is valid]. [If the woman] performed the rite of removing the shoe with a slipper, her performance of removing the shoe is valid. [If she did it] with a felt sock, her performance of removing the shoe is invalid. [If she did it] with a sandal which has a heel, it is valid. [If she did it] with a sandal which does not have a heel, it is invalid. [If the straps of the sandal were fastened] below the knee, her performance of removing the shoe is valid. [If the straps of the sandal were fastened] above the knee, it is invalid.

T. 12:9 The proper way to carry out the rite of removing the shoe is before three judges [M. Yeb. 12:1A] — and this is on condition that they know how to pronounce [Scriptures read in the rite].

T. 12:10 If she performed removing the shoe with a sandal which was damaged but held the larger part of the foot, with a slipper which was torn but which covered the larger part of the foot, with a sandal of cork, with a sandal of bast, with one of felt, and with the artificial leg of a cripple, and with a support for the feet, or with a leather sock — and she who performs the rite of removing the shoe with a sandal which is too big — whether he is standing or sitting or lying — and she who performs the rite of removing the shoe with a blind man — her performance of removing the shoe is valid. [If she does so] with a sandal which is damaged and does not hold the larger part of the foot, with a slipper which was torn and does not cover the larger part of the foot, with a hand-support, with a sock of cloth, and she who performs the rite of removing the shoe with a shoe which is too small — her performance of removing the shoe is invalid.

T. 12:12 A. A minor who performed the rite of removing the shoe should perform the rite of removing the shoe again when she grows up. If she did not perform the rite of removing the shoe, her performance of the rite of removing the shoe is valid.

T. 12:9 The proper way to carry out the rite of removing the shoe is before three judges [M. Yeb. 12:1A] — and this is on condition that they know how to pronounce [Scriptures read in the rite].

M. 12:2 [If] (1) she performed the rite of removing the shoe with a sandal which does not belong to him, or (2) with a sandal made of wood, or (3) with the sandal for the left foot on the right foot, her performance of removing the shoe is valid. [If] (1) she performed the rite of removing the shoe with a sandal too large in which [nonetheless] he is able to walk about, or (2) with one too small which [nonetheless] covers the larger part of his foot, her performance of removing the shoe is valid. [If] she performed the rite of removing the shoe by night, her performance of removing the shoe is valid. [If she did it] with the left [shoe], her performance of the rite of removing the shoe is invalid.

M. 12:3 [If] she removed the shoe and spit but did not pronounce the prescribed words, her performance of removing the shoe is valid. [If] she pronounced the prescribed words and spit but did not remove the shoe, her performance of removing the shoe is invalid. [If] she removed the shoe and pronounced the prescribed words but did not spit, the rite is valid.

T. 12:10 If she performed removing the shoe with a sandal which was damaged but held the larger part of the foot, with a slipper which was torn but which covered the larger part of the foot, with a sandal of cork, with a sandal of bast, with one of felt, and with the artificial leg of a cripple, and with a support for the feet, or with a leather sock — and she who performs the rite of removing the shoe with a sandal which is too big — whether he is standing or sitting or lying — and she who performs the rite of removing the shoe with a blind man — her performance of removing the shoe is valid. [If she does so] with a sandal which is damaged and does not hold the larger part of the foot, with a slipper which was torn and does not cover the larger part of the foot, with a hand-support, with a sock of cloth, and she who performs the rite of removing the shoe with a shoe which is too small — her performance of removing the shoe is invalid, he rite of removing the shoe is valid. [If] the straps of the slipper or of the sandal came out, or [if] the greater part of the foot came out, her performance of removing the shoe is invalid. If he wanted to revert [and marry her as his Levirate wife], he does not revert. [If] she removed the foot but did not spit and did not pronounce the required formula, her performance of removing the shoe is valid [M. Yeb. 12:3]. If he wanted to revert, he reverts. [If] she spit but did not pronounce the required formula and did no t remove the shoe, her performance of removing the shoe is invalid. [If] she pronounced the required formula but did not spit and did not remove the shoe, she has done nothing whatsoever. And he may retract.

T. 12:13 A rite of removing the shoe done under a false assumption is valid. [If] one performed the rite of removing the shoe with a woman — he with proper intention, and she not with proper intention, she with proper intention, and he not with proper intention, her rite of performance of removing the shoe is invalid. A rite of removing the shoe imposed by an Israelite court is valid. One imposed by a gentile court is invalid. Among gentiles they bind him and instruct him, "Do precisely what Rabbi so-and-so tells you to do!"

M. 12:4 **A deaf-mute boy with whom the rite of removing the shoe was carried out, a deaf-mute girl who performed the rite of removing the shoe, she who performs the rite of removing the shoe with a minor — her performance of removing the shoe is invalid. A minor girl who performed the rite of removing the shoe should perform the rite of removing the shoe again when she grows up. If she did not perform the rite of removing the shoe [later on], her performance of removing the shoe is invalid.**

M. 12:5 [If] she performed the rite of removing the shoe before two judges, or before three, one of whom turned out to be a relative or otherwise invalid, her performance of removing the shoe is invalid. A case: A certain man performed removing the shoe with his deceased childless brother's widow by themselves in prison. And when the case came before R. Aqiba, he validated the rite [without any valid witnesses present].

M. 12:6 The proper way to carry out the rite of removing the shoe [is as follows]: He and his deceased childless brother's widow come to court. And they offer him such advice as is appropriate for him, since it says, "Then the elders of the city shall call him and speak to him" (Deut. 25:8). "And she shall say, 'My husband's brother refuses to raise up for his brother a name in Israel. He will not perform the duty of a husband's brother to me'" (Deut. 25:7). "And he says, 'I do not want to take her'" (Deut. 25:7). And [all of this] was said in the Holy Language [of Hebrew]. "Then his brother's wife comes to him in the presence of the elders and removes his shoe from his foot and spits in his face" (Deut. 25:9) — spit which is visible to the judges. "And she answers and says, 'So shall it be done to the man who does not build up his brother's house.'" Thus far did they pronounce [the words of Scripture].

T. 12:14 They perform the rite of removing the shoe with a woman, even though they do not know her. They execute the right of refusal with a woman, even though they do not know her. A woman who claimed, "I have performed the rite of removing the shoe," brings evidence of her claim. [If she claimed,] "I have exercised the right of refusal," she brings evidence of her claim.

T.12:15 A. At first they wrote out a writ of removing the shoe: She came before us and removed his shoe from his right foot and she spit before us spit which was visible, and she said, Thus will be done, etc. (Deut. 25:9). It is a duty for the judges and not a duty for the disciples [M. Yeb. I 2:6L-M].

We proceed to two principal media for severing the marital bond, the rite of removing the shoe and the right of refusal. Both deal with anomalous situations. Some marital bonds to begin with are not firmly established; these may fall away of their own weight. But what do the rite of removing the shoe and the right of refusal bear in common? In both instances — and these form the center of the second half of the exposition — a flaw in the process of forming and confirming intentionality has taken over. The rite of removing the shoe is performed when the surviving brother refuses to confirm the deceased's intentionality to create life with this woman in particular. The right of refusal comes into play when the (now-)woman declares the bond null, as though it had never been; she was consecrated without a confirming act of intentionality, and the bond is dissolved without the husband's confirming act of intentionality. The cases involving the deaf-mute, male and female, which follow, underscore the issue: has a confirming act of intentionality taken place to effect the sanctification? The rules of conducting the rite of removing the shoe provide a systematic exegesis of the law, but contain no implications for larger questions such as have attracted our attention to this point.

VII. EXERCISING THE RIGHT OF REFUSAL. THE MINOR AND LEVIRATE MARRIAGE

A. THE RITE OF REFUSAL

M. 13:1 Those who are betrothed and those who are married exercise the right of refusal. [The right of refusal is exercised] against the husband, and against the Levir. It must be exercised in his presence. and not in his presence. in a court and not in a court.

T. 13:1 Aforetimes they would write writs of refusal: .She is not suitable for him or fond of him, nor does she wish to be married to him. In a court and not in a court — but on condition that there should be three [suitable witnesses]. How is the duty of refusal appropriately carried out? She testified, "I do not care for So-and-so, my husband. I reject the betrothal effected for me by my mother or my brothers." Even if she is sitting in a palanquin and went to the one who betrothed her to him, and said to him, "I do not care for this man, so-and-so, my husband" — there is no statement of refusal more powerful than that [statement].

M. 13:2 Who is the sort of girl who must exercise the right of refusal? Any girl whose mother or brothers have married her off with her knowledge and consent. [If] they married her off without her knowledge and consent, she does not have to exercise the right of refusal [but simply leaves the man].

T. 13:2 A minor who effected a betrothal in her own behalf, or who married herself off, while her father was yet alive — her betrothal is null, and her act of marriage is null [M. Yeb. 13:2A].

M. 13:3 Any hindrance [in the marriage] which derives from the man — it is as if she is his wife. And any hindrance [in the marriage] which does not derive from the man — it is as if she is not his wife.

M. 13:4 She who exercises the right of refusal against a man — he is permitted to marry her kinswomen, and she is permitted to marry his kinsmen. And he has not invalidated her for marriage into the priesthood. [If] he gave her a writ of divorce, he is prohibited from marrying her kinswomen, and she is prohibited from marrying his kinsmen. And he has invalidated her for marriage into the priesthood. [If] he (1) gave her a writ of divorce and (2) then took her back, [if] then she (3) exercised the right of refusal against him and (4) married someone else, and (5) was widowed or divorced — she is permitted to go back to him. [If] she (3) exercised the right of refusal and (2) he took her back, [if] he [then] (1) gave her a writ of divorce and she (4) married someone else and (5) was widowed or divorced, she is prohibited from going back to him. This is the general rule: In a case of a writ of divorce following the exercise of the right of refusal, she is prohibited from returning to him. In a case of exercise of the right of refusal after a writ of divorce, she is permitted to go back to him.

T. 13:3 A. She who exercises the right of refusal against a man does not collect a marriage-contract. [If] he gave her a writ of divorce, she has the right to collect a marriage-contract.

T. 13:5 A. She who exercises the right of refusal against a man who took her back and who died either performs the rite of removing the shoe or enters into Levirate marriage. [If] he divorced her and then took her back to him and died, she either performs the rite of removing the shoe or enters into Levirate marriage. This is the general principle: In the case of a writ of divorce following the exercise of the right of refusal she is prohibited from returning to him [M. Yeb. 13:4M]. In a case of the exercise of the right of refusal after a writ of divorce, she is permitted to go back to him [M. Yeb. 13:4N].

M. 13:5 She who exercises the right of refusal against a man [1] and was remarried to another, who divorced her [2] — [and who went and was assigned to yet] a third man, and she exercised the right of refusal against him, [and who went and was assigned to yet] a fourth, who divorced her, [and who went and was assigned to yet] a fifth, and she exercised the right of refusal against him — any of the men from whom she went forth with a writ of divorce [A2, C] — she is prohibited from going back to him. [And any of the men from whom she went forth] by exercising the right of refusal [A1, B, D] — she is permitted to go back to him.

If a man has entered into not only a betrothal but a consummated marriage with a girl under puberty, when she reaches puberty, she may simply up and walk out of the marriage. She requires no writ of divorce. She may do so even after coitus. She may walk out and declare the relationship null even in the husband's absence and even outside a rabbinical court. The upshot is simple. As soon as she reaches puberty, the girl may nullify the marriage. And, more to the point, the halakhah rules that it is as if she never had been married, so Mishnah-tractate Yebamot 13:4. All of these provisions yield a single result: this girl (not yet a woman) has never, ever been married to that man. And under what circumstances do we want such a rite to be carried out? It is when the girl has agreed to begin with to enter the marriage, M. Yebamot 13:2. She is no different from a girl who married herself off without her father's intervention, so Tosefta Yebamot 13:2. These and comparable provisions effectively nullify child-marriage on the part of the mother and brothers (but not the father) in ordinary circumstances, and that for a simple reason. They treat any such relationship, prior to puberty, as null: the girl can walk out on the "husband" and reject the "marriage" without any legal consequence whatever, and indeed, with only the most routine action: she has to tell three witnesses she's had it, so Tosefta Yebamot 13:1. Now where does the husband find himself? Whatever property transactions have taken place are null. If (not being a pedophile) he had in mind a union of family and heritage, he is disappointed. Through the entire span of time from the betrothal or marriage until the girl reaches puberty, the husband cannot enjoy the security of a long-term relationship. The upshot is, sages have set up conditions that nullify such a transaction between the mother and brothers and the groom. They have defined the outcome in such parlous terms that no rational man is going to want to take the risks built into the relationship. And in that way, the rabbis have done what they could do to abolish a relationship Scripture has ordained. True, the halakhah before us is clear that, if the father has married off the girl, the girl enjoys no right of refusal, since they explicitly assign that right only to the girl married off by those who bear responsibility but no authority. So the rabbis could not and did not legislate in such a way as to contradict the clear requirement of Scripture.

B. *THE MINOR AND LEVIRATE MARRIAGE*

M. 13:6 He who divorces his wife and took her back — [if he dies childless], she is permitted to a Levir. And so: He who divorces an orphan [not married off by her father, so whose marriage is not firm] and took her back — she is permitted to the Levir. A minor whose father married her off and who was divorced is deemed an orphan while her father is yet alive. [If] he took her back, the opinion of all parties is that she is prohibited to the Levir.

M. 13:7 Two brothers married to two sisters [who are] minor orphans, and the husband of one of them died [childless] — she [the widow] goes forth [without Levirate rites] on the count of being the sister of [his] wife. And so two deaf-mutes. An adult and a minor — the husband of the minor died [childless] — the minor goes forth on grounds of being the sister of his wife. [If] the husband of the adult died [childless].

T. 13:6 Two brothers married to two [sisters who were] orphans, one a minor and the other a deaf-mute — the husband of the minor dies — the deaf-mute goes forth through a writ of divorce. And the minor waits until she grows up, and then she performs the rite of removing the shoe. [If] the husband of the deaf-mute dies, the minor goes forth through a writ of divorce. And the deaf-mute is prohibited [from entering into Levirate marriage]. But if he [the Levir in any case] had sexual relations with her, she goes forth with a writ of divorce and is permitted [to remarry].

M. 13:8 He who was married to two minor orphans and who died — the act of sexual relations or the performance of the rite of removing the shoe on the part of one of them exempts her co-wife [from the Levirate connection altogether]. And so two deaf-mutes. [He who was married to] a minor and a deaf-mute — the act of sexual relations on the part of one of them does not exempt her co-wife. A woman of sound senses and a deaf-mute — the act of sexual relations of the woman of sound senses exempts the deaf-mute. But the act of the sexual relations of the deaf-mute does not exempt the woman of sound senses. An adult and a minor — the act of sexual relations of the adult exempts the minor. But the act of sexual relations of the minor does not exempt the adult.

M. 13:9 He who was married to two [unrelated] minor orphans and who died — the Levir came and had sexual relations with the first, and then he came and had sexual relations with the second — or another brother came and had sexual relations with the second — he has not invalidated the first [from marriage with him]. And so in the case of two deaf-mutes. A minor and a deaf-mute — the Levir came and had sexual relations with the minor, and then he came and had sexual relations with the deaf-mute — or another brother came and had sexual relations with the minor — he has not invalidated the minor. [If] the Levir came and had sexual relations with the deaf-mute, and then went and had sexual relations with the minor, or another brother came and had sexual relations with the minor — he has invalidated the deaf-mute.

M. 13:10 A woman of sound senses and a deaf-mute — the Levir came and had sexual relations with the woman of sound senses, then went and had sexual relations with the deaf-mute — or another brother came and had sexual relations with the deaf-mute — he has not invalidated the woman of sound senses. [If] the Levir came and had sexual relations with the deaf-mute, and then went and had sexual relations with the woman of sound senses, or another brother came and had sexual relations with the deaf-mute — he has invalidated the deaf-mute.

Y. 13:12 I:1 Even if he did not have sexual relations with the woman of sound senses, he invalidates the deaf-mute [for marriage with the Levir]. [The connection of the woman of sound senses to the Levir invalidates the deaf-mute. Since she was fully within the domain of the deceased, her connection to the Levir invalidates the deaf-mute, whose relation to the deceased was not so strong.] If the Levir did not have sexual relations with the woman of sound senses, and she had died, he would have been permitted to enter into Levirate marriage with the deaf-mute. Now that he has had sexual relations with her, if she then died, she invalidates the deaf-mute [from marrying the Levir]. [The Levir has the right to one of the widows, but not to both of them. The act of sexual relations sufficed to complete the transaction. The deaf-mute is not available to him.]

M. 13:11 An adult and a minor — the Levir came and had sexual relations with the adult, and then went and had sexual relations with the minor — or another brother came and had sexual relations with the minor — he has not invalidated the adult. [If] the Levir came and had sexual relations with the minor, and then came and had sexual relations with the adult — or another brother came and had sexual relations with the adult — he has invalidated the minor.

Y. 13:13 I:1 Even if he did not have sexual relations with the adult, he invalidates the deaf-mute [for marriage with him]. But if the Levir did not have sexual relations with the adult and she died, he would have been permitted to enter into Levirate marriage with- the minor. Now that he has had sexual relations with [the adult], if she then died, he invalidates the minor [from marrying him. The Levirate responsibility has now been carried out].

M. 13:12 A minor Levir who had sexual relations with a minor widow [of a deceased, childless brother] — they should grow up with one another. [If a minor Levir] had sexual relations with an adult widow, she should raise him. The deceased childless brother's widow who claimed within thirty days, "I have not yet had sexual relations [with my Levir]" — they force the Levir to perform the rite of removing the shoe with her. [If she so claimed] after the thirty days, they request from him that he perform the rite of removing the shoe for her. So long as he admits [her claim] even after twelve months, they force him to perform the rite of removing the shoe for her.

T. 13:7 He who was married to two minor orphans and who died — [If] the Levir went and had sexual relations with the first, and then he went and had sexual relations with the second — both of them are prohibited to him. And so is the rule with two deaf-mutes [M. Yeb. 13:9A-E]. A minor and a deaf-mute — [If] the Levir went and had sexual relations with the minor, then he went and had sexual relations with the deaf-mute — or one of the brothers had sexual relations with the deaf-mute — both of them are prohibited for him [M. 13:9F-I]. The deaf-mute goes forth with a writ of divorce and the minor goes forth with a writ of divorce and with the rite of removing the shoe.

She waits until she grows up and then she performs the required rite of removing the shoe. A woman of sound senses and a deaf-mute — the Levir went and had sexual relations with the woman of sound senses, then he went and had sexual relations with the deaf-mute — or one of his brothers went and had sexual relations with the deaf-mute — both of them are prohibited to him [M. Yeb. 13:10A-D]. The deaf-mute goes forth with a writ of divorce, and the woman of sound senses with a writ of divorce and a rite of removing the shoe. An adult and a minor — [If] the Levir went and had sexual relations with the adult, then he went and had sexual relations with the minor — or one of his brothers went and had sexual relations with the minor — both of them are prohibited to him [M. Yeb. 13:11A-D]. The minor goes forth with a writ of divorce, and the adult goes forth with a writ of divorce and the rite of removing the shoe. A deceased childless brother's widow who claimed within thirty days of Levirate marriage, "I have not yet had sexual relations with my Levir" [M Yeb. 13: 12D] — whether the Levir claimed, "I did have sexual relations with her," or whether he said, "I did not have sexual relations with her," they force him to perform the rite of removing the shoe for her [M. Yeb. 13:12E]. [If she so claimed] after thirty days [of the Levirate marriage had passed], they request him to perform the rite of removing the shoe for her [M. Yeb. 13: 12F-G]. [If] she claims, "I have had sexual relations," and he claims, "I did not have sexual relations with her," lo, this one goes forth with a writ of divorce. [If] he claims, "I had sexual relations with her," and she claims, "I did not have sexual relations with him," even though he retracts and claims, "I did not have sexual relations with her," lo, this one goes forth with a writ of divorce. R. Judah says, "[If] she vowed not to enter into Levirate marriage [with her husband's brother, should her husband die without children], even if this is in the lifetime of her husband [who then dies] — "they request [the Levir, after the brothers has died childless] to perform the rite of removing the shoe with her" [M . Yeb. 13:13E-F]. How does he put her away with a sign-language? He makes a sign and then gives to her her writ of divorce. A woman of sound senses married to a man of sound senses, who has a brother of sound senses — a woman of sound senses married to a deaf-mute, who has a brother of sound senses — he either performs the rite of removing the shoe or enters into Levirate marriage. A woman of sound senses married to a man of sound senses who has a brother who is a deaf-mute — he marries her and does not put her away for all time. A woman of sound senses married to a deaf-mute, who has a brother who is a deaf-mute, a deaf-mute woman married to a man of sound senses who has a brother of sound senses — a deaf-mute woman married to a man of sound senses who has a brother of sound senses — a deaf-mute woman married to a deaf-mute man who has a brother of sound senses — a deaf-mute woman married to a deaf-mute man who has a deaf-mute brother — [in all these cases] he marries the woman. And if he wants, he may put her away. If he wants to confirm the marriage, he confirms the marriage.

M. 13:13 She who vows against deriving benefit from her Levir — [if she does so] while her husband is yet alive, they force him [the Levir, after the husband dies without offspring] to perform the rite of removing the shoe with her. [If she so vows] after her husband's death, they request from him that he perform the rite of removing the shoe for her. And if that was her very intention, even [if she took the vow] while her husband was yet alive, they request him to perform the rite of removing the shoe for her.

The issue turns to another aspect of the marriage of a minor: changes in her status. The established rules sort out the ambiguities of the cases at hand.

VIII. THE MARRIAGE OF THE DEAF-MUTE AND THE PERSON OF SOUND SENSES

M. 14:1 A deaf-mute who married a woman of sound senses — or a man of sound senses who married a deaf-mute — if he wanted, he puts her away. And if he wanted, he confirms the marriage. Just as he marries her by means of sign language, so he puts her away by means of sign language. A man of sound senses who married a woman of sound senses, and the woman became a deaf-mute — if he wanted, he puts her away. And if he wanted, he confirms the marriage. [If] she became an idiot, he may not put her away. [If] he was made a deaf-mute or became an idiot, he may never put her away.

M. 14:3 Two deaf-mute brothers married to two deaf-mute sisters — or two sisters of sound senses — or two sisters, one a deaf-mute and the other of sound senses — or two deaf-mute sisters married to two brothers of sound senses — or to two deaf-mute brothers — or to two brothers, one a deaf-mute and one of sound senses — lo, these women are exempt from the rite of removing the shoe and Levirate marriage. But if they were unrelated to one another, they enter into marriage. And if they [the men in the several cases] wanted to put them away, they do put them away [M. 14:1E].

T. 13:8 A. Two brothers who were deaf-mutes married to two sisters of sound senses [M. Yeb. 14:3B] — or to two sisters who were deaf-mutes [M. Yeb. 14:3A] — or two sisters, one of sound senses and one a deaf-mute, and so: two sisters who were deaf-mutes married to two brothers of sound senses — or two brothers who were deaf-mutes, or two brothers, one of sound senses and one a deaf-mute

[M. Yeb. I 4:3C-F] — and so: two brothers, one of sound senses and one a deaf-mute, married to two sisters, one a deaf-mute and one of sound senses — a deaf-mute married to a man of sound senses and a woman of sound senses married to a deaf-mute — neither the rite of removing the shoe nor Levirate marriage applies here [M. Yeb. 14:3G]. But the [Levir's] wife remains with him. And the other goes forth as the sister of his wife. But if the women were unrelated to one another, he takes them in marriage. If he wanted to put her away, he puts her away [M. Yeb. 14:3H-J]. And if he wanted to confirm the marriage, he confirms the marriage.

M. 14:4 Two brothers — one deaf-mute and the other of sound senses [M. 14:3F] — married to two sisters of sound senses — the deaf-mute, husband of a sister of sound senses, died — what should the husband of sound senses who is married to the deaf-mute do? She [the deceased childless brother's widow] should go forth on the grounds of being the sister of his wife. [If] the husband of sound senses of a sister of sound senses died, what should the deaf-mute who is husband of the sister of sound senses do? He should put away his wife with a writ of divorce, and the wife of his brother is prohibited [for marriage to anybody at all] for all time. Two brothers of sound senses married to two sisters, one of them a deaf-mute and one of them of sound senses [M. 14:3C] — the husband of sound senses married to the deaf-mute died — what should the husband of sound senses married to the wife of sound senses do? She [the widow] should go forth on grounds of being the sister of his wife. If the husband of sound senses married to the wife of sound senses should die, what should the husband of sound senses married to the deaf-mute do? He puts away his wife with a writ of divorce, and the wife of his brother with a rite of removing the shoe. Two brothers, one of them a deaf-mute and one of sound senses [M. 14:3F], married to two sisters, one of them a deaf-mute and one of sound senses [M. 14:3C] — [If] the deaf-mute husband married to the deaf-mute wife should die, what should the husband of sound senses married to the sister of sound senses do? She [the widow] should go forth because of being the sister of his wife. [If] the husband of sound senses married to the wife of sound senses should die, what should the deaf-mute husband married to the deaf-mute sister do? He puts away his wife with a writ of divorce, and the wife of his brother is prohibited [to remarry] for all time. Two brothers, one a deaf-mute and one of sound senses [M. 14:3F], married to two women, not related to one another, of sound senses [M. 14:3H] — [if] the deaf-mute husband of the woman of sound senses should die, what should the husband of sound senses married to the woman of sound senses do? He either performs the rite of removing the shoe or takes the widow in Levirate marriage. If the husband of sound senses of the woman of sound senses should die, what should the deaf-mute husband of the woman of sound senses do? He marries [the widow] and does not put her away for all time. Two brothers of sound senses married to two women unrelated to one another, one of sound senses and one a deaf-mute [M. 14:3C+H] — [If] the husband of sound senses married to the deaf-mute dies, what should the husband of sound senses married to the woman of sound senses do? He should marry her, and if he wants to put her away, he puts her away. [If] the husband of sound senses married to the woman of sound senses should die, what should the husband of sound senses married to the deaf-mute woman do? He either performs the rite of removing the shoe or enters into Levirate marriage. Two brothers, one a deaf-mute and one of sound senses [M. 14:3F], married to two women unrelated to one another, one a deaf-mute and one of sound senses [M. 14:3C + H] — [if] the deaf-mute married to the deaf-mute woman should die, what should the husband of sound senses married to the woman of sound senses do? He should marry the widow, but if he wants to put her away, he puts her away. If the husband of sound senses married to the woman of sound senses should die, what should the deaf-mute man married to the deaf-mute woman do? He marries her and does not put her away for all time.

B. 14:4 I:1/112A A DEAF MAN OR AN IDIOT WHO MARRIED WOMEN OF SOUND SENSES, EVEN THOUGH THE DEAF MAN RECOVERED HIS HEARING OR THE IDIOT HIS SENSES — THE WIVES HAVE NO CLAIM WHATSOEVER ON THEM. IF THEY WANTED TO KEEP THE MARRIAGE GOING, HOWEVER, THE WIVES ARE ENTITLED TO A MARRIAGE SETTLEMENT OF A MANEH [A HUNDRED ZUZ]. A MAN OF SOUND SENSES WHO MARRIED A DEAF WOMAN OR AN IDIOT WOMAN, EVEN THOUGH HE WROTE FOR HER A MARRIAGE SETTLEMENT OF A HUNDRED MANEHS, HER MARRIAGE SETTLEMENT IS CONCERNED, SINCE HE WAS PREPARED TO ACCEPT THE DAMAGE TO HIS ESTATE [OF SUCH A HUGE SUM].

When the deaf-mute, otherwise fully in command of his senses, cannot unambiguously exercise an act of intentionality, that yields his or her interstitial status: mature in body, diminished in status. If he can use sign language, he functions like anyone else. But there are some restrictions, as are spelled out at M. 14:3ff.

IX. ASCERTAINING WHETHER THE HUSBAND HAS ACTUALLY DIED

A. WHEN THE HUSBAND IS MISSING

M. 15:1 The woman who went, she and her husband, overseas — there was peace between her and him, and the world was at peace — and she came and said, "My husband died" — she may remarry. "My husband died" — she may enter into Levirate marriage. [If] there was peace between her and him but war in the world — strife between him and her, but the world was at peace — and she came and said, "My husband died" — she is not believed.

M. 15:2 All the same are one who comes home from the grain harvest, and the one who comes home from harvesting olives, and one who comes from cutting grapes, and one who comes home from one province to another — sages spoke about the grain harvest only because that is commonplace.

We come to the final unit of this treatise on Heaven's intervention into the marital bond through death: cases where we do not know or cannot show that the husband has died. The problem is not required by the hermeneutics of the topic; the unit represents an appendix. How these are worked out is simple: evidence of any kind is acceptable to free the wife from the marriage-bond in the case of confirming the husband's death. Within some predictable limitations, persons ordinarily not able to give testimony in an Israelite court are allowed to do so in the extreme case at hand.

B. TESTIMONY THAT THE HUSBAND HAS DIED

M. 15:3 She [who testifies that her husband has died] remarries and collects her marriage contract [in the case of M. 15:1A-F].

B. 15:3 I.1/117A IF SHE ENTERS INTO LEVIRATE MARRIAGE, HER LEVIR TAKES OVER THE INHERITANCE [COMING TO HIM IN HIS LATE BROTHER'S ESTATE] ON THE STRENGTH OF HER TESTIMONY. FOR IF RABBIS HAVE INTERPRETED THE LANGUAGE OF THE MARRIAGE CONTRACT, SHOULD WE NOT INTERPRET THE LANGUAGE OF THE TORAH: "...SHALL SUCCEED IN THE NAME OF HIS BROTHER' (DEUT. 25:6) — AND HE HAS CERTAINLY SUCCEEDED."

M. 15:4 All are believed to testify in her behalf [that her husband has died], except for (1) her mother-in-law, (2) the daughter of her mother-in-law, (3) her co-wife, (4) her sister-in-law [who will enter Levirate marriage in case the husband has died childless], and (5) the daughter of her husband [by another marriage]. What is the difference between evidence for [severing a marital relationship] through a writ of divorce and [evidence for doing so] through death? The written document [of divorce] proves the matter. [If] one witness says, "He died," and she remarried, and then another witness comes and says, "He did not die," lo, this woman does not go forth [from the second marriage]. [If] one witness says, "He died," and two witnesses say, "He did not die," then even though she has remarried, she goes forth. Two witnesses say, "He died," and one witness says, "He did not die," even though she has not remarried, she may remarry.

T. 14:1 The woman who said, "My husband has divorced me," [or] "My Levir has performed the rite of removing the shoe with me," [or] "My Levir has entered into Levirate marriage with me and then died" — lo, this woman is not believed. All those who are not believed to testify concerning a woman [M. Yeb. 15:4A] — she too is not believed to testify concerning them. [If] one witness says, "He has died," and one witness says, "He has not died," a woman says, "He has died," and a woman says, "He has not died," lo, this one should not remarry [M. Yeb. 15:5E-G]. Two women [who contradict] one woman are like two male witnesses [who contradict] a single male witness. If two witnesses say, "He has died," and a hundred say, "He has not died," lo, the hundred are deemed equivalent [merely] to the two witnesses.

T. 14:3 The woman whose husband went overseas — and whom they came and told, "Your husband died," and he had a brother, who entered into Levirate marriage with her, and [the Levir] died — and afterward her husband returned home — he [the husband] is prohibited from marrying her [M. Yeb. 10:1] but permitted to marry her co-wife, he is prohibited from marrying her, but permitted to marry the wife of his brother [=E]. The woman who went — she and her husband — overseas, and who came home and said, "My husband died, "and the elder [the husband's father] was here in the country, and he too has died" — lo, this one is not believed [to force her mother-in-law into Levirate marriage with her late father-in-law's brother, M. Yeb. 15:4A]. The woman who went — she and her husband — overseas, and came and said, "My husband has died" — she is permitted [to remarry] but her co-wife is prohibited [from remarrying] [M. Yeb. 15:4A, 15:6]. If they entered into Levirate marriage and the Levirs died, they are prohibited from remarrying. Two women — this one has witnesses [to the effect that her husband has died] and children, and that one has no witnesses and no children [M. Yeb. 16:2E-H] — both of them are permitted [to remarry].

M. 15:5 [If] one woman [co-wife] says, "He died," and one [co-wife] says, "He did not die," this one who says, "He died," may remarry and collect her marriage contract, and that one who says, "He did not die," may not remarry and may not collect her marriage contract. [If] one witness says, "He has died," and one witness says, "He has not died," [or] a woman says, "He has died," and a woman says, "He has not died" — lo, this woman may not remarry.

M. 15:6 A woman who went, she and her husband, overseas, and came and said, "My husband has died," remarries and collects her marriage contract [M. 15:3]. But her co-wife is prohibited [from remarrying, for a woman is not believed concerning the death of her husband so as to free her co-wife from the marital tie, as at M. 15:4].

M. 15:7 [If] she said, "My husband died and afterward my father-in-law died," she may remarry and collect her marriage contract. But her mother-in-law is prohibited [from doing so]. [If] a man betrothed one of five girls and it is not known which one of them he betrothed, [and] each one of them says, "Me did he betroth" — he gives a writ of divorce to each one of them.

M. 15:8 The woman who went, she and her husband, overseas, and her son was with them — and she came and said, "My husband died, and afterward my son died" is believed. [If she said], "My son died, and afterward my husband died," she is not believed. But they scruple on account of her testimony, so that she performs the rite of removing the shoe, but she does not enter into Levirate marriage.

M. 15:9 "A son was given unto me overseas," and, she said, "My son died, and then my husband died," she is believed. "My husband died and afterward my son died" — she is not believed. But they scruple on account of her testimony, so that she performs the rite of removing the shoe, but she does not enter into Levirate marriage.

M. 15:10 "A Levirate brother-in-law was given unto me overseas," and, she said, "My husband died, and afterward my Levirate brother-in-law died" — "My Levirate brother-in-law died and afterward my husband died" — she is believed. [If] she went, she and her husband and her Levirate brother-in-law, overseas, and she said, "My husband died and afterward my Levirate brother-in-law died" — "My Levirate brother-in-law died and afterward my husband died" — she is not believed. For a woman is not believed to testify, "My Levirate brother-in-law has died," so that she may remarry. Nor is she believed to testify, "My sister has died," so that she may enter into his [her brother-in-law's] house. And a man is not believed to say, "My brother has died," so that he may enter into Levirate marriage with his [the brother's] wife. [Nor is he believed to testify,] "My wife died," so that he may marry her sister.

M. 16:1 A woman whose husband and co-wife went overseas and they came and said to her, "Your husband has died," should not remarry [without performing the rite of removing the shoe, or enter into Levirate marriage], until she ascertains whether her co-wife is pregnant. [If] she had a mother-in-law, [however] she does not have to scruple concerning her [the mother-in-law's possible pregnancy, which may bring forth a Levir, on whom she then would have to wait]. [And if] she [the mother-in-law] went away full [of child], she must scruple [concerning her].

M. 16:2 Two sisters-in-law [wives of two brothers] — this one says, "My husband died" — and that one says, "My husband died" — [each being believed about her own husband but not about the marital condition of the other,] this one is prohibited on account of the husband of that one [to whom she is bound in a Levirate connection], and that one is prohibited on account of the husband of this one. [If] this one has witnesses [who testify independently that the husband has died], and that one does not have witnesses — the one who has witnesses is prohibited. And the one who does not have witnesses is permitted. [If] this one [of A] has children and that one does not have children, the one who has children is permitted, and the one who does not have children is prohibited. [If] they entered into Levirate marriage and the Levirs died, they are prohibited from remarrying.

M. 16:3 They derive testimony [concerning the identity of a corpse] only from the appearance of the whole face with the nose, even though there are signs of the corpse's identity on his body or garments. They derive testimony [that a man has died] only after he has actually died [and has been seen dead], and even if they [the witnesses] saw him mortally wounded, crucified, or being eaten by a wild beast. They give testimony [about the identity of a corpse] only during a period of three days [after death].

M. 16:4 [If] he fell into a body of water, whether within sight of shore or not within sight of shore — his wife is prohibited [until the corpse turns up].

M. 16:5 Even if one heard the women saying, "So-and-so has died," it is sufficient [for him to go and testify in court that So-and-so has died].

M. 16:6 They give testimony [about the identity of a corpse which they have seen] by the light of a candle or by the light of the moon. And they permit a woman to remarry on the evidence of an echo [which is heard to say that her husband has died].

T. 14:4 [If] one fell into a lion's pit, they do not give testimony concerning him [in the assumption that he has died]. [If] he fell into a furnace of fire, they do give testimony concerning him [in the assumption] that he has died. [If] he was crucified, they do not give testimony concerning him [that he has died]. . [If] he was mortally wounded, they do give testimony concerning him [that he has died].

The composite presents no surprises; it bears all of the indicative traits of the Mishnah's formulation of the Halakhah. The principle announced at the outset is instantiated: evidence, however flimsy, however dubious, and however invalid under ordinary circumstances, here is accepted. The modulations of the principle all are predictable and accord with established principles, e.g., M. 15:5-8. I discern nothing of interest in the Tosefta's treatment of the same topic, and the two Talmuds present still less.

IV. DOCUMENTARY TRAITS

A. THE MISHNAH AND THE TOSEFTA

The principal documents cover the same ground in the same way. I do not see a point at which a different theory of interpretation enters into the one document but not the other. The proposition that the Tosefta bears its own hermeneutical approach to the Halakhic program — its own category-formations, or, dealing with extant ones, its own theory of how data are to be interpreted — finds no support to speak of. What we do find, here as elsewhere, is an interesting tendency on the part of persons engaged in producing compositions for utilization in what became the Tosefta. It is to translate cases into abstract principles, and to generate cases for another topic altogether out of those abstractions. Had that tendency prevailed, as I have noted many times now, the Halakhah would come to us in a very different construction — structure and system; its principal category-formations would find definition not in the intrinsic indicative traits of a topic, logically define, but in the governing generalizations that pertain to a variety of topics. I suppose, by way of example, someone can have organized a vast category-formation on the resolution of doubt in general (comparable to the category-formation on the resolution of doubt when it comes to the status of food and drink, set forth with exquisite clarity in Mishnah-tractate Tohorot). But the hermeneutics that identifies cogency in a-topical abstract principles, though surfacing here and there (and occasionally, even in the Mishnah) never dominated even in a single Halakhic document. And, it goes without saying, the received hermeneutics, the one that governs in large-scale Halakhic composites of the Pentateuch, e.g., the Priestly Code, also exercised remarkably limited authority.[2]

Even though the results are both paltry and one-sided, for the continuation of the present project I shall continue to take note of the data of this rubric and the next. It suffices to conclude that in asking about a distinctive hermeneutics of the Halakhah, embodied in category-formations and exegetical problematics therein, characteristic of one document and not another, I have produced a negative result.

B. THE YERUSHALMI AND THE BAVLI

The Talmuds' contributions to the hermeneutics of Yebamot prove negligible. The Bavli's presentation, constituting in the present case a large and in many ways profound and rich Talmud-tractate, full of important intellectual initiatives, serves in only a single way, and that is, as a commentary to the Mishnah-tractate of the same name. It has no other purpose, and that one purpose governs throughout. A search for an account of the other-than-Mishnaic components of the Rabbinic structure and system could well bypass this tractate, since, in its form and its program, it bears the character of a recapitulation of the Mishnah's ideas, within the Mishnah's framework. The hermeneutics that has framed the category-formation of as set forth in the Mishnah dictates the program of the Bavli as well. To be sure, the law of the Mishnah has been given more than a reprise; the framers have not merely clarified but have reshaped and deepened the received law of treated in the three components of the Mishnah-tractate. So, while everything appears to be the same, in fact, much has changed, as we move from the Mishnah into the writing that purports to do little more than, assigning the Mishnah a privileged standing, recapitulates the Mishnah's own statements in a clearer way than in the original.

As to the problem of comparative hermeneutics, the two Talmuds do not present a productive opportunity for comparison. Other, much more suggestive comparisons and contrasts, those that concern exegetical imagination and skill, have already emerged in other studies; but within the definitions that govern here, these have no bearing upon hermeneutics, so far as I can say.[3]

---

[2] I deal with that problem in my *Scripture and the Generative Premises of the Halakhah* (Binghamton, 1999: Global Publications of Binghamton University) I-IV, summarized and concluded in *From Scripture to 70. The Pre-Rabbinic Beginnings of the Halakhah*. Atlanta, 1999: Scholars Press for South Florida Studies in the History of Judaism.

[3] See the seven volume systematic work that follows *The Bavli's Unique Voice. A Systematic Comparison of the Talmud of Babylonia and the Talmud of the Land of*

V. THE HERMENEUTICS OF YEBAMOT

The category-formation, Yebamot, encompasses a considerable corpus of topics, and before we ask what holds the whole together, we do well to review the main topics, that are treated. This outline shows us how the document holds together: its problematics and topical articulation.

I. Heaven's Role in Establishing the Marital Bond [M. 1:1-6]
   A. Neither Levirate Marriage nor Rite of removing the shoe: consanguinity [M. 1:1-2:10]
   B. Rite of removing the shoe but no Levirate Marriage [M. 3:1-3:10]
   C. Levirate Marriage [M. 4:1-4:13]
   D. Reprise: Marriage, Divorce, Levirate Marriage, Rite of removing the shoe M. [5:1-6]

Israel. Volume One. *Bavli and Yerushalmi Qiddushin Chapter One Compared and Contrasted*. Atlanta, 1993: Scholars Press for South Florida Studies in the History of Judaism; *The Bavli's Unique Voice. A Systematic Comparison of the Talmud of Babylonia and the Talmud of the Land of Israel*. Volume Two. *Yerushalmi's, Bavli's, and Other Canonical Documents' Treatment of the Program of Mishnah-Tractate Sukkah Chapters One, Two, and Four Compared and Contrasted. A Reprise and Revision of The Bavli and its Sources*. Atlanta, 1993: Scholars Press for South Florida Studies in the History of Judaism; *The Bavli's Unique Voice. A Systematic Comparison of the Talmud of Babylonia and the Talmud of the Land of Israel*. Volume Three. *Bavli and Yerushalmi to Selected Mishnah-Chapters in the Division of Moed. Erubin Chapter One, and Moed Qatan Chapter Three*. Atlanta, 1993: Scholars Press for South Florida Studies in the History of Judaism; *The Bavli's Unique Voice. A Systematic Comparison of the Talmud of Babylonia and the Talmud of the Land of Israel*. Volume Four. *Bavli and Yerushalmi to Selected Mishnah-Chapters in the Division of Nashim. Gittin Chapter Five and Nedarim Chapter One. And Niddah Chapter One*. Atlanta, 1993: Scholars Press for South Florida Studies in the History of Judaism; *The Bavli's Unique Voice. A Systematic Comparison of the Talmud of Babylonia and the Talmud of the Land of Israel*. Volume Five. *Bavli and Yerushalmi to Selected Mishnah-Chapters in the Division of Neziqin. Baba Mesia Chapter One and Makkot Chapters One and Two*. Atlanta, 1993: Scholars Press for South Florida Studies in the History of Judaism; *The Bavli's Unique Voice. A Systematic Comparison of the Talmud of Babylonia and the Talmud of the Land of Israel*. Volume Six. *Bavli and Yerushalmi to a Miscellany of Mishnah-Chapters. Gittin Chapter One, Qiddushin Chapter Two, and Hagigah Chapter Three*. Atlanta, 1993: Scholars Press for South Florida Studies in the History of Judaism; *The Bavli's Unique Voice*. Volume Seven. *What Is Unique about the Bavli in Context? An Answer Based on Inductive Description, Analysis, and Comparison*. Atlanta, 1993: Scholars Press for South Florida Studies in the History of Judaism.

II. Under Heaven's Aspect. The Special Marital Bond: Marriage into the Priesthood [M. 6:1-9:6]
    A. When a Woman May Eat Priestly Rations [M. 6:1-6]
    B. Who May Eat Priestly Rations [M. 7:1-8:2]
    C. Miscellany [M. 8:3]
    D. The Eunuch [M. 8:4-6]
    E. Concluding Construction for Units I-II [M. 9:1-6]

III. Severing the Marital Bond Other than through Man's Intentionality and Intervention [M. 10:1-16:7]
    A. Marital Ties that are Subject to Doubt [M. 10:1-11:7]
    B. Severing the Marital Bond of the Deceased Childless Brother's Widow. The Rite of Removing the Shoe and How it is Performed [M. 12:1-6]
    C. Severing the Marital Bond of the Minor. Exercising the Right of Refusal [M. 13:1-13]
    D. The Infirm Marital Bond of the Deaf-Mute [M. 14:1-4]
    E. Severing the Marital Bond through the Death of the Husband. [1] The Woman's Testimony [M. 15:1-16:2]
    F. Severing the Marital Bond through the Death of the Husband [II] Identifying the Corpse [M. 16:3-7]

In line with our general theory of hermeneutics, involving analogical-contrasting reasoning in the definition of category-formations, what does this outline tell us about the present matter? What, specifically, are the generative analogies or contrasts that govern? Once asked in that way, the question answers itself. The topic is, the cessation of the marital bond, with attention also to marital bonds of an unconventional, therefore interstitial, character. The species are, death and the writ of divorce, which contrast: Heaven's as against man's action in effecting the same result. So the analogy is the given, the contrast defines the generative problematic. Let me spell out this way of seeing the matter.

The native category, Yebamot, deals with establishing a marital bond through Heaven's intervention and severing the marital bond through a means other than a writ of divorce issued by man, e.g., exercising the right of refusal on the part of a minor girl married off by her mother or her brothers, through the rite of removing the shoe, through the fact that the marital bond is not firm to begin with (by reason of doubt or the status of one of the participants) and through the death of the husband. The two divisions then match: [1] the beginning and [2] the end of a marriage when man through betrothal and a marriage contract has not effected the union or has not deliberately severed it through divorce. The middle part of the native category-formation concerns another aspect of marriage again from Heaven's perspective: the marital bonds of the priesthood and their special problems. Priests' wives and children eat priestly rations, which are holy, e.g., heave offering and the like. When we consider the impact of Heaven upon the marital bond, its formation and dissolution, we thus include the special problem of marriage with supernatural consequences. Since marriage under the aspect of Heaven is a subset of marriage effected through Heaven, the middle section fits tightly with the opening section. It follows that we have two principal parts of the whole.

The native category-formation, Yebamot, therefore deals with establishing the marital bond through Heavenly intervention, counterpart to doing so through man's intentionality, unit I; a marital bond subject to Heaven's particular supervision; and Heaven's provisions for severing the marital bond established by Heaven, not by man's and woman's intentionality (the rite of removing the shoe, the right of refusal). What the Halakhah wishes to say about exceptional marital ties, those brought about under Heavenly auspices through death rather than through the deliberate action of man and woman, and about severing those ties, is that there is a correspondence between Heaven's work and the ways of man. Both impose the marital bond and both sever it. Neither mode of joining nor means of loosening the bond is more holy than the other, and the consequences of each are identical with those of the other. A man's document removes the sanctity of a woman for that particular man, just as does the fulfillment of Heaven's rite of removing the shoe. Supernature sanctifies a woman to a man under the conditions of the Levirate connection; man sanctifies too; man, like God, can sanctify the relationship between man and woman and also effect the cessation of that same relationship.

A. WHAT FUSES THE HALAKHIC DATA INTO A CATEGORY-FORMATION?

With the outline in hand, we now ask, how does the whole hold together? The answer is, a theory of the full realization of the process of sanctification, by the criterion of intentionality, encompasses the bulk of the data and gives them their shape and structure. But that rather opaque formulation of matters takes much for granted. So let us start from the beginning.

Since marriage and the family, the second division, with their counterpart, the altar and its sacrifices, the fifth division, deal with sanctified relationships, the woman to the man, the beast to the altar, respectively, let us begin with the most fundamental question imaginable: what, exactly, do sages understand by the category — the status and the action — of sanctification, how is the status conferred, the action realized, and in what context? As sages read the Written Torah, the critical moment of sanctification takes place where life begins or is sustained, at the confluence of intentionality and deed modeled after God's intentionality and deed. "Let us make man in our image, after our likeness" (Gen. 1:26), states the intention. "So God created man in his own image, in the image of God he created him; male and female he created them" (Gen. 1:27) formulates the deed. "And God saw everything that he had made, and behold it was very good" states the judgment, the taxonomic effect (good, evil) of the realization of the intentionality, in the language of the hermeneutics spelled out here. When, as I said, man and woman act like God and create man, that action, like God's to begin with, realizes the intentionality of sanctification of the woman by the man, with the same result as in the beginning: the act of creation of life. The man's sanctification of the woman, then, forms a detail in the larger work of sanctifying the world, meaning, carrying forward God's work of creation that came to its climax in the repose of the Sabbath, sanctified at the conclusion of creation.

That accounts for the focus upon the Israelite household as much as upon the altar of God's household in Jerusalem, the one the setting for the creation of life, the other, the celebration thereof. The purpose of marriage is procreation, and the sanctification of the woman to the man comes about for that reason: man and woman, like God, create life. In the setting of the household, that means, not life in general but the life of the very next generation of the family of the husband in particular. It is for that purpose that the husband betroths the wife, and that purpose by its nature suffices to sanctify the union. The husband's intention and confirming action, confirmed by the wife's acquiescence, constitute the pertinent act of sanctification.

Now how is such a transaction effected and completed? And at what point is the process of sanctification brought to fruition? It is, self-evidently, when the intentionality has come to realization: [1] let us make..., [2] he created..., [3] and God saw.... That carries us to the particular transactions at hand. When we consider the Halakhah of betrothals, we shall realize that the woman enters the status of sanctification as does an animal, the one for the marital bed, the other for the altar. So, the matter is explicit, the Halakhah of the altar and that of the bed have to be drawn into juxtaposition for purposes of analogy. In the analogy of the cult, as we shall see in a moment, the answer to the question, when is sanctification fully realized *and so no longer affective*? is, when the intention has been accomplished. Then the same criterion will apply to the marital bond and its severance, and by that criterion we shall understand the special circumstance involving in the Levirate bond, which takes effect, as I shall explain, when the initial intentionality of the now-deceased childless husband has not been realized, leaving the widow still subject to that intentionality, hence the bond that it created.

That fact is established for the sanctification of the beast for the altar. A householder takes a secular beast and declares it to be sanctified for the altar for a particular purpose, e.g., "Lo, that animal is my sin-offering" (with a very particular sin in mind). The animal thus enters the status of a sin offering (and so throughout), and it is Holy Things. Until what point in the procedure is that status maintained, and Is there any point at which the animal or extant parts thereof are no longer sanctified but available for secular use, e.g., private benefit? Indeed there is. It is when the initial act of sanctification has come to its realization, *when the beast has accomplished the purpose for which it has been sanctified.* And, when a beast is sanctified to the altar, at what point is the act of sanctification realized? It is when the priest has collected the blood and tossed it onto the appropriate part of the altar, doing so with the correct intention (e.g., an animal designated as a sin offering being prepared and presented in the classification and by the rites of the sin offering, and so throughout).

What then happens to the remainder of the beast? Part or all of the meat may be burned up on the altar, depending on the classification of the offering; certain organs will be burned up on the altar; and so on. But what about the rest of the blood that has been collected in the act of slaughter — and that served for the sprinkling on the altar that effected atonement (where pertinent)? That residue of the blood is poured out as null, no longer being treated as consecrated; it flows into the gutters and downward and is sold to farmers for fertilizer. The Halakhah is explicit on that matter. That indicates the besought fact: when [1] the purpose of the act of sanctification has been fully realized, [2] the initial status of sanctification that has taken over the beast in question no longer affects (what remains of) the beast. Then the pertinent remnants are treated as secular. So as a general rule, we may posit, the intentionality to sanctify the beast lapses in the realization thereof with actualities of the rite at the altar. That explains why the extant parts of the beast are not subjected to on-going sanctification, having served their part in the event, now becoming secular.

Now — and only now — the facts of sanctification and secularization permit us to turn to the Halakhah of the desacralization of the bed. Man on his own may declare secular or common, available to anyone, the woman that he has consecrated. His initial act of sanctification has accomplished his purpose or has been nullified. For whatever reason, he no longer subjects the woman to that intentionality that effected her consecration to him. How does he so signify? He does so with a writ of divorce, which Heaven ratifies, as Heaven has ratified the initial act of sanctification (by her acceptance of a writ, or of a money-payment as token of the woman's acquiescence, or of an actual act of sexual relations, also as a token of her acquiescence). When the man declared the woman sanctified to himself and the woman acceded to his declaration, Heaven recognized the transaction, just as much as Heaven recognizes the sanctification for the altar of a beast that the farmer has declared holy for that purpose. Then if the woman violates her status of sanctification, she is punished. But when the man forms the intention of removing from her the status of sanctification (with her full knowledge, if not with her consent), and when that intention is realized in an appropriately prepared and delivered document, particular to the woman at hand, then the status of sanctification is removed from the woman. So one medium of desacralization of the marital relationship is the formal nullification of the initial intentionality and act of sanctification.

But Heaven on its own, not only in partnership with man has its purpose for a sacred union, and Heaven too may desacralize the marital union. Heaven intervenes when the husband dies, leaving the wife a widow. If she had children, the initial intentionality — that of the husband who sanctified the woman as his wife — has been realized. Death then severs the relationship of sanctification; no remnants of the original act of intentionality enthrall the wife. But what if there was no offspring in the union between that man and that woman? Then the man's initial intentionality has not been carried out. So, in the model of the sanctification of the beast that has not fulfilled the intentionality involved in the act of sanctification, the bond that Heaven recognized continues.[4] Then, to fulfill the original plan, Heaven on its own may arrange for the propagation of life through a particular woman. And that produces the Levirate relationship: either a consummated marriage, to carry forward the initial intent and attempt to accomplish the plan of procreation, or the rite of removing the shoe, counterpart to the writ of divorce.

The hermeneutics shaped within the theory of sanctification and intentionality just now spelled out for both the animal and the woman, then, finds its data in cases pertinent to how the intentionality of sanctification is realized or left unfulfilled. The hermeneutics finds place in the consequent category-formation for a wide range of cases. It has the power to extend the law to distant frontiers. Consider the contrast between the Levirate connection and its absence. If the husband dies having accomplished his goal of producing children, the union, now irrelevant to the propagation of life, is severed, which is to say, as with the residue of the blood of the offering, it is desanctified. The comparison of the woman and the sanctified beast — both of them subject to the laws of consecration, though also to be differentiated — yields an odd but telling result. Like the residual blood, now sold to farmers for manure, the woman is now utterly secular; she is free to marry anyone she chooses, within the limitations of the Torah (e.g., as a widow, she cannot marry a high priest).

---

[4] That is, the animal designated as a sin-offering that has not served its purpose is subject to the sanctification involved in that status and has to be appropriately disposed of, as the Halakhah of Zebahim makes abundantly clear.

There is no Levirate connection. But — so the same hermeneutics instructs — should Heaven intervene and the husband die childless, the union does not lose its sanctification, for life may yet be propagated in accord with the deceased's initial intentionality for this particular woman, and the same is so for the confirming act of sanctification. (To be sure, we take note that childless widow past the age of childbearing, the childless widow of a man who had children from her co-wife, and others will form exceptions to the basic conception that operates here. But they do not change the norm.) That provision, made by Heaven to realize the original intentionality and deed, is what carries us to the Levirate marriage. In such a marriage, the originally sanctified woman remains subject to the initial act of consecration by the particular man she married, and his original intentionality — to propagate life in his household — may yet be realized. That is through continuation of the sanctified relationship, now with a surviving brother of the childless deceased.

The upshot may be stated very simply. The bed is sanctified by the man's intention, together with the woman's acquiescence, ratified by a deed. It is desanctified by [1] the man's intention, communicated to a fully-sentient woman, ratified by the deed of drawing up and delivering the properly witnessed document of divorce. It also is desanctified [2] by the death of the husband, on the stipulation of his intention's having been realized in offspring. So intentionality may be nullified by contradictory intentionality or by the full accomplishment of the original intention — the one or the other. But death on its own does not always desanctify the relationship. Where there are surviving brothers, the relationship brought about by the generative intentionality and initial confirming deed overspreads the surviving brothers. Then the status of sanctification persists until resolved through Levirate marriage or the rite of removing the shoe, counterparts to the original betrothal and marriage, on the one side, and to the writ of divorce, on the other. So the principal way in which what is sanctified may by man's action be desacralized is the realization of the intentionality, confirmed by deed that motivated the original act of sanctification. The principal way by which Heaven may intervene and desacralize a relationship is through the death of the one who to begin with imparted the status of sanctification to that which has been made holy, that is, the woman.

B. THE ACTIVITY OF THE CATEGORY-FORMATION

The Halakhah of the Oral Torah takes for granted the categorical imperatives and principles of the Written Torah, commences not with the rules governing when or how Levirate marriage takes place, Scripture having defined the matter, but rather, with the rules that define why in accord with the law of the Torah it does not take place. Where the Written Torah is explicit and leaves no ambiguities, the Oral Torah falls silent. But even here, the surviving brother's refusal receives scant attention. Beyond Scripture's script for the woman's declaration in the rite of removing the shoe, he is a passive participant; we have no Halakhah that dictates a ritual for him to follow in declining to due his duty to his household. Not surprisingly, the Halakhah that does define the rite of removing the shoe is secondary and derivative, making no important points on its own, spun out of no generative problematic I can discern. Rather, following the Mishnah's authoritative statement of the normative law, we commence with the development of the established principle that Levirate marriage cannot and does not take place when the resulting union will violate the Torah's laws against consanguinity. Then no rite of removing the shoe is required; no union ever existed.

But that nullification of the relationship is not the sole way in which the Halakhah resolves matters. Much depends upon the grounds for the prohibition of the union. Here the general rule of M. 2:3 lays out the three possibilities. If the basis for the prohibition of the Levirate union is specified at Leviticus Chapter Eighteen, then the Levirate connection is null, no action being taken. If the prohibition is other than fundamental, e.g., by reason of a prohibition of marriage into a given caste, then the rite of removing the shoe is carried out, no Levirate marriage being possible. If her sister is also her sister-in-law (widow of her childless brother-in-law), the widow either executes the rite of removing the shoe or is taken into Levirate marriage. The Tosefta then amplifies how relationships of an interstitial character are sorted out, the entries of T. 2:3ff. being particularly lucid.

The critical issue at the initial level of analysis conducted by the Oral Torah is a subordinate question: if one of the co-wives of a polygamous union cannot enter into Levirate marriage with a surviving brother, how does that fact affect the other co-wives? Building a fence around the Torah, sages maintain that if one co-wife cannot marry any surviving brother, then all co-wives, legally married to the deceased at the moment of his death, are exempt from the Levirate connection with any one of all of the surviving brothers. In a polygamous society, such a blanket exemption is going to nullify Levirate connections in numerous cases, but I do not see a shred of evidence that sages intended to produce that result. Interstitial cases, involving matters of uncertainty, come to resolution in the rite of removing the shoe, which is performed formally to sever a relationship that may or may not exist. The sole practical result is that since the rite is tantamount to divorce, the widow then is classified as a divorcée and so may not marry into the priestly caste. Completing this matter is the counterpart-category: when a surviving brother does not participate in the Levirate marriage. The general rule is that a valid brother of any sort imposes the obligation of Levirate marriage; a valid offspring of any sort releases the widow from the Levirate connection. Once the exegetical process takes over, the exposition is simple and predictable, though, as we see with great effect in this category-formation, the problems for solution tax one's acumen.

The Halakhah relies upon the rite of removing the shoe to resolve cases that are subject to doubt or confusion, flawed betrothal or divorce, or mere error. In general the rite of removing the shoe serves to settle situations of confusion in such a way that no untoward results emerge from the transaction. In that way matters of doubt are resolved so that the Levirate connection is severed, and a consummated marriage, which can have the effect of producing children unable properly to marry within Israel, is prevented. So in various sequences of marriage, then death without children, the rite of removing the shoe is invoked to deal with a relationship, once legal, that now leads to law-violation. The Halakhah, as is its way, takes up interstitial cases, e.g., those where some confusion enters into the transaction. The relationship is properly severed — if it existed. And if not, not.

So if there was a valid marriage, the rite of removing the shoe frees the widow to marry outside of the family, and if there was not a valid marriage, there is no loss in performing said rite. What do we do in a case of betrothal, where the deceased has betrothed one of two sisters, does not know which one, and then dies childless? The deceased would have issued a writ of divorce had he survived, the brother goes through the rite of removing the shoe with both of them. Any brother may carry out the rite of Levirate marriage. But what if both surviving brothers enter into Levirate marriage with both of the childless deceased's widows? These and comparable cases find ample analysis in the Halakhah. So too, general principles of good order come to bear on the cases at hand. Some improprieties are penalized by the Halakhah, some not; some interested parties may nonetheless benefit from their engagement with a case, some not. In the present matter, for example, one may not testify to the validity of a writ of divorce and then marry the divorcée. A sage who forbade a woman to continue to live with her husband by reason of a vow she has taken and he has not remitted may not then marry the woman. But if he supervised a transaction in which he has no decision to make, e.g., if in the sage's presence the woman exercised the right of refusal or performed the rite of removing the shoe, he may marry her.

The Halakhah of Yebamot, having addressed marriages made in Heaven, turns to marriages absolutely forbidden by Heaven. The topic forms a natural next step in the present Halakhic exposition. These forbidden unions fall into several categories. First come marriages forbidden by reason of caste considerations, the widow to the high priest, the divorcée to an ordinary priest. Scripture is explicit in these matters, and the reason for introducing them in just the present context is not always compelling. In the case of the high priest, it is to clarify the sort of connection that he may establish with the widow of a deceased, childless brother: the rite of removing the shoe, not a Levirate marriage. So the requirement is met, but the intersecting law of the high priesthood is not violated.

The remainder of the Halakhah concerning marriages subject to confusion or to one or another flaw concerns the validation of a priest's mate to eat priestly rations (heave-offering) or the invalidation of a priest's daughter, by reason of matter, to do the same. So the predicate shifts, but the subject remains coherent with the remainder of the discussion at hand. The same class of dubious marriages extends to the infertile union. Sexual relations are carried on, even though it is clear that insemination is not going to come about. But the formulation underscores the prevailing conviction that marriage serves the purpose of procreation, which validates the sexual bond — indeed, necessitates and consecrates it. A third class of unions involves the deaf-mute and the boy nine years and a day old. The former cannot communicate in the conventional manner and so his act of sanctification is not of the same order as that of those possessed of sound senses. The latter no longer falls into the class of the pre-mature but is not yet deemed sexually mature, a classification attained at the appearance of pubic hair. A variety of special problems emerge by reason of the youngster's unclear status and capacity.

When it comes to others who also have some unclarity as to their marital unions, the physical act bears consequence, thus: "a deaf-mute, an idiot, and a minor who have had sexual relations have effected an act of acquisition. And they have freed the co-wives from the obligation of Levirate marriage. An idiot or a minor who married wives and who died — their wives are exempt from the requirement of performing the rite of removing the shoe. This is the general principle: Any act of sexual relations performed by them which requires articulated consciousness is not a valid act of sexual relations. But any which does not require articulated consciousness — lo, this is a valid act of sexual relations." It would not be possible to state matters with greater clarity than the Tosefta does here.

What unions are prohibited? Scripture specifies that the male Ammonite and Moabite may never marry Israelites, but the female may. The Egyptian and Edomite is forbidden for three generations. Mamzerim can never marry valid Israelites. All of these are excluded for reasons extrinsic to the marital bond. Others are forbidden because the purpose of marriage, procreation, cannot be realized, or cannot definitively be accomplished. The eunuch may not be deemed validly married, because his act of consecration has no bearing upon the relationship that is inaugurated thereby: he cannot produce offspring. So too is the case with the sterile woman. A eunuch by nature, a person exhibiting the traits of both sexes, a brother born of the same mother, a proselyte, and a freed slave do not perform the rite of removing the shoe and do not enter into Levirate marriage. With none of these does an Israelite woman contract a valid marriage. Nor does rape or seduction effect a marriage, the woman not having consented to the actuality of sanctification. A brother of the rapist may marry the woman, if she consents, even in the lifetime of the rapist.

One interesting detail of the law of performing the rite of removing the shoe registers. If the woman does the act but does not recite the formula, the rite is valid; if she recites the formula but does not do the deed of removing the shoe, the rite is invalid. Here is yet another way of dismissing intentionality unrealized by an actual deed, where required. But if intentionality plays no role — e.g., with the deaf-mute boy girl or the minor boy, none of whom is deemed capable of expressing intentionality and effecting it — the rite is equally null.

The Halakhah takes up two further topics pertinent to the theme of intentionality in severing the marital bond. The first involves the betrothal of a minor girl. Prior to the age of maturity, at which her intentionality takes effect so that she may agree to enter the consecrated relationship, the girl may be betrothed or married. But when she reaches the age of intentionality, she may refuse the action, and it is as if she was never sanctified. That is so if her mother or brothers have married her off with her knowledge and consent. If they did so without her agreement, she simply leaves the man to whom they have given her — no further rite being required. The upshot is, where deed is not joined to intentionality, the deed is null. The second involves the marriage of a deaf-mute and a person of sound senses. Here too, the issue of intentionality enters, since the deaf-mute cannot express intentionality in the unambiguous manner in which a person of sound senses can do so. Sign-language is not deemed a language equivalent to the conventional kind. Once a valid marriage is contracted, if the wife becomes an idiot, for the same reason the husband cannot divorce her.

The final composite addresses the topically, but not logically, pertinent problem of the cessation of marriage through death of the husband, the issue of Levirate connection not figuring. Here the question is whether or not, in the absence of the corpse, the evidence ascertains that the husband has died. The wife may testify that he has died, no reason existing to doubt her allegation. But if such a reason exists, e.g., marital strife, she cannot testify. Nearly any other party may testify that the husband has died. The main concern in the present set of rules concerns the power of the woman to bring word from overseas as to her own marital status.

C. THE CONSISTENCY OF THE CATEGORY-FORMATION

Once the category-formation has taken shape around the issues identified within the governing hermeneutics, the unfolding is coherent and uniform. Only the concluding topic, concerning the evidence that establishes the death of the husband, falls outside of the governing problematics, even though it is connected to the paramount theme.

D. THE GENERATIVITY OF THE CATEGORY-FORMATION

The most important datum of the Halakhah — what forms of the complex data a single coherent category-formation — is that the Levirate marriage, brought about by Heaven's intervention — death without offspring — is fully comparable to the marriage brought about by a man with a woman of his choice. The counterpart of the act of betrothal of a secular union is the act of "bespeaking" (my translation for the Hebrew word, *ma'amar,* act of speech) by which a surviving brother indicates his intention of entering into Levirate marriage. The Tosefta's formulation is lucid as always: What is "bespeaking"? If the Levirate husband says, "lo, thou art sanctified to me by money" or "by something worth money" or "by a writ." What is [the language to be used in a] writ? "I, So-and-so, the son of So-and so, take upon myself responsibility for Miss So-and so, my deceased childless brother's wife, to care for her and to supply maintenance for her in an appropriate way. This is with the proviso that the payment of her marriage-contract is the obligation of the estate of her [deceased] first husband." Just as the act of sanctification effects acquisition in the case of a woman only when both of them are agreed, so a statement of bespeaking effects acquisition of a sister-in-law only when both of them are agreed. The act of bespeaking sustains the original act of sanctification. The surviving brother confirms the intentionality of the deceased brother and quite properly proposes to realize the deceased's original act of will in consecrating that particular woman: to produce children.

This brings us to the positive side of matters, the actual Levirate connection. At each of its two stages of realization and at the stage of nullification, the Levirate relationship corresponds to the secular one. What is the difference between an act of sanctification via betrothal and the act of a brother's "bespeaking"? There is none. Once one brother has announced his intention to serve as Levir, the other brothers are no longer permitted to effect a relationship with the widow. So bespeaking, as I have stressed, is equivalent to an act of consecration; it serves to redirect, to extend the deceased's original act of sanctification, now to the surviving brother, him alone.

The act of consummation through sexual relations is the same. But that is not entirely so. Heaven has not only confirmed the intentionality and deed that inaugurated the transaction and assigned the woman to this now-deceased man, but now, willy-nilly, this woman to this surviving brother. The woman, remaining under the original bond of sanctification, can to begin with have rejected the now-deceased husband, but she cannot reject the brother. She remains in the status of sanctification, because the original intentionality, confirmed by deed, has not yet been realized. That explains why sexual relations in any circumstance — even inadvertence, even rape — now consummate the marriage. By contrast had the now-deceased husband originally raped the woman, she would not have automatically become his wife merely by reason of sexual relations performed without her consent. Indeed, the Halakhah makes that point explicitly. Party to the on-going relationship of sanctification, by contrast, she now continues the relationship with the surviving brother. And the surviving brother, too, has no choice once the matter of sexual relations, rather than the rite of removing the shoe, enters the picture. He too may be forced into having sex with the childless widow.

And here we identify the generative power of the hermeneutics, its capacity to identify a new range of issues out of its basic theory of matters. Now we make no distinctions as to intentionality — constraint, deliberation, consciousness or inadvertence. Why not? Because no one in the transaction possesses the power of intentionality. The widow has consented to begin with in the process of producing offspring for her husband's household. The surviving brother is subject to the deceased's act of will and can only accede or decline, but not redirect the course of the original transaction. He is given the right to decide only one matter: not whether he is to enter into a relationship with the widow, but how he is to dictate the course of the already-existing relationship that Heaven has imposed upon him. Only when the original act of sanctification, to which the woman did consent, has accomplished its purpose does the transaction conclude.

But, it goes without saying, when the woman has produced a child by the surviving brother, carrying forward the deceased, childless brother's intentionality, she remains wed to the Levir; no one imagines that at that point the marriage concludes. No marriage-contract pertains, since the original one, covering the deceased's union with the woman now widowed, remains in effect. The Levirate marriage, made in Heaven, once consummated, cannot be differentiated from a secular marriage, brought about by man. Property relationships are the same. Only the marriage-contract is charged against the estate of the original husband.

The surviving brother has the option of declining, as Scripture insists. But the relationship inaugurated by the intentionality and deed of the now-deceased husband remains in being until formally concluded, once more by an act of will on the part of the pertinent party. Accordingly, to sever the union, the rite of removing the shoe serves as counterpart to the writ of divorce. As noted, the documentary appurtenances of the betrothal, marriage, and divorce carried on in ordinary circumstances no longer are required, Heaven being fully informed of its own actions in realization of its own intentionality. So the connection yields Levirate marriage, brought about through a rite of bespeaking, then consummation. Or it concludes with an act of will and a confirming deed on the part of the Levir: the rite of removing the shoe. In the event of the rite of removing the shoe, the oldest brother must undergo the rite. The brothers must reach an immediate decision and may not keep the widow waiting. The Levirate husband does not lose his share in the deceased brother's estate. The husband who undergoes the rite of removing the shoe may not then marry the widow's relatives.

TO CONCLUDE: Like God, man intends to create life and so acts to realize his intentionality. But, unlike God, man dies. If his intentionality has been accomplished, the status of sanctification falls away from that which has been made holy. If not, as we realize, steps to accomplish that original plan are to be taken. Then, like divorce, when the intentionality is declared dead and so nullified, death marks the abrogation of the original act of will, resulting in the nullification of the status of sanctification. What man's intentionality has brought into being is either concluded when the intentionality is realized or is abrogated by the willful cessation of that same intentionality. Or the status of sanctification of the bed ceases with death. The difference between life and death should not be missed. Man's intentionality confirmed by deed brings about life. But death comes about willy-nilly.[5]

---

[5] Then, for the Halakhah to state matters in its way, uncleanness should come about whether man wills or does not will the pollution to take place. And, in theory at least, we should also learn from the Halakhah that pollution affects, in particular, what is subject to the will of man: what accomplishes man's purpose and is deemed by him to be useful. Life and will weigh in the balance against death and inevitability, thus also sanctification is set in the scales against uncleanness. So, at any rate, the Halakhah of the desacralization of the bed leads us to anticipate for the desacralization of the table. In later parts of this study we shall see that that anticipation is wholly realized.

2.
TRACTATE KETUBOT

I. THE DEFINITION OF THE CATEGORY-FORMATION

Ketubot and Yebamot form two matching species of a common genus: the marital union and that which pertains thereto. Ketubot deals with the beginning, middle, and end of the marriage through human action, Yebamot, the beginning, middle, and end of the marriage through supernatural action. That is to say, Yebamot addresses the marriage under the aspect of the death of the husband without children and disposition of the marital bond between the widow and the deceased's surviving brother. And by contrast, just as Yebamot traces the course of a marriage that does not completely fulfill the intentionality involved in the enterprise, so Ketubot follows the pattern of a marriage that does. Ketubot therefore presents the marital union from man's perspective, within the normal and routine course of human life, Yebamot, from God's perspective.

So while, as I shall explain, the hermeneutics that guides Rabbinic Judaism in its selection and interpretation of data that concern marriage on the surface takes shape not in a process of comparison and contrast but within the logic of a narrative, that view is superficial. When we have understood matters properly, we shall see that the logic of narrative defines only the means to the end of expounding the results of a process of comparison and contrast — one no less vivid than that of Yebamot.

But on first glance that is not how matters appear. How then does a narrative logic govern the exposition? In the Halakhic program of Ketubot — Mishnah-Tosefta-Yerushalmi-Bavli — we address first of all the document of marriage, the Ketubah, which provides for support for the wife by the husband and alimony in the event of divorce or the husband's death. This promises also restoration to the wife's family and patrimony of lands, goods and capital brought by the wife into the marriage and reserved for her male children by that husband (among the husband's children by his several wives). We then proceed to questions pertaining to the middle of the marriage, when the couple is living together, and finally at the end, we address the settlement of the marriage contract. The Halakhah therefore has its say in a marriage, from beginning, through middle, and to end. The logical organization by phases in the present instance means that we deal with the beginning of a marriage, effected by the deed, then the middle of the marriage, when the couple lives together, and then the end of the marriage so far as that is pertinent here, meaning, the settlement and payment of the marriage-contract.

That is what I mean when I say, the Halakhah tells the story of the tangible dimensions of a marriage, its beginning, middle, and end (in whether divorce or death). That category-formation then imposes its own tell-tale rationality, finding its topics for exposition in the sequence of the stages of a marriage: begin with the beginning, end with the end. That principle of selection of data explains why, viewed whole, the Halakhah of Nashim deals with the commencement of the marital bond with an act of sanctification of the woman to that man, confirmed by a document (tractates Qiddushin and Ketubot, respectively); aspects of the life of the marriage (an accusation if infidelity, Sotah, vows and special vows, Nedarim-Nazir); and the cessation of the marriage by reason of the husband's death without children (Yebamot) or divorce (Gittin).[6]

On the surface, then, that appeal to the order of a marriage, beginning, middle, and end, forms an altogether different principle of category-formation and bears in its wake a different hermeneutics from the ones that govern in the division of Appointed Times. There we found the key to the category-formation in a process of analogical-contrastive reasoning. Things are either like one another and fall into the same category so are subject to a rule in common, or they are unlike one another and fall into the opposite category, so are subject to opposed rules. That is how we were able to account for the character of the generative category-formations, e.g., Besah, Rosh Hashanah, Megillah, Hagigah, and the like, start to finish. But that preliminary impression, that we deal with a narrative hermeneutics, not an analytical-logical one, does not exhaust the matter by any means. As soon as we have in hand a full picture of the program of the Halakhah, we see the true correspondence: Yebamot with Ketubot!

To state the matter simply: the Ketubah is the work of man, and for its part, Heaven offers no contrasting, corresponding entity. Here — and in Qiddushin, as we shall see — we deal with a relationship between man and woman that accords to Heaven no entry into the transaction, and that Heaven nonetheless recognizes, honors, and reinforces with its own sanctions. The key to Ketubot and Qiddushin is Heaven's confirmation, above, of the properly-executed scribal labor, below. And what Heaven confirms is a transaction that imposes responsibilities on both parties to the relationship (and their families), while defining those responsibilities in accord with the teleology

---

[6] The wife's death without children is dealt with in the marriage-settlement, which adjusts the disposition of her dowry; no Halakhic problems are otherwise raised by her death, her husband or sons inherit her estate.

each party realizes: the husband to engender children, the wife to bear them, the husband to work to support his family, the wife to work to manage the domestic establishment, the husband to provide for the wife's sexual fulfillment, the wife for the husband's, as the Halakhah states explicitly.

If neither Scripture nor the Halakhic category-formations themselves offer us guidance in accounting for the hermeneutics of the category-formation, Ketubot, where do we find ourselves? The answer is, within the data themselves, the outline of the construction before us. That is what tells us the principle of cogency, the logic of coherent exposition, that guides the selection of, and holds together, the data that are assembled here and nowhere else. The formation, the duration, and the cessation of the marriage, with emphasis upon property-relationships where appropriate, personal ones where pertinent, define the sequential exposition, and since the sequence is beginning, middle, and end, we may state very plainly what I said at the outset: the hermeneutics of the story of the marriage is a sequential-topical one. But having said that, I raise more questions than I settle. What, exactly, defines the substance of the narrative? And why a story of one kind, rather than of another, told therein? It suffices at this stage to point to what we do not find, leaving for the exposition of the Halakhah the exposition of what we do find, and the meaning thereof. Absent from the account of Ketubot — the documentary embodiment of the marriage — is a place for Heaven's engagement and intervention. If we have Gittin and its counterpart, Yebamot, our starting point for the reading of each is in the contrast with the other, between man's and Heaven's mode of severing the marital bond. The document of divorce (*get*/Gittin) finds its match in the death of the husband, with or without children, such as Yebamot covers; but the document that embodies the marriage would seem to stand without a Heavenly equivalent. But for Ketubot (and Qiddushin) we have no corresponding corpus of Halakhah that organizes and systematizes Heaven's counterpart in realizing the same transaction. No corpus of Halakhah assembles the data on where and how Heaven realizes or brings about the embodiment of the marriage.

What is Heaven's counterpart to the Ketubah, the document that embodies the marital relationship, and, more broadly, to Ketubot, the native-category before us? Since Heaven has a very heavy stake in the marriage and its sanctity, relying upon the sanctification of Israelite woman by Israelite man for the propagation of holy Israel itself, that question certainly demands an answer. A moment of thought about the deepest sources of the Halakhic structure and system, which derive from Scripture's own narrative theology, points us toward that answer. It concerns the act of sanctification, with concomitant results for property relationships, by that man of that woman, and it focuses upon *whose* act of intentionality effects the act of sanctification. In the transaction of the marital bond, Heaven has a heavy stake but plays no role whatsoever. The whole enterprise depends upon man's and woman's will, but not God's active intervention. So there is no Heavenly counterpart to Ketubot — in the way in which Yebamot matches Gittin, for example — because there is no place for Heaven in the Halakhah, no role for Heaven to play, whether by analogy or by contrast. And why is that the case? Because where man's will works its power, Heaven's will gives way: man has free will, and, in the present context, so too does woman. In such a circumstance, Heaven confirms what man and woman affirm.

So the answer, specifically, to the question, why no place for Heaven in Ketubot, fits within the larger mythic framework of Judaism. Rabbinic Judaism, as we realize, embodies in the norms of behavior as much as of belief Scripture's account of man's and woman's power of intentionality, the autonomy and freedom of the human will. Of that power of will, as a matter of fact, the sanctification of the marital bond is a principal effect. And for human will to work its power, Heaven must leave ample space for human action. That explains why there is no room for a native category-formation on Heaven's counterpart to the man's and woman's act of creating a marriage, and that is why God cannot play a role in bringing about a marriage, comparable to his (demographically) primary role in bringing a marriage to its conclusion, with death.

While, accordingly, in the transaction that forms the heart of Ketubot, the marriage-document, its contents and its settlement, Heaven may have a heavy stake, Heaven still plays no role. The marriage is brought about by the act of man and the agreement of woman, both in full command of their senses and wholly in charge of the expression of their intentionality. Heaven confirms what man and woman have decided and reinforces the sanctification that has taken place. But Heaven cannot, as a matter of fact, intervene in the matter of intentionality when the initiative of man and the concurrence of woman are concerned. Man and woman enjoy entire autonomy, within the limits set by the Torah, which defines where and how the act of sanctification by a man of a woman takes effect to begin with. Why is this the case? It is because Heaven recognizes man's and woman's will as an independent power, countervailing to God's will. Man may or may not obey when God commands. But God then punishes disobedience, because God does not coerce. What confirms the ultimate freedom of man and woman to decide is God's just response to their disobedience; if they had no choice, then no justice would inhere in the penalty for disobedience.

Now, returning to the critical transaction of effecting the sanctification of the marital union, when it comes to an act of sanctification, man effects such an act through an expression of intentionality and will, just as God did and does. Accordingly, God has no place in the transaction, except to confirm what man and woman do of their own free will. Here, then, man and woman are like God, as free in their exercise of their will as God is free, as unimpeded in their realization of their intentionality just as God is, and the whole with the same end in mind: to create and sustain life, like God in the act of creation. And that explains why, since the act of sanctification by man over woman is an act wholly within the range of man's intentionality and will, Heaven finds no place in the entire transaction. These theoretical remarks do not exhaust the required analysis of the hermeneutics of Ketubot, but further inquiry must await consideration of the substance of the law. Then we shall gain a more detailed picture of the things that man controls in the formation of the marriage and why he controls them. We turn, therefore, to the systematic exposition of the pertinent verses of Scripture and of the Halakhah.

II. THE FOUNDATIONS OF THE HALAKHIC CATEGORY-FORMATIONS

Scripture figures only episodically, especially in two matters. First comes the fine for rape, which is paid to the father, so Dt. 22:28-29:

> If a man meets a virgin who is not betrothed and seizes her and lies with her and they are found, then the man who lay with her shall give to the father of the young woman fifty shekels of silver and she shall be his wife, because he has violated her; he may not put her away all his days.

Next comes Ex. 22:15-16:

> If a man seduces a virgin who is not betrothed and lies with her, he shall give the marriage present for her and make her his wife. If her father utterly refuses to give her to him, he shall pay money equivalent to the marriage-present for virgins.

Another aspect of the Halakhah to which Scripture contributes concerns conflicting claims as to the virginity of the bride, so Dt. 22:13-21:

> If any man takes a wife and goes in to her and then spurns her and charges her with shameful conduct and brings an evil name upon her, saying, 'I took this woman and when I came near her, I did not find in her the tokens of virginity,' then the father of the young woman and her mother shall take and bring out the tokens of her virginity to the elders of the city in the gate; and the father of the

> young woman shall say to the elders, 'I gave my daughter to this man to wife, and he spurns her, and lo, he has made shameful charges against her, saying, I did not find in your daughter the tokens of virginity. And yet these are the tokens of my daughter's virginity.' And they shall spread the garment before the elders of the city. Then the elders of that city shall take the man and whip him, and they shall fine him a hundred shekels of silver and give them to the father of the young woman, because he has brought an evil name upon a virgin of Israel; and she shall be his wife; he may not put her away all his days. But if the thing is true, that the tokens of virginity were not found in the young woman, then they shall bring out the young woman to the door of her father's house, and the men of her city shall stone her to death with stones, because she has wrought folly in Israel, by playing the harlot in her father's house; so you shall purge the evil from the midst of you.

But — and this is the main point — Scripture does not contribute the requirement of a marriage-agreement that provides for the woman's support in the event of divorce of death of the husband. These verses of Scripture figure in localized contexts but in no way prepare us for the program of the native category-formation.

The uneven and spare provision of Scripture accounts, in part, for the anomalous quality of the presentation of the Halakhah. When we come to the division of Women and Family, our task in identifying the like and the unlike presents a puzzle because Scripture does little of the work for us; our own intervention is required. For while Scripture supplies the lines of structure and order — the Sabbath is like and unlike the Festival; the Festival is like and unlike the intermediate days of the Festival, and the like — Scripture provides remarkably thin data on the stages of the marriage, the start and finish in particular. The data do not cohere, as they do for the Sabbath and Festivals.

Take for example the strikingly successful exercise of comparison and contrast of the two ways of severing the marital bond just now addressed in Yebamot in comparison and contrast with Gittin. The notion of comparing and contrasting the writ of divorce with the rite of removing the shoe — thus man's action in dissolving the sanctity of the marriage as against God's — does not derive from Scripture, which at Dt. 24:1ff., deals with the writ of divorce in a casual manner, en passant really, and at Dt. 25:5-10 with the cessation of the Levirate connection in its own terms. It is the analogical-contrastive hermeneutics of the sages that required them to compare and contrast like and unlike, here, the two media for dissolving a marriage. The genus is comprised by the severing of the marital bond, the secularization of the woman, the species, the circumstances of the husband at that moment, with or without offspring, respectively. So in working our way back from the Halakhah to its hermeneutics, in the Second Division we relied far more heavily on the Halakhah than on Scripture's own, established comparisons and contrasts. But the governing logic of analogy and contrast prevails, and the Halakhah on its own guides us to the comparison, therefore, the contrast, between the writ of divorce and the rite of removing the shoe, and that is what brought us to the much larger set of comparisons and contrasts between Heaven's and man's dissolving the marital bond. But where Scripture falls silent, a different source of truth, nature, takes over, and here the natural course of the marital bond dictates that narrative logic — beginning, middle, end of things — that exercises hegemony.

So we come to a category-formation that stands wholly out of relationship with Scripture, on the one side, and with contrasting category-formations, on the other. Ketubot, with its attention to the material rights of the parties to the marital union, constantly appeals to the principle of self-evident fairness, reciprocal responsibility in equal measure but different substance, — to a free-standing rationality of proportionality and balance and not to verses of Scripture. That is to say, Scripture does not guide the definition of a category-formation concerning marriage-contracts or marriage-settlements, such as is covered in Ketubot, nor for that matter does Scripture prepare us for the reading of the act of betrothal that is expounded in the category-formation, Qiddushin, as we shall see in due course. While the imagination and wit of the founders of the Halakhic system as we know it saw the intersection of Dt. 24:1ff. and Dt. 25:5-10 and so established the comparison of man's and Heaven's dealing with the end of a marriage and so the much broader treatment of that matter that makes of Yebamot such a remarkable native category-formation, here we find no counterpart. Not only does Scripture fail, but the Halakhah itself presents no counterpart to the present category-formation with some other.

III. THE EXPOSITION OF THE COMPONENTS OF THE GIVEN CATEGORY-FORMATION BY THE MISHNAH-TOSEFTA-YERUSHALMI-BAVLI

As always, I set forth the main points of **the Mishnah (in bold face type)**, then at the appropriate place add the Tosefta's own presentation not merely the clarification or amplification of the Mishnah's Halakhah (in ordinary type), thereafter *the Yerushalmi's (in italics)*, and finally, **THE BAVLI'S (IN BOLD FACE LOWER CASE TYPE)**. These are paraphrased and epitomized, they are not cited in full. I insert my observations on the points of special interest at the conclusion of each topical sub-unit. The units and sub-units derive from my own outline of the Mishnah-tractate, encompassing also the Tosefta-tractate; then the outline of the Yerushalmi, finally that of the Bavli.[7] Readers who compare the selections given here with the complete text will note that I omit disputed and schismatic opinion and discuss only the normative law.

I.   FOUNDATION OF THE HOUSEHOLD: THE MATERIAL RIGHTS OF THE PARTIES TO THE MARITAL UNION [1] THE WIFE

    A.   *THE MARRIAGE CONTRACT OF THE VIRGIN*

    M. 1:1 A virgin is married on Wednesday, and a widow on Thursday. For twice weekly are the courts in session in the towns, on Monday and on Thursday. So if he [the husband] had a complaint as to virginity, he goes early to court.

    T. 1:1 On what account did they rule, A virgin is married on Wednesday [M. Ket. 1:1A]? So that if he had a complaint against her virginity, he goes to court early on the next morning, when it is in session]. If so, she should [just as well] be married after the Sabbath [on Sunday]. But because the husband does his preparations [for the wedding feast] through the [three] weekdays, they arranged that he should marry her on Wednesday. From the time of the danger [Bar Kokhba's War] and thereafter, they began the custom of marrying her on Tuesday, and sages did not stop them. [If] he wanted to marry her on Monday, they do not listen to him. But if it is on account of constraint [a death in the family], it is permitted. On what account do they keep the husband apart from the bride on the night of the Sabbath for the first act of sexual relations? Because he makes a bruise. On what account did they rule, A widow is married on Thursday [M. Ket. 1:1A]?. For if he should marry her on any day of the week, he may leave her and go back to work. So they arranged that he should marry her on Thursday, so that he should remain away from work for three successive days, Thursday, the eve of the Sabbath [Friday], and the Sabbath — three days away from work.. He turns out to take pleasure with her for three days running.

    B. 1:1 I.11/4A LO, IF HIS BREAD WAS BAKED, MEAT SLAUGHTERED, WINE MIXED, AND WATER POURED ON THE MEAT, BUT THEN THE FATHER OF THE GROOM OR THE MOTHER OF THE BRIDE DROPPED DEAD, THEY PUT THE DECEASED INTO A ROOM AND THEN BRING THE GROOM AND BRIDE INTO THE MARRIAGE CANOPY, WHERE THE GROOM HAS SEXUAL RELATIONS WITH THE BRIDE IN FULFILLMENT OF THE RELIGIOUS DUTY, BUT THEN [THE BURIAL OF THE DECEASED

---

[7] These are cited with bibliographical data in the Introduction, Volume I.

TAKES PLACE, AND, OF COURSE, THE GROOM FOR THE MOURNING PERIOD] SEPARATES HIMSELF FROM HER. THE SEVEN DAYS OF BANQUETING ARE OBSERVED, THEN THE SEVEN DAYS OF MOURNING, AND DURING ALL THOSE DAYS, HE SLEEPS AMONG THE MEN, AND SHE AMONG THE WOMEN. AND SO, IF HIS WIFE HAD HER PERIOD, HE SLEEPS AMONG THE MEN AND SHE AMONG THE WOMEN. BUT THEY DO NOT WITHHOLD ANY FORM OF ORNAMENT FROM THE BRIDE FOR ALL THIRTY DAYS. ONE WAY OR THE OTHER, HE SHOULD NOT HAVE HIS FIRST ACT OF SEXUAL RELATIONS ON A FRIDAY OR SATURDAY NIGHT.

M. 1:2 A virgin — her marriage contract is two hundred [zuz]. And a widow, a maneh [one hundred zuz]. A virgin-widow, divorcée, and one who has severed the levirate connection through a rite of removing the shoe at the stage of betrothal — their marriage contract is two hundred [zuz]. And they are subject to the claim against their virginity. A convert, a woman taken captive, and a slave girl who were redeemed or who converted or who were freed at an age of less than three years and one day — their marriage contract is two hundred [zuz]. And they are subject to the claim against their virginity.

M. 1:3 An adult male who had sexual relations with a minor female, and a minor male who had sexual relations with an adult female — their marriage contract is two hundred zuz. The girl injured by a blow — her marriage contract is a maneh.

T. 1:2 An adult male who had sexual relations with a minor female, and a minor male who had sexual relations with an adult female, and a girl injured by a blow [so that her signs of virginity are destroyed] — their marriage-contract [for a marriage] to another is two hundred [zuz] [M. Ket. 1:3A-D].

M. 1:4 A virgin, a widow, a divorcée, or one who has severed the levirate connection through a rite of removing the shoe — at the stage of consummation of the marriage — their marriage contract is a maneh [a hundred zuz]. And they are not subject to a claim against their virginity. A convert, a girl taken captive, or a slave girl who were redeemed, or who converted, or who were freed at an age older than three years and one day — their marriage contract is a maneh. And they are not subject to a claim against their virginity.

T. 1:3 A man of sound senses who married a deaf-mute girl or an idiot — their marriage-contract is two hundred zuz, for he wants to gain a hold on their possessions. A deaf-mute or an idiot who married a woman of sound senses, even though the deaf-mute went and became sound in his senses, or the idiot regained his mind — they [these women of sound senses] do not receive a marriage-contract. [If after being healed] they went to confirm the marriage, they pay a maneh as the marriage-contract. A gentile or a slave who had sexual relations with an Israelite girl even though the gentile went and converted, the slave went and was freed, they [the women] do not have a marriage-contract. If they [the convert, the freed slave] wanted to confirm the marriage, they pay a maneh as the marriage-contract. An Israelite who had sexual relations with a slave-girl or with a gentile woman, even though the slave-girl went and was freed, or the gentile-girl went and converted — they [the women] do not have a marriage contract. [If] he wanted to confirm the marriage, he gives a maneh as the marriage contract. An adult woman and a barren woman — their marriage contract is two hundred zuz. [If she was married in the assumption that she is suitable and turned out to be barren, she has no marriage-contract. [If] he wanted to confirm the marriage, he gives a maneh as the marriage-contract. He who has sexual relations with a deaf-mute girl or with an idiot or with a mature woman or with a girl wounded by a blow — they are not subject to a claim of virginity. In the case of a blind woman or a barren woman, they are subject to a claim of virginity.

M. 1:5 He who lives ["eats"] with his father-in-law in Judah, not with witnesses, cannot lodge a claim against the girl's virginity, for he has been alone with her. All the same are the widow of an Israelite and the widow of a priest — their marriage contract is a maneh [a hundred zuz]. The priests' court would collect four hundred zuz for a virgin.

The act of sanctification bears with it material consequences, it is a tangible transaction. The status of the wife — virgin or otherwise — makes a difference in the husband's obligation in the marriage-settlement at death or divorce. The husband, then, also has the right to go to court with his claim.

B. *CONFLICTING CLAIMS FOR THE MARRIAGE-CONTRACT OF A VIRGIN*

M. 2:1 The woman who was widowed or divorced — she says, "You married me as a virgin" — and he says, "Not so, but I married you as a widow" — if there are witnesses that [when she got married], she went forth to music, with her hair flowing loose, her marriage contract is two hundred [zuz].

T. 1:4 [If] he married her in the assumption that she was suitable and she turned out to have had prior sexual relations, even though she was in private [with him], [or] there are witnesses that she was not alone with him for sufficient time to have sexual relations, the second has no claim of virginity against her. Therefore the marriage-contract on his account is only maneh.

T. 1:5 He who accuses [his bride of having had sexual relations with another man before marriage], and his witnesses against her turn out to be conspirators — he is scourged and pays four hundred zuz [to the accused woman]. And the conspiratorial witnesses are taken out for stoning. [If] she was an orphan, he is scourged, and her marriage-contract remains valid, and he pays her four hundred zuz [in addition to it]. And the conspiratorial witnesses are taken out for stoning. [If] he did not tell the witnesses to bear witness, but they came along on their own and testified against the girl [and they turned out to be conspirators] — he [the husband] is not scourged and does not pay her four hundred zuz. But the conspiratorial witnesses are taken out for stoning. [If] she committed fornication when she was a girl, and after she had matured, he accused her [of having done so], he is not scourged and does not pay four hundred zuz. And she or the conspiratorial witnesses against her are then taken out for stoning.

T. 2:1 Witnesses who said, "We testify about So-and-so, that he is the son of a divorcee, or the son of a woman who has performed the rite of removing the shoe, of a Samaritan, of a Netin, or a Mamzer" — [if] before their testimony was cross-examined in court, they said, "We were joking," lo, they are believed. If after their testimony was cross-examined in court, they said, "We are joking," they are not believed. This is the general principle of the matter: Witnesses who testified to declare someone unclean or clean, to bring someone near or to put someone afar, to prohibit or to permit, to exempt or to render liable — [if] before their testimony was cross-examined in court, they said, "We are joking," lo, these are believed. [If] after their testimony was cross-examined in court, they said, "We are joking," they are not believed.

T. 2:1 Greater is the power of a writ [document] than the power of witnesses, and [greater is the power of] witnesses than the power of a writ. Greater is the power of a writ, for a writ [of divorce] removes a woman from the domain of her husband, which is not the case with witnesses. Greater is the power of witnesses, for witnesses who said, "So-and-so has died," — his wife may remarry. But if it was written in a writ, "So-and-so has died," his wife may not remarry. If they said, "What is written in this document we in fact had heard but forgot," his wife may remarry. A man may write down his testimony in a document and give testimony on the strength of that document and continue even a hundred years after [the date of the document]. Greater is the power of a document than the power of money, and greater is the power of money than the power of a document. For a document allows one to collect from indentured [mortgaged] property, which is not the case with money. Greater is the power of money, for money serves for the redemption of things which have been given as valuations and as herem [to the sanctuary], things which have been sanctified, and second tithe, which is not the case with a document. Greater is the power of a document and of money than the power of possession, and greater is the power of possession than the power of a document and money. Greater is the power of a document and money, for a document or money serve to acquire a Hebrew slave, which is not the case with [mere] possession. Greater is the power of possession, for if one sold a man ten fields, as soon as he takes possession of one of them, he has acquired ownership of all of them. But if he gave him only the price of one of them, or wrote him a document only for one of them, he has acquired ownership of that field alone.

How to sort out conflicting claims in the marriage-contract, with special reference to the difference between virgin and otherwise, forms the next step in the exposition of the material transaction. All I see here are rules of resolving conflicting claims, but I discern no deeper layers of meaning. Nor does the Tosefta's brilliant exercise of comparison and contrast, T. 2:1, change the picture, with its comprehensive construction organizing information without vastly deepening our understanding of the conceptions that inhere.

C. *THE RULES OF EVIDENCE IN CONNECTION WITH THE VALIDATION OF THE MARRIAGE-CONTRACT*

M. 2:2 In the case of him who says to his fellow, "This field belonged to your father, and I bought it from him," he is believed. For the mouth that prohibited is the mouth that permitted. And if there are [other] witnesses that it had belonged to his father, and he claims, "I bought it from him," he is not believed.

M. 2:3 The witnesses who said, "This is our handwriting, but we were forced [to sign]," "...we were minors," "...we were invalid [as relatives] for testimony" — lo, these are believed, [and the writ is invalid]. But if there are witnesses that it is their handwriting, or if their handwriting was available from some other source, they are not believed.

M. 2:4 This one says, "This is my handwriting, and this is the handwriting of my fellow," and this one says, "This is my handwriting, and this is the handwriting of my fellow" — lo, these are believed. This one says, "This is my handwriting" and this one says, "This is my handwriting — they do not have to add another to them. But: A man is believed to say, "This is my handwriting."

M. 2:5 The woman who said, "I was married, and I am divorced," is believed. For the testimony that imposed a prohibition is the testimony that remitted the prohibition. But if there are witnesses that she was married, and she says, "I am divorced," she is not believed. [If] she said, "I was taken captive, but I am pure," she is believed. For the testimony that imposed a prohibition is the testimony that remitted the prohibition. But if there are

witnesses to the fact that she was taken captive, and she says, "I am pure," she is not believed. But if the witnesses appeared [to testify that she was taken captive] only after she had remarried, lo, this one should not go forth.

B. 2:5 I:5/22A IF TWO WITNESSES SAY THE HUSBAND HAS DIED, AND TWO SAY HE HAS NOT DIED, TWO SAY THE WIFE HAS BEEN DIVORCED, AND TWO SAY SHE HAS NOT BEEN DIVORCED, LO, THIS WOMAN MAY NOT REMARRY, AND IF SHE HAS REMARRIED, SHE ALSO DOES NOT HAVE TO LEAVE HER SECOND HUSBAND.

B. 2:5 I:8 22B IF TWO WITNESSES SAY SHE WAS BETROTHED AND TWO SAY SHE WAS NOT BETROTHED, SHE SHOULD NOT MARRY, AND IF SHE HAS MARRIED, SHE SHALL NOT GO FORTH. IF TWO SAY SHE WAS DIVORCED AND TWO SAY SHE WAS NOT DIVORCED, SHE SHALL NOT MARRY, AND IF SHE HAS MARRIED, SHE WILL GO FORTH.

M. 2:6 Two women who were taken captive — this one says, "I was taken captive, but I am pure," and that one says, "I was taken captive, but I am pure" — they are not believed. And when they give evidence about one another, lo, they are believed.

M. 2:7 And so two men — this one says, "I am a priest," and that one says, "I am a priest" — they are not believed. But when they give evidence about one another, lo, they are believed.

T. 2:2 The two hundred zuz owing to a virgin, the maneh owing to a widow, the compensation for damages and half-damages, double payment, and four- and five-times payment — all of them, even though they are not written in a document, do people collect from indentured property. The woman who said, "I am married," and then went and said, "I am not married" is believed. For the mouth which prohibited is the mouth which permitted [M. Ket. 2:5A-B]. [If] she said, "I was taken captive, but I am pure, and I have witnesses that I am pure," they do not say, "Let us wait until the witnesses come and render her permitted." But they permit her [to return to her husband] forthwith [M. Ket. 2:5E-F]. If once she has been permitted, witnesses come and say, "She was taken captive," lo, this one should not remarry. [If they say,] "She was taken captive and was contaminated," even though she has children, she should go forth [M. Ket. 2:5I]. One witness says, "She was taken captive and has been contaminated," and one witness says, "She was taken captive but is pure" — One woman says, "She was taken captive and is contaminated," and one woman says, "She was taken captive but is pure" — lo, this one should not remarry. But if she remarried, she should not go forth. Two women who were taken captive [M. Ket. 2:6H] — This one says, "I am unclean, but my girlfriend is clean," — she is believed. [If] she says, "I am clean, and my girlfriend is unclean," she is not believed.

"I and my girlfriend are unclean" — she is believed concerning herself, but she is not believed concerning her girlfriend. "I and my girlfriend are clean" — she is believed concerning her girlfriend but she is not believed concerning herself [M. Ket. 2:6E]. And so too with two men [M. Ket. 2:7A]: This one says, "My friend is a priest," and this one says, "My friend is a priest," — they give them [heave-offering] [M. Ket. 2:7E]. But as to confirming that they are priests [for genealogical purposes], they are not believed until there will be three of them, so that there will be two giving testimony about this one, and two giving testimony about that one.

T. 2:3 They raise to the priesthood [people thought to be] Levites or Israelites on the strength of the testimony of a single witness [M. Ket. 2:8C]. But they lower someone from the priesthood only on the evidence of two witnesses. How does one cast doubt about the matter? If they said, "How does Mr. So-and-so jump up into the priesthood, who never raised his hands to give the priestly blessing in his entire life, who never took his share [of heave-offering] in his entire life" — this is not a suitable casting of doubt. [If they said], "He is the son of a divorcee or of a woman who has performed the rite of removing the shoe, of a Samaritan, a Netin, or a mamzer," lo, this constitutes casting doubt about the matter.

T. 3:1 There are two presumptive grounds for a person's being deemed to be in the priesthood in the Land of Israel: Raising up hands [in the priestly benediction], and sharing heave-offering at the threshing floor. And in Syria: Up to the point at which the agents announcing the new moon reach, the raising of hands in the priestly benediction [constitutes adequate grounds], but not sharing heave-offering at the threshing floor. Babylonia is in the same status as Syria.

M. 2:9 The woman who was taken prisoner by gentiles — [if it was] for an offense concerning property, she is permitted [to return] to her husband. [If it was for] a capital offense, she is prohibited to her husband. A city which was overcome by siege — all the priest girls found therein are invalid [to return to their husbands]. But if they have witnesses, even a man slave or a girl slave, lo, they are believed. But a person is not believed to testify in his own behalf.

T. 3:2 All are believed to give testimony about her, even her son, even her daughter — except for her and her husband, for a man does not give testimony in his own behalf.

M. 2:10 And these are believed to give testimony when they reach maturity about what they saw when they were minors: A man is believed to say, (1) "This is the handwriting of Father," and (2) "This is the handwriting of Rabbi," and (3) "This is the handwriting of my brother" (4) "I remember about Mrs. So-and-

so that she went forth to music with her hair flowing loose [when she was married]" [M. 2:1] (5) "I remember that Mr. So-and-so would go forth from school to immerse to eat food in the status of priestly rations," (6) "That he would take a share [of food in the status of priestly rations] with us at the threshing floor" (7) "This place is a grave area" (8) "Up to here did we walk on the Sabbath." But a man is not believed to say, (9) "Mr. So-and-so had a right of way in this place," (10) "So-and-so had the right of halting and holding a lamentation in this place."

T. 3:3 A man is believed to say, "Father told me this family is unclean," "That family is clean," "We ate at the cutting off [ceremony marking the marriage of a man or woman to someone beneath his or her genealogical rank] of Mrs. So-and-so," "and that his teacher said to So-and-so, 'Go and immerse [to be clean for] your heave-offering," "We used to bring heave-offerings and tithes to So-and-so." They are believed so far as allowing the giving of heave-offerings and tithes to So-and-so, but not to confirm him in the priesthood [for genealogical purposes]. Or [if he said], "Others brought him [heave-offering and tithes]" — they are not believed. But if he was a gentile and converted a slave and was freed, lo, these are not believed. They are not believed to say, "I remember about So-and-so that he owes Mrs. So-and-so a maneh" — and "Such-and-such a road crosses such-and-such a field" — for this [right of way] is equivalent to property. Under what circumstances? When they gave testimony on the spot [about their own hometown]. But if they went forth and came back, they are not believed, for they may have stated matters only because of enticement or fear.

T. 3:4 All the same are men, women, slaves, and minors: they are believed to say, "This place is unclean," and "This place is clean" [M. Ket. 2:10E].

B. 2:10 IX.4/28B WHAT IS THE CUTTING-OFF CEREMONY? IF ONE OF THE BROTHERS MARRIED A WOMAN THAT WAS NOT APPROPRIATE IN GENEALOGY TO HIM, THE MEMBERS OF THE FAMILY COME AND BRING A JUG FULL OF PRODUCE, AND THEY BREAK IT IN THE MIDDLE OF THE STREET, AND THEY SAY, "OUR BRETHREN, HOUSE OF ISRAEL, GIVE EAR! OUR BROTHER, MR. SO-AND-SO, HAS MARRIED A WOMAN WHO IS NOT GENEALOGICALLY FIT FOR HIM, AND WE ARE AFRAID THAT HIS OFFSPRING WILL GET MIXED UP WITH OUR OFFSPRING. COME AND TAKE FOR YOU A TOKEN FOR FUTURE GENERATIONS, THAT HIS OFFSPRING IS NOT TO MIX UP WITH OUR OFFSPRING," AND THIS IS THE CUTTING-OFF CEREMONY CONCERNING WHICH A CHILD IS BELIEVED WHEN HE GIVES TESTIMONY.

The final unit does not materially change the picture. The rules of assessing evidence transcend the case at hand, the conflict of testimony being pertinent to a variety of claims. But I do not know what deeper issues in here in the cases. The governing principles — commonsensical throughout — are clear in context and do not point us toward any principles of interpretation that may come to expression in the cases at hand. I am inclined to suppose that the general applicability of the principles explains why the issues of the native category-formation — the material transaction of the marital bond — do not impinge.

II. THE FORMATION OF THE MARRIAGE: THE MATERIAL RIGHTS OF THE PARTIES TO THE MARITAL UNION [2] THE FATHER AND THE HUSBAND

A. THE FINE THAT IS PAID TO THE FATHER FOR RAPE OR SEDUCTION (DT. 21:22)

M. 3:1 These are the girls [invalid for marriage to an Israelite] who [nonetheless] receive a fine [from the man who seduces them]: He who has sexual relations with (1) a mamzer girl, (2) a netin girl, or (3) a Samaritan girl; he who has sexual relations with (4) a convert girl, and with (5) a girl taken captive, and (6) a slave girl who were redeemed, who converted, or who were freed [respectively] when they were at an age of less than three years and one day [and who remain in the status of virgins]; he who has sexual relations with (7) his sister, and with (8) the sister of his father, and with (9) the sister of his mother, and with (10) his wife's sister, and with (11) the wife of his brother, and with (12) the wife of the brother of his father, and with (13) the menstruating woman — they receive a fine [from the man who seduces them]. Even though [sexual relations with] them are subject to extirpation, one does not incur through having sexual relations with them the death penalty at the hands of an earthly court.

B. 3:1 III.19/35B-36A THOSE WHO STAND IN A CONSANGUINEOUS RELATIONSHIP WITH THE LOVER, AND THOSE FORBIDDEN TO HIM AT THE SECOND REMOVE, HAVE NO CLAIM ON PAYMENT OF A FINE IN THE CASE OF RAPE OR TO AN INDEMNITY IN THE CASE OF SEDUCTION. A GIRL WHO EXERCISES THE RIGHT OF REFUSAL HAS NO CLAIM ON PAYMENT OF A FINE IN THE CASE OF RAPE OR TO AN INDEMNITY IN THE CASE OF SEDUCTION. A BARREN WOMAN HAS NO CLAIM ON PAYMENT OF A FINE IN THE CASE OF RAPE OR TO AN INDEMNITY IN THE CASE OF

SEDUCTION. SHE WHO IS SENT OFF ON ACCOUNT OF A BAD REPUTATION HAS NO CLAIM ON PAYMENT OF A FINE IN THE CASE OF RAPE OR TO AN INDEMNITY IN THE CASE OF SEDUCTION.

M. 3:2 And these do not receive a fine [from the man who seduces them]: he who has sexual relations with (1) a convert, (2) a girl taken captive, or (3) a slave girl, who was redeemed, or who converted, or who was freed, when any of these was at an age of more than three years and one day — he who has sexual relations with (4) his daughter, (5) his daughter's daughter, (6) with the daughter of his son, (7) with the daughter of his wife, (8) with the daughter of her son, (9) with the daughter of her daughter — they do not receive a fine [from the man who seduces them], for he incurs the death penalty. For the death penalty inflicted upon him is at the hands of an earthly court, and whoever incurs the death penalty [at the hands of an earthly court] does not pay out a financial penalty [in addition], since it says, "If no damage befall he shall surely be fined" (Ex. 21:22).

T. 3:5 He who has sexual relations with a deaf-mute, or with an idiot, or with a mature woman, or with a woman injured by a blow [and so without a hymen] — they do not receive a penalty. For a blind girl and a barren girl they receive a penalty.

M. 3:4 The one who seduces a girl pays on three counts, and the one who rapes a girl pays on four: the one who seduces a girl pays for (1) the shame, (2) the damage, and (3) a fine, and the one who rapes a girl adds to these, for he in addition pays for (4) the pain [which he has inflicted]. What is the difference between the one who rapes a girl and the one who seduces her? (1) The one who rapes a girl pays for the pain, and the one who seduces her does not pay for the pain. (2) The one who rapes a girl pays the financial penalties forthwith, but the one who seduces her pays the penalties when he puts her away. (3) The one who rapes the girl [forever after] drinks out of his earthen pot, but the one who seduces her, if he wanted to put her away, does put her away.

T. 3:6 All the same are the one who rapes and the one who seduces [both of them pay fifty sheqels as a fine]. What is the difference between him who rapes and him who seduces? The one who rapes pays compensation for pain, and the one who seduces does not pay compensation for pain [M. Ket. 3:4E-F]. Even though they said, The one who rapes pays the penalty immediately [M. Ket. 3:4G], but if he should put her away, he pays nothing [in addition]. Even though they said, The one who seduces, if he should divorce her, pays a penalty [M. Ket. 3:4H], but the compensation for her shame and her injury he pays forthwith. What is the difference between paying forthwith and paying later on? As to paying forthwith, if the girl dies, her father inherits [her estate, inclusive of the fines]. But if he pays later on, if she should die, her husband inherits [her estate].

T. 3:7 All the same are the one who rapes and the one who spreads a bad story about a girl, who divorced [the woman they have raped or maligned, respectively]: they force him to bring her back. [If] they are priests, they incur forty stripes. All the same are the one who rapes and the one who seduces — either she or her father is able to dissent [from the required marriage], since it says, And if refusing, her father shall refuse [Ex. 22:16], and it further says, And she shall be a wife for him (Deut. 22:29) — with her consent. Him do you force, but you do not force the levir.

M. 3:5 How does he "drink from his earthen pot"? Even if she is lame, even if she is blind, and even if she is afflicted with boils, [he must remain married to her]. [If] a matter of unchastity turned out to pertain to her, or if she is not appropriate to enter into the Israelite congregation, he is not permitted to confirm her as his wife, [but, if he has married her, he must divorce her,] since it is said, "And she will be a wife to him" (Deut. 22:29) — a wife appropriate for him.

M. 3:7 What is the [mode of assessing compensation for] shame? All [is assessed] in accord with the status of the one who shames and the one who is shamed. [How is the compensation for] damage [assessed]? They regard her as if she is a slave girl for sale: How much was she worth [before the sexual incident], and how much is she worth now. The fine? It is the same for every person [fifty selas, Deut. 22:29]. And any [fine] which is subject to a fixed amount decreed by the Torah is equivalent for every person.

M. 3:8 In any situation in which there is a right of sale, there is no fine. And in any situation in which there is a fine, there is no right of sale. A minor girl is subject to sale and does not receive a fine. A girl receives a fine and is not subject to sale. A mature woman is not subject to sale and [does] not [receive] a fine.

M. 3:9 He who says, "I seduced Mr. So-and-so's daughter," pays the penalties of shame and damage on the basis of his own testimony. But he does not pay a fine. He who says, "I stole and I slaughtered and sold [an animal belonging to So-and-so]," pays back the principal on the basis of his own testimony, but he does not pay double damages or four- or fivefold damages. [If he says], "My ox killed So-and-so," or "the ox of So-and-so," lo, this one pays on the basis of his own testimony. [If he says], "My ox killed So-and-so's slave," he does not pay on the basis of his own evidence. This is the general principle: Whoever pays compensation greater than the damage he has actually done does not pay said damages on the basis of his own testimony [alone, and he cannot be assessed for such damages].

M. 4:1 A girl [twelve to twelve-and-a-half years of age] who was seduced – [the financial penalties] for her shame, damage, and fine belong to her father, and the [compensation for] pain in the case of a girl who was seized [(Deut. 22:28) and raped, also belongs to the father]. [If] she won in court before her father died, lo, they [the funds] belong to the father. [If] the father [then] died, lo, they belong to the brothers. [If] she did not suffice to win her case in court before the father died, lo, they are hers. [If] she won her case in court before she matured [at the age of twelve years and six months], lo, they belong to the father. [If] the father died, lo, they belong to the brothers. [If] she did not suffice to win her case in court before the father died, lo, they are hers. [As to] the fruit of her labor and the things which she finds, even though she did not collect [her wages] — [if] the father died, lo, they belong to the brothers.

From the wife's material rights in the marital union, we turn to the father's, which are indicated by Scripture. It is Scripture's provision that defines the sub-category and the determining principles. The father's scripturally-assigned rights to compensation depend on his legitimacy as father and of hers as his daughter.

B. *THE FATHER*

M. 4:2 He who betrothed his daughter, and he [the husband] divorced her, [and] he [the father] betrothed her [to someone else], and she was widowed — her marriage contract [in both instances] belongs to him [the father]. [If] he [the father] married her off, [however], and he [the husband] divorced her, he [the father] married her off, and she was widowed — her marriage contract belongs to her.

M. 4:3 The convert whose daughter converted with her, and she [the daughter] committed an act of fornication [when she was a betrothed girl] — lo, this one is put to death through strangling. She is not subject to the rule, "At the door of her father's house" (Deut. 22:21), nor to "a hundred selas" [Deut. 22:19, in the case of one who slandered her]. [If] her conception was not in a state of sanctity but her parturition was in a state of sanctity, lo, this one is put to death with stoning. She is not subject to the rule, "At the door of her father's house," nor to a hundred selas. [If] her conception and parturition were in a state of sanctity, lo, she is equivalent to an Israelite girl for every purpose. [If] she has a father but no "door of her father's house" [her father has no house], [or if] she has a "door of her father's house" but no father, lo, this one is put to death with stoning. "At the door of her father's house" is stated only as a duty [in addition to stoning].

The rights of the father to the bride-price that Scripture has provided depend, once more, on the authenticity of his paternity. If it is a case in which no family-ties are involved, e.g., a convert, who is classified from conversion as bearing no genealogy, no bride-price is claimed by the father.

C. THE FATHER AND THE HUSBAND

M. 4:4 The father retains control of his daughter [younger than twelve and a half] as to effecting any of the tokens of betrothal: money, document, or sexual intercourse. And he retains control of what she finds, of the fruit of her labor, and of abrogating her vows. And he receives her writ of divorce [from a betrothal]. But he does not dispose of the return [on property received by the girl from her mother] during her lifetime. [When] she is married, the husband exceeds the father, for he disposes of the return [on property received by the girl from her mother] during her lifetime. But he is liable to maintain her, and to ransom her, and to bury her.

T. 4:1 Greater is the power of the husband than that of the father, and [greater is] the power of the father than that of the husband. Greater is the power of the husband, for the husband disposes of the fruit of her labor during her lifetime, which is not so for the father [M. Ket. 4:4D].

T. 4:2 Greater is the power of the father, for the husband is liable to maintain her, to redeem her if she is taken captive], and to bury her [M. Ket. 4:4F], and, in a place in which it is customary to say a lamentation, to arrange for a lamentation for her, which is not incumbent on the father.

T. 4:3 Greater is the power of a wife than the power of the sister-in-law [the deceased, childless brother's wife], and [greater is the power of] the sister-in-law than of the wife. Greater is the power of the wife, for the wife eats heave-offering as soon as she enters the marriage canopy, even if she has not yet had sexual relations with the husband, which is not the case for the sister-in-law. Greater is the power of the sister-in-law, for he who has sexual relations with his sister-in-law [deceased, childless brother's widow], whether inadvertently or intentionally, whether under constraint or willingly, even if she is in her father's house, has acquired her as his wife, which is not the case with a wife.

Y. 4:4 I:7 Under no circumstances is the husband flogged, nor is he required to pay a hundred selas, unless [the contrary] witnesses are stoned to death [by being proved to be perjurers]. [Merely contradicting their testimony does not suffice.]

B. 4:4/VIII.1/47A IF THE FATHER WROTE A DEED FOR THE DAUGHTER ASSIGNING PRODUCE, CLOTHES, OR OTHER MOVABLES THAT SHE MAY TAKE WITH HER FROM HER FATHER'S HOUSE TO HER HUSBAND'S, AND SHE DIED [WHILE BETROTHED, NOT BRINGING THESE THINGS WITH HER TO THE HUSBAND'S HOUSEHOLD] — THE HUSBAND HAS NOT ACQUIRED THE TITLE OF THESE THINGS.

M. 4:5 Under all circumstances is she in the domain of the father, until she enters the domain of the husband through marriage. [If] the father handed her over to the agents of the husband, lo, she [from that point on] is in the domain of the husband. [If] the father went along with the agents of the husband, or [if] the agents of the father went along with the agents of the husband, lo, she is in the domain of the father. [If] the agents of the father handed her over to the agents of the husband, lo, she is in the domain of the husband.

T. 4:4 [If the father went along with her agents or with the agents of the husband. or if the agents of the father went along with the agents of the husband [M. Ket. 4:5C], (if she had a courtyard along the way and went in and spent the night in it or if [the husband] entered the marriage-canopy not for the purpose of consummating the marriage, and she died, even though her marriage-contract is with her husband, her father inherits it.. If the father gave her over to the agents of the husband, or the agents of the father gave her over to the agents of the husband [M. Ket. 4:5B-D], or if she had a courtyard on the way and went in there and spent the night in it, or if she entered the marriage-canopy for the purpose of consummating the marriage, and she died, even though her marriage-contract is with her father, her husband inherits it. Under what circumstances? In the case of her marriage-contract. But as to heave-offering, she does not eat heave-offering until she enters the marriage-canopy [M. Ket. 5:3].

M. 4:6 The father [while alive] is not liable for the maintenance of his daughter.

We come to the joint claims of father and husband, for the woman, daughter and wife, before maturity is not conceived prior to a valid marriage to stand wholly in her own stead (M. 4:5). The father retains control to the prepubescent daughter's property, the husband takes it over. The Tosefta's familiar exercise of comparison, T. 4:1-3, provides an admirable collection of well-classified facts.

D.   *THE HUSBAND*

M. 4:7 [If] he did not write a marriage contract for her, the virgin [nonetheless] collects two hundred [zuz in the event of divorce or widowhood], and the widow, a maneh, for this is [in all events] an unstated condition imposed by the court. [If] he assigned to her in writing a field worth a maneh instead of two hundred zuz, and did not write for her, *"All property which I have is surety for your marriage contract,"* he is nonetheless liable, for this is [in all events] an unstated condition imposed by the court.

M. 4:8 [If] he did not write for her, *"If you are taken captive, I shall redeem you and bring you back to my side as my wife,"* or, in the case of a priest girl, *"I shall bring you back to your town,"* he is nonetheless liable [to do so], for this is [in all events] an unstated condition imposed by the court.

B. 4:8 III.2/52A IF THE WOMAN WAS TAKEN CAPTIVE DURING THE LIFETIME OF HER HUSBAND, BUT THEN HE DIED, AND HER HUSBAND KNEW ABOUT HER SITUATION, HIS HEIRS HAVE TO RANSOM HER, BUT IF HER HUSBAND DID NOT KNOW ABOUT HER SITUATION, HIS HEIRS ARE NOT REQUIRED TO RANSOM HER.

B. 4:8 III 4/52A IF SHE WAS TAKEN CAPTIVE, AND THEY DEMANDED FROM HER HUSBAND TEN TIMES HER VALUE, HE STILL HAS TO RANSOM HER, AT LEAST ONCE. SUBSEQUENTLY, HOWEVER, HE MAY RANSOM HER IF HE WANTED, BUT HE DOES NOT HAVE TO DO SO IF HE DOESN'T WANT TO.

M. 4:9 [If] she was taken captive, he is liable to redeem her. And if he said, "Lo, here is her writ of divorce and [the funds owing on] her marriage contract, let her redeem herself," he has no right to do so. [If] she fell ill, he is liable to heal her. [If] he said, "Lo, here is her writ of divorce and [the funds owing on] her marriage contract, let her heal herself," he has the right to do so.

T. 4:5 [If] she was taken captive, he is not liable to redeem her. Under what circumstances? In the case of a girl taken captive by a government official. If she was taken captive by a thug, he redeems her. If [then] he wants to confirm the marriage, he confirms it. If not, he puts her away and pays her a maneh as her marriage-contract [M. Ket. 4:8C] [If] she was taken captive after her husband's death, the levirs are not liable to redeem her. And not only so, but even if she is taken captive while her husband was alive, and afterward her husband died, the levirs are not liable to redeem her. [If] she was maintained by his property and required medical attention, lo, that is equivalent to any other aspect of her support [M. Ket. 4:9D-E]. If there were years of famine, [if] he then said to her, "Take your writ of divorce and your marriage-contract, go and feed yourself," he has that right.

M. 4:10 [If] he did not write for her, *"Male children which you will have with me will inherit the proceeds of your marriage contract, in addition to their share with their other brothers,"* he nonetheless is liable [to pay over the proceeds of the marriage contract to the woman's sons], for this is [in all events] an unstated condition imposed by the court.

T. 4:6 [If] he did not write for her in her marriage-contract, "Male children which you will have from me will inherit the proceeds of your marriage-contract in addition to their share with their older brothers," he is liable for this is in all events an unstated condition imposed by the court on all marriage-contracts [M. Ket. 4:10]. All provinces wrote their marriage-contracts as did the Jerusalemites [M. Ket. 4:12D].

T. 4:7 A man marries a woman on condition of not having to maintain her and of not having to support her. And not only so, but he may make an agreement with her that she maintain and support him and teach him Torah.

M. 4:11 [If he did not write for her,] *"Female children which you will have from me will dwell in my house and derive support from my property until they will be married to husbands,"* he nonetheless is liable [to support her daughters], for this is [in all events] an unstated condition imposed by the court.

M. 4:12 [If he did not write for her,] *"You will dwell in my house and derive support from my property so long as you are a widow in my house,"* [his estate] nonetheless is liable [to support his widow], for this is [in all events] an unstated condition imposed by the court. So did the Jerusalemites write into a marriage contract. The Galileans wrote the marriage contract as did the Jerusalemites. The Judeans wrote into the marriage contract, "Until such time as the heirs will choose to pay off your marriage contract." Therefore if the heirs wanted, they pay off her marriage contract and let her go.

M. 5:1 Even though they have said, "A virgin collects two hundred zuz and a widow a maneh" [M. 4:7A], if [the husband] wanted to increase that sum, even by a hundred maneh, he may add to it. [If] she was widowed or divorced, whether at the stage of betrothal or at the stage of consummated marriage, she collects the full amount.

T. 4:14 A. The father of the groom who has made a pledge for the marriage contract of his daughter-in-law, if there are available possessions belonging to the son, they collect the marriage-contract from the property of the son. And if not, they collect from the property of the father. [If] the father wrote over a house or a field as a surety for the marriage-contract of his daughter-in-law, one way or the other, they collect from them. He who went abroad, and whom they told, "Your son has died," [and] who went and wrote over all his property as a gift, and afterward who was informed that his son was alive — his deed of gift is valid.

T. 4:15 If he was sick in bed, and they said to him, "To whom will your property go," and he said to them, "I had imagined that I should have a son. Now that I do not have a son, my property goes to So-and-so," and afterward he was informed that he had a son — he has not said anything [to annul the gift]. If he was sick in bed, and they said to him, "To whom will your property go?" and he said to them, "I had imagined that my wife would be pregnant, but now that she is not pregnant, my property goes to So-and-so," and afterward he was informed that his wife was pregnant — he has said nothing.

T.4:16 A proselyte who died, and whose property Israelites took over [assuming he had no Israelite heirs], and afterward it became known that he had had sons, or that his wife was pregnant — they all are liable to restore [to his legitimate heirs the property they took over]. [If] they returned it all, and the sons died, or his wife miscarried, he who took possession in the second go-around has acquired possession, but he who had taken possession in the first go-round has not acquired possession.

T. 4:17 The daughters, whether they were married before they reached full maturity, or whether they reached full maturity before they were married, lose their right to sustenance, but do not lose their right to dowry. What do they do? They hire husbands for themselves who collect their dowry for them.

Y 5:1 I:2 Just as the husband agrees to pay [a sum over and above the minimum amount of the marriage settlement], so the father agrees to a dowry [and thereby is obligated]. But the husband assigns ownership through a bond, while the father assigns ownership [of what he promises to give] only verbally. And that is on condition [that the matter subject to the pledge is] something which is acquired through a verbal declaration.

We proceed to the laws governing the husband's rights and obligations. The marriage-contract is a stipulation of the court and takes effect even though it is not written out. A variety of other conditions are enforced even when not articulated in a contract. The exposition of the rights, at the commencement of the marriage, of the bride, her father, and the groom has now concluded. The account presents no surprises; once a topic is selected, the issues are predetermined. I discern no analytical process at work, rather a fairly standard program of exegesis through a process of distinction and clarification of interstitial problems is at work. Now we turn to the exposition of the Halakhah governing the middle-period of a marriage, between its beginning and its end.

III. THE DURATION OF THE MARRIAGE. THE RECIPROCAL RESPONSIBILITIES AND RIGHTS OF THE HUSBAND AND WIFE

A. *THE WIFE'S DUTIES TO THE HUSBAND*

M. 5:2 They give a virgin twelve months to provide for herself from the time that the husband has demanded her. And just as they give [a time of preparation] to the woman, so they give a time of preparation to a man to provide for himself. And to a widow they give thirty days. [If the time came and he did not marry her,] she in any event is supported. And she eats heave-offering [if he is a priest, and she is not].

T. 5:1 Reaching maturity is equivalent to a demand [on the part of the prospective husband that the betrothed prepare herself for marriage] [M. Ket. 5:2A]. [And] they give her twelve months in which to prepare for marriage. If she was a minor, either she or her father can dissent.

M. 5:3 The levir [who is a priest] cannot feed heave-offering [to the sister-in-law [his deceased childless brother's wife] who is widowed at the stage of betrothal and is awaiting consummation of the levirate marriage (M. Yeb. 7:4)]. If she had waited six months for the husband [M. 5:2A], and six months awaited the levir, [or] even if all of them were waiting for the husband but only one day was spent waiting for the levir, or all of them were awaiting the levir, except one day awaiting the husband, she does not eat heave-offering. This is the first Mishnah. The succeeding court ruled: "The woman does not eat heave-offering until she enters the marriage canopy."

T. 5:2 What is the law as to providing food for the sister-in-law awaiting levirate marriage? So long as the husband is obligated [having supported her in his lifetime], the levirs are obligated. If] the husband is not obligated, the levirs are not obligated. Who controls the fruit of her labor? If she is supported by them, lo, they belong to them, and if not, lo they remain her own possession. What she inherits and what she finds, one way or the other, lo, they belong to her.

B. 5:2-3 I.4/57B HE WHO BETROTHS A VIRGIN, WHETHER THE HUSBAND NOW DEMANDS HER TO COMPLETE THE MARRIAGE AND SHE OBJECTS, OR SHE DEMANDS AND THE HUSBAND OBJECTS — THEY ASSIGN HER TWELVE MONTHS FROM THE MOMENT OF THE DEMAND, BUT NOT FROM THE MOMENT OF THE BETROTHAL. IF SHE REACHED PUBERTY, LO, IT IS AS THOUGH SHE WERE DEMANDED. HOW SO? IF SHE REACHED PUBERTY BY ONLY A SINGLE DAY AND THEN WAS BETROTHED, THEY GIVE HER TWELVE MONTHS, AND TO A BETROTHED GIRL, THIRTY DAYS.

M. 5:4 He who sanctifies to the Temple the fruits of his wife's labor [her wages], lo, this woman [continues to] work and eat [maintain herself].

M. 5:5 These are the kinds of labor which a woman performs for her husband: she (1) grinds flour, (2) bakes bread, (3) does laundry, (4) prepares meals, (5) gives suck to her child, (6) makes the bed, (7) works in wool. [If] she brought with her a single slave girl, she does not (1) grind, (2) bake bread, or (3) do laundry. [If she brought] two, she does not (4) prepare meals and does not (5) feed her child. [If she brought] three, she does not (6) make the bed for him and does not (7) work in wool. If she brought four, she sits on a throne.

T. 5:3 He who sanctifies to the Temple the fruit of his wife's labor [M. Ket. 5:4A] — lo, this one provides food for her from it [the fruit of her labor]. But the remainder is sanctified.

T. 5:4 The kinds of work which a woman does for her husband — seven basic categories of labor did they enumerate. And the rest did not require enumeration [M. Ket. 5:5A-B]. If she brought slaves to him, whether on his account or on her account, she does not spin or bake or do laundry [M. Ket. 5:5C]. He may not force her to work for his son, daughter, his brothers, or her brothers, or to feed his cattle. In a place in which it is not customary to do any one of these [listed at M. Ket. 5:5B], he cannot force her to do them.

The transaction commences with an earthly agreement between the bride and groom and their families, and the protracted middle — the course of the union itself — follows suit. Each party is obligated to the other. Two questions form the starting-point. The first is, once the act of betrothal has taken place, at what point is the consummation to be scheduled? The two parties are given time to prepare. At what point does the bride, once sanctified (betrothed), enter into the status of dependent of the groom, so able to eat priestly rations if the groom is a priest? For the duration of the marriage, the wife is obligated to perform domestic duties, M. 5:5. The Tosefta's gloss, T. 5:4, shows Tosefta as a secondary commentary, citing and glossing the Mishnah's rules and extending its logic to fresh problems.

B. *THE HUSBAND'S OBLIGATIONS TO THE WIFE*

M. 5:6 He who takes a vow not to have sexual relations with his wife may allow this situation to continue for one week. Disciples go forth for Torah study without [the wife's] consent for thirty days. Workers go out for one week.

T. 5:6 Workers [must engage in sexual relations] twice a week. If they were employed in another town, then they must have sexual relations at least once a week. Ass-drivers must have sexual relations once in two weeks, camel drivers once in thirty days, sailors once in six months [M. Ket. 5:6F].

M. 5:7 She who rebels against her husband [declining to perform wifely services (M. 5:5)] — they deduct from her marriage contract seven denars a week. How long does one continue to deduct? Until her entire marriage contract [has been voided]. And so is the rule for the man who rebels against his wife [declining to do the husband's duties (M. 5:4)] — they add three denars a week to her marriage contract.

T. 5:7 She who rebels against her husband, etc. [M. Ket. 5:7A] — this is the first Mishnah. Our rabbis ordained that a court should warn her four or five consecutive weeks, twice a week. [If she persists] any longer than that, even if her marriage-contract is a hundred maneh, she has lost the whole thing. All the same is the betrothed girl and the woman awaiting levirate marriage, and even a menstruating woman, or a sick woman.

M. 5:8 He who maintains his wife by a third party may not provide for her less than two qabs of wheat or four qabs of barley [per week]. And one pays over to her a half-qab of pulse, a half-log of oil, and a qab of dried figs or a maneh of fig cake. And if he does not have it, he provides instead fruit of some other type. And he gives her a bed, a cover, and a mat. And he annually gives her a cap for her head, and a girdle for her loins, and shoes from one festival season to the next, and clothing worth fifty zuz from one year to the next. And they do not give her either new ones in the sunny season or old ones in the rainy season. But they provide for her clothing fifty zuz in the rainy season, and she clothes herself with the remnants in the sunny season. And the rags remain hers.

T. 5:8 He who supports his wife by means of a third party [M. Ket. 5:8A] — all of them are measured out by Italian measure. Even a menstruating woman, and even a sick woman, and even a sister-in-law awaiting levirate marriage [receive the support specified at M. Ket. 5:8]. He gives her a cup, a plate, a bowl, an oil cruse, a lamp, and a wick. She has no claim for wine, for the wives of the poor do not drink wine. She has no claim for a pillow, for the wives of the poor do not sleep on pillows.

M. 5:9 He gives her in addition a silver ma'ah [a sixth of a denar] for her needs [per week]. And she eats with him on the night of the Sabbath. And if he does not give her a silver ma'ah for her needs, the fruit of her labor belongs to her. And how much work does she do for him? The weight of five selas of warp must she spin for him [M. 5:5B7] in Judea (which is ten selas weight in Galilee), or the weight of ten selas of woof in Judah (which are twenty selas in Galilee). And if she was nursing a child, they take off [the required weight of wool which she must spin as] the fruit of her labor, and they provide more food for her. Under what circumstances? In the case of the most poverty-stricken man in Israel. But in the case of a weightier person, all follows the extent of his capacity [to support his wife].

T. 5:9 The excess of food [beyond her needs] goes back to him. The excess of worn out clothing belongs to her. If he gets rich she goes up with him, but if he becomes poor, she does not go down with him.

M. 6:1 What a wife finds and the fruit of her labor go to her husband [M. 4:4]. And as to what comes to her as an inheritance, he has use of the return while she is alive. [Payments made for] shaming her or injuring her are hers.

If the wife owes the husband domestic service, the husband owes the wife more than support; he also is obligated to sexual relations. Since the premise of the Halakhah is polygamy, that is not a small matter. If the two parties to the relationship are remiss in the matter, each is penalized appropriately, and the marriage may be dissolved should the situation continue. The Halakhah specifies, also, the character of the husband's material provisions for the wife.

C. *THE DOWRY*

M. 6:2 He who agrees to pay over money [as a dowry] to his son-in-law, and his son-in-law dies can claim, 'To your brother was I willing to give [money], but to you [the levir] I am not willing to give money."

M. 6:3 [If a woman] agreed to bring into [the marriage for] him a thousand denars [ten manehs], he [the husband] agrees [to pay over in her marriage contract] fifteen manehs over against this. And over against the goods [which she agreed to bring in] estimated [to be at a given value], he agrees [to restore, as a condition of her marriage contract] a fifth less. [That is, if] the estimated value [to be inscribed in the marriage contract] is a maneh, and the actual value is [specified at] a maneh, he has [value] only for one maneh [and not a fifth more in value]. [If] the estimated value [to be inscribed in the marriage contract] is a maneh [but not specified at a maneh, as at D], she must give over thirty-one selas and a denar [= 125 denars in value of goods]. And [if the value to be written into the marriage contract is to be] four hundred, she must give over five hundred. What the husband agrees [to have inscribed in the marriage contract] he agrees to, less a fifth [than the appraised value].

T. 6:5 [If] she agreed to bring in to him two selas, they are treated as equivalent to six denars [M. Ket. 6:4A]. What the husband agrees to have inscribed in the marriage-contract he agrees to, less a fifth [M. Ket. 6:3G], except with regard to the two hundred zuz to be paid to the virgin, and the maneh to be paid to the widow [which are paid in full]. [If] she agreed to bring in to him gold, lo, gold is equivalent to utensils [and diminished from the estimated value]. [If] she stipulated to bring into him golden denars lo, the gold is then treated as equivalent to ready money [M. Ket. 6:3A-B. 6:4A]. [If] she brought in to him [things of value], whether estimated in value or ready money, and he contemplated divorcing her, [right after the marriage, before the capital and goods have been utilized], she may not say to him, "Give me the estimated value [of what I brought in to you]." And he may not say to her, "Take your money." But she takes everything which he has written over to her in her marriage-contract.

M. 6:4 [If] she agreed to bring in to him ready money, a silver sela is treated as six denars [instead of four]. The husband takes upon himself [responsibility to give] ten denars for pocket money ["for her basket"] in exchange for each and every maneh [which she brings in].

T. 6:6 If she agreed to bring in to him ready money, selas are treated as equivalent to six denars [M. Ket. 6:4A]. A bridegroom takes upon himself to provide ten denars per maneh for money for cosmetics. [If] she went to a place in which they were not accustomed to diminish the value of the estimate, or to increase the value over that of the ready money, they do not vary from the customs of the place. [If] she agreed to bring in to him five hundred denars of estimated value [of goods], and he wrote over to her a thousand denars in her marriage-contract, if she made her stipulation, she takes what he wrote over to her. And if not, he takes off three denars for each and every sela [written into the contract]. If she agreed to bring into him five hundred denars in ready money and he wrote over to her a thousand denars in her marriage-contract, if she made her stipulation, she takes what he wrote over to her. And if not, he takes off six denars for each and every sela [written into the contract]. If she brought into him a thousand denars in her marriage-contract, and he wrote over to her a field worth twelve manehs, if she made her stipulation, she takes what he wrote over to her. And if not, he should not pay less to a virgin than two hundred zuz and to a widow a maneh.

M. 6:5 He who marries off his daughter without specified conditions should not assign to her less than fifty zuz. [If] he agreed to bring her in naked, the husband may not say, "When I shall bring her into my house, I shall cover her with a garment belonging to me." But he clothes her while she is still in her father's house. And so: He who marries off an orphan girl should

not assign to her less than fifty zuz. If there is sufficient money in the fund, they provide her with a dowry according to the honor due her.

M. 6:6 An orphan girl [lacking a father], whose mother or brothers married her off [even] with her consent, for whom they wrote over as her portion a hundred zuz or fifty zuz, can, when she grows up, exact from them what should rightly have been given to her.

T. 6:7 He who married off his daughter and agreed with his son-in-law that she should stand naked and he, [the son-in-law] should clothe her, they do not say, "Let her stand naked and have him clothe her." But he covers her in a manner fitting to her. And so they who marry off an orphan girl should not provide for her less than fifty zuz. And if there is sufficient money in the fund, they provide her with a dowry according to the honor due her [M. Ket. 6:5D-E].

T. 6:8 An orphan girl whose mother or brothers married her off for whom they wrote over a hundred zuz or fifty zuz — [M. Ket. 6:6A-B] even though the husband wrote for them, "I have no judgment or claim with her," she can, when she grows up, exact from them what should rightly have been given to her [M. Ket. 6:6C]. A man makes an agreement in behalf of his daughter, but a woman does not make an agreement in behalf of her daughter. An orphan boy or an orphan girl who seek to be supported — they support the orphan girl first, then they support the orphan boy, for the orphan boy can go begging in any event, but the orphan girl cannot go begging in any event. An orphan boy and an orphan girl who seek to marry — they marry off the orphan girl first, and then they marry off the orphan boy, for the shame of a girl is greater than that of a boy. An orphan boy who seeks to marry — they rent a house for him, then they lay out a bed, and afterward they marry off a girl to him. since it is said, [But you shall open your hand to him] and lend him sufficient for his need, whatever it may be (Deut. 15:8) — even a slave, even a horse. For him — this refers to a wife, since it says elsewhere, I shall make for him a helpmate (Gen. 2:18) — Just as for him in the other context refers to a wife, so for him in this context refers to a wife.

T. 6:10 He who says, "Give over a sheqel from my property to my children for their maintenance for a week," but they are supposed to take a sela — they give over to them a sela. But if he said, "Give them only a sheqel," they give them only a sheqel. If he said, "If they die, let others inherit me," whether he said, "Give," and whether he did not say, "Give," they give them over to them only a sheqel. As to food for the widow and the daughters, whether he said, "Give," or said, "Do not give," they give to them a sela.

The rules governing the dowry present no surprises. The husband takes over the dowry but undertakes to return it to the wife or her family under specified conditions of the cessation of the marriage. If the marriage endures and he survives her, her marriage-contract specifies, her sons inherit in due course. So the property that she brings into the marriage remains within the legacy of her family and is not alienated therefrom.

D. *THE MARITAL RIGHTS AND DUTIES OF THE WIFE*

M. 7:1 He who prohibits his wife by vow from deriving benefit from him for a period of thirty days, appoints an agent to provide for her. [If the effects of the vow are not nullified] for a longer period, he puts her away and pays off her marriage contract.

M. 7:2 He who prohibits his wife by vow from tasting any single kind of produce whatsoever must put her away and pay off her marriage contract.

T. 7:2 A. [If] he prohibited her by vow from tasting any type [of produce whatsoever, M. Ket. 7:2A], whether it is foul or delectable food, even if she for her part had never tasted that sort of produce once in her entire life, he must put her away and pay off her marriage-contract.

M. 7:3 He who prohibits his wife by a vow from adorning herself with any single sort of jewelry must put her away and pay off her marriage contract.

M. 7:4 He who prohibits his wife by a vow from going home to her father's house — when he [father] is with her in [the same] town, [if it is] for a month, he may persist in the marriage. [If it is] for two, he must put her away and pay off her marriage contract. And when he is in another town, [if the vow is in effect] for one festival season he may persist in the marriage. [But if the vow remains in force] for three, he must put her away and pay off her marriage contract.

T. 7:3 [If] he prohibited her by vow from adorning herself with any sort of adornment [M. Ket. 7:4A], even if she is a young girl, and he prohibited her by vow from putting on the clothes of an old lady, even if she is an old lady, and he prohibited her by vow from putting on the clothes of a young girl, he must put her away and pay off her marriage-contract.

M. 7:5 He who prohibits his wife by a vow from going to a house of mourning or to a house of celebration must put her away and pay off her marriage contract, because he locks the door before her. But if he claimed that he took such a vow because of some other thing, he is permitted to impose such a vow. [If he took a vow,] saying to her, (1) "On condition that you say to So-and-so what you said to me," or (2) "what I said to you," or (3) "that you draw water and pour it out onto the ash heap," he must put her away and pay off her marriage contract.

T. 7:4 [If] he prohibited her by vow from lending a sieve or a strainer, millstones or oven [to her girlfriend], he must put her away and pay off her marriage-contract, because he gives her a bad name among her neighboring women. And so she who prohibited him by vow from lending a sieve or a strainer, millstones or oven, must go forth without payment of her marriage-contract, because she gives him a bad name in his neighborhood.

T. 7:5 [If] he prohibited her by vow from going to a house of mourning or to a house of celebration, he must put her away and pay off her marriage-contract, because sometime later she will be laid out [for burial] and not a single human being will come to pay respects to her.

T. 7:6 [If] he required her by vow to give a taste of what she was cooking to everybody [who came by], or that she draw water and pour it out onto the ash-heap [M. Ket 7:5D], or that she tell everybody about things which are between him and her [M. Ket. 7:5D], he must put her away and pay off her marriage-contract, because he has not behaved with her in accord with the law of Moses and of Israel.

M. 7:6 And those women go forth without the payment of the marriage contract at all: She who transgresses against the law of Moses and Jewish law. And what is the Law of Moses [which she has transgressed]? [If] (1) She feeds him food, which has not been tithed, or (2) has sexual relations with him while she is menstruating, or [if] (3) she does not cut off her dough-offering, or [if] (4) she vows and does not carry out her vow. And what is the Jewish law? If (1) she goes out with her hair flowing loose or (2) she spins in the marketplace, or (3) she talks with just anybody.

T. 7:6 And so she who goes out with her hair flowing loose [M. Ket. 7:6D], who goes out with her clothes in a mess, who acts without shame in the presence of her boy-slaves and girl-slaves and her neighbors, who goes out and spins wool in the marketplace [M. Ket. 7:6], who washes and bathes in the public bath with just anyone, goes forth without payment of her marriage-contract, for she has not behaved with him [her husband] in accord with the law of Moses and Israel [M. Ket. 7:6].

T. 7:7 What is a loudmouth? Anyone who, when she talks in her own house — her neighbors can hear her voice [M. Ket. 7:6P]. All these women who have transgressed the law must have fair warning, but [if they persist after fair warning], then they go forth without receiving payment of their marriage-contract. [If] one did not give them fair warning, he must put her away but pay off her marriage-contract — and one need not say it is two hundred to a virgin and a maneh to a widow. But as to more than this: Even if her marriage-contract is in the sum of a hundred manehs, she has lost the whole thing. She takes merely the old rags which are laid out before her [and leaves].

M. 7:7 He who betrothed a woman on condition that there are no encumbering vows upon her, and it turns out that there are encumbering vows upon her — she is not betrothed. [If] he married her without [further] specification and encumbering vows turned out to be upon her, she must go forth without payment of her marriage contract. [If he betrothed her] on condition that she had no blemishes on her, and blemishes turned up on her, she is not betrothed. [If] he married her without [further] specification and blemishes turned up on her, she must go forth without payment of her marriage contract. All those blemishes which invalidate priests also invalidate women.

T. 7:8 He who betroths a woman on condition that there are no encumbering vows upon her. and it turns out that there are encumbering vows upon her — she is not betrothed [M. Ket. 7:7A-B = M. Qid. 2:5]. [If] she went to a sage and he released her vow, lo, this woman is betrothed. If he married her without further specification and encumbering vows turned out to be upon her, she must go forth without payment of her marriage contract [M. Ket. 7:7C]. [If] she went to a sage and he released her vow, lo this one confirms the marriage. [If he betrothed her] on condition that she had no blemishes on her, and blemishes turned up on her, she is not betrothed [M. Ket. 7:7D]. [If] she went to a physician and he healed her, lo, this woman is betrothed. If he married her without further specification and blemishes turned up on her, she must go forth without payment of her marriage-contract [M. Ket. 7:7E]. Even though she went to a physician and he healed her, she goes out without receiving payment of her marriage contract. Of what sort of vows did they speak? For example, [if] she vowed not to eat meat, not to drink wine, or not to wear stylish clothing.

T. 7:9 All those blemishes which invalidate priests invalidate women [M. Ket. 7:7F]. In addition to them in the case of the woman are bad breath, a sweaty body odor, and a mole that has no hair on it.

T. 7:10 He who says to his fellow, "Betroth this daughter of yours to me on condition that there are no blemishes on her," [if] he [the father] said to him, "This daughter of mine is sick, is an idiot, is epileptic, is demented" — [if] there was some other sort of blemish on her, and he concealed it among these blemishes [which he did specify], lo, this is a purchase made in error [and null] [M. Ket. 7:7]. [If, however, he said], "There are these blemishes, and there is yet another [unspecified] blemish among them," this is by no means a purchase made in error.

M. 7:9 A man who suffered blemishes — they do not force him to put her away.

M. 7:10 And these are the ones whom they force to put her away: (1) he who is afflicted with boils, or (2) who has a polypus, or (3) who collects [dog shit], or (4) a coppersmith, or (5) a tanner — whether these [blemishes] were present before they were married or whether after they were married they made their appearance.

T. 7:11 Who is one who collects [M. Ket 7: 10A3]? This is a tanner. And some say, "This is one who collects dog-excrement." A coppersmith [M. Ket. 7:10A4] — this is a metal-pourer. Under what circumstances did they rule, He must put her away [M. Ket. 7:10A] and pay off her marriage-contract? When he wants, but she does not want, [or] she wants, but he does not want [to continue the marriage]. But if both want [to continue the marriage], they do continue the marriage. One who is afflicted with boils — even though both of them want [to continue the marriage], they may not continue the marriage [M. Ket. 7:10D-E].

We proceed from the dowry and the basic obligations of the marriage to secondary considerations. The husband's act of consecration and marriage does not give him absolute power over the wife. He may not take a vow that deprives her of her rights or that demeans her or that cuts her off from her family and friends. His act of consecration does not involve the right to control her life, only to share in it.

E. *PROPERTY RIGHTS OF THE WIFE*

M. 8:1 The woman to whom property came before she was betrothed sells or gives away [the property], and the transaction is valid. [If] they [goods or property] came to her after she was betrothed, she may not sell them. If she sold or gave away [goods or property], the transaction is valid.

M. 8:3 [If] ready cash fell to her, land should be purchased with it. And he [the husband] has the usufruct thereof. [If there fell to her] produce plucked up from the ground, [likewise] land should be purchased with its [proceeds]. And he has the usufruct thereof. And as to produce attached to the ground [which the wife inherits] [The value of the produce] attached to the ground belongs to him. [The value of that which is] plucked up from the ground is hers. And land is purchased with the [proceeds of the latter]. And he has the usufruct thereof.

T. 8:3 He who enters into an expropriated estate and heard a report that they [assumed to have died and left the estate] are returning — if he went ahead and plucked up produce from the ground in any measure at all, lo, this one is rewarded for his promptness. What is meant by the expropriated estate? Any whose father or brothers or one of those who leave him an inheritance went overseas and he heard that they had died, and he entered into his inheritance. What is an abandoned estate? It is any estate, the death of the owner of which has not been reported, but into which nonetheless one has entered for purpose of inheritance.

T. 8:4 The robber or the thief who grabbed from this one and gave to the other — what he has grabbed, he has grabbed, and what he has given he has given. The thief who grabbed from this one and gave to that one — what he has grabbed he has grabbed, and what he has given he has given. The Jordan River, which took from this one and gave to that one — what it has taken, it has taken, and what it has given it has given. If the river swept away wood, stones, and beams from this one and deposited them on the property of that one, if the owner has despaired of recovering his property, lo, these belong to him [on whose property they have been swept up]. And if the owner pursued [his property, as it flowed down the river], or if he was in some other place [and did not know about the flood], lo, this remains in the possession of the owner.

T. 8:6 He who acquires a field from his fellow as a sharecropper, and it is an irrigated field or an orchard, if there is produce attached to the ground, they make an estimate of its value.

T. 8:7 He who acquires a field from his fellow as a sharecropper and the year of release came, if there is produce attached to the ground, they make an estimate of its value. He who acquires a field from his fellow as a sharecropper, and the time came for him to quit the land [and make a final reckoning], if there is produce there attached to the ground, they make an estimate of its value. And in the case of all of them, they make an estimate as in the case of a sharecropper.

T. 8:9 A. He who takes over ruins belonging to someone else and rebuilt it without permission, [if] when he leaves them, he says, "Give me my wood and stones," they do not accept his claim.

T. 8:10 He who takes over ruins belonging to someone else and rebuilt them without permission, they estimate its value. But his hand is on the bottom. [If he did so] with permission, they estimate its value, and his hand is now on top. How is it that his hand is on the bottom? If the increase in value is greater than the outlay for the restoration, he [who retrieves his property] pays him his expenses. But if the expenses are greater than the increase in value, he pays him only the increase in value.

M. 8:5 [If] old slave men or slave women fell to her [possession], they are to be sold. And land should be purchased with their [proceeds]. And he [the husband] has the usufruct thereof.

[If] old olive trees or grapevines fell to her [possession], they are to be sold [for their value as] wood. And land should be purchased with their [proceeds]. And he has the usufruct thereof. He who lays out the expenses for [the upkeep of] the property of his wife — [whether] he laid out a great deal of money and received little usufruct, [or whether he laid out] a small amount of money and received much — what he has laid out, he has laid out, and the usufruct which he has enjoyed, he has enjoyed. [But] if he laid out [money for the upkeep of the estate] and did not enjoy the usufruct [at all, there being no return], he should take an oath [to verify] the amount which he has laid out [as expenses]. And that should he collect [in recompense, from her by deduction from her marriage contract].

M. 8:6 A woman awaiting levirate marriage with her deceased childless husband's brother to whom property came sells or gives away her property, and the transaction is valid. [If] she died, how should they dispose of her marriage contract and of the property which comes into the marriage with her and goes out of the marriage with her [=plucking property]? The property remains in the hands of its presumptive owners: the [value of the] marriage contract in the possession of the heirs of the husband, and the property which goes in and comes out with her in the possession of the heirs of the father.

M. 8:7 [If] the brother [the deceased husband] left ready cash, land should be purchased with it. And he [the levir] has the usufruct thereof. [If he left] produce plucked up from the ground, [it should be sold] and land should be purchased with the [proceeds]. And he has the usufruct thereof. [If he left] produce yet attached to the ground — produce attached to the ground belongs to him. Produce plucked up from the ground — whoever gets it first keeps it. [If] he got it first, he keeps it. [If] she got it first, land should be purchased with their [proceeds]. And he has the usufruct thereof. [If] he consummated the marriage with her, lo, she is deemed to be his wife for every purpose, except that her marriage contract is a lien on the estate of her first husband.

M. 8:8 [The levir] may not say to her, "There is [the repayment for] your marriage contract, lying on the table." But all of his property is subject to lien for the payment of her marriage contract. And so a man may not say to his wife, "There is [the repayment for] your marriage contract, lying on the table." But all of his property is subject to lien for the payment of her marriage contract. [If] he divorced her, she has a claim only on her marriage contract. [If] he remarried her, lo, she is equivalent to all women. And she has a claim only on her marriage contract alone.

T. 9:1 He who died and left his wife awaiting marriage with her deceased childless husband's brother, even if he left an estate worth a hundred manehs and the charge of her marriage-contract is only a maneh, the heirs cannot sell [his estate], for all of his property is encumbered for the payment of her marriage-contract [M. Ket. 8:8]. What should [the levir] do? He should consummate the marriage, then divorce her, and she gives him a quittance for her marriage-contract. [If] his brother left ready cash [M. Ket 8:7A], or the deceased childless brother's widow owed her husband money, he should not say, "Since I am going to inherit it anyhow, I take possession of it." But they seize it from him, and land is purchased for it, and he has the usufruct.

M. 9:1 He who writes for his wife, "I have no right nor claim to your property," lo, this one [nonetheless] has the usufruct during her lifetime. And if she dies, he inherits her estate. If so, why did he write to her, "I have no right nor claim to your property?" For if she sold or gave away [her property], her act is valid. [If] he wrote for her, "I have no right nor claim to your property or to its usufruct [consequent profits]," lo, this one does not have the usufruct in her lifetime. But if she dies, he inherits her estate, [If] he wrote for her, "I have no right nor claim to your property, to its usufruct, to the usufruct of its usufruct, during your lifetime and after your death," he neither has the usufruct in her lifetime, nor, if she dies, does he inherit her.

The property rights of the wife within the marriage encompass her control of what is hers outside the framework of the marriage-contract. The basic principle is, the husband enjoys the usufruct of, and manages, her property during the marriage, but she retains title. The Tosefta vastly expands the coverage of the principles established in the setting of the marriage.

IV. CESSATION OF THE MARRIAGE: THE COLLECTION OF THE MARRIAGE-CONTRACT

A. *IMPOSING AN OATH IN CONNECTION WITH COLLECTING THE MARRIAGE-SETTLEMENT*
M. 9:2 He who died and left a wife, a creditor, and heirs, and who had goods on deposit or a loan in the domain of others — they should be given over to the heirs. For all of them have to confirm their claim by an oath. But the heirs do not have to confirm their claim by an oath.

M. 9:3 [If] he left produce harvested from the ground, whoever gets them first has effected acquisition of them. [If] the wife made acquisition of an amount greater than the value of her marriage contract, or a creditor greater than the value of the debt owing to him — as to the excess [of the claims of these respective parties] — it should be given over to the heirs. For all of them have to confirm their claim by an oath. But the heirs do not have to confirm their claim by an oath.

M. 9:4 He who sets up his wife as a storekeeper, or appointed her guardian, lo, this one may impose upon her an oath [that she has not misappropriated any of his property], at any time he wants.

M. 9:5 If he wrote to her, "Neither vow nor oath may I impose upon you," then he cannot impose an oath on her. But he imposes an oath upon her heirs and upon those who are her lawful successors. [If he said], "Neither vow nor oath may I impose upon you, upon your heirs, or upon your legal successors," he cannot impose an oath upon her or upon her heirs or legal successors. But his heirs do impose an oath upon her, upon her heirs, or upon her legal successors. [If he said,] "Neither vow nor oath may I or my heirs or my legal successors impose upon you, upon your heirs, or upon your legal successors," neither he nor his heirs or legal successors can impose an oath upon her, her heirs, or her legal successors.

M. 9:6 [If] she went from her husband's grave to her father's house, or if she went back to her father-in-law's house and was not appointed guardian, the heirs do not impose an oath on her [that she has not misappropriated any property of the estate]. And if she was appointed guardian [of the estate], the heirs do impose an oath on her concerning time to come. But they do not impose an oath on her concerning past time.

T. 9:3 He who died and left movable property, and the marriage-contract of his wife and a creditor laid claim against whoever seizes it first has effected acquisition [of whatever he left] [M. Ket. 9:2-3]. And [there being nothing left for burial costs], he is buried by the philanthropic fund. Who are the heirs who are her legal successors [M. Ket. 9:5C]? Any to whom she sold [her property] or to whom she gave [her property] as a gift. [If] he wrote to her, "I have no claim to impose either a vow or an oath upon you" [M. Ket. 9:5A], the heirs [also] cannot impose an oath on her [that she has not misappropriated] items of which she made use after the death of her husband. Under what circumstances? When she went along from the grave of her husband to her father's house [M. Ket. 9:6A]. But if she went from the grave of her husband to her father-in-law's house, even if he wrote to her, "I have no claims to impose either a vow or an oath upon you," the heirs can impose an oath on her concerning items of which she made use after the death of her husband [M. Ket. 9:6D-E]. A husband cannot impose an oath on his wife unless he sets her up as a storekeeper or appoints her guardian [of his property] [M. Ket. 9:4A-C]. A sharecropper — so long as he is a sharecropper, [he is subject to an oath]. When he has gone forth from his position as sharecropper, lo, he is equivalent to any other person. A partner — so long as he is a partner, [he is subject to an oath]. When he has gone forth from his partnership, lo, he is equivalent to any other person. A guardian — so long as he is a guardian, [he is subject to an oath]. When he has gone forth from his guardianship, lo, he is equivalent to any other person. A member of the household of whom they spoke [at M. Sheb.. 7:8] — it is not this one who [merely] walks in and out, but the one who brings in produce and takes out produce, hires workers and dismisses workers. [If] one borrows from him on the eve of the Seventh Year and in the Seventh Year, and, in the year after the Seventh Year, he is made a partner of his, or a sharecropper, he is exempt [from the requirement of an oath]. But if he is made a partner or a sharecropper on the eve of the Seventh Year and in the Seventh Year, and in the year after the Seventh Year he went and borrowed from him, they obligate him for [an oath covering] all.

M. 9:7 She who impairs her marriage contract collects it only through an oath. [If] one witness testified against her that it had been collected, she collects it only through an oath. From (1) the property of the heirs [orphans], or from (2) property subject to a lien, or (3) in his [the husband's] absence should she collect [her marriage contract] only through an oath.

T. 9:4 She who claims less than the full value of her marriage-contract collects it without an oath. How so? [If] her marriage-contract had a value of a thousand zuz, and he said to her, "You have collected your marriage-contract," and she says, "I have not collected it, but it is of a value of only a maneh," she collects that amount without an oath [M. Ket. 9:7A, 9:8A-C]. As to [collecting what is owed to her by seizing] mortgaged property [M. Ket. 9:7C2], it is not necessary to say after her husband's death, but even while her husband is yet alive [does she collect only through an oath]. As to the property belonging to the orphans, it is not necessary to say, that of the adults [minors], but even that of the minors [adults] [does she collect only through an oath].

M. 9:8 "She who impairs her marriage contract" [M. 9:7A]: How so? [If] her marriage contract was worth a thousand zuz, and he said to her, "You have collected your marriage contract," but she says, "I have received only a maneh [a hundred zuz]," she collects [the remainder] only through an oath. [If] one witness testified against her that it had been collected: How so? [If] her marriage contract was worth a thousand zuz, and he [the witness] said to her, "You have collected the value of your marriage contract," and she says, "I have not collected it," and one

witness testified against her that it had been collected, she should collect the marriage contract only through an oath. "From property subject to a lien" [M. 9:7C2]: How so? [If the husband] sold off his property to others, and she comes to collect from the purchasers, she should collect from them only through an oath. From the property of the heirs [orphans] [M. 9:7Cl]: How so? [If the husband] died and left his property to the orphans, and she comes to collect [her marriage contract] from the orphans, she should collect from them only by an oath. "In his absence" [M. 9:7C3]: How so? [If the husband] went overseas, and she comes to collect [her marriage contract] in his absence, she collects [what is due her] only by an oath.

M. 9:9 [If] she produced a writ of divorce, and a marriage contract is not attached to it, she collects her marriage contract. [But if she produced] a marriage contract, and a writ of divorce is not attached to it, [and if] she claims, "My writ of divorce is lost," [while the husband] claims, "My quittance is lost" — and so, too, a creditor who produced a bill of indebtedness and a prosbol [securing the loan in the year of release] is not attached to it — lo, these [parties] may not collect [what they claim]. [If she produces] two writs of divorce and two marriage contracts — she collects [the value of] two marriage contracts. [If she produces] (1) two marriage contracts but only one writ of divorce, or (2) one marriage contract and two writs of divorce, or (3) a marriage contract and a writ of divorce and a death [certificate], she collects only one marriage contract. For he who divorces his wife and then remarries her — on the strength of the first marriage contract does he remarry her. And a minor boy whose father married him off — her [his wife's] marriage contract is confirmed [as valid after he reaches maturity]. For on the strength of that document he confirmed [the marriage when he came of age]. A proselyte who converted, and his wife alongside [did the same] — her [original] marriage contract is valid. For on the strength of that document he [the husband] confirmed [the marriage].

T. 9:5 [If] she produced a writ of divorce, and a marriage-contract is not attached to it [M. Ket. 9:9A] — a virgin collects two hundred zuz, and a widow, a maneh. [If she produced] a marriage-contract, and a writ of divorce is not attached to it [M. Ket. 9:9B], she collects nothing, because if she says, "My writ of divorce got lost," then he counters, "My quittance got lost" [M. Ket. 9:9C-D].

T. 9:7 [If] she gave him a quittance while she is subject to his authority, then he divorced her and remarried her and died, (and) she collects a maneh as her marriage-contract. But if he made a new document, she collects what he has made afresh. A minor-boy whose father married him off — the [wife's] marriage-contract is confirmed [as valid after he reaches maturity]. For on the strength of that document he confirmed the marriage [M. Ket. 9:9Q-R]. And if he made a new document, she collects what he has made afresh. And so: A proselyte who converted, and his wife alongside [did the same] — her [original] marriage-contract is valid. For on the strength of that document he [the husband] confirmed the marriage [after conversion] [M. Ket. 9:9S-U]. And if he made a new document, she collects what he made afresh.

The wife collects the property provided in her marriage contract at the death of the husband or at his divorcing her. The Halakhic repertoire takes up a number of special problems: multiple claims to the husband's estate and how these are sorted out; the wife's or creditors' seizure of more than is owing to them; the counterclaims of the heirs ("orphans"), e.g., that the wife has already taken money from the estate's property; the imposition of an oath on the wife; and the like.

B. *MULTIPLE CLAIMS ON AN ESTATE, INCLUDING THE WIVES' FOR THEIR MARRIAGE-SETTLEMENT*

M. 10:1 He who was married to two wives and died — the first [wife] takes precedence over the second, and the heirs of the first take precedence over the heirs of the second. [If] he married the first and she died, then he married the second, and he died, the second and her heirs take precedence over the heirs of the first.

T. 10:1 He who was married to two wives and died — the first [wife] takes precedence over the second, and the heirs of the first take precedence over the heirs of the second [M. Ket. 10:1A-C]. [If] he divorced the first and remarried her, and made a new marriage-contract for her, the first marriage-contract of the first wife takes precedence over the second and her heirs, then the second [wife] and her heirs take precedence over the second marriage-contract of the first wife. Under what circumstances? In the case of [the collection of] the marriage-contract. But as to maintenance, both of them are equal [and neither claims priority]. The wife and daughters — both of them enjoy equal claim. [If] he married the first and she died, then he married the second and he died [M. Ket. 10:1D], and there was there [the value of both marriage-contracts], plus one denar, then these collect the marriage-contract of their mother, and those collect the marriage-contract of their mother. And the rest do they divide [as an estate]. But if there is not there [the value of both marriage-contracts], plus one denar, the second wife or her heirs collect the marriage-contract of their mother, and the rest divide equally [the residuary estate].

Y. 10:1 I:3 [The Mishnah has] spoken [thus far] only of [the wife's] dying [at M. 10:1D]. [That is to say, the husband marries and the first wife dies. He therefore inherits her estate. Then he remarries. Then he dies. The second wife takes precedence over the heirs of the first. Why? Because in this case the property of the first wife has entered the husband's estate before he encumbered his estate with the debt constituted by the marriage contract of the second wife. The creditor takes precedence over the heir. So the second wife or her heirs take the value of the marriage contract, and then the estate is divided equally among the heirs.] Lo, if the wife was divorced, she is in the status of a creditor.

M. 10:2 He who was married to two wives and they died, and afterward he died, and the orphans claim the marriage contract of their mother — and there are [funds to pay] only two marriage contracts — they divide equally. [If] there was an excess of a denar [over the necessary funds], these collect the marriage contract of their mother, and those collect the marriage contract of their mother. [If] the orphans said, "We reckon the value of the estate of our father at one denar more," so that they may collect the marriage contract of their mother, they do not listen to them. But they make an estimate of the value of the property in court.

M. 10:3 [If] there was property which was going [to accrue to the estate], it is not deemed equivalent to that which is in [the estate's] possession.

B. 10:2-3 I:1/91A IF THE MARRIAGE CONTRACT OF ONE WIFE WAS FOR A THOUSAND ZUZ AND THE OTHER FIVE HUNDRED, IF THERE IS A SURPLUS OF A DENAR, THESE COLLECT THE MARRIAGE SETTLEMENT OWING TO THEIR MOTHER, AND THOSE COLLECT THE MARRIAGE SETTLEMENT OWING TO THEIR MOTHER. BUT IF NOT, THEY DIVIDE EQUALLY.

M. 10:4 He who was married to three wives and died, the marriage contract of this one was a maneh, and that of the next two hundred zuz, and that of the last three hundred — and there is there only a maneh — they divide it equally. [If] there are two hundred, the one who is owed a maneh takes fifty, and the ones who are owed two hundred and three hundred each take three golden denars [seventy-five zuz each]. [If] there were three hundred zuz there, the one who claims a maneh takes fifty zuz, and the one who claims two hundred takes a maneh, and the one who claims three hundred zuz takes six gold denars [one hundred fifty zuz]. And so [three who put their money into] a single purse — if the capital in the end was too little or too much [they made a loss or a profit], so would they divide up what was available.

M. 10:5 He who was married to four wives and who died — the first takes precedence over the second, and the second over the third, and the third over the fourth. The first is subjected to an oath by the second [that she has not yet collected her marriage contract], and the second to the third, and the third to the fourth, and the fourth collects without an oath. Ben Nannos says, "And is it on account of the fact that she is last that she is rewarded? "She, too, should collect only by means of an oath." [If] all of them [the marriage contracts] were issued on one day, whoever came before her fellow, by even a single hour, has acquired [the right of collection first]. And that is why, in Jerusalem, they write the hours of the day [in a marriage contract]. [If] all of them were issued at the same hour and there is only a maneh there, they divide it up equally.

M. 10:6 He who was married to two women, and who sold off his field and the first woman wrote to the purchaser, "I have no case or claim with you" — the second [wife] nonetheless seizes the field from the purchaser, and the first wife from the second, and the purchaser from the first, and they go around in a circle, until they make a compromise among them. And so in the case of a creditor, and so in the case of a woman who is a creditor.

T. 10:4 Three who put their money into one purse, which was stolen from them bring what is left to the middle [=divided equally] and divide it up. Two who put their money into one purse — this one puts in a maneh and this one put in two hundred zuz, and they did business — the profits are in the middle [divided equally]. [If] this one then took part of his, and that one took part of his, and they entered into partnership, this one then takes in accord with what he has put in. [If] three bills of debt went forth against him simultaneously, the first takes an oath to the second, and the second takes an oath to the third. [If] the second did not want to impose an oath on the first, the third can prevent him from [refraining from doing so]. [If] one borrowed from one person and sold his field to two others, and the creditor wrote to the second, "I have no case or claim against you, " he [the creditor] cannot collect what is owing to him, because he has left himself no place from which to make a collection. A proselyte who died and whose property Israelites took over, and the wife's marriage-contract and a debt were brought for collection to his property — they collect from the last who had taken over his property. [If] that one does not have enough, they collect from the one before him, and so they continue.

Multiple claims on an estate require the ordering of matters; priority rests on temporal sequence of the marriages.

C. *SUPPORT FOR THE WIDOW*

M. 11:1 A widow is supported by the property of the orphans. Her wages [the work of her hands] belong to them. But they are not liable to bury her. Her heirs who inherit her marriage contract are liable to bury her.

Y. 11:1 II:2: And they add extras to the food they supply to her. In the case of a married woman, she has no claim on wine. In the case of a widow, [if she used to have wine,] she has a claim on wine. In the case of a married woman, if she said, "Let the work of my hands be exchanged for my food," they do not listen to her [and allow her such a trade-off]. In the case of a widow who said, "Let the work of my hands be exchanged for my food," they do listen to her [and allow the trade-off].

B. 11:1 I:8/97A THE WOMAN MAY CONTINUE TO SELL OFF THE PROPERTY UNTIL WHAT IS LEFT IS WHAT IS OWING FOR HER MARRIAGE SETTLEMENT, AND THIS THEN IS A SUPPORT FOR HER SO THAT SHE MAY COLLECT HER MARRIAGE SETTLEMENT FROM WHAT IS THEN LEFT.

M. 11:2 A widow, whether [her husband died when she was] at the stage of betrothal or at the stage of marriage, sells [her husband's estate's property that was security for her marriage contract to realize her marriage contract or to purchase food] without court [permission].

M. 11:3 [If] she sold off her marriage contract or part of it, [or] pledged her marriage contract or part of it, [or] gave away her marriage contract to someone else, or part of it — she sells it even four or five times. And [in the meantime, before collecting her marriage contract] she sells [it] for support without court [permission], and writes, "I sold it for support." But a divorcée should sell only with court [permission].

T. 11:1 A widow who lays claim on her marriage-contract, and the heirs say to her, "You have received your marriage-contract" — [if] this is before she was married, they have to bring proof that her marriage-contract has been received [paid off]. [If] this is after she was married, she has to bring proof that her marriage-contract has not been received. [If] she sold off her marriage-contract, [or] pledged her marriage-contract, [or] set up her marriage-contract as a mortgage, she has lost her claim for support [from the estate of her husband]. One need not say that this is the rule [if she did so] after the death of her husband. But it is even the rule [if she did so] while her husband is yet alive.

M. 11:4 A widow whose marriage contract was two hundred, and who sold [land of her husband's estate] worth a maneh for two hundred zuz, or worth two hundred zuz for a maneh — her marriage contract has been received thereby. [If] her marriage contract was worth a maneh and she sold [land] worth a maneh and a denar for a maneh, her sale is void. Even if she says, "I shall return the denar to the heirs," her sale is void. [If] her marriage contract was worth four hundred zuz, and she sold [land] to this one for a maneh, and to that one for a maneh, [etc.,] and to the last [fourth] one, what was worth a maneh and a denar for a maneh, the sale to the last one is void. But all the others — their purchase is valid.

M. 11:5 [If] the estimate of the value made by judges was a sixth too little or a sixth too much, their sale is void. But if they drew up a deed of inspection, even if they sold what was worth a maneh for two hundred, or what was worth two hundred for a maneh, their sale is confirmed.

T. 11:2 Three who went down to estimate the value of a field — one says, "It is worth a maneh," and two say, "It is worth two hundred zuz" — one says, "It is worth two hundred," and two say, "It is worth a maneh" — the minority view is null. [If] one says, "It is worth a maneh [100 zuz]," and one says, "It is worth twenty [selas, 80 zuz]," and one says, "It is worth thirty [selas, 120 zuz]," they estimate its value at a maneh.

T. 11:3 What is a deed of inspection [M. Ket. 11:5D]? The time allotted for the estimate of the value of property accruing to orphans is thirty days. And the time allotted for the estimate of the value of property accruing to the sanctuary is sixty days. [If] they sold something worth a maneh for two hundred zuz, or something worth two hundred zuz for a maneh, the sale is confirmed. She who sold what was worth a maneh and a denar for a maneh, even if she says, "I shall return the denar to the purchaser's heirs" — her sale is null.

The widow is supported by the estate, in accord with the marriage-settlement, and relative to the widow's income, the estate enters into the status of the deceased. Her claim to the estate, defined by the marriage-contract, permits her to sell estate property to collect what is owing to her.

D. *RIGHTS TO, AND COLLECTION OF, A MARRIAGE CONTRACT: SPECIAL CASES*

M. 11:6 (1) A girl who exercised the right of the refusal, (2) a woman in a secondary remove of prohibited relationship [M. Yeb. 2:4], and (3) a sterile woman do not have a claim on a marriage contract, nor on the increase [on plucking property], nor on maintenance, nor on indemnity [for wear of clothing]. But if to begin with he married her as a sterile woman, she has a claim on a marriage contract. A widow married to a high priest, a divorced woman or one who has performed the rite of removing the shoe married to an ordinary priest, a mamzer girl and a netin girl married to an Israelite, an Israelite girl married to a netin or to a mamzer do have a marriage contract.

M. 12:1 He who marries a woman, and she stipulated with him that he support her daughter for five years — he is liable to support her for five years. [If] she [the wife, having been divorced] married someone else, and she stipulated with him [the second husband] that he support her daughter for five years, he is liable to support her for five years. The first may not say, "When she will come to my house, I shall support her." But he sends her food to the place where her mother is located. And so the two of them do not say, "Lo, we shall support her together [in partnership]." But one supports her and the other gives her the cost of her support [in addition].

T. 10:2 [If] he promised in writing to support the daughter of his wife and the son of his wife, lo, they are deemed equivalent to creditors and take precedence over all claimants. He may not say to them, "Go and do work, and I will support you." But they remain at home, and he provides food for them. [If] he promised in writing to support the daughter of his wife, and she [the wife] gave him a quittance — she has not the power to do so. For they provide an advantage to a minor, but they do not impose a disadvantage upon him [or her].

T. 10:3 A woman who said, "My husband has died," either derives maintenance or collects her marriage contract. [If she said], "My husband has divorced me," she is supported to the extent of her marriage-contract. What is the difference between [the severance of the marriage through] death and [the severance of the marriage through] divorce? In the case of death, she cannot deny [the facts]. But in the case of divorce, she can deny the facts of the matter. And she indeed may say right to his face, "You did divorce me" [M. Ket. 2:5].

Y. 12:1 I:2 As to the first five years [to which the husband referred] he supports her whether the cost of the food is high or low. If [he failed to provide food during that period] and the cost was high, but [at the end, when claim was laid against him], the cost had gone down, if he was the cause [of the nonpayment of support] he [now] pays at the highest price [prevailing during that period of years]. But if she was the cause [of the delinquency], he pays at the lowest cost [prevailing during that period of years]. [If, during the five years] the prices had been low but [at the point, at the end, at which claim was laid against the husband], the price had gone up, whether he was at fault or she was at fault, he pays the cost at the low prices [prevailing during the period for which he was obligated].

M. 12:2 [If the daughter, whom the two husbands have agreed to support] is married, the husband provides support. And they [the mother's successive husbands] pay her the cost of her support. [If] they died, their daughters are supported from unencumbered property, for she is in the status of a creditor. The smart ones would write, "...on condition that I support your daughter for five years, so long as you are [living] with me."

M. 12:3 A widow who said, "I don't want to move from my husband's house" — the heirs cannot say to her, "Go to your father's house and we'll take care of you [there]." But they provide for her in her husband's house, giving her a dwelling in accord with her station in life. [If] she said, "I don't want to move from my father's house," the heirs can say to her, "If you are with us, you will have support. But you are not with us, you will not have support." If she claimed that it is because she is a girl and they are boys, they do provide for her while she is in her father's house.

T. 11:5 She may make use of the old home just as she used it when her husband was alive, so, too, the boy slaves and girl slaves just as she did when her husband was alive, so, too, the pillows and blankets, silver and gold utensils, just as she did when her husband was alive, for thus does he write for her in her marriage contract, "You will dwell in my house and enjoy support from my property so long as you spend your widowhood in my house."

T. 12:3 If there is available only real property of the best quality, all of them [who are owed damages, debts, or marriage-contracts] collect what is due them from property of the best quality. [If there is available only] property of middling quality, all of them collect what is due them from property of middling quality. [If there is available only] property of poor quality, all of them collect what is due them from property of poor quality. [If there is] property of the best and of middling quality, then compensation for damages is collected from property of the best quality, and compensation for a debt and for the marriage-contract is collected from property of middling quality. [If there is] property of the best and of the poorest quality, then compensation for damages is collected from property of the best quality, and compensation for a debt and for the marriage-contract is collected from property of the poorest quality. [If there is available only] property of middling and of poorest quality, then compensation for damages and for debts is collected from property of middling quality, and compensation for the marriage-contract is collected from property of poor quality. [If the party who owes these monies] sold them [his properties] off to one person, or simultaneously three together, and they took over the property in place of the owner — then compensation for damages is collected from property of the best quality, for a creditor from property of middling quality, and for payment of the wife's marriage-contract from property of the poorest quality. [If] he sold them off to three people, one after the other in sequence, even compensation for damages, from property of the poorest quality, or payment for the wife's marriage-contract, from property of the finest quality, do they collect from the [land bought by] the last — f the three purchasers. [If] he does not have [enough], they collect from the one before him. [If] he does not have enough, they collect from the one before him. A widow who said, "I don't want to move from my husband's house" [M. Ket. 12:3A] — the heirs cannot stop her. For this is honor paid to her [deceased] husband. [If] she said, "I don't want to move from my father's house," the heirs can stop her. For the blessing of a house [is proportionate to its] size [the larger the household, the lower the individual's cost of living]. Just as she calls attention to her uncollected marriage-contract for a period of twenty-five years, so her heirs and her legal successors call attention to her uncollected marriage-contract for a period of twenty-five years [M. Ket. 12:4G]. But a creditor collects at any time [without limit], even though he has not [before] called attention [to the uncollected debt].

M. 12:4 So long as she is in her husband's house, she collects her marriage contract at any time. So long as she is in her father's house, she collects her marriage contract within twenty-five years. [If] she died, her heirs call attention [to her uncollected] marriage contract for twenty-five years.

T. 11:5 A woman whose husband has died dwells in her house just as she did when her husband was alive. She makes use of the man-slaves and women-slaves, silver utensils and golden utensils, just as she made use of them when her husband was alive. For thus does he write for her, "You will dwell in my house and enjoy support from my property so long as you spend your widowhood in my house."

T. 11:6 He who says, "Give over a house of widowhood to my daughter," "Give a house to So-and-so for a dwelling," and the house fell down — the heirs are liable to [pay to] rebuild it. He who says, "This house is a house for the widowhood of my daughter," "This house is for So-and-so for a dwelling" — then the heirs are not liable to rebuild it [if it fell down].

T. 11:7 He who says, "Give a house of widowhood for my daughter" — they give it over to her only if she took upon herself to live in it. The heirs can prevent her should she rent it to someone else. Therefore when she dies, they inherit the house.

T. 11:8 He who lends money to his fellow relying on a pledge, and the pledge is lost, collects the debt from other property [belonging to the debtor]. If he [the borrower] said to him, "On condition that you may make your collection only from this object," then he does not collect the debt from any other property belonging to the debtor. He who sets up his field as a mortgage for the marriage-contract of his wife, and the river washed it out — she collects from other property belonging to him. If he said to her, "On condition that you may make your collection only from this field," then she does not collect the debt from any other property belonging to her husband.

Some women have no claim on a marriage-contract and its provisions. The stipulations of the husband are enforceable.

E.   *TWO CASE-BOOKS*

M. 13:1 He who went overseas, and his wife [left at home] claims maintenance — let her take an oath at the end, but let her not take an oath at the outset [that is, she takes an oath when she claims her marriage contract after her husband's death, or after he returns, that she has not held back any property of her husband].

T. 12:4 He who went overseas and came back, and his wife claims support — if he said, "Pay out her wages in exchange for her support," he has the right to do so. But if a court had directed that support be provided for her, what [the court] has directed, it has directed [and he has no such claim]. He who makes an agreement to provide funds for his minor daughter and then showed the leg [defaulted] — they force him to provide [what he has promised]. For they impute an advantage to a minor, but they do not put him at a disadvantage.

M. 13:2 He who went overseas, and someone went and supported his wife – he [who did so] has lost his money.

M. 13:3 He who died and left sons and daughters, when the property is ample or negligible, the sons inherit, and the daughters receive support [from the estate].

T. 6:1 He who died and left sons and daughters — when the property is abundant, the sons inherit and the daughters are fed and maintained [from his estate] [M. Ket. 13:3]. How [do we interpret the statement], "The sons inherit"? We do not say, "If their father were alive, he would have given such-and-so to them." But we regard one as if he were the father present [for this purpose], and they give to them.

T. 6:2 How [do we interpret the statement], "The daughters are fed and maintained"? We do not say, "If their father were alive, he would have given such-and-so to them." But we regard how [women] who are equivalent to them in status are maintained, and we provide for them accordingly.

M. 13:4 He who claims that his fellow [owes him] jugs of oil, and the other party admitted that he owes him [empty] jugs — since he has conceded part of the claim, let him take an oath.

M. 13:5 He who agrees to give money to his son-in-law but then stretched out the leg [defaulted] — she can claim, "If I had made such an agreement in my own behalf, well might I sit until my head grows white. Now that father has made an agreement concerning me, what can I do? Either marry me or let me go!"

M. 13:6 He who contests [another's] ownership of a field, but he himself is a signatory on it [the documents of ownership] as a witness — he has lost every right. [If] he made his field a boundary mark for another person, he has lost every right.

M. 13:7 He who went overseas, and the right-of-way to his field was lost — let him purchase a right-of-way with a hundred manehs [if need be], or let him fly through the air.

M. 13:8 He who produces a bond of indebtedness against someone else, and the other brought forth [a deed of sale to show] that the other had sold him a field — this [first] man was smart in selling him the field, since he can take it as a pledge.

M. 13:9 Two who produced bonds of indebtedness against one another — this one collects his bond of indebtedness, and that one collects his bond of indebtedness.

M. 13:10 There are three provinces in what concerns marriage: (1) Judah, (2) Transjordan, and (3) Galilee. They do not remove [wives] from town to town or from city to city [in another province]. But in the same province, they do remove [wives] from town to town or from city to city, but not from a town to a city, and not from a city to a town. They remove [wives] from a bad dwelling to a good one but not from a good one to a bad one.

T. 12:5 There are three provinces in what concerns marriage: [l] Judah, [2] Transjordan, and [3] Galilee [M. Ket. 13:10A]: Under what circumstances does M's rule apply that women may be removed from one town to another, [M. 13:10C]? When the groom was from Judah and betrothed a girl from Judah, or was from Galilee and betrothed a girl from Galilee. But if he was from Judah and betrothed a girl from Galilee, or from Galilee and betrothed a girl from Judah, they force her to go away [M. Ket. 13: 10B], for it was on this assumption that she married him. If, however, he said, "I, So-and-so from Judah, have married a girl from Galilee," they do not force her to go away. But [if he writes, "I married a girl] in Galilee," they force her to go away. They remove a wife from a town which has a gentile majority to a town which has an Israelite majority, but they do not remove a wife from a town which has an Israelite majority to a town which has a gentile majority. [If] he wants to come to the Land of Israel, and she does not want to come, they force her to come. [If] she wants to come, and he does not want to come, they force him to come. [If] he wants to leave the Land of Israel, and she does not want to leave, they do not force her to leave. [If] she wants to leave, and he does not want to leave, they force her not to leave.

M. 13:11 All have the right to bring up [his or her family] to the Land of Israel, but none has the right to remove [his or her family] therefrom. All have the right to bring up to Jerusalem, but none has the right to bring down — all the same are men and women. [If] one married a woman in the Land of Israel and divorced her in the Land of Israel, he pays her off with the coinage of the Land of Israel. [If] he married a woman in the Land of Israel and divorced her in Cappadocia, he pays her off in the coinage of the Land of Israel. [If] he married a woman in Cappadocia and divorced her in the Land of Israel, he pays her off in the coinage of the Land of Israel. If he married a woman in Cappadocia and divorced her in Cappadocia, he pays her off in the coinage of Cappadocia.

T. 12:6 He who produces a writ [of indebtedness] in Babylonia collects on the strength of it in Babylonian coinage. [If he does so] in the Land of Israel, he collects on the strength of it in the coinage of the Land of Israel. [If] it was written without specification — [if] he produces it in Babylonia, he collects on the strength of it in Babylonian coinage. [If he produces it] in the Land of Israel, he collects on the strength of it in the coinage of the Land of Israel. [If] it was written on coinage without specification, lo, this one collects [in the coinage of] any place which he wants, which is not the case for the marriage-contract of a woman [paid only in Palestinian coinage under this circumstance]. [If he married a girl in the Land of Israel and divorced her in the Land of Israel, he pays her off in the coinage of the Land of Israel [M. Ket. 13:11 D]. [If he married her] in the Land of Israel and divorced her in Babylonia, he pays her off in the coinage of the Land of Israel. [If he married her] in Babylonia and divorced her in the Land of Israel, he pays her off in the coinage of the Land of Israel. The five selas for redemption of the first born, the thirty for a slave, the fifty paid by the one who rapes or seduces a girl, the hundred paid by one who spreads malicious rumors about a girl — all of them, even though they are in Babylonia, collect on their account in the coinage of the Land of Israel. The coinage concerning which the Torah speaks at every point, this is the coinage of Tyre. Tyrian coinage — this is the coinage of Jerusalem.

In light of established principles, the miscellany presents no surprises. The formation of composites on other-than-topical bases is rare indeed, and the result for the Halakhah of the formal principle of organization — cases associated with particular authorities' names, secondarily linked by common topics and even shared principles — is hardly compelling.

IV. DOCUMENTARY TRAITS

A. THE MISHNAH AND THE TOSEFTA

The Tosefta's relationship to the Mishnah is complex in all but one aspect: both documents follow a topical program in common, defining the category-formation at hand in exactly the same terms.

B. THE YERUSHALMI AND THE BAVLI

I do not see any detail at which the two Talmuds differ on their reading of matters; the category-formation is defined by the initial document and merely amplified and refined by the two principal commentaries.

C. THE AGGADAH: THE LITURGICAL CONTEXT OF KETUBOT

While the Bavli's presentation of the category-formation contains no Aggadic composites that vastly affect the interpretation of matters, the liturgy attached to the same transaction — the rite at the Huppah or marriage-canopy, at which the marriage-settlement is confirmed — certainly does. To identify the aggadic-liturgical statement on the same topic, we turn from the halakhic contexts and readings of the matter to the language of sanctification applying to the woman and man under the huppah or marriage-canopy. The reason is that, self-evidently, the rite of the marriage-canopy demands consideration in any religious commentary to the Halakhah of Ketubot, since the Ketubah is integral to that rite — it is read, start to finish, within the transaction under the marriage-canopy. That that is the fact is shown by the inclusion of the very un-liturgical language of the Ketubah in the very rite under the marriage-canopy. First the Ketubah is read. Then comes the liturgical moment.

The exact character of the liturgy of the Huppah in the time of the Mishnah and the Tosefta is not documented; the Bavli knows about the Seven Blessings under the marriage-canopy. Professor Guenter Stemberger comments, "We do not find any partial formulations of these *berakhot* earlier than the Bavli. The Yerushalmi just says that one has to recite the *birkat hatanim* for seven days, but does this mean seven blessings? We do not have earlier evidence — beyond the fact that there were berakhot for the newly-wed — as to what exactly was said in these berakhot. L. A. Hoffman, *The Canonization of the Synagogue Service* (Notre Dame 1979) pp. 144f, points to disputes regarding these blessings even in the Gaonic period."

The operative language, defining the transaction, is contained in the blessings that are said over the cup of wine of sanctification, which are as follows in contemporary liturgy:

>Praised are You, O Lord our God, King of the universe, Creator of the fruit of the vine.
>
>Praised are You, O Lord our God, King of the universe, who created all things for Your glory.
>
>Praised are You, O Lord our God, King of the universe, Creator of Adam.
>
>Praised are You, O Lord our God, King of the universe, who created man and woman in his image, fashioning woman from man as his mate, that together they might perpetuate life. Praised are You, O Lord, Creator of man.
>
>May Zion rejoice as her children are restored to her in joy. Praised are You, O Lord, who causes Zion to rejoice at her children's return.
>
>Grant perfect joy to these loving companions, as You did to the first man and woman in the Garden of Eden. Praised are You, O Lord, who grants the joy of bride and groom.
>
>Praised are You, O Lord our God, King of the universe, who created joy and gladness, bridge and groom, mirth, song, delight and rejoicing, love and harmony, peace and companionship. O Lord our God, may there ever be heard in the cities of Judah and in the streets of Jerusalem voices of joy and gladness, voices of bridge and groom, the jubilant voices of those joined in marriage under the bridal canopy, the voices of young people feasting and signing. Praised are You, O Lord, who causes the groom to rejoice with his bride.[8]

From the reading of the mundane, detailed, and this-worldly marriage-contract, with its talk of dowry and of the groom's selling the shirt off his back to maintain his wife, then, in line with the later reading of matters, we rise upward, surveying Israel's life with God. Now, at the new beginning represented by the household, we recall Eden. Israel's history begins with creation — first, the creation of the vine, symbol of the natural world. Creation is for God's glory. All things speak to nature, to the physical as much as the spiritual, for all things were made by God. In Hebrew, the blessings end, "who formed the *Adam.*" All things glorify God; above all creation is Adam. The theme of ancient paradise is introduced by the simple choice of the word *Adam,* so heavy with meaning. The myth of man's creation is rehearsed: man and woman are in God's image, together complete and whole, creators of life, "like God." Woman was fashioned from man together with him to perpetuate life. And again, "blessed is the creator of Adam." We

---

[8]*A Rabbi's Manual,* ed. by Jules Harlow (New York: The Rabbinical Assembly, 1965), p. 45. The "seven blessings: said at a wedding are printed in all classical Jewish prayer books.

have moved, therefore, from the natural world to the archetypal realm of paradise, backward to the mythic beginnings of Man, Woman, Eden, the household now transformed into something much beyond the young groom and his bride and the household they found. Before us we see not merely a man and a woman, but Adam and Eve. Whether the liturgy establishes the context for the Halakhah in the Mishnah and the Tosefta is hardly to be taken for granted. To these matters we return in due course.

V. THE HERMENEUTICS OF KETUBOT

We have now seen that the Halakhic category-formation follows the this-worldly course of a marriage from start to finish, with attention to personal and property rights of both parties and property rights of their families as pertinent. But the principle of interpretation of the topic, the selection of data deemed pertinent and the arrangement and exegesis of those data — these matters hardly surface in the exposition just now executed. Once again, an outline of the Halakhah as portrayed by the Mishnah, therefore also by the Tosefta, Yerushalmi, and — points us to the problematics of the topic, which guides us to the hermeneutical heart of the matter: what data, how interpreted?

I. Formation of the Marriage: The Material Rights of the Parties to the Marital Union. (1) The Wife (1:1-2:10)
    A. The Virgin and her Marriage-Contract (1:1-4)
    B. Conflicting Claims for a Marriage-Contrast for a Virgin (1:5-2:10)

II. The Formation of the Marriage: The Material Rights of the Parties to the Marital Union. (2) The Father and the Husband
    A. The Fine Paid to the Father (Dt. 21:22) for Rape or Seduction (3:1-4:1)
    B. The Father (4:2)
    C. The Father and the Husband (4:4-4:6)
    D. The Husband (4:7-5:1)

III. In the Duration of the Marriage. Reciprocal Responsibilities and Rights of the Husband and the Wife (5:2-9:1)
    A. The Wife's Duties to the Husband (5:2-5)
    B. The Husband's Duties to the Wife (5:6-6:1)
    C. The Dowry (6:2-7)
    D. The Marital Rights and Duties of the Wife (7:1-10)
    E. The Property Rights of the Wife (8:1-9:1)

IV. Cessation of the Marriage and Collection of the Marriage Contract (9:12-12:4 + 13:1-9)

A. Imposing an Oath in Collecting the Marriage Contract (9:2-9)
B. Multiple Claims on an Estate (10-1_6)
C. Support of the Widow (11:1-5)
D. Rights to, and Collection of, A Marriage Contract: Special Cases (11:6-12:4)
E. Two Case Books (13:1-9)

The outline leaves no unclarity as to the definition of the category-formation and the governing principles of interpreting it. As I said at the outset, the category-formation finds its logic of exposition, with principal reference to reciprocal obligations of a material and tangible order, in the temporal sequence of the marriage, and its coherence in the unfolding of the marriage stage by stage. I cannot point to comparisons or contrasts that generate the issues deemed to inhere in the topical program. I see no counterpart to the comparison of the circumstance of a fully-realized intentionality and one not entirely effected, such as imparted to Yebamot an active and vital energy. But that points us to what forms the center of the matter at hand. And that is, the marriage that follows its normal course, accomplishing the goals and intentionalities of all parties thereto: procreation, continuity in genealogy and in property.

If the category-formations of Yebamot and Gittin take up the disrupted, arrhythmic marriage — one that either does not accomplish the intentionality (procreation) of the husband, or that ends in a rupture — Ketubot calls our attention to what counts in a rhythmic, natural and normal one. That is a marriage that begins with a fully-consummated union between sexually mature persons of the opposite sex, brings about a joining of appropriate segments of two families' property, in accord with the basic aspirations and expectations of each, that produces children (heirs, "orphans") and an estate to be settled, and that concludes with the death of the husband, having had offspring, and issues of support of the wife from his estate and of the fulfillment of the conditions of the marriage-contract. It follows that the point of comparison and contrast is the unnatural versus the natural course of a marriage, in which case Ketubot can only have followed the narrative pattern that prevails: beginning, middle, and end of an ordinary marital transaction. Once we have decided to compare the abnormal to the normal marriage (to use somewhat imprecise adjectives), we set side by side Yebamot/Gittin and Qiddushin/Ketubot, each with its distinctive selection of data and forming of those data into its respective categorical message. The interpretative principle in play in Ketubot then is the same one that is in play in Yebamot — two means of effecting a marital union, the one abnormal, the other normal — just as, in due course, we shall see that

Yebamot must be situated in relationship with Gittin and Qiddushin, and so throughout.

If, then, we undertake the first part of the comparison — Ketubot's program against Yebamot's program as these deal with the same matters, what do we see? The following table summarizes the principal topics and their order, and we note exact correspondences.

YEBAMOT	KETUBOT
I. Heaven's Role in Establishing the Marital Bond [M. 1:1-6]	I. Formation of the Marriage: The Material Rights of the Parties to the Marital Union. (1) The Wife (1:1-2:10)
II. Under Heaven's Aspect. The Special Marital Bond: Marriage into the Priesthood [M. 6:1-9:6]	II. The Formation of the Marriage: The Material Rights of the Parties to the Marital Union. (2) The Father and the Husband
III. Severing the Marital Bond Other than through Man's Intentionality and Intervention [M. 10:1-16:7]	III. The Duration of the Marriage: Explicit Statement of the Reciprocal Responsibilities and Rights of the Husband and the Wife (5:2-9:1)
	IV. Cessation of the Marriage and Collection of the Marriage Contract (9:12-12:4 + 13:1-9)

In fact the analogical-contrastive programs of Yebamot and of Ketubot precisely correspond, topic for topic: Heaven's role versus Man's role; the marital bond as Heaven is involved in it, the marital bond as Man and Woman are engaged by it, and the considerations that affect the severing of the marital bond through Heaven's activity as against those that govern in this world. Then what differentiates Yebamot from Ketubot is quite clear: where Heaven's intentionality pertains, yields Yebamot, where Man's (and Woman's) plans and hopes are engaged produces Ketubot — and the nature of the details matches the generative problematics in each case, the one dealing with Heaven's unpredictable ways, the other, man's sense of what is fair and just. The hermeneutics of analogical-contrastive logic then dictates the selection of the data and the formulation thereof and accounts for the exegetical emphases of each category-formation.

At this point the governing principle of Ketubot demands attention, and that is the mutuality of responsibility, the self-evidence of principles deemed to embody fairness that is everywhere transparent. The self-evident realization of fairness — balance, proportionality, equivalence — comes to the surface in the account of the middle of the marriage: what the husband owes, given his teleology, what the wife owes, given hers. Then what contrast does Yebamot present? Heaven's role involves anything other than "fairness," the husband having died without children, having undertaken an enterprise, critical to his existence, without realizing it. But what of the exegetical program, counterpart to Ketubot's middle section? There, as if to underscore the contrast between analogous species, Heaven's interest in the marriage involves only the matter of caste status.

So Heaven attends to severance of the marital bond other than through man's intentionality, on the one side, or intervention, on the other. Ketubot's program takes on its own inevitable logic: man and woman undertake mutual responsibilities, along with the other parties to the marriage, the father and the families that are united; man and woman owe mutual obligations of dignity; when the marriage ends by man's action or in the natural course of events — a death that is suitably public and attested — the contract takes effect and the woman's rights are balanced against those of the estate.

Then the analogical-contrastive hermeneutics works itself out in a massive labor of categorical comparison. That is why there is no reading of Ketubot as a problem in hermeneutics without the comparison afforded by the counterpart reading of Yebamot. The two match, and the differences are to be explained within a single, encompassing theory of matters. The marital union defines the genus, Heaven's as against Man's and Woman's respective engagements therein, the two species thereof. Now that we understand the generative hermeneutics of Ketubot in its correct context, let us turn to the concrete results of the matter. Here is the marital union from man's perspective.

A. WHAT FUSES THE HALAKHIC DATA INTO A CATEGORY-FORMATION?

Now that we have explained the Halakhic hermeneutics, we understand why, in the analogical-contrastive process, we examine the way in which man realizes his intentionality in bringing the marriage into being: the data and the way they fuse. But here the comparisons with Yebamot fall away, as we follow how the narrative logic takes over and dictates the data to be selected and the way they are to be portrayed. The main point throughout concerns fairness, balance, and proportion among the contracting parties within the framework of Scripture where pertinent. The premise is, what man and woman intend is for a relationship of justice, a transaction with equal outcomes for all parties in realizing, at the intersection, a common intentionality: procreation and continuation of families.

The basic question facing the Halakhah is how to spell out the reciprocal and corresponding rights and obligations of all parties to the marriage as it unfolds. The marriage-contract defines the locus for working out those rights and obligations; each party has an interest in the orderly formation of the social and economic fact of the marriage — and in its fair and orderly dissolution as well. Here the dissolution involves collecting the marriage-settlement from the husband's estate; as noted, elsewhere we deal with other aspects of the dissolution of the marriage (which may involve the dissolution of the household as well). That document and the arrangements it represents have no foundations in Scripture and constitute a contribution of the Oral part of the Torah alone. As we have seen, the topic of marriage-contracts takes as its generative problem reciprocal and corresponding rights and obligations of all parties to the marriage, at each point in the unfolding of the marriage. These parties are the girl, the boy, and the girl's family (father). The marriage-contract then defines the locus for the negotiation of the rights and obligations of each. All parties have an interest in the orderly formation of the social and economic fact of the marriage — the foundation, after all, of the household — and in its orderly dissolution as well. In the present context, that means, collecting the settlement from the husband's estate.

The Halakhah in its exposition and generative problematic scarcely alludes to the change in relationships embodied in the Ketubah, which takes its place in a process to which the language of sanctification is applied. Nonetheless, even the details of the law contribute to the main point: through this piece of writing, stating the intentionality and commitment of a man and implicitly bearing the woman's consent, a woman becomes sacred to a particular man; without the document (at least in implicit form), the relationship is not legitimated. That is why the Ketubah is integral to the transaction by which there takes place the sanctification of the woman to a particular man, in the analogy of the sanctification of an animal to the altar. The language of Qiddushin, the rules and conceptions of the marital bond in general — these require that we ask, what has the marriage-document to do with the process of sanctification of the relationship of the wife to the husband, how is the woman transformed, in part, through this document and the procedures to which the contract is critical?

Through the Halakhic language of Qiddushin and of Ketubot a woman formerly free to mate with any Israelite is restricted, for the duration, to a particular man. And that restriction is recognized by God ("Heaven") and deemed sacred by him. So we deal with other than an ordinary legal document, e.g., a bill of sale of a piece of property or a will. Not all formulaic legal documents effect sanctification; this one does. The contracts and deeds we meet in the Babas, for example, do not transform the status of the property and land they cover, so if one steals the one or invades the other, he only an actionable offense, but not a sin against Heaven that Heaven punishes. But if a man takes another man's consecrated woman, that is a sin against Heaven, and the offspring of the union are irreparably tainted for all time. Not only so, but at specific points the Halakhah itself confirms the transformative power of the language and writing at hand. How come language exercises such power, and what analogies or models define the context?

To answer that question, we recall the power of language to effect sanctification in the two other critical contexts of the Halakhah, the separation of heave-offering from the crop and the designation of an animal for the offering. The involves the rations for the priesthood to be separated out of the crop. These rations constituted God's share and are holy; the rest of the crop, once the rations have been taken out, is deemed available for ordinary use. When the farmer evinced the desire to utilize the produce, then God responded by imposing the requirement of separating his share; at that point, the crop became liable to tithing and the separation of other offerings. Then a portion of the crop shared by the farmer and God grown on land ownership of which is invested in the farmer and God was to be removed, leaving the rest free for the farmer's use. And the act of separation took the form of a statement, a formulaic act of transformation. To accomplish that end, the farmer recited a formula that serves to designate as holy to the priesthood a portion of the grain at the threshing floor. That part of the whole crop, called variously "heave-offering" or "the priestly ration" enters into the status of sanctity — is sanctified — when the farmer says something along the lines of, "The heave-offering of this heap [of produce] is in its northern portion" [M. Ter. 3:5C]. At that point, the designated portion of the grain enters the status of sanctity, with the result that a non-priest who eats that grain incurs severe punishment. The effect of language is not to convey a generalized desire to designate any portion of the crop, but a particularized intentionality governing the status of a specified segment thereof: "that which is there is...."

Second comes the consecration of an animal for the altar. Language once more serves the purpose of particularizing the intentionality, which concerns a specific sin, and a designated beast to expiate for that sin. The householder who wishes to make an offering has first to designate an animal for the purpose of that offering, and that designation, the act of consecration, involves stating something along the lines of, "This lamb is a sin-offering for such-and-such an inadvertent sin that I have committed." So too, if someone says, "This beast is instead of that beast, a sin-offering," the beast to which he makes reference is consecrated, even while the one to which he made reference remains consecrated. And that language effects even parts of the beast, so M. Tem. 1:3: "he who says, 'The foot of this is a burnt offering' — the whole beast is a burnt offering." And, it goes without saying, we recall full well from the Halakhah of Qiddushin, if a woman agrees when one who says, "Lo, you are sanctified to me on the strength of this coin," the formula, along with the woman's agreement, constitutes the act of consecration. She then is transformed, and if she violates the rules governing her status of sanctity, God expects the holy community to inflict appropriate punishment.

It is in that context that the Ketubah, too, finds its place. Even though the Halakhah frames the topic in other than mythic language and terms, the Ketubah forms an integral component in the process by which, through the evocation of certain language, a woman's status as to all men in the world radically shifts. Before the recitation of the correct formula, including (as in the case at hand) a written record, the woman was free to marry any appropriate Israelite (excluding male relatives); afterward she is not. The upshot is, the Ketubah represents the formula of sanctification. It too is specific and particular to the transaction at hand. And (to jump ahead) that fact pertains, too, to the writ of divorce that effectively ends the sanctification of a marital bond: it must be written for that particular man, woman, and transaction.

That the document bears its own significance, beyond the language that is used in it, is shown by a simple, much-explored fact. The Ketubah's power is fully present even when the requisite language is not written and properly articulated, just as much as the formula of Qiddushin commences the process of sanctification, the formula of designating priestly rations changes the status of both the portion of the crop so designated and the remainder of the crop, no longer containing inherent sanctification, and the formula of designating an animal for the altar. The upshot is, in the transaction represented by, as much as in the language used in, the Ketubah inheres the power of sanctification, such that the status of the woman is redefined and transformed. That explains why clauses take effect even when not written out. Before us is language that evokes conditions and establishes facts not through what is said, but through the transformative power of what is evoked.

Heaven responds to and confirms that same language. Say the right words and Heaven hears. Then what happens upon earth is affected — in that order. And, it goes without saying, Heaven takes seriously the language of human transactions, in oaths and vows as other formularies in which Heaven has a special interest, so that if man violates his commitment to man, God intervenes. Where does language evoke Heaven's interest in particular? What is important is, when we ask where, in the entire corpus of the Halakhah, we find the greatest weight placed upon the language of human transactions in which Heaven involves itself, the answer is, in transactions of the Israelite household. The entire relationship of betrothal and marriage, fidelity in marriage on the part of the woman, and the dissolution of marriage — all of these transactions are effected through Heavenly-supervised formularies, and all are deemed consecrated in a way in which transactions involved in Israel's social order are not. When the language of consecration occurs, it finds its location in two of the three dimensions of Israel's existence, in relationships with God in Heaven and within the Israelite household on earth — but rarely in the Israelite social order acted out in the streets and marketplaces, in transactions of commerce and real estate; there, under specified circumstances, an oath corresponds. And, when it comes to relationships with God in Heaven, where the language of consecration proves effective, it is ordinarily in the context of the household, e.g., providing God with his share of the household's product.

In that context of divine supervision fall [1] the formulary of betrothal, [2] the Ketubah, and [3] the Get. But what defines Heaven's interest, and why should the use of the specified language attract Heaven's attention? Must the relationship of man to woman invariably involve documents that embody the sanctity of the relationship and effect sanctification? To understand the answer, we have to ask, is there a transformation that takes place in a woman's status as to sanctification to a given man? Can a woman's status in relationship to all men but one change without the provision of a particular document, meaning, without the recitation of a specified formula, properly witnessed? Of course there is, and of course it can. A particular man may be singled out as the sole man in the world to whom a given woman is available for marriage and procreation, and no documentary media for the transaction of transformation are required. I refer to the transaction covered by the levirate connection (Dt. 25:1-5), when a man dies and his childless widow forthwith becomes consecrated to a surviving brother. Before the man died, she was forbidden to the brother, and had the man had children, she would have remained forbidden to him. But now, by reason of the decedent's childlessness, she is automatically deemed to have entered into a consecrated relationship with her brother-in-law. On what basis? Heaven has imposed that relationship; then no document by man is required. And to respond to that relationship, one of two things must happen. Either the surviving brother states in advance his intention of entering into levirate marriage with the sister-in-law and then has sexual relations with her — the counterpart to the act of betrothal and the consummation of the marriage, respectively — or he goes through a rite of "removing the shoe," prescribed by Scripture to sever the levirate connection. In neither case is a document essential to the transaction.

What is the difference, and why is a document required, then, in the case of a betrothal and marriage and divorce in other-than-levirate circumstances but not in the levirate one? We have come far enough into this inquiry to identify the answer without difficulty. What God does — by his free will — requires no documentary confirmation effected by man, what man does — exercising his free will, with the woman's consent — requires transformative language, whether or not in written form; and — more to the point — the actions of God find their counterpart in the documents of man. Specifically, God has established the levirate connection, and man merely proceeds through the rites that will either realize or sever that connection. The connection comes about because of the death of the childless husband. No document is called for. The woman is automatically restricted to the decedent's brother. God does it all, having created the conditions that transfer the woman from one man to another. In an ordinary act of betrothal and marriage by contrast, man — the offer of the man, the acceptance by the woman — effects that other connection, the ordinary one between the man and the woman where no intervention on Heaven's part, e.g., in the form of childlessness and death, has taken place.

The upshot is that when Heaven intervenes, documents representing the enactment of formulary language of transformation play no role. When man acts on his own account and enters into a relationship of sanctity through an act of sanctification, then man must speak the words that articulate and make real his intention in that circumstance for the object of his intentionality, whether grain, whether beast, whether woman. God acts by speaking, as in creation. Man speaks but then confirms in writing the announced intention: *let there be*.... Then the document lends palpability to the intention, not so much confirming it as realizing it in an exact sense of the word, just as much as the statement in connection with a specific animal accomplishes the same goal. Sanctity overtakes the animal of which man has spoken; no further documentation in the context of the cult is necessary. Sanctity overtakes the woman in the agreed-upon transaction of betrothal and marriage, but, in the context of the household, documents do play their part. In that context the Ketubah or the Get forms a statement, in material form, of the intentionality of the man, to consecrate the woman or to suspend and annul the status of consecration, as the case may be. The documents form concrete representations of intentionality. To those representations, to that intentionality, the conditions and clauses of the contract of marriage form mere details; they state the consequences of the realization of the intentionality to consecrate the woman to that particular man, or to release the woman to all men.

What, finally, defines the religious meaning of the Ketubah in particular, and what statement did sages choose to make through the Halakhah of Ketubot and only there? The answer is, sages wished to define the actualities of the condition of the consecrated woman not in mythic terms but in those pertinent to the household, and it was only through the Halakhah, with its preoccupation with the small and the intimate, that they could make their comment. To understand the entire implicit statement made by sages through the Halakhah, we have to revert to the liturgical statement of the aggadic view of Man and Woman in consecrated union. Only having scaled the heights of the aggadah in its liturgical formulation, cited earlier, do we grasp the proportionate response: the humility of sages' framing of the ordinary and the everyday context of sanctification. In no detail does the Halakhah of Ketubot demand interpretation in the mythic context evoked at the very point at which the Ketubah is proclaimed in public and takes effect. Unlike the Halakhah of Qiddushin, when we consider the Halakhah of Ketubot, none of the points of amplification, sources of problems requiring analysis, or issues of protracted consideration, requires us to ask questions of a religious character. The language of sanctification does not enter in, and considerations of God's stake in the transaction never arise. And yet the power of language to sanctify remains at the heart of matters. The language at hand has that power. Ketubot flows from Qiddushin, the requirement of the (verbal) documentation of the marital bond from the (verbal) act of sanctification of the woman to the man and her (verbal) assent. It is the simple fact that without completion in documentation, including a Ketubah, the act of Qiddushin is incomplete, the marital union premature. The act of sanctification takes place through the exchange of a token of betrothal, or a writ, or sexual intercourse, we recall, and the next step is the provision of the Ketubah, at which point the relationship of sanctity is established. So what connection can we identify between the act of sanctification and the provision of a document specifying the conditions of the relationship — between religion and law, in gross categories?

Let me now answer the question in a simple way: what connection does the Halakhah identify between the status of sanctification and the use of language, whether oral or written, to declare and establish said status? Why of the three media of sanctification of a woman specified at Mishnah-tractate Qiddushin 1:1, [1] the exchange of a token, [2] the provision of a writ, and [3] the act of sexual relations — all of which, after all, effect the marital bond and bring about the sanctification of the woman to the man — does the provision of the Ketubah take priority? The reason, in the context now established, is self-evident. The Ketubah, declaimed under the marriage-canopy, takes over the rite of the marriage-canopy and defines its this-worldly venue. The marriage-rite invokes the creation of the world, Adam and the creation of Eve in God's image, after God's likeness. The rite compares bride and groom to the loving companions of Eden, invoking too the ultimate return of Israel to Zion, the eschatological restoration of Adam and Eve to Eden. So much for large and public matters. Why should the Ketubah know nothing of all this? That is precisely the wrong question, for everyone knows that the Ketubah is read just moments before we evoke Adam and Eve in Eden and Israel's future return to the Land, its Eden, and before the initial act of sexual relations takes place.

So what has taken place in the legal-liturgical transaction at hand? Viewed at the outcome, at the end of the formation of the Halakhah of the Mishnah-Tosefta-Yerushalmi-Bavli, the matter may be seen in this way. The Ketubah at that very moment of the marital union under the marriage-canopy serves to define the interior dimensions of Eden, explains what makes the groom into Adam and the bride into Eve, specifies the worldly meanings of paradise — so completing the public realm of the aggadah with the private preserve of the Halakhah. Israel in the household realizes Eden through the relationships defined as norms by the Halakhah, portrayed as ideals by the aggadah. The one makes its full and complete statement only in dialogue with the other. Under the marriage-canopy, the *huppah*, therefore, the Halakhah turns exalted matters upside down and draws them down to earth. The Halakhah in that unique setting makes its statement, and it is only through Halakhah on this particular subject — the topic before us — that our sages can have delivered their message. For the Halakhah declares, if you want to know Eden, come to the Israelite household, where the woman is fairly and considerately provided for, and where the man's obligation to found a household in Israel is diligently carried out by the wife. Of that Eden consists. To more than that let no man aspire, therein is the consecrated relationship realized.

B. THE ACTIVITY OF THE CATEGORY-FORMATION

We now understand why the category-formation, Ketubot, addresses the mundane details that occupy its program. The Halakhah takes as its problem the balancing of the rights and obligations of the two household-families that are united, the girl's and her father's, the boy's and his family's. The one contributes a dowry, to be utilized by the groom but subject to restoration to the household of the bride under specified conditions or, more commonly, handed on to the male children of the bride (in a polygamous society, an important consideration indeed). The other undertakes to support the bride and to treat her honorably. How that fair exchange of persons and property plays itself out in the details of the document and the relationships it represents then forms the burden of the Halakhah.

In the formation of the marriage three parties, wife and husband and wife's father, enjoy material rights, the father to certain fees and fines under conditions specified by Scripture, and, more to the point, the wife to protection and support in the event of divorce or widowhood, the husband to the dowry. Scripture's component of the Halakhah, suitably honored and expounded, proves not entirely symmetrical to the main body of the Halakhah, with its interest in the document and what rests upon it. There we find the focus of the Halakhah, and, as we shall note in the next section, that is with good reason.

The Ketubah, the husband's undertaking of obligations to the wife, forms the principal components of the transaction outlined in the Halakhah at hand. We begin with the basic sum of money represented by the document, that is, minimum alimony in the case of a divorce or death. The distinction between the widow and the virgin makes a difference because of the greater alimony paid to the virgin should the husband die or divorce her. The virgin gets about two years of maintenance, two hundred zuz,[9] the widow, about six months, a maneh or one hundred zuz. That leads to the adjudication of conflicting claims and the rules of evidence adduced in support of said claims. The father is accorded the ownership of the woman's bride-price and hence has an interest in her virginity, which accounts for the Halakhah concerning the fine that is paid to the father for rape or seduction. The father further owns the marriage-settlement in cases in which he will continue to support the woman should she be divorced or widowed, e.g., in the case of betrothal. When the girl is under-age, that is, younger than twelve and a half, the father retains control as well, and for the same reason. She will return to his household. Throughout the issue is, who is liable to maintain, ransom, and bury the woman. It is the father until consummation of the marriage, the husband thereafter, and the woman herself if in her mature years she is divorced or widowed. That will then account for the disposition of the marriage-settlement. The Ketubah further assigns to the husband a considerable stake in the success of the marriage; he alone can issue a writ of divorce, but, if he does so, he pays a meaningful indemnity in the form of alimony. All of this is the minimum commitment that he makes to the marriage; the dowry and further add-ons, the provision of luxuries for the wife — these represent further provisions by which the husband responds to the dowry handed over as the bride's inheritance from her father's estate.

Clearly, the Ketubah represents a transaction that vastly transcends the document itself, and, while the writing out of the document and its proclamation under the marriage-canopy form part of the rite of marriage, the

---

[9] Two hundred zuz are about the yearly income of an unskilled worker and should support a family, so that should suffice the girl for two years on her own.

legal relationship that the Ketubah establishes does not depend upon the jot and tittle of the document; in this regard the divorce-document, the *Get,* differs radically. If that document is improperly prepared, there is no divorce. Here, by contrast, the document symbolizes a set of conditions that pertain whether articulated or not, whether correctly documented or not. How explain the difference? The sanctification of the wife and the consummation of the marriage involve several procedures, as we know from Qiddushin, while the divorce rests only on the document. The Ketubah finds its confirmation in the relationship it inaugurates; the couple lives together in accord with its conditions. So by deed the couple embodies the contract. The *Get,* by contrast, has on its own to validate the right of the woman to return to her father's house for good, until she chooses to remarry; everything depends upon the effect of the writing, and the cessation of her previous condition as a married woman, now radically changed, finds its confirmation and legitimation only in the correctly-prepared writing. The upshot is, the writ of divorce stands on its own, and the Ketubah forms only one component of a composite of transactions that accomplish a single coherent goal.

That explains why, unlike the writ of divorce, the marriage-settlement or Ketubah is effective even if the document is not written out; it is an unstated condition "imposed by the court," meaning, valid even when not documented. The protections of the settlement extend to all details normally written in the contract itself. The mutual obligations that apply through the course of the marriage present no surprises. The wife is obligated to work for the upkeep of the household, though if she brought in her dowry slave-girls able to do the work, she is relieved of these obligations. The household work carried out by the wife involves provision of food, clothing, and child-care. The husband's obligations are spelled out in the marriage-settlement; he must provide food, clothing, shelter, and the like. The one important obligation over and above the practical ones concerns sexual relationships; the husband must have sexual relations on a weekly basis, no matter how many wives he may have. The dowry represents the woman's share in her father's estate, collected at the point at which ownership of the woman is transferred to the husband. If the marriage is dissolved, the dowry reverts to the household of the father and his male heirs. The husband may not use the power of the vow to disrupt the wife's normal conduct of her life. Such a vow is treated as a form of abuse of the wife. For her part the wife may not violate her unstipulated obligations, e.g., she must feed him proper food and conduct herself with piety and modesty. During the course of the marriage the husband controls the wife's property, enjoying the usufruct; but the property reverts to the wife, that is, to her family's household, when the marriage has run its course, or it is inherited by her male children. As to collecting the marriage-settlement, e.g., in the event of divorce or widowhood, the matter is complicated by the existence of other claims, besides the widow's or divorcee's, to the husband's property. The widow is supported by the husband's estate, but then her wages belong to the estate ("the orphans").

C. THE CONSISTENCY OF THE CATEGORY-FORMATION

It suffices to say that the points of differentiation emerge not at the boundaries of documents but at the frontier between the Halakhah and the Aggadah. The category-formation as defined in the first of the documents retains its fixed structure and program in the last of them.

D. THE GENERATIVITY OF THE CATEGORY-FORMATION

In theory a category-formation has the power to extend its boundaries to new territory, to generate new problems and to solve them; that is what I mean by "generativity." Does the hermeneutical program of Ketubot — self-evidently proportionate and fair reciprocal obligations between husband and wife, from the provision at the outset of the marriage of the marriage-agreement, to the instructions at the end of the fulfillment of the promises of that agreement — expand? The criterion for the answer lies in whether the topical program proves varied or monotonous, and the answer then is self-evident. The breadth and diversity of the details that are covered at any given point indicate that the principles of selection accommodate an open-ended body of data.

The history of the Halakhah, so far as the documents portray that history, shows us a progress from this world to the next, from the Ketubah to its liturgical setting. In the heightened reality of high mythic being embodied in the powerful imagery of the marriage-canopy, Eden in the here and now, the Ketubah does more than bring matters down to earth. It declares, here on earth, in the household in particular, is where the sanctified relationship governs. So from the exalted re-embodiment of Adam and Eve in Eden, the Ketubah reminds all parties to the transaction of what really is at stake in the holy union of man and wife, the woman consecrated to this particular man. The most humble and hidden activities register. Thus: "He who takes a vow not to have sexual relations with his wife may allow this situation to continue for one week. She who rebels against her husband declining to perform wifely services — they deduct from her marriage contract seven denars a week. And those women go forth without the payment of the marriage contract at all: She who transgresses against the Law of Moses and Jewish Law." How better define Eden than the marital relationship where obligations such as these are honored. The Halakhah for the interiority of Israel's being, with its attention to the workaday details of documents, turns the Ketubah into not only a transformative formulary, but also a powerful, wry commentary to what is truly at stake. Most formularies turn the secular into the sacred. The Ketubah turns the sacred on high into the sacred here on earth, identifying the dimensions of consecration that take the measure of the marriage.

3.
TRACTATE NEDARIM

I. THE DEFINITION OF THE CATEGORY-FORMATION

Man has the power to use language to express the intentionality of sanctifying persons and things, and Heaven confirms and puts into effect his intentionality and language. That fact — the power of language to transform will into intentionality, and intentionality into actuality — forms the genus. But that power of language takes two forms, the one public, the other personal. In the former category is language used conventionally and undifferentiatedly, affecting all persons. In the latter is language used idiosyncratically, transforming the status and relationships principally of the person who uses that language, leaving unaffected all others. Specifically, two species afford the occasion of analogical-contrastive analysis of the genus. First comes the use of sanctifying language with effects for the world at large, that is, sanctification for an objective, public purpose. Second is the use of sanctifying language with results only for the person who has used that language, that is, sanctification for a subjective purpose. The one serves God's purpose for all Israel, the other exploits Heaven's power for personal expression and aggrandizement. In the comparison and contrast of the two species of the one species we identify the hermeneutics of Nedarim: its theory of interpretation of the category-formation of vows.

We start with the genus. The language of sanctification — hierarchical classification effected through human intentionality and action — to Heaven concerns how language affects the tangible, objective, public world of wine and grain and oil. Their status is established for all persons and under every circumstance. By contrast, the language of imposition of the status of sanctification limited to the person himself concerns the intangible but very real world of a particular person's standing in the sight of Heaven and Israel alike. The status of food and persons remains the same for everyone but the person who by language has transformed his relationships thereto. By using certain language, a man or woman effects an alteration in his or her condition, e.g., in relationships with other people, or in food that may or may not be eaten, or situations that may or may not be entered into. Therein lies the analogical-contrastive analysis that defines the hermeneutics of Nedarim. All the rest is exegesis.[10]

Tractate Nedarim, carrying in its wake Nazir, thus explores the issues that arise when a person uses public language for a private purpose: the effects of idiosyncratic exercise of the power of language. The generative problematic works itself out within the hermeneutics of language that affirms the objective meaning of words; words stand for real things; language corresponds to that of which it speaks. What is at stake is this: now personal nuance has no bearing on Heaven's response to man's words. Therefore at the exegetical level, problems of the precise meanings of words, for all persons and under all circumstances, come to the fore. Then philosophical issues take over; theological ones concerning God and man's relationship through language, having set the category-formation and its problematics, now give way.

That man's declarations of intentionality find confirmation in Heaven and so affect the status of that concerning which he speaks is self-evident. Up to this point we have dealt, and at many native category-formations to come, we shall deal, with the first of the two species, the use of public language for public purposes. In that species of the genus, "the sanctifying power of language," what a person says affects for everybody, not only for himself, the status of that of which he speaks. Man has the power to sanctify to the Temple animals and produce, and he has the power to sanctify a woman to himself (with the condition that she concurs). In such matters relationship to God what is at issue is the designation of what belongs to God or God's surrogates.

But the second species of the same genus yields the category-formation, the power of a man to use language to affect only himself. The language that he uses is public but has no bearing upon the world beyond the private universe of which the man speaks. That category-formation is in two parts, Nedarim, vows, and Nazir, the special vow of the Nazirite, the latter dealt with in its own framework but set forth, so far as I can see, without fresh hermeneutical initiatives. The native category-formation, Nedarim, takes up statements man makes that bear consequences for his own status vis à vis himself alone: *to him* are sanctified things that are secular to everyone else. He therefore may not derive secular benefit from persons or objects of which all others are perfectly free to make use. Accordingly, if someone uses appropriate formulations, so far as he himself is concerned, he imposes upon that of which he speaks but only for himself alone the status of sanctification.

---

[10] To be sure, the exegetical issues fall into several categories, not all of them generated by the hermeneutics of the category-formation or particular to that category-formation, as I shall explain.

Then he may not derive benefit from those persons or that property. That is the upshot of taking a vow; it is what vow-taking does.

The contrast between the public vow, affecting Heaven and earth, and the self-centered vow, affecting only the one who expresses it, may be drawn because the point in common is well-established: Heaven hears and responds to man's statement of his intentionality. Then at issue is, does Heaven not only hear but also respond to man's idiosyncratic formulation of his private intentionality, or is there a framework of objective, universal meanings imputed to the words man uses? The question flows from a more fundamental one, as I have already hinted: do words possess objective meanings, everywhere uniform, or do we take account of the subjective sense that a person may impart to his usage?

The question is legitimate, since implicit in the analogical-contrastive analysis is the recognition of the legitimacy of the autonomous person, who may take upon himself obligations and restrictions not incumbent on the objective world round about. So if a person may invoke the taxonomic category of sanctification in his own regard alone, it is quite logical to ask whether language too serves for a private universe of meaning. The Halakhah answers that question negatively. It does so by investigating the objective properties of words, eliminating from Heavenly purview the notional and ad hoc senses that an individual may conceivably have in mind.

This is done in two ways. First, euphemisms are not explained away but encompassed within the objective law, so private usage is objectified. Second, general rules of classifying things are applied to specific cases of language, so language is shown to conform to the laws of natural history and of physics. How is this demonstrated? Two fundamental media of philosophical analysis, differentiation between genus and species and among species, differentiation between primary cause and secondary effect, execute the investigation, with enormous success. Then the hermeneutics of Nedarim concerns itself with the objective interpretation of language in accord with common usage, and consequently the native category-formation selects as its data the meanings of words and phrases, finding its exegetical program in the meanings of specific formulations of matters within a standard philosophical framework.

What is at stake in the exercise? When a person speaks of his own situation, then, the net of common language and established usage holds him within the public, social order. Here at stake is an exercise of "objectification," here meaning, the treating, in accord with established, social norms, of language of the personal status set forth within the subjective framework of the person himself. He indeed possesses the power to declare that that thing that he has sanctified, of which he speaks, remains as it was. It is, by reason of his formulation, secular to everyone in the world, except to him. So, on the one side, the use of language produces not objective results for everyone, as a statement of consecration of an animal or of a woman does, but only for the person who uses the language. But, on the other side, language retains its common and objective meanings — that is the recurrent point that is demonstrated in numerous, particular circumstances.

That explains how the vow serves as the medium for idiosyncratic expression. The fact that the vow produces direct effects only for the person who takes the vow (though it contains within itself consequences for those around him) renders paradoxical the hermeneutics of the tractate: the interpretation of the topic that dictates the selection of data and the exegesis thereof. The hermeneutical principle in play comes to the surface in cases such as these representative ones:

> M. 3:6 He who vows [not to gain benefit] from those who go down to the sea is permitted [to enjoy benefit] from those who dwell on dry land.
> M. 6:1 He who takes a vow not to eat what is cooked is permitted [to eat what is] roasted or seethed.

So too, the rules of the genus and the species are embodied in formulations of vows:

> M. 6:10 [He who takes a vow not to eat the genus,] cabbage is forbidden from asparagus [deemed a species of the cabbage genus]. [He who takes a vow not to eat] asparagus is permitted to have cabbage.

Implicit and governing throughout is the principle: a man even when he alone is the focus may not effectively use language other than in public and objective senses. From Heaven's viewpoint, any idiosyncratic meanings he may have in his heart represent gibberish. Euphemisms count and cannot be explained away as utterly private. We therefore do not ask what the man personally means; only what the language that he has used actually says. Then the (philosophical) rules of close reading of language take over, and the exegesis of case proceeds within the established principle that words mean what they say, and they say what the generality of persons assumes that they say. What is the consequence? Language is exclusionary: this not that; it is precise, "cooked" is not the same thing as "roasted." The consequent exegetical program viewed whole then concerns how we interpret the language that is used for a vow, the common meanings to be imputed to the idiosyncratic declaration of the one who singles himself out thereby. Only in one specific circumstance do we ask about the man's personal intent and reach a practical decision based upon his answer; that is when we engage in the discovery-process to find out whether, in fact, the vow has taken effect or was null to begin with. But the meaning of the vow is unaffected.

Then what the Halakhah accomplishes in the present category-formation is a massive, detailed study of the public and objective meanings of words. That study furthermore embodies in cases the principles of hierarchical classification, of the genus and the species for one principal example. And, in that context, what establishes the common usage is the correct analysis of the definitive traits of things, their inherent, indicative qualities. Indeed, if we wished to teach lessons concerning hierarchical classification as these are embodied in the working of language, we could find no better exposition of the analytical rules of differentiation of classes of things on the basis of their definitive qualities. That is how we discern the like from the unlike. In the body of data selected and systematically arrayed in the present category-formation sages teach the rules of natural history. Take for example the classification of Israel among the nations of the world. Here is how, in the present exercise, the matter is laid out:

> M. 3:11 [If a man said,] "Qonam if I have benefit from the children of Noah" — he is permitted [to enjoy benefit] from Israelites and prohibited [to enjoy benefit] from the nations of the world. "...if I have benefit from the seed of Abraham," he is prohibited [to enjoy benefit] from Israelites, and permitted [to enjoy benefit] from the nations of the world....[If he said,] "Qonam if I derive benefit from the uncircumcised," he is permitted [to derive benefit] from uncircumcised Israelites but prohibited [from deriving benefit] from circumcised gentiles. "Qonam if I derive benefit from the circumcised" — he is prohibited [to derive benefit] from uncircumcised Israelites and permitted [to derive benefit] from circumcised gentiles. For the word "uncircumcised" is used only as a name for gentiles.

At stake is the standing of the children of Noah: are they all humanity after the flood and where does Israel fit in? The answer is, the children of Noah are all but Israel, who are classified as children of Abraham. So too "circumcision" is treated as not physical but taxonomical, a synonym for Israel, of whom circumcision is typical.

Generalizing on the case at hand recapitulates the elementary rules of natural history. Or we go over standard distinctions between primary and subordinate causes or effects (such as will preoccupy us when we reach the first of the Babas). The upshot, time and again, is to conduct an exercise in taxonomy in accord with the rules of natural history and of physics, as I said.

Now it is with special reference to the objective facts that indicate the status of things, which facts then correspond in actuality to the meanings imputed to language, the taxic differentiation contained therein. So we see how the exegetical problems that form the shank of the tractate are generated by the principle that language bears objective meanings, corresponding to the reality of things. It must follow, the use of language for entirely subjective purposes by the man who has taken an oath so far as the Halakhah is concerned conforms to rules that the private person does not set. Language is never private, even when used for wholly private purposes.

If the species of the genus, the power of language to realize intentionality, covered by Nedarim is as I have said it is, then what about a theoretical counterpart and its hermeneutics? Where do we find the analogical-contrastive exercise as it extends to the other species of the same genus — rules for using language, with effect, in accord with public, not personal intentionality? To answer that question, we must ask ourselves, in other transactions involving the evocation of Heaven's engagement in the business of individuals, do we find an equivalent preoccupation with the rules that govern all cases, the laws of language viewed as objective and real? The answer is, no counterpart to the linguistic analysis before us pertains to language a private person uses in sanctifying objects for Heaven, effective for all persons and not for himself alone. There no issue arises concerning the meaning of language, no idiosyncratic circumstance having intervened. A simple fact shows the Halakhic reality: when one sanctifies an animal or a handful of meal for that matter, we look in vain for analytical exercises that establish the objective sense of what he individually says, differentiating the autonomy of usage from the private intent of the one who uses that language. That is stated in so many words in numerous contexts but in no encompassing native category-formation. Here is one such formulation of the principle that, in acts of sanctification, language is effective only when it is used in accord with universal rules:

A. [He who says,] "Lo, I pledge myself [to bring] a meal offering made of barley," [in any case] must bring one made of wheat. [Free will meal offerings have to be made of wheat.]

B. [He who says,] "Lo, I pledge myself to bring a meal offering made of meal," must bring one made of fine flour.

C. [He who says,] "Lo, I pledge myself to bring a meal offering without wine and frankincense," must bring one with oil and frankincense.

D. [He who says,] "Lo, I pledge myself to bring a meal offering made of a half-tenth," must bring one made of a whole tenth.

E. [He who says,] "Lo, I pledge myself to bring a meal offering made of a tenth and a half-tenth," brings one made of two [whole] tenths [of an ephah of fine flour].
F. R. Simeon declares free [of the obligation to bring a meal offering in any of the foregoing cases], for [in so specifying,] he has not volunteered [a freewill meal offering] in the way in which people volunteer [to make a freewill meal offering].

Mishnah-tractate Menahot 12:3

"Sanctified" is sanctified for everybody, by the rules that apply to everybody. Whatever one says, he must do the thing in accord with the prevailing rule and rite. Language possesses objective meanings, imposes universally applicable obligations. That is because when one speaks of the sanctity of animals or produce to Heaven, all persons are affected by his action; the status of that of which he has spoken changes. When he speaks of the sanctify of animals or produce or persons *so far as he himself is concerned* — and that is what the Halakhah understands by a vow — then the uncertainties and variables of idiosyncratic usage naturally present a problem. Now the issue is, what meaning can one intend? And the answer is, thus and so are the limits of language.

The Halakhah then rarely will take account of utterly private usages but will impose the generality of meaning upon the diverse cases that require sorting out. In a system of analogies and contrasts, why then do we find no category-formation of the Halakhah to serve in contrast to Nedarim? If someone uses appropriate language, with appropriate intentionality for sanctifying to Heaven a given beast or vegetable, why not take account of the possibilities of variation in intent and usage, such as preoccupy us when it comes to sanctifying the same to that particular man alone and uniquely, meaning, he may not derive benefit therefrom but everyone else may? Asking the question in that form answers it: when the effect of language is public and undifferentiated, all persons being forbidden secular benefit from what has now been sanctified, no distinctions and points of differentiation arise.

The matter of the use of language to substitute a secular beast for an already-sanctified one shows the reality. Lev. 27:10 provides a fine model: if one declares one beast as a substitute for a consecrated beast, the beast that is already consecrated remains so, and the beast consecrated as a substitute therefor enters the classification of sanctification as well. The Halakhah admits to no unclarity or imprecision in the matter: "sanctified to Heaven" forms an undifferentiated and unnuanced category. Personal qualifications of intent mean little. The objective focus — "to Heaven" — then forms the contrast to the subjective one — "to me." Then the former context generates no category-formation; there is nothing to analyze, no rule to be established out of the exegesis of data. But the latter setting self-evidently does. Then, to conclude, what hermeneutics governs? It is a theory of language that maintains, words correspond to things. Objective meanings inhere. Classes of things bear an autonomous standing. They form not negotiable and personal or private realms of idiosyncratic preference but rather fixed and public classes into which data are readily assigned. In a religious construction that values language as the medium of communication between God and man and that maintains God speaks to the corporate community, only rarely and then episodically to the private person, the hermeneutics of public discourse governed by universal and objective rules is logically required. And, were the character of the native category-formation, Nedarim, insufficient to establish that fact, the Halakhic provision of the language of public prayer would prove it.

To conclude: what we shall now see is a detailed exposition of how vows are a means used on earth by weak or subordinated person to coerce the more powerful person by invoking the power of Heaven. They are taken under emotional duress and express impatience and frustration. They are not to be predicted. They do not follow a period of sober reflection. They take on importance principally in two relationships, [1] between friends (e.g., host and guest), [2] between husband and wife. They come into play at crucial, dangerous points, because they disrupt the crucial relationships that define life, particularly within the household: marriage, on the one side, friendly hospitality, on the other. They jar and explode. By admitting into human relationships the power of intentionality, they render the predictable — what is governed by regularities — into a source of uncertainty, for who in the end will penetrate what lies deep in the heart, as Jeremiah reflected, which is beyond fathoming? But language brings to the surface, in a statement of will best left unsaid, what lurks in the depths, and the result, Heaven's immediate engagement, is not to be gainsaid. That is why vows form a source of danger. What should be stable if life is to go on is made capricious. So far as marriage is concerned, vows rip open the fabric of sacred relationships.

II. THE FOUNDATIONS OF THE HALAKHIC CATEGORY-FORMATIONS

Scripture evokes a different hermeneutics for the interpretation of the same data, those concerning the vow. The Written Torah, in line with the interests of the Pentateuch in Numbers and Deuteronomy in general, treats the matter as principally one involving women — wives and daughters — while the Halakhah of the Oral Torah presents it as a sex-neutral one, involving vows by man or woman alike. What is nearly the whole story of the topic in Numbers is handled in Nedarim as subordinate and secondary. Rather, the Halakhah of the Oral part of the Torah wants to know about the language that makes the vow effective, the results of vows, the release of vows — topics implicit, but not explored, within the Scripture's account of the matter. Scripture supplies relevant verses but not the generative concerns of the Halakhah. The pertinent verses of Scripture, which are as follows (Numbers 30:1-16), scarcely prepare us for the present category-formation, because the hermeneutics that governs the exposition of the topic takes up other considerations altogether:

> Moses said to the heads of the tribes of the people of Israel, This is what the Lord has commanded. When a man vows a vow to the Lord or swears an oath to bind himself by a pledge, he shall not break his word; he shall do according to all that proceeds out of his mouth.
> Or when a woman vows a vow to the Lord and binds herself by a pledge, while within her father's house in her youth, and her father hears of her vow and of her pledge by which she has bound herself and says nothing to her, then all her vows shall stand, and every pledge by which she has bound herself shall stand. But if her father expresses disapproval to her on the day that he hears of it, no vow of hers, no pledge by which she has bound herself, shall stand; and the Lord will forgive her, because her father opposed her. And if she is married to a husband while under her vows or any thoughtless utterance of her lips by which she has bound herself, and her husband hears of it, and says nothing to her on the day that he hears, then her vows shall stand, and her pledges by which she has bound herself shall stand. But if, on the day that her husband comes to hear of it, he expresses disapproval, then he shall make void her vow which was on her and the thoughtless utterance of her lips, by which she bound herself; and the Lord will forgive her. But any vow of a widow or of a divorced woman, anything by which she has bound herself, shall stand against her.
> And if she vowed in her husband's house or bound herself by a pledge with an oath, and her husband heard of it, and said nothing to her and did not oppose her, then all her vows shall stand, and every pledge by which she bound herself shall stand. But if her husband makes them null and void on the day that he hears them, then whatsoever proceeds out of her lips concerning her vows or concerning her pledge of herself shall not stand; her husband has made them void. But if her husband says nothing to her from day to day, then he establishes all her vows or all her pledges that are upon her; he has established them, because he said nothing to her on the day that he heard of them. But if he makes them null and void after he has heard of them, then he shall bear her iniquity.

These are the statues that the Lord commanded Moses, as between a man and his wife, and between a father and his daughter, while in her youth, within her father's house.

The generalization, that a person is not to break his word but keep "all that proceeds out of his mouth," meaning, his vows, plays little part in the Halakhic category-formation, Nedarim. The power of the father, then the husband, over the daughters, then the wife's, vows does define a set of exegetical problems, but these are tacked on and play no consequential role in the shank of the Halakhic exposition. So, as is often the case, what Scripture defines as the problematic that generates exegetical issues hardly points us toward the generative problematics of the Halakhah. But who can doubt that Scripture's account of how God and man communicate in language forms the foundation for our category-formation? That is the given of every account, from the act of creation onward, of the meeting of God and man.

III. THE EXPOSITION OF THE COMPONENTS OF THE GIVEN CATEGORY-FORMATION BY THE MISHNAH-TOSEFTA-YERUSHALMI-BAVLI

As always, I set forth the main points of **the Mishnah (in bold face type)**, then at the appropriate place add the Tosefta's own presentation not merely the clarification or amplification of the Mishnah's Halakhah) (in ordinary type), thereafter *the Yerushalmi's (in italics)*, and finally, **THE BAVLI'S (IN BOLD FACE LOWER CASE TYPE)**. These are paraphrased and epitomized, they are not cited in full. I insert my observations on the points of special interest at the conclusion of each topical sub-unit. The units and sub-units derive from my own outline of the Mishnah-tractate, encompassing also the Tosefta-tractate; then the outline of the Yerushalmi, finally that of the Bavli.[11] Readers who compare the selections given here with the complete text will note that I omit disputed and schismatic opinion and discuss only the normative law.

I. THE LANGUAGE OF VOWS

  A. *EUPHEMISMS*
  M. 1:1 All euphemisms [substitutes for language used to express] (1) vows are equivalent to vows, and [all euphemisms] for (2) bans (herem) are equivalent to bans, and [all euphemisms] for (3) oaths are equivalent to oaths, and [all euphemisms] for (4) Nazirite vows are equivalent to Nazirite vows. He who says to his

---

[11] These are cited with bibliographical data in the Introduction, Volume I.

fellow [euphemisms such as], (1) "I am forbidden by vow from you," (2) "I am separated from you," (3) "I am distanced from you," "if I eat your [food]," [or] "if I taste your [food]," is bound [by such a vow]. [He who says], "As the vows of the evil folk," has made a binding vow in the case of a Nazir, or in the case of [bringing] an offering, or in the case of an oath. [He who says,] "As the vows of the suitable folk" has said nothing whatsoever. "As their [suitable folks'] freewill-offerings" ...he has made a binding vow in the case of a Nazir or in the case of [bringing] an offering.

T. 1:1 [He who says,] "By the right hand," — lo, this is an oath. "By the left hand" — lo, this is an oath. "By the Name" — lo, this is an oath. "For the Name" — lo, this is a qorban. [If he said:] "Like the freewill-offering of evil folk" — he has said nothing, for evil people do not bring freewill-offerings.

T. 1:2 He who says, "I do not vow," — lo, this one is permitted. [He who says], "I already should have vowed" — lo, this one is prohibited. "It is [not] qorban if I taste it" — he is permitted. "It is not qorban, and I shall not taste it" — he is prohibited.

M. 1:2 He who says to his fellow, "Qonam," "Qonah," "Qonas" — lo, these are euphemisms for the Qorban [a vow to bring a sacrifice, and are valid]. [He who says to his fellow,] "Hereq," "Herekh," "Heref," lo, these are euphemisms for a herem [ban]. [He who says to his fellow,] "Naziq," "Naziah," "Paziah" — lo, these are euphemisms for Nazirite vows. [He who says,] "Shebutah," "Shequqah," [or if he] vowed [with the word] "Mohi," lo, these are euphemisms for "shebuah" [oath].

M. 1:3 He who says, "Not-unconsecrated produce shall I not eat with you," "Not-valid [food]," and, "Not-pure," "[Not]-clean [for the altar]," or "Unclean," or "Remnant," or "Refuse" — is bound. [If he said, "May it be to me] like the lamb [of the daily whole-offering]," "...like the [temple] sheds," "...like the wood," "...like the fire," "...like the altar," "...like the sanctuary," "...like Jerusalem" — [if] he vowed by the name of one of any of the utensils used for the altar, even though he has not used the word qorban — lo, this one has vowed [in as binding a way as if he had vowed] by qorban.

T. 1:3 A. [He who says,] "Jerusalem," "To Jerusalem," "In Jerusalem," "Hekhal," "To the Hekhal," "In the Hekhal," "Altar," "To the altar," "In the altar," "Lamb," "To the lamb," "In the lamb," "Sheds," "To the sheds," "In the sheds," "Wood," "To the wood," "In the wood," "Fires," "To the fires," "On the fires," "Dishes [of frankincense]," "To the dishes," "On the dishes" — any one of these — "if I eat with you" is prohibited [M. Ned. 1:3C-F]. [He who says,] "That I shall not eat with you [any of these]" is permitted. [He who says,] "Unconsecrated food," "For unconsecrated food," "With unconsecrated food," whether he said, "That I shall eat with you," or whether he said "That I shall not eat with you," is permitted. [He who says,] "Not-unconsecrated-food if I shall eat with you," is prohibited. [He who says,] "Unconsecrated food if I shall eat with you," "If I shall not eat with you," is permitted. [If he said,] "If I shall not eat with you," he is permitted. He who says, "Lo, it is unto me," even if he did not mention the word qorban, lo, this is a vow. "It is qorban like my mother's flesh," "Like my sister's flesh," "Like a foreskin," "Like mixed seeds in a vineyard," he is permitted. For he has not declared anything to be sanctified [which actually is subject to sanctification].

M. 1:4 He who says, "An offering [be what I eat with you]," "A whole-offering [be what I eat with you]," "A meal-offering [be what I eat with you]," "A sin-offering [be what I eat with you]," "A thank-offering [be what I eat with you]," "Peace-offering be what I eat with you" — he is bound [prohibited from eating with the other party]. [If he says, "May what I eat of yours be] the qorban," "Like the qorban [be what I eat with you]," "[By] a qorban [do I vow] be what I eat with you," he is bound. [If he says,] "For a qorban shall be what I eat with you," he is bound. He who says to his fellow, "Qonam be my mouth which speaks with you," or "My hand which works with you," or "My foot which walks with you," is bound.

M. 2:1 And these [vows] are not binding [at all]: [He who says,] "May what I eat of yours be unconsecrated food," "[May what I eat of yours be] like pig meat," "[May what I eat of yours be] like an idol," "[May what I eat of yours be] like hides pierced at the heart," "[May what I eat of yours be] like carrion," "[May what I eat of yours be] like terefah meat," "[May what I eat of yours be] like abominations," "[May what I eat of yours be] like creeping things," "[May what I eat of yours be] like the dough-offering of Aaron," or "[May what I eat of yours be] like his heave-offering" — it is not binding. He who says to his wife, "Lo, you are like mother to me" — they open for him a door [for the unbinding of his oath] from some other source, so that he may not behave lightly in such a matter. [He who says,] "Qonam if I sleep," or, "...if I speak," or, "...if I walk" — he who says to his wife, "Qonam if I have sexual relations with you" — Lo, this is a case to which applies the law, "He shall not break his word" (Num. 30:2). [If he said], "By an oath that I shall not sleep," "that I shall not speak," "that I shall not walk" — it is binding

T. 1:4 He who vows "by the Torah" — lo, this is not binding. He who vows "by what is written in the Torah" — lo this is binding. He who vows " by what is in the Torah and by what is written in it" — it is binding [cf. M. Ned. 2:1]. What is a vow which prohibits [that which is written] in the Torah? [Num. 30:3]. He who says, "Lo, I take upon myself that I shall not eat meat, " and "that I shall not drink wine," "as on the day on which I saw Jerusalem in ruins," or "as on the day on which So-and-so was slain" — it is binding.

B. 2:1A-M III.2/14B HE WHO TAKES A VOW BY THE TORAH HAS SAID NOTHING AT ALL. [IF HE TOOK THE OATH] "BY WHAT IS WRITTEN THEREIN," HIS WORDS ARE CONFIRMED. "BY IT AND BY WHAT IS WRITTEN IN IT," HIS WORDS ARE CONFIRMED.

M. 2:2 He who says, "For qorban I shall not eat with you!" "Qorban be what I eat with you!" "Not-qorban be what I do not eat with you!" — He is not bound. "By an oath, I shall not eat with you!" "By an oath, if I shall eat with you," "Not by an oath I shall not eat with you," he is bound. This rule is therefore more strict in the case of oaths than in the case of vows. But [there is] a more strict rule which applies to vows than applies to oaths. How so? [If] he said, "Qonam be the Sukkah [hut for the festival of Tabernacles] which I am making!" "The lulab which I am taking!" "The tefillin which I am laying on" — in the case of vows, it is binding. In the case of oaths, it is not binding. For an oath is not taken to transgress the commandments [of the Torah].

T. 1:5 A more strict rule applies to vows than to oaths, and to oaths than to vows [M. Ned. 2:1-2]. For vows apply to matters which are a matter of choice as well as to those which are subject to commandment, which is not the case with oaths [M. Ned. 2:2H-K]. A more strict rule applies to oaths. For oaths apply to something which is of substance and to something which is not of substance, which is not the case of vows. In the case of vows, how so [A-C]? [If] one said, ' Qonam is the Sukkah which I am making," "the lulab which I am taking," "the tefillin which I am putting on" — it is binding in the case of vows and not binding in the case of oaths [M. Ned. 2:2]. How so? If he said, "Qonam if I sleep," if I speak, ' if I walk, [M. Ned. 2:1 F], it is binding in the case of oaths and not binding in the case of vows. "Qonam is my mouth if it speaks with you," "my hands if they work with you," "my feet if they walk with you" — it is binding in the case of vows and binding in the case of oaths [M. Ned. 1:4J-K].

M. 2:3 There is a vow within a vow, but there is no oath within an oath. How so? [If] he said, "Lo, I am a Nazir if I eat," "Lo, I am a Nazir if I eat," [and if] he ate, he is liable for each such statement [and observes two spells of Naziriteship]. [If he said], "By an oath I shall not eat," "By an oath I shall not eat," and he ate, he is liable for one count only.

M. 2:4 Vows which are not spelled out are subject to a more stringent rule, and [vows] which are spelled out are subject to a more lenient rule. How so? [If] he said, "Lo, it is to me like salted meat," "Like wine used for idolatrous worship," if his vow referred to things belonging to Heaven, it is binding. If it is of things belonging to idolatry that he vowed, it is not binding. But if he vowed without specification, it is binding. [If he said,] "Lo, it is to me like a devoted thing," if he said, "Like a thing devoted to Heaven," it is binding. If [he said,] "Like a thing devoted to priests," it is not binding. And if he said it without further specification, it is binding. [If he said,] "Lo, it is unto me like tithe," if he vowed that it was like tithe of cattle, it is binding. If it was like tithe of the threshing floor, it is not binding. And if he said it without further specification, it is binding.

T. 1:6 Vows which are not spelled out are subject to a more stringent rule [M. Ned. 2:4A]: "Why did you take an oath?" If he said, "I do not know. But I saw my buddies taking oaths that way" — it is binding.

M. 2:5 [If] one vowed by "herem," but then he said, "I vowed only concerning that which is a herem [a net] of the sea," [or if he vowed] by "qorban," but then he said, "I vowed only concerning qorban [offerings] to kings," [if he said,] "Lo, *asmi* [my bone] is qorban," and explained, "I vowed only concerning the *esem* [bone] which I placed before me by which to vow," [if he said,] "Qonam is that benefit which my wife derives from me," and he said, "I vowed only concerning my first wife, whom I have already divorced" — they find an opening for them in some other place [by some pretext]. And they instruct them that they not treat vows lightly.

That the vow is personal and idiosyncratic, the oath public and governed by the law of the Torah, is made explicit at M. 2:2. One cannot take an oath to transgress the commandments of the Torah; Israel's oath to keep the Torah takes priority. But one may take a vow concerning all manner of things. The issue of private language is settled: any euphemism, anything remotely resembling a vow, is classified as a vow; little space is left for negotiation about individual intent. The ambiguities of language are sorted out, M. 2:5, as well. The negative judgment on vow-taking ("for suitable folk do not take vows") is noteworthy. The setting of the vow, time and again, is conflict in the household, e.g., an overbearing host is resisted by a vow-taking guest, someone loses his temper and takes an oath, and the like. We note the Tosefta's complementary amplification; no new ideas occur that I discern. The rulings on ineffective formulations, M. 2:1/T. 1:4, present no surprises.

B.   LANGUAGE OF NO EFFECT

M. 3:1 Four [types of] vows did sages declare not binding: (1) Vows of incitement, (2) vows of exaggeration, (3) vows made in error, and (4) vows [broken] under constraint. Vows of incitement: How so? [If] one was selling something and said, "Qonam if I chop the price down for you to under a sela," and the other says, "Qonam if I pay you more than a sheqel," [then] both of them agree at three denars.

M. 3:2 Vows of exaggeration: [If] he said, "Qonam if I did not see [walking] on this road as many as went out of Egypt," "...if I did not see a snake as big as the beam of an olive press." Vows made in error: "...if I ate," or "...if I drank," and he remembered that he ate or drank; "...if I shall eat," or "...if I shall drink" and he forgot and ate and drank. [If] he said, "Qonam be any benefit my wife gets from me, for she stole my purse" "...for she beat up my son," and he found out that she had not beaten up his son, or he found out that she had not stolen it. [If] he saw people eating figs [belonging to him] and said, "Lo, they are qorban to you!" and they turned out to be his father and brothers, and there were others with them — these and those [men] are permitted [to eat the figs].

M. 3:3 Vows [broken] under constraint: [If] one's fellow imposed a vow on him to eat with him, but he got sick, or his son got sick, or a river [overflowed and] stopped him — lo, these are vows [broken] under constraint.

M. 3:4 They take a vow to murderers, robbers, or tax collectors that [produce] is heave-offering, even though it is not heave-offering; that [property] belongs to the state, even though it does not belong to the state, even in the form of an oath. One [voluntarily] takes a vow at the outset. [One takes a vow] only in the matter concerning which the vow is imposed also: Concerning that in which the vow is not imposed. How so? [If] they said to him, "Say: 'Qonam be any benefit my wife has with me!'" and he said, "Qonam be any benefit my wife and children have with me!" — these and those are permitted.

M. 3:5 [He who says], "Lo, these plants are qorban, if they are not cut down," "This cloak is qorban if it is not burned" — they are subject to redemption. "Lo, these plants are qorban until they are cut down," "This cloak is qorban until it is burned" — they are not subject to redemption.

T. 2:2 A. They attribute [produce subject to seizure] by assessors and tax-collectors to heave-offering, or to gentile ownership, or to the ownership of the government [M. Ned. 3:4A-C]. But they do not attribute ownership to another Israelite.

T. 2:3 [He who says], "Lo, these plants are qorban until they are cut down, This cloak is qorban until it is burned," [M. Ned. 3:5D-E] "This cow is qorban, until it is slaughtered," once they have been cut down, burned, or slaughtered, they have gone forth to the status of unconsecrated objects.

Because vows embody an act of bad temper, sages have further to place broad limits on what to begin with can be classed as an effective statement; a person need not claim in his own behalf, I said such and so merely as incitement, because such language is null to begin with. The four types that are null include two self-evident types, vows made under constraint, which then do not represent the vow-taker's own intentionality, and vows made in error, which do not embody his intentionality either. The other two — those of incitement and of exaggeration — are dismissed as trivial abuse of language, e.g., a vow made in the context of buying or selling. These are conventional and not particularizations of the intent of the one who makes them. So too vows taken under duress, M. 3:4, are null. The Tosefta's complement raises no new issues.

C. *LANGUAGE OF LIMITED EFFECT*

M. 3:6 He who vows [not to gain benefit] from those who go down to the sea is permitted [to enjoy benefit] from those who dwell on dry land. [He who vowed not to enjoy benefit] from those who dwell on dry land is prohibited [to enjoy benefit] from those who go down to the sea, for those who go down to the sea are part of the generality of those who live on dry land. [Those who go down to the sea includes] not the like of those who go from Acre to Jaffa but the one who sails out of sight of land.

M. 3:7 He who vows [not to enjoy benefit] from those who see the sun is prohibited even [to enjoy benefit] even from the blind. For he intended [to separate himself] only from the one whom the sun sees.

M. 3:8 He who vows [not to enjoy benefit] from black haired men is prohibited [to enjoy benefit] from bald people and from white haired people. But he is permitted [to enjoy benefit] from women and children for only men are called black haired.

M. 3:9 He who vows [not to enjoy benefit] from creatures that are [already] born is permitted [to enjoy benefit] from those creatures who may be born [thereafter]. [If he vowed not to enjoy benefit] from those who may be born [thereafter], he is prohibited [to enjoy benefit] from those who are born. This one intended [to separate himself] only from anyone [whose nature it is to be] brought forth [living creatures]."

M. 3:10 He who vows [not to enjoy benefit] from those who rest on the Sabbath is prohibited [to enjoy benefit] both from Israelites and from Samaritans. [If he vowed not to enjoy benefit] from garlic eaters, he is forbidden [to derive benefit] from Israelites and Samaritans. [If he vowed not to enjoy benefit] from those who ascend to Jerusalem, he is forbidden [to enjoy benefit] from Israelites but permitted [to enjoy benefit] from Samaritans.

M. 3:11 [If a man said,] "Qonam if I have benefit from the children of Noah" — he is permitted [to enjoy benefit] from Israelites and prohibited [to enjoy benefit] from the nations of the world. "...if I have benefit from the seed of Abraham," he is prohibited [to enjoy benefit] from Israelites, and permitted [to enjoy benefit] from the nations of the world. [If he said, "Qonam] if I have benefit from Israelites," he buys for more and sells for less. "...If Israelites enjoy benefit from me," he buys for less and sells for more — (if anyone will pay attention to him!). "... If I derive benefit from them and they from me" — he derives benefit from gentiles. [If he said,] "Qonam if I derive benefit from the uncircumcised," he is permitted [to derive benefit] from uncircumcised Israelites but prohibited [from deriving benefit] from circumcised gentiles. "Qonam if I derive benefit from the circumcised" — he is prohibited [to derive benefit] from uncircumcised Israelites and permitted [to derive benefit] from circumcised gentiles. For the word "uncircumcised" is used only as a name for gentiles, as it is written. "For all the nations are uncircumcised, and the whole house of Israel is uncircumcised at heart" (Jer. 9:26). And it says, "This uncircumcised Philistine" (1 Sam. 17:36). And it says, "Lest the daughters of the Philistines rejoice, lest the daughters of the uncircumcised triumph" (2 Sam. 1:20).

T. 2:4 He who vows not to derive benefit from Israelites is prohibited from deriving benefit from proselytes. He who vows not to derive benefit from proselytes is permitted to derive benefit from Israelites. He who vows not to derive benefit from Israelites is prohibited from deriving benefit from priests or Levites. He who vows not to derive benefit from priests and Levites is permitted to derive benefit from Israelites. He who vows not to derive benefit from priests is permitted to derive benefits from Levites. He who vows not to derive benefit from Levites is permitted to derive benefit from priests. He who vows that Israelites will not derive benefit from him buys for less and sells for more [M . Ned. 3:11 D].

The rules of correct classification dictate the course of the composition at hand. Language is deemed precise, and a person says what he means; any private sense is dismissed as null, and the common sense of language prevails, e.g., M. 3:8: "only men are called...." various classifications of persons, e.g.,

Israelites and Samaritans, are compared and contrasted, common genus, different species, the whole lucidly instantiated. The Tosefta's small gloss, T. 2:4, presents no puzzle.

II.   THE BINDING EFFECTS OF VOWS

   A.   *VOWS NOT TO DERIVE BENEFIT*
   M. 4:1 There is no difference between him who forbids himself by vow from enjoying any benefit from his fellow and him who is forbidden by vow from deriving food from him, except for setting foot in his [the fellow's] house and [using his] utensils in which food is not prepared. He who is forbidden by vow from deriving food from his fellow — [the fellow] should not lend him a sifter, a sieve, a millstone, or an oven. But he may lend him a shirt, a ring, a cloak, earrings, or anything in which food is not prepared. But in a place in which such things as these are rented out [for money or food], it is forbidden to do so.
   [Y. 4:1 I:2 But he may lend him cups, plates, and dishes, for they do not enhance the food but merely hold it. Frying pans and pots are prohibited. Milling or pressing is forbidden. As to reaping, there is a question. As to cutting olives, there is a question.
   M. 4:2 He who is prohibited by vow from deriving benefit from his friend — he [the friend] nonetheless (1) pays out his sheqel [half-sheqel tax to the Temple], (2) pays back his debt, and (3) returns to him something which he [the one who took the vow] has lost. But in a place in which for this action a reward is paid out, the benefit [of the reward] should fall to the sanctuary.
   M. 4:3 (1) And he takes up his heave-offering or his tithes with his permission. (2) And he offers in his behalf bird-offerings for (1) Zab men or (2) Zab women, (3) bird-offerings for women who have just given birth, (4) sin-offerings, and (5) guilt-offerings. (3) And he teaches him exegetical rules, laws, and stories. But he does not teach him Scripture. But he teaches his sons and daughters Scripture. (4) And he takes care of his wife and children, even though he [who is subject to the vow] is liable for their care. (5) But he should not take care of his domesticated animal, whether unclean or clean.
   M. 4:4 He who is prohibited by vow from enjoying benefit from him — he [the fellow] goes in to visit him when he is sick, remaining standing but not sitting down. And he heals him himself but not what belongs to him. He washes with him in a large bathtub but not in a small one. He sleeps with him in the same bed. And he sits with him on the same couch, and eats with him at the same table but not from the same bowl. But he eats with him from the same bowl which is passed around. He may not eat with him

from the same feeding bowl that is set before workers. He works with him but at a distance.

T. 2:7 There is no difference between him who is forbidden by vow from enjoying any benefit from his fellow without specification, and him who is forbidden by vow from deriving food from him, except for selling foot in his house and using utensils with which food is not prepared [M. Ned. 4:1A-B]. He who is forbidden by vow from deriving benefit from his fellow and who died — he [the fellow] brings a coffin and shrouds for him, wailing pipes and wailing women, for the dead get no benefit [from these things]. He gives testimony in his behalf in property cases and in criminal cases. If he fell ill, he [the fellow] goes into visit him [M. Ned. 4:4A]. But if [the one who took the vow] has someone ill [in his house], [the fellow] does not go in to visit him or inquire after his welfare. [If] he [the fellow] was a priest, he tosses the blood of his [the one subject to the vow] sin-offering in his behalf, and the blood of his guilt offering, for the sake of peace [M. Ned. 4:3B]. He washes with him in the same bathtub and sleeps with him in the same bed [M. Ned. 4:4D-E].

M. 4:5 He who is forbidden by vow from enjoying benefit from his fellow, [if this was] before the Seventh Year, he may not go down into his field, and he may not eat produce that hangs over [from the property of the other]. But [if this was] in the Seventh Year [when all produce is deemed ownerless and free for all], while he may not go down into his field, he may eat the produce that hangs over [from the property of the other]. [If] he vowed that he would not derive food from him, [if this was] before the Seventh Year, he goes down into his field but does not eat the produce. And [if this was] in the Seventh Year, he goes down [into the field] and eats the produce.

T. 2:8 He who is forbidden by vow from enjoying benefit from his fellow before the Seventh Year does not go down into his field and may not eat what is planted there [M. Ned. 4:5A-B]. In the Seventh year, he does go down into his field and eats what is planted there.

M. 4:6 He who is forbidden by a vow from deriving benefit from his fellow — should not lend him [his fellow] anything, nor should [the one who took the vow] borrow anything from him. He should not lend him money nor should he borrow money from him. He should not sell him anything, nor should he buy anything from him. [If] he said to him, "Lend me your cow" [and] he said to him, "It is not available," and he said to him, "Qonam be my field if I ever again plough my field with it [the cow]" — If he [himself] usually ploughed, while he is prohibited, everyone else is permitted [to plough his field with that cow]. If he did not usually plough his own field, then he and everyone else in the world are prohibited [from ploughing the field with that cow].

M. 4:7 He who is forbidden by vow from deriving benefit from his fellow and has nothing to eat — He [the fellow] goes to a storekeeper and says, "Mr. So-and-so is forbidden by vow from deriving benefit from me, and I don't know what I can do about it." And he [the storekeeper] gives food to him [who took the vow] and then goes and collects from this one [against whom the vow was taken]. [If] he [against whom the vow was taken] had to build his house [that of the one prohibited by vow from deriving benefit], or to set up his fence, or to cut the grain in his field, he [the fellow] goes to the workers and says to them, "Mr. So-and-so is forbidden by vow from deriving benefit from me, and I don't know what I can do about it." [Then] they [the workers] do the work with him [who took the vow] and come and collect their salary from this one [against whom the vow was taken].

M. 4:8 [If] they were going on a journey and he [who had forbidden himself by a vow from deriving benefit from his fellow] had nothing to eat, he [against whom the vow was taken] gives something to another as a gift, and the other [who took the vow] is permitted to make use of it. If there is no one else with them, he [against whom the vow was taken] leaves it on a rock or on a fence and says, "Lo, these things are ownerless property for anyone who wants them." Then the other [who is prohibited by vow from deriving benefit from his fellow] takes what he wants and eats it.

M. 5:1 Partners who prohibited themselves by vow from deriving benefit from one another are prohibited from entering the common courtyard [ownership of which they share]. And both of them are prohibited from setting up a millstone and oven there, or from raising chickens. [If] one of them was prohibited by vow from deriving benefit from his fellow, he should not enter into the common courtyard. And they force the one who has taken the vow to sell his share [to the other].

M. 5:2 [If] a third party ["someone from the market"] was prohibited by vow from deriving benefit from one of them, he should not enter into the common courtyard.

M. 5:3 He who is prohibited by vow from deriving benefit from his fellow, and he [the fellow] has a bathhouse or an olive press in town which is hired out [to other people] — If he [the fellow] has rights therein, it [the bathhouse or olive press] is prohibited [to the other]. [If] he has no rights therein, he [the other] is permitted. He who says to his fellow, "Qonam if I enter your house," or "...if I buy your field," [if the other party] died or sold them to a third party, he [the one who took the vow, now] is permitted [to enter the house or the field]. [If he said], "Qonam if I enter this house" or "...if I purchase this field" — [if the other party] died or sold it to a third party, it is [nonetheless] forbidden.

M. 5:4 [If one said to his fellow,] "Lo, I am *herem* unto you," the one against whom the vow is made is prohibited [from using what belongs to the other, who made the vow]." [If he said,] "Lo, you are *herem* unto me," the one who takes the vow is prohibited [from benefiting from the other] — [If he said,] "Lo, I am unto you and you are unto me [*herem*]," both of them are prohibited. But both of them are permitted [to make use of property belonging to] the immigrants from Babylonia [i.e., inalienable property, which is deemed ownerless]. And they are forbidden [to make use of property] belonging to that town [which each citizen owns jointly with all others].

M. 5:5 What is something which belongs to the immigrants from Babylonia? For example, the Temple mount and courtyards, and the well which is in the middle of the way. And what are things which belong to that town? For example, the town square, the bathhouse, the synagogue, the ark, and the scrolls. And he who writes over his share to the patriarch [of the court allows the fellow, prohibited by vow, to derive benefit from those things which are deemed to be held jointly by the town's citizens].

T. 2:9 Just as both of them [the two men who have prohibited themselves by a vow from deriving benefit from one another] are prohibited from dwelling in the same courtyard [M. Ned. 5:1A], so they are prohibited from living in the same alleyway. Just as both of them are prohibited from raising chickens [M. Ned. 5:1C], so both of them are prohibited from raising small cattle [in the common courtyard]. [If] one of them was accustomed to prohibiting others by vow from deriving benefit from his share, they force the one who is accustomed to do so to sell his share [M. Ned. 5:IF]. A public square through which the public way passes, lo, this belongs to the immigrants from Babylonia. [But if] the public way does not pass through, lo, it belongs to the men of that town [M. Ned. 5:5].

M. 5:6 He who is forbidden by vow from deriving benefit from his fellow and who has nothing to eat — he [the fellow] gives it [food] to someone else as a gift, and this one [prohibited by vow] is permitted [to make use of] it. A precedent: There was someone in Bet Horon whose father was prohibited by vow from deriving benefit from him. And he [the man in Beth Horon] was marrying off his son, and he said to his fellow, "The courtyard and the banquet are given over to you as a gift. But they are before you only so that father may come and eat with us at the banquet." The other party said, "Now if they really are mine, then lo, they are consecrated to Heaven!" He said to him, "I didn't give you what's mine so you would consecrate it to Heaven!" He said to him, "You did not give me what's yours except so that you and your father could eat and drink and make friends again, and so the sin [for violating the oath] could rest on his [= my] head!" Now the case came before sages. They ruled, "Any act of donation which is not so [given] that, if one sanctified it to Heaven, it is sanctified, is no act of donation."

T. 2:10 He who is prohibited by vow from deriving benefit from his town or from the people of his town, and someone came from the outside and lived there for thirty days — he [who took the vow] is permitted to derive benefit from him. [But if he was prohibited by vow from deriving benefit] from those who dwell in his town, and someone came from the outside and lived there for thirty days, he is prohibited [from deriving benefit from him. He who is prohibited by vow from deriving benefit from his fellow [in a vow made] in his presence — they accept inquiry [for absolution from the vow] from him only in his presence. But if he vowed not to derive benefit from his fellow not in his presence, they accept inquiry from him either in his presence or not in his presence.

One who is forbidden by a vow from deriving food from another may set foot in the other's house and use things not connected with food preparation; if he is forbidden any benefit, these too are cut off, T. 2:7. But there are services that one may perform for the one prohibited by vow, M. 4:2-5, by contrast to M. 4:6. Various ways of working around the situation created by the vow are spelled out, M. 4:7-8, M. 5:1ff.

B. *VOWS NOT TO EAT CERTAIN FOOD*

M. 6:1 He who takes a vow not to eat what is cooked is permitted [to eat what is] roasted or seethed. [If] he said, "Qonam if I taste cooked food," he is prohibited from eating what is loosely cooked in a pot but permitted to eat what is solidly cooked in a pot. And he is permitted to eat a lightly boiled egg or gourds prepared in hot ashes.

T. 3:1 He who vows not to eat what is cooked is prohibited from eating what is roasted and what is seethed and what is boiled [M. Ned. 6:1B]. And he is prohibited from eating soft biscuits, because sick people eat their bread with them. He who vows not to eat what goes down into a pot is prohibited from eating what goes down into a pan. [He who vows not to eat] what goes down into a pan is permitted to eat what goes down into a pot.

M. 6:2 He who takes a vow not to eat what is cooked in a pot is prohibited only from what is boiled [therein]. [If] he said, "Qonam if I taste anything which goes down into a pot" he is prohibited from eating anything which is cooked in a pot.

M. 6:3 [He who takes a vow not to eat] what is pickled is prohibited only from eating pickled vegetables. [If he said, "Qonam] if I taste anything pickled," he is prohibited from eating anything which is pickled. [If he took a vow not to eat what is] seethed, he is forbidden only from eating seethed meat. [If he said, "Qonam] if I taste anything seethed," he is prohibited from eating anything which is seethed. [If he said, "Qonam] if I taste anything roasted," he is prohibited from eating anything which is roasted. [He who takes a vow not to eat] what is salted is prohibited only from eating salted fish. [If he said, "Qonam] if I eat anything salted," then he is prohibited from eating anything at all which is salted.

M. 6:4 He who says, "Qonam if I taste fish or fishes," is prohibited [to eat] them, whether large or small, salted or unsalted, raw or cooked. But he is permitted to eat pickled chopped fish and brine. He who vows not to eat small fish is prohibited from eating pickled chopped fish. But he is permitted to eat brine and fish brine. He who vowed [not to eat] pickled chopped fish is prohibited from eating brine and fish brine.

M. 6:5 He who vows not to have milk is permitted to eat curds. [If he vowed not to eat] curds, he is permitted to have milk.

T. 3:2 [He who vows not to eat] what is prepared in a pot is permitted [to eat] what is prepared in a pan. [He who vows not to eat] what is prepared in a pan is permitted [to eat] what is prepared in a pot. [He who vows not to eat what] goes down into an oven is prohibited [from eating] only bread alone. [He who vows not to eat] what is prepared in an oven is prohibited [from eating] anything which is prepared in an oven. He who vows [not to eat] what is curdled is permitted to eat cheese. He who vows [not to eat] cheese is prohibited from eating what is curdled [M. Ned. 6:5]. He who vows not to eat the meat sediment is permitted to eat the broth. He who vows not to eat the broth is permitted to eat the sediment.

M. 6:6 He who takes a vow not to eat meat is permitted to eat broth and meat sediment.

M. 6:7 He who vows not to drink wine is permitted to eat a cooked dish which has the taste of wine. [If] he said, "Qonam if I taste this wine," and it fell into a cooked dish, if there is sufficient [wine] to impart a flavor, lo, this is prohibited. He who takes a vow not to eat grapes is permitted to drink wine. [He who takes a vow not to eat] olives is permitted to have olive oil. [If] he said, "Qonam! if I eat these olives or grapes," he is prohibited to eat them and what exudes from them.

M. 6:8 He who takes a vow not to eat dates is permitted to have date honey. [He who takes a vow not to eat] winter grapes is permitted to have the vinegar made from winter grapes.

M. 6:9 He who takes a vow not to have wine is permitted to have apple wine. [He who takes a vow not to have] oil is permitted to have sesame oil. He who takes a vow not to have honey is permitted to have date honey. He who takes a vow not to have vinegar is permitted to have the vinegar of winter grapes. He who takes a vow not to have leeks is permitted to have shallots. He who takes a vow not to have vegetables is permitted to have wild vegetables, since they have a special name.

T. 3:3 [He who takes a vow not to eat] oil is permitted to eat sesame-oil [M. Ned. 6:9B]. But in a place in which they make use of sesame-oil as a staple he is prohibited even from using sesame-oil.

M. 6:10 [He who takes a vow not to eat the genus,] cabbage is forbidden from asparagus [deemed a species of the cabbage genus]. [He who takes a vow not to eat] asparagus is permitted to have cabbage. [He who takes a vow not to have] grits is forbidden to have grits pottage. [He who takes a vow not to eat] grits pottage is permitted to have grits. [He who takes a vow not to eat] grits pottage is forbidden to eat garlic. [He who takes a vow not to eat] garlic is permitted to eat grits pottage. [He who takes a vow not to eat] lentils is forbidden from eating lentil cakes. [He who takes a vow not to eat] lentil cakes is permitted to eat lentils. [He who says, "Qonam] if I taste [a grain of] wheat or wheat [ground up in any form]" is forbidden from eating it, whether it is ground up or in the form of bread. [If he said, "Qonam if I eat] a grit [or] grits in any form," he is forbidden from eating them whether raw or cooked.

T. 3:6 He who in the Seventh Year takes a vow not to eat vegetables is prohibited from eating wild vegetables. [If he vowed not to eat] gourds, he is prohibited only from eating Greek gourds alone. If he vowed not to eat cabbage, he is prohibited from eating asparagus. If he vowed not to eat asparagus, he is permitted to eat cabbage [M. Ned. 6:10A-B]. If he vowed not to eat leeks, in a place in which they call shallots leeks, he is prohibited to eat shallots. [If he vowed not] to eat shallots, he is permitted to eat leeks [M. Ned. 6:9E.] [If he vowed not to eat] onions, he is prohibited from eating scallions. If he vowed not to eat scallions, he is permitted to eat onions. If he vowed not to eat lentils, he is prohibited from eating lentil-cakes. [If he vowed not to eat] grits-porridge, he is permitted to eat garlic [M. Ned. 6:10:F-G].

T. 4:1 He who vows not to eat the produce of a given year is prohibited from eating all the produce of that year. But he is permitted to eat [meat of the] calves, lambs and sheep, and milk, and pigeons [produced that year]. If he said, "[Qonam if I taste what is] produced in this year," he is prohibited from eating all of them. He who vows not to eat summer fruit is prohibited only from eating figs alone.

M. 7:1 He who vows not to eat vegetables is permitted to eat gourds. And [if he vowed not to eat vegetables] he is prohibited from eating Egyptian beans when they are fresh, but he is permitted to eat them when they are dried.

M. 7:2 He who vows not to eat grain prohibited only from eating the five varieties [wheat, barley, spelt, goat grass, and oats]. But he is permitted to eat fruit of trees and vegetables.

T. 4:3 He who vows not to eat pe'ah is prohibited from eating cucumbers, gourds, and chate-melons, but permitted to eat fruit which grows on trees. He who vows not to drink fruit-juice is prohibited from drinking all kinds of sweet juice, but permitted to drink wine. He who vows not to use spices is prohibited from using raw spices but permitted to eat cooked spices. If he said, "Lo, they are prohibited to my mouth," "Lo, they are incumbent on me," he then is prohibited from eating them whether they are raw or cooked. He who vows not to eat bread is prohibited only from eating bread which comes from the five varieties [of grain of the Land] [M. Ned. 7:2B]. He who vows not to eat grain is prohibited from eating Egyptian beans when they are fresh but permitted to eat them when they are dried [M. Ned. 7:1F]. And he is permitted to eat rice, split grain, groats of wheat, and barley-groats. He who vows not to wear clothing is prohibited from putting on a belt or a fascia. But he is permitted to put on a leather coat, a spread, shoes, pants, and a hat.

B. 7:2 II.3/55B HE WHO TAKES A VOW NOT TO EAT GRAIN IS FORBIDDEN TO EAT EGYPTIAN BEAN WHEN IT IS DRY, BUT PERMITTED TO EAT IT WHEN GREEN, AND HE IS PERMITTED TO EAT RICE, COARSE MEAL, PULSE PORRIDGE, AND PEARL BARLEY. HE WHO VOWS NOT TO EAT THE PRODUCE OF A GIVEN YEAR IS PROHIBITED FROM EATING ALL OF THE PRODUCE OF THAT YEAR, BUT IS PERMITTED TO EAT THE MEAT OF GOATS, LAMBS, MILK, EGGS, AND FLEDGLINGS OF THAT YEAR. BUT IF HE VOWED, "WHATEVER GROWS OF THIS YEAR IS FORBIDDEN TO ME," ALL OF THEM ARE FORBIDDEN.. HE WHO VOWS NOT TO EAT THE FRUITS OF THE EARTH IS FORBIDDEN TO EAT ALL THE FRUITS OF THE EARTH BUT PERMITTED TO EAT MUSHROOMS AND TRUFFLES. BUT IF HE VOWED, "THAT WHICH GROWS FROM THE EARTH IS FORBIDDEN TO ME," ALL OF THEM ARE FORBIDDEN TO HIM.

Here and in the next rubric we revert to the investigation of the implications of word-choices. The prevailing principle is, language bears fixed, objective meanings. One therefore means what he says, not more, not less, and the common sense of the meaning of language governs throughout. Thus if one vows not to eat what is pickled, that vow is taken to refer to vegetables, which are what is commonly pickled. We further distinguish, M. 6:6, between what is primary and what is derivative, what causes and what is caused, meat is primary, broth and sediment, derivative, and so for the rest. If the vow refers to the genus, the species of the genus are covered; if he refers to the species, the other species of the same genus are not covered. In this way an exercise in the analysis of the relationship of genus to species and in correct rules of speciation is easily constructed.

C. *VOWS NOT TO USE CERTAIN OBJECTS*

M. 7:3 He who vows not to wear clothing is permitted to wear sacking, curtains, or hangings. [If] he said, "Qonam if wool touches me," he is permitted to wear wool shearings. [If he said, "Qonam if] flax touches me," he is permitted to wear stalks of flax.

T. 3:4. He who takes a vow not [to wear anything made of] wool is permitted [to wear something made of] flax. [If he took a vow not to wear anything made of] flax, he is permitted [to wear something made of] wool [M. Ned. 7:3].

M. 7:4 He who vows not to enter a house is not permitted to enter the upper room," for the upper room is covered by the category of the house [and he is prohibited from entering it]. He who vows not to enter the upper room is permitted to enter the house.

T. 4:5 He who says, "Qonam be this loaf of bread which I am tasting if I go to such and such a place tomorrow" — if he ate it, lo, he is subject to not going to that place. And if he went to that place, he is subject to [violation of] the rule, "He shall not profane his word" (Num. 30:2).

M. 7:5 He who vows not to use a bed is not permitted to use a couch, for couch is covered by the category of the bed [and he is prohibited from making use of a couch]. He who vows not to make use of a couch is permitted to make use of a bed. He who vows not to enter a city is permitted to enter into the border of the city but prohibited from entering into its confines. But he who vows not to enter a house is prohibited from entering beyond the jamb of the door and inwards.

T. 3:5 He who takes a vow not to eat meat is prohibited from eating every kind of meat. He [also] is prohibited from eating the head, feet, and windpipe, and fowl . But he is permitted to eat the gills of fish and locusts.

The same problem — the genus and the species — is carried forward in the present subset, M. 7:5 providing a perfect example of how the analysis is to be done.

D. SECONDARY AND DERIVATIVE EFFECTS; THE TEMPORAL LIMITATION IN VOWS

M. 7:6 He who says, "Qonam be these pieces of fruit for me," "They are qonam for my mouth," "They are Qonam to my mouth" — he is prohibited from eating whatever he may exchange for those pieces of fruit and whatever grows from them too. If he says, "Qonam if I eat these pieces of fruit," "Qonam if I taste them," he is permitted to eat whatever he may exchange for those pieces of fruit and whatever grows from them. This is the case of something the seed of which perishes. But in the case of something the seed of which does not perish, even what grows from it is prohibited.

M. 7:7 He who says to his wife, "Qonam be the results of the work of your hands for me," "They are qonam for my mouth," "They are qonam to my mouth" — he is prohibited to make use of things exchanged for them or things which grown from them as well. If he said, "Qonam that I shall not eat," or "...that I shall not taste," then he is permitted to eat or taste things exchanged for them and things that grow from them. This is the rule for something the seed of which perishes in the ground. But in the case of something the seed of which does not perish, even things that grow from the things that grow from them are prohibited.

M. 7:8 He who says, "Qonam be what you are making if I eat it until Passover," "...Be what you are making if I wear it until Passover" — If she prepared these things before Passover, he is permitted to eat or to wear what she made after Passover. If he said, "Qonam be to me what you are making until Passover, if I eat it," "...what you are making until Passover if I wear it," if she prepared these things before Passover, he is prohibited after Passover from eating or wearing what she has made.

M. 7:9 [He who says, "Qonam] be what you enjoy on my account before Passover if you go to your father's house before the Festival of Sukkot," [if] she went before Passover, she is prohibited from deriving benefit from him until Passover. [If she went] after Passover, he is subject to the rule, "He shall not profane his word" (Num. 30:2). [He who says, "Qonam] be what you enjoy on my account up to the Festival of Sukkot if you go to your father's house before Passover," and she went to her father's house before Passover, she is prohibited from deriving benefit from him up to the Festival of Sukkot. But she is permitted to go to her father's house after Passover.

M. 8:1 [He who says,] "Qonam if I taste wine today," is prohibited only to nightfall. [If he referred to] "this week," he is prohibited the entire week and the Sabbath [which is coming is included] in that past week. [If he referred to] "this month," he is prohibited that entire month, but the day of the New Month [is assigned] to the coming month. [If he referred to] "this year," he is prohibited that entire year, but the New Year['s day] is assigned to the year which follows. [If he referred to] "this septennate," he is prohibited that entire septennate, and the Seventh Year is assigned to the last septennate [and is included] in the vow. And if he said, "One day," "One week," "One month," "One year," "One septennate," he is prohibited from that day until the same day [or month, year, or septennate following].

M. 8:2 [If he said], "To Passover," he is prohibited until it comes. [If he said,] "Until it will be [Passover]," he is prohibited until it is over.

M. 8:3 [If he said,] "Until harvest," "Until vintage," "Until olive gathering," he is forbidden only until it comes. This is the general principle: As to any occasion whose time is fixed, if he said, "Until it comes," he is prohibited until it comes. [If] he said, "Until it will be," he is prohibited until it is over. But as to any occasion whose time is not fixed, whether he said, "Until it will be," and whether he said, "Until it comes," he is prohibited only until it comes.

M. 8:4 [If he said,] "Until summer [harvest]," "Until it will be summer [harvest]" it applies until the people will begin to bring in produce in baskets. [If he said,] "Until summer [harvest] is over," it applies until the knives are put away. [If he said], "Until the harvest," it applies until the people begin to harvest the wheat crop but not the barley crop. All is in accord with the place in which he takes his oath: If it was in the mountain, [we follow conditions in] the mountain. And if it was in the valley, [we follow conditions in] the valley.

M. 8:5 [If he said,] "Until the rains," "Until the rains will come," it applies until the second shower has fallen [in November]. [If he said,] "Qonam be wine if I taste it this year," and the year received an intercalated month, he is prohibited during the year and the added month. [If he said,] "Until the beginning of Adar," it applies until the beginning of the first Adar [not the intercalated one]. [If he said], "Until the end of Adar," it applies until the end of the first Adar.

T. 4:6 Even though there are vows which we have said are not binding how do we know that one should not make such a vow with the plan of annulling it? Scripture says, "He shall not profane his word" (Num. 30:2). That is to say, he should not treat his words as profane [and unconsecrated]. Another matter: He should not profane his word — even a sage does not annul his vow for himself. [If] he said to him, "Lend me your spade," [and the other said, "Qonam be this spade] if it is mine," "Qonam be these things to me if I have a spade [at all]," one may be sure that [now] he has no spade at all.

T. 4:7 He who makes a vow up until the summer [in the mountains of Galilee] and went down into the valleys, even though the summer came in the valleys, he is prohibited until the summer comes to Galilee [M. Ned. 8:4D-F]. This is the general principle: As to any occasion whose time is fixed, and he said, "... until it," he is prohibited until "before it" [M. Ned. 8:2C]. [If he said], "Until the rains end," he is prohibited until the first night of Passover [M. Ned. 8:5C — D]. [If he said], "Until the Sukkot are torn down," he is prohibited until the last night of the Festival [of Sukkot]. [If he said], "Until Adar," it means, the first. And if the year was intercalated with the addition of a second Adar, he is prohibited until the second Adar [M. Ned. 8:5F-G].

M. 8:6 [If] he said, "Qonam be meat if I taste it until there will be the fast," he is prohibited only up to the night of the fast. For this man intended to refer only to the time at which people usually eat meat.

If one refers to specific pieces of fruit, not only they but whatever derives from them fall under the vow, that is, secondary effects of the primary object are covered. The same rule is in effect at M. 7:7. At M. 7:8 we deal with temporal limitations of vows. I see no surprises here; the clarifications simply identify what is implicit in the statement that is made. The Tosefta at T. 4:6 makes an original and important contribution: we do not allow for the abuse of vowing through too-clever formulations that leave ambiguity.

III.   THE ABSOLUTION OF VOWS

A.   GROUNDS FOR THE ABSOLUTION OF VOWS

M. 8:7 He who says to his fellow, "Qonam be benefit I derive from you, if you do not come and collect for your child a kor of wheat and two jugs of wine" — lo, this one [the fellow] can annul his vow without consultation with a sage, and say to him, "Did you not speak only to do me honor? But this [not taking your wheat and wine for my children] is what I deem to be honorable!" And so: He who says to his fellow, "Qonam be benefit you derive from me, if you do not come and give my son a kor of wheat and two jugs of wine" — this one can annul his vow without consultation with a sage, and one [who made the vow] says to him, "Lo, it is as if I have received what I demanded' [If] they were nagging him to marry the daughter of his sister and he said, "Qonam be what she enjoys which is mine for all times" — and so he who divorces his wife and says, "Qonam be what my wife enjoys of mine for all time — lo, these are permitted to derive benefit from him. For this man intended [his vow] only with reference to [actual] marriage with them. [If] one was nagging his friend to eat with him [and the other] said, "Qonam be your house if I enter it," "If I drink a single drop of cold water of yours," he is permitted to enter his house and to drink cold water of his. For this man intended [his vow] only with reference to eating and drinking [but not merely coming into the house or taking a glass of cold water].

T. 4:8 He who says to his fellow, "Qonam if I derive any benefit whatsoever from you, if you do not come and collect for your child a kor of wheat and two jugs of wine, [M. Ned. 8:7A] — And [between times] an occasion of mourning befell him, or he was prevented by constraint, or he had an occasion for a banquet, or there were rains — he is permitted [the vow is not binding]. And so: He who says to his fellow, "Qonam if you derive benefit from me, if you do not come and give my son a kor of wheat and two jugs of wine [M. Ned. 8:7D]. [If] one was nagging his fellow to eat with him during a banquet [and] said, Qonam be your house if I enter it" [M. Ned. 8:7L] — during the banquet, he is prohibited from going in there. After the banquet, he is permitted to go in there.

T. 4:9 If one was nagging his fellow to eat with him during a banquet and said to him, "Qonam be your house if I enter it," during the banquet, he is prohibited from going in there. After the banquet he is permitted to go in there. [If] he said, "Qonam be your house if I enter it," "If I drink a single drop of cold water of yours," [M. Ned. 8:7L], he is permitted to enter his house [M. Ned. 8:7L], and to wash with him in cold water. But he is prohibited from eating or drinking with him.

M. 9:1 In a matter which is between him and his mother or father, they unloose his vow by [reference to] the honor of his father or mother.

M. 9:5 They unloose a man's vow by reason of the wife's marriage contract.

M. 9:6 They unloose [vows] by reference to festival days and Sabbaths. At first they said, "On those particular days [the vows] are not binding, but for all other days they are binding." But then R. Aqiba came along and taught that the vow part of which is unloosed is wholly unloosed.

M. 9:7 How so? [If] he said, "Qonam be what I enjoy from any one of you" — [if] his vow with reference to any one of them was declared not binding, the vow with reference to all of them was declared not binding. [If he said, "Qonam] be what I enjoy from this one and from that one," [if] the vow pertaining to the first was declared not binding, all of them are no longer subject to the vow. [If] the vow pertaining to the last one of them was declared not binding, the last one is permitted [to give benefit to the man] but the rest of them are prohibited. [If the vow] was declared not binding for one in the middle, from him and onward, it is not binding, but from him and backward, it is binding. [If he said,] "Let what I enjoy of this one's be qorban, and of that one's be qorban, " they require an opening [absolution] for each and every one of them.

T. 5:2 If he says, "Qonam be what I enjoy from any one of you," and [if] his vow with respect to one of them is declared not binding, then the vow with reference to all of them is declared not binding [M. Ned. 9:7A-C]. [If] he said, "Qonam be what I enjoy from this one and from that one, and from the other one," and the vow pertaining to the one in the middle was declared not binding, then from him and onward, it is not binding, but from him and backward, it is binding [M. Ned. 9:7G]. [If he said,] "Qonam be what I enjoy from So-and-so," and then he hesitated for a time sufficient to say something and went and said, "Also for So-and-so," he is prohibited in the case of the first, but permitted in the case of the second. How much is an interval sufficient to say something? Time enough for a master to ask after the welfare of his disciple. [If he said,] "Qonam be what I enjoy from Mr. So-and-so, and further, from Mr. Such-and-such," [or if he said], "For Mr. So-and-so and Mr. Such-and-such, Qonam be what I derive benefit," lo, these are deemed to be two separate and distinct vows. [If] the first is declared not binding, then the second is not binding. [If] the second is not binding, the first has not been declared not binding [and has to be unloosed on its own] [M. Ned. 9:7E, F].

T. 5:5 He who takes a vow not to derive benefit from a town (and) seeks absolution from a sage in that town, and one does not scruple that he grants absolution for his own interest. [If he takes a vow not to derive benefit] from an Israelite, he seeks absolution from a sage who is an Israelite, and one does not scruple that he grants absolution in his own interest.

M. 9:8 [If he said,] "Qonam be wine, because it is bad for the belly" [and] they told him, "But isn't old wine good for the belly?" He is permitted to drink old wine. And not old wine alone is permitted, but all wine [is permitted]. [If he said,] "Qonam be an onion if I taste it, for onions are bad for the heart," then Cyprus onions are permitted for him. And not Cyprus onions alone are permitted, but all onions [are permitted].

M. 9:9 They unloose a vow for a man by reference to his own honor and by reference to the honor of his children. They say to him, "Had you known that the next day they would say about you, 'That's the way of So-and-so, going around divorcing his wives,' "and that about your daughters they'd be saying, 'They're daughters of a divorcée! What did their mother do to get herself divorced' [would you have taken a vow]?" And [if] he then said, "Had I known that things would be that way, I should never have taken such a vow," lo, this [vow] is not binding.

M. 9:10 [If one said,] "Qonam if I marry that ugly Miss So-and-so," and lo, she is beautiful, "...dark...," and lo, she is light, "...short...," and lo, she is tall, he is permitted [to marry] her, not because she was ugly and turned beautiful, dark and turned light, short and turned tall, but because the vow [to begin with] was based on erroneous facts.

T. 5:1 He who prohibits himself by a vow from deriving benefit from a house [and] an upper room, and finds out that, before his vow, they had fallen to him by inheritance or had been given to him as a gift [and said], "If I had known that that was the case, I should never have taken such a vow," — lo, this [vow] is not binding.

T. 5:2 [If he said,] "Qonam be benefit I derive from So-and-so and from anyone from whom I may obtain absolution for him" — they go and obtain absolution in respect to the first and then go and gain absolution in respect to the second.

T. 5:3 [If] he intended to take a vow by a whole-offering and took a vow as a Nazirite, by an offering, and took a vow by an oath, it is not binding. [If] he intended to take a vow by a whole-offering and took a vow by an offering, by a herem and took a vow by that which is sanctified [to the Temple], it is binding.

T. 5:4 [If] he took a vow as a Nazir, by an offering, and by an oath, they unloose his vow by a single pretext covering all of them. If he said, "I have taken a vow but I do not know by which of these two I have taken a vow," they unloose his vow through a single pretext covering all of them.

While when it comes to the interpretation of the language used in a vow, objective standards govern, that is not the case when we ask about the validity, to begin with, of the vow. There the mental condition of the person who takes the vow and his initial intentionality do register. That is only reasonable, since the vow affects only the one who takes it himself, though its secondary effects are taken into account. So the idiosyncratic dimension of the transaction does take effect in one aspect, if not in the other. Vows, specifically, may be absolved on grounds that, to begin with, they were never valid; we have already noted grounds for deeming a vow ineffective to begin with. A sage ordinarily is consulted in the nullification of the vow, but M. 8:7 commences with a case in which even that formality is not required. The reason is critical: we take account of the intention that is implicit in the context or situation in which the language is used. But then, as before, we deal not with a person's private reading of matters, but what the Halakhah deems the prevailing attitude or intentionality. We note that the Tosefta at T. 4:8-9 serves only to complement the Mishnah. The grounds for unloosing vows that generally govern, e.g., when a sage is involved in the process of nullification, are by appeal to the unstated, implicit intention: "would you have vowed if you knew...," to which the man replies in the negative. Or if the man has taken a vow for a reason, which he has made explicit, and the reason is null, the vow is as if it never were. Once a vow is released in one aspect, it is null in all regards.

B. *THE ANNULMENT OF THE VOWS OF A DAUGHTER*

M. 10:1 A betrothed girl — her father and her husband annul her vows. [If] the father annulled her vow, but her husband did not annul her vow, [or if] her husband annulled her vow, but her father did not annul her vow, it is not annulled. And it is not necessary to say, if one of them confirmed her vow [and the other did not, that it is not confirmed].

M. 10:2 [If] the father died, [his] authority does not pass to the husband. [If] the husband died, [his] authority passes to the father. In this regard the power of the father is greater than the power of the husband. In another regard, however, the power of the husband is greater than the power of the father. For the husband annuls the vows in the case of a grown-up woman, but the father does not annul the vows of a grown-up woman.

T. 6:2 Under what circumstances did they rule that if the husband died, his power passes to the father [M. Ned. 10:2B]? When he [the husband] did not hear [the vow], and annulled it, and died on that very day. But if he [the husband] heard the vow and remained silent, [or] heard it and confirmed it, and died on the next day, he [the father] has not got the power to annul it. [If] the husband heard the vow and did not annul it, and the father did not suffice to hear the vow before the husband died, this [too] is the case concerning which they ruled, If the husband died, his power [to] annul the vow passes to the father.

T. 6:3 [If] her father heard the vow before the father died, this is the sort of case concerning which they ruled, [If] the father died, the right to annul her vows does not pass to the husband [M. Ned. 10:2A]. [If] her husband heard the vow and annulled it, but the father did not suffice to hear the vow before he died, lo, this is a case in which annulment is prohibited. For the husband has the power to annul the vow only in conjunction with the father [M. Ned. 10:2C]. [If] her father heard the vow and annulled it for her, but the husband did not suffice to hear the vow before he died, let the father go back and annul the share of the husband.

M. 10:3 [If] she took a vow while she was betrothed and was divorced on that very day [and] betrothed again on that same day [and repeated the process], even a hundred [times] her father and her last husband annul her vows. This is the general principle: In the case of any girl who has not gone forth to her own domain for a single moment, her father and her last husband annul her vows.

M. 10:4 The way of a disciple of sages [is this]: Before his daughter goes forth from his home, he says to her, "All vows which you vowed in my house, lo, they are annulled." And so the husband, before she enters his domain, says to her, "All vows which you vowed before you came into my domain, lo, they are annulled." For after she enters his domain, he cannot annul [those prior] vows any more.

T. 6:4 A betrothed girl — her father and her last husband annul her vows [M . Ned. 10:3]. [If] the father heard the vow and annulled it for her, but the husband did not suffice to hear the vow before he died, and she then was betrothed, even to ten [further] men — this is the case concerning which they ruled, her father and her last husband annul her vows. [If] her father heard the vow and annulled it, but the husband did not suffice to hear the vow before he died, and she was betrothed to another, let her second husband go and annul the share [in the vow] of the first husband. Under what circumstances? When he divorced her that day and remarried her that day [M. Ned. 10:3C], or he divorced her that day, and she was betrothed to someone else.

Now Scripture's foci recast matters. Once Scripture enters in, the theoretical hermeneutics I have outlined cease to pertain, and other considerations govern the topic; then the issue shifts, the exegetical program defines a different set of problems. But the Mishnah's own veneer — its filigreed surface of distinctions and nuances — covers all topics that are expounded. Specifically, Scripture specifies that the father or the husband annuls the vows of the daughter or the wife, as the case may be. To expound that principle, the Halakhah — in line with the Mishnah's universal mode of analysis — takes up the problem of interstitiality, e.g., when the girl is neither wholly a daughter nor completely a wife, M. 10:1-4. The sages make provision for nullifying all vows the daughter may have taken while under their roof, the husband doing the same at the appropriate time.

C. *THE ANNULMENT OF THE VOWS OF A WIFE*

M. 10:5 A grown-up [= pubescent] woman who waited twelve months, and a widow who waited thirty days — the husband does not annul her vows until she enters his domain.

M. 10:7 He who says to his wife, "All vows which you will vow from this time until I return from such-and-such a place, lo, they are confirmed," has said nothing whatsoever. [If he says], "Lo, they are annulled" — it is not annulled.

T. 6:1 How [do they annul vows]? [If] his wife was subject to five vows, or he had five wives and each had taken a vow, and he said, "It is annulled," all of them are annulled. [If he said, "It is annulled for you," he has annulled the vow only pertaining to her. [If he said] "This vow [is annulled]," he has annulled only that particular vows. [If he said] "Now why did you take a vow?" "I don't what you to take a vow," "This is not a vow," he has said nothing whatsoever. [If he said] "This is annulled," "This is cancelled," lo, this is cancelled. [If he said,] "It is confirmed for you," "You did very nicely," "So may I be like you," "If you had not vowed as you did, I should have imposed a vow upon you," he has no power to annul that vow.

M. 10:8 The annulment of vows [may be done] all day long. There is in this matter a basis for a lenient ruling and for a stringent ruling. How so? [If] she vowed on the night of the Sabbath, [the husband] annuls the vow on the night of the Sabbath and on the Sabbath day, down to nightfall. [But if] she vowed just before nightfall, he annuls the vow only until it gets dark. For if it should get dark and he should not annul the vow, he cannot annul the vow [any longer].

T. 6:7 A. [If one said], "This ox will be sanctified once I have purchased it," "This house will be sanctified once I have purchased it," "This ox will be sold to you, once I have purchased it," "This house is sold to you, once I have purchased it," "Give this divorce to my wife, once I have betrothed her," he has said nothing. [If he said], "The ox which I shall inherit from father is sold to you," "What will come up in my trap is sold to you," he has said nothing. [If he said,] "What I shall inherit from father today is sold to you," "What will come up in my trap this day is sold to you," his statements are confirmed [and put into force] [cf. M. Ned. 10:8A].

Once the girl has grown up, the father has no more power to annul her vows; the husband may not nullify vows before they have been taken; he has no power to nullify vows he has confirmed, even implicitly, T. 6:1.

D. THE HUSBAND'S POWER TO ANNUL THE WIFE'S VOWS: SPECIAL RULES

M. 11:1 And these are the vows that he annuls: matters of inflicting self-punishment [= afflicting the soul (Num. 30:13)], for example: "...If I shall wash," or "If I shall not wash," "...If I shall adorn myself," or "...If I shall not adorn myself."

T. 7:1 Any matter in which there is inflicting of self-punishment [M. Ned. 11:1B], whether it involves something between him and her, or between her and other people, he annuls. But a matter in which there is no inflicting of self-punishment [if it is] between him and her, he annuls it. [If it is] between her and other people, he does not annul it. How so? [If] she said, "Qonam if I work for father," ". . . for your father, . . . for my brother,. . . for your brother" [M. Ned. 11:4A], "if I feed your cattle," he has not got the power to annul [such vows], because these are between her and other people. [If she said, "Qonam] if I put on eye-shadow," ". . . if I put on rouge," ". . . if I adorn myself," " . . . if I have sexual relations with you," lo, this one annuls such vows as these, because they relate to matters which are between him and her. [If she said, "Qonam] if I lay out the bed," ". . . if I wash your feet," ". . . if I mix the cup for you," he does not have to annul [such a vow] but forces her to do these services against her will.

T. 7:2 [If] she vowed not to taste a particular sort of produce, whether it be inedible or edible, even if she had never in her life tasted that sort of produce [which she had vowed not to taste], he annuls the vow. [If] she said, "Qonam be pepper which I taste," ". . . be white bread which I taste," even if she had never had that sort of thing in her entire life, he annuls that vow

T. 7:3 [If] she said, "Qonam be the produce of the Land of Israel for me," if he has a share in them, he annuls that vow. But if not, let him provide produce for her from other countries. [If she said,] "Qonam be the produce of this hyparchy for me," . if he has a share in them, he annuls that vow. But if not, let him provide produce for her from some other province. [If] she said, "Qonam be the produce of this stall for me," if there is there another stall, he does not annul that vow, but if not, he does annul that vow.

M. 11:3 [If she said,] "Qonam if I derive benefit from anybody," he has not got the power to annul that vow. And she may derive benefit from Gleanings, the Forgotten Sheaf, and the Corner of the Field (Lev. 19:9, Deut. 24:19). [If she said], "Qonam be the benefit priests and Levites derive from me," they collect their dues by force. [If she said,] "Qonam be the benefit these [particular] priests and Levites derive from me," others collect [the priestly dues from her].

M. 11:4 [If she said,] "Qonam if I work for father," or "For your father," or "...For your brother," he cannot annul that vow. [If she said, "Qonam if I work for you," he need not annul [that vow, which is null to begin with].

M. 11:5 [If] his wife took a vow and he thought that his daughter had taken a vow, [if] his daughter took a vow and he thought that his wife had taken a vow, [if] she vowed a Nazirite

vow and he thought she had vowed by Qorban, [if she vowed by] Qorban, and he thought that she had vowed a Nazirite vow, [if] she vowed not to eat figs, and he thought she had vowed not to eat grapes, [if] she vowed not to eat grapes and he thought she had vowed not to eat figs — lo, this one should go back and annul [the vow again].

M. 11:6 [If] she said, "Qonam be these figs and grapes if I taste [them]," [if] he confirmed the vow concerning figs, the whole is deemed confirmed. [If] he annulled the vow concerning figs, it is not deemed annulled until he annuls the vow concerning grapes too. [If] she said, "Qonam be figs if I taste them, and grapes if I taste them," lo, these are deemed two distinct vows.

T. 7:4 [If] she said, [Qonam if I derive benefit from anybody," he has not got the power to annul that vow. But she can derive benefit from Gleanings, the Forgotten Sheaf, and the Corner of the Field [M. Ned. 11:3A-B], and from the tithe set aside for the poor. If his wife took a vow, and he annulled it for her, and he thought that his daughter had taken a vow, or if his daughter took a vow, and he annulled it for her, and he thought that his wife had taken the vow [M. Ned. 11:5A, B], lo, this one may confirm the vow. But if he wanted to annul it, he annuls it. [If] his wife took a vow, and he confirmed it for her and he thought that his daughter had taken the vow, [if] his daughter took a vow, and he confirmed it for her, and he thought that his wife had taken the vow, lo, this one annuls the vow. But if he wanted to confirm it, he confirms it. [If] she vowed not to eat figs and grapes [and] he annulled the vow confirming figs but did not annul the vow concerning grapes, she is prohibited from eating figs and grapes [M. Ned. 11:6C]. [If] he annulled the vow not to eat grapes but did not annul the vow not to eat figs, she is prohibited from eating grapes and figs [M. Ned. 11:6C]. [If] he annulled the vow concerning the figs and it got dark, she is prohibited from eating figs and grapes [cf. M. Ned. 10:8A]. [If] he annulled the vow concerning grapes and it got dark, she is prohibited from eating grapes and figs. If she said, "Qonam be a fig which I eat, and furthermore Qonam be grapes which I eat," lo, these are deemed two distinct vows [M. Ned. 11:6D]. He annuls whichever one he wants and confirms whichever one he wants, since it is said, "Her husband will confirm it [regarding this one], and her husband will annul it [regarding the other one]."

M. 11:7 [If he said,] "I was aware that there are vows, but I was not aware that there is the possibility of annulling them," he may annul [the vow]. [If he said], "I was aware that there is the possibility of annulling vows, but I was not aware that this particular statement was a vow," he may annul the vow.

M. 11:8 He who was prohibited by vow from imparting any benefit to his son-in-law but who wants to give his daughter some money says to her, "Lo, this money is given to you as a gift, on condition that your husband has no right to it, but you dispose of it for your own personal use."

T. 7:5 A more strict rule applies to confirming vows than applies to annulling vows, and a more strict rule applies to annulling vows than applies to confirming vows. For silence [on the part of the husband who hears a vow] is tantamount to confirmation, but it is not tantamount to annulment. The husband may confirm a vow in his heart, but he may not annul the vow in his heart [but must say so explicitly]. And there is a rule governing confirmation of vows which does not apply to annulling them, and there is a rule applying to annulling vows which does not apply to confirming vows. Once the husband has confirmed a vow, he cannot annul it. Once he has annulled a vow, he has not got the power to confirm it.

What vows of the wife does the husband annul? They are vows that the wife takes to her own detriment, if (Tosefta adds) the vow affects relationships between him and her. Vows that are null to begin with, e.g., by reason of their contradicting the law of the Torah, he need not annul; they are null to begin with. If the husband does not annul the vow in a timely manner because of ignorance of his own power, he may do so when he discovers he is able to nullify it.

E. *VOWS OF A WOMAN THAT ARE NOT SUBJECT TO ABROGATION*

M. 11:9 "But the vow of a widow or a divorcée shall stand against her" (Num. 30:9): How so? [If] she said, "Lo, I shall be a Nazir after thirty days," even though she was married during the thirty days, he [whom she married] has not got the power to annul her vow. [If] she took a vow and she was in the domain of the husband, he annuls the vow for her. How so? [If] she said, "Lo, I shall be a Nazir after thirty days," [if] the husband abrogated [the vow], even though she was widowed or divorced within thirty days, lo, this [vow] is annulled. [If] she took a vow on that very day and was divorced on the same day and remarried to the same man on the same day, he cannot annul the vow. This is the general principle: [In the case of] any woman who has gone forth into her own domain for a single moment [M. 10:3C] — he has not got the power to annul the vows.

M. 11:10 In the case of nine [sorts of] girls, their vows are valid [and not subject to abrogation]: a girl [who vowed when] past maturity who is an orphan [in her father's lifetime]; a girl who [vowed as] a minor girl and then passed maturity and is an orphan [in her father's lifetime]; a girl who [vowed] before she reached maturity and is an orphan [in her father's lifetime]; a girl [who vowed] past maturity whose father died; a girl who [vowed as] a minor and then passed maturity whose father died; a girl who [vowed] before she reached maturity and whose father died; a girl whose father died, and [who vowed and] after the death of her father, she passed maturity; a girl [who vowed] past maturity whose father is alive; a girl who passed maturity [and then vowed] and whose father is alive.

M. 11:11 [If she said,] "Qonam be any benefit I have of father...," "Of your father..., if I do any work for you," "...if I derive benefit from you, if I work for my father," "...if I work for your father," lo, this one he annuls.

M. 11:12 In times past they did rule: Three sorts of women go forth and collect their marriage contract: she who says, "I am unclean for you," "Heaven [knows] what is between you and me [namely, your impotence], "I am removed from [having sexual relations with] all the Jews." They reverted to rule: so that a woman should not covet someone else and spoil [her relationship with] her husband, but: she who says, "I am unclean for you," must bring proof for her claim. [She who says], "Heaven [knows] what is between you and me" — let them find a way to appease her. [She who says], "I am removed from all the Jews," let him annul his share [in the vow], so that she may have sexual relations with him, but let her be removed from all the other Jews.

The vows of women who are free of the authority of the father and the husband are not subject to abrogation. That principle presents no surprises.

IV. DOCUMENTARY TRAITS

A. THE MISHNAH AND THE TOSEFTA

I see no important differences in the definition of the category-formation and in its articulation between the two primary statements of the Halakhah. Once more a single conclusion presents itself: the Halakhah — the native category-formation — is prior to its documentary formulation. The presentation by the documents, the Mishnah, then the Tosefta, furthermore bears the distinctive mark that the documents make upon the Halakhah — the Mishnah's preoccupation with problems of interstitiality or of causality or of the differentiation of the genus and the species, for instance — while they work out the exegetical problems precipitated by the governing hermeneutics of the topic to which the respective tractates are devoted. In the interplay between the particularity of the native category-formation and the universalizability of the documentary exegetical programs, whether the Mishnah's or the Yerushalmi's, the concretization of the Halakhah in its detailed exposition takes shape.

B. THE YERUSHALMI AND THE BAVLI

The contribution of the two Talmuds to the Halakhic repertoire (as distinct from its exegesis) is too slight to permit comparison. We see how paltry are the Talmuds' contributions to the formation of the Halakhah. Even if I were to reproduce the baraita-corpus of the two Talmuds and attribute it to the Talmuds in which it occurs, that would not change the picture. The baraita-corpus is independent of the Mishnah and the Tosefta though in formal and attributive traits comparable to them. Nonetheless, that corpus, viewed from afar, generally takes up secondary and derivative questions and rarely contains Halakhic statements of a fundamental and generative character, such as we find in the Mishnah and (sometimes also) in the Tosefta. But that is a matter to be dealt with in a systematic study of the intellectual and formal traits of the baraita-corpus that is independent of the Mishnah and the Tosefta, along the lines of my systematic study of the detailed relationship of the compositions and composites of the Mishnah and the Tosefta in my *History of the Mishnaic Law*.

C. THE AGGADAH AND THE HALAKHAH IN THE BAVLI

The Bavli's presentation of the Halakhah is greatly expanded by the repertoire of Aggadic materials that it inserts alongside. Some of these affect the reading of the category-formation, not merely the clarification of details in its connection. The reference-system pertains to my *Talmud of Babylonia. An Academic Commentary*, where readers will find the passages classified here.

I:D: COMPOSITE Of SAYINGS
by R. Giddal-Rab on the General Theme
of Personal Acts of Piety

XIV:C: Topical Appendix in the Matter of Adultery
XV:B: Topical Composite on Losing One's Temper, Deemed the Basis for Taking Vows
XXX:B: Topical Composite on Abraham
XXXIV:D: Topical Appendix on the Correct Way of Writing and Reading Scripture
XXXVI:B: Topical Composite on the Matter of Korach and His Sect
XLV:D: Topical Composite Concerning Eating Various Types of Food
XLV:F: Miscellany Concerning Food: Marks of Poverty or Wealth

LX:A: Free-Standing Problem, to which the Foregoing Makes a Factual Contribution
LXII:C: Not Utilizing the Torah and Commandments for an Inappropriate Purpose

What the Halakhah states in its way, the aggadah expresses in its manner too. Here is the Bavli's topical composite on losing one's temper, which is deemed the basis for taking vows:

> B. 3:1A-D I.14/22A Said R. Samuel bar Nahman said R. Yohanan, "Whoever loses his temper — all the torments of Hell rule over him: 'Therefore remove anger from your heart, thus will you put away evil from your flesh' (Qoh. 11:10), and the meaning of 'evil' is only Hell: 'The Lord has made all things for himself, yes, even the wicked for the day of evil' (Prov. 16:4). Moreover, he will get a belly ache: 'But the Lord shall give you there a trembling heart and failing of eyes and sorrow of mind' (Deut. 28:65). And what causes weak eyes and depression? Stomach aches."
>
> B. 3:1A-D I.16/22b Said Rabbah bar R. Huna, "Whoever loses his temper — even the Presence of God is not important to him: 'The wicked, through the pride of his countenance, will not seek God; God is not in all his thoughts' (Ps. 10:4)."
>
> B. 3:1A-D I.17/22b A. R. Jeremiah of Difti said, "[Whoever loses his temper] — he forgets what he has learned and increases foolishness: 'For anger rests in the heart of fools' (Qoh. 7:9), and 'But the fool lays open his folly' (Prov. 13:16)."
> B. R. Nahman bar Isaac said, "One may be sure that his sins outnumber his merits: 'And a furious man abounds in transgressions' (Prov. 29:22)."
> B. 3:1A-D I.18/22b Said R. Ada b. R. Hanina, "If the Israelites had not sinned, to them would have been given only the Five Books of the Torah and the book of Joshua alone, which involves the division of the Land of Israel. *How come?* 'For much wisdom proceeds from much anger' (Qoh. 1:18)."

Sages leave no doubt as to their view of matters, which they express with the usual explicit clarity; that is how the Halakhah gains weight and clarity in the Aggadah, the Aggadah specificity and effect in the Halakhah.

Two points of interest capture our attention, first, the extended statement on how losing one's temper causes vow-taking, surely implicit in the Mishnah-tractate itself but nicely articulated; and, second, the insertion of a free-standing demonstration of a proposition with no bearing on our tractate but utilizing facts thereof for its own purpose, a kind of composition or composite we find here and there. The former shows the Bavli's resort to the Aggadah to underscore the judgment of the Halakhic subject-matter at hand. That dismissive judgment of the Halakhah upon the vow is fully exposed in the rule, "He who says, 'As the vows of the suitable folk' has said nothing whatsoever." Such a statement does not constitute a euphemism for a vow. Why not? "Because suitable folk (*kesherim*) do not take vows." And the rest follows. But what a commentary, then, on the very subject-matter of the category-formation!

V. THE HERMENEUTICS OF NEDARIM

The native category-formation, Nedarim, encompasses the most fundamental workings of the Rabbinic system, characterized as it is at many points by deep thought about the interplay of intentionality and reality brought about through the transformative power inherent in the use of language. The Halakhah deems language to mirror the soul; words expose the heart, because they articulate and give effect to intentionality. And, as we have seen time and again, intentionality exposed through language greatly matters. The key to the entire system comes to expression in language, therefore, which realizes and embodies intentionality in affective form. Take, for example, the rule that an act of consecration done in error is not binding. What man intends here is shown to make all the difference in actuality. God responds to what man wants, more than to what he does, as the Torah's distinction between murder and manslaughter shows in an obvious way. In contexts such as vow-taking, the critical dialectics of the Torah embodies the conflict between God's and man's will. That focus upon the definitive, taxonomic power of intentionality explains, also, why if a man says to a woman, "Lo, you are consecrated...," and the woman acquiesces, the intentionalities matching, the woman is thereby sanctified to that man and forbidden to all others; Heaven then enforces what man and woman have accomplished in the realization through language of their intentionalities. That is because the act of intention formulated in words bears the power of classification upon which the entire system builds. But — self-evidently — not all intentionality finds Heaven's approval, and that is so even though Heaven confirms and acquiesces therein. And that brings us to the vow, which realizes in words the intentionality of the person who takes the vow and imposes upon himself restrictions of various kinds.

The vow is the weapon of the weak, the wife over the husband or vice versa, the peddler over the purchaser or vice versa — the way by which the lesser party to a transaction exercises power over the greater. If the wife says to the husband, "By a vow, I shall not derive benefit from you," or the guest to the host, "What food you feed me is qorban," she removes from herself her husband's control, so too, the guest to the host. But the vow also stands for the release of discipline, it is an expletive and an outcry, an act of temper, and no wonder sages do not respect those that take vows. Now we see matters in more general, theoretical terms. The power of the word to change the status of persons and things defines and sustains the household above all, which rests in the last analysis upon the foundations of commitment, responsibility, and trust — all to begin with embodied in language. Classifying vows as a chapter in the life of the household, with special reference to the sanctification of marriage, therefore presents no surprise. The sanctity of one's word forms a corollary of the proposition that the language we use bears the power of classification, and, in the present context, of therefore effecting sanctification. If, after all, by declaring a woman consecrated to a man, or an animal to the altar or a portion of the crop to the priesthood, one brings about the sanctification of the woman or the beast or the grain, then what limits to the power of language to affect the everyday world are to be set? In that same framework, after all, God communicates and is communicated with: in the present age, with the Temple in ruins, worship is through prayer, which takes the form of words whether spoken or not.

A. WHAT FUSES THE HALAKHIC DATA INTO A CATEGORY-FORMATION?

Language by definition ought to express reflected-upon intentionality — like the designation of an animal to expiate an inadvertent, newly-realized sin. Here it conveys the outcome of temper and frustration, not ratiocination worthy of the creature "in our image, after our likeness." Designating a beast as consecrated realizes a noble, godly intention; designating benefit one receives from one's spouse as "qorban" uses language to embody a lowly and disreputable intention. It is to humiliate and reject and disgrace the other. Sages' message registers that language is dangerous because it realizes intentionality, which had best, therefore, be expressed with probity and restraint. And these virtues form the opposite of the traits of mind and character of the vow-taking Israelite, wife or husband, host or guest, salesman or customer, as the exemplary cases of Nedarim have shown us. The hermeneutical center, as we noted at the outset and then saw in the repertoire of the Halakhah, focuses on the public and objective character of language even when used in a private context.

What are the classes of data and how do they fuse in the category-formation, Nedarim? Here we must distinguish three distinct dimensions of the category-formation.

First is the definition of the category-formation itself, which I have spelled out in the opening unit; the hermeneutics of analogical-contrastive reasoning defines a category-formation, namely, uses of public language for private purposes.

Second is the identification of exegetical problems consequent upon the definition of said category-formation. Here the exegetical program yields large generalizations, [a] some on the fixed and public meanings of words; [b] some on the principles of hierarchical classification of the species of a genus; [c] some on problems of interstitiality (causation, e.g., primary and derivative classes) and how these are to be resolved in the case at hand. The two philosophical issues that predominate are, first, the relationship of genus and species, and, second, the relationship between direct and indirect causation.

Third is the judgment of the Halakhic construction *upon* its subject-matter. That is stated only occasionally, but with effect, not only in the explicit judgment, but in the implicit contempt contained within the formulas for releasing the vow.

These types of data do not compare in proportion. Of the three, the second is the largest but the least particular to the category-formation; the first is the most important but accorded the least systematic exposition; and the third is the most consequential for the larger system, the most pervasive within the category-formation itself, but the least detailed and articulated.

The exposition of the category-formation proves comprehensive and fundamental: the topic defined through analogical-contrastive reasoning; the exegetical problematics inherent in the topic or imposed thereon by the documentary preferences of the Mishnah and, where autonomous, of the Tosefta; the judgment of the Halakhah upon matters, the "message" (in our terms) drawn by the Halakhah, along with the Aggadah,[12] from the matter at hand. The data of language and its uses and effects in the setting of the individual's existence fuse at the level of definition: how the individual's exercise of his intentionality intersects with the rules of public discourse. From there, everything flows. But when it comes to the details that fill the shank of the tractate of the Mishnah-Tosefta-Yerushalmi-Bavli, the principal energy that animates the detailed exposition comes from the philosophical tensions, genus and species, primary and secondary causation, respectively. That is to say, the Mishnah imposes upon the received category-formations of the Halakhah the stamp of its intellect and thereby defines the exegetical task of the Halakhists of the Tosefta, Yerushalmi, and Bavli.

---

[12] It is self-evident that the interplay of the Aggadah and the Halakhah awaits systematic analysis.

B. THE ACTIVITY OF THE CATEGORY-FORMATION

The category-formation Nedarim exercises the power to define rules for the particular and the subjective, first, in the use of language, then in the unfolding of the diverse relationships among persons. The Halakhah of vows concerns matters of personal status: what may a person do or not do by reason of a self-imposed vow? But, as I have stressed, the category-formation expands to encompass the systematic ordering of language: does the individual's intent change the effect of words? The answer, that it does not, places firm limits on the power of intentionality to classify. A person's intentionality, and the language he uses to convey it, must conform to the repertoire of publicly-shared rules and may not appeal to utterly private and individual meanings. No wonder, then, that the category-formation encompasses at its center family ties (father to daughter) marital bonds (husband and wife), which are at once the most private and the most public of transactions.

The presentation of the Halakhah starts with the definition of a vow and proceed to consider the affects of a vow upon what a person may or may not do, mainly, eat. We conclude with close attention to how one may gain absolution from a vow, releasing its binding character by reason of diverse grounds or pretexts. That is the whole story, beginning, middle, and end, a structure that is simple and logical — and familiar from numerous other category-formations of the Halakhah. That vows principally locate themselves within the household — the premise of the Scripture's statements and the Halakhah's presentation throughout — guides the articulation of the details of the law.

The Halakhah spreads a broad net over the language people use, treating every sort of euphemism as effective in imposing the vow. The Halakhah of definition yields the principle, richly instantiated, that any sort of language that resembles the language of a vow takes effect. The upshot is, no one can say, "I had some other meaning in mind than the one potentially present in my language." The essay on language that the Halakhah embodies proceeds to language that is null, because the euphemism itself contradicts reality, such as "the dough-offering of Aaron," for the priesthood does not separate dough-offering; hides pierced at the heart fall into the category of idolatry, which is null; double-negatives do not count. Language that refers to idolatry is not affective. More to the point, there are entire categories of vows that are null, meaning, types of language that do not bear the authority of the vow. These are vows that to begin with represent language of no effect or language used without adequate reflection, e.g., vows of incitement, on the one side, vows of exaggeration, on the other. In both cases the vow does not follow much thought. Or, more to the point, the intention behind the language is inappropriate. Vows of incitement — to purchase an object at a given price — embody inappropriate intentionality; they are meant to influence the other only. Vows made in error, like acts of consecration made in error, do not stand for the intentionality of the speaker, and so are null. Finally, vows broken under constraint are null. Along these same lines, one may intentionally take a false vow to save life or limb or to deceive the thief and the tax-collector (regarded as one and the same).

The second important problematics provides a systematic exercise in differentiating the genus from the species, embodied in the distinction between a vow against deriving benefit from the genus, which encompasses all the species of that genus (the genus, house, the species, upper chamber), and a vow against deriving benefit from a particular species, which leaves available the other species of the same genus (upper chamber, house). That exercise is worked out in vast detail, repeating the same point throughout. The difference between genus and species (wool, shearings) and between two distinct genera (clothing, sacking) accounts for a broad range of the issues dealt with here, and the matter of speciation covers much of the rest. Thus we differentiate cooking from roasting or seething. So too, language that is general is interpreted in minimal ways, "pickling" applying only to vegetables. In all, the exercise of speciation and its effects accounts for many of the concrete Halakhic problems that are set forth, and a few generalizations, even given in abstract terms, would encompass much of the Halakhah in its details. A philosophical formulation could have stated the entire repertoire of cases in a simple general rule: if the genus is covered, so are all the species; but if one species is covered, other species of the same genus are unaffected.

If speciation explains a broad range of rules, the matter of causation accounts for another. Specifically, the third type of problem addressed by the Halakhah concerns the effects of vows, e.g., the result of general statements about deriving benefit for specific types of benefit. A vow against deriving benefit from his friend leaves the friend free to perform certain general actions, e.g., paying the man's half-sheqel tax to the Temple and restoring what he has lost. The distinction between forbidden and permitted benefit is subtle, and so far as I can see rests upon the difference between efficient cause and proximate cause, benefit deriving from actions in the category of efficient causes being forbidden, the other kind permitted.

That that distinction governs is shown, among other cases, by the rule that allows the fellow, forbidden by the man's vow to give him any benefit, to hire a storekeeper to give what the man cannot directly give himself. The rule is worth reviewing: The fellow goes to a storekeeper and says, "Mr. So-and-so is forbidden by vow from deriving benefit from me, and I don't know what I can do about it." And the storekeeper gives food to him who took the vow and then goes and collects from this one against whom the vow was taken. [If] he against whom the vow was taken had to build the house of the one prohibited by vow from deriving benefit, or to set up his fence, or to cut the grain in his field, the fellow goes to the workers and says to them, "Mr. So-and-so is forbidden by vow from deriving benefit from me, and I don't know what I can do about it." Then the workers do the work with him who took the vow and come and collect their salary from this one against whom the vow was taken. Clearly, the difference between direct and indirect action governs. But if we differentiate indirect from direct cause, we also focus upon direct cause in its own terms, e.g., fruit, what is exchanged for the fruit, what grows from the fruit. So from an exercise on the difference between genus and species we here proceed to one on the difference between direct and indirect causation.

Vows are remitted or lose effect when the conditions specified in them have been realized or proved null. They also are remitted when the purpose of the vow is shown spurious, e.g., "Did you not speak only to do me honor? But this not taking your wheat and wine for my children is what I deem to be honorable!" Further, vows cannot in the end take effect so as to bring about the violation of existing obligations or contracts. A vow against what is written in the Torah is null; one that violates the marriage-contract is ineffective; one that requires dishonoring parents is null. Vows that contradict the facts explicitly invoked in making them are null. The point is then obvious: language takes effect only when the facts embodied in the language to begin with are valid.

The power of the husband or the father, as the case may be, to annul the vows of the wife or the daughter presents no surprises. We deal with the familiar range of cases, e.g., the interstitial status of the betrothed girl, over which both father and husband enjoy power. Once the woman is on her own, it goes without saying, no man may nullify her vows. The husband may annul the vows of the wife once she comes into his domain. The action must take place on the spot, through the day in question; it cannot be done in advance. The Halakhah clearly makes provision for the autonomous woman, not subject to father or husband, and treats as valid whatever vows she makes on her own account.

C. THE CONSISTENCY OF THE CATEGORY-FORMATION

The category-formation recapitulates a few simple conceptions, which have already been specified. In the successive documents, the same issues, worked out in accord with the same principles, are refined; the whole is integrated and cogent, start to finish.

D. THE GENERATIVITY OF THE CATEGORY-FORMATION

Within its basic premise, the outreach of the category-formation knows few limits. The Halakhah of Nedarim investigates is the power of a person through invoking the name of Heaven to affect the classification in which he or she individually is situated and so, consequently, his or her concrete and material relationships with other people. This is done by stating, "May what I eat of your food be prohibited to me as is a sacrifice prohibited to me," all conveyed in the word "Qorban." Having said that, the person may not eat the food of the other. The reason is that the other person's food has been declared by the individual who took the vow to be in the status of a sacrifice. Yet the rules of the Temple do not apply, the food need not be suitable for the altar, for example. It is wholly a matter of status, something fictive and imaginary, but here rendered real, and that is why the outreach of Nedarim runs far and wide.

What we are dealing with is the use of Temple-language in an analogical sense: this is like that. As I have already said, one may appeal to Lev. 27:10 for a model of what is in play: this is a substitute for that yields, that remains holy, but this enters the status of that. We know that what makes an ordinary beast into a holy beast, subject to the laws of sacrilege and set aside for the alter, is a verbal designation as a sacrifice. Here too what makes ordinary food into food in the status of Holy Things, *so far as the given individual is concerned,* is the verbal designation of that ordinary food as Holy Things. The difference is that designating an animal as a beast for sacrifice is a public act, affecting society at large. No one then can make use of said animal. Declaring that a dish of oatmeal is in the status of a qorban by contrast, has no affect upon the cereal, except for the person who made that declaration.

What lies at the foundation of this conception? If I had to point to a social reality that precipitates the imaginary transaction at hand, — the effective use of public language for private circumstances — it would be to the conception that a layman may eat his food in accord with the rules governing the priests' eating their rations. Here is a case in which the individual invokes the uncleanness laws of the Temple to affect the table at home. The Halakhah accords systematic recognition to the pretense of the private person or a group of individuals. That is why one may consequentially prepare one's domestic meals in accord with the purity-laws of the Temple, that is, the conceptions active at M. Hag. 2:7-9, M. Tohorot 2:2-3, M. Demai 2:2-3, and so on and so forth through the many passages of the Halakhah that accord to the individual the power to impose upon himself a status and a discipline that do not, in tangible, material reality, pertain. If a layman at home may pretend to be a priest in the Temple and so prepare and consume his meals in accord with the rules for preserving the cultic cleanness of food set forth in Lev. 11-15, then what stops anyone from declaring "Qorban" whatever he wishes? Nothing whatsoever. And that fact underscores the gap between what Scripture finds important in Nedarim, which is, keeping one's vows and the like, and what the Halakhah deems critical, which is, the power of language to sanctify for a single person what is not subject to sanctification at all in any objective sense.

Language then conforms to, and confirms, an underlying actuality: the power of imagination to impose discipline where it otherwise would not pertain by any objective rule. The reason is that language conveys in intelligible form the intentionality of the person who uses it. So we have this sequence: [1] the power of will to impose a fictive status, [2] the power of intentionality to effect that will, and [3] the power of language to embody intentionality and give it consequence.

That language confirms and conveys the intentionality to effect the man's will, e.g., to sanctification, hardly presents a surprise; it is, after all, the governing principle of Qiddushin for the spoken word and Ketubot for the written word, the legal document. But what sages wish to say in the Halakhah before us differs from their message concerning language in the contexts set by Qiddushin and Ketubot, even though all four tractates — Nedarim, Nazir, Qiddushin, Ketubot — take up the power of language to bring about changes in status. Sages revere the language that brings about sanctification of a woman to a man, and they treat with great punctiliousness the language of the marriage-contract, which, indeed, they subject to the closest exegetical processes of reading and interpretation. If they wished to say, language bears its own power (for the reason stated earlier, its capacity to embody intentionality), they could have no superior choice of topic than the Halakhah of Qiddushin and Ketubot (and Gittin, as we shall see presently).

But what if they wanted to say, language bears power even for purposes of which we (and Heaven) disapprove? And what if their intent was to warn, watch what you say, hold your tongue and keep your temper, because in expressing intentionality, your words give effect to your will, and you will be unable to retract? The subjective will is then made into objective fact! In other words, if sages wanted to make the point that language possesses power *eo ipse* so people had best use in a wise and astute manner the power of language lest it produce unwanted results, how would they best say so? The present category-formation presents itself as the obvious choice. Within the framework of the Halakhah, vows, inclusive of the special vow of the Nazirite, present the particular and appropriate medium for such a message.

That is not only because sages want to tell people to watch their words and not pretend to joke (using euphemisms for instance) when it comes to matters where intentionality makes a difference as to personal status. That is also because sages to begin with take a negative view of vowing. While of oaths taken in court with full deliberation, invoking the name of God, they approve, vows they despise. They are explicit on that matter: people who take vows show their weakness, not their strength. Vows represent the power of the weak and put-upon, the easy way to defend oneself against the importunities of the overbearing host, the grasping salesman, the tormenting husband or wife. But sages do not honor those who take the easy way, asking God to intervene in matters to which on our own we ought to be able to attend.

But, we must take note, because the Halakhah begins and ends with the conviction that language is power, the Halakhah also takes account of the sanctifying effect of even language stupidly used. That is the message of the Halakhah, and it is only through the Halakhah at hand that sages could have set forth the message they had in mind concerning the exploitation and abuse of the power of language. What is private and personal — and what is more personal than temper! — is a disreputable use of the holy. And language is holy because language gives form and effect to intentionality — the very issue of the Halakhah at hand! That is why we do admit intentionality — not foresight but intentionality as to honor — into the repertoire of reasons for nullifying vows, as we note in the Halakhah of Nedarim:

> M. 9:1 In a matter which is between him and his mother or father, they unloose his vow by [reference to] the honor of his father or mother.
> M. 9:9 They unloose a vow for a man by reference to his own honor and by reference to the honor of his children. They say to him, "Had you known that the next day they would say about you, 'That's the way of So-and-so, going around divorcing his wives,' "and that about your daughters they'd be saying, 'They're daughters of a divorcée! What did their mother do to get herself divorced' [would you have taken a vow]?" And [if] he then said, "Had I known that things would be that way, I should never have taken such a vow," lo, this [vow] is not binding.

The normative law rejects unforeseen events as a routine excuse for nullifying a vow; foresight on its own ("had you known...would you have vowed?") plays a dubious role. But when it comes to the intentionality involving honor of parents or children, that forms a consideration of such overriding power as to nullify the vow.

By using formulary language man or woman invoke the response of Heaven more really by throwing up words toward Heaven and so provoking a response in Heaven. That is how patterns of behavior and relationship, such as are defined by the vow, the Nazirite-vow, the act of sanctification of a woman to a particular man or a marriage contract, are subjected to Heaven's concerned response. Relationships and deeds are subjected to Heaven's engagement by the statement of the right words, and the wrong ones.

4.
TRACTATE NAZIRITE

I. THE DEFINITION OF THE CATEGORY-FORMATION

The genus, vow, is divided into two species, the general vow, set forth in Nedarim, and the Nazirite vow, the special vow described at Numbers 6. That Scripture treats the former casually and generally and the latter in acute detail makes little impact upon the Halakhic presentation of the two, which are treated in an analogical-contrastive process as two species of a single genus.[13] The comparison and contrast of the two help us identify the hermeneutical theory that is particular to the Nazirite vow as distinct from the theory that is general to vowing overall. And here, for the first time in this project, we come face to face with the three quite distinct sources of interpretative theory that govern in the presentation of any Halakhic category-formation:

[1] Scripture and its reading of the topic (where available);

[2] the hermeneutics of the Halakhah in general, principles of interpretation of all data and all category-formations equally; and

[3] the hermeneutics of the particular category-formation.

Up to this point we have concentrated on the third component of the complex hermeneutics that governs in any given category-formation. Because of the intimate relationship between Nedarim and Nazir, we readily recognize the first and the second components as well. And that recognition, a product of the analogical-contrastive hermeneutics that I identify within Halakhah and consequently impose thereon, will illuminate the study of the subsequent problems of this project, that is, the hermeneutics of the category-formations of Neziqin, Qodoshim, and Tohorot.

---

[13] So much for any conception of the Halakhah as essentially spun out of Scripture. The Halakhah defines its own categorical structure, responding to Scripture's categorical structure but not to Scripture's hermeneutical prescriptions for its category-formations. That is the burden of the present demonstration. At its deepest conceptual and categorical strata the Halakhah bears its own autonomy, drawing upon Scripture but always as an autonomous partner of Scripture. I have examined each of the category-formations of the Halakhah (for the Mishnah-Tosefta-Yerushalmi-Bavli) in my *Scripture and the Generative Premises of the Halakhah* (Binghamton, 1999: Global Publications of Binghamton University) I-IV.

The Nazirite vow, spelled out at Numbers 6, contrasts with the generic vow treated in Nedarim (and in a fragmentary way at Numbers 30), because although it too is a private vow, it is publicly acknowledged. While it is a special vow, a subset of the vow in general, it is not idiosyncratic and does not require the study of how private persons are restricted to the public meanings of the language that they use. If we compare the programs of the two logically-paired category-formations side by side, we see how the special vow of the Nazirite compares and contrasts with the general vow set forth in Nedarim.

Nedarim	Nazir

I. THE LANGUAGE OF VOWS
  A. Euphemisms
  B. Language of No Effect
  C. Language of Limited Effect
	I. THE SPECIAL VOW OF THE NAZIRITE
	  A. The Language of the Vow to be a Nazirite

II. THE BINDING EFFECTS OF VOWS
  A. Vows Not to Derive Benefit
  B. Vows Not to Eat Certain Food
  C. Vows Not to Use Certain Objects
  D. Secondary and Derivative Effects; The Temporal Limitation in Vows
	B. Stipulations and the Nazirite Vow
	C. The Duration of the Nazirite Vow
	D. Annulling the Nazirite Vow
	
	II. THE SPECIAL OFFERINGS OF THE NAZIRITE
	  A. Designation and Disposition of the Nazirite's Offerings

III. THE ABSOLUTION OF VOWS
  A. Grounds for the Absolution of Vows
  B. The Annulment of the Vows of a Daughter
  C. The Annulment of the Vows of a Wife
  D. The Husband's Power to Annul the Wife's Vows: Special Rules
  E. Vows of a Woman that Are Not Subject to Abrogation
	III. SPECIAL RESTRICTIONS ON THE NAZIRITE SET FORTH BY SCRIPTURE
	  A. The Grape
	  B. Cutting Hair
	  C. Corpse-Uncleanness
	  D. Doubts in the Case of a Nazirite

Nazirite follows the same plan as Nedarim, analyzing affective formulations, stipulations, the duration of the vow, and annulling the vow. Not only so, but the exposition of Nazirite follows the same logical sequence — beginning, middle, end — that governs at Nedarim (and elsewhere). On the surface the only points at which Nazirite goes its own way, tacked on at the end, derive from Scripture.[14] The exposition of Scripture, so as not to disrupt the topical presentation, can have come only at the beginning or at the end, and, as we have seen elsewhere, the logic of the whole category-formation determines the position of Scripture's concerns and requirements figure as a coherent agenda, whether at the outset, as at Yebamot, or at the end, as here. Here, first in order of presentation comes the program of the Halakhah autonomous of Scripture, then the secondary exposition of Scripture's Halakhic proscriptions. The single most critical question at Yebamot is the harmonizing of Scripture's conflicting instructions; it marks the beginning, from which everything else flows. Here the counterpart — the primary question that demands attention — is how the Nazirite vow is like the vow in general, so it comes at the outset. Here, then, the first task is to establish the genus, then to accomplish speciation. That certainly stands to reason, for the logic of comparison and contrast, as I have noted many times now, is, first we establish likeness, then difference. Any other order would disrupt the work of comparison and contrast and produce unintelligible facts, rather than well-considered explanations of cogent information, such as our category-formation (I would say, self-evidently) yields. The upshot is simple. The correspondence of the topical plans of the respective category-formations points toward a shared exegetical program, and, working back, ought to lead us to a common hermeneutics governs.

But that is only in part. Where Scripture intervenes, at Nazir Units II and III, just as at Nedarim unit III, there Scripture's interests dictate the characteristics of the category-formation, the issues that will govern. Then at its sector, Scripture has defined the topic. At many points, moreover, the topic on its own elicits, in the Halakhic presentation of the Mishnah (consequently, of the Tosefta, in large measure, and in the two Talmuds in entire measure), interest in a standard set of exegetical questions, e.g., concerning interstitiality, e.g., of causation, or of intentionality (where appropriate), characteristic of the Mishnah. We have already identified the ubiquitous presence of that analytical program, which is not particular to any topic or, as a matter of fact, to the Mishnah itself.

So what we learn, from the comparison of Nedarim and Nazir, about the hermeneutics of the category-formations at hand is illuminating. We see three distinct hermeneutical principles in play, one pertinent to Scripture's data,

---

[14] Compare the counterpart phenomenon in Nedarim!

one applicable to all category-formations equally, and one particular to the case at hand. Specifically, these are as follows:

[1] SCRIPTURE'S CASES AND CONSEQUENT RULES: Where Scripture defines a principal category-formation for the Halakhah, its details will attract systematic analysis, not episodic, ad hoc exegesis of this or that. That analysis, specifically, is aimed at identifying the general traits that logically inhere in cases, which are treated as exemplary and subject to generalization. So the hermeneutics focuses upon the possibilities of universalizing details into rules for example, the secondary, generalizing amplification of matters. The hermeneutics of a scripturally-defined category-formation will identify data that may (or may not) yield generalizations, governing principles for other cases. The Halakhic hermeneutics then seeks to translate cases and examples into laws, and ultimately, laws into principles that transcend the limitations of category-formations altogether. Of Sifré to Deuteronomy engages in the exercise of universalization of particulars, their transformation into governing principles pertinent to diverse types of cases altogether).[15] One principal component of the Halakhic hermeneutics in intersection with Scripture will find definition in the matter of universalizability.

[2] THE HALAKHAH'S ANALYTICAL PROGRAM FOR ALL CATEGORY-FORMATIONS: The Halakhic category-formations without much distinction as to particulars raises a set of analytical questions deemed everywhere pertinent and nowhere particular. These questions produce a coherent set of answers, without regard to the topic on which they are brought to bear. Not only so, but, so far as pertinent, that set of questions will focus, indeed, on Halakhic compositions of Scripture as much as those of the category-formations of the Mishnah-Tosefta-Yerushalmi-Bavli. These, too, aim at universalization of particulars. The hermeneutics that governs the interpretation of these (consequent) rules will focus in one way or another upon the excluded middle, or, in my language, problems of interstitiality. At issue may be problems of causation or of mixtures or of intentionality, as we have seen many times. What is important is, to every native category-formation an analytical program independent of all category-formations comes to bear, yielding results that concern abstract problems of a mainly philosophical character.

[3] THE HALAKHIC PROGRAM FOR A PARTICULAR CATEGORY-FORMATION: In addition to [1] Scripture's definition of what requires analysis in a given category-formation and [2] the Halakhah's program

---

[15] See my *Sifré to Deuteronomy. An Introduction to the Rhetorical, Logical, and Topical Program.* Atlanta, 1987: Scholars Press for Brown Judaic Studies.

of logical analysis for all category-formations, the Halakhah may, and ordinarily does, respond to a hermeneutics that defines in a particular category-formation what is at issue and what is at stake. These we have systematically identified in the completed parts of this project and will continue to investigate. In general, the hermeneutics of the particular category-formations, as we have seen to this point, takes shape in a process of analogical-contrastive reasoning, for example, the cessation of a marriage by Heavenly as against human intervention for Yebamot and Gittin, the Heavenly as against the human program for the course of a marriage for Yebamot and Ketubot, and the language of sanctification for the generality of humankind as against for a particular person, for Nedarim. Accordingly, two (or more) category-formations, time and again find their interpretative principles in the comparison and contrast of the species of a common genus.

To expand on this point: seen on its own, a particular category-formation is difficult to place into hermeneutical context. That is because we cannot see the choices that have been made between or among the interpretative possibilities that have been considered. Stated simply: we do not know "why this, not that," without access to both "this and that." It is not sufficient to work our way back from a given exegetical program to its generative hermeneutics. An explanation requires more than what is in the end merely sophisticated recapitulation, and pretentious paraphrase.

Accordingly, lacking the possibility of comparison and contrast, we can merely paraphrase, but not actually explain, the issues. And we certainly cannot account for the generative problematics, let alone the primary hermeneutics that precipitate the exegetical program of a given category-formation. We are able to identify, but not explain the choice of, the generative issues. Only in the *Auseinandersetzung* of comparison and contrast with a comparable but different species of a common genus, by contrast, are we able to identify the interpretative principles that account for and explain the entire matter. To state matters differently, out of the work of comparison and contrast of the species of a genus a process of dialectics — thesis, antithesis — is to be reconstructed. Thereby a sequence of steps of thought is (theoretically) recapitulated. We make the move from a description of the exegesis that is before us to an analysis of the hermeneutics that has generated the exegesis at hand.[16] In due course, the descriptive and analytical work having come to

---

[16] Or, more to the point, that large segment of the exegetical work that responds to the dictates of hermeneutics, not to the data of Scripture or to the built-in Halakhic process itself, entries [1] and [2] above.

fruition, we shall be ready to undertake the labor of interpretation.[17]

These general observations now allow us to place Nazirite into its three hermeneutical context(s): Scripture, the documentary logic of the Mishnah-Tosefta,[18] and the topical hermeneutics of the special vow of the Nazirite, as compared with the general vow. We start with Scripture.

[1] SCRIPTURE: As is common in the Priestly Code, so here too, Scripture focuses upon the offerings presented by the Nazirite either in the case of uncleanness or in the event of the successful completion of his vow in a state of cleanness. Hence we deal with a component of the cultic program of the Temple. The Nazirite vow, moreover, forms a subdivision of the category, vows, and is treated as continuous with the exposition of that topic. That is because the right of the husband to annul his wife's vows extends to the Nazirite vow that she may take. That is surely the formal reason that justifies situating the tractate where it is.

[2] GENERIC AND PARTICULAR HERMENEUTICS: But what about the Nazirite vow in its generic context, and what about the particular hermeneutics that takes shape within the comparison and contrast of the two species: the general vow (Nedarim) and the special vow of the Nazirite (Nazirite)? The Nazirite vow invokes God's special interest in the one who takes it, so the topic addresses an Israelite's relationship with God. With that formulation, Scripture can readily make its peace. But a closer look at the Halakhah in its own terms suggests otherwise. We find ourselves with a program of interpretation of the category-formation that closely follows that of Nedarim in general. For the special vow of the Nazirite, like the vow in

---

[17] I have already hinted at my present intuition, that the work of interpretation of the results of description and analysis of the Halakhic hermeneutics is going to have to encompass the Aggadic hermeneutics as well. But only when the Halakhic work is completely done and the intersection of the Halakhah in the Aggadah and of the Aggadah in the Halakhah is fully exposed will we have some clues on how to proceed.

[18] The two Talmuds inherit the results of the analytical program, but their documentary tasks differ so radically from those of the Mishnah and the Tosefta that it would mislead to speak of a common documentary logic among the four principal Halakhic media. For an account of the dialectics of the Talmuds, see my systematic account in *Talmudic Dialectics: Types and Forms*. Atlanta, 1995: Scholars Press for South Florida Studies in the History of Judaism. I. *Introduction. Tractate Berakhot and the Divisions of Appointed Times and Women; Talmudic Dialectics: Types and Forms*. Atlanta, 1995: Scholars Press for South Florida Studies in the History of Judaism. II. *The Divisions of Damages and Holy Things and Tractate Niddah*, the results of which are reworked and expanded in my *Jerusalem and Athens: The Congruity of Talmudic and Classical Philosophy*. Leiden, 1997: E. J. Brill. *Supplements to the Journal for the Study of Judaism,*

general, draws in its wake consequences for the life of the family of which that individual that takes the vow is (by definition) a key member: the householder, his wife, children, and slaves. Not only so, but a woman can accept the restrictions of the Nazirite vow, and that fact distinguishes the Nazirite condition from the condition of the priests! So the Israelite who takes the Nazirite vow is different from the Israelite who takes some other sort of vow, not this particular one.

To understand the speciation under way with the Nazirite vow, we have to ask, to whom is the Nazirite comparable? To whom is the one who says "Qorban" comparable? The latter is comparable to any Israelite; he is forbidden to partake of what is sanctified, as any other Israelite would be. But the Nazirite turns out to be like the priest in particular, since he or she accepts some of the disciplines of the priesthood — that sector of the priesthood ready to serve at the altar. The Nazirite has to keep himself or herself suitable for service at the altar and at the climax of the vow, the hair cutting and the offering attendant thereon, he or she is as much like a priest ready for altar-service as a lay Israelite or as a woman ever can be. He or she cannot drink wine, since a drunken priest cannot serve. He or she cannot contract corpse-uncleanness. Corpse-contamination is the principal source of uncleanness that keeps the priest away from the Temple. And he is subject to rules as to his appearance as well. An unkempt priest cannot serve; a Nazirite must cut his hair at the end of the standard spell, thirty days. At that moment, at the point of presenting the hair-offerings, then, the Nazirite (male or female!) is in the condition of the priest ready to serve at the altar. Then the hair-offering is a counterpart to the consecration offering of the priesthood. So he or she is not like ordinary Israelites vis à vis the Holy Things, he or she is like the priests in that same context, subject to special rules of a caste, not general rules of an entire community. The Nazirite cannot attend to the deceased, cannot drink wine with the family, and subjects himself or herself to his or her own rule when it comes to his or her appearance. As is the priest to the family of Israel, so is the Nazirite to the household of Israel, a particular classification of persons, distinguished in consequential and practical ways as to nourishment and comportment. But if the Nazirite is like a priest in certain restrictions, he or she vastly differs from the priest in every significant criterion of ordinary life: a woman, a layman, with no access to the altar at all!

So the comparison of the Nazirite to the priest yields contrasts as well. He or she is like a priest, but only by his own act of will. His or her offerings are not like those of ordinary Israelites but like Israelites who have contracted uncleanness. That is, while other votive acts of service, e.g., the thank-offering or the peace-offerings, engage the priesthood in the Temple at the altar, the offerings brought in consequence of the Nazirite vow do not. Having completed the Nazirite vow, the Israelite who has spent a month acting more like a priest than a layman brings about offerings given to the priest at the door of the tent of meeting. That is, he completes the process in the manner of the offerings of the person afflicted with the skin ailment described in Leviticus Chapters 13 and 14; the formerly-unclean person comes to the door of the tent of meeting and there he stays. The Nazirite, an Israelite who has assumed obligations of the working priesthood, in the end is kept outside of the Temple and classified, when the vow has been fully carried out (all the more so when not) as an outsider, no different in situation from the one who has attained cleanness from the skin ailment.

Having drawn these contrasts, we must ask ourselves, have we identified not only [1] a Scriptural foundation for the Halakhah and [2] the standard Mishnaic program for analytical presentation of the Halakhah, but also — and especially — [3] a hermeneutics particular to the category-formation, Nazirite? The answer to that question must await a systematic review of Scripture's treatment of the topic, in unit II, the Halakhic repertoire, unit III, and the quick reprise of the several documents' treatment of the topic, unit IV.

II. THE FOUNDATIONS OF THE HALAKHIC CATEGORY-FORMATIONS

Scripture deals with two topics, the restrictions self-imposed by the vow, and the offerings required in connection therewith. The relevant verses of Scripture are as follows (Num. 6:10-21):

RESTRICTIONS

And the Lord said to Moses, "Say to the people of Israel: when either a man or a woman makes a special vow, the vow of a Nazirite, to separate himself to the Lord, he shall separate himself from wine and strong drink; he shall drink no vinegar made from wine or strong drink, and shall not drink any juice of grapes or eat grapes fresh or dried. All the days of his separation he shall eat nothing that is produced by the grapevine, not even the seeds or the skins. "

"All the days of his vow of separation no razor shall come upon his head; until the time is completed for which he separates himself to the Lord, he shall be holy; he shall let the locks of hair of his head grow long. "

"All the days that he separates himself to the Lord, he shall not go near a dead body. Neither for his father nor for his mother nor for brother or sister, if they died, shall he make himself unclean, because his separation to God is upon his head; all the days of his separation he is holy to the Lord. "

Not drinking wine, not cutting the hair, and not contracting corpse-uncleanness constitute the restrictions accepted by the Israelite man or woman who takes the vow to be a Nazirite. Scripture says nothing more about the condition of the Nazirite when subject to the vow, but turns directly to the offerings that are required at the end of the vow, either in a state of uncleanness when the vow is ended and a new spell undertaken, or in a state of cleanness.

OFFERINGS

And if any man dies very suddenly beside him and he defiles his consecrate head, then he shall shave his head on the day of his cleansing; on the seventh day he shall bring two turtledoves or two young pigeons to the priest to the door of the tent of meeting, and the priest shall offer one for a sin-offering and the other for a burnt-offering, and make atonement for him, because he sinned by reason of the dead body. And he shall consecrate his head that same day and separate himself to the Lord for the day of his separation, and bring a male lamb a year old for a guilt-offering, but the former time shall be void, because his separation was defiled.

And this is the law for the Nazirite, when the time of his separation has been completed; he shall be brought to the door of the tent of meeting, and he shall offer his gift to the Lord, one male lamb a year old without blemish for a burnt-offering, and one ewe lamb a year old without blemish as a sin-offering, and one ram without blemish as a peace-offering, and a basket of unleavened brad, cakes of fine flour mixed with oil and unleavened wafers spread with oil, and their cereal-offering and their drink-offerings. And the priest shall present them before the Lord and offer his sin-offering and his burnt-offering, and he shall offer the ram as a sacrifice of peace-offering to the Lord, with the basket of unleavened bread; the priest shall offer also its cereal-offering and its drink-offering. And the Nazirite shall shave his consecrated head at the door of the tent of meeting and shall take the hair from his consecrated head and put it on the fire that is under the sacrifice of the peace-offering. And the priest shall take the shoulder of the ram, when it is boiled, and one unleavened cake out of the basket, and one unleavened wafer; and he shall put them upon the hands of the Nazirite, after he has shaven the hair of his consecration, and the priest shall wave them for a wave-offering before the Lord; they are a holy portion for the priest, together with the breast that is waved and the thigh that is offered; and after that the Nazirite may drink wine.

This is the law of the Nazirite who takes a vow. His offering to the Lord shall be according to his vow as a Nazirite, apart from what else he can afford; in accordance with the vow that he takes, so shall he do according to the law of his separation as a Nazirite.

The exposition of the law set forth by Scripture, which preoccupies the Halakhah of the Oral Torah in the present case, explicitly concerns husband-wife relationships at M. 4:4-7, the husband's annulling the vows of the wife, the affect upon the wife of the husband's sudden death without an act of nullification, and the like. Not only so, but the tractate commences with a formulation modeled upon that of Mishnah-tractate Nedarim. But the center of matters is not at Scripture.

III. THE EXPOSITION OF THE COMPONENTS OF THE GIVEN CATEGORY-FORMATION BY THE MISHNAH-TOSEFTA-YERUSHALMI-BAVLI

As always, I set forth the main points of **the Mishnah (in bold face type)**, then at the appropriate place add the Tosefta's own presentation not merely the clarification or amplification of the Mishnah's Halakhah (in ordinary type), thereafter *the Yerushalmi's (in italics),* and finally, **THE BAVLI'S (IN BOLD FACE LOWER CASE TYPE)**. These are paraphrased and epitomized, they are not cited in full. I insert my observations on the points of special interest at the conclusion of each topical sub-unit. The units and sub-units derive from my own outline of the Mishnah-tractate, encompassing also the Tosefta-tractate; then the outline of the Yerushalmi, finally that of the Bavli.[19]

I.   THE SPECIAL VOW OF THE NAZIRITE

    A.   *THE LANGUAGE OF THE VOW TO BE A NAZIRITE*
    M. 1:1 All euphemisms for [the form of words for] a Nazirite vow are equivalent to a Nazirite vow [and binding]. He who says, "I will be [such]" — **lo, this one is a Nazirite. Or: "I shall be comely"** — **he is a Nazirite. [If he says,] "Naziq " or "Naziah " or "Paziah "** — **lo, this one is a Nazirite. [If he says,] "Lo, I shall be like this one," "Lo, I shall curl [my hair]," "Lo, I shall tend [my hair]," "Lo, it is incumbent on me to grow [my hair] long"** — **lo, this one is a Nazirite. [If he says,] "Lo, I pledge myself [to offer] birds"** — **he is not a Nazirite.**
    M. 1:2 [He who says,] "Lo, I shall be an abstainer [Nazirite] from grape pits" or "from grape skins" or "from haircuts" or "from uncleanness [of corpses]" — **lo, this one is a Nazir-**

---

[19] These are cited with bibliographical data in the Introduction, Volume I.

ite [in all regards]. And all the details of a Nazirite vow pertain to him. [He who says,] "Lo, I shall be like Samson" or "like the son of Manoah" or "like the husband of Delilah" or "like the one who tore down the gates of Gaza" or "like the one whose eyes the Philistines plucked out" — lo, this one is a Nazirite in the status of Samson. What is the difference between a lifelong Nazirite and a Nazirite in the status of Samson [also a Nazirite for life]? A lifelong Nazirite: [If] his hair gets too heavy, he lightens it with a razor and brings three [offerings of] cattle (Num. 6:14). And if he is made unclean, he brings an offering on account of uncleanness. A Nazirite in the status of Samson: [if] his hair gets too heavy, he does not lighten it. And if he is made unclean, he does not bring an offering on account of uncleanness.

T. 1:5 Just as euphemisms for Nazirite-vows are equivalent to Nazirite-vows, so euphemisms for Samson-vows are equivalent to Samson-vows [M. Naz. 1:2C]. Naziriteship applies in the Land and abroad, whether the man has hair or does not have hair. Even though it is said, "And the Nazirite shall shave his consecrated head at the door of the tent of meeting and shall take the hair from his consecrated head land put it on the fire" (Num. 6:18). And it applies whether or not he has hands, even though it is said,"[And the priest shall take the shoulder of the ram ...and one unleavened cake out of the basket, and one unleavened wafer, and shall put them upon the hands of the Nazirite" [Num. 6:19].

M. 1:3 A Nazirite vow that is unspecified [as to length] is for a period of thirty days. [If] he said, "Lo, I shall be a Nazirite for one long spell," "Lo, I shall be a Nazirite for one short spell," [or] even "From now until [for as long as it takes to go] the end of the world" — he is a Nazirite for thirty days. [If he said,] "Lo, I shall be a Nazirite and for one day [more]," " "Lo, I shall be a Nazirite and for one hour [more]," "Lo, I shall be a Nazirite for one spell and a half" — lo, he is a Nazirite for two spells [of thirty days]. [If he said,] "Lo, I shall be a Nazirite for thirty days and for one hour," he is a Nazirite for thirty days and for one day, for Nazirite vows are not taken by the measure of hours.

T. 1:2 [If he said,] "Lo, I am a Nazirite and one," lo, this one is a Nazirite for two spells [M. Naz. 1:3D]. [If he said,] "...And more," lo, he is a Nazirite for three spells. [If he said,] "...One and more and again," lo, this one is a Nazirite for four spells.

M. 1:4 [He who said,] "I will be a Nazirite like the hairs of my head" or "like the dust of the earth" or "like the sand of the sea" — lo, this one is a lifetime Nazirite. But he cuts his hair once every thirty days. [He who says,] "Lo, I am a Nazirite, a jugful" or "a basketful" — they examine his intention. And if he said, "I intended to take a Nazirite vow for one long period," he is a

Nazirite for thirty days. But if he said, "I took a Nazirite vow without specification," they regard the basket as if it is full of mustard seeds. And he is a Nazirite for the rest of his life.

T. 1:4 [If he said], "Lo, I am a Nazirite like the hairs of my head," "...like the dust of the earth," "...like the sand of the sea," lo, this one is a lifelong Nazirite. And he cuts his hair once in thirty days. [If he said,] "Lo, I am a Nazirite from now until the border," "...from the earth to the firmament," lo, this one is a lifelong Nazirite. [If he said,] "Lo, I am a Nazirite all my days," "Lo, I am a lifelong Nazirite," lo, this one is a lifelong Nazirite. [If he said, "Lo, I am a Nazirite] for a hundred years," or "...for two hundred years," this one is not a lifelong Nazirite.

M. 1:5 [If he said,] "Lo, I shall be a Nazirite from here to such-and-such a place," they make an estimate of how many days it takes to go from here to such-and-such a place. If it is less than thirty days, he is a Nazirite for thirty days. And if not, he is a Nazirite in accord with the number of days [required to go to such-and-such a place]. [If he said,] "Lo, I shall be a Nazirite according to the number of days of the year," he counts his Nazirite spell in accord with the number of days of the year.

T. 1:3 [He once said,] "Lo, I am a Nazirite, if I do not [reveal] the families [which are impure]," let him be a Nazirite and let him not reveal the families [which are impure]. "Lo, I am a Nazirite in accord with the hours of the day," "...in accord with the months of the year," lo, this one is a Nazirite for twelve spells. "...in accord with the days of the week," "...in accord with the years of the septennate," "...in accord with the years of release of a Jubilee," lo, this one is a Nazirite for seven spells. "Lo, I am a Nazirite in accord with the days of the solar year," he is a Nazirite for three hundred sixty-five spells of Naziriteship, in accord with the number of days of the solar year. "...in accord with the days of the moon," "...in accord with the number of the days of the moon," — he is a Nazirite for three hundred fifty-four spells of Naziriteship, in accord with the number of the days of the lunar year. [If he said, "Lo, I am a Nazirite] ...a jarful," or "...a basketful" [M. Naz. 1:5A], lo, this one is a lifetime Nazirite. And he shaves once in thirty days. [This is so] unless he says to them, "It was not to that purpose [that I intended in taking a vow]."

T. 1:6 A more strict rule applies to the Nazirite than applies to the mesora' [one who is afflicted with the skin ailment of Lev. 13], and to the mesora' that does not apply to the Nazirite. A Nazirite, if he shaved on the day of completion of his vow, incurs forty stripes, which is not the case with the mesora'. A mesora' shaves his head, his beard, and his eyebrows, which is not the case with the Nazirite.

T. 1:7 A more strict rule applies to Nazirite-vows than applies to oaths, and to oaths than to Nazirite-vows. For a Nazirite-vow may be found within another such vow, but an oath is not contained within another oath [M. Ned. 2:3]. A more strict rule applies to oaths, for an oath made inadvertently is binding, but a Nazirite-vow made inadvertently is not binding.

The same issue with which the Halakhah of Nedarim commences, the status of private formulations, e.g., euphemisms, produces the same result. Language is affective only in its public contexts. Private meanings are not taken into account; anything that resembles the acknowledged, official formulation suffices to establish one's status as a Nazirite. None can claim, "That is not exactly what I meant." Not only so, but the special vow of the Nazirite is always subject to the same requirements, e.g., M. 1:3's thirty days (or more). One cannot define the terms of his abstention.

With the matter treated as an actuality, the question arises: how literally do we take the terms? At issue is both the general prohibition against contracting corpse uncleanness and the specificities of details of the rite. Must a person who takes the vow be able to avoid corpse-uncleanness, meaning, be resident in the Land of Israel, and must he have the necessary body parts to do, literally, what is required by the vow, e.g., hands to present the offering, hair on his head to be shaved off? The Tosefta introduces a matter of its own: is the Nazirite vow pertinent only to the Land, which alone is suitable for entering the status of cultic cleanness, and only to those who have hair and other perquisites for going through the rite? The answer is, the Nazirite vow may take place even outside of the Land, where one is infected by definition with corpse-uncleanness, and it may take effect for persons who cannot in fact carry out the offerings in the conventional manner. The Tosefta answers a question not raised by the Mishnah and does so with great perspicacity. Since, as I shall point out, the Nazirite vow has an ordinary Israelite pretend to be a priest ready for service at the altar — not drunk, not unclean with corpse-uncleanness — the issue of the reality of pretense takes over. The judgment of the Halakhah is, once one — man or woman — undertakes the pretense of being a priest ready for service, the language bears its own discipline, autonomous of the actualities: he or she must do what he or she has said. That is without regard to the realities of the person's individual situation; once more, the principle of the power of language to take over and reshape the everyday condition of a person applies.

The vow lasts for a month, the length of time required for growing hair that requires cutting. The language one uses is subject to interpretation by standard rules of ordinary usage. The Tosefta in another triumphant composition articulates the necessary comparisons between the Nazirite vow and comparable species of the common genus, oaths and vows to heaven. We return to that matter presently.

    B.   *STIPULATIONS AND THE NAZIRITE VOW*
        M. 2:1 [He who says,] "Lo, I am a Nazirite as to dried figs and pressed figs" — he is not a Nazirite.
        Y. 2:1 I:2 *All sorts of linguistic usages serve as an expression of Naziriteship, except for language used to say [that something is forbidden to him] as an offering. All sorts of linguistic usages serve as an expression [of a vow not to derive benefit from something, because to him it has the status of] an offering, except for the language used as an expression of Naziriteship. If one has said to a grape cluster, "I am finished with you," "I am separate from you," "I am held back from you," "Lo, I am a Nazirite from you" — lo, this one is a Nazirite. [If he said,] "Lo, incumbent on me as an offering [is the grape cluster]", he has not rendered it prohibited for himself, except for the sake of a [vow using the language of prohibition as an] offering. If he said to a loaf, "I am finished with you," "I am separate from you," "I am held back from you," "Lo, incumbent on me as an offering [is the loaf]," he has prohibited the loaf for himself only on account of its being an offering. If he said, "Lo, I am a Nazirite from you," lo, he is a Nazirite. Thus we see that a usage such as "restrained from" serves to express both the Nazirite vow and the vow of a prohibition on account of an offering. So too the language of "grape cluster" contains implications both for the Nazirite vow and for the [vow of prohibition on account of its being] — an offering. If one has said to the grape cluster, "I am finished with you," if he then comes [to seek permission from a sage to eat it,] one says to him, "As to its value, it is holy [and] one has to redeem it." And if he then comes to seek permission to eat it, one says to him, "No, you are a Nazirite." All sorts of linguistic usages serve as an expression of deconsecration, except for the language of substitution. All sorts of linguistic usages serve as an expression of substitution, except for the language of deconsecration. If one said of Holy Things consecrated for use on the altar, "Lo, this is in place of that," "This is substituted for that," "This is exchanged for that," "Lo, this is an exchange; this is deconsecrated for that," it does not constitute a substitution, [for a beast that has been consecrated for the altar does not suffer deconsecration and cease to be holy. It also is not a statement of substitution, because the language of deconsecration bears no effects for substitution.] All sorts of linguistic usages serve as an expression of fixed valuations except for language limited to the meaning of one's actual market value [in general]. All sorts of linguistic usages serve as an expression of the pledge of one's actual market value in general, except for language limited to the meaning of pledging one's fixed valuation in particular. If one has said of someone, "His worth is*

incumbent on me," "His value is incumbent on me," "The estimate of his worth is incumbent on me," "His valuation is incumbent on me" — *one pays his valuation. "His price is incumbent on me"* — *he pays his market price. Thus the language of estimate of value serves both as an expression of estimated market value and of fixed valuation.*

M. 2:2 [If] one said, "This cow says, 'Lo, I am a Nazirite if I stand up,' "This door says, 'Lo, I am a Nazirite if I am opened'" — he is not a Nazirite."

M. 2:3 [If] they mixed a cup for someone, and he said, "Lo, I am a Nazirite from it," lo, this one is a Nazirite.

M. 2:4 [If one said,] "Lo, I am a Nazirite on condition that I shall drink wine and become unclean with corpse uncleanness," lo, this one is a Nazirite. But he is prohibited to do all of these things [that he has specified as conditional upon his vow]. [If he said,] "I recognize that there is such a thing as Naziriteship, but I do not recognize that a Nazirite is prohibited from drinking wine," lo, this one is bound [by the Nazirite oath]. [If he said,] "I recognize full well that a Nazirite is prohibited to drink wine, but I was thinking that sages would permit me to do so, because I cannot live without wine," or "because I am in the work of burying the dead," lo, this one is not bound.

T. 2:2 A. [If he said], "Lo, I am a Nazirite on condition that I shall be drinking wine and making myself unclean with corpse-uncleanness" lo, this one is a Nazirite [M. Naz. 2:4A-B]. But his prior stipulation is null. For he has made a condition contrary to what is written in the Torah, and whoever makes a condition contrary to what is written in the Torah — his condition is null.

T. 2:3 "I recognize that there are Nazirs, but I do not recognize that Nazirs are prohibited from drinking wine" [M. Naz. 2:4D] "that it is prohibited to drink wine and to become unclean with corpse-uncleanness" — you have no greater pretext than such a statement [for annulling the vow]" [M. Naz. 2:4F].

M. 2:5 [If one said,] "Lo, I am a Nazirite, and I take it upon myself to bring the hair offering of another Nazirite," and his friend heard and said, "So am I, and I take it upon myself to bring the hair offering of another Nazirite," if they are smart, they each bring the hair offering of the other, and if not, they bring the hair offering of other Nazirs.

T. 2:5 [If one said,] "Lo I am a Nazirite, and it is incumbent upon me to bring the hair-offering of another Nazirite" [M. Naz. 2:5A], and if he [first] offered his own hair-offering, he has not fulfilled the terms of his pledge.

T. 2:6 "Lo, I pledge myself to offer half of the hair-offering of a Nazirite," and he further said, "Lo, I am a Nazirite," if he [first] offered his own hair-offering, he has not fulfilled the terms of his pledge. [If he said], "These are the offerings an account of which I shall separate [myself as a Nazirite]," he has said nothing, since it says, "His offering for the Lord on account of his Nazirite-vow" (Num. 6:21), and not his Nazirite-vow on account of his offering.

T. 2:7 "Lo, I pledge myself to offer the sin-offering or the guilt-offering owed by Mr. So-and-so" — if he said so with the other's knowledge, the other has fulfilled his obligation . [If he said so] not with the other's knowledge, he has not fulfilled his obligation . "Lo, this is the sin-offering or the guilt-offering owed by Mr. So-and-so and the other went and brought offerings in his own behalf"— lo, these [brought by the first party] are in the status of a sin-offering or a guilt-offering, the owner of which has effected atonement [through some other animal].

M. 2:6 [If one said,] "Lo, I pledge myself to bring half of the hair offering of a Nazirite," and his friend heard and said, "And I too pledge myself to bring half the hair offering of a Nazirite," this one brings half the hair offering of a Nazirite, and that one brings half the hair offering of a Nazirite.

M. 2:7 [If one said,] "I will be a Nazirite when a son is born to me," and a son was born to him, lo, this one is a Nazirite. [If] a daughter, a child of unclear sexual traits, [or] a child bearing the sexual traits of both sexes is born to him, he is not a Nazirite. If he said, "When I see that a child is born to me, [I shall be a Nazirite,]" even if a daughter, a child bearing unclear sexual traits, [or] a child bearing the sexual traits of both sexes, is born to him, lo, he is a Nazirite.

M. 2:8 [But if] his wife miscarried, he is not a Nazirite. [If] she went and gave birth again, lo, this one is a Nazirite.

M. 2:9 [He who said,] "Lo, I am a Nazirite, and [again] a Nazirite if a son is born to me," [if] he began counting out the Nazirite days covering his own vow, and afterward a son was born to him, he completes the days of his own vow and afterward counts out the days of the vow pertaining to his son. [If he said,] "Lo, I am a Nazirite when a son will be born to me, and [again] a Nazirite," [if] he began to count out the days covering his own vow, and afterward a son was born to him, he puts aside [the observance of the days of] his own [vow] and counts out the days covering the vow he made for his son. And afterward he completes the days required for his own vow.

M. 2:10 [If he said,] "Lo, I am a Nazirite when a son will be born to me and a Nazirite for a hundred days," [if] a son was born to him before seventy days [had passed], he has lost nothing. [If the son was born] after seventy days, he loses the seventy days he has observed, for there is no cutting of hair in less than thirty days [from the beginning of the observance of the vow].

T. 2:10 "Lo, I am a Nazirite after twenty days, a Nazirite from now for a hundred days," he counts twenty, and afterward he counts thirty, and he counts eighty to complete his first Nazirite-vow [cf. M. Naz. 2:10].

The Nazirite vow is specific and particular: not a model in general, but a prescription in particular. So we ask, Can a person redefine the Nazirite vow, e.g., by undertaking a discipline comparable to the terms of the vow but not corresponding to the details, e.g., refraining from figs not grapes? Or by setting his own conditions for the vow (M. 2:4)? No, he or she cannot do so. The Nazirite vow represents an objective condition, beyond all negotiation, unlike the vow in general, which conforms to individual intent and involves no objective transformation such as the Nazirite vow effects. The Nazirite vow bears none of the subjectivity of the ordinary vow. The Torah has distinguished this vow from the generality of vows, the familiar principle being stated in the present context: For he has made a condition contrary to what is written in the Torah, and whoever makes a condition contrary to what is written in the Torah — his condition is null In this regard, the Nazirite vow is different from the ordinary vow, which can pertain to anything. One who takes an ordinary vow may declare sanctified — as to himself — whatever he wishes, including things that never can enter the objective status of sanctification at all. That is, the ordinary vow functions entirely in relationship to the one who takes it, an expression of his will alone. By contrast, the Nazirite vow conforms to an objective standard and in no way responds to the preferences of the one who takes it. The Torah has defined it, and that closes all further questions. Not only so, but the context in which the language of the Nazirite vow is used is taken into account.

The result is, someone cannot claim to have meant by the Nazirite language something other than the ordinary sense. Euphemism are affective, transformative, just as in the case of vows, but subject to the special conditions that pertain. The context then is everything, as M. 2:3 makes clear. And then, as we noted, with the vow in effect, all of its conditions govern, even those a person explicitly rejects. The upshot is, the Nazirite vow considerably differs from the ordinary vow.

A vow may last indefinitely. If it is nullified by a sage, it is as if it never took effect. No rite of any kind marks its nullification, and if it was subject to a term-limit, the advent of that limit is not celebrated. Clearly, what makes the Nazirite vow noteworthy is the elaborate procedure involved in winding it up. No counterpart rite — at the door of the Temple no less — marks the conclusion of a vow. In that context — the focus on the hair-offering — the possibility of a Nazirite's undertaking to bring not only his, but another's, hair-offerings finds its place. The Tosefta as is its way pursues at T. 2:7 the same matter in other contexts altogether.

The Mishnah's ubiquitous analytical problem takes over at M. 2:7, introducing the interstitial issues as these pertain. While some of the problems are particular to the case of the Nazirite vow, e.g., M. 2:9, most of them can be worked out in other contexts altogether.

C.   THE DURATION OF THE VOW

M. 3:1 He who said, "Lo, I am a Nazirite," cuts his hair on the thirty-first day. But if he cut it on the thirtieth day, he has fulfilled his obligation. [If he said,] "Lo, I am a Nazirite for thirty days," if he cut his hair on the thirtieth day, he has not fulfilled his obligation.

M. 3:2 He who took a Nazirite vow for two spells cuts his hair for the first on the thirty-first day and for the second on the sixty-first day. And if he cut his hair for the first on the thirtieth day, he cuts his hair for the second on the sixtieth day. But if he cut his hair on the sixtieth day less one, he [nonetheless] has fulfilled his obligation. For the thirtieth day counts for him among the number [of days of the second Nazirite vow].

T. 2:11 He who took two successive vows to be a Nazirite, the first a vow to be a Nazirite without specification [as to length], and the second a vow to be a Nazirite for thirty days, cuts his hair for the first oath on the thirty-first day and for the second on the sixty-first day [M. Naz. 3:2A]. But if he cut his hair for the first on the thirtieth day, he cuts his hair for the second on the sixtieth day [M. Naz. 3:2B], [and] he has fulfilled his obligation. [If the time specified for] for the first Nazirite-vow was thirty days and for the second vow was not specified, he cuts his hair for the first vow on the thirty-first day and for the second on the sixty-first day. And if he cut his hair on the sixtieth day, he has not fulfilled his obligation.

Y. 3:2 I:1 *[If] he completed his first spell as a Nazirite, [then designated the offerings required on that account,] and came to lay hands on the offerings designated for the second spell, [and he came to ask a sage whether or not his vows indeed were binding, there being some pretext on the basis of which to nullify them,] and [the sages who were consulted] did not find for him a pretext for releasing the former vow before they found a pretext for releasing the second vow, [so he has the animal set aside for the second vow available, and he wants to offer that for the offering owing by reason of the first vow and indeed does so] — the offering set aside in fulfillment of the second vow does indeed serve in fulfillment of the animal required in completion of the first vow.*

M. 3:3 He who said, "Lo, I am a Nazirite," [if] he was made unclean on the thirtieth day, he loses the whole [thirty days he already has observed]. [If he said,] "Lo, I am a Nazirite for thirty [whole] days," [and] was made unclean on the thirtieth day, he loses the whole [thirty days he already has observed].

T. 2:12 He who said, "Lo, I am a Nazirite," and was made unclean on the thirtieth day loses the whole thirty days which he already has counted in accord with the rules of being a Nazirite. If he said, "Lo, I am a Nazirite for thirty days," and was made unclean on the thirtieth day, he loses the whole thirty days already observed.

M. 3:4 "Lo, I am a Nazirite for a hundred days, [if] he was made unclean on the hundredth day, he loses the whole [hundred days already observed]. [If] he was made unclean on the hundred-and-first day, he loses thirty days.

M. 3:5 He who vowed to be a Nazirite while in a graveyard, even if he was there for thirty days — those days do not count for him toward the number [of days owing under the vow]. Nor does he bring an offering for his uncleanness [for being in the graveyard]. [If, however] he went out and then came back [into the graveyard], they do count for him toward the number [of required days]. And he does bring an offering for his uncleanness.

T. 2:14 He who was unclean and took an oath as a Nazirite is prohibited from cutting his hair and from drinking wine and from contracting corpse-uncleanness. And if he cut his hair, drank wine, or contracted corpse-uncleanness, he receives forty stripes. He is sprinkled and repeats the process [on the third and seventh days of becoming unclean with corpse-uncleanness]. The days on which he is unclean do not count toward the fulfillment of his vow. But also: the seventh day does count toward the fulfillment of his vow. All cases concerning which they have said, "He does not begin to count [the clean days for the purposes of his Nazirite-vow] until he becomes clean"-the seventh day does not count toward the fulfillment of the vow. All cases concerning which they have said, "He begins to count [the clean days for the purposes of his Nazirite-vow] forthwith"-the seventh day does count toward the fulfillment of his vow [cf. M. Naz. 7:2]. [If] he counted out the days in fulfillment of his Nazirite-vow but did not bring his offerings, he is prohibited from cutting his hair, from drinking wine, and from contracting corpse-uncleanness. And if he cut his hair, drank wine, or contracted corpse-uncleanness, lo, this one receives forty stripes.

M. 3:6 He who [while overseas] took a vow to be a Nazirite for a long spell and completed his spell as a Nazirite, and afterward came to the Land [of Israel] — he is a Nazirite as from the very beginning.

M. 3:7 He concerning whom two groups of witnesses gave testimony — these testify that he took a vow to be a Nazirite for two spells, and these testify that he took a vow to be a Nazirite for five spells in the sum of five are two spells. So let him serve out two spells of Naziriteship.

The generic analytical program of the Halakhah defines the issue at M. 3:1, the interpretation of the formulas the people use. We note that while the vow pertains abroad, its actualization begins with entry into the Land, M. 3:6.

D. *ANNULLING THE VOW*
M. 4:1 He who said, "Lo, I am a Nazirite," and his friends heard and said, "Me too," "Me too," "Me too" — all of them are Nazirs. [If] the vow of the first was declared not binding, the vows of all of them are deemed not binding. [If the vow of the] last of them was declared not binding, the last of them is not bound, but all the rest of them remain bound. [If] he said, "Lo, I am a Nazirite," and his friend heard and said, "Let my mouth be like his mouth, and my hair like his hair," lo, this one is a Nazirite [= M. 1:1A]. [If he said,] "Lo, I am a Nazirite," and his wife heard and said, "Me too" — he annuls her vow, but his stands. [If the wife said,] "Lo, I am a Nazirite," and her husband heard and said, "Me too," he cannot annul [her vow].

T. 2:15 He who took two vows as a Nazirite, counted out the first but did not bring his offerings, and afterward sought absolution for the first from a sage to declare it not binding for him — the second vow to be a Nazirite goes forth with the loosening of the first. [If] he counted out the days required for both of them, and brought the offerings for both of them at one time, he gets credit only for one of them. [If] he set aside the offerings for one of them by itself and the offering for the other by itself and went and offered this one in place of that one, he has not fulfilled his obligation.

T. 3:2 He who said, "Lo, I am a Nazirite," and then hesitated for a time sufficient for a break in conversation, and his friend heard and said, "And me too" [M. Naz. 4:1A-B] — he is bound [by the oath], but his friend is not bound by it. And how long is a time sufficient for a break in conversation? Sufficient time to ask after someone's welfare.

T. 3:3 "Lo, I am a Nazirite," and his friend heard and said, "Let my mouth be like his mouth, and my hair like his hair," lo, this one also is a Nazirite [M. Naz. 4:1E]. [If he said], "Let my hand be like his hand." "my foot like his foot," lo, this one is a Nazirite. [If he said], "My hand is a Nazirite," "My foot is a Nazirite," he is not a Nazirite. "My head is a Nazirite," "My liver is a Nazirite," — lo, this one is a Nazirite. This is the general principle: [If he spoke of] something upon which life depends, he is a Nazirite. [If he spoke of] something on which life does not depend, he is not a Nazirite.

Y. 4:1 I:4 One party who said, "Lo, I am a Nazirite for a hundred days," and his fellow heard and said, "And me too, for a hundred days," and the first party then went and said, "Me too" — the one that had been principal is treated as secondary. [That is to say, the first party took his oath, the second followed suit, then the first party reverted and accepted the formulation of the second party. In this case, if the vow of the second party is nullified, that taken by the first party is automatically nullified as well, for obvious reasons.] If one party said, "Lo, I am a Nazirite," and another said, "Me too" during the span of time of the first party's statement, and another party heard and said, "Me too," during the span of time of the second party's statement — if the first party is released from his vow, the second party is released. If the second party is released from his vow, the third party is not released. If he is released from his vow, they are released from theirs. If they are released from their vow, he is not released from his. Two who said, "Lo, we are Nazirs," and one other person heard and said, "And I shall be in the place of the two of them" — is he liable for two spells as a Nazirite, or is he liable for a single spell as a Nazirite, covering each one of them? If they are released from their vow, he is released. If he is released from his vow, they are not released from theirs.

Y. 4:1 I:5 If someone has said, "My mouth is prohibited from wine," "My hair from being cut," "My hands from touching corpse uncleanness," "My feet from walking in corpse uncleanness," "My head is a Nazirite," "My liver is a Nazirite," "My walking about is a Nazirite," "My speaking is a Nazirite," he has said nothing at all. Why not? Because he treated the Nazirite vow as dependent upon something which life does [not] depend [in the case of mouth, hands, feet]. "When a man vows a vow to the Lord" (Num 30:2) — just as the language of a vow to which reference is made later on speaks of a matter upon which life depends, so "vow," concerning which reference is made here [with regard to the Nazirite], speaks of something on which life depends.

M. 4:2 "Lo, I am a Nazirite, — and you?" and she said, "Amen" — If he annuls hers, his is null. [If she said] "Lo, I am a Nazirite, and you?" and he said, "Amen" — he has not got the power to annul her vow.

T. 3:4(5) He who says to his wife, "Lo, I am a Nazirite, and you?" If she said, "Yes," both of them are bound by his oath. If he wanted to annul her vow, he annuls her vow, because [his] vow came before [her acceptance and his] confirmation [M. Naz. 4:2]. If not, he is bound by his vow, and she is not bound by his vow. He who says to his wife, "Lo, I am a Nazirite, and [if] you [are]?" If she said, "Yes," both of them are bound by his oath. And if not, both of them are not bound, because he makes his vow contingent upon her vow.

T. 3:6 [If] his wife said to him, "Lo, I am a Nazirite, and you?" [If] he said, "Yes," both of them are bound by her oath. If he wanted to annul her vow, he cannot annul it, because his confirmation [of her vow] came before his vow. If not, she is bound and he is permitted.

T. 3:7 [If] his wife said to him, "Lo, I am a Nazirite, [if] you are?" If he said, "Yes," both of them are bound by her vow. If not, both of them are not bound, because she made her vow contingent upon his vow.

T. 3:8 He who said to his friend, "Lo, I am a Nazirite, and you?" If he said, "Yes," both of them are bound. If not, he is bound, and his friend is not bound.

T. 3:9 He who says to his friend, "Lo, I am a Nazirite, and [if] you [are]?" If he said, "Yes," both of them are bound. And if not, both of them are not bound, because he made his vow contingent upon the vow of his [friend]. [If] his friend said to him, "Lo, are you a Nazirite?" [If] he said to him, "Are you?" If he said to him, "Yes," he is bound, and his friend is not bound. [If] his friend said to him, "Lo, are you Nazirite?" If he said to him, "And you?" If he said to him, "Yes," then both of them are bound. And if not, both of them are not bound, because he made his vow continent upon the vow of his [friend].

T. 3:10 The woman who took a vow and her girl-friend heard and said, "And me too," and afterward the husband of this one [who originally took the vow] came and annulled it for her — she is not bound by her vow, but her girl-friend is bound by it.

M. 4:3 A woman who took a vow as a Nazirite but nonetheless went around drinking wine and contracting corpse uncleanness — lo, this one receives forty stripes. [If] her husband annulled the vow for her, but she did not know that her husband had annulled it for her and nonetheless continued to go around drinking wine and contracting corpse uncleanness, she does not receive forty stripes.

T. 3:11 [If she said], "By an oath that I not enter this house," and she made a mistake and went into it — he is not bound as to the past but is bound as to the future.

T. 3:14 The woman who took a vow to be a Nazirite — her husband annulled the vow for her, but she did not know that her husband had annulled the vow — she went around drinking wine and contracting corpse-uncleanness [M. Naz. 4:3A-C] — lo, this one receives forty stripes [vs. M. Naz. 4:3D].

T. 3:15 He who took a vow to be a Nazirite but went around drinking wine and contracting corpse-uncleanness, and afterward sought absolution from a sage, and the sage absolved him of the vow, does not receive forty stripes.

The final topic shared with Nedarim concerns the nullification of the vow. We begin with the case of several vows taken in close succession (as defined at T. 3:2) and viewed as a totality: if one is released, all the later ones are null as well. That problem derives from the larger generic concern with sequences and mixtures and is not particular to our category-formation. M. 4:3 makes the distinction between actuality and intentionality. The woman violated a nullified vow that she thought was valid; she is not punished, since the facts override her intentionality. So too, T. 3:15 adds, if the vow never took **effect, what he has done is null.**

II. THE SPECIAL OFFERINGS OF THE NAZIRITE

A. DESIGNATION AND DISPOSITION OF THE NAZIRITE'S OFFERINGS

M. 4:4 A woman who took a vow to be a Nazirite and set aside her beast [for the required sacrifice], but afterward her husband annulled her vow for her — now if the beast [set aside for her] belonged to him, it goes forth and pastures in the corral. But if the beast [set aside for her] belonged to her, the animal designated as a sin offering is left to die. And the animal designated as a burnt offering is offered as a burnt offering. And the animal designated as a peace offering is offered as a peace offering. It is eaten for one day [like a Nazirite's peace offering], but it does not require bread offering, [unlike a Nazirite's offering]. [Now if] she had coins that she had not designated for any specific purpose, they fall to a free-will offering. [If the] coins [were] designated [for a specific purpose] — those designated for a sin offering are to go off to the Dead Sea. They are not available for benefit, but the laws of sacrilege do not apply to them. The coins set aside for the purchase of a burnt offering are used for the bringing of a burnt offering. And they are subject to the laws of sacrilege. The coins set aside for the purchase of a peace offering are used [for the bringing of a peace offering]. And [the animal] is eaten for one day and does not require a bread offering.

T. 3:16 [If] he sets aside coins for the purchase of offerings for his Naziriteship, they are not available for benefit but are not subject to the laws of sacrilege, for all of them [the coins which have been set aside] are suitable to serve for bringing peace-offerings. [If] he died, coins which have not been designated for the purchase of a particular sacrifice fall for the purchase of a freewill-offering [M. Naz. 4:4F]. Coins which have been designated [for the purchase of a particular sacrifice are dealt with as follows]: Those which have been set aside for the purchase of a sin-offering go off to the Salt Sea. They are not available for benefit but are not subject to the laws of sacrilege. Those which have been set aside for the purchase of a burnt-offering are used for the bringing of a burnt-offering. And they are subject to the laws of sacrilege. Those which are set aside for the purchase of a peace-offering are used for the offering of a peace-offering, which is eaten for one day and which does not require a bread-offering [M. Naz. 4:4A-M]. [If he said,] "These are for my burnt-offering, and the rest of the money is for the purchase of the rest of the offerings for my Naziriteship," and then he died, with the money set aside for the purpose of a burnt-offering, let [the executor] bring a burnt-offering. And the rest of the money falls for the purchase of a freewill-offering. [If he said that] these are for his peace-offering, and the rest is for the remainder of the offerings for his Naziriteship, and then died, with the money set aside for the purchase of a peace-offering, let one bring a peace-offering. And the rest of the money falls for the purchase of a freewill-offering. [If he said,] "These [coins] are for the purchase of my burnt-offering, and these for the purchase of my sin-offering, and the rest are for the purchase of the rest of the offerings for my Naziriteship," and then he died, the money set aside for the sin-offering goes off to the Salt Sea. It is not available for benefit but is not subject to the laws of sacrilege. [If he said,] "These are for my sin-offering, and these are for my burnt-offering, and these are for my peace-offering," and the coins got mixed up together, Lo, this one should purchase with them three beasts, whether from one part [of the mixture] or from three distinct [parts of the mixture of coins]. He renders the coins set aside for the purchase of a sin-offering unconsecrated on account of the animal to be used for the sin-offering [which he now has purchased], and the coins set aside for the purchase of a burnt-offering [are rendered] unconsecrated on account of the burnt-offering, and the coins set aside for the purchase of a peace-offering [are rendered] unconsecrated on account of the peace-offering. And he pays the coins over to the owners of the several animals. He should not pay out the money to the owners until he renders the coins unconsecrated by means of each of the animals [which he is purchasing].

Y. 4:4 II:3 There will be a guilt offering after the abrogation of the vow. [That is, the woman became unclean as a Nazirite and so owes a guilt offering, but the husband then abrogates the vow; she brings the guilt offering anyhow.] But if she should die, the guilt offering is not offered. [But since there is no guilt offering after death,] if she should die, the beast set aside as a guilt offering is not offered. If the husband should [merely] abrogate the vow [as we just noted], her guilt offering will be offered. If she should die, her guilt offering will not be offered, because you have no guilt offering that is prepared after the death of the sacrifier. If the husband should abrogate her vow, however, the animal designated as her guilt offering will be offered, for you have no guilt offering brought needlessly, as this one is.

[That is, a guilt offering normally would not be offered if the sacrifier already has atoned for the cause that the obligation applied to bring such a guilt offering. But in this case the guilt offering is offered.]

M. 4:5 Once the blood of any one of the offerings has been tossed for her, he cannot any longer annul the vow. Under what circumstances? In the case of the hair offering of a woman who has remained clean. But it was the hair offering of a woman who has become unclean, he may annul her vow. For he has the power to say, "I don't want a disgraceful wife."

M. 4:6 A man imposes a Nazirite vow upon his son, but a woman does not impose a Nazirite vow upon her son. How so? [If] he cut his hair, or his relatives cut his hair, he objected [and would not keep the vow] or his relatives objected — [If] he had a beast set apart [for his offering], the beast set aside as a sin offering is left to die. And the beast set aside as a burnt offering is offered as a burnt offering, and the one set aside as a peace offering is offered as a peace offering and eaten on one day and does not require a bread offering. [If] he had set aside coins [for the purchase of his offerings, and they] had not yet been designated, they fall to the purchase of a free-will offering. [If] the coins had been set aside and designated for particular purposes, the coins set aside for the purchase of a sin offering go off to the Salt Sea. They are not available for benefit, but they are not subject to the laws of sacrilege. The coins set aside for the purchase of a burnt offering are used for the bringing of a burnt offering, and they are subject to the laws of sacrilege. The coins set aside for the purchase of a peace offering are used for the bringing of a peace offering, which is eaten on one day and does not require a bread offering. A man brings a hair offering [with offerings set aside] for the Naziriteship of his father, but a woman does not bring a hair offering [with offerings set aside] for the Naziriteship of her father. How so? He who had a father who was a Nazirite, who had set aside coins for the purchase of his sacrifices, which had not been designated for his particular Naziriteship offerings, and whose [father] died, and he said, "Lo, I am a Nazirite on condition that I may bring a hair offering with the coins [set aside by my] father" — Lo, these coins fall to the purchase of a free-will offering. This one does not bring a hair offering [with money set aside] for the Naziriteship of his father. And what is the case in which one brings a hair offering [with money set aside] for the Naziriteship of his father? He who, along with his father, was a Nazirite, and his father set aside coins that were not designated for the purchase of particular animals for the fulfillment of his Nazirite vow and his father then] died — this is a case in which one brings a hair offering [with offerings set aside] for the Naziriteship of his father.

T. 3:17 A man does impose a Nazirite-vow on his son" [M. Naz. 4:6A]. [If] he imposed such a vow on him while he was a minor, [if] he then shaved, or produced two pubic hairs, the Nazirite vow imposed on him by his father is null.

M. 5:1 [An act of] consecration done in error is not binding [consecrated]. How so? [If] one said, "The black ox that goes out of my house first, lo, it is consecrated," and a white one went out — it is not consecrated. "The gold denar that comes into my hand first, lo, it is consecrated," and one of silver came up [into his hand] — it is not consecrated. "The jug of wine that comes up into my hand first, lo, it is consecrated," but one of oil came up — it is not consecrated.

M. 5:2 He who vowed to be a Nazirite and sought absolution of a sage, who declared his vow to be binding, counts out the days from the moment at which he took the vow. [If] he sought absolution from a sage, who declared him nor bound, if he had a cow set aside, it goes forth and pastures with the herd [never having been consecrated].

T. 3:19 He who vowed to be a Nazirite and sought absolution from a sage, who declared his vow to be binding, he counts out the days from the moment at which he treated the vow as not binding. [If] he sought absolution from a sage, who declared his vow to be not binding, these and those concur that if he had a beast set aside for his offerings, it should go forth and pasture in the herd [M. Naz. 5:2D-E].

M. 5:3 He who vowed to be a Nazirite and went to bring his beast [for the sacrifice] and found that it had been stolen, if before his beast was stolen he took the vow as a Nazirite, lo, this one is a Nazirite. And if after his beast was stolen [but he had not known it] he took the vow as a Nazirite, he is not a Nazirite. [It was a vow taken in error.]

M. 5:4 [If people] were going along the way and someone was coming toward them — one of them said, "Lo, I am a Nazirite if this is so-and-so," and one of them said, "Lo, I am a Nazirite if this is not so-and-so." "Lo, I am a Nazirite if one of you is a Nazirite." "Lo, I am a Nazirite if neither one of you is a Nazirite," "if both of you are Nazirs," "if all of you are Nazirs" — a Nazirite is only one whose statement was not confirmed. [If] one saw a koy and said, "Lo, I am a Nazirite if this is a wild beast. " "Lo, I am a Nazirite if this is not a wild beast." "Lo, I am a Nazirite if this is a domesticated beast." "Lo, I am a Nazirite if this is not a domesticated beast." "Lo, I am a Nazirite if this is a wild beast and a domesticated beast." "Lo, I am a Nazirite if this is not a wild beast and a domesticated beast." "Lo, I am Nazirite if one of you is a Nazirite." "Lo, I am a Nazirite if none of you is a Nazirite." "Lo,

I am a Nazirite if all of you are Nazirs" — lo, all of them are Nazirs.

Scripture provides for an elaborate rite at the conclusion of the Nazirite vow; the Halakhah, for its part, finds its own problems in amplifying the matter. First, what do we do if the beasts set aside for the offering are not needed for that purpose? That problem is generic, arising also in the case of sin-offerings not needed for the designated sin, for instance. Second, at what point does the husband's power to nullify the vow lapse? It is at the point at which the blood of one of her offerings at the end of the vow has been validly tossed against the altar. At that late point, the husband's power falls away, the vow being confirmed at the moment of its fulfillment. The meaning of "impose a Nazirite vow upon" at M. 4:6 is clearly, impose the requirement of observing the vow including that of presenting the offerings. The father then designates the animal offerings at the point of imposing the vow; the power of the initial "imposition" concerns the beasts the father has designated: they have to be properly disposed of. The father cannot impose the restrictions of the vow against the adult son's will.

The Halakhah generically concerns itself with the power of intentionality, and here at issue is an act of consecration carried out in error, M. 5:1. Since the motivating intentionality rests on a mistake, it is not carried out and produces no effect. That principle does not require the special vow of the Nazirite for its instantiation, and M. 5:1 concerns act of sanctification in general, only M. 5:3 introducing the particular details of that vow.

III. RESTRICTIONS ON THE NAZIRITE

A. *THE GRAPE*
M. 6:1 Three things are prohibited to a Nazirite: [corpse] uncleanness, cutting the hair, and anything that goes forth from the grapevine. And anything that exudes from the grapevine joins together with anything else that exudes from the grapevine [to form a volume prohibited for use]. And one is liable only if he will eat about an olive's bulk of grapes.

T. 4:1 A Nazirite who ate anything which is prohibited to him or drank anything which is prohibited to him, [if he was subject] to a single admonition not to do so, he is liable on only one count. [But if] people admonished him and he nonetheless ate, people admonished him and he nonetheless drank, he is liable for each and every count [cf. M. Naz. 6:4]. And what is the measure [to impose liability] for them? In the volume of an olive's bulk [M. Naz. 6:1C]. And all of them join together to form the requisite volume of an olive's bulk [M. Naz. 6:1B]. Wine and vinegar follow suit. What does he do [to reckon the liquid-volume of an olive]? He brings a cup filled with wine, and he brings a summer olive, and he puts it into the cup and lets it spill over.

Y. 6:1 II:5 If one has eaten five ants at once, in a single spell of inadvertence, he is liable on each count because in each instance it was a creature unto itself. But if he mashed them up and ate them, he is liable on only one count. But that law applies when they constitute the bulk of an olive. If he ate what was mashed up, and it completes the measure to an olive's bulk, he is liable. If he ate from what is mashed up in the bulk of an olive, and an additional ant, he is liable on two counts. If that is the case, then if he ate from what is mashed up but forms less than the olive's bulk, and he added to the mash a whole ant, he should be liable on two counts. If so, then if he ate an ant of the bulk of an olive, he should be liable on two counts. So is the rule covering the joining together of what is prohibited to a Nazirite. If he ate from a mixture of diverse prohibited materials that adds up to the bulk of an olive, he is liable. If he ate from such a mixture of forbidden materials in the bulk of an olive, and in addition he ate the stalk of a grape, he is liable on two counts. If that is the case, then if he ate the branch of a grape that is an olive's bulk, he should be liable on two counts.

M. 6:2 And he is liable for wine by itself, for grapes by themselves, for grape pits by themselves, and for grape skins by themselves.

M. 6:3 A Nazirite vow for an unspecified period of time is [to apply] for thirty days. [If] he cut his hair, or thugs forcibly cut his hair, he loses thirty days. A Nazirite who cut his hair, whether with scissors or with a razor, or who pulled out any hair whatsoever, is liable. A Nazirite shampoos and parts his hair [with his fingers], but he does not comb his hair.

T. 4:3 A Nazirite who shaved or who rubbed his head or who pulled out a hair with a scissors in any amount at all, lo, this one is liable. But he loses [the days he already has observed] only if he does so with a razor to the greater part of his head.

Y. 6:3 I:4 You rule with regard to an unclean Nazirite: Failure to cut off even two hairs invalidates his hair cutting. Removal of as many as two hairs causes him to lose days he already has observed. And along these same lines with regard to a clean Nazirite: Failure to cut off two hairs invalidates the hair cutting. Cutting off as few as two hairs causes him to lose days already observed.

M. 6:4 A Nazirite who was drinking wine all day long is liable only on one count. [If] they said to him, "Don't drink it! Don't drink it!" and he continues drinking, he is liable on each and every count [of drinking]. [If] he was cutting his hair all day

long, he is liable only on a single count. [If] they said to him, "Don't cut it! Don't cut it!" and he continued to cut his hair, he is liable for each and every count [of cutting]. [If] he was contracting corpse uncleanness all day long, he is liable on only one count. If they said to him, "Don't contract corpse uncleanness! Don 't contract corpse uncleanness!" and he continued to contract corpse uncleanness, he is liable for each and every count.

Y. 6:4 I:2 *If there were set before a Nazirite two flasks, one containing water, and one containing wine, and he drank the one containing water, and they said to him, "You should know that, what you are drinking is water, but if you drink the wine, there are ten olive's bulks in volume of wine, and you will be liable for ten floggings" — he has not received an admonition on that assumption. But if there was one flask of wine, and he began to drink it, and they said to him, "You should know if you drink the whole of it, that it contains in volume ten olive's bulks of wine, and you will be liable for ten floggings," he has received an admonition on that assumption [and will be flogged ten times if he drinks the whole flask]. If there were before a man two spits of meat, one containing properly slaughtered meat, the other containing carrion meat, if he then took the one containing properly slaughtered meat, and they said to him, "What you are now eating is properly slaughtered meat. If you should eat the one containing carrion, there are ten olive's bulks of carrion on it, and you will be liable for ten floggings," he has not thereby received a warning on that assumption. But if there was a single spit, containing only carrion meat, and he began to eat it, and they said to him, "You should know that if you should eat the whole thing, it contains ten olive's bulks in volume of carrion meat, and you will thereby become liable for ten floggings," he thereby has received suitable admonition in that assumption [and will be liable should he proceed as planned].*

M. 6:5 Three things are prohibited to a Nazirite: [corpse] uncleanness, cutting the hair, and anything that goes forth from the grapevine. A more strict rule applies to corpse uncleanness and haircutting than applies to that which comes forth from the grapevine. For corpse uncleanness and haircutting cause the loss of the days already observed, but [violating the prohibition against] that which goes forth from the vine does not cause the loss of the days already observed. A more strict rule applies to that which goes forth from the vine than applies to corpse uncleanness and haircutting. For that which goes forth from the vine allows for no exception, but corpse uncleanness and haircutting allow for exceptions, m the case of [cutting the hair for] a religious duty and in the case of finding a neglected corpse [with no one else to provide for burial, in which case, the Nazirite is absolutely required to bury the corpse]. A more strict rule applies to corpse uncleanness than to haircutting. For corpse uncleanness causes the loss of all the days previously observed and imposes the liability for an offering. But haircutting causes the loss of only thirty days and does not impose liability for an offering.

T. 4:4 A more strict rule applies to the cutting of the hair. For the cutting of the hair is subject to no limit. And [the law] treats the one who cuts the hair as equivalent to the one whose hair is cut, which is not the case for the other two things [M. Naz. 6:5]. How is it so that for that which goes forth from the vine there is no exception [M. Naz. 6:5E]? A Nazirite who drank wine in the status of heave-offering in the status of second tithe — one who said, "By an oath! I shall not drink wine," but drank it — such as these are liable for each and every such action. How is it so tsshat cutting of the hair is allowed an exception in the case of a religious duty [M. Naz. 6:5F]? A man who had been certified as a mesora", lo, this one cuts his hair. One need not say that he cuts his hair in connection with his sara'at, but he even does so also to allow for the inspection-sign of his boil-to see whether or not it spread. Whether he was made unclean or others made him unclean, whether inadvertently or deliberately, whether under constraint or willingly, he loses all the days already observed, and is liable for an offering [M. Naz. 6:5H]. Whether he cut his own hair or others cut his hair, whether inadvertently or deliberately, whether under constraint or willingly, he loses only thirty days [M. Naz. 6:5H].

T. 4:5 Under what circumstances did they rule, Cutting the hair causes the loss of thirty days [already observed] [M. Naz. 6:5]? When he had no more days to count. But if he had yet more days to count, lo, this one does not lose any days. [If] he cut his hair on account of a sacrifice, and it turned out to be invalid, he loses thirty days.

Here the Halakhah's generic hermeneutics dictates the topical exposition. Once more at issue is the problem of mixtures, here: the difference between a single, protracted spell of law-violation, and a sequence of distinct spells. The former imposes a single count, the latter, many. Reading M. 6:1 in line with M. 6:2, the Tosefta at T. 4:1 introduces the general issue. M. 6:4 goes over the same ground.

B. *CUTTING HAIR*

M. 6:6 Cutting off the hair on account of contracting corpse uncleanness: how [is it done]? One would sprinkle [with purification water] on the third and seventh day and cut off his hair on the seventh day [the purification process having been completed] and bring his offerings on the eighth day. But if he cut off his hair on the eighth day, he brings his offerings on that same day.

M. 6:7 The cutting of hair in the case of [completing the vow in a state of] cleanness: How is it done? [It is an ordinary rite, carried out at the Temple.] One would bring three beasts, a sin offering, a burnt offering, and a peace offering [Num. 6:14].

M. 6:8 He would take "the hair of the head of his separation " (Num. 6:18) and cast it under the cauldron [in which the peace offering is cooked]. And if he cut it off in the provinces, he would [in any event] cast it under the cauldron. Under what circumstances? In the case of [completing the vow and] cutting the hair in a state of cleanness. But in the case of cutting the hair in a state of uncleanness, he would not cast it under the cauldron.

T. 4:6 All cast hair under the cauldron, except for someone who cut his hair in the provinces on account of uncleanness [M. Naz. 6:8H], because his hair is to be buried. How does one cast it under the cauldron? One puts some broth on it and casts it under the cauldron of the peace-offering. But if one cast it under the cauldron of the sin-offering or of the guilt-offering, he has fulfilled his obligation.

M. 6:9 He would cook the peace offerings or seethe [the offering]. The priest takes "the cooked shoulder of the ram and one unleavened cake out of the basket and one unleavened wafer and puts them into the hand of the Nazirite" (Num. 6:19). And he waves them. And afterwards the Nazirite is permitted to drink wine and to contract corpse uncleanness.

M. 6:10 [If] he cut off his hair after a sacrifice and the sacrifice turned out to be invalid, his cutting of the hair is invalid, and his sacrifices have not gone to his credit. [If] he cut his hair after a sin offering made not for its own name [under an incorrect designation], and afterward he brought his [other] offerings under their proper designation, his cutting of the hair is invalid, and his sacrifices have not gone to his credit. [If] he cut his hair after the burnt offering or the peace offering improperly designated and afterward he brought his [other] offerings under their proper designation, his cutting of the hair is invalid, and his sacrifices have not gone to his credit. And if he cut his hair after all three of them and one of them turned out to be valid, his cutting of the hair is valid, and be brings the other sacrifices.

T. 4:8 A Nazirite who was made unclean and again was made unclean and again was made unclean brings a single offering for the whole spell of uncleanness.

T. 4:9 That which is appropriate to be brought at the age of one year which he brought at the age of two years, at the age of two years which he brought at the age of one year or if one of the animals which he brought had committed bestiality with a human being, or had suffered bestiality with a human being, or had been set aside for idolatrous worship, or had actually been worshipped, or was the fee paid to a harlot or the price paid for a dog, or had one hip larger than the other, or had not cloven hoofs — his cutting of the hair is invalid, and his sacrifices have not gone to his credit [M. Naz. 6:10A]. And as to the remainder of the peace-offering of a Nazirite which he brought not in accord with its requirement, it is eaten for one day and the following night, and it does not require either a bread offering or the giving of the shoulder to the priest. He in whose behalf one of the drops of blood was properly tossed and who was made unclean brings the rest of his offerings when he is clean [M. Naz. 6:11A-C]. because the hair already has been sanctified by the blood.

T. 4:11 He who took two vows of Naziriteship, counted out the first but did not bring his offerings, is prohibited from cutting his hair and from drinking wine and from contracting corpse-uncleanness.

M. 6:11 He in whose behalf one of the drops of blood has been properly tossed and who [then] is made unclean — let him bring the rest of his offerings when he becomes clean.

I see nothing more than a systematic recapitulation of facts on how the hair offering is carried out.

C. *CORPSE-UNCLEANNESS*

M. 7:1 A high priest and a Nazirite do not contract corpse uncleanness on account of [burying even] their close relatives. [But they do contract corpse uncleanness on account of a neglected corpse]. [If] they were going along the way and found a neglected corpse — let a Nazirite contract corpse uncleanness, but let a high priest not contract corpse uncleanness, for his sanctification is not a permanent sanctification, but let a priest not contract corpse uncleanness, for his sanctification is a permanent sanctification.

M. 7:2 On account of what sorts of uncleanness does the Nazirite cut his hair [and bring an offering for having become unclean]? On account of a corpse, and on account of an olive's bulk of flesh from a corpse, and on account of an olive's bulk of corpse matter, and on account of a ladleful of corpse mould; on account of the backbone, and on account of the skull, and on account of a limb of a corpse, and on account of a limb cut from a living human being on which is still proper flesh; and on account of a half-qab of bones, and on account of a half-log of blood — on account of touching them, and on account of carrying them, and on account of overshadowing them; and on account of a bone the bulk of a barley seed — on account of touching it and on account of carrying it. On account of these, the Nazirite cuts his hair and is sprinkled on the third and seventh day [after contamination].

And he loses the days that he has already observed. And he begins to count [clean days] only after he is made clean and brings his offerings.

T. 5:1 All those concerning whom they have ruled, "He does not begin to count the days of his Nazirite-vow until he becomes clean" [M. Naz. 7:2J] — if he becomes unclean, he does not bring an offering on account of his uncleanness. All those concerning whom they have ruled, "He begins to count and counts his Nazirite days forthwith," [M. Naz. 7:3E], if he is made unclean he does bring an offering on account of uncleanness. A bit of corpse-uncleanness which is located above the wall, even half on one side and half on the other — and so too: living rows of cattle, wild beasts, or fowl, which were walking one after the other, even if the head of one is between the hind-legs of the other — a Nazirite does not cut his hair on account of [their having overshadowed both him and a bit of corpse-matter]. And people [affected by their overshadowing] who enter the Temple or touch its Holy Things are not liable for contaminating the Temple and its Holy Things [M. Naz. 7:4A-C].

M. 7:3 But as to [uncleanness contracted by overshadowing] interlaced foliage, projecting stones, a grave area, foreign land, the sealing stone and the buttressing stone [of a grave], a quarter log of blood, and a tent, and a quarter qab of bones, and utensils that touch a corpse, and because of the days of counting [after producing a symptom of sara'at (Lev. 14:8)] and the days during which he is certified [unclean with sara'at] — on account of these, the Nazirite does not cut his hair or sprinkle himself on the third and seventh days and he does not lose the prior days [observed m cleanness]. And he begins to count forthwith [after immersion and sunset]. And he is not subject to bringing an offering. Truly did they rule: The days [of uncleanness] by reason of being a zab or zabah (Lev. 15:2, 25, 28), and the days of being shut up as mesora' (Lev. 13:4-10, these [nonetheless] go to his credit [in counting out his Nazirite days].

Not only is the Nazirite comparable to a priest, he is comparable to a high priest, in that both the Nazirite and the high priest may not contract corpse uncleanness even to bury their close relatives. That underscores the comparison of the standing of the two vis à vis a neglected corpse, the burial of which overrides the prohibitions affecting the high priest and the Nazirite. What we have is speciation and hierarchization of status as to sanctification — a perfectly familiar exercise in the Halakhah. M. 7:2-3 go over equally familiar ground, defining for the present purpose the character of contaminating corpse matter.

D. *DOUBTS IN THE CASE OF A NAZIRITE*

M. 8:1 Two Nazirs, to whom someone said, "I saw one of you made unclean, but I don't know which one of you it was" — [they cut their hair] and bring an offering [owed by a Nazirite] because of uncleanness and an offering because of cleanness. And each one of them says, "If it was I who was unclean, the offering because of uncleanness is mine, and the offering because of cleanness is yours. And if it was I who was the clean one, then the offering of cleanness is mine, and the offering of uncleanness is yours." Then they count out thirty days and bring an offering because of cleanness. And each one of them says, "If it was I who was unclean, the offering because of uncleanness was mine and the offering of cleanness was yours, and this offering is now because of my being clean. But if it was I who was the clean one, the offering because of uncleanness was mine, and the offering because of cleanness was yours, and this offering now is because of your being clean."

T. 5:3 Two Nazirs, to whom someone said, "I saw one of you made unclean, but I do not know which one of you it was" — they count out thirty days and bring an offering for uncleanness and an offering for cleanness. And they say, "If I was the unclean one, then the offering for uncleanness is mine and the offering for cleanness is yours, and if I am the clean one, then the offering for cleanness is mine, and the offering for uncleanness is yours." And they count out thirty days more and bring an offering for cleanness. And one says, "If I am the unclean one, then this offering for uncleanness was mine and the offering for cleanness is yours, and this is the offering for my state of cleanness. But if I was the clean one, then the offering for cleanness was mine, and the offering for uncleanness was yours, and this offering is for your state of cleanness" [M. Naz. 8:1A-E].

M. 8:2 A Nazirite who was subject to doubt as to being made unclean [on the day he took the vow] and subject to doubt as to being a confirmed [victim of sara'at] eats Holy Things after sixty days [= two Nazirite periods]. And he drinks wine and contracts corpse uncleanness after a hundred-and-twenty days [four Nazirite periods]. For cutting of the hair in the case of a nega [sara'at] overrides [the prohibition against] cutting the hair of the Nazirite [only] when [the [sara'at] is certain. But in a case when it is subject to doubt, it does not override [the other].

T. 6:1 [If] it is a matter of doubt whether a Nazirite was unclean or clean, but it is certain that he was a Nazirite, if it is a matter of doubt whether a mesora' was unclean or clean, but it is certain that he was a mesora', he eats Holy Things after sixty days, drinks wine and contracts corpse-uncleanness after one hundred and twenty days [M. Naz. 8:2A-C]. How so? [If] they said to him, "You are an unclean Nazirite, and an unclean Nazirite cuts his hair only after seven days, so go and count out seven days," and he was sprinkled and the sprinkling-process was repeated, and he cut his hair and brought an offering, [if] he counted out seven days and sought to cut his hair, and they said to him, "You are a clean Nazirite, and a clean Nazirite cuts his hair only after thirty days, go and count out twenty-three more days to complete the required thirty days," he cut his hair and brought his offering, [if] he counted out thirty days and sought to cut his hair and they said to him, "You are a clean Nazirite, and a clean Nazirite cuts his hair only after the blood has been tossed," what should he then do? He brings a burnt-offering in the form of a beast and makes the following stipulation concerning it, saying, "Now if I am clean, lo, this is brought in fulfillment of my obligation, and if not, lo, this is a freewill-offering." How should it be done for him to impose the more stringent ruling upon him [as a possibly-confirmed mesora']? He brings a new clay jug and puts into it a quarter-log of spring water and brings two wild birds and slaughters one of them over the earthenware utensil into the spring water. He digs a hole and buries it in his presence, and it is prohibited for the benefit [of anybody]. Then he brings a sin-offering in the form of a bird and makes the following stipulation concerning it, saying, "Now if I am unclean, the sin-offering is in fulfillment of my obligation, and the burnt-offering is a freewill-offering. But if I am clean, then the burnt-offering is in fulfillment of my obligation and the sin-offering is subject to doubt." And he cuts the hair on his head, beard, and eyebrows, just as mesora's cut their hair, and he brings the burnt-offering of a beast and makes the following condition concerning it, saying, "Now if I was unclean, the first burnt-offering was a freewill offering, and this one is in fulfillment of my obligation. And the sin-offering in the form of fowl is on account of my obligation. But if I am clean, then the first burnt-offering was a fulfillment of my obligation. And this one is a freewill-offering. And the sin-offering in the form of a bird is subject to doubt." And he cuts off the hair of his head, beard, and eyebrows, just as the mesora's cut off their hair. This guilt-offering then is slaughtered on the north side of the altar. And its blood has to be placed on the thumbs and big toes of the man, and it requires laying on of hands, and drink-offerings, and the waving of the breast and thigh, and it is eaten by the male priests. To offer a sin-offering of a beast is something he cannot do, because a sin-offering in the form of a beast is not offered in a case of doubt. To offer a sin-offering in the form of a bird is something he cannot do. For a rich man who brought the offering of a poor man has not fulfilled his obligation [M. Neg. 14:12]. So what should he do? Let him write over his property to someone else and then bring the offering of a poor man. It turns out that the poor man brings a sin-offering in the form of a bird, and makes the following condition concerning it, saying, "If I was a Mesora' — lo, this is in fulfillment of my obligation. And if not, lo, this is given because of the doubt concerning me." And he is permitted to eat Holy Things forthwith. But as to drinking wine and contracting corpse-uncleanness, these are things he has not got the power to do. For the days of his Nazirite-vow are not credited on account of the days in which he is subject to sara'at. Under what circumstances? When he took the vow of a Nazirite for thirty days. But if he took the vow as a Nazirite for twelve months, he eats Holy Things only after two years have passed. And he drinks wine and contracts corpse-uncleanness after four years have passed. If one was in doubt as to being unclean but certainly shut up as a mesora', he eats Holy Things after eight days. He drinks wine and contracts corpse-uncleanness after sixty-seven days. If he was certainly unclean but subject to doubt as to whether he was a mesora', he eats Holy Things after thirty-seven days, he drinks wine and contracts corpse-uncleanness after seventy-four days. If he was unclean of a certainty and determined to be a mesora' of a certainty, he eats Holy Things after eight days. And he drinks wine and contracts corpse-uncleanness after forty-four days.

M. 9:1 Gentiles are not subject to the Nazirite vow. Women and slaves are subject to the Nazirite vow. A more strict rule applies to women than to slaves. For a master forces his slave [to be subject to a Nazirite vow], but a husband does not force his wife [to be subject to a Nazirite vow]. A more strict rule applies to slaves than to women. For the husband has the right to annul the vows of his wife, but he does not [permanently] annul the vows of his slaves. [If] he annulled [the vow] of his wife, it is annulled for all time. [If] he annulled [the vow] of his slave, [if] the slave went forth to freedom, he has to complete his Nazirite vow.

T. 6:4 A more strict rule applies to a man's wife and his daughter which does not apply to his boy-servant or his girl-servant, [and a strict rule applies] to his boy-servant and girl-servant which does not apply to his wife and his daughter. For as to his wife and his daughter, he annuls their vows. And he cannot force them to drink wine or to contract corpse-uncleanness [M. Naz. 9:1D]. But as to his boy-servant or his girl-servant, he does not annul their vows. But he does force them to drink wine or to contract corpse-uncleanness [M. Naz. 9:1F]. And they drink wine only when in his presence, and they contract corpse-uncleanness only in his presence [M. Naz. 9:1L].

M. 9:2 A Nazirite who cut his hair and then [before he brought his offerings] learned that he had been unclean — if it was a known uncleanness he loses [all the days he has counted in cleanness]. But if it was an uncleanness located in the nethermost deep, he does not lose the days he already has counted out. If

before he had cut his hair he learned that he had been made unclean, one way or the other, he loses the days he already has observed. How so? [If] he went down to immerse in a cave and a bit of corpse matter turned out to be floating at the mouth of the cave, he is unclean. [If] it was located imbedded in the floor of the cave — [if] he had gone down only to cool himself in the water, he is deemed still clean. [If he had gone down] to clean himself from corpse uncleanness, he is yet unclean. For the unclean person is confirmed in the presumption of being unclean, and the clean one is confirmed in the presumption of being clean. For there are grounds for such a decision [in either case].

T. 6:2 For all offerings of the community and the individual, the priestly frontlet effects expiation for uncleanness of the blood and for uncleanness of the body [of the owner], except for the case of the Nazirite and the one who prepares the Passover. For in these cases the priestly frontlet effects expiation for uncleanness of the blood, but it does not effect expiation for uncleanness of the body. But if he is made unclean by reason of uncleanness of the nethermost depths, lo, it does effect uncleanness in his behalf. How so? [If] he was going along to slaughter his Passover or to circumcise his son, and they said to him, "There was a corpse with you in that house which you entered," or "...under the stone on which you were sitting," and if he was informed of this fact, whether he had already prepared his Passover or whether he had not already prepared his Passover, he has to prepare a second Passover. But [if] they told to him, "There was a grave in the nethermost depths with you in that house into which you entered," or "...under that stone on which you were sitting," if he was so informed of that fact before he had prepared his Passover, then he has to prepare a second Passover [in a state of cleanness]. But if he was so informed after he had prepared his Passover, he does not have to prepare a second Passover.

T. 6:3 And so is the rule in the case of a Nazirite who went to offer his offerings, and they said to him, "There was a corpse with you in that house which you entered," or "...under the stone on which you were sitting," and he was so informed, whether this was before or after he brought his offerings, he has to bring an offering on account of uncleanness. But [if] they told him, "There was a grave in the nethermost depths with you in that house which you entered," or "...under that stone on which you were sitting," and he was so informed before he had brought his offerings, he has to bring an offering on account of uncleanness. But if this was told to him after he had brought his offerings, he does not have to bring an offering on account of uncleanness [M. Naz. 9:2A-E].

Y. 9:2 I:2 [If the Nazirite] had completed observing his vow as a Nazirite but did not suffice to cut off his hair before he was informed concerning his having been made unclean as a matter of doubt by reason of a grave in the nethermost deep, he loses the days he already has observed. If, however, he had designated animals for his offerings, but had not then sufficed to cut off his hair before he was informed concerning his having been made unclean as a matter of doubt by reason of a grave in the nethermost deep, [how do rabbis, B, deal with this case? Does the fact that he has designated the animals for his offerings constitute a decisive turning as against the mere doubt represented by the buried grave?] In the view of sages it makes no difference whether the blood had already been tossed in his behalf or had not in fact been tossed in his behalf.

M. 9:3 He who finds a corpse in the first instance lying in usual fashion removes it and the earth affected by it. [If] he found two, he removes them and the earth surrounding them. [If] he found three, if there are between one and the other from four to eight amahs, lo, this is deemed a graveyard. He examines the dirt twenty amahs from it. [If] he found a corpse at the end of the twenty amahs, he examines the dirt another twenty amahs from that corpse. For there are grounds for such a decision. But if he had found it at the outset, he would have removed it and the dirt affected by it.

M. 9:4 Any matter of doubt concerning nega's at the outset is ruled as clean before a decision has been made in favor of uncleanness. [But if] a decision has been made in favor of uncleanness, a matter of doubt in its regard is deemed unclean [M. Neg. 5:4]. In seven ways do they examine the zab [of Lev. 15] before he has been confirmed to be subject to zibah: In regard to food, drink, carrying things, jumping up and down, sickness, something he had seen, and something in his fantasy. Once he has been confirmed as to zibah, they do not examine him. Any flux he produces through constraint, or which is subject to doubt, or his semen is unclean. For there are grounds for such a decision.

M. 9:5 He who hits his fellow, whether with a stone or with his fist, and they diagnosed him as likely to die, [but] he got better than he was, and afterward he got worse and died — he is liable.

We take up yet another conventional Halakhic issue, pertinent to a broad variety of category-formations: cases of doubt, a subset of the problem of mixtures. Here we ask how we sort out a situation in which one of two Nazirites is certainly unclean, but we do not know which one (M. 8:1). The Tosefta, T. 6:1, refines the classifications at hand but goes over the same principles.

The difference between the slave and the woman, M. 9:1, is that the slave is subject to the master's will, but the woman in this case is not. Where the husband has the power to dispose of the wife's will, he exercises that power.

IV. DOCUMENTARY TRAITS

A. THE MISHNAH AND THE TOSEFTA

We have noted a number of points at which the Tosefta improves upon the Mishnah's presentation of the Halakhah. But the only program of interpreting the category-formation at hand that I discern is the Mishnah's. We have no reason to anticipate significant results in the contrast of the Tosefta to the Mishnah.

B. THE YERUSHALMI AND THE BAVLI

The Talmuds' contribution to the framing of the category-formation is negligible.

C. THE AGGADAH AND THE HALAKHAH IN THE BAVLI

I identify these asymptotic entries in the Bavli's presentation of the category-formation of Nazir:

XIV.B	free-standing exposition of a problem, inserted here because the Mishnah-rule at hand is invoked in the solution of the problem
XXIV.B	composite on the theme of intentionality, expounded because of the Mishnah-rule that concerns the case of someone who intends to violate the law but actually does not do so; with a sub-set on a specific problem in that connection
XXV.D	free-standing exposition of a problem, inserted here because the Mishnah-rule at hand is invoked in the solution of the problem
XXXVIII.C	topical appendix: when priests contract corpse uncleanness, inserted here because the Mishnah-rule deals with Nazirites' contracting corpse uncleanness
XLVII.D	topical composite on corpse-mould, inserted because the Mishnah-rule introduces that topic
LI.C	topical composite on the theme of cutting the hair, head and body alike, inserted here because the Mishnah-rule deals with that topic

LXI.B composite on reciting a blessing, completely irrelevant to the context but part of the subscript for the entire tractate

The program of the Mishnah has dictated the character of the Talmud throughout. The composites that do not take up the task of Mishnah-exegesis, narrowly construed, turn out to deal with the Mishnah in one of two ways: either a Mishnah-rule is invoked in a discussion that is otherwise not relevant to the problem of the exegesis of Mishnah-tractate Nazir (XIV.B, XXV.D), or a composite on a theme is inserted because the Mishnah, for its part, has touched upon that theme. I cannot point to any anomalous composition or composite — one that is not devoted to Mishnah-exegesis — that does not fit into one or the other category, except for LXI.B. Now the issue is, have these entries changed the face of the Bavli-tractate's re-presentation of the Mishnah-tractate and its topic? The answer is, they have in no way revised the Mishnah-tractate's presentation of the subject, the Nazirite vow. There is one composite of interest, which follows:

XXIV. MISHNAH-TRACTATE NAZIR 4:3
A. **A woman who took a vow as a Nazirite but nonetheless went around drinking wine and contracting corpse uncleanness — lo, this one receives forty stripes. [If] her husband released the vow for her, but she did not know that her husband had released it for her and nonetheless continued to go around drinking wine and contracting corpse uncleanness, she does not receive forty stripes. R. Judah says, "If she does not receive forty stripes, nonetheless, she should receive punishment for disobedience."**

1. [I.1] *Our rabbis have taught on Tannaite authority:* "Her husband has made them void and the Lord shall forgive her" (Num. 30:13) — Of whom does Scripture speak? It speaks of a woman who took a vow to be a Nazirite, **[and] her husband annulled the vow for her, but she did not know that her husband had annulled it for her and nonetheless continued to go around drinking wine and contracting corpse uncleanness [M. Naz. 4:3C].**, for she requires atonement and forgiveness."

B. TOPICAL APPENDIX ON THE THEME OF INTENTIONALITY [1:1]. *When R. Aqiba would come to this verse, he wept, saying,* "If someone intended to eat ham and really had in hand veal, yet the Torah has said that he requires atonement and forgiveness, one who intends to eat ham and really had in hand ham — all the more so!"

1. [I.2] *Said Rabbah bar bar Hannah said R. Yohanan, "What is the meaning of the verse of Scripture, 'For the paths of the*

Lord are straight, that the righteous shall pass along them, but the transgressors will stumble in them' (Hos. 14:10)? The matter may be compared to the case of two men who roasted their Passover offerings. One of them ate it for the sake of performing the religious duty, and the other one ate it to stuff himself with a big meal. The one who ate it for the sake of performing a religious duty — 'the righteous shall pass along them.' And as to the one who ate it to stuff himself with a big meal — 'but the transgressors will stumble in them'"

1. SUBSET ON LOT AND ABRAHAM

a. [I.3] Said R. Yohanan, "The entire verse of Scripture is formulated to express the intention of committing a transgression, as it is said, 'And Lot lifted his eyes and saw the entire plain of the Jordan that it was well watered' (Gen. 13:10).

b. [I.4] Rabbah expounded, "What is the meaning of the verse of Scripture: 'A brother offended the mighty city, and contention is like the bars of a castle' (Prov. 18:19)? 'A brother offended the mighty city:' this refers to Lot, who took his leave from Abraham in order to sin with his daughters.

c. [I.5] *Raba, or some say, R. Isaac, expounded, "What is the meaning of the verse of Scripture:* 'To lust is a separatist drawn, and of any wisdom will he be contemptuous' (Prov. 18:1)?"

d. [I.6] Said Ulla, "Tamar committed an act of prostitution, and Zimri committed an act of prostitution."

2. [I.7] Said R. Nahman bar Isaac, "A transgression committed for its own sake, in a sincere spirit, is greater in value than a religious duty carried out not for its own sake, but in a spirit of insincerity.

a. [I.8] [Reverting to the body of the foregoing:] Said R. Judah said Rab, "A person should always be occupied in study of the Torah and in practice of the commandments, even if this is not for its own sake [but in a spirit of insincerity], for out of doing these things not for their own sake, a proper spirit of doing them for their own sake will emerge."

The amplification of the rule that the wife who has deliberately violated an oath thinking it is valid when in fact it is null is not subject to sanctions. This leads to a broader inquiry into the relationship between intentionality and deed. I see no way in which the category-formation is vastly recast by this excellent Aggadic amplification.

V. THE HERMENEUTICS OF NAZIR

A. WHAT FUSES THE HALAKHIC DATA INTO A CATEGORY-FORMATION?

The generic vow imparts to secular persons, actions, and materials the status of the sacred — but that is so only for the person who takes the vow. The special vow of the Nazirite imparts but only to the person that takes that vow — a man or a woman — the pretend-status of a priest at the altar, indeed, of a high priest. It would be difficult to point to a more blatant case of the taxonomic power of language to transform the character and status of persons — or a more paradoxical one. For at the foundations of the power of language to make real the pretense that is involved — and that engages Heaven in the acting out of the pretense — is the priority of the individual's intentionality. If a person intends to treat as consecrated what is secular or to spend a month (or a lifetime) pretending to be at the ready as a priest or a high priest, and if he or she states that intentionality in language however approximate, Heaven confirms the transaction.

At Nedarim and Nazir alike, the governing hermeneutics is the same. It is the principle that language matters because of what it represents and conveys, which is, the solemn intentionality of the one who uses the language, and that is the key to all else. Language makes public and attracts public attention to the intentionality of the private person, forms the point of intersection ("the interface") between the individual and the community. That personal intentionality is transformed into an objective, affective fact of nature and society. When it comes to the theme and problem at hand — the interplay of intentionality and language — the Halakhah uniformly explores the matter in its impact upon Israel's relationship with God, Israel's social order, and Israel's life within the household, all three. That is the hermeneutics particular to the category-formation before us and its companion, Nazir and Nedarim.

Having identified what is distinctive, we immediately turn to the two other sources of interpreting and selecting the data of the category-formation: Scripture and the generic hermeneutics of the Halakhah. We cannot ask either Scripture or the documentary hermeneutics of the Mishnah to explain the particular hermeneutics of Nazir. When we ask what is particular to Nazir, however, we find little result from the appeal to analogical-contrastive reasoning. The classical writings themselves demonstrate that fact. At a number of points in the Halakhah we noted the difference between the generic vow and the Nazirite vow. Moreover, the Tosefta and the Mishnah at M. Neg. 14:4 contribute comparisons of the Nazirite to comparable categories of persons who cut the hair. The Tosefta compares the Nazirite and the mesora, and the Nazirite vow to the oath:

> T. 1:6 A more strict rule applies to the Nazirite than applies to the mesora' [one who is afflicted with the skin ailment of Lev. 13], and to the mesora' that does not apply to the Nazirite. A Nazirite, if he shaved on the day of completion of his vow, incurs forty stripes, which is not the case with the mesora'. A mesora' shaves his head, his beard, and his eyebrows, which is not the case with the Nazirite.
> T. 1:7 A more strict rule applies to Nazirite-vows than applies to oaths, and to oaths than to Nazirite-vows. For a Nazirite-vow may be found within another such vow, but an oath is not contained within another oath [M. Ned. 2:3]. A more strict rule applies to oaths, for an oath made inadvertently is binding, but a Nazirite-vow made inadvertently is not binding.

M. Neg. 14:4 compares the Nazirite to the mesora and the Levite:

> There are three who must cut their hair, and their hair-cutting is a religious duty: the Nazirite, the person afflicted with the skin ailment [mesora'], and Levites. And in the case of all of them, if one cut the hair without a razor, or left two hairs, he has accomplished nothing.
> M. Negaim 14:4

Neither comparison does more than sift and organize facts; I see no point that the comparison means to articulate. The Bavli's amplification, at B. Naz. 39b-40a, does little more than clarify details. But these comparisons and contrasts do not much shape the category-formation at hand.

Yet none can deny that the category-formation holds together and makes a coherent statement about its topic. The comparison with which we commenced, between Nedarim and Nazir, leaves no reasonable doubt that the whole is coherent; the data have been selected to make a distinctive point, one that, as a matter of fact, is quite distinct from Scripture's on the same topic. But that same comparison underscores that we cannot discuss the hermeneutics of Nazir outside of the framework of that of Nedarim. So let us consider them as a coherent category-formation, two species of a common genus that bear so much in common as to form a single, if complex, construct.

In both cases the hermeneutics takes up the use of language to single out a person vis à vis Heaven. In the one, the person declares "as if sanctified to Heaven" various goods and services that he receives from or supplies to others, and, as we saw in Nedarim, these are consequently deemed forbidden as sanctified. In the other, the person declares himself "as if a priest," indeed, "as if a high priest." Important prohibitions pertinent to the priesthood or to the high priesthood then apply. So language serves to sanctify, to enchant, even in the special circumstances of the private person who uses it — or especially in those circumstances. For however public and objective the interpretation of the effects of speech, nonetheless, we address the domestic circumstances of home and family, not public bodies, not the Temple, not the priesthood.

The larger part of the consequences of the use of special language — the illustrative materials of both bodies of Halakhah, Nedarim and Nazir — concerns relations of husbands and wives, or parents and children, hosts and guests, or the localized transactions of the household and the service-economy round-about (the shop-keeper or the peddler, for example), thus the household and the conduct of life therein. Only rarely does the language, e.g., of the vow or of the special vow of the Nazirite, spill over into the public affairs of Israel in general. Being private, the vow and the Nazirite vow have no consequences for the relationship of Israel to God in general; breaking the vow or failing to observe what is pledged concerns the individual and God, the community being a bystander to the transaction and bearing no stake therein. The category-formations involved in vows and Nazirite vows do not encompass public transactions within the social order, never alluding to a Nazirite's cow that gored the cow of a woman, or a man subject to a vow who struck another and injured him; the compensation is unaffected by the status of the Nazirite or the person who has taken a vow, in the way in which compensation is shaped by the status, e.g., of the slave, the minor, or the idiot:

> A. A deaf-mute, idiot, and minor — meeting up with them is a bad thing.
> B. He who injures them is liable.
> C. But they who injure other people are exempt.
> D. A slave and a woman — meeting up with them is a bad thing.
> E. He who injures them is liable.
> F. And they who injure other people are exempt.
>
> M. Baba Qamma 8:4

No such provision in public law ever takes account of the status of the Nazirite or the person subject to a vow; these do not define classifications of persons for which the social order publicly makes provision. The exemplary cases in Nedarim-Nazirite reinforce the essentially private circumstance of matters, their restriction to the household or the village formed by households. The matter of accepting gifts or hospitality hardly registers as a social event. In two of the three dimensions of Israel's world order, its public relationship with God and the conduct of its social order, vows and special vows make no material difference.

But, balancing the personal setting with the objective medium of language and its taxonomic power, the hermeneutics that governs here treats language used in private contexts as public and objective in effect. Language on its own is a public event, not subject to private manipulation. That is why "qorban"-language imparts sanctification to things that can never really serve in the Temple, and that is why euphemisms serve to impose the status of the Nazirite on one who uses them.

Intentionality matters in many category-formations of the Halakhah, but in connection with vows and the Nazirite vow in particular do sages localize their statement on the matter. Here they say, people bear direct, personal responsibility for what they say, and while statements made in error are null, those made in jest bear real consequences. That is why, as we have seen in the consideration of both bodies of Halakhah, euphemisms form so central a concern. There is no fooling around with God, no language exempt from God's hearing. What makes the Nazirite vow effective is language that an individual has used for his own subjective purpose. If he forms the intentionality and makes it public by expressing it in intelligible language, that suffices. It is the power of language to objectify matters, to bring about profound change in the status of a person who has used language in a strange way, speaking of ordinary things in the extraordinary setting of his own situation. This he does idiosyncratically by singling himself out before Heaven through "qorban"-language or through adopting priestly restrictions, as if eligible for service at the altar. Once he or she says that that is how things are willed, that is how, from Heaven's viewpoint, for that person, they must be.

B. THE ACTIVITY OF THE CATEGORY-FORMATION

[1] SCRIPTURE'S HERMENEUTICS: The Written Torah finds two points of interest in the present topic, the prohibitions upon the Nazirite, the offerings that come as the climax of the vow. The Nazirite then is comparable to a *kohen* or priest: subject to certain prohibitions and is assigned a particular position in the conduct of the Temple cult. The priest cannot serve if he is drunk or contaminated by a corpse or bald (a bald-headed man is invalid to serve as a priest, so M. Bekh. 7:2A). A single paradigm pertains, a single analogy governs. From the perspective of Scripture, once the Nazirite vow takes effect, prohibitions are invoked against wine, hair-cutting, and corpse-uncleanness; the other point of interest is the offerings that are required if the Nazirite is made unclean with corpse-uncleanness and when the Nazirite completes the vow in a state of cleanness.

All this the Halakhah both takes for granted and in the main simply ignores. What Scripture holds does not require detailed analysis, by contrast, is the process by which the woman or man becomes a Nazirite, that is to say, the vow itself. To that problem fully half of the Halakhah as defined by the Mishnah with the Tosefta is devoted.[20] So while the triple taboo is merely restated by the Halakhah of the Oral Torah, it is the exposition of the vow that defines the tough problems, generates interesting conundrums, and entails the rich exposition that the Tosefta and two Talmuds would ultimately provide.

[2] THE HALAKHAH'S GENERIC HERMENEUTICS: But in the Oral Torah, the Halakhah, for its part, characteristically ignores what is securely classified and instead takes up interstitial problems, generated by intersecting rules or classes of data. In the present case, the Halakhah focuses upon not the black-and-white language that invokes the vow, but on euphemisms that may or may not pertain, just as we saw with Nedarim. Language that is similar in sound or in sense takes effect. What about stipulations that might affect the vow, conditions under which the vow is or is not invoked, the taking of sequences of Nazirite-vows at a single moment? That is the next problem. The duration of the vow, undefined in Scripture, occupies attention. Then comes the intervention of the husband into the applicability of the vow his wife has taken. We turn, further, to designating the diverse animals that are to serve as the Nazirite's offerings at the end of the vow, with special attention to situations in which the animals are not used in accord with the original language of sanctification.

When it comes to the offerings of the Nazirite, the Halakhah — as at Pesahim and elsewhere — takes special interest in the interstitial case of the beast that has been consecrated but cannot be offered in fulfillment of the intent of the sacrifier: what to do with a beast designated for a given purpose that no longer is needed for that purpose? That involves the general rules that pertain. If a beast is designated as a burnt offering, it is presented in that designation; so too, a peace offering, differentiated from the Nazirite's peace-offering as to accompanying gifts. When it comes to the disposition of the coins that are designated for the purchase of an animal to be consecrated for the stated purpose, the rules follow the same lines. The upshot is, the language that is used to designate the animal or the coins takes effect, even though the purpose for which the animal or coins is required is nullified by circumstance. What is the stopping point? It is the tossing of the blood. At that point, the vow has been fully carried out and can no longer be annulled.

---

[20]As usual, the contribution of the Talmuds to the formulation of Halakhah proves negligible. Their interest is in analysis, not legislation. The Yerushalmi's formulations show little augmentation of the law, much amplification; I give no indication of the speculative problems explored therein, which are as usual imaginative and rich, but add nothing to the Halakhah in its classical formulation except refinements.

This brings us to the problem of mixtures, cast in appropriate terms. When it comes to the restrictions upon the Nazirite, which the Written Torah has defined, the Oral Torah devotes its Halakhah to the familiar problem of differentiating among a sequence of actions of a single type, that is, the general theme of the many and the one, the one and the many, that preoccupies the Halakhah in one topic after another. This routine problem comes to expression in the language, A Nazirite who was drinking wine all day long is liable only on one count. If they said to him, "Don't drink it! Don't drink it!" and he continues drinking, he is liable on each and every count of drinking. The problem is particular, the resolution and consequent rule not. So too the conundrum about the high priest and the Nazirite, both of them subject to the same restriction against corpse-uncleanness, who share the obligation to bury a neglected corpse requires us to hierarchize the sanctity of each in relationship to that of the other. This too represents a particular form of a general problem of the Halakhah in its work of hierarchical classification, here of competing sanctities: who is holier than whom, and so what? For the same reason, we need not be detained by the Halakhah covering cases of doubt. They merely illustrate prevailing principles on how cases of doubt are to be resolved; another tractate provides the systematic statement of governing principles of the matter, the present one, merely concrete problems for solution.

[3] THE HALAKHAH'S PARTICULAR HERMENEUTICS OF NEDARIM-NAZIR: It is no surprise that the problematics of the Halakhah, then, finds acute interest in the working of euphemisms. But that is not only because of the unclear status of euphemistic language — does it mean what it seems or not? A deeper consideration comes into play. Language, the Halakhah recognizes, conveys sense and meaning in many ways. Language stands for what is intensely personal and private. But language also conveys meanings of general intelligibility. It is by definition always a public act. With what result for the Halakhah? What is private (mumbled, unintelligible, gibberish) bears no consequence, what is intelligible by a common-sense standard takes effect. That is how the Halakhah sorts matters out. Thus, when it comes to euphemisms, all of them take effect; for what matters about language is not adherence to the governing formula, though it matters. What makes all the difference is the perceived and publicly comprehensible intent. If the intent conveyed by the language is clear and unmistakable, then the language has done its task of embodying intentionality. And then the language is affective. If the intentionality is not vividly conveyed, however indirectly, then the language is null. The power of language lies in its capacity to convey, to embody, inchoate intentionality, to realize in the shared world of public transactions the individual and private attitude or intentionality that motivates action.

And that accounts for the Halakhah's recognition of the special status of a Samson-Nazirite: the language that is used signals the intentionality to accept the model of Samson, and hence fully exposes the will of the one who takes the special vow. Whether or not the Oral Torah has invented the category of the Samson-Nazirite to build upon the implications of its theory of the relationship of language to intentionality — the necessary connection between language and intention, public metaphor and private attitude and will — we cannot surmise. It is the simple fact that once the important questions pertinent to the topic at hand center upon the power of language to embody and realize, confirm and convey the attitude, the (mere) details of language will precipitate the formation of specificities of the Halakhah. The main problem addressed by the Halakhah pertaining to the language of the vow to be a Nazirite is how to standardize matters, so that private meanings and personal stipulations do not corrupt discourse. Then the prevailing solution is to identify what is general and intelligible and dismiss the rest. One example serves. That is why if someone specifies a detail as incumbent, then all the details of a Nazirite vow pertain to him. Nothing remains private, personal, idiosyncratic, once language serves. Even what affects the household in particular is framed for effect for all Israel.

The Tosefta's contribution to all this is predictably, expansive: Just as euphemisms for Nazirite-vows are equivalent to Nazirite-vows, so euphemisms for Samson-vows are equivalent to Samson-vows. The vow applies in the Land and abroad, to hirsute and bald alike, and — it goes without saying — whether or not the Temple is standing. The intention is the key, not the limitations of circumstance. And that same governing principle accounts for the interpretation of the language, "I will be a Nazirite like the hairs of my head" or "like the dust of the earth." That is taken to mean, for an unlimited period of time. The net effect of the Halakhah is to generalize upon specific and idiosyncratic usages. Individual conditions are null, e.g., If one said, "Lo, I am a Nazirite on condition that I shall drink wine and become unclean with corpse uncleanness," lo, this one is a Nazirite. But he is prohibited to do all of these things that he has specified as conditional upon his vow. If he said, "I recognize that there is such a thing as Naziriteship, but I do not recognize that a Nazirite is prohibited from drinking wine," lo, this one is bound by the Nazirite oath. But legitimate stipulations bear consequences, e.g., conditions that do not violate the law of the Torah: "...if my wife bears a son" or "a daughter."

Because the husband has the power to nullify the vows of the wife (or the father of the daughter), the Halakhah attends to the case of nullification. But I see nothing of special interest in the laws, except that while the husband may nullify the wife's vow, he may not nullify his own. If his vow is contingent upon her vow, by contrast, neither is subject to the Nazirite rule. Limits are set upon intentionality; if one intended to violate the vow but in fact was not subject to the vow, there is no penalty: If her husband annulled the vow for her, but she did not know that her husband had annulled it for her and nonetheless continued to go around drinking wine and contracting corpse uncleanness, she does not receive forty stripes. So too, someone who violated the vow but had a sage annul it is not penalized; the vow never took effect. Here intention to violate the vow is insufficient to precipitate sanctions; the actualities intervene. Or, to put it otherwise, improper intention not confirmed by improper deed is null. Mere intention on its own is null — language and action decide everything, and, when it comes to the vow, the language constitutes the act.

C. THE CONSISTENCY OF THE CATEGORY-FORMATION

I see no component of the category-formation as revealed in the exegetical program at hand that cannot find its place within one of the three hermeneutical resources we have identified. I should not want to have to specify the proportions contributed by each.

D. THE GENERATIVITY OF THE CATEGORY-FORMATION

The present dual category-formation, Nedarim and Nazir, is capable of extension and expansion without limit. The two formations jointly embody profound reflections on the meaning and affects of language. If a man or woman says a certain set of words, expressive of an appropriate intentionality, Heaven hears. The man or woman thereby adopts certain restrictions or prohibitions, whether, as in Nedarim, not to eat certain foods of any sort or to derive benefit from a given person, or, as in Nazirite, not to eat grapes in particular, cut hair, or attend funerals (something the husband cannot ever prevent the wife from doing, but the Nazirite vow prevents the Nazirite from doing). These restrictions, that language, serve to provoke Heaven's interest in, and intervention into, the conduct of the man or the woman. That is why Nedarim and Nazir form a continuous exposition of the Halakhah, even though, in Scripture, the framer of the book of Numbers does not recognize continuity between the Nazirite vow, Num. 6, contiguous with the woman accused of unfaithfulness, Num. 5, and the vow in general, Num. 30. But from the perspective of the Oral Torah, with its focus upon the sanctifying power of language, it is no surprise that Nedarim and Nazir fit together so well as they do, or that both belong comfortably within the framework of the division of women.

5.
TRACTATE SOTAH

I. THE DEFINITION OF THE CATEGORY-FORMATION

For Sotah, concerning the ordeal inflicted on the wife accused of adultery, the inquiry into the particular hermeneutics of a native category-formation within the Halakhic framework produces nothing. Scripture at Numbers 5 sets forth its theory of the category-formation. The Halakhah of the Mishnah-Tosefta-Yerushalmi-Bavli (Chapters One through Six) for its part conducts principally those generic exercises of analysis with which we are familiar elsewhere. These are the ones, for example, that respond to the philosophical hermeneutics of interstitiality, and related general questions. But, as we shall see at some length, when we examine the exegetical program of Sotah, we find no traces of a hermeneutics distinctive to the topic at hand. But that is only half of the story. When we turn to the Aggadic approach to the same category-formation — especially the Aggadah deeply embedded within the Halakhic documents under study here — we confront a systematic hermeneutics, particular to the category-formation and critical to the larger structure and system of Rabbinic Judaism.[21]

We know exactly how the framers of the category-formation, Sotah, have selected their data and chosen to interpret it, yielding such exegetical problems as logically follow. It is a hermeneutics that identifies data concerning injustice and justice in order to demonstrate God's justice and that episodically forms exegetical problems in the articulation of that hermeneutics. The injustice done to the innocent wife, by the husband's whim required to undergo the humiliating ordeal of the bitter water, serves as the Halakhic documents' occasion to make their definitive statement on the matter. It is that God's justice is perfect: the wicked get their exact punishment, the righteous, their precise reward. For the sages that statement becomes possible uniquely here — but only in the Aggadic framework, rarely spilling over from normative beliefs to normative behavior. In accord with the governing hermeneutics it is not enough to show that sin or crime provokes divine

---

[21] I leave for discussion below, at the section on "what fuses the Halakhic data into a category-formation," the problem of how the entire corpus of Halakhah treated at Sotah holds together, whether or not we have here a single category-formation at all. Here I deal only with Chapters One through Six, as readers will note in the reprise of the Halakhah.

response, that God penalizes evil-doers. Justice in the here and now counts only when the righteous also receive what is coming to them. Scripture's accused wife then is treated as a case illustrative of a rule, as is commonly the trait of mind of the Aggadic reading of Scripture. Therefore Scripture's casual remark that the woman found innocent will bear more children provokes elaborate demonstration, out of the established facts of history that Scripture supplies, that both righteous and wicked are subject to God's flawless and exact justice.

A powerful hermeneutics emerges, reading all the data that are chosen to make one and the same point. It is this: not only must the penalty fit the crime, but the reward must fit the virtue (a point much amplified in the Talmuds' treatment of the category, zekhut, which the Halakhic documents introduce casually). Thus, on both sides of the equation, measure must match measure, and the more exact the result to the cause, the more compelling the proof of immediate and concrete justice. Then history — that is, Scripture's historical facts read as atemporal paradigms — identifies God's justice as the building block of world order that sages would put forth. That is the point at which justice is transformed from a vague generality — a mere sentiment — to a precise and measurable dimension of the actual social order of morality. The actualities are meant to show how things hold together when subject to tension, at the pressure-points of structure, not merely how they are arrayed in general.

Here we have a kind of "physics" of the moral universe, a treatise on causation and commensurability that takes the measure of things in reward and punishment rather than cause and effect. Here, at the category-formation, Sotah, in fact, is made manifest how God made the world, what is good about the creation that God pronounced good. That explains why, to make that point, sages select a rite that reeks of injustice, the case of the wife accused of adultery and the ordeal to which she is subjected. Their presentation of the rite, in the setting of home and family, is framed so as to demonstrate God's perfect justice — not only in the public life of Israel's social order, but in the here and now of that same home and family. It is hard to find a less likely candidate for service in demonstrating that proposition than the subject before us. But, for reasons that are now clear, sages identified the topic as the ideal occasion for saying just that.

Now we must ask ourselves the question, how come the Aggadah, not the Halakhah, serves as the primary medium for the hermeneutical message that infuses sages' reading of the category-formation, the accused wife? It is the fact that, while as I shall show, within the Halakhah are provisions aimed at righting the balance between accused wife and aggrieved husband, the Aggadah within the very Halakhic exposition is where justice, reward and punishment form the principal motif. To this point we have not had to resort to extra-

Halakhic discourse in our inquiry into the principles of interpretation that govern the reading of native category-formations, and beyond this point, we shall not have to. So we come to an anomalous circumstance, one that, to our advantage, permits a verification of our basic method of identifying the hermeneutics in play.

To take advantage of the occasion, we revert to our general observation concerning the analogical-contrastive foundations of the Rabbinic hermeneutics. At each point we have identified the generative hermeneutics by identifying alternatives and explaining why this, not that. Are we able to do the same here? That is to say, time and again we have found in the comparison and contrast of two species of the same genus the generative logic of a category-formation as set forth by the Halakhah. The categorical identification of the genus, the speciation thereof — these have brought to the surface that particular hermeneutics, the one of comparison and contrast, that guided the formation and the interpretation of a given category-formation. In case after case a theory of interpretation has been shown to take shape always in a dialectical relationship with a counterpart and corresponding one. Hence our hermeneutical inquiry takes as its starting point the question, why this, not that? And from there we proceeded to the comparison and contrast of the species of a genus. Now, if that general procedure has produced good results in our inquiry in sequence, then, what happens when we come to a category-formation that is *sui generis*, lacking a corresponding and contrasting category-formation for purposes of comparison? A genus, not a species of a genus matched against another species of the same genus, does not present a favorable occasion for the identification of the prevailing theory of interpretation as I expound matters. If my general approach matches the labor at hand, then, absent the possibilities of analogical-contrastive analysis, we ought to find ourselves precisely where we now are. That is to say, where we have a category-formation that is *sui generis*, lacking a counterpart to form a paired species of a common genus, we should be stymied in our effort to penetrate from the surface of Halakhic details to the exegetical program effected therein, and from the exegesis to the hermeneutics, interpretative foundations upon which the exegetical superstructure rests.

Here I find no corresponding, contrasting category-formation, no counterpart to the Sotah, another species of the common genus. Why not? To answer a question with a question, I ask: what native category-formation of the Halakhah can claim to match the Sotah as portrayed by Scripture, so as to form that besought, analogous species of a common genus?

[1] THE FAITHFUL WIFE/THE UNFAITHFUL WIFE: The Halakhah does not contemplate as corresponding species for the accused wife others in a marital or familial relationship. Surely, one may object, the genus,

"the wife," produces the contrasting species, "the faithful wife," "the unfaithful wife." Alas, we must immediately exclude the faithful wife, for her proposed counterpart and opposite, the Sotah, is not unfaithful, only subject to an accusation. That is the very point of the ordeal. By definition, the Sotah is neither faithful nor unfaithful, only subjected to a charge of unfaithfulness!

[2] THE UNFAITHFUL WIFE/THE WAYWARD AND REBELLIOUS SON: Then — remaining within the range of family relationships — what about the wayward and rebellious son? The Sotah and the wayward and rebellious son have in common that they are part of a family-relationship predicated on faithful obedience, the one to the husband, the other to the parents. And if the Sotah as a wife put on trial for something she may or may not have done — hence for an indeterminate cause, and that by definition — so the rebellious and wayward son is brought to court (so the Halakhah tells us) not for what he has done. Rather, he too is put on trial for something other than what he has done, namely, for something he is accused of being capable of doing! He is punished, the Halakhah insists, not for what he has done but for what he is likely to do, and that point, made explicitly as we shall see in due course, is wildly off the mark here.

[3] GOOD FAITH/BAD FAITH: If not familial relationships, then what about others accused of unfaith in transactions subject to trust? How — to pursue the question — about those who violate contracts, workers who do not show up, deceitful peddlers and land-grabbers — all topics we shall address in Volume III of this study, on the hermeneutics of Neziqin? They too hardly compare with the Sotah, but for a different reason. They form a genus that excludes the Sotah, because Heaven has not the same stake in their transactions, which are not classified as sanctified. The fact that Heaven does not intervene forms the point of categorical differentiation.

[4] THE UNFAITHFUL WIFE/THE ONE WHO TAKES A FALSE OATH: And, finally, if Heaven's engagement in a transaction involving both Heaven and good faith is the key, then what about comparing the Sotah with the one who takes a false oath, such as is under analysis in the category-formation, Shebuot? Heaven there indeed is invoked, and the oath (not the vow) therefore engages Heaven's immediate interest. But the critical element here — accusation, not conviction — is absent. The oath validates the claim; it is not tested, it itself represents the test, and taking the oath subjects the oath-taker to recompense without a further ordeal. So, while topically proximate, the Halakhah of the oath does not form a sufficient match to lay foundations for

comparison, therefore contrast, and our basic approach to the solution of the hermeneutical problem fails.[22]

But if not in the Halakhah, then, as we shall see, in the Aggadah we find a rich field of inquiry. The genus is, God's justice and the evidence therefor, the corollaries that spin out its implications, the refinements and details thereof. The matched, contrasting species are, God's justice and rewards to the virtuous person, God's justice and penalties to the sinful person. Now in the precedents and cases of Scripture, generalized into laws of reading events in general, the hermeneutics of the ordeal of the Sotah generalizes the case of the accused wife into the universal rule of God's perfect justice. Here is a category-formation that finds ample data for interpretation in accord with a clear and explicit principle of interpretation. A single question governs, which is, how does a case prove the rule of God's justice? And what, about God's justice, does a given case teach us? And then, as we shall see presently, a massive corpus of evidence serves. The hermeneutical principle thus derives from a reading of the Aggadah deemed integral to the Halakhic category-formation exactly as Scripture sets forth the norms of procedure. That principle can come to exegetical instantiation only in the facts, provided by Scripture, of other cases in which Heaven rewards good faith and punishes bad faith, and they are many.

How — it may be objected — does so obvious a reading of what Scripture says explicitly qualify as an autonomous hermeneutical principle at all — one that Scripture does not impose in its own terms and framework? Surely the hermeneutics of the category-formation, Sotah, represents a recapitulation of Scripture's own view, not a choice and an alternative particular to the sages whose work produced the Mishnah-Tosefta-Yerushalmi-Bavli. After all, that Heaven rewards faithfulness and punishes unfaithfulness is the articulated statement of Numbers 5 itself. We did not have to turn to the Rabbinic Aggadah, but only to Scripture, to find out how Rabbinic Judaism would interpret the category-formation of the Sotah. That objection would represent a more considerable obstacle, were there no other possibilities for the interpretation of the category-formation, Sotah — indeed, were Scripture itself to provide no alternative readings of the matter, the unfaithful wife. But as soon as the category-formation, the unfaithful wife, comes to the fore, in

---

[22] All I have done here is follow the model of Sifra's critique of hierarchical classification (yielding analogical-contrastive analysis) based on category-formations defined by intrinsic traits, as against the same reasoning based Scripture's divinely-designated category-formations. This is spelled out in *Uniting the Dual Torah: Sifra and the Problem of the Mishnah*. Cambridge and New York, 1989: Cambridge University Press.

addition to the hermeneutics of God's justice, a separate and quite different way of interpreting the category presents itself, also within Scripture. It is a hermeneutics of God's mercy.

Specifically, an alternative hermeneutics of the topic is best formulated by Hosea's account of the faithless mother of his children. For Hosea the category-formation, the faithless wife, serves as a model for corporate-Israel's relationship with God, not for God's relationship with innocent and guilty persons. The consequent hermeneutics for the category-formation, the faithless wife, would then take shape around grace, unearned and unmerited love, and not justice, merited reward or punishment. The data selected for interpretation would embody cases of God's unearned mercy, not his perfect justice, and the exegesis would inquire into how cases show God rewards those without merit, not those who earn God's recompense for righteousness. Specifically, Hosea reads our category-formation under the aspect not of justice but of mercy. The category-formation, the faithless wife, becomes the occasion for systematic exposition of the capacity of man to love even the faithless wife — and of God to love even faithless Israel. The exegesis then would choose different data to make interpret matters in a different framework altogether, not private but public and corporate, involving cases and acts not of individuals but of all Israel. And the consequent exegetical problems would take up an altogether different agenda.

On the surface, therefore, and in the grossest terms, the Aggadah therefore finds before itself a choice: two ways of interpreting species of what can be formed into a common genus. The genus, the wife accused of adultery, divides into two species, the one who may or may not be guilty, the Sotah, and the one who is guilty, the wife in Hosea. The speciation follows. The guilty-Sotah is meted justice. (It goes without saying, the innocent-Sotah, to use the language required in this context, is recognized and rewarded with more children.) The guilty-Sotah in Hosea, by contrast, is meted mercy beyond all deserts. So we have (in theory at least) a process of analogical-contrastive analysis, and sages in Sotah clearly have made a choice for themselves: how to read these data in one way, not in some other.

I underscore: these rough and approximate remarks serve only to establish that the hermeneutics of the category-formation, Sotah (Chapters One through Six), represented by the Halakhic documents (but within their Aggadic components alone) represents a choice: this, not that. Having come this far, we may therefore ask, why have the sages chosen a hermeneutics of justice, not one of unearned mercy, for their interpretation of the category-formation? This choice means they speak only of the wife as a concrete figure, not of the wife as metaphor for Israel, and it means that, in their exposition of the category-formation, they will not explore the theme of God's unlimited capacity for forgiveness of Israel. In choosing the hermeneutics of divine justice and selecting data to illustrate God's reliable recompense for those who do justice and keep faith — wives with their husbands, Israel with God[23] — the sages delivered the only message that, as the men responsible for Israel's condition, they could set forth. God rewards good and punishes evil. To deliver the alternative message, however fitting to Israel's condition in the world and among the nations, would have represented an act of utter social irresponsibility. That explains why, in the heart of the Halakhic documents, an Aggadic corpus is situated, there to underscore the doctrines of personal responsibility for personal action, Israel at home defining the Halakhic focus here as everywhere else.[24]

II. THE FOUNDATIONS OF THE HALAKHIC CATEGORY-FORMATIONS

The ordeal imposed on the woman accused of unfaithfulness, spelled out in the Written Torah, elicits from the sages of the Oral Torah no searching inquiry. The Halakhah of the Mishnah narrates the rite, and the Tosefta and two Talmuds fill in some minor details. The tractate expands to cover other rites conducted in Hebrew or in other languages as well. The pertinent verses of Scripture are as follows (Num. 5:1-31):

UNCLEANNESS, BREAKING FAITH

The Lord said to Moses, "Command the people of Israel that they put out of the camp every leper and everyone having a discharge and everyone that is unclean through contact with the dead; you shall put out both male and female, putting them outside the camp, that they may not defile their camp, in the midst of which I dwell." And the

---

[23] For Israel as feminine in this age, masculine in the age to come, see my *Androgynous Judaism. Masculine and Feminine in the Dual Torah*. Macon, 1993: Mercer University Press.

[24] Israel among the nations will engage the Aggadah, as we have already seen See the Introduction to my *The Halakhah: An Encyclopaedia of the Law of Judaism*. Volume I. *Between Israel and God*. Part A. *Faith, Thanksgiving, Enlandisement: Possession and Partnership*. Leiden, 1999: E. J. Brill. And note also *The Native Category-Formations of the Aggadah*. I. *The Later Midrash-Compilations*. Atlanta, 1999: Scholars Press for South Florida Studies in the History of Judaism, and *The Native Category-Formations of the Aggadah*. II. *The Earlier Midrash-Compilations*. Atlanta, 1999: Scholars Press for South Florida Studies in the History of Judaism.

people of Israel did so and drove them outside the camp as the Lord said to Moses, so the people of Israel did.

And the Lord said to Moses, "Say to the people of Israel, When a man or woman commits any of the sins that men commit by breaking faith with the Lord and that person is guilty, he shall confess his sin that he has committed, and he shall make full restitution for his wrong, adding a fifth to it, and giving it to him to whom he did the wrong. But if the man has no kinsman to whom restitution may be made for the wrong, the restitution for the wrong shall go to the Lord for the priest, in addition to the ram of atonement with which atonement is made for him. And every offering, all the holy things of the people of Israel, which they bring to the priest, shall be his; and every man's holy things shall be his; whatever any man gives to the priest shall be his."

THE UNCLEANNESS OF THE WIFE ACCUSED OF BREAKING FAITH:
THE ORDEAL IN THE TEMPLE

And the Lord said to Moses, "Say to the people of Israel, If any man's wife go astray and act unfaithfully against him, if a man lie with her carnally and it is hidden from the eyes of her husband, and she is undetected though she has defiled herself and there is now witness against her, since she was not taken in the act, and if the spirit of jealousy comes upon him, and he is jealous of his wife who has defiled herself; or if the spirit of jealousy comes upon him and he is jealous of his wife, though she has not defiled herself, then the man shall bring his wife to the priest, and bring the offering required of her, a tenth of an ephah of barley meal; he shall pour no oil upon it and put no frankincense on it, for it is a cereal offering of jealousy, a cereal offering of remembrance, bringing iniquity to remembrance. "

"And the priest shall bring her near and set her before the Lord, and the priest shall take holy water in an earthen vessel and take some of the dust that is on the floor of the tabernacle and put it into the water. "

"And the priest shall set the woman before the Lord and unbind the hair of the woman's head and place in her hands the cereal offering of remembrance, which is the cereal offering of jealousy. "
And in his hand the priest shall have the water of bitterness that brings the curse. Then the priest shall make her take an oath, saying, 'If no man has lain with you, and if you have not turned aside to uncleanness, while you were under your husband's authority, be free from this water of bitterness that brings the curse. But if you have gone astray, though you are under your husband's authority, and if you have defiled yourself, and some man other than your husband has

lain with you, then (let the woman take the oath of the curse and say to the woman) 'the Lord make you an execration and an oath among your people, when the Lord makes your thigh fall away and your body swell; may this water that brings the curse pass into your bowels and make your body swell and your thigh fall away.' And the woman shall say, 'Amen, Amen.'

"Then the priest shall write these curses in a book and wash them off into the water of bitterness; and he shall make the woman drink the water of bitterness that brings the curse, and the water that brings the curse shall enter into her and cause bitter pain. And the priest shall take the cereal offering of jealousy out of the woman's hand and shall wave the cereal offering before the Lord and bring of the woman's hand and shall wave the cereal offering before the Lord and bring it to the altar; and the priest shall take a handful of the cereal offering as its memorial portion and burn it upon the altar, and afterward shall make the woman drink the water. And when he has made her drink the water, then, if she has defiled herself and has acted unfaithfully against her husband, the water that brings the curse shall enter into her and cause bitter pain, and her body shall swell, and her thigh shall fall away, and the woman shall become an execration among her people. But if the woman has not defiled herself and is clean, then she shall be free and shall conceive children. "

"This is the law in cases of jealousy, when a wife, though under her husband's authority, goes astray and defiles herself, or when the spirit of jealousy comes upon a man and he is jealous of his wife; then he shall set the woman before the Lord, and the priest shall execute upon her all this law. The man shall be free from iniquity, but the woman shall bear her iniquity."

The woman accused of unfaithfulness finds her place in the Torah's presentation of those excluded from the camp, the ones who are subject to the uncleanness specified at Lev. 13-15 in particular. Then comes the matter of breaking faith, and, finally, the special case of the accused wife. Scripture speaks both of the wife who has actually committed adultery, and whose husband is made jealous and the woman whose husband expresses jealousy but who is guiltless. As anticipated, Scripture focuses, then, upon the rite at the Temple that accommodates the situation. The Halakhah raises its customary questions as well, working its way through its familiar general-philosophical agendum alongside its particular-theological one.

III. THE EXPOSITION OF THE COMPONENTS OF THE GIVEN CATEGORY-FORMATION BY THE MISHNAH-TOSEFTA-YERUSHALMI-BAVLI

As always, I set forth the main points of **the Mishnah (in bold face type)**, then at the appropriate place add the Tosefta's own presentation not merely the clarification or amplification of the Mishnah's Halakhah) (in ordinary type), thereafter *the Yerushalmi's (in italics)*, and finally, **THE BAVLI'S (IN BOLD FACE LOWER CASE TYPE)**. These are paraphrased and epitomized, they are not cited in full. I insert my observations on the points of special interest at the conclusion of each topical sub-unit. The units and sub-units derive from my own outline of the Mishnah-tractate, encompassing also the Tosefta-tractate; then the outline of the Yerushalmi, finally that of the Bavli.[25]

I. INVOKING THE ORDEAL

M. 1:1-2 He who expresses jealousy to his wife [concerning her relations with another man (Num. 5:14)] how does he express jealousy to her? [If] he stated to her before two witnesses, "Do not speak with Mr. So-and-so," and she indeed spoke with him, she still is permitted to have sexual relations with her husband and is permitted to eat heave-offering. [If] she went with him to some private place and remained with him for sufficient time to become unclean, she is prohibited from having sexual relations with her husband and [if the husband is a priest,] she is prohibited from eating heave-offering. And if he [her husband] should die, she performs the rite of *rite of removing the shoe* [removing the shoe, which severs her relationship to the childless husband's surviving brother, in line with the law of Dt. 25:5-10] but is not taken into levirate marriage.

T. 1:2 What is the character of the first testimony [M. Sot. 1:2]? This is the testimony concerning her going off alone [with such and such a person]. The second [testimony]? This is testimony concerning her having been made unclean. And how long is the time required for becoming unclean? Sufficient time to have sexual relations. And how much is sufficient time for having sexual relations? Sufficient time for sexual contact.

M. 1:3 And these women [married to priests and accused of unfaithfulness] are prohibited from eating heave-offering: (1) She who says, "I am unclean to you," and (2) she against whom witnesses testified that she is unclean; and (3) she who says, "I shall not drink the bitter water," and (4) she whose husband will

---

[25] These are cited with bibliographical data in the *Introduction*, Volume II.

not force her to drink it; and (5) she whose husband has sexual relations with her on the way [up to Jerusalem for the rite of drinking the water]. What should he do in respect to her? He brings her to the court in that place [in which they live], and [the judges] hand over to him two disciples of sages, lest he have sexual relations with her on the way.

The Halakhah wants to know at what point the wife's status has been called into question, so that we are not certain she retains her position as wife, e.g., for purposes of eating priestly rations. Scripture does not provide details of the juridical process that protects wives from unfair accusations. There has to be a formal notification and also evidence that the husband's warning has been defied. Once she has done a deed, her status indeed is subject to doubt. If the conditions of M. 1:3 are met, there is no longer doubt as to her status — one way or the other. So the Halakhah narrowly defines the circumstance of doubt that the rite is meant to resolve.

II. NARRATIVE OF THE ORDEAL

    A. THE WIFE IS SUBJECTED TO THE ORDEAL
    M. 1:4 They would bring her up to the high court which is in Jerusalem and admonish her as they admonish witnesses in a capital crime. They say to her, "My daughter, much is done by wine, much is done by joking around, much is done by kidding around, much is done by bad friends. For the sake of the great Name which is written in holiness, do it so that it will not be blotted out by water [Num. 5:23]." and they tell her things which neither she nor the family of her father's house should be hearing.
    T. 1:6 And just as the court admonishes her to repent [M. Sot. 1:4], so they admonish her not to repent. Therefore they say to her, "Now my daughter, if it is perfectly clear to you that you are clean, stand your ground and drink. For these waters are only like a dry salve which is put on living flesh and does no harm. If there is a wound, it penetrates and goes through [the skin, and if there is no wound, it has no effect]." Two accused wives are not made to drink simultaneously, so that one not be shameless before the other.
    B. 1:4 III.1 7B AND THEY TELL HER THINGS... [M. 1:4C]: HE TELLS HER LESSONS OF NARRATIVE AND EVENTS THAT TOOK PLACE [AND ARE RECORDED] IN THE EARLIER WRITINGS [OF THE PENTATEUCH]. FOR EXAMPLE "WHICH WISE MEN HAVE TOLD AND HAVE NOT HID FROM THEIR FATHERS [BY CONFESSING THEIR SIN]" (JOB 15:18). SPECIFICALLY: JUDAH CONFESSED AND WAS NOT ASHAMED TO DO SO. WHAT WAS HIS DESTINY? HE INHERITED THE WORLD TO COME. REUBEN

CONFESSED AND WAS NOT ASHAMED TO DO SO. WHAT WAS HIS DESTINY? HE INHERITED THE WORLD TO COME. WHAT WAS THEIR REWARD? WHAT WAS THEIR REWARD?! RATHER, WHAT WAS THEIR REWARD IN THIS WORLD? "TO THEM ALONE THE LAND WAS GIVEN, AND NO STRANGER PASSED AMONG THEM" (JOB 15:19).

M. 1:5 [Now] if she said, "I am unclean," she gives a quittance for her marriage-contract [which is not paid over to her], and goes forth [with a writ of divorce]. And if she said, "I am clean," they bring her up to the eastern gate, which is at the entrance of Nicanor's Gate. There it is that they force accused wives to drink the bitter water, and they purify women after childbirth and purify lepers. And a priest grabs her clothes — if they tear, they tear, and if they are ripped up, they are ripped up — until he bares her breast. And he tears her hair apart [Num. 5:18].

T. 1:7 Priests cast lots among themselves. Whoever won the lottery, even a high priest, goes out and stands next to the accused wife. And a priest grabs her clothes — if they tear, they tear, and if they are ripped up, they are ripped up — until he bares her breast. And he tears her hair apart

M. 1:6 [If] she was clothed in white clothing, he puts black clothes on her. [If] she had gold jewelry, chains, nose-rings, and finger rings on, they take them away from her to put her to shame. Then he brings a rope made out of twigs and ties it above her breasts. And whoever wants to stare at her comes and stares, except for her boy-slaves and girl-slaves, since in any case she has no shame before them. And all women are allowed to stare at her, since it is said, "That all women may be taught not to do after your lewdness" (Ezek. 23:48).

The Tosefta's complement, T. 1:6/M. 1:4, makes an important point, once more orienting the Halakhic narrative to the principle of justice. If the woman has been falsely accused, she most certainly should go through the ordeal; if not, as the Mishnah's formulation has it, she should confess up-front. If she confesses, the procedure is over with the end of the marriage. If not, the rite is carried on at the gate of the Temple.

B. *HOW THE PUNISHMENT FITS THE CRIME*

M. 1:7 By that same measure by which a man metes out [to others], do they mete out to him: She primped herself for sin, the Omnipresent made her repulsive. She exposed herself for sin, the Omnipresent exposed her. With the thigh she began to sin, and afterward with the belly, therefore the thigh suffers the curse first, and afterward the belly. But the rest of the body does not escape [punishment].

T. 3:2 And so you find that with regard to the accused wife: With the measure with which she measured out, with that measure do they mete out to her. She stood before him so as to be pretty before him, therefore a priest stands her up in front of everybody to display her shame, as it is said, And the priest will set the woman before the Lord (Num. 5:18).

T. 3:3 She wrapped a beautiful scarf for him, therefore a priest takes her cap from her head and puts it under foot. She braided her hair for him, therefore a priest loosens it. She painted her face for him, therefore her face is made to turn yellow. She put blue on her eyes for him, therefore her eyes bulge out.

T. 3:4 She signaled to him with her finger, therefore her fingernails fall out. She showed him her flesh, therefore a priest tears her cloak and shows her shame in public. She tied on a belt for him, therefore a priest brings a rope of twigs and ties it above her breasts, and whoever wants to stare comes and stares at her [M. Sot. 1:6C-D]. She pushed her thigh at him, therefore her thigh falls. She took him on her belly, therefore her belly swells. She fed him goodies, therefore her meal-offering is fit for a cow. She gave him the best wines to drink in elegant goblets, therefore the priest gives her the bitter water to drink in a clay pot.

T. 4:1 I know only with regard to the measure of retribution that by that same measure by which a man metes out, they mete out to him [M. Sot. 1:7A]. How do I know that the same is so with the measure of goodness [M. Sot. 1:9A]? Thus do you say: The measure of goodness is five hundred times greater than the measure of retribution. With regard to the measure of retribution it is written, "Visiting the sin of the fathers on the sons and on the grandsons to the third and fourth generation" (Ex. 20:5). And with regard to the measure of goodness it is written, "And doing mercy for thousands" (Ex. 20:6). You must therefore conclude that the measure of goodness is five hundred times greater than the measure of retribution.

M. 1:8 Samson followed his eyes [where they led him], therefore the Philistines put out his eyes, since it is said, And the Philistines laid hold on him and put out his eyes (Judges 16:21). Absalom was proud of his hair, therefore he was hung by his hair [II Sam. 14:25-26]. And since he had sexual relations with ten

concubines of his father, therefore they thrust ten spear heads into his body, since it is said, "And ten young men that carried Jacob's armor surrounded and smote Absalom and killed him" (II Sam. 18:15). And since he stole three hearts — his father's, the court's, and the Israelite's — since it is said, "And Absalom stole the heart of the men of Israel" (II Sam. 15:6) — therefore three darts were thrust into him, since it is said, "And he took three darts in his hand and thrust them through the heart of Absalom" (II Sam. 18:14).

M. 1:9 And so is it on the good side. [The remainder of these materials is cited below.]

Here is the point at which the Halakhah underscores the match of punishment to crime, detail to detail. The Tosefta greatly improves on matters. It is at Tosefta, specifically T. 4:1, that the contrary result — vindication — is introduced. Now we insist on the perfect match not only of punishment to crime, but reward to virtue (here: restraint).

C. *THE RITE, CONTINUED*

M. 2:1 He [the husband (Num. 5:15)] would bring her meal-offering in a basket of palm-twigs and lay it into her hands to tire her out. All meal-offerings at the outset and at the end are in a utensil of service. But this one at the outset is in basket of palm-twigs, and [only] at the end is in a utensil of service. All meal-offerings require oil and frankincense, But this one requires neither oil nor frankincense. All meal-offerings derive from wheat. But this one derives from barley. As to the meal-offering of the first sheaf ('omer), even though it [too] derives from barley, it would derive from sifted flour. But this one derives from unsifted flour. Just as she acted like a cow, so her offering is food for a cow.

T. 1:9 Priests are permitted to put wine, oil, and honey into the residue of meal-offerings, but they are prohibited from allowing them to leaven.

T. 1:10 All meal-offerings which are specified in the Torah require oil and frankincense, except for the meal-offering of a sinner and the meal-offering of jealousy, since it is said, "He will not pour oil into it, and he will not put frankincense in it" (Num. 5:15).

M. 2:2 He [the husband] would bring a clay bowl and put in it a half-log of water from the laver. And he [the priest] goes into the hekhal and turns to his right. Now there was a place, an *amah* by an *amah*, with a marble flagstone, and a ring was attached to it. And when he raised it [the stone], he took the dirt from under it and put it [into the bowl of water], sufficient to be visible on the water, since it says, "And of the dust that is on the floor of the tabernacle the priest shall take and put it into the water" (Num. 5:17).

T. 1:8 Three things must be visible on the water: the dust of the red cow, the dust of the accused wife, and the blood of the bird [used to purify a mesora' (Lev. 14:6)]. The dust of the red cow — sufficient to be visible on the surface of the water. The dust of the accused wife — sufficient to be visible on the surface of the water [M. Sot. 2:2G]. The blood of the bird of a mesora' — sufficient to be visible on the surface of the water. The spit of a deceased childless brother's wife — sufficient to be visible to the sight of the elders.

M. 2:3 He came to write the scroll. From what passage [in Scripture] did he write? From "If no man has lain with thee... but if thou hast gone aside with another instead of thy husband..." (Num. 5:19f.). But he does not write, "And the priest shall cause the woman to swear" (Num. 5:21). And he writes, "The Lord make thee a curse and an oath among thy people... and this water that causeth the curse shall go into thy bowels and make thy belly to swell and thy thigh to fall away." But he does not write, "And the woman shall say, Amen, Amen!"

M. 2:4 He writes (1) neither on a tablet, (2) nor on papyrus, (3) nor on unprepared hide, but only on [parchment] scroll, since it is written, In a book (Num. 5:23). And he writes (1) neither with gum, (2) nor with coppera, (3) nor with anything which makes a lasting impression [on the writing-material], but only with ink, since it is written, And he will blot it out — writing which can be blotted out.

T. 2:1 He would take her scroll and bring it into the ulam. Now there was a gold flagstone set up there by the wall of the hekhal. And it was visible from the ulam. At that point he sees it, and he writes, neither leaving out anything nor adding anything. He goes out and stands by the accused wife. He reads it aloud and explains it and spells out every detail of the pericope. And he says it to her in whatever language she understands, so that she will know for what she is drinking the bitter water and for what incident she is drinking it, on what account she is accused of being unclean, and under what circumstances she is accused of being unclean. And he says to her, "I invoke an oath upon you — And may it come upon you." "And may they come upon you" — this is the curse. "I invoke an oath upon you" — this is an oath.

M. 2:5 To what does she say, Amen, Amen? (1) "Amen to the curse" [Num. 5:21], (2) "Amen to the oath" [Num. 5:19]. (3) "Amen that it was not with this particular man" (4) "Amen that it was with no other man." (5) "Amen that I have not gone aside while betrothed, married, awaiting Levirate marriage, or wholly taken in Levirate marriage." (6) "Amen that I was not made unclean, and if I was made unclean, may it [the bitter water] enter into me."

M. 2:6 All concur that he [the husband] may make no stipulation with her about anything which happened before she was betrothed or after she may be divorced. [If after she was put away], she went aside with some other man and became unclean, and afterward he [the first husband] took her back, he makes no stipulation with her [concerning such an event]. This is the general principle: Concerning any situation in which she may have sexual relations in such wise as not to be prohibited [to her husband], he [the husband] may make no stipulation whatsoever with her.

M. 3:1 He would take her meal-offering from the basket made of twigs and put it into a utensil of service and lay it into her hands. And a priest puts his hand under hers and waves it [the meal-offering].

M. 3:2 He waved it [Num. 5:25] and brought it near the altar. He took a handful [of the meal-offering] and burned it up [on the altar]. And the residue is eaten by the priests. He would give her the water to drink. And [only] afterward he would offer up her meal-offering.

M. 3:3 [If] before the scroll is blotted out, she said, "I am not going to drink the water," her scroll is put away, and her meal-offering is scattered on the ashes. But her scroll is not valid for the water-ordeal of another accused wife. [If] her scroll was blotted out and then she said, "I am not going to drink it," they force her and make her drink it against her will.

T. 2:2 He goes in and writes the scroll, comes out and blots it out. If before the scroll is blotted out, she says, "I am not going to drink it" [M. Sot. 3:3A], or if she said, "I am unclean," or if witnesses came and testified that she is unclean, the water is poured out. And no sanctity adheres to it. And the scroll written for her is hidden under the hekhal, and her meal offering is scattered [M. Sot. 3:3A].

T. 2:3 [If] the scroll is blotted out and she said, "I am unclean," the water is poured out, and her meal-offering is scattered on the ashes. And her scroll is not valid for the water-ordeal of another accused wife [M. Sot. 3:3C, B]. If her scroll is blotted out and then she said, "I am not going to drink it," they force her and make her drink it against her will [M. Sot. 3:3D].

M. 3:4 She hardly sufficed to drink it before her face turns yellow, her eyes bulge out, and her veins swell. And they say, "Take her away! Take her away!" so that the Temple-court will not be made unclean [by her corpse]. [But if nothing happened], if she had merit, she would attribute [her good fortune] to it. There is the possibility that merit suspends the curse for one year, and there is the possibility that merit suspends the curse for two years, and there is the possibility that merit suspends the curse for three years.

M. 3:6 [If] her meal-offering was made unclean before it was sanctified in a utensil, lo, it is in the status of all other such meal-offerings and is to be redeemed. And [if this takes place] after it is sanctified in a utensil, lo, it is in the status of all other such meal-offerings and is to be burned. And these are the ones who meal-offerings are to be burned: (1) the one who says, "I am unclean to you," and (2) the one against whom witnesses come to testify that she is unclean; (3) the one who says, "I am not going to drink the water," and (4) the one whose husband does not want to make her drink it; and (5) the one whose husband has sexual relations with her on the way to Jerusalem [M. 1:3]. (6) And all those who are married to priests — their meal-offerings are burned.

T. 2:4 For every act of sexual relations which her husband had with her, lo, he is liable on her account. If her meal-offering was made unclean before it was sanctified in a utensil, lo, it is in the status of all other such meal-offerings. it is redeemed [M. Sot. 3:6A-B] and eaten. [If] her meal-offering was made unclean] after it was sanctified in a utensil [M. Sot. 3:6C-D], its appearance is allowed to rot, and it goes out to the place of burning.

T. 2:5 [If] the meal-offering was offered, but there was not time to offer up the handful before her husband died, or if she died, the residue is prohibited. [If] the handful was offered, and afterward she died, or the husband died, the residue is permitted. For to begin with it was brought in a case of doubt. Her doubt has been atoned for and gone its way.

T. 2:6 [If] witnesses came against her to testify that she was unclean, one way or the other the meal-offering is prohibited. [If] they turned out to be conspiring witnesses, one way or the other her meal-offering is treated as unconsecrated. In the case of any woman married to a priest, whether she is a priest-girl, or a Levite-girl, or an Israelite-girl, her meal-offering is not eaten, for he has a share in it. But the offering is not wholly consumed in the fire, because she has a share in it. What should he do? The handful is offered by itself, and the residue is offered by itself. A priest stands and makes offerings at the altar, which is not the case of a priest-girl [cf. M. Sot. 3:7].

The Halakhic details continue to organize the facts into clear patterns and to underscore the degrading character of the ordeal. The one interesting point is at M. 2:5f., which breaks into the narrative. Here the generic analytical program takes over and clarifies matters of language.

D. *SPECIAL RULES FOR PRIESTS AND THEIR WIVES*

M. 3:7 An Israelite girl who is married to a priest — her meal-offering is burned. And a priest-girl who is married to an Israelite — her offering is eaten [by the priests]. What is the difference between a priest and a priest-girl? The meal-offering of a priest-girl is eaten, the meal-offering of a priest is not eaten. The priest-girl may be deconsecrated [declassed], but a priest may not be deconsecrated [declassed]. A priest-girl contracts corpse-uncleanness [e.g., to bury the dead], and a priest does not contract corpse-uncleanness. A priest eats Most Holy Things, but a priest-girl does not eat Most Holy Things.

M. 3:8 What is the difference [along these same lines of comparing and contrasting the male priest and the female priest] between a man and a woman? A man goes around with unbound hair and torn garments, but a woman does not go around with unbound hair and torn garments [Lev. 13:44-5]. A man imposes a Nazirite-vow on his son, and a woman does not impose a Nazirite-vow upon her son [M. Naz. 4:6]. A man brings the hair-offering for the Nazirite-vow of his father, and a woman does not bring a hair-offering for the Nazirite-vow of her father [M. Naz. 4:7]. The man sells his daughter, and the woman does not sell her daughter [Ex. 21:6]. The man arranges for a betrothal of his daughter, and the woman does not arrange for a betrothal of her daughter [M. Qid. 2:1]. A man [who incurs the death-penalty] is stoned naked, but a woman is not stoned naked. A man is hung [after being put to death], and a woman is not hung [M. San. 6:3-4]. A man is sold [to make restitution] for having stolen something, but a woman is not sold to [make restitution] for having stolen something [Ex. 22:2].

T. 2:7 A man has control over his daughter and has power to betroth her through money. a writ, or an act of sexual relations, and he controls what she finds, the produce of her labor, and the abrogation of her tows [M. Ket. 4:4], which is not the case of a woman [cf. M. Sot. 3:8].

T. 2:8 A man is subject to punishment for the transgression of a commandment which has to be performed at a particular time [M. Qid. 1:7], which is not the case with a woman. A man is subject to the transgression of the commandment not to trim the beard and not to remove the beard and [in the case of a priest] not to contract corpse-uncleanness [M. Sot. 3:7F], which is not the case with a woman. A man is subject to the trial as a rebellious son, but a woman is not subject to trial as a rebellious daughter [M. San. 8:1].

T. 2:9 A man wraps himself in a cloak [if he is a mesora'] and he proclaims, ["Unclean, unclean,"], but a woman does not wrap herself in a cloak and so proclaim [cf. M. Sot. 3:8B]. A man may be sold repeatedly, but a woman may not be sold repeatedly. A man is sold as a Hebrew slave, but a woman is not sold as a Hebrew slave. A man is subjected to the ceremony of the awl [having his ear pierced to the door if he refuses to go free], but a woman is not subject to the ceremony of the awl. A man acquires a Hebrew slave, and a woman does not acquire a Hebrew slave.

The special case of the marriage of a woman to a priest concerns the disposition of the meal-offering, as spelled out at M. 3:7. Then further contrasts are drawn, not having to do with the case at hand alone. This kind of generic contrast, as distinct from one particular to the topic before us, is uncommon in the Halakhah. We note that the Tosefta amplifies the Mishnah's rule, giving more examples of the same phenomenon.

III. RULES OF THE ORDEAL

    A.   *EXEMPTIONS AND APPLICABILITY*

M. 4:1 A betrothed girl and a deceased childless brother's widow awaiting levirate marriage neither undergo the ordeal of drinking the bitter water nor receive a marriage-contract, since it is written, "When a wife, being subject to her husband, goes astray" (Num. 5:29) — excluding the betrothed girl and the deceased childless brother's widow awaiting levirate marriage. A widow married to a high priest, a divorcee and a woman who has undergone the rite of removing the shoe married to an ordinary priest, a Mamzer-girl and a Netinah-girl married to an Israelite, an Israelite-girl married to a Mamzer or to a Netin neither undergo the ordeal of drinking the bitter water nor receive a marriage-contract.

T. 5:1 He who expresses a warning of jealousy to his betrothed or to his deceased childless brother's widow awaiting Levirate marriage with him [cf. M. Sot. 4:1A] — if after she entered into marriage with him, she went in secret [with the man against whom the prospective husband had warned her not to go], she either undergoes the ordeal of drinking the water or does not receive her marriage-contract.

T. 5:4 A priest-girl, a Levite-girl, and an Israelite-girl, who married a priest, a Levite, or an Israelite, a Netinah-girl married to a Netin, a Mamzeret-girl married to a Mamzer, the wife of a proselyte, a freed slave, and a barren woman either undergo the ordeal of drinking the bitter water or do not receive a marriage-contract. But he who expresses jealousy to his betrothed or to the deceased childless brother's widow awaiting Levirate marriage with him — [if] before he married her, she went in secret [with the man against whom she was warned], she does not undergo the ordeal of drinking the bitter water and does not collect a marriage contract [M. Sot. 4:1A-C].

Y. 4:1 I:4 What would be an example of the rule, A betrothed girl and a deceased childless brother's widow awaiting levirate marriage neither undergo the ordeal of drinking the bitter water nor receive a marriage-contract]? [In fact M. 4:1A applies only if the entire ordeal is completed with the woman m the stated status.] [If, however,] the husband expressed jealousy to her when she was still betrothed, consummated the marriage, and she went aside with the named man, then he makes her drink the water by reason of the original expression of jealousy. [So this exemplifies the other side of the rule, the point at which the status specified at M. 4:1A does not exempt the woman from undergoing the ordeal.] [Again:] if he expressed jealousy to her while she was yet awaiting marriage with the levir, then he consummated the marriage, then he requires her to drink the water by reason of the original expression of jealousy. If he expressed jealousy to her while she was yet betrothed, and he married her, and then she went aside, and only thereafter did he have sexual relations, then she goes forth along with collecting her marriage settlement. [This is in line with M. 4:2E: because of his having sexual relations with her, she loses the opportunity to undergo the ordeal, hence collects.] But if not, she goes forth without collecting her marriage settlement. If her husband expressed jealousy to her, then died, and she fell before the levir [for levirate marriage], and he married her, and she went aside with the man originally named by the now-deceased husband, the levir requires her to drink the water by reason of the expression of jealousy of the original husband [the levir's brother]. If her husband did not express jealousy to her, and he died, and she fell before the levir, and he, for his part, expressed jealousy to her about the named man, and he had not consummated the marriage to her before he too died, and then she fell before his brother [yet a further levir], he does not have the right to impose on her the ordeal of the water, for she has fallen to him [as a wife] only because of the relationship to the first brother, [her original husband, who never issued an expression of jealousy to begin with]. But if the levir [the second brother] had expressed jealousy to her and married her and then died, and she then fell before the second levir, and he married her, and she went aside with the named man, he has every right to impose the rite of drinking the water upon her by reason of the expression of jealousy of the second brother.

M. 4:2 And these do not undergo the ordeal of drinking the bitter water or receive a marriage-contract: She who says, "I am unclean," or against whom witnesses came to testify that she is unclean; and she who says, "I will not drink." [If, however,] her husband said, "I will not make her drink, or [if] her husband had

sexual relations with her on the way [to Jerusalem], she receives her marriage-contract and does not undergo the ordeal of drinking the bitter water. [If] their husbands died before they drank the bitter water — do not undergo the ordeal of drinking the bitter water and do not receive the marriage-contract.

M. 4:3 A barren woman and a woman past menopause, and a woman who cannot give birth do not undergo the ordeal of drinking the bitter water and do not receive the marriage-contract. And all other woman either undergo the ordeal of drinking the bitter water or do not collect the marriage-contract.

T. 5:2 A young man who married a barren woman or a woman past menopause, and who has another wife and children — she either undergoes the ordeal of drinking the bitter water or does not receive her marriage-contract [M. Sot. 4:3].

T. 5:3 A. A woman made pregnant by the husband himself or who gives suck to the child of the husband himself either undergoes the ordeal of drinking the bitter water or does not receive payment of her marriage-contract [M. Sot. 4:3A, E].

T. 5:5 A. A young man who married a barren woman or a woman past menopause and who does not have another wife and children — she does not undergo the ordeal of drinking the bitter water and does not collect a marriage-contract [cf. M. Sot. 4:3C-D]. A woman who was pregnant by another husband [who died or divorced [the woman] and a woman who was giving suck to a child by another husband do not undergo the ordeal of drinking the bitter water and do not receive the marriage-contract [M. Sot. 4:3A].

M. 4:4 The wife of a priest drinks the bitter water and [if proved innocent] is permitted [to go back] to her husband. The wife of a eunuch undergoes the ordeal of drinking the bitter water. On account of [men in] all sorts of prohibited relationships [to the woman] are wives subject to warning, except for a minor, and for one who is not human.

T. 5:6 With any sort of man is a woman made unclean, except for a minor and for one who is not human [cf. M. Sot. 4:4C-E].

M. 4:5 And these are the women whom a court subjects to warning [in behalf of the husband]: A woman whose husband became a deaf mute or an imbecile, or was imprisoned — not to impose upon her the ordeal of drinking the water did they state the rule, but to invalidate her for receiving her marriage-contract.

M. 5:1 Just as the water puts her to the proof, so the water puts him [the lover] to the proof, since it is said, "And it shall come...," "And it shall come..." (Num. 5:22, 5:24). Just as she is prohibited to the husband, so she is prohibited to the lover, since it is said, "And she will be unclean...," "And she will be unclean..." (Num. 5:27, 29).

Y. 5:1 II:1 Just as she is forbidden to the husband, so she is forbidden to the lover: Just as she is forbidden to the brother of her husband [should he die childless], so she is forbidden to the brother of her lover [under the same circumstances]. [Consequently, her lover's brother cannot marry her.] Just as the water puts her to the test for each act of sexual relations which she has with her husband after she has had sexual relations with her lover, so they put him to the test.

We turn from a composite made up principally of narratives of the rite to one that is comprised by analysis of interstitial cases, e.g., the woman who is neither fully wed nor entirely available to any man, M. 4:1. Then the issue of other infirm marital bonds follows, with a fine amplification at T. 5:1 and exemplifications added by the Yerushalmi. When a woman does not undergo the rite, she may or may not lose her marriage-settlement; but the husband by his actions may impose upon himself the obligation to pay it. Others involved in the ordeal who lose the marriage-settlement are listed as well, M. 4:2-3. Another unclear situation involves a marriage where the husband is unable to subject the wife to a warning; then the court does so. But that has an effect only on the marriage-settlement, not on her having to go through the ordeal, which only the husband can do.

B. *TESTIMONY AND EXEMPTIONS FROM THE ORDEAL*

M. 6:1 He who expressed jealousy to his wife, but she went aside in secret, even if he heard [that she had done so] from a bird flying by — he puts her away, but pays off her marriage-contract.

M. 6:2 [If] one witness said, "I saw that she was made unclean," she would not undergo the ordeal of drinking the bitter water. And not only so, but even if it was a boy-slave or a girl-slave, lo, these are believed even to invalidate her [from receiving payment of] her marriage-contract. As to her mother-in-law and the daughter of her mother-in-law, her co-wife, and the husband's brother's wife, and the daughter of her husband, lo, these are believed [cf. M. Yeb. 15:4] — not to invalidate her from receiving payment of her marriage-contract, but that she should not undergo the ordeal of drinking the bitter water.

M. 6:3 For logic might dictate as follows: Now, if, in the case of the first kind of testimony [that she has been warned not to get involved with such-and-such a man], which does not impose upon her a permanent prohibition [but only until she has undergone the ordeal of the bitter water], [the accusation] is not sustained by less than two witnesses, in the case of the second kind of testimony [that she has indeed been made unclean], which does impose upon her a permanent prohibition [against remaining wed to her husband], surely [the accusation] should not be sustained by less than two witnesses. But Scripture says, "And there is no witness against her" (Num. 5:13) — [meaning], any sort of testimony which there is against her. On these grounds we may now construct an argument from the lesser to the greater with reference to the first kind of testimony: Now if the second kind of testimony, which imposes upon her a permanent prohibition, lo, is sustained by a single witness, the first kind of testimony, which does not impose upon her a permanent prohibition, surely should be sustained by means of a single witness. But Scripture says, 'Because he has found some unseemly matter in her' (Deut. 24:1), and elsewhere it says, 'At the mouth of two witnesses shall a matter be established" (Deut. 19:15) — just as matter spoken of there requires two witnesses, so matter spoken of here requires two witnesses.

M. 6:4 [If] one witness says, "She was made unclean," and one witness says, "She was not made unclean," [if] one woman says, "She was made unclean," and one woman says, "She was not made unclean," she would undergo the ordeal of drinking the bitter water. [If] one witness says, "She was made unclean," and two witnesses say, "She was not made unclean," she would undergo the ordeal of drinking the bitter water. [If] two say, "She was made unclean," and one says, "She was not made unclean," she would not undergo the ordeal of drinking the bitter water.

T. 5:8 One witness says, "She was made unclean." and one witness says, "She was not made unclean," — a woman says, "She was made unclean," and a woman says, "She was not made unclean" [M. Sot. 6:4] — she either undergoes the ordeal of drinking the water or does not collect her marriage-contract.

The generic analysis now takes up another interstitial situation, one in which the woman is subject to conflicting testimony (e.g., M. 6:4) or by testimony of an inadequate character, M. 6:2-3. The two-stage process of warning and then an evidentiary action then is fully analyzed. The Halakhic presentation of the matter concludes here. What follows is an account of other rites, besides the one affecting the accused wife, that are conducted in the Hebrew language

IV. RITES CONDUCTED IN ANY LANGUAGE, AND THOSE CONDUCTED ONLY IN HEBREW

A. *A CATALOGUE*

M. 7:1 These are said in any language: (1) the pericope of the accused wife [Num. 5:19-22], and (2) the Confession of the tithe [Deut. 26:13-15], and (3) the recital of the Shema, [Deut. 6:4-9], and (4) the Prayer, (5) the Grace after Meals, (6) the oath of testimony [imposed by the judges], and (7) the oath concerning a bailment.

T. 7:1 The oath of witnesses and judges is said in any language [M. Sot. 7:1]. If one has imposed an oath upon them five times in any language which they understand, and they replied to him, "Amen," lo, they are liable.

T. 7:2 The oath imposed by judges — how so? Lo, he who is obligated to take an oath to his fellow — they say to him, "Know that the whole world trembled on the day on which it was said, You shall not take the name of the Lord your God in vain (Ex. 20:7)." With reference to all the transgressions which are mentioned in the Torah, it is written, "And he shall be acquitted," but with reference to this one, it is written concerning it, "And he shall not be acquitted." In regard to all the transgressions which are mentioned in the Torah, they exact retribution from the man himself. But with reference to this one, they exact retribution from the man and from the entire world, so that the transgression of the entire world is blamed on him, since it is said, "Swearing and lying . . . therefore does the land mourn, and every one who dwells therein does languish" (Hos. 4:2-3). In regard to all the transgressions which are mentioned in the Torah, they exact retribution from the man himself, but in this case, they exact retribution from him and from his relatives, as it is said, "Suffer not your mouth to bring your flesh into guilt" (Qoh. 5:5), and flesh refers only to one's relative, as it is said, "From your flesh do not hide yourself" (Is. 58:7). All transgressions which are mentioned in the Torah do they suspend punishment for two or three generations, but in this case, they impose punishment forthwith, since it is said, "I cause it to go forth, says the Lord of hosts, and it shall enter into the house of the thief and into the house of him who swears falsely by My name and it shall abide in the midst of this house and shall consume it with the timber thereof and the stones thereof" (Zech. 5:4). "I cause it to go forth" — forthwith. "And it comes into the house of the thief" — this is one who swears falsely, knowing that he does not have it, and who deceives [steals the mind of] people. And into the house of him who swears falsely by My name — according to its plain meaning. All transgressions which are mentioned in the Torah apply to one's property. But this one applies to his property and to his own person, as it is said, And it will abide [spend the night]. Come and see how things which fire cannot consume a false oath destroys.

B. 7:1-5 I:1/32B [THE PRIESTS] INFORM THE WOMAN IN ANY LANGUAGE THAT SHE GRASPS ON WHAT ACCOUNT SHE DRINKS THE BITTER WATER, AND IN WHAT SORT OF UTENSIL SHE DRINKS IT, ON WHAT ACCOUNT SHE IS DEEMED TO HAVE BECOME UNCLEAN, AND IN WHAT CIRCUMSTANCES SHE IS DEEMED TO HAVE BECOME UNCLEAN. "ON WHAT ACCOUNT SHE DRINKS:" BECAUSE OF THE MATTERS OF THE [HUSBAND'S] EXPRESSION OF JEALOUSY AND [HER] HAVING GONE ASIDE [WITH THE NAMED MAN]. "IN WHAT SHE DRINKS IT:" IN A POTSHERD. "ON WHAT ACCOUNT SHE IS DEEMED TO HAVE BECOME UNCLEAN:" BECAUSE OF MATTERS OF LIGHTHEADEDNESS AND CHILDISHNESS. "AND IN WHAT CIRCUMSTANCES SHE IS DEEMED TO HAVE BECOME UNCLEAN:" WHETHER INADVERTENTLY OR INTENTIONALLY, UNDER CONSTRAINT OR WILLINGNESS. AND WHY ALL THIS? SO AS NOT TO BRING THE BITTER WATER INTO DISREPUTE.

M. 7:2 And these are said [only] in the Holy Language: (1) the verses of the first-fruits [Deut. 26:3-10], (2) the rite of rite of removing the shoe [Deut. 25:7,9], (3) blessings and curses [Deut. 27:15-26], (4) the blessing of the priests [Num. 6:24-26], (5) the blessing of a high priest [on the Day of Atonement], (6) the pericope of the king [Deut. 17:14-20]; (7) the pericope of the heifer whose neck is to be broken [Deut. 21:7f.], and (8) [the message] of the anointed for battle when he speaks to the people [Deut. 20:2-7].

T. 7:7 Blessings, Hallel, the Shema', [and] the Prayer are said in any language. The blessing of the priests [M. Sot. 7:2A4, 7:6A] — this refers to the blessing which is said when the priests stand on the steps of the ulam.

M. 7:3 The verses of the first fruits [M. 7:2A1] — how so? "And you will answer and say before the Lord thy God" (Deut. 26:5). And later on it says, "And the Levites will answer and say" (Deut. 27:14). Just as answering which is said in that later passage is in the Holy Language, so answering which is said here [in reference to the first fruits] is in the Holy Language.

M. 7:4 The rite of removing the shoe [M. 7:2A2] — how so? "And she will answer and say" (Deut. 25:9). And later on it says, "And the Levites will answer and say" (Deut. 27:14). Just as later on answering is to be in the Holy Language, so there answering is to be said in the Holy Language.

M. 7:5 Blessings and curses [M. 7:2A3] — how so? When Israel came across the Jordan and arrived before Mount Gerizim and before Mount Ebal in Samaria, near Shechem, beside the oak of Moreh, — as it is written, "Are not they beyond the Jordan..." (Deut. 11:30) and elsewhere it says, "And Abram passed through the land to the place of Shechem to the oak of Moreh (Gen. 12:6) — just as the oak of Moreh spoken of there is at Shechem, so the oak of Moreh spoken of here is at Shechem —) six tribes went up to the top of Mount Gerizim, and six tribes went up to the top of Mount Ebal. And the priests and Levites and ark of the covenant stood at the bottom, in the middle [between two mountains]. The priests surround the ark, and the Levites [surround] the priests, and all Israel are round about, since it says, "And all Israel and their elders and officers and judges stood on this side of the ark and on that..." (Joshua 8:33). They turned their faces toward Mount Gerizim and began with the blessing: "Blessed is the man who does not make a graven or molten image." And these and those answer, "Amen." They turned their faces toward Mount Ebal and began with the curse: "Cursed is the man who makes a graven or molten image" (Deut. 27:15). And these and those answer, "Amen." [And this procedure they follow] until they complete the blessings and the curses. And afterward they brought stones and built an altar and plastered it with plaster. And they wrote on it all the words of the Torah in seventy languages, as it is written, "Very plainly" (Deut. 27:8). And they took the stones and came and spent the night in their own place [Josh. 4:8].

T. 8:1 The blessings and the curses [M. Sot. 7:5A] — these are the ones which the Israelites spoke when the Israelites crossed the Jordan, as it is said, And on the day you pass over the Jordan to the land which the Lord your God gives you, you shall set up large stones (Deut. 27:2). How did the Israelites cross the Jordan? Every day the ark would journey behind two standards, but this day it journeyed first, as it is said, Behold, the ark of the covenant of the Lord of all the earth passes over before you (Josh. 3:11).

T. 8:2 Every day the Levites would carry the ark, but this day the priests carried it, as it is said, And it shall come to pass, when the soles of the feet of the priests that bear the ark of the Lord (Josh. 3:13).

T. 8:9 How did the Israelites say the blessings and the curses? Six tribes went up to the top of Mount Gerizim, and six tribes went up to the top of Mount Ebal. And the priests and the Levites and the ark of the covenant stood at the bottom in the middle [M. Sot. 7:5C-D]. The priests surround the ark, and the Levites [surround] the priests, and all Israel are round about, since it says, "And all Israel and their elders and of elders and judges stood on this side of the ark and on that" (Josh. 8:33) [M. Sot. 7:5C-E]. What is the meaning of the Scripture, "...Half of them in front of Mount Gerizim and half of them in front of Mount Ebal" (Josh. 8:33)? This teaches that the part which was before Mount Gerizim was greater than that before Mount Ebal, since the part of the tribe of Levi was below.

B. 7:1-5 XII:1/37A-B THERE IS A BLESSING IN GENERAL AND A BLESSING IN PARTICULAR, A CURSE IN GENERAL AND A CURSE IN PARTICULAR. TO LEARN, TO TEACH, TO OBSERVE, AND TO DO (DEUT. 5:1, 11:19) — LO FOUR [DUTIES WITH EACH COMMANDMENT]. FOUR AND FOUR ARE EIGHT, AND EIGHT AND EIGHT ARE SIXTEEN [EIGHT BLESSINGS AND CURSES WITH THE GENERAL COMMANDMENT, AND EIGHT WITH THE PARTICULAR COMMANDMENTS], WITH THREE COVENANTS FOR EACH ONE — LO, FORTY-EIGHT COVENANTS FOR EACH COMMANDMENT, AND SO AT MOUNT SINAI, AND SO IN THE PLAINS OF MOAB [T. SOT. 8:10A-D], AS IT IS SAID, "THESE ARE THE WORDS OF THE COVENANT WHICH THE LORD COMMANDED MOSES" (DEUT. 28:69), AND IT IS WRITTEN, "KEEP THEREFORE THE WORDS OF THIS COVENANT" (DEUT. 29:8). THUS THERE ARE FORTY-EIGHT COVENANTS WITH EACH COMMANDMENT [SIXTEEN IN EACH OF THE THREE PLACES].

M. 7:6 The blessing of the priests [M. 7:2A4] — how so? In the provinces they say it as three blessings, and in the sanctuary, as one blessing. In the sanctuary one says the Name as it is written, but in the provinces, with a euphemism. In the provinces the priests raise their hands as high as their shoulders, but in the sanctuary, they raise them over their heads, except for the high priest, who does not raise his hands over the frontlet.

M. 7:7 The blessing of the high priest [M. 7:2A5] — how so? The minister of the assembly takes a scroll of the Torah and gives it to the head of the assembly, and the head of the assembly gives it to the prefect, and the prefect gives it to the high priest. And the high priest stands and receives it and reads in it: "After the death..." (Lev. 16:1ff.) and "Howbeit on the tenth day" (Lev. 23:16-32). Then he rolls up the Torah and holds it at his breast and says, "More than I have read for you is written here." "And on the tenth..." which is in the Book of Numbers (Num. 29:7-11) did he recite by heart. And afterward he says eight blessings: (1) ... for the Torah, (2) and... for the Temple-service, (3) and... for the Thanksgiving, (4) and for the forgiveness of sin, (5) and for the sanctuary, (6) and for Israel, (7) and for the priests, (8) and the rest of the Prayer.

M. 7:8 The pericope of the king [M. 7:2A5] — how so? At the end of the first festival day of the Festival [of Sukkot], on the eighth year, [that is] at the end of the seventh year, they make him a platform of wood, set in the courtyard. And he sits on it, as it is said, "At the end of every seven years in the set time" (Deut. 31:10). The minister of the assembly takes a scroll of the Torah and hands it to the head of the assembly, and the head of the assembly hands it to the prefect, and the prefect hands it to the high priest, and the high priest hands it to the king, and the king stands and receives it. But he reads sitting down. Agrippa the King stood up and received it and read it standing up, and sages praised him on that account. And when he came to the verse, "You may not put a foreigner over you, who is not your brother" (Deut. 17:15), his tears ran down from his eyes. They said to him, "Do not be afraid, Agrippa, you are our brother, you are our brother, you are our brother!" He reads from the beginning of "These are the words" (Deut. 1:1) to "Hear O Israel" (Deut. 6:4), "Hear O Israel" (Deut. 6:4), "And it will come to pass, if you hearken" (Deut. 11:13), and "You shall surely tithe" (Deut. 14:22), and "When you have made an end of tithing" (Deut. 26:12-15), and the pericope of the king [Deut. 17:14-20], and the blessings and the curses [Deut. 27:15-26], and he completes the whole pericope. With the same blessings with which the high priest blesses them [M. 7:7F], the king blesses them. But he says the blessing for the festivals instead of the blessing for the forgiveness of sin.

M. 7:1 is tacked on because of the first item, which is handsomely amplified at B. 7:1-5 I:1, as indicated. Then its match, M. 7:2, items said only in Hebrew, follows, and each of these is subjected to a systematic amplification.

B. *THE ANOINTED FOR BATTLE AND THE DRAFT-EXEMPTIONS*

Deut. 20:1-9: "When you go forth to war against your enemies and see horses and chariots and an army larger than your own, you shall not be afraid of them, for the Lord your God is with you, who brought you up out of the Land of Egypt. And when you draw ear to the battle, the priest shall come forward and speak to the people and shall say to them, 'Hear O Israel, you draw near this day to battle against your enemies. Let not your heart be faint, do not fear nor tremble nor be in dread of them, for the Lord your God is he that goes with you, to fight for you against your enemies, to give you the victory.' Then the officers shall speak to the people, saying, 'What man is there that has built a new house and has not dedicated it? Let him go back to his house, lest he die in battle and another man dedicate it. And what man is there that has planted a vineyard and has not enjoyed its fruit? Let him go back to his house lest he die in the battle and another man enjoy its fruit. And what man is there that has betrothed a wife and has not taken her? Let him go back to his house, lest he die in the battle and another man take her.' And the officers shall speak further to the people and say, 'What man is there that is fearful and faint-hearted? Let him go back to his house, lest the heart of his fellows melt as his heart.' And when the officers have made an end of speaking to the people, then commanders shall be appointed at the head of the people."

M. 8:1 The anointed for battle, when he speaks to the people, in the Holy Language he did speak, as it is said, "And it shall come to pass when you draw near to the battle, that the priest shall approach" (this is the priest anointed for battle) "and shall speak to the people" (in the Holy Language) "and shall say to them, Hear, O Israel, you draw near to battle this day" (Deut. 20:203) — "against your enemies" (Deut. 20:3) — and not against your brothers, not Judah against Simeon, nor Simeon against Benjamin. For if you fall into their [Israelites'] hand, they will have mercy for you, as it is said, "And the men which have been called by name rose up and took the captives and with the spoil clothed all that were naked among them and arrayed them and put shoes on their feet and gave them food to eat and something to drink and carried all the feeble of them upon asses and brought them to Jericho, the city of palm trees, unto their brethren. Then they returned to Samaria" (II Chron. 28:15). "Against your enemies" do you go forth. For if you fall into their hand, they will not have mercy upon you. "Let not your heart be faint, fear not, nor tremble, neither be afraid" (Deut. 20:3). "Let not your heart be faint" — on account of the neighing of the horses and the flashing of the swords. "Fear not" — at the clashing of shields and the rushing of the tramping shoes. "Nor tremble" — at the sound of the trumpets. "Neither be afraid" — at the sound of the shouting. For the Lord your God is with you" (Deut. 20:4) — they come with the power of mortal man, but you come with the power of the Omnipresent. The Philistines came with the power of Goliath. What was his end? In the end he fell by the sword, and they fell with him. The Ammonites came with the power of Shobach [II Sam. 10:16]. What was his end? In the end he fell by the sword, and they fell with him. But you are not thus: "For the Lord your God is he who goes with you to fight for you" (— this is the camp of the ark).

Y. 8:1 I:3 At the frontier you must say, the officer listens to what the priest says and he repeats it in all the languages [spoken by the troops]. But in the battle lines [the priest speaks, without having his message repeated, because the troops are busy] providing water and food for themselves and repairing the lines of communication.

B. 8:1 III.1/42A-B LET NOT YOUR HEART BE FAINT, FEAR NOT [M. 8:1I]: TWO TIMES DOES HE SPEAK TO THEM, ONCE ON THE BORDER, AND ONCE ON THE BATTLEFIELD. ON THE BORDER WHAT DOES HE SAY? "OBEY THE WORDS OF THOSE WHO LAY OUT THE RULES OF BATTLE AND GO HOME [IF YOU ARE NOT REQUIRED TO BE PRESENT, IN LINE WITH DEUT. 20:5-9]." ON THE BATTLEFIELD WHAT DOES HE SAY? "LET NOT YOUR HEART BE FAINT, FEAR NOT, NOR TREMBLE, NEITHER BE AFRAID" (DEUT. 20:3). [THESE FOUR COMMANDMENTS] MATCH THE FOUR THINGS THAT IDOLATORS DO [ON THE BATTLEFIELD]. THEY CRASH THEIR SHIELDS, BLAST ON TRUMPETS, SHOUT, AND TRAMPLE WITH THEIR HORSES.

M. 8:2 "And the officers shall speak to the people, saying 'What man is there who has built a new house and has not dedicated it? Let him go and return to his house' (Deut. 20:5)." All the same are the ones who build a house for straw, a house for cattle, a house for wood, and a house for storage. All the same are the ones who build it, who purchase it, who inherit it, and to whom it is given as a gift. "And who is the man who has planted a vineyard and has not used the fruit thereof" (Deut. 20:6) — All the same are the ones who plant a vineyard and who plant five fruit-trees, and even if they are of five different kinds. And all the same are the ones who plant such a tree, who sink them into the ground, and who graft them. And all the same are the ones who buy a vineyard, and who inherit it, and to whom it is given as a gift. "And who is the man who has betrothed a wife" (ibid.) — All the same are the ones who betroth a virgin and who betroth a widow — and even a deceased childless brother's widow who awaits the Levir. And even if one heard during the battle that his brother had died, he returns and comes along home. All these listen to the words of the priest concerning the arrangements of battle and go home. And they provide water and food and keep the roads in good repair.

T. 7:18 Two times does he go out and talk with them, once on the boundary [before invading the enemy's territory] and once on the battlefield. On the boundary what does he say? "Hear the words of the priest['s war-regulations] and return [home]." On the battlefield what does he say? "What man is there that has built a new house and has not dedicated it?" (Deut. 20:5) [If] his house fell down and he built it up again, lo, this one goes home.

T. 7:19 "And what man is there that has betrothed a wife and has not taken her? Let him go back to his house, lest he die in the battle and another man take her" (Deut. 29:7). All the same is he who betroths and he who enters into Levirate marriage, and even if there is a woman awaiting Levirate marriage with one of five brothers, and even if there are five brothers who heard that their brother has died in battle, all of them return and come home [M. Sot. 8:2J-K].

T. 7:20 I know only that the law applies to one who builds his house but has not dedicated it, planted a vineyard but has not eaten the fruit, betrothed a wife but has not taken her. How do we know that if one has built a house and dedicated it, but has not lived in it twelve months, planted a vineyard and eaten its fruits, but has not had the use of it for twelve months, betrothed a wife and taken her, but has not dwelt with her for twelve months — how do we know that these [stay home and] do not move from their place [M. Sot. 8:4A-B]? Scripture says, When a man is newly married, he shall not go out with the army or be charged with any business; he shall be free at home one year, to be happy with his wife whom he has taken (Deut. 24:5). This matter was covered by the general principle, and why has it been explicitly stated? To allow for the imposition of an analogy on its basis, so teaching you: Now just as this one is distinguished in having betrothed a wife and taken her but in not having lived with her for twelve months, that he does not move from his place, so all of them are subject to the same rule. Torah thereby has taught a rule of conduct: When a man gains a portion for his support, he buys himself a house. If he gains yet a further portion for his support, he takes a wife for himself, as it is said, What man is there that has built a new house...And what man is there that has planted a vineyard...And what man is there that has betrothed a wife ... (Deut. 20:5,6,7).

M. 8:3 And these are the ones who do not return home: He who builds a gate-house, a portico, or a porch; he who plants only four fruit-trees or five barren trees; he who remarries a woman whom he has divorced, or [he who marries] a widow in the case of a high priest, a divorcee or a woman who has undergone the rite of rite of removing the shoe in the case of an ordinary priest, or a mamzeret or a Netinah in the case of an Israelite, or an Israelite girl in the case of a mamzer or a Netin — such a one did not go home.

M. 8:4 And these are the ones who [to begin with] do not move from their place: He who had [just now] built a house and dedicated it, who had planted a vineyard and used its fruits, who had married the girl whom he had betrothed, or who had consummated the marriage of his deceased childless brother's widow, since it is said, "He shall be free for his house one year" (Deut. 24:5) — "For his house" — this is his house. "Will be" — this refers to his vineyard. "And shall cheer his wife" — this applies to his own wife. "Whom he has acquired" — to include

even his deceased childless brother's widow. These do not [even] have to provide water and food and see to the repair of the road.

M. 8:5 "And the officers shall speak further unto the people [and they shall say, What man is there who is fearful and fainthearted? Let him return to his home]" (Deut. 20:8). He cannot stand in the battle-ranks or see a drawn sword.

M. 8:6 "And it shall be when the officers have made an end of speaking to the people that they shall appoint captains of hosts at the head of the people" (Deut. 20:9), and at the rear of the people. They station warriors at their head and others behind them, and iron axes are in their hand. And whoever wants to retreat — he has the power to break his legs. For the start of defeat is falling back, as it is written, "Israel fled before the Philistines and there was also a great slaughter among the people (1 Sam. 4:17). And further it is written, "And the men of Israel fled from before the Philistines and fell down slain" (1 Sam. 31:1).

M. 8:7 Under what circumstances [do the foregoing rules apply]? In the case of an optional war. But in the case of a war subject to religious requirements, everyone goes forth to battle — even a bridegroom from his chamber, and a bride from her marriage-canopy.

T. 7:24 All those concerning whom they have said, "They do not go forth at all," for example, he who builds a house and dedicated it but has not lived in it for twelve months, planted a vineyard and eaten the fruit but not made use of it for twelve months, betrothed a wife and taken her in marriage and has not remained with her twelve months [M. Sot. 8:4B] — these do not pay their share of the taxes of the town, and do not provide water and food for the battle. And they do not repair the roads. But in the case of a war imposed by obligation, everyone goes forth, even a bridegroom from his chamber and a bride from her canopy [M . Sot. 8:7].

C.   *THE RITE OF THE HEIFER*

Deut. 21:1-9: "If in the land that the Lord your God gives you to possess, any one is found slain, lying in open country, and it is not known who killed him, then your elders and your judges shall come forth, and they shall measure the distance to the cities that are around him that is slain; and the elders of the city that is nearest to the slain man shall take a heifer that has never been worked and that has not pulled in the yoke. And the elders of that city shall bring the heifer down to a valley with running water, which is neither plowed nor sown, and shall break the heifer's neck there in the valley. And the priests, the sons of Levi, shall come forward, for the Lord your God has chosen them to minister to him and to bless in the name of the Lord, and by their word every dispute and every assault shall be settled. And all the elders of that city nearest to the slain man shall wash their hands over the heifer whose neck was broken in the valley; and they shall testify, 'Our hands did not shed this blood, neither did our eyes see it shed. Forgive, O Lord, thy people Israel, whom thou hast redeemed, and set not the guilt of innocent blood in the midst of thy people Israel; but let the built of blood be forgiven them.' So you shall purge the guilt of innocent blood from your midst, when you do what is right in the sight of the Lord."

M. 9:1 The rite of the heifer whose neck is to be broken is said in the Holy Language, since it is said, "If one be found slain in the land lying in the field..." "Then your elders your judges shall come forth" (Deut. 21:1-2). Three from the high court in Jerusalem went forth.

T. 9:1 If it [a neglected corpse] was found on the other side of the Jordan, they would go through the rite of breaking a heifer's neck, since it is said, If in the land which the Lord your God gives you to possess, any one is found slain — to include the other side of the Jordan. [If] it was found in the entrance to a town, they nonetheless would measure. It is a religious duty to do the work of measuring. How did they do it for him? The agents of the court go forth and take markers, and they dig a hole and bury him, and they mark off his place, until they come to the high court in the hewn-stone chamber, and then they measure out. [If] it is he is found nearer the frontier, to a town in which there are gentiles, or to a town in which there is no court, they do not measure [M. Sot. 9:2E]. They measure only for a town in which there is a court. If there was a town of gentiles in between, or [if it was] near Jerusalem, they did not measure [M. Sot. 9:2E], but they left it and measured around it. The area of its winepress and its environs, lo, this is prohibited. And how large is its environs? Forty amahs.

Y. 9:1 I:3 If the slain was found at the entrance to a town [where there can be no doubt as to the nearest place], they nonetheless measure, so as to carry out in this regard the religious duty of engaging in the act of measuring.

M. 9:2 [If] it was found hidden under a heap of rocks or hanging from a tree or floating on the surface of water, they did not break the neck of a heifer. since it is said, On the ground [Deut. 21:1] — not hidden under a pile of rock. Lying — not hung on a tree. In the field — not floating on the water. [If] it was found near the frontier, near a town which had a gentile majority, or near a town which had no court, they did not break a heifer's neck. They measure only from a town which has a court. And Jerusalem does not have to bring a heifer whose neck is to be broken.

M. 9:5 The elders of Jerusalem took their leave and went away. The elders of that town bring "a heifer from the herd with which labor had not been done and which had not drawn the yoke"

(Deut. 21:3). But a blemish does not invalidate it. They brought it down into a rugged valley (and rugged is meant literally, hard, but even if it is not rugged, it is valid). And they break its neck with a hatchet from behind. And its place is prohibited for sowing and for tilling, but permitted for the combing out of flax and for quarrying stones.

Y. 9:5 I:4 *Just as in the case of the yoke stated with regard to the heifer, Scripture has treated all other sorts of labor as equivalent to pulling on the yoke, so in the case of the yoke stated with regard to the red cow Scripture has treated all other sorts of labor as equivalent to pulling on the yoke. Just as in the case of "yoke" stated with regard to the heifer, an act of labor invalidates the heifer, whether or not done with the owner's knowledge and consent, so "yoke" stated with regard to the red cow means that an act of labor done with it invalidates it, whether this is or is not with the knowledge and consent of the owner. Just as in the case of "yoke" stated with regard to the red cow the yoke [itself] invalidates the cow, so "yoke" stated with regard to the heifer [means that] the yoke invalidates it.*

M. 9:6 The elders of that town wash their hands in the place in which the neck of the heifer is broken, and they say, "Our hands have not shed this blood, nor did our eyes see it" (Deut. 21:7). Now could it enter our minds that the elders of a court might be shedders of blood? But [they mean:] He did not come into our hands so that we sent him away without food. And we did not see him and let him go along without an escort. And [it is] the priests [who] say, "Forgive, O Lord, your people Israel, whom you have redeemed, and do not allow innocent blood in the midst of your people, Israel" (Deut. 21:8). They did not have to say, "And the blood shall be forgiven them" (Deut. 21:8). But the Holy Spirit informs them, "Whenever you do this, the blood shall be forgiven to you."

M. 9:7 [If] the murderer was found before the neck of the heifer was broken, it [simply] goes forth and pastures in the herd. [If the murderer is found] after the neck of the heifer is broken, it is to be buried in its place. For to begin with it was brought in a matter of doubt. It has atoned for the matter of doubt on which account it was brought and which has gone its way. [If] the neck of the heifer was broken and afterward the murderer was found, lo, this one is put to death.

M. 9:8 [If] one witness says, "I saw the murderer," and one witness says, "You did not see him." [If] one woman says, "I saw him," and one woman says, "You did not see him," they would go through the rite of breaking the neck of the heifer. [If] one witness says, "I saw," and two say, "You did not see," they would break the neck of the heifer. [If] two say, "We saw," and one says to them, "You did not see," they did not break the neck of the heifer.

M. 9:9 When murderers became many, the rite of breaking the heifer's neck was cancelled. [This was] when Eleazar b. Dinai came along, and he was also called Tehinah b. Perishah. Then they went and called him, "Son of a murderer." When adulterers became many, the ordeal of the bitter water was cancelled. And Rabban Yohanan b. Zakkai cancelled it, since it is said, "I will not punish your daughters when they commit whoredom, nor your daughters-in-law when they commit adultery, for they themselves go apart with whores" (Hosea 4:14). When Yosé b. Yoezer of Seredah and Yosé b. Yohanan of Jerusalem died, the grape-clusters were cancelled, since it is said, "There is no cluster to eat, my soul desires the first ripe fig" (Micah 7:1).

M. 9:10 Yohanan, high priest, did away with the confession concerning tithe. Also: He cancelled the rite of the Awakeners and the Stunners. Until his time a hammer did strike in Jerusalem. And in his time no man had to ask concerning doubtfully-tithed produce.

T. 13:10 The knockers [M. Sot. 9:10B] — these are those who knock the calf between its horns, just as they stun a beast to be sacrificed for idolatry. Said to them Yohanan the high priest, "How long are you going to feed terefah-meat to the altar?" Until his time a hammer did strike in Jerusalem [M. Sot. 9: 10C] on the intermediate days of the festival. Also: he decreed concerning the confession [concerning tithes] and annulled [the rules of] doubtfully-tithed produce.

M. 9:11 When the Sanhedrin was cancelled, singing at wedding feasts was cancelled, since it is said, "They shall not drink wine with a song" (Is. 24:9).

M. 9:12 When the former prophets died out, the Urim and Tummim were "cancelled. When the sanctuary was destroyed, the Shamir-worm ceased and [so did] the honey of supim. And faithful men came to an end, since it is written, "Help, O Lord, for the godly man ceases" (Ps. 12:2).

T. 13:2 When the first Temple was destroyed, the kingship was removed from the House of David. The Urim and Thummim ceased [M. Sot. 9:12A]. The cities of refuge came to an end, as it is said, The governor told them that they were not to partake of the most holy food until there should be a priest to consult the Urim and Thummim (Ezra 2:63). This is like a man who says to his friend, "Until the dead will live," or, "Until Elijah will come.

M. 9:14 In the war against Vespasian they decreed against the wearing of wreaths by bridegrooms and against the wedding-drum. In the war against Titus they decreed against the wearing of wreaths by brides. And [they decreed] that a man should not teach

Greek to his son. In the last war [Bar Kokhba's] they decreed that a bride should not go out in a palanquin inside the town. But our rabbis [thereafter] permitted the bride to go out in a palanquin inside the town.

T. 15:8 In the war against Vespasian they decreed concerning the wearing of wreaths by bridegrooms [M. Sot. 9:14A]. And what are the sorts of bridegroom's wreaths [against which they decreed]? Those made of salt or brimstone. But those made of roses and myrtles they permitted. In the war against Titus [better: Quitus] they made a decree against crowns for brides. And what are the sorts of crowns for brides against which they made their decree? Gold-embroidered silks. But she may go forth in a cap of fine wool . And that a man should not teach Greek to his son [M. Sot. 9:14C].

T. 15:9 And that a man should not plaster his house with plaster — that is with the egg of plaster. But if he put straw or sand into the mixture, it is permitted. After the last war, they made a decree against the marriage-canopy of bridegrooms. Against what sort of marriage-canopy of bridegrooms did they make such a decree? It is against those made of gold. But he may make a framework of laths and hang on it anything he wants. And that a bride should not go forth in a palanquin in the town. But our rabbis permitted a bride to go forth in a palanquin in the town [M. Sot. 9:14D, E].

M. 7:2's final two items, the rite of the heifer whose neck is broken at the discovery of a neglected corpse and the address of the priest anointed for battle switch places. That allows the compositor of the tractate in the Mishnah (therefore, in suite, the Tosefta, Yerushalmi, and Bavli) to end with the homiletic materials of M. 9:12ff. The Mishnah shifts to an exegetical mode, citing the pertinent verses at drawing lessons from them, at M. 8:1-6, M. 9:5-6. M. 9:1-2, 7-8, by contrast, revert to the analytical presentation. The historical materials add nothing to the Halakhah.

IV. DOCUMENTARY TRAITS

A. THE MISHNAH AND THE TOSEFTA

While, as is commonly the case, the Tosefta enriches and amplifies the Halakhah as set forth in the Mishnah, here and there going its own way, the Tosefta's reading of the topic(s) in no way departs from the Mishnah's model.

B. THE YERUSHALMI AND THE BAVLI

Neither Talmud contains Halakhic materials framed around a hermeneutics of the topic other than the Mishnah's, nor should we expect otherwise.

C. THE AGGADAH AND THE HALAKHAH IN THE BAVLI

These are the Bavli's topical composites or massive miscellanies, introduced into the Talmud even though they do not constitute Mishnah-commentary, that require attention

I.E: The exposition of the themes of faithfulness; the power of sin; the effects of a single action puts into perspective the topic of the tractate, which is, the accusation of adultery. Faithfulness is the opposite; the power of sin explains the act; and the result of a single action is then underscore. The composite then draws that moral conclusion that the legal exercise requires, placing the whole into a higher plane than merely legal formalities would suggest.

I.F: continuous with the foregoing.

I.H: The treatment of adultery in more general terms picks up the immediately adjacent Mishnah-rule. The general theme of I.H is not well-constructed, but I.I leaves no doubt about the point of the whole. It is that sin is a result of arrogance, and right deed is a result of humility. The power of the whole, then, is to underscore the governing virtues and vices of the Torah, which are one set of matched opposites: humility vs. arrogance. Then the topic of the tractate is situated in that larger theological and moral framework that holds together a wide variety of specific sins and concrete virtues. What we have here is an explanation of why adultery takes place — which is the same explanation as serves for most other sins.

VI:B: The introduction of Judah and Tamar alongside the story of Samson and Delilah derives from a merely formal connection, as is made explicit. But the comparison is substantive, since the exposition makes the point that Judah was humble, Samson, arrogant.

VI:E: This massive composite underscores the arrogance of Pharaoh and the faithfulness of Israel — a proposition Scripture itself introduces into its narrative. I cannot claim that the purpose of the composite is exhausted by that one proposition, but it certainly forms a dominant motif.

IX.B: Zekhut [a lien on Heaven's grace] is attained through acts of self-abnegation, e.g., Abraham says he is dirt, the children gain zekhut through the use of dirt. The relevance here is the dirt used for the accused wife.

XIII.A: The composite here contributes to the exposition of the theme of the Mishnah. The observation that God is so humble as to permit his name to be blotted out to restore amity between husband and wife plays no role here.

XV.A and B: here we have a large theoretical essay on whether the woman requires a warning if she is to be deprived by her action of payment of her marriage-settlement. The deeper questions concern whether the outcome depends on the husband's objection to the wife's conduct, or whether we impute to the husband an attitude that he does not necessarily express. How much power does the husband have in the outcome of the transaction? This is a systematic essay in legal theory on the husband's rights and power.

XV:L: This composition fits into the context of marriage to a woman who stands in a prohibited relationship to the man; the issue is subordinate to its context.

XVIII.C: One should speak in a low voice and not in a loud voice when it comes to claiming credit or announcing failure, respectively; a subset on the theme of arrogance.

XVIII:L: The theme of the spies and the land of Canaan is introduced in the setting of Israel's successful crossing into the land, because these form the contrasting events, the former, the result of lack of faith, the latter, the consequence of an act of faith. The contrast is necessary to make the point that the Talmud's framers wish to make, which is, the crossing into the land, to which the Mishnah makes reference, forms a great act of faith and faithfulness, and this is shown by the systematic contrast to the conduct of the spies in the generation of the wilderness.

XIX.B, C, D: The topical miscellany belongs in the setting in which the Mishnah takes up the theme; Joshua b. Levi's sayings on the subject then form a subset of the former, and his sayings on generosity were joined to his other sayings before the whole was introduced. That accounts for the agglutination of D to C and the introduction of C-D along with B; and B's exposition is entirely within the rationality of Mishnah-commentary.

XXI.F: The theme of flattery is invited by the contents of the Mishnah, which refer to sages' flattering Agrippa.

XXVII.H, I, J, K: The theme of providing an escort is required by the topic of the Mishnah, the neglected corpse. The reason that the man was murdered is that those responsible for him did not provide an escort. Then providing an escort for travelers is taken up as a free-standing theme, with H, I, as systematic expositions of verses and the general theme; then J, a specific case, with K, a subset of the specific case. The principle of composite-formation and agglutination is self-evident, and there in no irrationality here.

We identify large-scale composites formulated and included in our tractate for a purpose other than Mishnah-commentary. These in general take shape around a problem, such as the husband's role in the rite, or a theme, as in the cases of Judah and Tamar, Pharaoh, Zekhut, the spies' conduct in Israel's first entry into the land, generosity, flattery, providing an escort, and the like. Two principles explain the selection of such massive miscellaneous composites. One is, to pursue a theme that the Mishnah and its exposition have required, and that explains the matter of Judah and Tamar, the spies' conduct, the matter of flattery, and the like. These composites then form a secondary but quite reasonable expansion on the exposition of the Mishnah's contents.

The second principle is the more interesting one, since the face of the Mishnah-tractate has been transformed by the materials that have been inserted in compliance with this other principle. It is, to introduce into the topic of the Mishnah-tractate a dimension of interpretation that deepens and reshapes matters. In our tractate the Talmud introduces this question: why does adultery take place, and what is the basis for jealousy? The answer is, adultery is an expression of arrogance, and so too is jealousy. A larger theory of sin and virtue then takes over this topic, among many others: sin is an expression of arrogance, and virtue, of humility. The marital bond expresses that same faithfulness that is required of Israel in relationship to God. Sin contrasts with faithfulness, since the opposite of faithfulness is arrogance, the opposite of sin, humility. A single action suffices. Judah contrasts with Samson. Pharaoh forms the very model of arrogance. Zekhut — the heritage of acts of humility performed by one's ancestors or oneself — opposes arrogance, self-abnegation, self-aggrandizement. God is humble, Pharaoh is arrogant. A low voice is used to record one's virtue, a loud voice, one's failure. The faithfulness of Israel in crossing the Jordan (and the Sea) is contrasted with the faithlessness of the spies. Flattery is a form of manipulation of the other, thus arrogance; accepting flattery is a form of self-praise.

It follows that composites that do not relate to Mishnah-exegesis, extending to the topics touched upon by the Mishnah, impose upon the theme of the Mishnah-tractate a proposition that the Mishnah-tractate lacks but invites. It is the proposition that the opposite of the vice of adultery and jealousy, imputed to the wife and the husband, respectively, is faithfulness and humility. Then the Mishnah-tractate, concerning the private affairs of home and family, is here transformed into a statement on the public condition of Israel, the people. What the framers of the Talmud say in their own behalf, and not in the setting of Mishnah-commentary, is that Israel's humility defines that virtue that God prizes, and that humility takes the form of faithfulness. Hosea could not have said it better.

V. THE HERMENEUTICS OF SOTAH

A. WHAT FUSES THE HALAKHIC DATA INTO A CATEGORY-FORMATION?

To answer this question, we go over the issues raised at the very outset, now with the entire repertoire in hand. So far as the category-formation, Sotah, in Chapters One through Nine, holds together at all, it is a compilation concerning the use of language, that is, Hebrew as against any other language, as is made explicit at M. 7:1-2:]

> M. 7:1 These are said in any language: (1) the pericope of the accused wife [Num. 5:19-22], and (2) the Confession of the tithe [Deut. 26:13-15], and (3) the recital of the Shema, [Deut. 6:4-9], and (4) the Prayer, (5) the Grace after Meals, (6) the oath of testimony [imposed by the judges], and (7) the oath concerning a bailment.
>
> M. 7:2 And these are said [only] in the Holy Language: (1) the verses of the first-fruits [Deut. 26:3-10], (2) the rite of rite of removing the shoe [Deut. 25:7,9], (3) blessings and curses [Deut. 27:15-26], (4) the blessing of the priests [Num. 6:24-26], (5) the blessing of a high priest [on the Day of Atonement], (6) the pericope of the king [Deut. 17:14-20]; (7) the pericope of the heifer whose neck is to be broken [Deut. 21:7f.], and (8) [the message] of the anointed for battle when he speaks to the people [Deut. 20:2-7].

In that context, the first six chapters are devoted to M. 7:1(1), and the remainder to M. 7:2 (8), (7), with adequate exposition of the other items, as we noted.[26]

A category-formation on language-conventions and rules can have encompassed a sizable corpus of Halakhah, involving not only the items listed here, in the category of cultic and court rites, but others that are omitted. Wherever we find fixed formulas, e.g., in writs of divorce, deeds and bonds, and the like, usages in the Temple of a formulaic character beyond those listed above, the language of social conventions, e.g., how people greet one another, and the indicators of social standing and of categorization and classification and hierarchization (father/master for son/disciple for instance) — all contain within themselves the possibility of generating language-laws, beyond

---

[26] To the present analysis, literary criticism is irrelevant. In any case it is carried out in the pertinent discussion in my *History of the Mishnaic Law of Women* (Leiden, 1979: E. J. Brill).

the catalogue given here. And the items at hand — fifteen in all — certainly can have sustained secondary amplification and clarification, following the generic hermeneutics of the Halakhah over all. So the category-formation of "the Halakhah of language and its effects, for the Temple, for the village and for the household and the family" (the three venues of the Halakhah) can be conceived and, in theory, constructed even out of the data before us. Why the Halakhah did not bring into being such a category-formation, selecting and interpreting the data within an autonomous hermeneutics such as we find for the other category-formations, I cannot say.[27]

But that formal definition of the category-formation — "Sotah: the Halakhah of language rules, both [1] Hebrew and other languages and [2] formulaic conventions in Hebrew, Aramaic, and other languages" — ignores the matter of proportion and hence cannot serve. While possible and even plausible, such a reading of what is before us hardly compels assent. And even if it did, who can imagine out of the data before us what theory of interpretation has motivated the selection of the data — this, not that, on linguistic conventions — and the interpretation thereof? I cannot, the exposition of Chapters Seven through Nine contains no hints I am able to utilize in proposing a hermeneutics other than the Scriptural and generic ones that yield so little.

What of the obvious alternative, regarding Chapters One through Six as for all intents and purposes the category-formation, the rest as an add-on? That theory of matters, which I think the framers of the Halakhah as we know it in the Mishnah-Tosefta-Yerushalmi-Bavli actually adopted, leaves open its own obvious questions of coherence and proportion. Few compilations of the Halakhah in the Mishnah-Tosefta-Yerushalmi-Bavli accommodate so disproportionately large a topical appendix for so paltry a Halakhic exposition — six chapters to three, in the rough but handy proportions at hand. Where

---

[27] I can readily conceive the design of a project on Halakhic category-formations that might have been effected. The data would derive not only from the Mishnah but also, and especially, from the Tosefta. At issue would be other modes of category-formation entirely, besides the topical ones; other modes of organizing existing Halakhic compositions and composites besides the present definition; and even other theories of conglomeration of existing, discrete Halakhic formations — Scriptures for instance — besides the governing ones. It would be a work of sustained, disciplined imagination, that is to say, a reconsideration of the Halakhic data from entirely fresh perspectives. All re-presentations of the Halakhah undertaken from the Bavli forward, e.g., codes of the law, culminating in Maimonides' total reconstruction of the Halakhah, embody such exercises in disciplined imagination. At this time, however, I myself do not contemplate undertaking such a project.

topics prove multiple and diverse, as at Yebamot, we have had no difficulty accounting for the cogency of the several components of the whole. Where there is a blatant shift in interest, e.g., Yoma Chapter Eight from Chapters One through Seven and Pesahim Chapter Ten from Chapters One through Nine, or a whole series of shifts, as at Shabbat-Erubin, viewed whole or in part, we readily identify the thick threads that run through the entire fabric of the Halakhah, start to finish. The category-formation of Shabbat-Erubin, after all, is the unitary one: the Halakhah of the Sabbath — and so for the rest. But here we deal with an anomaly, since if we were to deem "the Halakhah of language-conventions" as the unifying topic, the disproportions would be reversed: too little for the main theme, too much for one subordinate component thereof, that is, Chapters Seven through Nine as against Chapters One through Six![28]

The problem of the particular hermeneutics of Sotah Chapters One through Nine, which I cannot solve, should not obscure a simple fact. For the tractate viewed whole — accepting what we have without trying to explain how the whole holds together — we have no difficulty in defining the principle of interpretation that governs. They are two, each generic in its context, [1] the general rules of Scriptural interpretation in the Halakhic framework, [2] the general rules of philosophical analysis in the Halakhic context. Whether for the bulk of the Chapters One through Six, or for the exposition of Chapters Seven through Nine, Scripture's presentation of matters defines the data and how they are read, which is through the routine exegetical procedures of clarification and extension that, in general, Scripture is deemed to generate on its own. The usual temporal-ordinal sequence takes over, beginning, middle, and end, for one obvious example. And, for the rest, the component of the hermeneutical composite before us that does not derive from Scripture finds its definition in the generic hermeneutics of the Halakhah, as that hermeneutics pertains throughout.

So to answer the question, what fuses the Halakhic data into a category-formation, let us revert to Chapters One through Six and concentrate on what data have been selected and how these are interpreted. Now, as I said at the outset, the hermeneutics is blatant — but only implicit in the Halakhah, articulated principally in the Aggadah, whether within the Halakhic compilations or otherwise. What we have is a hermeneutics focused upon the perfect justice of Heaven.

Now to spell this out. Justice defines the problematics of the topic, the wife accused of adultery, and the theme of how the righteous are rewarded and the wicked punished through the reliable working of God's justice permeates

---

[28] And who is to evaluate the wildly-irrelevant materials with which Chapter Nine concludes!

the Oral Torah's exposition of the topic at hand. And, still more to the point, the sages choose this particular topic — Sotah read as an exercise of justice in the household, justice for the accused wife — as the centerpiece of its presentation of evidence that, in the end, God does justice for all to see. Sages recapitulate the rite only to recast it into a juridical transaction, one involving procedures that protect the woman's right and secure, so far as possible, her dignity under the burden of her husband's accusation. They do not allow the husband lightly to sever the marriage without paying the marriage-settlement, they hold the male participant equally culpable, though, in the nature of things, not equally at risk, and they do insist on the normal rules of evidence, so far as these pertain.

As the sages re-present the ordeal imposed on the accused wife, they underscore the exact justice that the ordeal executes. The exposition of the topic in the Mishnah and the Tosefta, therefore also in the Talmuds, lays heavy emphasis upon how, measure for measure, the punishment fits the crime — but the reward matches the virtue as well. What the guilty wife has done, the law punishes appropriately; but also, they point to cases in which acts of merit receive appropriate recognition and reward. In this way sages make the point that, within the walls of the household, rules of justice prevail, with reward for goodness and punishment for evil the standard in the household as much as in public life. Why sages have chosen the Halakhah of the accused wife as the venue for their systematic exposition of the divine law of justice is not difficult to explain.

The law of the accused wife renders urgent the question of whether and how justice governs in the household. Scripture, as we note, imposes the ordeal not only upon the adulteress but on the faithful wife. A spirit of jealousy suffices, whether or not the wife warrants the husband's suspicion. Surely the entire procedure reeks of injustice, and the promise of future offspring hardly compensates for the public humiliation that the innocent wife has undergone. It is in that context that, in the very presentation of the Halakhah, the Oral Torah systematically lays out the evidence that, here, especially here, justice prevails. And that means not only that the wicked woman is punished, but that the righteous one is rewarded. What for Scripture is tacked on as an afterthought in the Oral Torah becomes a principal focus of exposition.

If we turn from Sotah's (first six chapters') Halakhah to the Aggadah associated therewith, we find precisely the same focus on how God's perfect justice is embodied in the very rite of the accused wife. In sages' view, which animates every line in the Oral Torah, the will of the one, unique God, made manifest through the Torah, governs, and, further, God's will, for both private life and public activity, is rational. That is to say, within man's understanding of reason, God's will is just. And by "just," sages understood the commonsense meaning: fair, equitable, proportionate, commensurate. In place of fate or impersonal destiny, chance, or simply irrational, inexplicable chaos, God's plan and purpose everywhere come to realization. So the Oral Torah in the Aggadic representation of the Halakhic topic identifies God's will as the active and causative force in the lives of individuals and nations.

But the coherence of the theology hardly presents a surprise. The more urgent question is, how do sages know that God's will is realized in the moral order of justice, involving reward and punishment? Sages turned to Scripture for the pertinent facts; that is where God makes himself manifest. But of the various types of scriptural evidence — explicit commandments, stories, prophetic admonitions — that they had available to show how the moral order prevailed in all being, what type did the prefer? The one bearing the greatest probative weight derived from the exact match between sin and punishment. Here is their starting point; from here all else flows smoothly and in orderly fashion. World order is best embodied when sin is punished, merit rewarded — both; one without the other does not suffice.

That body of evidence, the facts, that Scripture supplied recorded human action and divine reaction, on the one side, and meritorious deed and divine response and reward, on the other. It was comprised by consequential cases, drawn from both private and public life, to underscore sages' insistence upon the match between the personal and the public, all things subject to the same simple rule. That demonstration of not only the principle but the precision of measure for measure, deriving from Scripture's own record of God's actions, takes priority of place in the examination of the rationality of sages' universe. That is because it permeates their system and frames its prevailing modes of explanation and argument. The principle that all being conforms to rules, and that these rules embody principles of justice through exact punishment of particular sin, precise reward of singular acts of virtue defined the starting point of all rational thought and the entire character of sages' theological structure and system. What we see in the topic at hand is of special interest: when sages wish to show the justice of God, they turn to the case before us.

It is here, in particular, that sages identify the sources for their conviction of the order of society, natural and supernatural alike. What captures our interest is not the conviction but the way in which sages set forth that conviction. What they found to overcome the doubt that everyday life surely cast upon their insistence upon the governing of a moral order was the facts of Scripture as they ordered those facts. Now, were we on our own to open Scripture and locate pertinent evidence that God is just and the world he made conforms to rules of equity, we should find Scripture states it in so many words. It is not merely that when God contemplated the world that he had made, he pronounced it good; Scripture leaves no doubt about God's definitive trait of justice, justice understood as man does, in a different context altogether.

That is why, when sages examined the facts of Scripture to establish that principle of rationality and order in conformity to the requirements of justice and equity, what impressed them was not the inevitability but the precision of justice. Scripture portrays the world order as fundamentally just and reasonable, and it does so in countless ways. But Scripture encompasses the complaint of Job and the reflection of Qoheleth. Sages for their part identified those cases that transcended generalities and established the facticity of proportionate justice, treating them as not only exemplary but probative. They set forth their proposition and amassed evidence in support of it. And, to underscore the point that sages demonstrate in the present Halakhic category: when God judges and sentences, not only is the judgment fair but the penalty fits the crime with frightening precision. But so too, when God judges and awards a decision of merit, the reward proves equally exact. These two together, the match of sin and penalty, meritorious deed and reward, then are shown to explain the point and purpose of one detail after another, and, all together, they add up to the portrait of a world order that is fundamentally and essentially just — the starting point and foundation of all else.

Here is sages' account of God's justice, which is always commensurate, both for reward and punishment, in consequence of which the present permits us to peer into the future with certainty of what is going to happen, so M. Sot. 1:7ff. What we note is sages' identification of the precision of justice, the exact match of action and reaction, each step in the sin, each step in the response, and, above all, the immediacy of God's presence in the entire transaction. They draw general conclusions from the specifics of the law that Scripture sets forth, and that is where systematic thinking about takes over from exegetical learning about cases, or, in our own categories, philosophy from history, noted earlier:

    A. By that same measure by which a man metes out [to others], do they mete out to him:

    B. She primped herself for sin, the Omnipresent made her repulsive.

    C. She exposed herself for sin, the Omnipresent exposed her.

MISHNAH-TRACTATE SOTAH 1:7

We begin with sages' own general observations based on the facts set forth in Scripture. The course of response of the woman accused of adultery to her drinking of the bitter water that is supposed to produce one result for the guilty, another for the innocent, is described in Scripture in this language: "If no man has lain with you...be free from this water of bitterness that brings the curse. But if you have gone astray...then the Lord make you an execration...when the Lord makes your thigh fall away and your body swell; may this water...pass into your bowels and make your body swell and your thigh fall away" (Num. 5:20-22). This is amplified and expanded, extended to the entire rite, where the woman is disheveled; then the order, thigh, belly, shows the perfect precision of the penalty. What Scripture treats as a case, sages transform into a generalization, so making Scripture yield governing rules. The same passage proceeds to further cases, which prove the same point: where the sin begins, there the punishment also commences; but also, where an act of virtue takes its point, there divine reward focuses as well. Merely listing the following names, without spelling out details, for the cognoscenti of Scripture will have made that point: Samson, Absalom, Miriam, Joseph, and Moses. Knowing how Samson and Absalom match, also Miriam, Joseph, and Moses, would then suffice to establish the paired and matched general principles.

Justice requires not only punishment of the sinner or the guilty but reward of the righteous and the good, and so sages find ample, systematic evidence in Scripture for both sides of the equation of justice:

    A. And so is it on the good side:
    B. Miriam waited a while for Moses, since it is said, "And his sister stood afar off" (Ex. 2:4), therefore, Israel waited on her seven days in the wilderness, since it is said, "And the people did not travel on until Miriam was brought in again" (Num. 12:15).

MISHNAH-TRACTATE SOTAH 1:9

    A. Joseph had the merit of burying his father, and none of his brothers was greater than he, since it is said, "And Joseph went up to bury his father...and there went up with him both chariots and horsemen" (Gen. 50:7, 9).
    B. We have none so great as Joseph, for only Moses took care of his [bones].
    C. Moses had the merit of burying the bones of Joseph, and none in Israel was greater than he, since it is said, "And Moses took the bones of Joseph with him" (Ex. 13:19).
    D. We have none so great as Moses, for only the Holy One blessed he Be took care of his [bones], since it is said, "And he buried him in the valley" (Deut. 34:6).

E. And not of Moses alone have they stated [this rule], but of all righteous people, since it is said, "And your righteousness shall go before you. The glory of the Lord shall gather you [in death]" (Is. 58:8).

MISHNAH-TRACTATE SOTAH 1:10

Scripture provides the main probative evidence for the anticipation that when God judges, he will match the act of merit with an appropriate reward and the sin with an appropriate punishment. The proposition begins, however, with general observations as to how things are, M. 1:7, and not with specific allusions to proof-texts; the character of the law set forth in Scripture is reflected upon. The accumulated cases yield the generalization.

Sifré to Numbers, a systematic exegesis of the biblical book of Numbers, takes up the Mishnah's proposition concerning Numbers 5:23ff., that, when God punishes, he starts with that with which the transgression commenced, which sages see as a mark of the precision of divine justice:

SIFRÉ TO NUMBERS XVIII:I.1:
1. A. "And when he has made her drink the water, [then, if she has defiled herself and has acted unfaithfully against her husband, the water that brings the curse shall enter into her and cause bitter pain,] and her body shall swell, and her thigh shall fall away, [and the woman shall become an execration among her people. But if the woman has not defiled herself and is clean, then she shall be free and shall conceive children]" (Num. 5:23-28).
   B. I know only that her body and thigh are affected. How do I know that that is the case for the rest of her limbs?
   C. Scripture states, "...the water that brings the curse shall enter into her."
   D. So I take account of the phrase, "...the water that brings the curse shall enter into her."
   E. Why [if all the limbs are affected equally] then does Scripture specify her body and her thigh in particular?
   F. As to her thigh, the limb with which she began to commit the transgression -- from there the punishment begins.

But the sages represented by Sifré to Numbers, exegetes of Scripture and the Mishnah, like the commentators whom we shall meet in the Tosefta that follows, wish to introduce their own cases in support of the same proposition:

G. Along these same lines:
H. "And he blotted out everything that sprouted from the earth, from man to beast" (Gen. 7:23.
I. From the one who began the transgression [namely Adam, the punishment begins.

Adam sinned first, therefore the flood began with Adam. Now comes a different sort of proportion: the exact match. The Sodomites are smitten with piles:

J. Along these same lines:
K. "..and the men who were at the gate of the house they smote with piles" (Gen. 19:11).
L. From the one who began the transgression the punishment begins.

In the third instance, Pharaoh is in the position of Adam; with him the sin began, with him the punishment starts:

M. Along these same lines:
N. "...and I shall be honored through Pharaoh and through all of his force" (Ex. 14:4).
O. Pharaoh began the transgression, so from him began the punishment.
P. Along these same lines:
Q. "And you will most certainly smite at the edge of the sword the inhabitants of that city" (Deut. 134:15).
R. From the one who began the transgression, the punishment begins.
S. Along these same lines is the present case:
T. The limb with which she began to commit the transgression -- from there the punishment begins.

Here comes a point important to the system: God's mercy vastly exceeds his justice, so the measure of reward is far greater than the measure of punishment — and, if possible, still more prompt:

U. Now does this not yield an argument *a fortiori:*
V. If in the case of the attribution of punishment, which is the lesser, from the limb with which she began to commit the transgression -- from there the punishment begins,

W. in the case of the attribute of bestowing good, which is the greater, how much the more so!

Punishment is rational in yet a more concrete way: it commences with the very thing that has sinned, or with the person who has sinned. So the principles of reason and good order pervade the world. We know that fact because Scripture's account of all that matters has shown it. But the exposition of justice commences with the topic at hand.

The Tosefta as usual takes a fresh look at matters and asks questions left open by the Mishnah. It thus contributes further cases illustrating the exact and appropriate character of both divine justice and divine reward. What is important here is what is not made explicit; it concerns a question that the Mishnah does not raise: what about the gentiles? Does the principle of world order of justice apply to them, or are they subject to chaos? The answer given through cases here is that the same rules of justice apply to gentiles, not only Israelites such as are listed in the Mishnah's primary statement of the principle. That point is made through the cases that are selected: Sennacherib, who besieged Jerusalem after destroying Israel comprised by the northern tribes, Nebuchadnezzar, who took and destroyed Jerusalem in the time of Jeremiah. Now the sin is the single most important one, arrogance or hubris, and the penalty is swift and appropriate, the humbling of the proud by an act of humiliation:

A. Sennacherib took pride before the Omnipresent only through an agent, as it is said, "By your messengers you have mocked the Lord and you have said, "With my many chariots I have gone up the heights of the mountains . . . I dug wells and drank foreign waters, and I dried up with the sole of my foot all the streams of Egypt" (11 Kings 19:23-24).

B. So the Omnipresent, blessed be He, exacted punishment from him only through an agent, as it is said, "And that night the messenger of the Lord went forth and slew a hundred and eighty-five thousand in the camp of the Assyrians" (2 Kings 19:35).

C. And all of them were kings, with their crowns bound to their heads.

TOSEFTA TRACTATE SOTAH 3:18

A. Nebuchadnezzar said, "The denizens of this earth are not worthy for me to dwell among them. I shall make for myself a little cloud and dwell In it," as it is said, "I will ascend above the heights of the clouds, I will make myself like the Most High" (Is. 14:14).

B. Said to him the Omnipresent, blessed be He, "You said in your heart, 'I will ascend to heaven, above the stars of God I will set my throne on high' — I shall bring you down to the depths of the pit" (Is. 14:13, 15).
C. What does it say? "But you are brought down to Sheol, to the depths of the pit" (Is. 14:15).
D. Were you the one who said, "The denizens of this earth are not worthy for me to dwell among them"?
E. The king said, "Is not this great Babylon, which I have built by my mighty power as a royal residence and for the glory of my majesty? While the words were still in the king's mouth, there fell a voice from heaven, O King Nebuchadnezzar, to you it is spoken, The kingdom has departed from you, and you shall be driven from among men, and your dwelling shall be with the beasts of the field, and you shall be made to eat grass like an ox" (Dan. 4:29-32).
F. All this came upon King Nebuchadnezzar at the end of twelve months (Dan. 4:28-29).

TOSEFTA TRACTATE SOTAH 3:19

As in the Mishnah, so here too, we wish to prove that justice governs not only to penalize sin but also to reward virtue. To this point we have shown the proportionate character of punishment to sin, the exact measure of justice. The first task in this other context is to establish the proportions, now of reward to punishment.

Is reward measured out with the same precision? Not at all, reward many times exceeds punishment. So if the measure of retribution is exactly proportionate to the sin, the measure of reward exceeds the contrary measure by a factor of five hundred. Later on we shall see explicit argument that justice without mercy is incomplete; to have justice, mercy is the required complement. Here we address another aspect of the same matter, that if the measure of punishment precisely matches the measure of sin, when it comes to reward for merit or virtue, matters are not that way:

A. I know only with regard to the measure of retribution that by that same measure by which a man metes out, they mete out to him [M. Sot. 1:7A]. How do I know that the same is so with the measure of goodness [M. Sot. 1:9A]?
B. Thus do you say:'
C. The measure of goodness is five hundred times greater than the measure of retribution.
D. With regard to the measure of retribution it is written, "Visiting the sin of the fathers on the sons and on the grandsons to the third and fourth generation" (Ex. 20:5).

E. And with regard to the measure of goodness it is written, "And doing mercy for thousands' (Ex. 20:6).

F. You must therefore conclude that the measure of goodness is five hundred times greater than the measure of retribution.
TOSEFTA TRACTATE SOTAH 4:1

Having made that point, we revert to the specifics of cases involving mortals, not God, and here, we wish to show the simple point that reward and punishment meet in the precision of justice.

Before proceeding to the Tosefta's extension of matters in a quite unanticipated direction, let us turn to further amplifications of the basic point concerning the exact character of the punishment for a given sin. The fact is, not only does the sinner lose what he or she wanted, but the sinner also is denied what formerly he or she had possessed, a still more mordant and exact penalty indeed. At T. Sotah 4:16, the statement of the Mishnah, "Just as she is prohibited to her husband, so she is prohibited to her lover" [M. Sot. 5:1], is transformed into a generalization, which is spelled out, and then demonstrated by a list lacking all articulation; the items on the list serve to make the point. The illustrative case — the snake and Eve — is given at T. 4:17-18. The list then follows at T. 4:19.

A. Just as she is prohibited to her husband, so she is prohibited to her lover:
B. You turn out to rule in the case of an accused wife who set her eyes on someone who was not available to her:
C. What she wanted is not given to her, and what she had in hand is taken away from her.
TOSEFTA SOTAH 4:16

The poetry of justice is not lost: what the sinner wanted he does not get, and what he had he loses:

A. And so you find in the case of the snake of olden times, who was smarter than all the cattle and wild beasts of the field, as it is said, 'Now the serpent was smarter than any other wild creature that the Lord God had made'" (Gen. 3:1).
B. He wanted to slay Adam and to marry Eve.
C. The Omnipresent said to him, "I said that you should be king over all beasts and wild animals. Now that you did not want things that way, 'You are more cursed than all the beasts and wild animals of the field' (Gen. 3:14).

> D. "I said that you should walk straight-up like man. Now that you did not want things that way, 'Upon your belly you shall go' (Gen. 3:14).
> E. "I said that you should eat human food and drink human drink. Now: 'And dust you shall eat all the days of your life' (Gen. 3:14).
>
> TOSEFTA SOTAH 4:17
>
> A. "You wanted to kill Adam and marry Eve? 'And I will put enmity between you and the woman' (Gen. 3:15)."
> B. You turn out to rule, What he wanted was not given to him, and what he had in hand was taken away from him.
>
> TOSEFTA SOTAH 4:18

Sages' mode of thought through classification and hierarchization to uncover patterns does not require the spelling out of the consequences of the pattern through endless cases. On the contrary, sages are perfectly happy to list the other examples of the same rule, knowing that we can reconstruct the details if we know the facts of Scripture that have been shown to follow a common paradigm:

> A. And so you find in the case of Cain, Korah, Balaam, Doeg, Ahitophel, Gahazi, Absalom, Adonijah, Uzziah, and Haman, all of whom set their eyes on what they did not have coming to them.
> B. What they wanted was not given to them, and what they had in hand was taken away from them.
>
> TOSEFTA SOTAH 4:19

Were we given only T. 4:19A, a construction lacking all explanation, we should have been able to reach T. 4:19B! Here is a fine example of how a pattern signals its own details, and how knowing the native categories allows us to elaborate the pattern with little further data. But whether we should have identified as the generative message, What he wanted was not given to him, and what he had in hand was taken away from him, is not equivalently clear, and I am inclined to think that without the fully-exposed example, we could not have done what the compositor has instructed us to do: fill out the *et cetera*. What a passage of this kind underscores is sages' confidence that those who would study their writings saw the paradigm within the case and possessed minds capable of generalization and objective demonstration.

As to Tosefta Sotah 4:1, which we considered above, sages both distinguish the realm of the Torah from the realm of idolatry, Israel from the gentiles, but also treat the two realms as subject to one and the same rule justice. But then what difference does the Torah make for holy Israel, the Torah's sector of humanity? As the Tosefta's passage that we first met just now proceeds, discussion shades over into a response to this very question. The point concerning reward and punishment is made not at random but through the close reading of Scripture's record concerning not only the line of Noah — the Generation of the Flood, the men of Sodom and Gomorrah, the Egyptians — but also the founder of God's line on earth, Abraham. Abraham here, often head of the line with Isaac and Jacob, is deemed the archetype for Israel, his extended family. What he did affects his heirs. His actions form models for the right conduct of his heirs. What happened to him will be recapitulated in the lives and fate of his heirs.

So from retributive justice and the gentiles, the discourse shifts to distributive reward, shared by the founder and his heirs later on. Reward also is governed by exact justice, the precision of the deed matched by the precision of the response:

> G. And so you find in the case of Abraham that by that same measure by which a man metes out, they mete out to him.
> H. He ran before the ministering angels three times, as it is said, "When he saw them, he ran to meet them" (Gen. 18:2), "And Abraham hastened to the tent" (Gen. 18:6), "And Abraham ran to the herd" (Gen. 18:7).
> I. So did the Omnipresent, blessed be He, run before his children three times, as it is said, 'The Lord came from Sinai, and dawned from Seir upon us; he shone forth from Mount Paran" (Deut. 33:2).
>
> TOSEFTA TRACTATE SOTAH 4:1

Justice extends beyond the limits of a single life, when the life is Abraham's. Now justice requires that Abraham's heirs participate in the heritage of virtue that he has bequeathed. Point by point, God remembers Abraham's generous actions in favor of Abraham's children into the long future, an intimation of a doctrine involving a heritage of grace that will play a considerable role in the theological system, as we shall see in due course. Here, point by point, what Abraham does brings benefit to his heirs:

> A. Of Abraham it is said, "He bowed himself to the earth" (Gen. 18:2).
> B. So will the Omnipresent, blessed be He, respond graciously to his children in time to come, "Kings will be your foster-fathers, and their queens your nursing mothers. With their faces to the ground they shall bow down to you and lick the dust of your feet" (Is. 49:23).
> C. Of Abraham it is said, "Let a little water be brought" (Gen. 18:4).

D. So did the Omnipresent, blessed be He, respond graciously and give to his children a well in the wilderness, which gushed through the whole camp of Israel, as it is said, "The well which the princes dug, which the nobles of the people delved (Num. 21:18) teaching that it went over the whole south and watered the entire desert, which looks down upon the desert" (Num. 2 1 :20).

E. Of Abraham it is said, "And rest yourselves under the tree" (Gen. 18:4).

F. So the Omnipresent gave his children seven glorious clouds in the wilderness, one on their right, one on their left, one before them, one behind them, one above their heads, and one as the Presence among them.

TOSEFTA TRACTATE SOTAH 4:2

The same theme is expounded in a systematic way through the entire account; it is worth dealing with the complete statement:

A. Of Abraham it is said, "While I fetch a morsel of bread that you may refresh yourselves" (Gen. 18:5).

B. So did the Omnipresent, blessed be He, give them manna in the wilderness, as it is said, "The people went about and gathered it... and made cakes of it, and the taste of it was like the taste of cakes baked with oil" (Num. 11:8).

TOSEFTA TRACTATE SOTAH 4:3

A. Of Abraham it is said, "And Abraham ran to the herd and took a calf, tender and good" (Gen. 18:7).

B. So the Omnipresent, blessed be He, rained down quail from the sea for his children, as it is said, "And there went forth a wind from the Lord, and it brought quails from the sea, and let them fall beside the camp" (Num. 11:31).

4:5 A. Of Abraham what does it say? "And Abraham stood over them" (Gen. I 8:8).

B. So the Omnipresent, blessed be He, watched over his children in Egypt, as it is said, "And the Lord passed over the door" (Ex. 12:23).

4:6 A. Of Abraham what does it say? 'And Abraham went with them to set them on their way" (Gen. 18:16).

B. So the Omnipresent, blessed be He, accompanied his children for forty years, as it is said, "These forty years the Lord your God has been with you" (Deut. 2:7).

TOSEFTA TRACTATE SOTAH 4:4

The evidence is of the same character as that adduced in the Mishnah: cases of Scripture. But the power of the Tosefta's treatment of Abraham must be felt: finding an exact counterpart in Israel's later history to each gesture of the progenitor, Abraham, shows the match between the deeds of the patriarchs and the destiny of their family later on. Justice now is given dimensions we should not have anticipated, involving not only the individual but the individual's family, meaning, the entire community of holy Israel. Once more, we note, a systematic effort focuses upon details. Justice is not a generalized expectation but a very particular fact, bread/manna, calf/quail, and so on. There is where sages find the kind of detailed evidence that corresponds to the sort suitable in natural history.

The focus now shifts shift from how justice applies to the actions of named individuals — Samson, Absalom, Sennacherib and Nebuchadnezzar — to the future history of Israel, the entire sector of humanity formed by those whom God has chosen and to whom he will give eternal life. It is a jarring initiative. The kinds of instances of justice that are given until that point concern sin and punishment, or the reward of individuals for their own actions. And these cases surely conform to the context: justice as the principle that governs what happens to individuals in an orderly world. But now we find ample evidence of the fundamental position in sages' system, the generative character in their consideration of all issues that, as the first principle of world order, that justice governs.

For sages not only accept the burden of proving, against all experience, that goodness goes to the good and evil to the wicked. They have also alleged, and here propose to instantiate, that the holy people Israel itself, its history, its destiny, conform to the principle of justice. And if claim that justice governs in the lives and actions of private persons conflicts with experience, the condition of Israel, conquered and scattered, surely calls into question any allegation that Israel's story embodies that same orderly and reasonable principle. Before us sages take one step forward in their consideration of that very difficult question, how to explain the prosperity of the idolaters, the gentiles, and the humiliation of those who serve the one true God, Israel. That step consists only in matching what Abraham does with what happens to his family later on.

If sages had to state the logic that imposes order and proportion upon all relationships — the social counterpart to the laws of gravity — they would point to justice: what accords with justice is logical, and what does not is irrational. Ample evidence derives from Scripture's enormous corpus of facts to sustain in sages view that the moral order, based on justice, governs the affairs of men and nations. But justice begins in the adjudication of the affairs of men and women in the Israelite household and from there radiates outward, to the social order of Israel, and thence, the world order of the nations. It is from the Halakhah before us that sages commence their exposition of God's perfect justice, in rewarding the innocent and punishing the guilty, because only there could they state their deepest conviction concerning justice: all things start in the Israelite household, the smallest whole social unit of creation.

B. THE ACTIVITY OF THE CATEGORY-FORMATION

Before the ordeal is invoked, the Oral Torah wants some sort of solid evidence [1] of untoward sexual activity and also [2] of clear action on the part of the wife: at least the possibility, confirmed through a specific case, that adultery has taken place. Scripture leaves everything to the husband's whim, the "spirit of jealousy." So here if the husband gives his statement of jealousy and the wife responds by ignoring the statement, the ordeal does not apply. By her specific action the wife has to indicate the possibility that the husband is right. This is a far cry from Scripture's "spirit of jealousy." For the Written Torah, the ordeal settles all questions. For the Oral Torah, the ordeal takes effect only in carefully defined cases where [1] sufficient evidence exists to invoke the rite, but [2] insufficient evidence to make it unnecessary: well-established doubt, so to speak.

The Halakhah of the Oral Torah further introduces the clarification that the marriage must be a valid one; if the marriage violates the law of the Torah, e.g., the marriage of a widow to a high priest, the rite of the ordeal does not apply. The rite does not apply at the stage of betrothal, only of a fully consummated marriage. If the fiancé expressed jealousy to the betrothed or the levir to the deceased childless brother's widow, no rite is inflicted. Sages severely limited the range of applicability of the rite. Not only so, but the marriage may well be severed without the ordeal's being inflicted, if the wife confesses, if there are witnesses to the act, if the wife declines to go through the ordeal, if the husband declines to impose it, or if the husband has sexual relations with her en route to the performance of the ordeal. In such cases the marital bond is called into question, so the wife loses her status as wife of a priest, should the husband be a priest. If in the preliminaries to the ordeal she confesses, she is given a writ of divorce, losing her marriage-settlement. Only if she continues to plead purity is the ordeal imposed. The details of the rite are meant to match the sequence of actions that the unfaithful wife has taken with the paramour, beautifully expounded at M. 1:7 and its accompanying Tosefta-composite, cited in the interpretive section of this account.

The Halakhah makes provision for the cancellation of the rite, down to the point at which the scroll is blotted out, with the divine names inscribed therein. At that point, the accused wife can no longer pull out of the ordeal. That moment matches, in effect, the moment of death of the sacrifier, when we have to dispose of the animals that he has sanctified for his offering. But if at that point she confesses, the water is poured out, and she loses her marriage-settlement but otherwise is left alone. So too, if witnesses come, or if she refuses to drink, or if the husband pulls out, the meal offering is burned. The exposition of the other rites follows the standard program of the Mishnah's analysis of the Halakhah, and generic Halakhic exposition need not detain us.

C. THE CONSISTENCY OF THE CATEGORY-FORMATION

If we read the category-formation in light of all nine chapters of the Halakhah, we find a diffuse and disproportionate reading of one topic. If we read the category-formation as fully exposed in Chapters One through Six, we come up with a cogent narrative. Nothing in the second reading disrupts the smooth unfolding of the topic, reading within a single generative hermeneutics, one quite appropriate and particular to the topic.

D. THE GENERATIVITY OF THE CATEGORY-FORMATION

Having come this far, we must wonder, how is it possible that while the Aggadic exposition of the category-formation focuses so sharply on the reading of the data in light of God's perfect justice both in punishing and in rewarding, the Halakhic presentation should in no way invoke the same hermeneutics? The Written Torah appears superficially to have set forth the program of the Oral Torah's Halakhah, but in fact, sages have redefined the entire program of the topic. In their way, in the small shifts and subtle details, they too re-present the category-formation within the same hermeneutics. The category-formation in action, as distinct from articulation, imparts to the data the imprint of sages' theory of matters.

The Halakhah takes the ordeal and encases it in juridical procedures, rules of evidence, guidelines meant to protect the woman from needless exposure to the ordeal to begin with. The Halakhah radically revises the entire transaction, when it says, if the husband expresses jealousy by instructing his wife not to speak with a specified person, and the wife spoke with the man, there is no juridical result: she still is permitted to have sexual relations with her husband and is permitted to eat heave-offering. But if she went with him to some private place and remained with him for sufficient time to become unclean, she is prohibited from having sexual relations with her husband and if the husband is a priest, she is prohibited from eating heave-offering.

The Halakhah thus conceives of a two-stage process, two kinds of testimony. In the first kind, she is warned not to get involved, but she is not then prohibited to the husband. In the second kind of stage, witnesses attest that she can have committed adultery. Not only so, but the Halakhah wants valid evidence if it is to deprive the wife of her marriage-settlement. If a single witness to the act of intercourse is available, that does not suffice. People who ordinarily cannot testify against her do not have the power to deprive her if her property rights in the marriage, e.g., her mother-in-law and the daughter of her mother-in-law, her co-wife, and the husband's brother's wife, and the daughter of her husband. She still collects her settlement. But because of their testimony, she does not undergo the rite; she is divorced in course and the transaction concludes there.

If I had to summarize in a single sentence the main thrust of the Halakhah of Sotah, it is to create the conditions of perfect, unresolved doubt, so far as the husband is concerned, alongside perfect certainty of innocence, so far as the wife is concerned. Despite the humiliation that awaits, she is willing to place her marriage-settlement on the line, so sure is she that she is innocent. His doubt is well-founded, but remains a matter of doubt, so uncertain is he of her status. Then, and only then, the ordeal intervenes to resolve the exquisitely-balanced scale of her certainty against his doubt. In the balance sages do justice to both aggrieved parties, the one whose grievance is legitimate, the one whose grievance is dubious — as the case may be.

6.
TRACTATE GITTIN

I. THE DEFINITION OF THE CATEGORY-FORMATION

How in the case of Gittin does analogical-contrastive thinking shape the interpretation of the transaction and the selection of the data? Gittin principally concerns severing the relationship that consecrates a woman to a man. The divorce is accomplished by means of a document that the man at his sole initiative prepares, the woman at her entire discretion and awareness receives, and Heaven confirms. Everything depends upon the document, which, properly done on earth, is ratified in Heaven. The critical stage in the process comes with the intentionalities of each party to the transaction. The hermeneutics that comes to concretization in the exegetical program emerges at those points at which the husband and the wife, respectively, are assigned responsibility for the correct realization of the matter, each able at a critical turning to exercise his or her particular will. That is at the outset for the husband, at the end for the wife. Then, to answer the question with which we started, what are compared are the transactions of sanctification at the outset of the relationship and of desanctification at the end. At the betrothal the man initiated, the woman consented to the relationship. At the end, the woman reenters secular status of the unattached woman, regaining that complete freedom of will that she relinquished in accepting, in betrothal, the status of sanctification to a given man. Here the key is, just as both parties participate in establishing the relationship of sanctification, both participate in ending it. But each has a distinctive responsibility and role.

If that is the principal point, there is a quite other contrast to be drawn, and that is, between the two ways of ending a marriage, death and the writ of divorce, the former not subject to the intentionality of either party to the marriage, the latter subject to that of both. Then — at this second level of analogical-contrastive analysis, the counterpart to Heaven's sundering the union through death is man's provision of a proper piece of writing. The contrast is jarring: death and a document produce the same result in this context. But a moment of thought shows the rationality of the comparison. In a system that identifies in a properly-prepared piece of writing the principal medium for God's communication with man, the Torah being the embodiment of the covenant between God and Israel, the writ of divorce functions in an analogous way. That is to say, at the second level of analogical-contrastive analysis the writ of divorce compares with the written Torah as writing representing Heaven's engagement with Israel, the one public, the other private, the one establishing, the other dissolving a consecrated union, God with Israel, husband with wife, respectively. That is the point at which the issue of intentionality becomes acute.

Then at what point does the wife's intentionality actually register? To jump ahead and identify the Halakhic statement on the matter: when the husband determines that he wishes to deconsecrate the wife, he has the power to do so only in such a manner that the wife is fully informed and takes an active role in the transaction, receiving the writ of divorce — initiated solely on the husband's volition to be sure — on terms that she has the power to dictate. The Halakhah states eloquently that she must play a fully conscious role in the transaction when it says she may not be asleep when the writ is handed over to her, and she may not be misinformed as to its character. Thus she must know that the document is a writ of divorce; she must be awake; if she sets conditions for the reception of the document, these must be met. In these fundamental ways, then, she accedes to the process of deconsecration, to the secularization of her status within the Israelite household.

So much for the analogy. But, predictably, the analogy carries alongside its own point of contrast. The writ of divorce is wholly the work of man. Heaven's will intersects with Israel's, the Israelite's will, properly documented, invokes Heaven's concurrence — not a very exact correspondence. But at one point the analogical-contrastive hermeneutics captures with great precision what is at stake in the category formation. That involves the analogy between God's and Israel's freely-entered covenant and the husband's and the wife's counterpart: each party to the transaction has the power of intentionality, God and Israel, husband and wife. Specifically, God offered the Torah, Israel accepted it, the husband offered the token of betrothal, the wife accepted it. And when it comes to the reversal of the results of that transaction, not only must the husband initiate the transaction, as before, but the wife — as before! — must in full consciousness and deliberation participate by receiving the writ.[29] The upshot is, at Gittin we deal with a document that Heaven puts into effect, one that affects the status, as to consecration, of a relationship. Consequently, the hermeneutics will work out the results of a process of analogical-contrastive reasoning that at critical turnings we ought to be able to reconstruct.

---

[29] How Israel and God undertake a comparable transaction is not pertinent; the analogy works when it works. But in a moment, we shall revert to the same analogy in another context.

What specifically is to be compared, then contrasted? In line with what has just been said, we start with the husband's and the wife's respective roles. Here the comparability is critical: each must bear responsibility for a component of the transaction, therefore each must exercise the power of intentionality at some stage thereof — but neither dominates throughout. How does this negative process work in fact? If [1] the husband does not give instructions, or if [2] the wife does not acknowledge the properly-executed process, Heaven deems the transaction null, the couple still consecrated. What we shall see is, at the heart of the category-formation is a hermeneutics focused on the exercise of intentionality, therefore the assignment of the responsibility, of the several parties within the transaction, the husband, the wife, the agents of each, and the scribe, for the successive stages and results thereof. No wonder that logically, not just circumstantially, a critical issue should focus upon the law of agency.

The analogical-contrastive exercise thus compares the wife's and the husband's respective roles — intentionality, responsibility — in the transaction, with some secondary interest in comparing the wife's and the slave's situations, the one at divorce, the other at emancipation. The following outline shows the articulation of the category-formation.

  I. THE WRIT OF DIVORCE
     A. Transmitting the Writ of Divorce
     B. The Writ of Divorce and the Writ of Emancipation of Slaves
     C. Preparing a Writ of Divorce
 II. RULES OF AGENCY AND WRITS OF DIVORCE
III. RULINGS PERTINENT TO THE WRIT OF DIVORCE MADE FOR GOOD ORDER OF THE WORLD, AND OTHER RULINGS IN THE SAME CLASSIFICATION
 IV. THE SLAVE
  V. THE WIFE'S RECEIPT OF THE WRIT OF DIVORCE
 VI. THE HUSBAND'S INSTRUCTIONS ON THE PREPARATION & DELIVERY OF THE WRIT
     A. Instructing Agents to Prepare the Writ
     B. The Conditional Writ of Divorce
VII. THE IMPAIRED WRIT OF DIVORCE
     A. The Writ of Divorce that is Subject to Doubt
     B. The Writ of Divorce that is Subject to Flaws or Imperfections
     C. An Invalidating Restriction in a Writ of Divorce

D. Confusing Writs of Divorce

The usual logical order — beginning, middle, end — does not govern. The only logically situated unit is at the end; that is to say, first comes the valid, then the impaired, writ of divorce. Any other order would confuse. The topics on the surface seem to double back, transmitting the writ, I.A, preparing the writ, I.C; the wife's receipt of the writ, V; the husband's instructions concerning preparation and delivery, VI; and then the impaired writ of divorce. It would appear that we go over transmitting and preparing and receiving the writ of divorce twice, at units I and V, then VI. If that somewhat odd order bears consequence, then we have a hermeneutics that compares and contrasts the wife's and the husband's roles in the transaction. But that is not an exact reading of matters. That the wife plays an active role at the cessation of the marriage, in specified circumstances bearing responsibility for the outcome of the process, corresponds — comparing and contrasting — with her power of assent to the act of consecration.

In fact I see these three distinct processes of analogical-contrastive analysis before us, yielding also some important exegetical exercises. The first and third define the category-formation at hand, the generative problematic concerning the definition of the wife's power of intentionality at the beginning and end of the marital bond.

1. COMPARING THE ACT OF CONSECRATION OF THE MARITAL BOND WITH THE ACT OF DISSOLUTION OF THAT SAME BOND (QIDDUSHIN/GITTIN): The relationship between a man and woman becomes holy with the consecration of the woman to that man. The purpose of the act of consecration of a woman is to produce children whose paternity and caste status are known and valid. The formation, transmission and preservation of life in conditions of sanctity define the critical issue of the Halakhah. But to realize that intentionality, the Halakhah takes for granted, both parties must concur, the woman being sanctified to the man when she agrees to the betrothal and therefore commits herself to carry out her half of the transaction that the betrothal is meant to make possible. The sanctification of a woman accordingly takes place when the woman, available for that man (meaning, not otherwise consecrated, and also not prohibited by rules of consanguinity or incest) consents. Designating a woman as "holy" or set apart for a particular man, requires the woman's participation through assent. Unlike a beast sanctified for the altar, a woman enters the relationship of sanctification only when she agrees to do so. The animal does not possess the power of will or intentionality, the woman does, though she surrenders a proportion thereof by agreeing to be betrothed. The consecrated relationship thus involves affirmative intentionality on the part of both parties. That is not so when it comes to the desacralization of the relationship, at which point the

woman is no longer consecrated to that particular man but becomes available to any other man of her choice (within certain restrictions, e.g., the prohibitions of incest). One of two parties — man or God, but not woman — at his own initiative intervenes. It is only logical that the husband should initiative the dissolution, since he is the one who to begin with undertook the act of sanctification. That is why the husband acts to desanctify what he has sanctified. His initiative, resulting from his intentionality, is dissolved at his own will. Exercising its will too, Heaven may intervene; the husband dies, leaving the wife free to remarry. In very unusual circumstances, covered at Yebamot, Heaven intervenes to bring to a conclusion one relationship of consecration but immediately impose another.

    2.   CONTRASTING THE WRIT OF DIVORCE WITH THE ACT OF MANUMISSION, THE EMANCIPATION OF THE WIFE AND THE SLAVE: Here the analogical-contrastive process takes up the sanctified with the secular relationship: wife to husband, slave to master. The wife and the slave are comparable, because by reason of the relationship to the householder, both of them surrender in some measure, partial or entire, their power of intentionality, their unfettered power of free will. But then the contrast has also to be drawn. The slave is never "holy" to the master, and the contrast between the route by which he returns to his prior condition, as a man possessed of free will and no longer subject to the will of another, and the route by which the woman does so, is explicitly drawn. This is not a principal component of the category-formation before us, but, as the precis above has shown, it does provide the occasion to make explicit the difference between the wife's and the slave's respective powers of intentionality.

    3.   CONTRASTING THE HUSBAND'S AND WIFE'S ROLES IN SEVERING THE MARITAL BOND: Obviously, when Heaven cancels the existing relationship of sanctification through the husband's death, neither the husband nor the wife participates; when Heaven creates the special circumstance involving levirate connection, no party on earth plays a role. What about the husband's and wife's roles when Heaven does not intervene? The husband ordinarily has the right at any time and for any reason to issue a writ of divorce and pay off what he owes on that account. Now what role — meaning, what power of intentionality — does the wife possess? None, so far as the Written part of the Torah is concerned. But — as with the woman's ordeal when accused of unfaithfulness — that matter is considerably reshaped in the Halakhah. Scripture does not contemplate a role for the woman in its account of how the relationship of sanctification to a particular man is secularized, that is, nullified.

Even though only the husband may initiate the writ of divorce and have it written and handed over, the Halakhah provides the wife with important occasions of participation in the process of ordinary divorce. And the woman's stake in the process correspondingly gains enormous consequence. She has the right, specifically, to dictate the conditions of delivery. She has the right to be correctly informed, to participate in the transaction as an active player, determining how her half of the matter will be conducted by dictating the circumstances under which she will receive the document. As she was alert in the beginning, so she must be engaged at the end. And, above all, because the Halakhah also imposes the most severe and long-lasting penalties upon a woman whose writ of divorce turns out to be impaired and so invalid, and who on the strength of such a document remarries, the woman must thoughtfully exercise her power within the transaction. That is the key point: *above all players, the woman must make certain that the scribe does his job right.* So the woman not only is given a role in the process but also a very heavy responsibility in the correct implementation of the transaction. For that reason, she takes any but a passive role in the matter.

That is why the Halakhah may be said to accord the wife the power of intentionality within the transaction of divorce. For to bear responsibility for a transaction, one must have the power of intentionality. Here therefore the analogy to the rite of sanctification (betrothal) to that man comes into play. Just as the woman is sanctified only by her act of consent, so at specific points in the process she is given the power of an active will to decide upon the circumstance (if not the result) of the action. For example, if she is not aware of the transaction (e.g., asleep) or if the document is misrepresented or if it is drawn up improperly, e.g., for some other person or circumstance, it is null, — and the consequences exacting their toll from her in particular, the Halakhah makes it her responsibility to see to it that the document is correctly represented and drawn up punctiliously. So if the transaction of divorce expresses the husband's, not the wife's intentionality and will — he initiates it, she cannot — the Halakhah nonetheless assigns to the wife a measure of responsibility and concomitantly a right to make decisions in the process at hand.

Within these exercises of analogical-contrastive analysis in mind, we identify what I conceive to form the hermeneutics of the category-formation, writs of divorce. Since the exegetical focus, time and again, is establishing responsibility for the meticulous performance of the transaction,[30] and since, as I just said, responsibility comes in consequence of the power to make decisions, the rest follows. The exegesis will focus on problems of correct procedure, time and again making certain of who is responsible for what

---

[30] The scribe's role will come to the fore presently.

condition and its consequence. Then, as I said, what we have before us is a massive exercise in the balancing of responsibility for a transaction among the parties thereto.

II. THE FOUNDATIONS OF THE HALAKHIC CATEGORY-FORMATIONS

Scripture is explicit that at the cessation of the marital bond (for which, in Scripture, the language of sanctification does not enter) a writ of divorce be handed to the woman. The pertinent verse of Scripture, Dt. 24:1-4, is as follows:

> When a man takes a wife and marries her, and it happens that she finds no favor in his eyes because he has found some uncleanness in her and he writes her a certificate of divorce, puts it in her hand and sends her out of his house, when she has departed from his house and goes and becomes another man's wife, if the latter husband detests her and writes her a certificate of divorce, puts it in her hand and sends her out of his house, or if the latter husband dies who took her as his wife, then her former husband who divorced her must not take her back to be his wife after she has been defiled; for that is an abomination before the Lord, and you shall not bring sin on the land that the Lord your God is giving you as an inheritance.

Scripture lays emphasis upon the prohibition of a divorced woman, once remarried, to return to the husband who has divorced her. From this statement we have no means of anticipating what will concern the Halakhah. Here we see the radical disjuncture between the Halakhic hermeneutics of the topic and Scripture's presentation of the same topic (we can hardly dignify Scripture's rather casual treatment of the subject, the writ of divorce, by invoking the august category, "hermeneutics").

III. THE EXPOSITION OF THE COMPONENTS OF THE GIVEN CATEGORY-FORMATION BY THE MISHNAH-TOSEFTA-YERUSHALMI-BAVLI

As always, I set forth the main points of **the Mishnah (in bold face type)**, then at the appropriate place add the Tosefta's own presentation not merely the clarification or amplification of the Mishnah's Halakhah) (in ordinary type), thereafter *the Yerushalmi's (in italics)*, and finally, THE BAVLI'S (IN BOLD FACE LOWER CASE TYPE). These are paraphrased and epitomized, they are not cited in full. I insert my observations on the points of special interest at the conclusion of each topical sub-unit. The units and sub-units derive from my own outline of the Mishnah-tractate, encompassing also the Tosefta-tractate; then the outline of the Yerushalmi, finally that of the Bavli.[31]

I. THE WRIT OF DIVORCE

A. VALIDATING THE WRIT OF DIVORCE

M. 1:1 He who delivers a writ of divorce from overseas must state, "In my presence it was written, and in my presence it was signed." He must state, 'In my presence it was written, and in my presence it was signed,' only in the case of him who delivers a writ of divorce from overseas, and him who takes [one abroad]. And he who delivers [a writ of divorce] from one overseas province to another must state, "In my presence it was written, and in my presence it was signed."

Y. 1:1 1:3 *He who delivers a writ of divorce from overseas must state, "In my presence it was written by day, and in my presence it was signed by day."*

Y. 1:4 *"In my presence it was written especially for her, and in my presence it was signed especially for her."*

M. 1:3 He who delivers a writ of divorce in the Land of Israel does not have to state, "In my presence it was written, and in my presence it was signed." If there are disputants against [the validity of the writ], it is to be confirmed by its signatures. He who delivers a writ of divorce from overseas and cannot say, "In my presence it was written, and in my presence it was signed," if there are witnesses [inscribed] on it – it is to be confirmed by its signatures.

T. 1:1 He who delivers a writ of divorce by boat is equivalent to him who delivers it from abroad [M. Git 1:1A]. He has to state, "In my presence it was written, and in my presence it was signed." [He who delivers a writ of divorce] from Transjordan is equivalent to one who delivers a writ of divorce in the Land of Israel, and he does not have to state, "In my presence it was written and in my presence it was sealed" [M. Git. 1:3A]. He who delivers a writ of divorce from overseas lands cannot state, "In my presence it was written, and in my presence it was signed," — if he can confirm it through its signatures, it is valid. And if not, it is invalid [M. Git. 1:3C-E]. One must conclude: They have ruled, He must state, "In my presence it was written, and in my presence it was signed," not to impose a stringent ruling, but to provide for a lenient ruling. He who delivers a writ of

---

[31] These are cited with bibliographical data in the Introduction, Volume I.

divorce from overseas, and it was not written in his presence, and it was not signed in his presence, lo, this one sends it back to its place, and he calls a court in session for that matter, and has it confirmed through its signatures. Then he delivers it again, and states, "I am an agent of a court." In the Land of Israel an agent appoints another agent. At first they would rule, "[He who brings a writ of divorce must testify that in his presence it was written and in his presence it was signed, if he brought it] from one province to another. Then they ruled, From one neighborhood to another.

T. 1:2 A more strict rule applies to [writs of divorce deriving from] overseas than to [writs of divorce deriving from] the Land of Israel, and to [writs of divorce deriving from] the Land of Israel then to [writs of divorce deriving from] overseas. For he who delivers a writ of divorce from overseas must state, "In my presence it was written, and in my presence it was signed." Even though there are disputants [against its validity], it is valid.

T. 1:3 He who brings a writ of divorce from the Land of Israel [and] cannot state, "In my presence it was written, and in my presence it was signed," — if there are witnesses, it is confirmed through its signatures [M. Git. 1:3B-E]. In what way have they ruled, "Let it be confirmed through its signatures?" Witnesses who stated, "This is our handwriting" — it is valid. [If they said], "It is our handwriting, but we do not know either the man or the woman," it is valid. [If they said], "This is not our handwriting," but others give testimony concerning them, that it is their handwriting, or if an example of their handwriting was forthcoming from some other source, it is valid.

M. 1:4 Any sort of writ on which there is a Samaritan witness is invalid, except for writs of divorce for women and writs of emancipation for slaves. All documents which are drawn up in gentile registries, even if their signatures are gentiles, are valid, except for writs of divorce for women and writs of emancipation for slaves.

Y. 1:4 As regards monetary matters [Samaritans] are suspect, and, [consequently,] as regards their testimony in monetary matters they are deemed invalid [witnesses]. They are not deemed suspect in regard to observing the laws of forbidden connections. And testimony in capital cases is equivalent to testimony in cases involving prohibited connections. [Samaritan testimony is accepted in capital cases.]

M. 2:1 He who delivers a writ of divorce from overseas and said, "In my presence it was written," but not, "In my presence it was signed," "In my presence it was signed," but not, "In my presence it was written," "In my presence the whole of it was written, but in my presence only part of it was signed," "In my presence part of it was written, but in my presence the whole

of it was signed" – it is invalid. [If] one says, "In my presence it was written," and one says, "In my presence it was signed," it is invalid. [If] two say, "In our presence it was written," and one says, "In my presence it was signed," it is invalid. [If] one says, "In my presence it was written," and two say, "In our presence, it was signed," it is valid.

T. 2:1 He who delivers a writ of divorce from overseas and gave it over to the woman, but did not say to her, "In my presence it was written and in my presence it was signed," lo, this one takes it back from her even after three years, and then goes and gives It to her, saying to her, "In my presence it was written, and in my presence it was signed."

T. 2:2 A woman is believed to state, "This is the writ of divorce which you gave to me." [If] it was torn, it is valid. [If] it was ripped up [torn in many places], it is invalid. [If] there is in it a tear made by a court, it is invalid. If one wrote it in this town, he should not sign it in another town. But if he signed it [elsewhere], it is valid. [If] he wrote it in the Land and signed it abroad, he must state, "In my presence it was written, and in my presence it was signed." [If] one wrote it abroad and signed it in the Land of Israel, he does not have to say, "In my presence it was written, and in my presence it was signed."

T. 2:3 If he wrote it with nut shells or pomegranate husks, with congealed blood or congealed milk, on olive leaves or pumpkin leaves, on carob leaves, or on anything which lasts, it is valid [cf. M. Git. 2:3A-G]. [If he wrote it] on leaves of lettuce or onion, on leaves of fenugrec or on vegetables' leaves, on anything which does not last, it is invalid. This is the general principle: [If] he wrote it in anything which lasts on something which does not last, or in something which does not last on something which lasts, it is invalid. [It is not valid] unless he wrote it with something which lasts on something which lasts.

M. 2:6 [If] a minor received [the writ of divorce from the husband,] and then passed the point of maturity, a deaf-mute and he regained the power of speech, a blind man and he regained the power of sight, an idiot and he regained his senses, a gentile and he converted, [it remains] invalid. But [if it was received from the husband] by one of sound senses who then lost the power of speech and then regained his senses, by one who had the power of sight and who was blinded but then recovered the power of sight, by one who was sane and then became insane and regained his sanity, it is valid. This is the governing principle: In any case in which the agent at the outset and at the end was in full command of his senses, it is valid.

M. 2:7 Even women who are not deemed trustworthy to state, "Her husband has died" [M. Yeb. 15:4], are deemed trustworthy to deliver her writ of divorce: her mother-in-law, the daughter of her mother-in-law, her co-wife, her husband's brother's wife, and her husband's daughter. What is the difference between [testifying] when delivering a writ of divorce and [testifying that the husband has] died? For the writing serves as ample evidence [in the case of a writ of divorce]. A woman herself delivers her writ of divorce [from abroad], on condition that she must state, "In my presence it was written, and in my presence it was signed."

From the perspective outlined above, a hermeneutics concerned with who is responsible for what aspect of the transaction, the starting point is not difficult to explain. We begin with agents who deliver the writ of divorce; they turn out to serve not only as agents but as witnesses to the validity of the document. It is not enough for them to bring the document, they must assert that in their presence the document was written and signed, which is to say, they must validate the document, which depends for its effect on correct witnessing. Once validated in this way, the husband cannot later on allege for any reason that the writ is invalid, so this is a protection for the wife. The witnesses and agents must be of sound senses, possessed of the power of intentionality.

B. *THE WRIT OF DIVORCE AND THE WRIT OF EMANCIPATION OF SLAVES*

M. 1:4 All the same are writs of divorce for women and writs of emancipation for slaves: They have treated in the same way the one who takes [it] and the one who delivers it. This is one of the ways in which writs of divorce for women and writs of emancipation for slaves are treated as equivalent.

B. 1:3-4 II.1/9A-B: IN THREE ASPECTS WRITS OF DIVORCE FOR WOMEN AND DOCUMENTS OF EMANCIPATION FOR SLAVES ARE EQUIVALENT: IN THE RULE GOVERNING THEIR BEING TAKEN FROM THE LAND OF ISRAEL TO OVERSEAS LOCATIONS OR BRINGING BROUGHT TO THE LAND OF ISRAEL FROM OVERSEAS; IN THE FACT THAT ANY WRIT THAT BEARS THE SIGNATURE OF A SAMARITAN WITNESS IS INVALID EXCEPT FOR WRITS OF DIVORCE FOR WOMEN AND DOCUMENTS OF EMANCIPATION FOR SLAVES; AND ALL DOCUMENTS THAT DERIVE FROM GENTILE ARCHIVES, EVEN THOUGH THE WITNESSES THERETO ARE GENTILES, ARE VALID, EXCEPT

FOR WRITS OF DIVORCE FOR WOMEN AND DOCUMENTS OF EMANCIPATION FOR SLAVES.

M. 1:5 Any sort of writ on which there is a Samaritan witness is invalid, except for writs of divorce for women and writs of emancipation for slaves. All documents which are drawn up in gentile registries, even if their signatures are gentiles', are valid, except for writs of divorce for women and writs of emancipation for slaves.

M. 1:6 He who says, "Give this writ of divorce to my wife, and this writ of emancipation to my slave," if he wanted to retract in either case, he may retract for writs of divorce for women but not for writs of emancipation for slaves. For they act to the advantage of another person not in his presence, but they act to his disadvantage only in his presence. For if he wanted not to support his slave, he has the right to make such a decision. [But if he wanted] not to support his wife, he has not got the right [to make such a decision]. He who says, "Give this writ of divorce to my wife and this writ of emancipation to my slave," and who then died – they [to whom he gave the charge] should not give over the documents after his death. [If he said], "Give a maneh to Mr. So-and-so," and then he died, let them give over the money after the man's death.

T. 1:6 He who says, "Give this maneh to So-and-so, which I owe him," "Give this maneh to So-and-so, a bailment which he has in my hands," "Take this maneh to So-and-so, a bailment which he has in my hands, " — if he wanted to retract, he may not retract. And he is responsible to replace it should it be lost, up to that point that he [to whom it is owing] receives that which belongs to him.

T. 1:7 [He who says], "Take this maneh to So-and-so," "Give this maneh to So-and-so," — if he wanted to retract, he may retract. [If] he went and found him dead, let him return the money to the one who gave it. If he [the one to whom the money is given] should die, let him hand over the money to the heirs [of the one who originally gave it].

T. 1:8 [He who said,] "Receive this maneh in behalf of So-and-so," "Acquire this gift in behalf of So-and-so," "Receive this writ of gift for So-and-so," "Acquire this writ of gift for So-and-so," — if he wanted to retract, he may not retract. [If] he went and found him dead, let him give it to the heirs. But if after the death of the donee he made acquisition, he should restore it to the heirs [of the donor], for they do not acquire an advantage for a deceased person once death has taken place.

T. 1:9 [If he said], "Carry this maneh to So-and-so," "Take this to So-and-so," "Let this maneh for So-and-so be in your hand," and he died, if the heirs [of the sender] wanted to force him [not to deliver it], they cannot do so. And one need not say, in the case of one who says, "Acquire possession for him," or who says, "Receive it for him" [that the rule is the same].

The reason that the comparison is made between the writ of divorce and the writ of emancipation of a slave is clear at M. 1:4: the same rules govern the delivery of the document, and that leads to the exposition of other points in common. The Bavli's formulation at B. 1:3-4 II.1 is particularly lucid. What the two classes of document have in common is that, in both cases, the husband/master restores the power of intentionality to the recipient, the wife or slave. For the prior spell, the former had surrounded part, and the latter all, of that power. So the documents produce the same effect and, it follows, fall under the same rule, as specified. Where they differ, as at M. 1:6, the difference is explained, and the explanation turns out to invoke the consideration of the will or intentionality of the recipient and whether that enters into consideration.

C. PREPARING A WRIT OF DIVORCE
M. 2:2 [If] it was written by day and signed by day, by night and signed by night, by night and signed by day [on the next morning], it is valid. [If it was written] by day and signed by night, it is invalid.

M. 2:3 With all sorts of things do they write [a writ of divorce]: with (1) ink, (2) caustic, (3) red dye, (4) gum, (5) copperas, or with anything which lasts. They do not write [a writ of divorce] with (1) liquids, or (2) fruit juice, or with anything which does not last. On anything do they write [a writ of divorce]: (1) on an olive's leaf, (2) on the horn of a cow, (but he gives the woman the cow) (3) on the hand of a slave, (but he gives the woman the slave).

T. 2:3 If he wrote it with nut shells or pomegranate husks, with congealed blood or congealed milk, on olive leaves or pumpkin leaves, on carob leaves, or on anything which lasts, it is valid [cf. M. Git. 2:3A-G]. [If he wrote it] on leaves of lettuce or onion, on leaves of fenugrec or on vegetables' leaves, on anything which does not last, it is invalid. This is the general principle: [If] he wrote it in anything which lasts on something which does not last, or in something which does not last on something which lasts, it is invalid. [It is not valid] unless he wrote it with something which lasts on something which lasts.

T. [If] he wrote it for her on the horn of a cow and gave her the cow, or on the hand of a slave and gave her the slave, she has acquired possession of these [M. Git. 2:3H-K]. [If] he then said to her, "Lo, this is your writ of divorce," and the rest of it [the cow, the slave] is in compensation for the marriage-contract," she has received her writ of divorce, and she has received her payment of her marriage-contract. [If he said to her], "Lo, this is your writ of divorce, on condition that you give me back the paper," lo, this one is deemed to have been divorced. " . . . On condition that the paper is mine," or if he gave her the paper itself [so that the paper was hers to being with], or if she wrote it on her hand, she is not deemed to have been divorced.

T. 2:5 All are valid to receive a woman's writ of divorce [in her behalf], except for a deaf-mute, an idiot, and a minor.

M. 2:4 They do not write [a writ of divorce] on something which is attached to the ground. [If] one wrote it on something attached to the ground, then plucked it up, signed it, and gave it to her, it is valid.

M. 2:5 All are valid for the writing of a writ of divorce, even a deaf-mute, an idiot, or a minor. A woman may write her own writ of divorce, and a man may write his quittance [a receipt for the payment of the marriage contract], for the confirmation of the writ of divorce is solely through its signatures [of the witnesses]. All are valid for delivering a writ of divorce, except for a deaf-mute, an idiot, and a minor, a blind man, and a gentile.

M. 3:1 Any writ of divorce which is written not for the sake of this particular woman [for whom it is intended] is invalid. How so? [If] one was passing through the market and heard the voice of scribes dictating [to students], "Mr. So-and-so is divorcing Mrs. So-and-so from such-and-such a place," and said, "Why this is my name and the name of my wife" – it is invalid therewith to effect a divorce. Moreover: [If] one wrote a writ of divorce for divorcing his wife therewith and then changed his mind, [and] a fellow townsman found it and said to him, "My name is the same as yours, and my wife's name is the same as your wife's name," it is invalid therewith to effect a divorce. Moreover: [If] one had two wives, and their names were the same, [if] he wrote a writ of divorce to divorce therewith the elder, he shall not divorce the younger with it. Moreover: [If] he said to a scribe, "Write for whichever one I shall decide to divorce," it is invalid therewith to divorce a woman.

T. 2:7 The writ of divorce for a woman which one wrote not for her own name is invalid [cf. M. Git. 3:1A], since it says, And he shall write for her (Deut. 24:1) for her in particular. The writ of emancipation of a slave which one wrote not for his own name is invalid, since it says, And not yet ransomed or given her freedom (Lev. 19:20). And below it says, And he shall write to her (Deut. 24:1). Now just as to her stated elsewhere means that it must be for her in particular, so to her stated here must mean that it must be for her in particular. The scroll for a woman accused of adultery which one wrote not for her own name is invalid, since it says, And the priest shall prepare for her this entire Torah (Num. 5:30) — that is all the rites concerning her must be [done] for her sake in particular. [If] the scribe wrote it for her sake, and the witnesses signed it for her sake [in particular], even though they wrote it and signed it and gave it to him and he gave it to her, it is invalid. It is valid only if he [the husband] will say to the scribe, "Write," and to the witnesses, "Sign."

T. 2:8 And not only so, but even if he wrote it in his own hand to the scribe, saying, "Write," and to the witnesses, "Sign," even though they wrote it and signed it and gave it to him and he gave it to her, it is invalid. It is valid only if they hear his [the husband's] voice saying to the scribe, "Write," and to the witnesses, "Sign."

M. 3:2 He who writes out blank copies of writs of divorce must leave a space for the name of the man, for the name of the woman, and for the date. [If he does so] for bonds of indebtedness, he must leave a space for the lender, the borrower, the sum of money, and the date. [If he does so] for deeds of sale, he must leave a space for the purchaser, the seller, the sum of money, the field, and the date – for good order.

M. 3:3 He who is bringing a writ of divorce and lost it – [if] he found it on the spot, it is valid. And if not, it is invalid. [If] he found it in a satchel or a bag, if he recognizes it, it is valid. He who is bringing a writ of divorce and left him [the husband] aged or sick hands it over to the woman in the assumption that he [the husband] is [still] alive. An Israelite girl married to a priest, and her husband went overseas, eats heave-offering in the assumption that [her husband] is alive. He who sends his sin-offering from overseas – they offer it up in the assumption that he is alive [cf. M. Tem. 4:1].

T. 2:6 All are believed to deliver a woman's writ of divorce, even her son, even her daughter, and even the five women who are in such a relationship to her that they are not believed to testify that her husband has died are believed to deliver her divorce. her mother-in-law, the daughter of her mother-in-law, her co-wife, her husband's brother's wife, and the daughter of her husband [by another marriage] [M. Git. 2:7A-B].

M. 3:4 Three things did R. Eleazar b. Parta say before sages and they confirmed his opinion concerning (1) [those who live in] a besieged city, (2) [those who are aboard] a storm-tossed ship, and (3) he who goes out to judgment –   that they are assumed to be alive. But (1) [those in] a town conquered in a siege, (2) a ship lost at sea, and (3) he who goes forth to be put to death – they apply to them the stringent rules applicable to the living and the stringent rules applicable to the dead: An Israelite girl married to a priest, or a priest girl married to an Israelite [in cases like these] does not eat heave-offering.

M. 3:5 He who brings a writ of divorce in the Land of Israel and got sick – lo, this one sends it on by means of someone else. But if he [the husband] had said to him, "Get from her such-and-such an object," he should not send it by means of someone else, for it is not the wish [of the husband] that his bailment should fall into someone else's hands.

T. 2:13 [If the husband said to] bring this writ of divorce to his wife on condition that she give "to my father, or to my brother, two hundred zuz." He [the messenger] has the power to appoint a [messenger]. [If he said,] ". . . on condition that she give you two hundred zuz," he cannot appoint an agent. For he has relied upon none except this one. [If] he said to him, "Bring this writ of divorce to my wife," he has the power to appoint an agent. [If he said,] " You bring this writ of divorce to my wife," then he does not have the power to appoint an agent [for the husband] has relied upon no one except this particular man [M. Git. 3:5].

M. 3:6 He who brings a writ of divorce from overseas and got sick appoints a court and sends it [the writ, with someone else]. And he says in their presence, "In my presence it was written, and in my presence it was signed." And the latter does not have to say, "In my presence it was written, and in my presence it was signed." But he merely states, "I am the agent of a court."

T. 2:11 A writ of divorce which one lost, and which he found after a while, even though he recognizes its distinguishing traits, is invalid. since [the law of] distinguishing traits does not apply to writs of divorce. What is the meaning of "after a while"? Sufficient time for someone else to come to that same location. But [if] he handed it over to him in a box, chest, or cupboard, and he locked the door thereof, and then the key was lost even though he found it only after a while it [the writ of divorce] remains valid.

T. 2:12 And three more [cases] did they add [to M. Git. 3:4]: [if] a wild beast was mauling him, or a river was sweeping him away, or a house fell on him, they apply to him the strict rulings applicable to the living and the strict rulings applicable to the dead. An Israelite girl married to a priest, or a priest-girl married to an Israelite does not eat heave-offering [M. Git. 3:4F]. The slave of a priest who fled, and the wife of a priest who rebelled against him [and ran away], lo, these continue to eat heave-offering [in the assumption that the master or husband is yet alive]. A person guilty of manslaughter should not go outside of the frontier of a city of refuge, but should assume that the high priest is yet alive.

M. 3:7 He who lends money to a priest or to a Levite or to a poor man so that he may set apart [what would be] their [share as heave-offering, tithe, or poor man's tithe, respectively, and sell the heave-offering to another priest or eat the tithe or poor man's tithe, in compensation for this loan] separates the produce in their behalf in the assumption that they are alive. And he does not take account of the possibility that the priest has died, or the Levite, or that the poor man has gotten rich. [If] they died, he has to get permission from [their] heirs [to continue in this way to collect what is owing]. If he lent them this money in the presence of a court, he does not have to get permission from the heirs.

T. 3:1 He who lends money to a priest and a Levite and a poor man and they died has to get permission from the heirs [of the man to whom he lent the money to continue to collect what is owing to him from heave-offering, tithe, or poorman's tithe] [M. Git. 3:7D].

M. 3:8 He who put aside produce, so that he may set apart heave-offering and tithes on its account [reckoning that it will serve for these purposes], ...coins, so that he may set apart second tithe on its account, he designates produce [as unconsecrated] relying upon them in the assumption that they remain available.

T. 2:9 [If] one borrowed from him a thousand denars with a bond of indebtedness and paid him back, and he now proposes to borrow from him a second time, he should not give him back the first bond of indebtedness, for he weakens the claim of the purchasers.

T. 2:10 [If he] mortgaged a house to him [or] mortgaged a field to him, and he paid him back and proposes to borrow from him a second time — lo, this one should not return him the first bond of mortgage, because he weakens the claim of those who follow him.

T. 3:2 [If] he put aside produce so that he may set apart heave-offering and tithes on its account [reckoning that it will serve for these purposes, coins so that he may set apart second-tithe on its account, he designates produce [as unconsecrated] relying upon them in the assumption that they remain available [M. Git. 3:8A-C]. He does not take account of the possibility that the produce has rotted, that the wine has turned into vinegar, that the coins have gotten rusty. [If] he went and found them rotted, turned into vinegar, or rusted, lo, this one then does take into account that fact. He takes into account the possibility of grain's having rotted during a time sufficient that it rot, for wine, during a time sufficient that it turn into vinegar, for money, during a time sufficient that it rust.

The document must be the work of a single day, that is, from sunset to the following sunset; otherwise the date is wrong. It must be written on what lasts, something that can be handed over to the woman. Anyone may write the document; the critical consideration is the character of the witnesses to it. They must be able to say that the husband has acted of his own free will in instructing the scribe to prepare the document. They must also insure that the document was written for this particular woman. Why the heavy stress on the particularity of the document? That is because it is the woman in particular who receives back her power of intentionality and reassumes entire responsibility for herself. Just as the act of consecration, at which she surrendered part of that power, had to concern her in particular — sanctification, like atonement, is an exceedingly specific transaction — so the act of dissolution must concern her in particular.

II. RULES OF AGENCY AND WRITS OF DIVORCE

> M. 4:1 He who sends a writ of divorce to his wife, and overtakes the messenger, or who sent a messenger after him, and said to him, "The writ of divorce which I gave you is null" – lo, this is null. [If] he [the husband] got to his wife first, or [if] he sent a messenger to her, and said to her, "The writ of divorce which I sent to you is null" – lo, this is null. If [this took place] after the writ of divorce reached her possession, he no longer has the power to annul it.
> *Y. 4:1 I:2 If one has appointed an agent to bring the writ of divorce, he must hand it over to the wife before two witnesses, and the agent does not count as one of the two. If the agent went to nullify the writ of divorce, he has to do so before two witnesses, and the agent counts as one of the two.*

Here the husband's intentionality governs until the wife is takes possession of the writ of divorce. That is why the husband may nullify the writ up to the point at which she has taken possession of it.

III. RULINGS PERTINENT TO THE WRIT OF DIVORCE MADE FOR GOOD ORDER OF THE WORLD, AND OTHER RULINGS IN THE SAME CLASSIFICATION

> M. 4:2 At first [the husband] would set up a court in some other place and annul it. Rabban Gamaliel ordained that people should not do so, for the good order of the world. At first he used to change his name and her name, the name of his town and the name of her town [i.e., to give an adopted name]. And Rabban Gamaliel ordained that one should write, "Mr. So-and-so, and whatever alias he has," "Mrs. So-and-so, and whatever alias she has," for the good order of the world.

T. 3:3 [If the husband] got to his wife first, or sent a messenger to her [M. Git. 4:1E-F], [and] said to her, "as to the writ of divorce which I sent you, I don't want you to be divorced with it," lo, this is null [M. Git. 4:1G-H]. At first the husband would set up a court in another place and declare it null [M. Git. 4:2A].

M. 4:3 **A widow collects [her marriage contract] from the estate of the orphans only by means of an oath. They held back from imposing the oath on her. Rabban Gamaliel the Elder ordained that she should take any vow the heirs wanted and collect her marriage contract. The witnesses sign the writ of divorce, for the good order of the world. Hillel the Elder ordained the prosbol, for the good order of the world.]**

M. 4:7 **He who puts his wife away because she has a bad name should not take her back. [If he did so] because of a vow [which she had made], he should not take her back.**

T. 3:4 A slave who is taken captive, and they redeemed him as a slave is to be subjugated, and his master is to pay his value. [If he was redeemed] as a free man, he is not to be subjugated, and his master does not pay his value.

T. 3:5. What is the sort of vow which requires the examination of a sage? If one said "Qonam be what my wife enjoys of mine, for she has stolen my wallet," ". . . for she has beaten up my son," [if] he found out that she had not hit him or that she has not stolen it, [he must undergo the examination of a sage for the absolution of his vow]. Under what circumstances? In a case in which he vowed and then divorced her. But if he divorced her and afterward took the vow, he is permitted [to remarry her]. [If] he took a vow to divorce her and changed his mind, he is permitted [to remarry her]. [If] he took a vow to be a Nazirite, or by an offering [Qorban], or by an oath, he is permitted [to remarry her]. On what account did they rule, "He who puts away his wife because of her having a bad name may not remarry her" [M. Git. 4:7A]? For if one puts away his wife because of her having a bad name, and then she is married to someone else and produces a child, and afterward the things said about the first wife turn out to be a joke — if he said, "If I had known that these things were a joke, even if someone had given me a hundred manehs, I should never have divorced her," [then, if he has the power to nullify the divorce and remarry her] the writ of divorce turns out to be invalid, and the offspring [of the second marriage] to be a mamzer. And on what account did they rule, "He who puts away his wife because of a vow may not remarry her" [M. Git. 4:7B]? For, if one puts away his wife because of a vow, and she is married to someone else and she produces a child, . and then the vow should turn out to be null, [if] he said, "If I had known that the vow was null, if someone had given me a hundred manehs, I should never have divorced her," it will turn out that the writ of divorce is invalid, and the offspring a mamzer.

M. 4:8 He who divorces his wife because of sterility may remarry her." [If] she was married to someone else and had children by him, and she then claims payment for her marriage contract – they say to her, "Your silence is better for you than your talking."

M. 4:9 He who sells himself and his children to a gentile — they do not redeem him, but they do redeem the children after their father's death. He who sells his field to a gentile and an Israelite went and purchased it from him — the purchaser brings the fist fruits, on account of the good order of the world.

M. 5:1 As to compensation for damages — they pay out of the highest quality of real estate, and [they pay] a debt out of middling quality of real estate, and [they pay] the marriage contract of a woman out of the poorest quality of real estate.

M. 5:2 They do not exact payment from mortgaged property in a case in which there also is unencumbered property, even if it is of the poorest quality. They exact payment from the property of an estate ["orphans"] only from the poorest quality [real estate].

M. 5:3 They do not exact indemnity for produce consumed ["food eaten by cattle"], or for the improvements made on land, or for the maintenance of a widow or daughters, from mortgaged property – for the good order of the world. He who finds a lost object is not subjected to an oath, for the good order of the world.

M. 5:4 Orphans who boarded with a householder, or for whom their father appointed a guardian — he [who provides for their keep] is liable to separate tithe from their produce. A guardian whom a father of orphans has appointed is to be subjected to an oath. He who imparted uncleanness [to the clean food of someone else], and he who mixed heave-offering into the produce of someone else, and he who mixed another's wine with libation wine — if he did so inadvertently, he is exempt [from punishment]. And if he did so deliberately, he is liable. And priests who deliberately imparted the status of refuse to a sacrifice in the sanctuary are liable.

T. 3:7 At first they ruled, He who causes uncleanness to the clean things of someone else, and he who mixes heave-offering in the produce of someone else — they reverted to rule, Also: he who mixes wine used for idolatrous purposes [in acceptable wine of his fellow] — if he did so inadvertently, he is exempt. If he did so deliberately, he is liable [M. Git. 5:4G-I], for the good order of the world. A. Priests who made a sacrifice refuse [by their improper intention, at the time of slaughtering it, to eat it at the wrong time or in the wrong place], [if they did so] inadvertently, are exempt [M. Git. 5:4J]. [If they did so] deliberately, they are liable, for the good order of the world. A messenger of a court who inflicted a blow by the authority of the court and did bodily harm, [if he did so] inadvertently, he is exempt. [If he did so] deliberately, he is liable, for the good order of the world. An expert physician who prescribed a cure by the authority of a court and did damage, [if he did so] inadvertently, he is exempt. [If he did so] deliberately, he is liable, for the good order of the world.

T. 3:9 He who cuts up the foetus in the womb of the mother did damage — doing so by the authority of the court, [if he did so] inadvertently, he is exempt. [if he did so] deliberately, he is liable, for the good order of the world.

M. 5:5 Testified R. Yohanan b. Gudeggedah concerning (1) a deaf-mute, whose father married her off, that [if she should be divorced], she goes forth with a writ of divorce; and (2) concerning a minor Israelite girl who was married to a priest, that she eats heave-offering, and if she died, her husband inherits her estate; and (3) concerning a stolen beam which one built into his house, that the original owner collects its value — on account of the good order of those who repent; and (4) concerning a stolen sin-offering, that was not publicly known, that it effects atonement — for the good order of the altar.

M. 5:6 The law concerning the usurping occupant did not apply in Judah in the case of those slain in the war. From the time of those slain in the war and thenceforward the law of the usurping occupant did apply. How [does the law apply]? [If] one purchased a property [first] from the usurping occupant and [then] went and [also] purchased it from the householder, his purchase is null. [If he purchased it first] from the householder and [then] went and purchased it from the usurping occupant, his purchase is confirmed. [If] a man purchased it from a man and then purchased it from a woman, his purchase is null. [If] he purchased it from a woman and then purchased it from a man, his purchase is confirmed. This is the first Mishnah. The court after them ruled: He who purchases a property from a usurping occupant pays the owner a fourth of the value. Under what circumstances? When he [the original owner] has not got the means to buy it. But [if] he has got the means to buy it, he takes precedence over all other people. Rabbi called a court into session and they voted that if the property had remained in the hands of the usurping occupant for twelve months, whoever comes first has the right to purchase it. But he pays the owner a quarter of the value.

T. 3:10 The law concerning the usurping occupant does not apply to the Land of Judah, for the sake of securing the settlement of the province [by permitting purchasers freedom from claims against their title to the land bought from a usurper]. ('. Under what circumstances? In the case of those who were slain before the war and in the time of the war [of Bar Kokhba]. But in the case of those who were slain from the war and onward the law of the usurping occupant does apply [M. Git. 5:6B]. As to Galilee, it is always subject to the law of the usurping occupant. He who purchases a field from a usurping occupant and went and purchased it afterward from the householder — his purchase is valid [vs. M. Git. 5:6D-E]. [If he first purchased it] from the householder and then went and purchased it from the usurping occupant, his purchase is null [vs. M. Git. 5:6F]. If the householder made him responsible for it, his purchase is valid. This i., the first Mishnah. L The court which was after them ruled. He who purchased [a property] from a usurping occupant pays to the owner a quarter [M. Git. 5:61-J] — a quarter [of the value, to be paid] in real estate, a quarter in ready money — N and the claim of the owner is uppermost [to decide which he prefers]. /f he has sufficient funds to purchase the field, he takes precedence over anyone else. Rabbi called a court into session, and they voted that, if the field had remained in the possession of the usurping occupant for twelve months, then whoever comes first has the right to purchase it. [Nonetheless the purchaser] pays the owner a quarter of the value [M. Git. 5:6N-O], [either] a quarter in land, [or] a quarter in ready money. And the claim of the owner is uppermost. If [the one from whom the field was seized] has sufficient funds to purchase the field he takes precedence over anyone else.

T. 3:11 Share-croppers, tenant-farmers, and guardians are not subject to the law of the usurping occupant. He who takes over a field in payment of a debt, [or] in payment of a tax-debt payable in installments — they are not subject to the law of the usurping occupant. As to the collection of the tax itself: they wait for the owner [to redeem it] for twelve months.

M. 5:7 A deaf-mute makes signs and receives signs. in the case of movables. And as to little children: Their purchase is valid and their sale is valid in the case of movables.

T. 3:12 As to children. their purchase is valid, and their sale is valid in the case of movables [M. Git. 5:7D-E], but not in the case of real estate.

M. 5:8 And these rules did they state in the interests of peace: A priest reads first, and afterward a Levite, and afterward an Israelite — in the interests of peace. They prepare an meal of commingling for purposes of the Sabbath in the house where it was first placed — in the interests of peace. A well nearest to the

stream is filled first — in the interests of peace. Traps for wild beasts, fowl, and fish are subject to the rules against stealing — in the interests of peace. Something found by a deaf-mute, an idiot, and a minor is subject to the rule against stealing — in the interests of peace. A poor man beating the top of an olive tree — what is under it [the tree] is subject to the rule against stealing — in the interests of peace. They do not prevent poor gentiles from collecting produce under the laws of Gleanings, the Forgotten Sheaf, and the Corner of the Field — in the interests of peace.

  T. 3:13 A poor man who takes them [olives which he gleans from a tree] in his hand and throws them down one by one — what is under it [the tree] is wholly subject to the prohibition against thievery [cf. M. Git. 5:81-K]. A city in which Israelites and gentiles live — the collectors of funds for the support of the poor collect equally from Israelites and from gentiles, for the sake of peace. They provide support for the poor of the gentiles along with the poor of Israel, for the sake of peace.

  T. 3:14 They make a lament for, and bury, gentile dead, for the sake of peace. They express condolences to gentile mourners, for the sake of peace.

  M. 5:9 A woman lends a sifter, sieve, handmill, or oven to her neighbor who is suspected of transgressing the law of the Seventh Year, but she should not winnow or grind wheat with her. The wife of an associate meticulous about cultic purity at home [haber] lends the wife of an outsider a sifter and sieve. She sifts, winnows, grinds, and sifts wheat with her. But once she has poured water into the flour, she may not come near her, for they do not give assistance to transgressors. And all of these rules they stated only in the interests of peace. They give assistance to gentiles in the Seventh Year but not Israelites. And they inquire after their welfare — in the interests of peace.

The power of the husband to nullify the writ of divorce, M. 4:1, accounts for the inclusion of M. 4:2 and the composite that depends on it, only a few of the entries of which I include. If the husband could issue the writ in one place and nullify it elsewhere, the wife, having received the writ after it was nullified in some other place, may assume on the basis of incorrect facts that she is free to remarry. What is important at M. 4:3 is the provision for the witnesses' validation of the writ. The considerations of M. 4:7 involve the husband's validly changing his mind on the basis of new facts, with the same possibility of the wife's assuming she is free to remarry when she is not. Under the stated arrangement that cannot happen. The remainder of the provisions "for the good order of the world" and "in the interests of piece" do not pertain to our category-formation.

IV. THE SLAVE

> M. 4:4 A slave who was taken captive, and they redeemed him – if as a slave, he is to be kept as a slave; if a freeman, he is not to be enslaved. A slave who was made over as security for a debt by his master to others and whom the master [then] freed – legally, the slave is not liable for anything. But for the good order of the world, they force his master to free him. And he [the slave] writes a bond for his purchase price.
>
> Y. 4:4 I:4 A proselyte who died, whose estate Israelites took over — if there were slaves in the estate, whether adult or minor, they go forth to freedom. [They are freed when the owner dies, prior to Israelite entry into the property.]
>
> M. 4:5 He who is half-slave and half-free works for his master one day and for himself one day for the good order of the world, they force his master to free him. And he [the slave] writes him a bond covering half his value.
>
> M. 4:6 He who sells his slaves to a gentile, or to someone who lives abroad – he [the slave] has gone forth a free man. They do not redeem captives for more than they are worth, for the good order of the world. And they do not help captives to flee, for the good order of the world.
>
> M. 4:9 He who sells himself and his children to a gentile – they do not redeem him, but they do redeem the children after their father's death. He who sells his field to a gentile and an Israelite purchased it from him – the purchaser brings the first fruits, on account of the good order of the world.

How the ordinances made for the good order of the world pertain to the slave is self-evident, and the whole forms a single, protracted composite formed on the basis of an anomalous redactional principle. Once formed, the composite makes its way through the successor-documents.

V. THE WIFE'S RECEIPT OF THE WRIT OF DIVORCE

> M. 6:1 He who says, "Receive this writ of divorce for my wife," or, "Take this writ of divorce to my wife," if he wanted to retract, may retract. The woman who said, "Receive my writ of divorce in my behalf," if he [the husband] wanted to retract, he may not retract. Therefore if the husband said to him, "I do not want you to receive it for her, but bring and give it to her," if he wanted to retract, he may retract.

T. 4:1 [The woman who said to a messenger], "Receive my writ of divorce in my behalf," and [the messenger said to the husband], "Your wife said, 'Receive my writ of divorce in my behalf,"' "Bring [my writ of divorce to me]," and, [the messenger reported to the husband that she had said,] " Bring it to her," . "Receive it for her," and, "Make acquisition of it for her" — . if he wanted to retract, he may not retract [cf. M. Git. 6:1].

M. 6:2 **The woman who said, "Receive my writ of divorce in my behalf," requires two sets of witnesses: two who say, "In our presence she made the statement," and two who say, "In our presence he [the messenger] received and tore it up." Even if the first set of witnesses are the same as the second set of witnesses, or there was one of the first set of witnesses and another in the second set of witnesses with one joined with each of them. A betrothed girl – she and her father receive her writ of divorce.**

T. 4:2 [If the wife said], "Receive my writ of divorce for me," and "Your wife said, 'Receive my writ of divorce for me,"' "Receive it for me," and, "Your wife said, 'Bring me my writ of divorce. " ' . "Take it," "Carry it," and, "Give it to her," "Receive it in her behalf," and "Make acquisition of it in her behalf," if he wanted to retract, he may retract. [If she said], "Carry my writ of divorce to me," "Take my writ of divorce to me," "Let my writ of divorce be in your hand for me," it is equivalent to her saying, "Receive my writ of divorce in my behalf." [He who says], "Bring a writ of divorce of your wife," " . . . a writ of divorce of your daughter," ". . . a writ of divorce of your sister," and he [to whom it is said] went and gave it to her, it is invalid. [If] they said to him, "Shall we write a writ of divorce for your wife," "Here is a writ of divorce for your wife," ". . .a writ of divorce for your daughter," ". . .a writ of divorce for your sister," and he went and delivered it to her, it is valid. Even if the first witnesses are the same as the last ones, or there was one of the first and one of the last even if they are brothers, and a third party joins together with them [M. Git. 6:2E-F]. A minor who knows who to take care of her writ of divorce, lo, this one may be divorced [cf. M. Git. 6:2K]. But she does not [have the power to] appoint a messenger until she produces two pubic hairs.

T. 4:3 What is the sort of minor who knows how to take care of her writ of divorce [M. Git. 6:2K]? This is any girl to whom they give her writ of divorce or some other object and who returns it after a while.

M. 6:3 **A minor girl who said, "Receive my writ of divorce for me" – it is not a valid writ of divorce until it reaches her hand. Therefore if the husband wanted to retract, he may retract. for a minor cannot appoint a valid messenger. But if the girl's father said to him, "Go and receive my daughter's writ of** divorce in her behalf," if he [the husband] wanted to retract, he may not retract. He who says, "Give this writ of divorce to my wife in such-and-such a place," and he [the messenger] delivered it to her in some other place – it is invalid. [If he said], "Lo, she is in such-and-such a place," and he gave it to her in some other place, it is valid. The woman who said, "Receive my writ of divorce for me in such-and-such a place," and he [the messenger] received it for her in some other place – it is invalid.

T. 4:4 The woman who said, ' 'Receive my writ of divorce for me in such and such a place," and he received it for her in some other place — it is invalid. "Bring me my writ of divorce from such and such a place," and he brought it to her from some other place — it is valid [M. Git. 6:3K-0]. But in the case of all of them she is divorced, unless [the husband said], "I want you to receive it for her only in such-and-such a place."

M. 6:4 [If she said to an agent,] "Bring me writ of divorce," she retains the right to eat food in the status of heave-offering until the writ of divorce reaches her. "Receive my writ of divorce in my behalf," she is prohibited from eating food in the status of heave-offering from that point. "Receive my writ of divorce for me in such-and-such a place" – she continues to have the right to eat food in the status of heave-offering until [the messenger with a writ of divorce] reaches that place.

Now we deal with the wife's and the husband's equal power to govern the receipt and the transmission of the document, respectively. Either party may appoint messengers for receiving or delivering the writ. If the husband appoints an agent using the language "receive" or "take," it makes no difference; he may retract. If the woman appoints the agent to receive the writ, once her agent has received the document, it is as if she has received it, and the husband may retract. But the husband may then override the wife's instructions and appoint the messenger to bear the writ, not to receive it in behalf of the wife. The wife has the power to establish the conditions in which her writ will be received, M. 6:2, within the proviso that her agents must be able to bear witness to the transaction. But, underlining the criterion of the power of intentionality, the law denies the same power to the minor; her father acts in her behalf. M. 6:4 adds the usual consideration of the status of the priest's wife as to eating priestly rations.

VI.   THE HUSBAND'S INSTRUCTIONS ON THE PREPARATION & DELIVERY OF THE WRIT

    A.   *INSTRUCTING AGENTS TO PREPARE THE WRIT*

M. 6:5 He who says, "Write a writ of divorce and give it to my wife," "Divorce her," "Write a letter and give it to her," lo, these [to whom he spoke] should write and give it to her. [If he said,] "Free her," "Feed her," "Do what is customary for her," "Do what is appropriate for her," he has said nothing whatsoever. At first they ruled, "He who goes out in chains and said, 'Write a writ of divorce for my wife' – lo, these should write and deliver it to her." They reverted to rule, "Also: He who is taking leave by sea or going forth in a caravan [may give the same valid instructions]."

B. 6:5AA-I I:1/65B [IF HE SAID,] "SEND HER OUT," "LET HER GO," "DRIVE HER OUT," THEY SHOULD GO AND WRITE IT AND GIVE IT TO HER. IF HE SAID, "RELEASE HER," "PROVIDE FOR HER," "DO WHAT IS CUSTOMARY FOR HER," HE HAS SAID NOTHING.

M. 6:6 He who had been cast into a pit and said, "Whoever hears his [my] voice – let him write a writ of divorce for his [my] wife" – lo, these should write and deliver it to her. A healthy man who said, "Write a writ of divorce for my wife" – his intention was to tease her. There was the case of a healthy man who said, "Write a writ of divorce for my wife," and then went up to the rooftop and fell over and died – if he fell because of his own action, lo, this is a writ of divorce. If the wind pushed him off, it is no writ of divorce.

T. 4:8 A. [If a man] was afraid and shouting from the top of a mountain saying, "Whoever hears my voice — let him write a writ of divorce to my wife," lo, these should write it and hand it over [cf. M. Git. 6:5-6]. A healthy man who said, " Write a writ of divorce for my wife," and who went up to the roof-top and fell down — they write and hand it over to her so long as he is yet breathing.

M. 6:7 [If] he said to two men, "Give a writ of divorce to my wife," or to three, "Write a writ of divorce and give it to my wife," lo, these should write and give it to her. If he said to ten men, "Write a writ of divorce for my wife," one should write it, and two should sign it as witnesses. [If he said], "All of you write it," one of them writes it, and all of them sign it. Therefore if one of them died, lo, this is an invalid writ of divorce.

T. 4:5 He who says, "Banish my wife," — they write and hand over to her a writ of divorce. [If he said], "Lo, this is your writ of divorce," and she said, "Hand it over to so-and-so," — she is not divorced. . [If she added,] ". . .so that he may receive it in my behalf," lo, she is divorced.

T. 4:6 [If] he said to two, "Give a writ of divorce to my wife, " or to three, "Write a writ of divorce and give it to my wife," "Write and give a writ of divorce to my wife," they write and hand it over to her [M. Git. 6:7A-C]. If they do not know how to write it, let them learn how to do so.

T. 4:7 [If] they know the man but do not know the wife, they write and hand it over. [If] they know the wife and do not know the man, they write it but do not hand it over. [If] he said, "Write it," but did not say, "Give it over," even though they know both of them, they write it but do not hand it over.

M. 7:1 He who was seized by delirium and said, "Write a writ of divorce for my wife," has said nothing whatsoever. [If] he said, "Write a writ of divorce for my wife," and [then] delirium seized him, and then he said, "Do not write it," his second statement is nothing. [If] he lost the power of speech, and they said to him, "Shall we write a writ of divorce for your wife," and he nodded his head, they test him three times. If he said for no, "No," and for yes, "Yes," lo, these should write and deliver the writ of divorce to his wife.

T. 5:1 [If a man] was crucified or hacked up, and he gave a sign to write a writ of divorce to his wife, they write and hand it over to her, so long as he is breathing [cf. M. Git. 6:6]. [If] he was ill and struck dumb, and they said to him "Shall we write a writ of divorce for your wife," and he nodded his head, they test him three times. If he said for no, "No, " and for yes, " Yes" [M . 7:1 D — F], his words are valid. Just as they test him as to a writ of divorce, so they test him as to purchases, gifts, inheritances, and statements of testimony.

M. 7:2 [If] they said to him, "Shall we write a writ of divorce for your wife?" and he said to them, "Write," [if] they then instructed a scribe and he wrote it, and witnesses and they signed it, even though they wrote it and signed it and delivered it to him, and he handed it over to her, lo, this writ of divorce is null, unless he himself says to the scribe, "Write," and to the witnesses, "Sign."

The oral instructions to prepare the writ of divorce and hand it over must represent an act of deliberation, of intentionality, so M. 7:1, 2. One important purpose of a writ of divorce is to free the wife from the requirement of levirate marriages, which accounts for the oral instructions of M. 6:5-6 and the interesting analysis set forth at T. 4:8. That euphemisms serve when precise but not when inexact presents no surprise.

B. THE CONDITIONAL WRIT OF DIVORCE

M. 7:3 [If he said], "This is your writ of divorce if I die," "This is your writ of divorce if I die from this ailment," "This is your writ of divorce effective after death," he has said nothing. [If he said, "This is your writ of divorce] effective today if I die," "Effective now if I die," lo, this is a valid writ of divorce. [If he said, "Lo, this is your writ of divorce] effective now and after death," it is a writ of divorce and not a writ of divorce. If he dies, [the widow] performs the rite of removing the shoe but does not enter into levirate marriage. [If he said,] "This is your writ of divorce effective today if I die from this illness," and then he arose and went about in the market, then fell ill and died – they make an estimate of his situation. If he died on account of the first ailment, lo, this is a valid writ of divorce. And if not, it is not a valid writ of divorce.

T. 5:2 "This is your writ of divorce, effective today, if I die from this illness " [M. Git. 7:3H], "If I die from this illness, lo, this is your writ of divorce effective today," his statement is confirmed [M. Git. 7:3E]. "This is your writ of divorce effective today if I die from this illness," if a house fell on him, or a snake bit him, it is not a writ of divorce. For he did not die of that particular ailment. [If he said, "Lo, this is your writ of divorce], if I do not arise from this ailment," if the house fell on him, or a snake bit him, lo, this is a valid writ of divorce. For in point of fact he did not arise from that illness.

M. 7:4 She should not afterward continue together with him except in the presence of witnesses, even a slave, even a girl servant, except for her own slave girl, because she is shameless before her slave girl.

T. 5:4 If they saw that she continued to be with him alone in the dark, or that she slept with him at the foot of the bed, even if he was awake and she was asleep, or he was asleep and she was awake, they do not take account of the possibility that they did some other sort of business, but they do take account solely of the possibility of their having had sexual relations, and they do not take account of the possibility of sexual relations for betrothal.

M. 7:5 "Lo, this is your writ of divorce on condition that you pay me two hundred zuz," lo, this one is divorced, and she should pay the money. ". . . on condition that you pay me within thirty days from now," if she paid him during the period of thirty days, she is divorced. And if not, she is not divorced.

T. 4:9 [If] he said to two men, "Give a writ of divorce to my wife on condition that she wait for me two years [without remarrying]," and then he went and said to two others, "Give a writ of divorce to my wife on condition that she pay me two hundred zuz," the instructions which he gave at the end do not nullify the instructions he gave at the outset. But the choice is hers: If she wanted, she may wait two years, and if she wanted, she may pay off the two hundred zuz [cf.: M. Git. 7:5A-B].

T. 4:10 [If] he said to two men, "Give a writ of divorce to my wife on condition that she wait for me two years," and then he went and said to two others, "Give a writ of divorce to my wife on condition that she wait for me three years," the instructions which he gave at the end do nullify the instructions he gave at the outset. And one of the former group and one of the latter group do not join together to deliver her writ of divorce to her. [If he said], "Lo, this is your writ of divorce, on condition that you not have sexual relations with so-and-so," lo, this is a valid writ of divorce, and he does not have to take account of the possibility that she will go and have sexual relations with him. [If he said, "Lo, this is your writ of divorce] on condition that you will marry and have sexual relations with father," or, "with my brother," lo, this one should not remarry, [but if she did remarry], she should not go forth. ". . . on condition that you have sexual relations with so-and-so," if she had sexual relations with him, lo, this is a valid writ of divorce, and if not, it is not a valid writ of divorce.

T. 5:5 [If the husband said,] "Lo, this is your writ of divorce, on condition that you pay me two hundred zuz"' [M. Git. 7:5A], and he died, if she paid the money, she is not subject to the Levir. And if not, she is subject to the Levir. "Lo this is your writ of divorce, on condition that you pay me two hundred zuz," and the writ of divorce was ripped up or lost — lo, this is a valid writ of divorce. For he who says, "On condition . . .," is equivalent to one who says "Effective immediately." But she should not remarry before she pays the money. ". . .when you will pay me two hundred zuz," and the writ of divorce was ripped up or lost, if she had paid over the money, lo, this is a valid writ of divorce. And if not, it is not a valid writ of divorce. [If he said,] "Lo, this is your writ of divorce on condition that you pay me two hundred zuz," and he went and said to her, "Lo, this is your writ of divorce effective immediately," he has said nothing whatsoever. What should he do? Let him take it back from her and go and hand it over to her again and say to her, "Lo, this is your writ of divorce effective immediately."

M. 7:6 "Lo, this is your writ of divorce on condition that you serve my father" – "...on condition that you give suck to my son" – how long must she give suck to him [for the writ to remain valid]? Two years. If the son died, or the father died, lo, this is a valid writ of divorce. [If he said,] "Lo, this is your writ of divorce on condition that you serve my father for two years," "On condition that you give suck to my son for two years," if the son

died, or if the father died, or if the father said, "I don't want her to serve me," [if this is] not because of provocation [on the woman's part], it is not a writ of divorce.

T. 4:11 "Lo, this is your writ of divorce on condition that you eat pork," and, if she was a non-priest, "On condition that you eat heave-offering," and, if she was a Nazirite-girl, "On condition that you drink wine," if she ate or drank [what he specified] lo, this is a valid writ of divorce. And if not, it is not a valid writ of divorce.

T. 5:6 ' 'Lo, this is your writ of divorce, on condition that you serve father, " [M. Git. 7:6A-B], or ". . . on condition that you give suck to my son," [if] she served him a single hour or gave suck to him a single hour, lo, this is a valid writ of divorce. . ". . .on condition that you give suck to my son."

M. 7:7 "Lo, this is your writ of divorce, if I do not return within thirty days," and he was going from Judah to Galilee, [if] he reached Antipatris and came home, his condition is null. "Lo, this is your writ of divorce, if I do not return within thirty days," and he was going from Galilee to Judah, [if] he reached Kepar Otenai and came home, his condition is null. "Lo, this is your writ of divorce, if I do not return within thirty days," and he was going overseas, [if] he reached Akko and came home, his condition is null. "Lo, this is your writ of divorce if I remain away from your presence for thirty days," if he was coming and going, coming and going, since he did not continue together with her, lo, this is a writ of divorce.

T. 4:12 He who says to his wife, "Lo, here is your writ of divorce [effective] one hour before his [my] death," and so, he who says to his servant-girl, "Lo, here is your writ of emancipation [effective] one hour before his [my] death," lo, these women [if married to or owned by a priest] should not eat food in the status of heave-offering, lest the man die an hour later.

T. 4:13 [If] he said to ten men, "Give a writ of divorce to my wife," one of them takes it in behalf of all of them. . [If he said,] "All of you take it, one of them hands it over in the presence of all of them. Therefore if one of them died, lo, this is an invalid writ of divorce [M. Git. 7:7G].

T. 5:7 Kepar 'Otenai is in Galilee. Antipatris is in Judah. As to the area between them, they assign it to its more stringent status: she is divorced and not divorced. If he said, "For I am going from Judah to Galilee," if he reached Antipatris and went back, his condition is null. "... I am going from Galilee to Judah," and he reached Kepar 'Otenai and went back, his condition is null. ". . .1 am going overseas," and he reached Akko and came back his condition is null. ". . .1 am sailing on the Great Sea," and he reached the place at from which the ships sail and went back, his condition is null [cf. M. Git. 7:7].

T. 5:8 "Lo, this is your writ of divorce, if I am apart from your presence for thirty days," [if] he was coming and going, coming and going, since he did not continue with her, lo, this is a writ of divorce [M. Git. 7:7M-P]. But she should not remarry until he is absent for thirty days

M. 7:8 "Lo, this is your writ of divorce, if I do not come back within twelve months," and he died within twelve months, it is no writ of divorce. "Lo, this is your writ of divorce effective now, if I do not come back here in twelve months," and he died within twelve months, lo, this is a valid writ of divorce.

T. 5:9 "Lo this is your writ of divorce if I do not come back in twelve months," and he died during the twelve months [M. Git. 7:8A-B] — she should not remarry [without dealing with the levir]. And our rabbis instructed her to remarry. But if the writ of divorce was torn up or lost during the twelvemonth-period, it is not a writ of divorce. [If this happened] after the twelve month period, lo, this is a valid writ of divorce.

T. 5:10 "Lo this is your writ of divorce, on condition that you give me two hundred zuz," and then he went and said to her, "Lo, they are forgiven you," he has said nothing. What should he do? He should take them from her and then go and return them to her, and at that point he should say to her, "Lo, they are forgiven to you."

T. 5:11 "Lo, this is your writ of divorce, on condition that you never again go to your father's house," "On condition that you never again drink wine," — it is not a writ of divorce, for she might go to her father's house or drink wine. " . . . On condition that you not go to your father's house for thirty days," "On condition that you not drink wine for thirty days," — lo, this is a valid writ of divorce. And one does not take account of the possibility that she might go or might drink. "Lo, this is your writ of divorce on condition that you not climb this tree," and " . . . on condition that you not go over this wall," if the tree was cut down or the wall torn down, lo, this is a valid writ of divorce. " . . . on condition that you climb this tree," or, "that you climb over this wall," if the tree was cut down or the wall torn down, lo, this is not a valid writ of divorce.

T. 5:12 " . . on condition that you not fly in the air," ". . .on condition that you not cross over the Great Sea by foot," lo, this is a writ of divorce. . ". . . on condition that you cross the Great Sea by foot," it is not a valid writ of divorce.

M. 7:9 If I do not come back within twelve months, write and hand over a writ of divorce to my wife" – [if] they wrote a writ of divorce during twelve months and handed it over at the end of the twelve months, it is not a valid writ of divorce. "Write

and hand over a writ of divorce to my wife, if I do not return within twelve months," [if] they wrote it during the twelve months and handed it over after twelve months, it is not a valid writ of divorce. [If] they wrote a writ of divorce after twelve months and handed it over after twelve months, and then he died, if the writ of divorce came before death, lo, it is a valid writ of divorce. But if the death came before the writ of divorce, it is not a valid writ of divorce. And if the facts are not known, this is the case of which they have said, "She is divorced and not divorced."

T. 7:7 A writ which has no witnesses, but which they gave to her in the presence of witnesses, is valid.

Freeing the wife from the levirate connection, e.g., before the husband goes off on a long trip, accounts for the conditional writ of divorce set forth at M. 7:3ff., 7:7-9, but also for the problems of confusion that result, M. 7:4. The power of the husband is shown at M. 7:5-6; he may establish enforceable conditions for the validity of the writ of divorce. But the conditions must be subject to fulfillment, so T. 5:11.

VII. THE IMPAIRED WRIT OF DIVORCE

A. THE WRIT OF DIVORCE THAT IS SUBJECT TO DOUBT

M. 8:1 He who threw a writ of divorce to his wife, and she was in her own house or in her own courtyard – lo, this one is divorced. [If] he threw it to her in his house or in his courtyard, even if it [the writ] is with her in bed, she is not divorced. [If he threw it] into her bosom or into her basket, she is divorced.

M. 8:2 [If] he said to her, "Take this bond of indebtedness," or if she found it behind him and read it, and lo, it is her writ of divorce, it is not a valid writ of divorce – until he says to her, "Here is your writ of divorce." [If] he put it into her hand while she is sleeping, [then] she woke up, read it, and lo, it is her writ of divorce, it is not a valid writ of divorce – until he will say to her, "Here is your writ of divorce." [If] she was standing in public domain and he threw it to her, [if] it is nearer to her, she is divorced. [If] it is nearer to him, she is not divorced. [If] it is exactly halfway, she is divorced and not divorced.

M. 8:3 And so is the rule with regard to betrothals. And so is the rule with regard to a debt. [If] the creditor said to him, "Throw me [what you owe] me [as a debt]," and he threw it to him, [if] it is closer to the lender, the borrower has the advantage. [If] it is closer to the borrower, the borrower is liable. [If] it is exactly in between, both of them divide [the sum, should it be lost]. [If the wife] was standing on the rooftop and he threw it to her, once it has reached the airspace of the roof, lo, this woman is divorced. [If] he is above and she is below and he threw it to her, once it has left the domain of the roof, [even if] it should be blotted out or burned, lo, this woman is divorced.

T. 6:2 A. If she was standing on the roof-top and he threw it to her, once it has reached the airspace of the roof, lo, she is divorced. [If] he is above and she is below, and he threw it to her, once it has gone forth from the domain of the roof, [if it should be] blotted out or burned, lo, she is divorced [M. Git. 8:3G-L]. [If he said to her,] "Lo, this is your writ of divorce," and she took it from his hand and tossed it into the sea or a river, and he then went and said to her, "It really was an invalid writ," "It was blank paper," he has not got the power to prohibit her [from remarrying].

The writ of divorce may be impaired by reason of doubt as to its validity. In the first instance, the wife must take possession of the writ, and the situation in which it is delivered must be one in which that can take place. More important — indeed, critical to the entire procedure — is the rule at M. 8:2. The writ is valid only if it is correctly described to her as she receives it. If the husband says it is a bond of indebtedness and she receives it and it turns out to be her writ of divorce, it is null; she has not received it with the correct intentionality. If it is left with her and she discovers its character, it is null. The husband must correctly describe the document, and on that condition, the wife receives it, for the writ to be valid. The provisions of M. 8:2 are explicitly compared at M. 8:3 to those of a betrothal, which also requires an articulate act of intentionality.

B. *THE WRIT OF DIVORCE THAT IS SUBJECT TO FLAWS OR IMPERFECTIONS*

M. 8:5 [If] he wrote [the writ of divorce dating it] according to an era which is not applicable, for example, according to the era of the Medes, according to the era of the Greeks, according to the building of the Temple, according to the destruction of the Temple, [if] he was in the east and wrote, "In the west," in the west and wrote, "In the east," she goes forth from this one [whom she married on the strength of the divorce from the former husband] and from that one [the first husband]. And she requires a writ of divorce from this one and from that one. And she has no claim on the payment of her marriage contract, or on the usufruct [of plucking property], or to alimony, or to indemnity [for loss on her plucking property], either against this one or against that one. If she collected [such payment] from this one or from that one, she must return what she has collected. And the offspring from either marriage is a mamzer. And neither one nor the other contracts uncleanness from her [if they are priests, and she should die and require burial]. And neither this one nor the other gains possession of what she may find, or of the fruit of her labor, or is vested with the right to abrogate her vows. [If] she was an Israelite girl, she is invalidated from marrying into the priesthood. [If she was] a Levite girl, [she is invalidated] from eating tithe. [If she was] a priest girl, she is invalidated from eating heave-offering. And the heirs neither of this one nor of that one inherit her marriage contract. And if they died, the brothers of this one and the brothers of that one perform the rite of rite of removing the shoe but do not enter into levirate marriage. [If] he changed his name or her name, the name of his town or the name of her town, she goes forth from this one and from that one. And all these [above] conditions apply to her.

T. 6:4 [If] he wrote it in accord with the date of a province, in accord with the dating of a hyparchy, or if there were two kings in power, and he wrote the writ of divorce bearing the date of only one of them, it is valid. [If he wrote it in accord] with the date of the father of his [the reigning emperor's] father, it is valid. If he wrote it in accord with the date of the founder of the dynasty [e.g., Arsaces], it is invalid. If they were called by the same name as the founder of the dynasty [e.g., Arsaces IX], it is valid.

T. 6:4 A male convert who changed his [Israelite] name for a gentile name — it is valid. And so you rule in the case of a female convert. Writs of divorce which come from abroad, even though the names written in them are gentile names, are valid, because Israelites overseas use names which are gentile names [cf. M. Git. 8:5R].

T. 6:5 [If] a man has two wives, one in Judah and one in Galilee, and he has two names, one used in Judah and one used in Galilee [if] he divorced his wife in Judah by the name he uses in Galilee, and his wife in Galilee by the name he uses in Judah, it is invalid. If [however] he said, "1, Mr. So and so, from Judah, with the name I use in Galilee, and married to a woman in Galilee," or if he was somewhere else [than Judah or Galilee] and wrote it in the name [used in either one of them], it is valid.

M. 8:6 All those prohibited relationships of which they have said that their co-wives are permitted [to remarry without levirate marriage], [if] these co-wives went and got married and this [woman who is in a prohibited relationship] turns out to be barren – she goes forth from this one and from that one. And all the above conditions apply.

M. 8:7 He who marries his deceased childless brother's widow, and her co-wife went off and married someone else, and this one turned out to be barren – she [the co-wife] goes forth from this one and from that one. And all the above conditions apply.

M. 8:8 [If] the scribe wrote a writ of divorce for the man and a quittance [receipt given to the husband for her marriage contract payment] for the woman, and he erred and gave the writ of divorce to the woman and the quittance to the man, and they then exchanged them for one another, and [if] after a while, lo, the writ of divorce turns up in the hand of the man, and the quittance in the hand of the woman – she goes forth from this one and from that one. And all the above conditions apply. [If] he wrote [a writ of divorce] to divorce his wife and changed his mind, even though he gave it to her on a condition, and the condition was not carried out [so that she is not divorced], he has not invalidated her from marrying into the priesthood.

M. 8:9 He who divorced his wife and spent a night with her in an inn – she requires a second writ of divorce from him. Under what circumstances? When she was divorced following consummation of the marriage. But they concur in the case of one divorced after betrothal alone, that she does not require a second writ of divorce from him. For he is not yet shameless before her. If he married her on the strength of [her having been divorced from a former husband] by a "bald" [defectively witnessed] writ of divorce, she goes forth from this one and from that one. And all the above conditions apply.

Y. 8:9 I:2 *He who divorces his wife — she should not live alongside him either in the same courtyard or in the same locale. If the courtyard belonged to the wife, the man moves out. If it belonged to the husband, the wife moves out. If it belonged to both of them, who moves out because of the other? The woman moves out because of the man. But if they are able to do so, [rather than moving out,] this one makes an opening [in the courtyard] in one direction, and that one makes an opening in the other direction. Under what circumstances? In a case in which they were actually married. But if they were not married, it is not called for. And in the case of a priest girl, even if they were not married, [they may not live side by side].*

The juxtaposition of M. 8:5 to M. 8:2-3 underscores the wife's involvement in the procedure. If the writ is improperly drawn up and the wife remarries on the strength thereof, the most severe penalties follow, not only for her but for her offspring in the second marriage. That fact places a heavy burden of responsibility on the wife to supervise the work of the scribe and to make certain that the writ is properly drawn up when she receives it. If she acts on the strength of the invalid writ, it is her own fault. But that fact underscores the active intentionality that the Halakhah accords to the wife. She has willingly accepted the invalid writ and willfully acted upon it, so she is held fully responsible for the consequences. The further cases, M. 8:6-8, underscore the same assignment of responsibility for the wife's situation to her own actions, and as I have stressed, where we find responsibility, there by definition we find imputed to the responsible party also the power of intentionality.

    C.   *AN INVALIDATING RESTRICTION IN A WRIT OF DIVORCE*

M. 9:1 He who divorces his wife and said to her, "Lo, you are permitted [to marry] any man except for So-and-so" – sages forbid it. What should he do [in such a circumstance]? He should take it back from her and go and give it to her again, and say to her, "Lo, you are permitted to marry any man." But if he wrote it into the body of the writ, it is invalid.

M. 9:2 [If the husband said,] "Lo, you are permitted to any man, except for my father, and your father, my brother, your brother, a slave, or a gentile," or any man to whom she cannot become betrothed – it is valid. "Lo, you are permitted to any man, except, in the case of a widow, to a high priest, in the case of a divorcée or a woman who has undergone the rite of removing the shoe, to an ordinary priest, a mamzer girl or a netin girl to an Israelite, an Israelite girl to a mamzer or to a netin," or any man to whom she can become betrothed, even though it is in transgression [for her to do so] – it is invalid.

M. 9:3 The text of the writ of divorce [is as follows]: "Lo, you are permitted to any man." The text of a writ of emancipation [is as follows]: "Lo, you are free, lo, you are your own [possession]" [cf. Deut. 21:14].

M. 9:4 There are three writs of divorce which are invalid, but if the wife [subsequently] remarried [on the strength of those documents], the offspring [nonetheless] is valid: [If] he wrote it in his own handwriting, but there are no witnesses on it – if there are witnesses on it, but it is not dated; if it is dated, but there is only a single witness – lo, these are three kinds of invalid writs of divorce, but if the wife [subsequently] remarried, the offspring is valid.

The husband may set some conditions in the writ. The wife must be free to remarry anyone of her choice. On the other hand, he may forbid her from marrying someone she may not, in any event, marry, as specified at M. 9:2.

    D.   *CONFUSING WRITS OF DIVORCE*

M. 9:5 Two [with identical names] who sent [to their wives, also bearing identical names] two writs of divorce [which were] identical, and which were mixed up – they give both of them to this one and both of them to that one. Therefore if one of them was lost, lo, the second one is null. Five who wrote jointly in one [and the same] bill of divorce [bearing a single date]: "Mr. So-and-so divorces Mrs. Such-and-such," "Mr. So-and-so divorces Mrs. Such-and-such," [..., and so on, five times], and there are witnesses below – all of them are valid. And let it be given over to each one. [If] the formula was written [anew in full] for each of them, and there are witnesses below – that with which the names of the witnesses are read is valid.

B. 9:5 II.2 87A FIVE MEN WHO WROTE JOINTLY IN A WRIT OF DIVORCE, "WE, MR. SO-AND-SO, AND MR. SO-AND-SO, AND MR. SO-AND-SO, AND MR. SO-AND-SO, AND MR. SO-AND-SO, DIVORCE OUR WIVES, MRS. SUCH-AND-SUCH, AND MRS. SUCH-AND-SUCH, AND MRS. SUCH-AND-SUCH, AND MRS. SUCH-AND-SUCH, AND MRS. SUCH-AND-SUCH, WITH MR. SO-AND-SO DIVORCING MRS. SUCH-AND-SUCH, AND SO FOR THE REST, AND THE WHOLE HAS A SINGLE DATE, WITH WITNESSES SIGNING BELOW, ALL ARE VALID, AND THE DOCUMENT IS HANDED OVER TO EACH ONE. IF THERE IS A SEPARATE DATE FOR EACH ONE, OR SPACE BETWEEN ONE ANOTHER, WITH THE WITNESSES SIGNED AT THE BOTTOM, THE ONE WITH WHICH THE SIGNATURES ATTACHED ARE READ IS VALID.

M. 9:6 Two writs of divorce which one wrote side by side, and [the signatures of] two witnesses, [written in] Hebrew, run from under this one [on the right] to under that one [on the left], and [the signatures of] two witnesses, [written in] Greek, run from under this one [left] to under that one [right], that with which the first witnesses' [signatures] are read is valid. [If the signatures of] one, [written in Hebrew], and one [written in] Greek, one [written in] Hebrew and one witness [written in Greek] run from under this one to under that one, both of them are invalid.

T. 7:11 [If] the names of the witnesses were separated from the body of the writ of divorce by a distance of two lines, it is invalid. [If the space between the body of the writ and the signatures of the witnesses is] less than this, it is valid [cf. M. Git. 9:6]. A writ of divorce on which five witnesses signed and of which the first three turn out to be invalid — the testimony [of the document] is confirmed by the remainder of the witnesses. A writ of divorce which was written in five languages, and which five witnesses signed in five languages, is invalid. [If] it was torn, it is valid. [If] it was torn with the sort of tear made by a court, it is invalid.

T. 7:12 [If] it was eaten by moths or rotted or was made as full of holes as a sieve, it is valid. [If] it was erased or faded but its impression remains, [if] one can read it, it is valid. . If not, it is invalid.

T. 7:13 "I witness it," "I signed it as a witness," if an example of their handwriting is available from some other source, it is valid. And if not, it is invalid.

M. 9:7 [If] one left over part [of the text of] the writ of divorce and wrote it on the second page, and the witnesses are below, it is valid. [If] the witnesses signed at the top of the page, on the side, or on the backside, in the case of an unfolded writ of divorce, it is invalid. [If] one joined the top of this [writ of divorce] alongside the top of that writ of divorce, and the witnesses are in the middle, both of them are invalid. [If he joined] the bottom of this one with the bottom of that one, with the witnesses in the middle, that with which the names of the witnesses are read [alone] is valid. [If he joined] the head of this one alongside the bottom of that one, with the witnesses in the middle, that with which the witnesses' names are read at the end is valid.

T. 7:8 A writ of divorce on which there is an erasure or an interlinear insertion, [if this was in] the body of the document, is invalid. [If this is] not in the body of the document, it is valid. If one restores [the erasure] at the bottom, even in the body of the document, it is valid.

T. 7:9 A writ of divorce on which the witnesses signed after an interval sufficient to inquire after one's welfare is invalid. For they have signed only concerning the asking after their welfare. [If] one replied a word or even two words relating to the writ of divorce, it is valid.

T. 7:10 [If] one wrote it on one side of the page, and the witnesses signed on the other side of the page, it is invalid [M. Git. 9:7A-B]. [If] one restored to it some one thing or two things dealing with a writ of divorce, it is valid.

M. 9:8 A writ of divorce which one wrote in Hebrew with its witnesses' signing in Greek, [or which he wrote in] Greek, with its witnesses' signing in Hebrew, [or which] one witness [signed] in Hebrew and one in Greek, [or which] the scribe wrote which one witness [signed, with the scribe as the second witness], is valid. [If it was written,] "Mr. So-and-so, a witness," it is valid; "The son of Mr. So-and-so, a witness," it is valid; "Mr. So-and-so, son of Mr. So-and-so," but he did not write, "A witness," it is valid. And thus did the scrupulous in Jerusalem do. [If] he wrote [only] his family name and her family name, it is valid. A writ of divorce imposed by a court – in the case of an Israelite court, it is valid. And in the case of a gentile court, it is invalid. In the case of

gentiles, they beat him and say to him, "Do what the Israelites tell you to do," and it is valid.

M. 9:9 [If] the word goes around town, "She is betrothed" – lo, she is [deemed] betrothed. "She is divorced" – lo, she is [deemed] divorced, on condition that there should not be some reason to doubt it. And what would be a reason to doubt it? "Mr. So-and-so has divorced his wife conditionally." "He tossed her her tokens of betrothal" – it is a matter of doubt whether it landed nearer to him or nearer to her – lo, these are grounds for doubt.

M. 9:10 A man should divorce his wife only because he has found grounds for it in unchastity, even if she spoiled his dish.

We end with the anticipated rules covering cases of confusion, that is, the generic hermeneutics of the law, now concerning cases of doubt, e.g., mixtures, here, writs of divorce that are confused or joined and run on.

IV. DOCUMENTARY TRAITS

A. THE MISHNAH AND THE TOSEFTA

The Tosefta goes its own way from time to time, but the hermeneutics of the principal documents of the Halakhah remains constant. The category-formation defined by the Mishnah governs throughout.

B. THE YERUSHALMI AND THE BAVLI

In the presentation of the Halakhah, so far as they participate at all, the two Talmuds exhibit differences only in detail.

V. THE HERMENEUTICS OF GITTIN

A. WHAT FUSES THE HALAKHIC DATA INTO A CATEGORY-FORMATION?

The data that comprise the category-formation prove somewhat diffuse, but they cohere around the role of the document — writing, delivering, receiving it by scribe, husband, and wife, and their agents, respectively — in the deconsecration of the marital bond. It is the particularity of the document, its exact correspondence to the wishes and circumstances of those to whom it pertains, that the Halakhah underscores. Making sure that there is an exact match between the document and those that it serves — the husband and the wife — realizes the hermeneutical interest in balancing the beginning with the end of the consecrated relationship. The responsibility, deriving from the implicit but active intentionality of both parties, comes to actuality in the points of Halakhic stress, as we have seen.

How does the issue of particularity figure? Our inquiry into how the halakhic data fuse into a category-formation invites yet another analogy. This one is to the cultic counterpart of sanctification of a wife, namely, a farmer's sanctification of an animal for the altar. When a farmer consecrates an animal as a sin-offering, the transaction involves a very specific process. He must

[1] the particular sin that is to be expiated by
[2] the particular animal (or in the case of what is unclear, designate an animal in a way that takes account of his uncertainty as to the sin he has committed). He must then make certain
[3] the officiating priest makes the offering (toss the blood against the altar) "in the proper name," meaning, the sacrifice must fall into the category of offering that is required and no other; the act of tossing the blood must be performed with the correct, appropriate, particular intentionality for that particular beast.

If the farmer does not utilize the animal he has designated, or consecrated, to the altar for his particular sin, he must undertake the appropriate process of disposing of the still-consecrated beast in a manner appropriate to its status and, more to the point, to the purpose that, by his act of will, he has planned to use the beast. When it comes to the transformation of the woman's status, from secular and available to any appropriate Israelite to sacred to a single, specified individual male, the process of sanctification is equally particular, and the result equivalently decisive.

The analogy and contrast concerning sanctification and desanctification in the cult finds its counterpart in Gittin at one fundamental point. It is a point of contrast. The man's act of will in consecrating the beast cannot be nullified by a corresponding act of will to deconsecrate the beast. Scripture is very clear on that point, when it forbids even an act of substitution of one beast for another (Lev. 27:11). If the man should decide he wishes to offer beast B rather than beast A, beast B is consecrated, but beast A retains its prior status. That is because — so it seems to me — an additional participant in the transaction has had his say and cannot now be dismissed, and that, of course, is Heaven. Once the beast has been consecrated, therefore, it leaves the status of consecration only with Heaven's assent, meaning, by following the procedures that the Halakhah deems appropriate. But man by an act of will can effect the deconsecration of the woman. That is because Heaven has a different relationship to the marriage, and other parties enter in. Heaven confirms the realization of the husband's act of sanctification of the woman and the wife's consent — a critical point of contrast with the consecration of a beast for the altar.

If the husband has power in deconsecration to which, in the cult, the sacrifier has no counterpart, then a further question arises. What about Heaven? Does Heaven here take an equivalent role to its engagement in the disposition of the sanctified beast and if so, where and how does that engagement take effect? The answer is, predictably, that Heaven, not only the husband and wife, concerns itself with the change in the woman's status as holy. In the logic of the system, no other answer is possible. Where, then, in the repertoire of the Halakhah, does that concern express itself? It is in the valid preparation of the document itself. That document — properly written, properly witnessed, properly handed over — serves to deconsecrate the woman, as surely as the rites of disposition of the consecrated animal not used for its correct purpose deal with the change in status of that beast. So it is the document that is the medium of effecting, or of annulling, the status of consecration. We have already commented on the role of meticulously prepared documents in realizing the covenant between God and Israel.

Here what gives the document effect? The answer is in two parts.

First, we know, the witnesses are the key-element in the process; the document is validated by valid witnesses, and lacking valid witnesses, even though it is correctly written and delivered, it has no effect at all. In the end the particular witnesses attest not only to the facts of what is incised in the writing but also to the specificity of the writing: this man, this woman, *this very particular document*. Then what is to be said about the witnesses to the preparation of the document, for whom do they stand? Given Heaven's stake in the transaction and the witnesses' status as non-participants, we may offer only one answer: the witnesses validate the document and give it effect because they stand as Heaven's surrogates. Israelite males not related to the parties, the witnesses accord cognizance on earth in behalf of Heaven to that change in intentionality and status that the document attests. And to what do they testify? When the witnesses to the validity of the writ prepared overseas say, "Before us it was written and before us it was signed" (that is, by the witnesses to the document itself), they confirm what is at stake in the entire transaction: Heaven has been informed of the change of intention on the part of this particular husband, releasing this particular wife from her status of sanctification to him. So the change in intentionality in very particular terms must be attested on earth in behalf of Heaven. And that which is certified by the witnesses is not only the validity of the writing of the document but the explicit transaction that has brought about the writing: the husband has instructed the scribe to write the writ of divorce, that particular writ of divorce, for his wife, for the named wife and no other woman (even of the same name).

When he has done that, pronouncing his intent to nullify the relationship of sanctification that he proffered and the woman accepted, then all else follows.

But, second, Heaven wants something else as well. Not only must the intention be articulated, and explicitly in the transaction at hand and no other. The document itself must give evidence of corresponding specificity. What makes all the difference? The Halakhah specifies irregularities of two classes, first, those that do not fundamentally invalidate the transaction, second, those that so completely invalidate the transaction that the original status of sanctification retains effect, despite what the husband has said, despite what the wife has correctly received by way of documentary confirmation of the change of intentionality and therefore status, his and hers, respectively. That represents a most weighty result, with long-term consequences. What conditions do not nullify the transaction? Confusing the writ of divorce of two couples bearing the same names presents a situation that can be sorted out. If the two writs of divorce are written side by side, so that the signatures have to be assigned to the respective writs, that is a problem that can be solved. The document may be spread over two sheets: If one left over part [of the text of] the writ of divorce and wrote it on the second page, and the witnesses are below, it is valid.

On the other hand, we have two explicit situations that produce the catastrophe of a totally invalid exchange, such that the woman remains sanctified to the husband who has indicated the intention of divorcing her. That is to say, in two circumstances the husband's intentionality does not register with Heaven. These are at M. 8:5 and M. 8:8, as follows, to review:

> M. 8:5 If he wrote the writ of divorce dating it according to an era which is not applicable, for example, according to the era of the Medes, according to the era of the Greeks, according to the building of the Temple, according to the destruction of the Temple, [if] he was in the east and wrote, "In the west," in the west and wrote, "In the east," she goes forth from this one [whom she married on the strength of the divorce from the former husband] and from that one [the first husband]. And she requires a writ of divorce from this one and from that one.
>
> M. 8:8 If the scribe wrote a writ of divorce for the man and a quittance [receipt given to the husband for her marriage contract payment] for the woman, and he erred and gave the writ of divorce to the woman and the quittance to the man, and they then exchanged them for one another, and if after a while, lo, the writ of divorce turns up in the hand of the man, and the quittance in the hand of the woman – she goes forth from this one and from that one.

The two rules produce this question: who then has the power to nullify even the effect of the intentionality of the husband? It is the scribe. If he errs in dating the document, or if he errs and writes down the wrong location of the participant, then, whatever the husband's intentionality and whatever the wife's state of alertness — her (wrong) impression of what has taken place — the writ is null, and the result is as specified, chaotic. So too if the scribe made a mistake in transmitting the documents that are to be exchanged, the transaction is null.

Then the question presses: why does the scribe possess so critical a role in the transaction that he can utterly upset the intentionality of the one and the consequent conclusion drawn by the other party, husband and wife, respectively? The reason is clear: the Halakhah attributes to the scribe a role in the transaction as critical, in its way, as the role of the husband in commissioning the document and the wife in receiving it. And what is it that the scribe can do to ruin the transaction? He can do two things. First, he can commit the unpardonable sin of not delivering the document to the correct party at the husband's instructions. That is, the husband has told him to deliver the writ of divorce to the wife, but he has given her the quittance instead. The woman has never validly received the writ. The scribe must realize and not thwart the husband's intentionality.

But what about the other matter, mis-dating the document, mis-identifying the parties? Here what has happened is that the writ no longer pertains to those mentioned in it. The scribe has placed the parties in a different period from that in which they live, dating them, by reason of the document, in some other time; or he has placed them in a different locale from the one where they are situated. He has set forth a document for some others than the ones before him, and he has given to those before him a spurious time and place. So the Halakhah raises yet again its requirement on the acute localization and particularization of the piece of writing: this woman, here and now, her and her alone, this man, here and now, him and him alone. That is to say, the Halakhah has underscored the conception, the conviction really, that the moment and act of sanctification are unique, specific, not to be duplicated or replicated in any way or manner. When God oversees this holy relationship, he does not wish it to be confused with any other. That is why, when God is informed of the change of intentionality that has brought about the consecration of the woman to the man, he must be given exact information.

The Halakhah spins out a hermeneutics expressed in [1] the power of a valid piece of writing before Heaven and [2] the character of intentionality and its effects. Of the former we have already taken note. As to the latter, what the law ascertains encompasses not only the intentionality and will of the husband, not only the conscious, explicit cognizance of the wife, but the facts of the case. Specifically, the Halakhah insists that the husband's act of will carries effect only when confirmed by valid action. Intention on its own is null. The full realization of the intention, involving valid provision for all required actions, alone carries effect. Not only so, but a third party, the scribe, intervenes in the realization of the husband's will. That means, facts beyond the husband's control and the wife's power to secure a right to supervise and review matters take over — with truly dreadful and permanent results.

So the wife, with the best will in the world having acted on the writ invalidated by the scribe's, not her or her husband's actions or intentionality, emerges as the victim of circumstances quite in contradiction to anybody's will. The upshot is, by the rule of the Halakhah, she may not then claim that her intention — in this case, the acquiescence in a successive relationship of consecration — has been thwarted by the actions or errors of a third party and so ought to be honored in the breach. The Halakhah rejects that claim. She acted in accord with the rules of intentionality and in good faith — and it makes no difference. And the first husband, with all good will, cannot confirm that he intended to divorce the woman, and her actions fully accord with his initiative and his intentionality. The Halakhah dismisses that allegation as well. Neither bears material consequence in the validation of what is, by reason of the facts of the case, an invalid transaction.

But the scribe possesses no intentionality in the transaction (other than the will we assume motivates his practice of his profession, that is, professionalism). The very role accorded to the scribe, not to the contracting parties, underscores the position of the Halakhah. It is that intentionality not confirmed by the correct deeds in the end does not suffice. The scribe's errors stand athwart the realization of the intentionality of the husband and the responsible participation (where possible) of the wife; but the scribe obviously did not intend to make mistakes. So what stands in judgment of intentionality and its effect are the facts of the case: the objective actions taken by third parties. In a legal system that has made a heavy investment in the priority of intentionality and the power of will, the statement made by the Halakhah of Gittin sounds a much-needed note of warning. Good will and proper intentionality do not govern when facts intervene.

What one means to do contradicted by what one has done, which, willy-nilly changes no facts, nonetheless makes no difference at all. That is because Heaven still insists upon something more than the correct will. It does, in the end, scrutinize actions, and these alone serve not only to confirm, but also to carry out, the will of the principals in any transaction. And, if we refer to the generative myth of the Torah, where to begin with the power of man to form and exercise intentionality is set forth, we find the reason why. The man and the woman — in the account of the calamity in Eden — enter the excuses that they gave way to the will of another, so their actions should be set aside. But God punishes all the parties to the act of rebellion, the snake, the woman, and the man. Then the lesson at the origin of all things — the power of humanity's will to stand against Heaven's will — finds its complement in its companion: what matters in the end is the deed, not only the intention.

That fact is underscored by another. Death too severs the marital bond. But on the occasion of death no document is involved, no scribe, no act of preparation, delivery, and attestation. The man's will to be confirmed by a deed plays no role whatever. God's will supersedes. Heaven intervenes, without the man's or the woman's consent. So what man accomplishes through a statement of intentionality confirmed by a documentary action, the writ of divorce, Heaven effects through the husband's death. Then the wife gains the right to enter a new consecrated relationship. That fact affords perspective on the deconsecration of the union that man accomplishes. Specifically, the document serves to attest in a tangible manner to the man's intentionality, the correct conditions of receipt of the document to the woman's conscious knowledge of what has happened. Neither can then claim not to have known that the relationship has been severed, and Heaven confirms the act of intentionality embodied in the document.

That is not what happens when the husband dies. Here, since Heaven's will is done without man's consent or woman's articulated awareness, the Halakhah sees no need for documentary confirmation, in palpable form, of the desacralization of the marital bond. The widow automatically is free to marry some other man. No one ever articulates that fact, which is everywhere taken for granted. But it does represent a choice, the alternative — keeping the widow "sacred" to the deceased until her own death — never presenting itself in either law or narrative as an option worthy of consideration. No writ of severance is involved; God's decisive action suffices. So much for man's power to bring about the deconsecration of the marital bed. What about God's? He has his own stake in the consecration or deconsecration of the conjugal bond.

B.   THE ACTIVITY OF THE CATEGORY-FORMATION

With the primary comparisons and contrasts in hand, we proceed to secondary ones. For reasons already set forth, the principal subordinate exercise of analogical-contrastive analysis concerns the writ of emancipation (manumission). The writ of divorce is compared with the writ of emancipation for a slave, because both represent documents that bring about a radical change in the status of a person in respect to her or her freedom of will or intentionality. In both instances, the person acquires full freedom of will, no longer being subject, wholly (for the slave) or in part (for the wife) to the will of another, the master or the husband, respectively. The point in common is documentary, because the shift is brought about through the preparation of a writ. Heaven has a heavy stake in the wife's writ, but not in the slave's. For while the slave's status shifts in relationship to his worldly master, the wife's changes in the view of Heaven as well. Specifically, she had been in the status of sanctification to a particular man and forbidden to all others. Now she reenters the ordinary condition of availability to any man of her choice; that shift represents an act of secularization.

What about the comparison of the writ of divorce to death as media for severing the marital bond? One main motivation for issuing a writ of divorce involves the law of the levirate connection. Since, when a childless man dies, his widow is bound to one of his surviving brothers, betrothed as of the moment of death for subsequent consummation of the marriage, a childless dying man might well provide a writ of divorce for his wife, to sever the connection and avoid the levirate procedure. That accounts for the interest in instructions issued by dying men. But a further consideration should register. Since the husband can issue the writ but the wife cannot, what happens if the husband is lost at sea or disappears? The wife is then unable to remarry. So the conditional writ, specifying a span of time after which, in the husband's absence, the writ takes effect, further accommodates the conditional writ, that is, "Lo, this is your writ...if I do not return..." in a specified span of time; it is then assumed that the husband may have died, and his wife is then free to remarry. She is not chained to him, without the possibility of release. That further explains, in part, why women who may not testify to the death of the husband may assert that he has ordered the writ of divorce to be issued; so too people who may not testify to the wife's affairs in other contexts may deliver the writ of divorce.

We turn, third, to the systematic exposition of the law of agency in connection with the writ of divorce. The Halakhah takes as its principal problem the delivery of the writ of divorce to the wife. The husband may send it through his agents, in which case they must give testimony that they have witnessed the writing and the signing, by witnesses, of the document. That guarantees one of the main requirements of the matter has been met, as I have already stressed, the document has been prepared for this particular woman, by this particular man. The husband must know what he is doing; instructions given in delirium are null. He must explicitly instruct the scribe to write. He may, moreover, set conditions for the validity of the document, and these must be met.

Consideration of agency raises the issue of a change of heart during the process of delivery. If the writ of divorce has not come into the wife's domain, the husband may retract; once she is in possession, he has no further power over her. That concern extends to attesting the wife's designation of her agents; witnesses must validate the transaction. They must attest that the wife has appointed the agents, and witnesses must attest that the messenger did receive the writ and dispose of it in the proper manner. So it is the moment of delivery of a valid writ that severs the former relationship of sanctification.

What about the sustained concern with the correct dating of the document? That is a subset of the concern for the specificity, the particularity, of this document. The preparation of the writ, including its signing by witnesses, must be completed within a given span of time, whether one night or one day. What is at stake in such a rule? Sages want not only that the writ serve that particular woman, but also that it be a fresh document, not made stale through the passage of time: that woman, those witnesses, on that particular occasion. It must represent a current, effective statement of the husband's will and respond to his attitude toward this particular moment toward this specific woman. Who writes it makes slight difference, by contrast, since the operative conditions are the timely preparation, on the one side, and the correct attestation by valid witnesses, on the other: both marking the particularity of the transaction. The husband may instruct whom it may concern, without knowing the identities of his agents, if circumstances warrant. So the principal concern involves the writ's preparation, in a finite span of time, for that particular woman and no other — even another woman of the same name. Not only so, but the writ is validated by its witnesses, and these make all the difference; the specific identity of the witnesses to the procedure has to be established (even though the husband does not know who they are, as noted).

Contrast the document of emancipation! No such conditions as to time, the particular identity of the recipient, and other considerations important to the preparation of the writ of divorce pertain to the slave's writ of emancipation. The difference is fundamental. The slave was never classified as "holy to his master," the relationship was functional and secular, a business transaction by which the slave in exchange for a fee sold his labor, if also his rights of intentionality, to the master. The slave may work for anyone designated by the master; the husband cannot assign the woman's wifely services to another party. And God has a stake in the relationship of husband and wife that he does not indicate in the relationship of master and slave. Heaven will even take account of the husband's deteriorating attitude toward his wife and supervise the ordeal of the bitter water. The wife is subjected to considerations of a supernatural character, with attention to the timing of the document and its being written specifically for her. What is at issue is not the form but the substance: the name of the man and the woman and the date. And that is no mere formality, as we observed at M. 3:1: the mere coincidence of names does not suffice to meet the requirement of particular preparation. If one wrote a writ of divorce for divorcing his wife therewith and then changed his mind, and a fellow townsman found it and said to him, "My name is the same as yours, and my wife's name is the same as your wife's name," it is invalid therewith to effect a divorce. These and comparable rules show what is meant by the rule of specificity.

What is at stake in these requirements? They serve to make certain the writ is valid and takes effect, so that all parties to the transaction know that the woman's status has changed irrevocably. But that means, even an imperfection without any bearing on the substance of the transaction, such as mis-dating or mis-identifying the writ (using the wrong date, or mis-identifying the locale of the husband, suffices to invalidate the writ. So too, if the scribe erred and gave the writ of divorce to the woman and the quittance to the man, rather than giving the writ to the man to give to his wife and vice versa, it is a complete disaster. Both cases and comparable ones bring to bear the most severe penalties. Then, if she should remarry on the strength of the impaired writ of divorce, her entire situation is ruined. She has to get a new writ of divorce from the first husband and from the second; she loses her alimony; she loses many of the benefits and guarantees of the marriage-settlement. And the offspring from the marriage fall into the category of those whose parents are legally unable to wed, e.g., the offspring of a married woman by a man other than her husband. Everything is lost by reason of the innocent actions of the wife in remarrying on the strength of an impaired writ, and that means, the wife has an acute interest in, and bears full responsibility for, the validity of the writ. The husband's only unique power is to direct the writing and delivery of the writ; otherwise, the wife bears equal responsibility for the accurate preparation of the document, the valid delivery (hence insistence that she be alert to the transaction), and the fully-correct details inscribed therein.

C. THE CONSISTENCY OF THE CATEGORY-FORMATION

The comparisons and contrasts we have drawn produce consistent results. The rules for validating the writ, the conditions that invalidate it — these cohere in the pattern we have identified throughout.

D. THE GENERATIVITY OF THE CATEGORY-FORMATION

What marks the generativity of the category-formation is its capacity to shape the law to the logic thereof. Once the category-formation takes shape around the comparison of beginnings and endings, betrothal and divorce, it is faced with the central problem, how is the wife's role at the end in any way comparable to the woman's role at the outset, if betrothal depends on the woman's consent but divorce does not? To answer that question, the category-formation dwells on the wife's responsibility at the end, which compares with her responsibility at the outset — in both instances, responsibility for her own condition and fate. If a single point marks the category-formation, Gittin, as distinctive, distinguishing the category-formation from its counterpart in the processes of desanctification, it is the stress that the wife must be alert and aware of the character of the document, that she dictates how it is handed over, and that she has a very heavy stake in the correct drafting of the writ. These critical components of the Halakhic category-formation all represent ways of securing for the wife a principal part in the transaction. And they mark the distinctive point of generativity of the category-formation. Not only must the document be particular to that woman, but it must also accommodate her preferences as to its delivery. Since the document must conform to the law or yields no effect and leaves her sanctified to that particular man, she has to make sure it is validly prepared at its critical points. That is why she dictates the conditions of the writ's delivery. While she cannot initiate the procedure — Scripture has accorded her no role in the transaction but the passive one of receiving the document — her will governs where and how the writ will be handed over to her. She is responsible for the outcome, so she is given a critical part in the exchange.

That is how the Halakhah assigns to her a part by allowing her to dictate the conditions under which she receives the document; she may appoint an agent, specify the circumstance of delivery to her agent, and otherwise take an active role in severing the marital bond. Not only so, but the husband must explicitly identify the document as a writ of divorce, and the wife must receive it as such. Thus: If he put it into her hand while she is sleeping, [then] she woke up, read it, and lo, it is her writ of divorce, it is not a valid writ of divorce – until he will say to her, "Here is your writ of divorce." Here again, the transaction requires the wife's full participation, on the one side, and an explicit exchange, understood by both parties, for the marital bond to be severed. These rules represent significant ways of realizing the hermeneutics the results of which are before us. When we work our way back from the exegesis of particular problems to the hermeneutics of the category-formation, we find the center of analogical-contrastive analysis: the correspondence of the end with the beginning of the marriage, the end with the beginning of the condition of sanctification. If I had to identify the single fixed principle that animates the entire system, it is that the Halakhah holds no one responsible for an act he did not deliberately carry out in the way in which he is responsible to do so, and, consequently, an unintended act bears few actual consequences and in many contexts, none. The hermeneutics of Rabbinic Judaism in the various native category-formations works out that principle time and again, and in the case before us the issue of responsibility and intentionality pervades the exegetical program and defines the regnant hermeneutics.

7.
TRACTATE QIDDUSHIN

I. THE DEFINITION OF THE CATEGORY-FORMATION

Israel is sanctified in two ways: by nature, through genealogy; and by conviction realized in deed, through adherence to the Torah. Sanctification by nature comes about when an Israelite man consecrates an Israelite woman who is available to him, and when the woman consents to becoming sanctified to him. That is, she is one not married or betrothed to someone else, the governing analogy being the consecration of the offering, as we shall note. She also is not forbidden to him by reason of incest taboos or caste regulations, the governing analogy being the consecration of the priesthood. Then sanctification by nature is passed on when that union produces offspring. In these two conditions for a valid betrothal, we discern the analogical-contrastive hermeneutics of Qiddushin, as will be seen presently. Sanctification by actualized conviction, on which we dwell elsewhere (e.g., Ketubot, Sotah) but not here, takes place when through those actions specified in connection with, e.g., correct food-selection and preparation, the Israelite sustains life as life is sustained at the altar. So in creating and sustaining life Israel both *is* holy and *acts* — behaves — so as to sanctify itself. In other words, Israel both is genealogically holy and also nourishes itself in the manner required by holiness.

Here we focus on the former of the two media of sanctification, the genealogical one. To undertake the required analogical-contrastive analysis of the category-formation, Qiddushin, we begin not with the abstraction conveyed by the title, Qiddushin, "sanctification," but with the concrete matters encompassed within the native category. We work our way from these surfaces to the subterranean, interior sources of the Halakhah. The data coalesce in two matters: the procedures of betrothals and the rules of marriage between Israelite castes, with the usual heavy component of the Halakhah's generic exegesis, e.g., cases of doubt, impaired documents, and other standard issues:

    I.   BETROTHALS
           A.   Rules of Acquisition of Persons and Property

B. Procedures of Betrothal: Agency, Value, and Stipulations
C. Impaired Betrothal
D. Stipulations
E. Cases of Doubt

II. CASTES FOR THE PURPOSES OF MARRIAGE
A. The Status of the Offspring of Impaired Marriages
B. Castes and Marriage Between Castes
C. Cases of Doubt

We deal with [1] a transaction (betrothal) and [2] its outcome (intermarriage between Israelite castes, e.g., priest to Israelite). These extend outward to the comparison and contrast of acquiring a woman and acquiring (other) property, procedures, and the usual generic-exegetical concerns with impaired results, stipulations and the fulfillment thereof, and cases of doubt; then the issue of intra-Israelite marriage across caste-lines. At stake therefore is the formation of valid marital unions, such that Heaven approves the outcome, the progeny as suitable for holy Israel. That is in two aspects: [1] correct procedure, and [2] correct partnerships, the "how" and the "who" in the formation of a marriage for the procreation of holy Israel.

What happens when the Halakhah registers is not that Israel is sanctified, but that Israelites through procreation activate and transmit their *pre-existing* condition of sanctification. Then — within the hermeneutics of analogical-contrasting analysis — to what genus and what species of said genus do the categorical data belong? For answers to that question I see two candidates. Both serve. Neither excludes the other. They work together to form of the data an integrated system of interpretation. The "how" of the formation of the marital bond that will yield holy progeny finds its Halakhic formulation in the first of the two candidates that follow, and, self-evidently, the "who" in the second, The "who" and the "how" form components of the still larger genus: sustaining and transmitting life in conditions of holiness. In both genera, holiness is understood as incarnate, physical, whether in the natural media of nourishment and procreation, whether in the social media of Israel's own genealogy and that of the nations.

[1] NATURE: PROCREATION/NOURISHMENT: The first is the genus, "the preservation and transmission of the status, sanctification through processes of nature." The comparison and contrast between species of the genus, sanctification, encompasses [A] procreation, that is, the marital bond at outset and end (as Gittin has already shown us), the act of sanctifying a woman to an Israelite man and [B] nourishment, modeled on an offering to the altar (the one requiring intentionality of both parties, the other not), and the like. The hermeneutics yielded by the analogy produces the comparison and contrast

of sanctifying a beast for the altar and a woman for a man. The outcome presents no surprises, recapitulating much that we learned in our encounter with Gittin. Fundamental to the first, and the more important, genus then are activities for sustaining life and how these are conducted in conditions of sanctification. These activities — the species of the genus — are only two, eating and sex. What is compared is the table and the bed, and what is contrasted are rules of sanctifying acts of nourishment with rules of sanctifying acts of procreation. In a moment we shall address a concrete comparison of the species of this genus, the table and the bed as media for sanctification of the woman and the crop, respectively. The language of sanctification in the present analogical-contrastive exercise thus overspreads the household in its principal functions, creating and sustaining life, in the bed as much as the table.

[2] SOCIETY: GENEALOGICAL ISRAEL AND THE NATIONS: A distinct, but correlative, genus accommodating analogy and contrast is, the genealogy of humanity, encompassing Israel and the nations: how the correct participants in procreation transmit the status of sanctification. The species of the genus, humanity, Israel, and the other species, "everybody else" ("the nations"), form a striking contrast, each linked to its respective ancestors and descendants. Here we compare and contrast holy Israel with the generality of mankind. The genus is easily speciated: one species being heavily differentiated (sub-speciated by castes, as we shall see), the other not. Then the primary task is contrastive: how are these classifications of data different? That will encompass those classes of gentiles that can enter Israel, differentiated from those that cannot; those classes of Israelites that through marriage can enter the priesthood or the Levitical caste or Israel, differentiated from those that cannot; and the like. Then the contrastive process takes two parallel paths with entry into Israel the common goal, the one differentiating among nations, the other, among Israel.

In both sets of comparisons and contrasts, "holy seed," the incarnation of the status, sanctification, figures. How in the exercises of analogical-contrastive analysis does genealogy ("the bed") in fact enter in? Transmission of caste-status provides the model. The sanctification of the priesthood is passed on through the male line, a principal consequence of genealogy. But, more broadly speaking, the Halakhah imputes to birth to an Israelite mother the caste-status of the offspring within holy Israel. If Israel is to form a kingdom of priests and a holy people, and if belonging to the holy people (without speciation in caste-status) comes about "naturally," that is, by birth to a Jewish mother, as the Halakhah everywhere takes for granted, then genealogy will take its place beside theology as arbiter of the validity of acts of betrothal.

So the native-category, Qiddushin, bears an apt and appropriate name, sanctification, in reference to its subject matter, the formation of the Israelite family, securing the transmission of Israel's sanctification genetically. The category is formed by [1] the woman who consents [2] to the man at hand and agrees to enter into a sacred relationship with him, to maintain the domestic order of the household and bear and raise children in the condition of holiness. When that relationship is characterized as holy and the result of an act of sanctification, the man's of the consenting woman, the act then confirmed by Heaven, the intent is not figurative or merely symbolic but material and concrete, and for its part genealogy is physical, genetic, not merely symbolic or "figurative," whatever that might mean. Within the walls of the Israelite household through betrothal an act of incarnate sanctification takes place that bears as weighty consequences as does an act of sanctification of an animal for an offering to God in the Temple. The transaction at hand defines the locus at which Israel attains the sanctity that God proposes to bestow on it.

What links the issue of the preservation of Israel's sanctity through the consecrated seed of Israelites together with the issue of Israel's unique genealogy and standing among the nations? It is the activity of sexuality, defined by the conditions under which sexuality is legitimately carried on. And that leads to the more encompassing question, how is sanctification "physicalized" or made incarnate within Israel? Both nourishment and procreation serve. Then how to explain in particular terms the focus on genealogy, that is, to say why genealogy (sexuality properly governed) forms the medium for transmission of Israel's holy condition? To answer that question we shall have to cross the boundaries of the Halakhah and turn to an Aggadic category, and that we shall do in due course. It suffices here to note that we deal with yet another category-formation that can be fully understood, its hermeneutics entirely set forth, only when the Aggadah and the Halakhah join together.

But, remaining entirely within the limits of the Halakhah, we ask how and where, precisely, does the transformative act of sanctification take place? Gittin has already prepared us for the answer: sanctification is always particular, this woman to this man, just as the writ of divorce must correspond to the specificities of the exchange. The governing principle of Qiddushin, comparable to that of Gittin, focuses upon the singularity of the transaction of betrothal that is compared to one with the altar and the individuality of its effects. In the Halakhah what is at issue is sanctifying a particular woman to a particular man, comparable to sanctifying a given beast to the Lord for a given, particular purpose, e.g., this animal for this classification of offering, and, in the case of a sin-offering, for this specific sin committed inadvertently in particular.

That is because in the Halakhah to "sanctify" means "in full deliberation to select in a concrete way, for a distinctive sacred purpose, not in a general way or for a generic purpose." Precision of intentionality finds its match in precision of language. The act of selecting a beast for sacrifice on the altar involves setting that beast aside from all others and designating it for the unique purpose of an offering for the sacrifier (the one who benefits, e.g., expiates sin, through the offering) carried out by the priest. The animal must be designated ("consecrated") for an offering for a singular purpose; it must be a specific type of offering, e.g., sin-offering; and the particular sin that the sacrifier has in mind must be articulated, there being no such thing as a sin-offering in general. So the act of sanctification finds its definition in the specificity of the selection, designation for a unique purpose, and performance of those rites that effect the selection and designation and carry out the purpose. Out of these concrete exchanges of intentionality matched to circumstance the transaction of sanctification produces a relationship of sanctity. Here one exercise in analogical-contrastive analysis modifies the result of another, sanctification through deed confirming intentionality being imposed on sanctification through correct genealogy. The latter, status within holy Israel, sets the necessary condition for the procreation of sanctification through genealogy. But it is not sufficient. It is the intentionality of the Israelite man that realizes the potential of sanctity inhering in the woman's capacity to procreate with him, and the consent of the Israelite woman to that realization.

The upshot is simply stated. The man possesses the power to effect consecration when he wishes to do so; his will determines. The woman is potentially sacred to any appropriate Israelite; her will decides which one, among those that present themselves. She is then made actually holy to that particular one when he asks and she agrees. So according to the details at hand by an act of will what is potential becomes real. The transaction of Qiddushin therefore involves the actualization, by the Israelite man, of the potential of sanctification inherent in the Israelite woman. If this reading of matters is valid, then the hermeneutics of analogical-contrastive analysis has produced a very particular result, and what we wish to know is whether that result — the actualization, through an act of will, of what is potential — is unique to the case or more broadly present in the system throughout? More simply stated, the question is, does the Halakhah afford other cases in which Israelite man's specific intentionality evokes in that which is subject to his will an inherent, but latent, holiness? These are the conditions we have identified: [1] the woman is subject to sanctification, but [2] until the man sanctifies her as his own and she affirms his act, her inherent status is not actualized; then it is. Not only so, but [3] the woman contains within herself the potentiality of producing holy Israel, but [4] until the man contributes the holy seed, her potentiality is not realized. To what, then, is the transaction comparable?

The realization of a potential of sanctification through an act of will finds its counterpart when we turn to the disposition of the crops of the Land of Israel raised by Israelite householders. It is the act of will confirmed by specific deeds by the Israelite householder that imparts the status of sanctification to the crop and imposes the obligation upon the householder to remove God's share in the crop, so secularizing the remainder of the crop for private use. Within the analogy afford by that Halakhic category-formation — tithing, Maaserot, and its companions, e.g., Terumot, Hallah, and the like — the Israelite householder through his act of will realizes in the Israelite woman her potential for sanctification, with the proviso that she join in the willful transaction by consenting. In the one case, the produce is made holy by the householder's will and made available by his separating the holy part for God; in the other, the woman is already holy, being Israel, but her sexuality is sanctified by the man's act of will to which she responds.

To spell out the comparable Halakhic category-formation: when Israel — the Israelite householder — asserts rights of possession of the crop of the Land of Israel, God's interest is aroused and he as the owner of the Land lays claim to his share in the crop, the ownership of which is held in partnership between God and the Israelite farmer. Then the rest follows, a vast exercise in how the will of God and the will of the Israelite meet in concord, Israel obeying God's laws about the disposition of the abundance of the Land. The basic principle is that when the produce is suitable for use by its owner, then it becomes subject to tithing and may not be used until it is tithed. The halakhah then indicates the point in the growth of various species at which tithes may be removed. That is the moment at which the produce is deemed edible. If someone picks and eats unripe produce, that does not impose the obligation to tithe, since the commonality of people do not regard unripe produce as food and do not eat it. Only when people ordinarily regard the produce as edible does consideration of tithing arise. Then there are two stages in the process, votive and obligatory. Crops *may* be tithed when the produce ripens. Then the produce becomes useful, and it is assumed that the farmer values the produce. But crops *must* be tithed when, by his action confirming his attitude, the farmer claims the produce as his own.

So what makes the difference? It is not the condition of the produce at all, but, rather, the attitude toward the produce that is taken by the farmer who has grown it. That attitude takes effect through the farmer's act of ownership, beyond possession. Asserting ownership takes place when he brings untithed produce from the field to the courtyard or prepares it for sale in the market. At that moment, the farmer having indicated his claim to the produce and intent to use it for his own purposes, God's interest is aroused, his share then is due. God responds to man, specifically, God's attitudes correspond to those of man: when (Israelite) man wants to own the crop and dispose of it as he wishes, then, God demands his share. God asserts his ownership when Israel proposes to exercise its rights of usufruct: when the tenant takes his share of the crop, he must also hand over to the Landowner (and to those designated by him to receive his share) the portion of the crop that owing. And until the tenant, in possession of the Land, does pay his rent, he may not utilize the crop as owners may freely do. Human actions that reveal human intentions provoke God: when the farmer indicates that he plans to dispose of the fruit, God wants his share. Martin Jaffee expresses this matter in the following *language (The Mishnah's Theology of Tithing*, p. 5):

> The fundamental theological datum of Ma'aserot...is that God acts and wills in response to human intentions. God's invisible action can be discerned by carefully studying the actions of human beings...the halakhah of Maaserot locates the play of God's power...in an invisible realm immune from the hazards of history...the realm of human appetite and intentions...God...acts and wills...only in reaction to the action and intention of his Israelite partner on the Land...Those who impose upon themselves the task of reconstructing the human and social fabric of Israelite life make effective the holiness of the Land and make real the claims of its God.

From these remarks, the point of the analogy is clear. The inherent sanctification is actualized when God responds to man's will. The specific analogy is readily drawn:

[1] The woman's sexuality compares with the Land's fecundity, both bearing latent sanctity;

[2] the woman's status as a medium of sanctification is comparable to the Land of Israel's equivalent status, both bearing the power to make manifest what is latent;

[3] the man's intentionality to sanctify this woman is like the householder's intentionality to make his own the produce of the Land, and

[4] God's confirmation of the woman's sanctification to that man is comparable to the God's sanctification of the produce that the householder has designated as God's share.

God by an act of will — claiming his share — and the Israelite man by an act of will — declaring his desire — accomplish the same transformation of status, from secular to sacred. But there is an important, indeed a decisive contrast. The Land need not consent for its crops to be sanctified. But the woman must consent to enter into the relationship of sanctification to this man. So in a critical component, Israel's power of the realization of sanctity is vested in both the man and the woman. And from that contrast flows much of the Halakhah of Qiddushin that is particular to the category-formation and not generic to the Halakhah.

We see then the ultimate result of analogical-contrastive analysis: in attitude and emotion, Israelite man possessed of the power of intentionality (what he wants makes a difference) is like God. In the concrete case, the Israelite farmer and God see matters in exactly the same way when it comes to assessing the value and use of the Land and its crops, the woman and her offspring. Both parties — Israel and God — value the Land. Both furthermore regard the Israelite woman as embodying (latent) sanctification. Man's desire for the crop precipitates God's interest and effects the sanctification of the crop. Man's intentionality to sanctify that woman precipitates God's confirmation that the potential for sanctification in that woman has been realized and is now actual.

II. THE FOUNDATIONS OF THE HALAKHIC CATEGORY-FORMATIONS

No Halakhic passage of Scripture contributes to the Halakhic transaction described here.

III. THE EXPOSITION OF THE COMPONENTS OF THE GIVEN CATEGORY-FORMATION BY THE MISHNAH-TOSEFTA-YERUSHALMI-BAVLI

As always, I set forth the main points of **the Mishnah (in bold face type)**, then at the appropriate place add the Tosefta's own presentation not merely the clarification or amplification of the Mishnah's Halakhah) (in ordinary type), thereafter *the Yerushalmi's (in italics),* and finally, THE BAVLI'S (IN BOLD FACE LOWER CASE TYPE). These are paraphrased and epitomized, they are not cited in full. I insert my observations on the points of special interest at the conclusion of each topical sub-unit. The units and sub-units derive from my own outline of the Mishnah-tractate, encompassing also the Tosefta-tractate; then the outline of the Yerushalmi, finally that of the Bavli.[32]

---

[32] These are cited with bibliographical data in the Introduction, Volume I.

I. BETROTHALS

A. *RULES OF ACQUISITION OF PERSONS AND PROPERTY*

M. 1:1 A woman is acquired [as a wife] in three ways, and acquires [freedom for] herself [to be a free agent] in two ways. She is acquired through money, a writ, or sexual intercourse. And she acquires herself through a writ of divorce or through the husband's death. The deceased childless brother's widow is acquired through an act of sexual relations. And acquires [freedom for] herself through a rite of removing the shoe or through the levir's death.

T. 1:1 A woman is acquired [as a wife] in three ways, and acquires herself to be a free agent in two ways. She is acquired through money, a writ, and sexual intercourse [M. Qid. 1:1A-B]. By money — how so? [If] he gave her money or something worth money, saying to her, "Lo, you are consecrated to me," "Lo, you are betrothed to me," "Lo, you are a wife to me," lo, this one is consecrated. But [if] she gave him money or something worth money and said to him, "Lo, I am betrothed to you," "Lo, I am sanctified to you," "Lo, I am a wife to you," she is not consecrated.

T. 1:2 By a writ [— how so?] Must one say it is a writ which has a value of a perutah? But even if one wrote it on a shard and gave it to her, on waste paper and gave it to her, lo, this one is consecrated.

T. 1:3 By sexual intercourse [— how so?] By any act of sexual relations which is done for the sake of betrothal is she betrothed. But if it is not for the sake of betrothal, she is not betrothed.

T. 1:4 A man should not marry a wife until the daughter of his sister grows up or until he will find a mate suitable for himself, since it is said, "[Do not profane your daughter by making her a harlot lest the land fall into harlotry and the land become full of wickedness" (Lev. 19:29).

B. 1:1 III.51/8B [A WRIT:] A WRIT: HOW SO? IF ONE WROTE ON A PARCHMENT OR ON A POTSHERD, EVEN THOUGH THEY THEMSELVES WERE OF NO INTRINSIC VALUE, "LO, YOUR DAUGHTER IS BETROTHED TO ME," "YOUR DAUGHTER IS ENGAGED TO ME," "YOUR DAUGHTER IS A WIFE FOR ME" — LO, THIS WOMAN IS BETROTHED.

M. 1:2 A Hebrew slave is acquired through money and a writ. And he acquires himself through the passage of years, by the Jubilee Year, and by deduction from the purchase price [redeeming himself at this outstanding value (Lev. 25:50-51)]. The Hebrew slave girl has an advantage over him. For she acquires herself [in addition] through the appearance of tokens [of puberty]. The slave whose ear is pierced is acquired through an act of piercing the ear (Ex. 21:5). And he acquires himself by the Jubilee and by the death of the master.

T. 1:5 How does [he redeem himself] by deduction from the purchase price [at his outstanding value] [M. Qid. 1:2B]? [If] he wanted to redeem himself during these years, he reckons the value against the years [left to serve] and pays off his master. And the hand of the slave is on top [in estimating the sum to be paid]. How is usucaption [established in the case of] real estate? [If] he locked, made a fence, broke down a fence in any measure at all, lo, this is usucaption. How is usucaption [established in the case of] slaves? [If] he [the slave] tied on his [the master's] sandal, or loosened his sandal, or carried clothing after him to the bathhouse, lo, this is usucaption.

M. 1:3 A Canaanite slave is acquired through money, through a writ, or through usucaption. By money paid by himself or by a writ taken on by others, on condition that the money belongs to others.

B. 1:3 I.5/22B HOW IS A SLAVE ACQUIRED THROUGH AN ACT OF USUCAPTION? IF THE SLAVE FASTENED THE SHOE OF THE MAN OR UNDID IT, OR IF HE CARRIED HIS CLOTHING AFTER HIM TO THE BATHHOUSE, OR IF HE UNDRESSED HIM OR WASHED HIM OR ANOINTED HIM OR SCRAPED HIM OR DRESSED HIM OR PUT ON HIS SHOES OR LIFTED HIM UP, THE MAN ACQUIRES TITLE TO THE SLAVE.'

M. 1:4 Large cattle are acquired through delivery [of the bit or bridle]. Small cattle are acquired through an act of drawing [the beast by force majeure].

T. 1:8 What is an act of delivery [M. Qid. 1:4A]? Any act in which he handed over to him the bit or the bridle — lo, this is an act of delivery. Under what circumstances did they rule, Movables are acquired through drawing? In the public domain or in a courtyard which does not belong to either one of them. But if it is the domain of the purchaser, once he has taken upon himself [to pay the agreed upon sum], he has acquired the thing. [And if it is] in the domain of the seller, once he has raised up the object or after he has taken it out from the domain of the owner [it has been acquired]. In the domain of this one in whose hands the bailment is located, an act of acquisition is carried out when he [the owner] will have taken it upon himself [to allow the buyer a portion of the premises to effect an acquisition] or when he [the purchaser] will have rented their place for himself.

M. 1:5 Property for which there is security is acquired through money, writ, and usucaption. And that for which there is no security is acquired only by an act of drawing [from one place to another]. Property for which there is no security is acquired along with property for which there is security through money, writ, and usucaption. And property for which there is no security imposes the need for an oath on property for which there is security.

M. 1:6 Whatever is used as payment for something else — once this one has effected acquisition [thereof] the other has become liable for what is given in exchange. How so? [If] one exchanged an ox for a cow, or an ass for an ox, once this one has effected acquisition, the other has become liable for what is given in exchange. The right of the Most High is effected through money, and the right of ordinary folk through usucaption. One's word of mouth [dedication of an object] to the Most High is equivalent to one's act of delivery to an ordinary person.

T. 1:9 If one exchanged with another person real estate for other real estate, movables for other movables, real estate for movables, movables for real estate, once this one has made acquisition, the other has become liable for what is given in exchange [M. Qid. 1:6B-C]. The right of the Most High is effected through money [M. Qid. 1:6G] — how so? The Temple-treasurer who paid over coins of the Sanctuary for movables — the Sanctuary has made acquisition wherever [the movables] may be located. But an ordinary person has not made acquisition until he will have drawn [the object]. One's word of mouth [dedication of an object to the Most High is equivalent to one's act of delivery to an ordinary person [M. Qid. I:6H] — how so? "This ox is sanctified," "This house is sanctified" — even if it is located at the end of the world, the Sanctuary has made acquisition wherever it is located. But in the case of an ordinary person, he makes acquisition only when he will effect usucaption.

T. Arakhin 4:4 If a common person performed the act of drawing when the beast was worth a maneh but did not suffice to redeem the beast, paying the money, until the price rose to two hundred zuz, he must pay the two hundred. How come? Scripture says, "And he will pay the money and depart," meaning, if he has given the money, lo, these belong to him, but if not, they do not belong to him. If he performed the act of drawing when it was worth two hundred zuz but did not suffice to redeem it before the price fell to a maneh, he still has to pay two hundred zuz. How come? So that the rights of a common person should not be stronger than those of the sanctuary. If he redeemed it when it was worth two hundred but did not suffice to draw the beast before the price went down to a maneh, he has to pay the two hundred zuz. How come? Scripture says, "And he will pay the money and depart." If he redeems it at a maneh and did not suffice to perform the act of drawing before it went up to two hundred zuz, what he has redeemed is redeemed, and he pays only a maneh.

M. 1:7 For every commandment concerning the son to which the father is subject — men are liable, and women are exempt. And for every commandment concerning the father to which the son is subject, men and women are equally liable. For every positive commandment dependent upon the time [of year], men are liable, and women are exempt. And for every positive commandment not dependent upon the time, men and women are equally liable. For every negative commandment, whether dependent upon the time or not dependent upon the time, men and women are equally liable, except for not marring the corners of the beard, not rounding the corners of the head (Lev. 19:27), and not becoming unclean because of the dead (Lev. 21:1).

T. 1:10 What is a positive commandment dependent upon the time [of year, for which men are liable and women are exempt (M. Qid. 1:7C)]? For example, building the Sukkah, taking the lulab, putting tefillin. What is a positive commandment not dependent upon the time [of year (M. Qid. 1:7D)]? For example, restoring lost property to its rightful owner, sending forth the bird, building a parapet, and putting on *sisit*.

T. 1:11 What is a commandment pertaining to the son concerning the father to which men and women are equally liable (M. Qid. 1:7B)]? Giving him food to eat and something to drink and clothing him and covering him and taking him out and bringing him in and washing his face, his hands, and his feet. All the same are men and women. But the husband has sufficient means to do these things for the child, and the wife does not have sufficient means to do them, for others have power over her. What is a commandment pertaining to the father concerning the son [M . Qid. 1:7A]? To circumcise him, to redeem him [if he is kidnapped], and to teach him Torah, and to teach him a trade, and to marry him off to a girl. And there are those who say, "Also: to row him across the river."

M. 1:8 [The cultic rites of] laying on of hands, waving, drawing near, taking the handful, burning the fat, breaking the neck of a bird, sprinkling, and receiving [the blood] apply to men and not to women, except in the case of a every commandment which is dependent upon the Land applies only in the Land, and which does not depend upon the Land applies both in the Land and outside the Land, except for 'orlah [produce of a fruit tree in the first three years of its growth] and mixed seeds [Lev. 19:23, 19:19], the meal-offering of an accused wife and of a Nazirite girl, which they wave.

M. 1:10 Whoever does a single commandment — they do well for him and lengthen his days. And he inherits the Land. And whoever does not do a single commandment — they do not do well for him and do not lengthen his days. And he does not inherit the

Land. Whoever has learning in Scripture, Mishnah, and right conduct will not quickly sin, since it is said, "And a threefold cord is not quickly broken" (Qoh. 4:12). And whoever does not have learning in Scripture, Mishnah, and right conduct has no share in society.

T. 1:17 Whoever occupies himself with all three of them, with Scripture, Mishnah, and good conduct, concerning such a person it is said, And a threefold cord is not quickly broken (Qoh. 5:12) [cf. M. Qid. 1:10E-G].

Once more the comparison of the situation of the woman to that of the slave (Hebrew, Canaanite) figures in the Halakhah, with M. 1:1 compared to M. 1:2. The analogy is, both voluntarily surrender their will to the householder, the difference, the one is sanctified, the other merely acquired as a worker. The exposition proceeds to other classifications of the acquisition of property, now to animals and real estate and movables. Once the genus, acquisition, has been speciated into its species, woman, Hebrew slave, Canaanite slave, animals, real and movable property, we proceed to the woman's status as to her husband's and God's will. The issue is liability to keep the commandments, and these are immediately divided. The key is that for man, God's will is unmediated, but for woman, God's will and man's will both come into play. Negative commandments apply equally, positive ones do not, because a woman has obligations that take priority over commandments dependant upon a particular time or occasion, namely, caring for her children and feeding her family. M. 1:8 is tacked on, but, as my account of the comparability of woman to the Land has suggested, it is pertinent in its way.

    B.   *PROCEDURES OF BETROTHAL: AGENCY, VALUE, STIPULATIONS*

M. 2:1 A man effects betrothal on his own or through his agent. A woman becomes betrothed on her own or through her agent. A man betroths his daughter when she is a girl on his own or through his agent. He who says to a woman, "Be betrothed to me for this date, be betrothed to me with this," if [either] one of them is of the value of a penny, she is betrothed, and if not, she is not betrothed. [If he said to her,] "By this, and by this, and by this" — if all of them together are worth a penny, she is betrothed, and if not, she is not betrothed. [If] she was eating them one by one, she is not betrothed, unless one of them is worth a penny.

T. 2:1 Just as a man does not effect a betrothal for his son, either on his own or through his agent, so a woman does not effect a betrothal for her daughter, either on her own or through her agent [cf. M. Qid. 2:1C].

T. 2:3 "Be betrothed to me with this and this," and she was eating [the pieces of fruit] one by one [M. Qid. 2:1H-I], if there remained in his possession produce worth a perutah, she is betrothed, and if not, she is not betrothed. "Be betrothed to me with this cup," if the value of the cup and of what is in it is a perutah, she is betrothed, and if not, she is not betrothed. And she has acquired both it and what is in it. "With what is in this cup," if what is in it is worth a perutah, she is betrothed, and if not, she is not betrothed . And she has acquired only what is in it alone.

M. 2:2 "Be betrothed to me for this cup of wine," and it turns out to be honey — "...of honey" — and it turns out to be of wine, "...with this silver denar" — and it turns out to be gold, "...with this gold one" — and it turns out to be silver — "...on condition that I am rich" — and he turns out to be poor, "...on condition that I am poor" — and he turns out to be rich — she is not betrothed.

T. 2:5 "Be betrothed with a sela," and after she took it from his hand, she said, "I was thinking that you were a priest, but you are only a Levite," "...that you were rich, but you are only poor," lo, this woman is betrothed. This is the principle: Once the tokens of betrothal have fallen into her hand, whether he deceived

T. 2:6 "Be betrothed to me with this sela, with this cow, with this cloak," once she has taken the sela, and drawn the cow, and made use of the cloak, lo, this woman is betrothed.

T. 2:7 "Collect this sela for me," and at the moment at which it was given over, he said to her, "Lo, you are betrothed to me," lo, this woman is betrothed. [If this happened] after she has taken it from his hand, [however,] if she agrees, then she is betrothed, but if she does not agree, she is not betrothed . "Here is this sela which I owe you," [if] at the moment of giving it over, he said to her, "Lo, you are betrothed to me," if she concurs, she is betrothed, and if she does not concur, she is not betrothed. [If this happened] after she has taken it from him, even though both of them concur, she is not betrothed. "Be betrothed to me with the sela of mine which is in your hand" — she is not betrothed. What should he do? He should take it from her and then go and give it back to her and say to her, "Lo you are betrothed to me."

T. 2:8 "Be betrothed to me with this sela," [if] after she took if from his hand, she tossed it into the ocean or into the river — she is not betrothed. "Be betrothed to me with this maneh," and she said to him, "Give it to so-and-so" — she is not betrothed. ["Give it to Mr. So-and-so,] who will receive it for me," lo, she is betrothed. [If] he gave her her tokens of betrothal but did not say to her, "Lo, you are betrothed unto me," "Be betrothed to me with this maneh," and it turns out to be a maneh lacking a denar — she is not betrothed. [If] it was a bad denar, let him exchange it for a good one.

T. 3:10 "...with this silver denar," and it turns out to be gold, she is not betrothed [cf. M. Qid. 2:2]. What should he do? He should take it back from her and go and give it to her again and say to her, "Lo, you are betrothed to me."

Y. 2:1 IV:8 *"Be betrothed to me with this maneh," and it turns out to lack a denar — she is not betrothed [since she expected a whole maneh]. If there was a counterfeit denar in it, lo, this woman is betrothed, on condition that he exchange the counterfeit for a valid coin. If he was counting out the coins one by one into her hand, she has the right to retract until he completes counting out the entire sum.]*

M. 2:3 "...On condition that I am a priest," and he turns out to be a Levite, "...on condition that I am a Levite," and he turns out to be a priest, "...a Netin," and he turns out to be a mamzer, "...a mamzer," and he turns out to be a Netin, "...a town dweller," and he turns out to be a villager, "...a villager," and he turns out to be a town dweller, "...on condition that my house is near the bath," and it turns out to be far away, "...far," and it turns out to be near: "...On condition that I have a daughter or a slave girl who is a hairdresser'" and he has none, "...on condition that I have none," and he has one; "...on condition that I have no children," and he has; "...on condition that he has," and he has none — in the case of all of them, even though she says, "In my heart I wanted to become betrothed to him despite that fact," she is not betrothed. And so is the rule if she deceived him.

T. 2:2 He who says to a woman, "Lo, you are betrothed to me, on condition that I am [called] Joseph," and he turns out to be [called] Joseph and Simeon, "...on condition that I am a perfumer," and he turns out to be a perfumer and a tanner, "...on condition that I am a town-dweller," and he turns out to be a town-dweller and a villager [M. Qid. 2:3E-F], lo, this woman is betrothed. [If he said, "Lo, you are betrothed to me, on condition that] I am only Joseph," and he turned out to be Joseph and Simeon, "...that I am only a perfumer," and he turned out to be a perfumer and a tanner, "...that I am only a town-dweller," and he turned out to be a town dweller and a villager, she is not betrothed.

T. 2:4 [If a man said to a woman, "Be betrothed to me] on condition that I am poor," and he was poor but got rich, "...on condition that I am rich" and he was rich and became poor, "...on condition that I am a perfumer," and he was a perfumer but became a tanner, "...on condition that I am a tanner," and he was a tanner but became a perfumer, "...on condition that I am a town-dweller," and he was a town dweller but he moved to a village, "...on condition that I am a villager," and he was a villager, but he moved to a town, "...on condition that I have children," and he had children, but then they died, "...on condition that I have no children," and he had no children, and afterward children were born to him — lo, this woman is betrothed. [If he said, however,] that he was only poor, and he was rich and became poor, that he was only rich, and he was poor and became rich, ". . .that I am only a perfumer," and he was a tanner and became a perfumer, "...that I am only a tanner," and he was a perfumer and became a tanner, "...that I am only a town-dweller," and he was a villager and became a town-dweller, "...that I am only a villager," and he was a town-dweller and became a villager, that he had no children, and he had children, but afterward they died, that he had children, and he did not have any, but afterward children were born to him, she is not betrothed. This is the principle: In the case of any condition which is valid at the moment of betrothal, even though it was annulled afterward, lo, this woman is betrothed. And in the case of any condition which is not valid at the moment of betrothal, even though it was validated afterward, lo, this woman is not betrothed.

M. 2:4 He who says to his messenger, "Go and betroth Miss So-and-so for me, in such-and-such a place," and he went and betrothed her for him in some other place, she is not betrothed. [If he said,] "...lo, she is in such-and-such a place," and he betrothed her in some other place, lo, she is betrothed.

T. 4:2 He who says to his agent, "Go and betroth for me Miss So-and-so in such-and-such a place," and he went and betrothed her in some other place — she is not betrothed. "...lo, she is in such and such a place," and he went and betrothed her in some other place, lo, this woman is betrothed [M. Qid. 2:4].

M. 2:5 He who betroths a woman on condition that she is not encumbered by vows, and she turns out to be encumbered by vows — she is not betrothed. [If] he married her without specifying and she turned out to be encumbered by vows, she goes forth without collecting her marriage contract. ...On condition that there are no blemishes on her, and she turns out to have blemishes, she is not betrothed. [If] he married her without specifying and she turned out to have blemishes, she goes forth without collecting her marriage contract. All blemishes which invalidate priests [from serving in the Temple] invalidate women.

T. 2:9 [If] he was counting out and putting into her hand one by one, she has the power to retract up to the time that he completes [counting out the specified sum]. [If in a dispute about how much was specified for a betrothal,] this one says, "With a maneh," [a hundred zuz] and this one says, "With two hundred zuz," and this one went home and that one went home and afterward they laid claim against one another and effected betrothal, if the man laid claim against the woman let the claims of the woman be carried out. And if the woman laid claim against the man, let the claim of the man be carried out. And so in the case of him who sells an object, and he was counting out [the objects] into the hand of the buyer, he has the power to retract. [If] this one claims, "[You sold it for] a maneh," and that one claims, "[You bought it for] two hundred zuz," and this one went home and that one went home, and afterward they laid claim against one another, if the purchaser laid claim against the seller, let the claim of the seller be done, and if the seller laid claim against the purchaser, let the claim of the purchaser be done.

We proceed to the generic analytical program of the Halakhah. We start with issues of procedure and agency. The token of betrothal has to bear a specific, minimal value, hence the issues of M. 2:1. The inclusion of stipulations in the husband's language, familiar from Gittin, is then addressed, M. 2:2-3; here the wife must have given consent to the actuality, and if the language of the husband has misrepresented the facts, it is an act of sanctification that has taken place in error and is null. The rules of agency recur at M. 2:4, once more with reference to the husband's statement. M. 2:5 introduces other stipulations that the husband imposes, now on the condition of not himself but his prospective wife.

C. IMPAIRED BETROTHAL
M. 2:6 He who betroths two women with something worth a penny, or one woman with something worth less than a penny, even though he sent along [additional] presents afterward, she is not betrothed, since he sent the presents later on only because of the original act of betrothal [which was null]. And so in the case of a minor who betrothed a woman.

T. 4:4 He who betroths a woman in error, or with something of less than the value of a perutah, and so a minor who effected an act of betrothal — even though he sent along presents afterward, she is not betrothed. For it was on account of the original act of betrothal that he sent the gifts [M. Qid. 2:6].

M. 2:7 He who betroths a woman and her daughter, or a woman and her sister, simultaneously — they are not betrothed.

M. 2:8 He [who was a priest] who betroths a woman with his share [of the priestly gifts], whether they were Most Holy Things or Lesser Holy Things — she is not betrothed.

T. 4:5 He who effects an act of betrothal by means of something which is stolen, or with a bailment, or who grabbed a sela' from her and betrothed her with it — lo, this woman is betrothed. [If] he said to her, "Be betrothed to me with the sela' which is in your hand," she is not betrothed. What should he do? He should take it from her and go and give it back to her, and say to her, "Lo, you are betrothed to me."

T. 4:6 He who betroths a woman with meat of cattle of tithe, even if it is after slaughter — she is not betrothed. [If he does so] with its bones, sinews, horns, hooves, blood, fat, hide, or shearings, lo, this woman is betrothed.

T. 4:7 He who betroths a woman, whether with Most Holy Things or Lesser Holy Things — she is not betrothed [M. Qid. 2:8A-B].

M. 2:9 He who betrothed a woman with (1) orlah fruit, (2) with fruit which was subject to the prohibition against Mixed Seeds in a vineyard, (3) with an ox which was to be stoned, (4) with a heifer the neck of which was to be broken, (5) with birds set aside for the offering of a person afflicted with the skin ailment [Lev. 13-14], (6) with the hair of a Nazir, (7) with the firstborn of an ass, (8) with meat mixed with milk, (9) with unconsecrated animals [meat] which had been slaughtered in the courtyard [of the Temple] — she is not betrothed. [If] he sold them off and betrothed a woman with the money received in exchange for them, she is betrothed.

M. 2:10 He who consecrated a woman with food in the status of heave-offering, tithe, or gifts [to be given to the priest], purification water, purification ash — lo, this woman is betrothed, and even if she is an Israelite.

T. 4:8 He who betroths a woman by means of libation-wine, an idol, a city and its inhabitants which are slated for destruction [for rebellion], hides with a hole cut out at the heart, an asherah and its produce, a high place and what is on it, a statue of Mercury and what is on it, and any sort of object which is subject to a prohibition by reason of deriving from idolatry — in the case of all of them, even though he sold them and betrothed a woman with their proceeds — she is not betrothed [cf. M. Qid. 2:9A-C]. [If he did so] with purification-water and with purification-ash, she is betrothed [cf. M. Qid. 2:10A]. [The Israelite may not benefit from the proceeds, hence the use of the proceeds for the act of betrothal is null.]

M. 3:1 He who says to his fellow, "Go and betroth Miss So-and-so for me," and he went and betrothed her for himself — she is betrothed [to the agent]. And so: He who says to a woman, "Lo, you are betrothed to me after thirty days [have passed]," and someone else came along and betrothed her during the thirty days — she is betrothed to the second party. [If] it is an Israelite girl betrothed to a priest, she may eat heave-offering. [If he said,] "...as of now and after thirty days," and someone else came along and betrothed her during the thirty days, she is betrothed and not

betrothed. [If it is either] an Israelite girl betrothed to a priest, or a priest girl betrothed to an Israelite, she should not eat heave-offering.

T. 4:2 And he who says to his fellow, "Go and betroth for me Miss So-and-so," and he went and betrothed her for himself, she is betrothed [M. Qid. 3:1A-B] to the second man.

T. 4:3 [He who says, "Lo, you are betrothed to me retroactively from now after thirty days," and a second party came along and betrothed her during the thirty days — she is betrothed [M. Qid. 3:1 F-G] to the second party [or: to both of them]. How should they arrange matters? One gives a writ of divorce, and the other marries her. If they were two brothers, she is invalidated from marrying the one or the other

T. 4:4 A creditor and an heir, one of whom went ahead and took over movable goods — lo, this one is prompt and rewarded on that account. He who says to his fellow, "Go and betroth for me Miss So-and-so," [if] he [the fellow] then went and betrothed her for himself — [or if he said to his fellow,] "Go and buy me such-and-such an item," [if] he went and bought it *for* himself, what he has done is done. But he has behaved deceitfully.

Betrothals may be impaired for various reasons. The first is that the token of betrothal must be of adequate value and must be theoretically accessible to the woman (M. 2:8-9), the second, that the woman must be free to marry him, M. 2:7. The agent must carry out the instructions. But if the agent does not but instead acts in his own account, the agent's action is valid (M. 3:1). The interstitial situations further fabricated at M. 3:1 present no surprises.

D. *STIPULATIONS*

M. 3:2 He who says to a woman, "Behold, you are betrothed to me, on condition that I pay you two hundred zuz" — lo, this woman is betrothed, and he must pay [her what he has promised]. "...On condition that I pay you within the next thirty days," and he paid her during the thirty days, she is betrothed. And if not, she is not betrothed. "...On condition that I have two hundred zuz," lo, this woman is betrothed, and [if] he has that sum. "...On condition that I shall show you two hundred zuz," lo, this woman is betrothed, and [if] he will show her that sum. But if he showed her the money on the table of a money changer, she is not betrothed.

T. 3:1 He who says to a woman, "Lo, you are betrothed to me through the bailment which I have in your hand," [if] she went off and found that it had been stolen or had gotten lost if [of that bailment] there was left in her possession something worth a perutah, she is betrothed, and if not, she is not betrothed. But [if it concerned] a loan, even though there was something worth a perutah left in her possession, she is not betrothed.

T. 3:2 [If he said,] "On condition that I speak in your behalf to the government," if he spoke in her behalf as people generally do it, she is betrothed, and if not, she is not betrothed. "... through the value of my speaking in your behalf to the government," if he spoke in her behalf to the value of a perutah, she is betrothed, and if not, she is not betrothed. "...through the act of labor which I shall do in your behalf," if he worked in her behalf to the value of a perutah, she is betrothed, and if not, she is not betrothed. "...on condition that I shall work with you," "...on condition that I shall labor with you tomorrow," if he did work in her behalf value to the extent of a perutah, she is betrothed, and if not she is not betrothed. "... on condition that I have two hundred zuz," lo, this woman is betrothed [M. Qid. 3:2E], for he may have that sum on the other side of the world. "...on condition that I have two hundred zuz in such-and-such a place, ' if he has the money in that place, she is betrothed, and if not, she is not betrothed.

M. 3:3 "...On condition that I have a kor's space of land," lo, this woman is betrothed, and [if] he has it. "...On condition that I have that land in such-and-such a place," if he has it in that place, she is betrothed, and if not, she is not betrothed. "...On condition that I show you a kor's space of land," lo, this woman is betrothed, and [if] he will show it to her. But if he showed her [land] in a plain [which was not his], she is not betrothed.

T. 3:3 "...on condition that I have [money] in the hand of Mr. so-and- so even though [the other party] said, "He has no money in my hand," she is betrothed. For they might have conspired to defraud her. "...until he will say that he has the money in my hand," if he said, "He has money in my hand," she is betrothed, and if not, she is not betrothed. "...on condition that I show you two hundred zuz, " if he showed her the money on the table [of a money-changer], she is not betrothed. For he stated that he would show her only what in fact belonged to him.

T. 3:4 ".. .on condition that I have a kor of land," lo, this woman is betrothed [M. Qid. 3:3A-B], for he might have such land on the other side of the world. "...on condition that I have it in this place," if he has it in that place she is betrothed, and if not, she is not betrothed. ". . .on condition that I show you a kor of land " if he showed it to her in a plain [of public property], she is not betrothed [M. Qid. 3:3E-G]. For he stated that he would show her only what in fact belonged to him.

M. 3:5 He who betroths a woman and said, "I was thinking that she is a priest, and lo, she is a Levite," "...a Levite, and lo, she is a priest," "A poor girl, and lo, she is a rich girl," "A rich girl, and lo, she is a poor girl," lo, she is betrothed, for she has not deceived him. He who says to a woman, "Lo, you are betrothed to me after I convert to Judaism," or "after you convert," "...after I am freed" or "after you are freed," "...after your husband died," or "...after your sister dies," "after your levir will have performed the rite of removing the shoe with you" — she is not betrothed. And so he who says to his fellow, "If your wife gives birth to a girl-child, lo, [the baby] is betrothed to me" — she is not betrothed. If the wife of his fellow indeed was pregnant and the foetus was discernible, his statement is confirmed, and if she produced a girl-child, the baby is betrothed.

T. 4:9 He who says to a woman, "Lo, you are betrothed [to me] after I convert, ' "...after you convert," "...after I am freed," "...after you are freed," "...after your husband will die," "...after your sister will die," "...after your Levir will perform the rite of halisah with you," even though the condition is met, she is not betrothed [M. Qid. 3:5].

M. 3:6 He who says to a woman, "Lo, you are betrothed to me, on condition that I speak in your behalf to the government"' or, "That I work for you as a laborer," [if] he spoke in her behalf to the government or worked for her as a laborer, she is betrothed. And if not, she is not betrothed. "...On condition that father will concur," [if] father concurred, she is betrothed. And if not, she is not betrothed. [If] the father died, lo, this woman is betrothed. [If] the son died, they instruct the father to state that he does not concur.

T. 3:5 "...on condition that So-and-so will concur, "even though he said "I do not concur," she is betrothed. For he may concur a while later. "...unless he will say, 'I concur,"' if he says, "I concur," she is betrothed, and if not she is not betrothed.

T. 3:6 "...on condition that father agrees" [M. Qid. 3:6D], even though his father did not agree, she is betrothed. Perhaps he may agree some other time. [If] the father died, lo, this woman is betrothed. [If] the son died — this was a case, and they came and instructed the father to say, "I do not concur" [so that the woman is exempt from the Levirate connection] [M. Qid. 3:6F-G].

Stipulations in the action of betrothal are enforceable, M. 3:2-3. If the husband claims that his stipulations have not been met and the wife is not responsible for his disappointment, the betrothal remains valid.

E. *CASES OF DOUBT*

M. 3:7 "I have betrothed my daughter, but I don't know to whom I have betrothed her," and someone came along and said, "I have betrothed her," he is believed. [If] this one said, "I betrothed her," and [at the same time], that one said, "I betrothed her," both of them give her a writ of divorce. But if they wanted, one of them gives her a writ of divorce and one of them consummates the marriage.

T. 4:10 "I betrothed my daughter, but I do not know to whom I betrothed her," and someone came along and said, "I betrothed her" — he is believed [M. Qid. 3:7A-C] to consummate the marriage. [If] after he has consummated the marriage, someone else came along and said, "I betrothed her," he has not got the power to prohibit her [from remaining wed to the husband who got there first].

M. 3:8 [If the father said,] "I have betrothed my daughter," "...I have betrothed her and I have accepted her writ of divorce when she was a minor" — and lo, she is yet a minor — he is believed. "I betrothed her and I accepted her writ of divorce when she was a minor," and lo, she is now an adult — he is not believed. "She was taken captive and I redeemed her," whether she is a minor or whether she is an adult, he is not believed. He who said at the moment of his death, "I have children," is believed. [If he said,] "I have brothers," he is not believed. He who betroths his daughter without specification — the one past girlhood is not taken into account.

T. 4:11 [If a man said], "I betrothed my daughter," the minors are subject to his statement, but the adults are not subject to his statement. "My daughter has been betrothed," — the adults are subject to his statement, but the minors are not subject to his statement. "I received the writ of divorce for my daughters" — the minors are subject to his statement, but the adults are not subject to his statement. "My daughter has been divorced" — the minors are not subject to his statement [cf. M. Qid. 3:8K].

T. 4:12 "She was taken captive and l'redeemed her" [M. Qid. 3:8G], or, "She was invalidated by one of those who are invalid" [for marriage with a priest] — he has not got the power to prohibit her [from marrying a priest]. [If he said], "I have betrothed my daughter," and he had ten daughters, all of them are prohibited by reason of doubt [from remarrying without a writ of divorce]. If he said, "The oldest one," only the oldest one is deemed to have been betrothed. If he said, "The youngest," only the youngest is deemed to have been betrothed [cf. M. Qid. 3:9]. And so two brothers who betrothed two sisters — this one does not know which one of them he betrothed, and that one does not know which one of them he betrothed — both of them are prohibited by reason of doubt. But if they were engaged in the betrothal of the older girl to the older man, and the younger girl to the younger man [if] the older one says, "I was betrothed only to the older brother," then the younger sister has been betrothed only to the younger brother.

M. 3:10 He who says to a woman, "I have betrothed you," and she says, "You did not betroth me" — he is prohibited to marry her relatives, but she is permitted to marry his relatives. [If] she says, "You betrothed me," and he says, "I did not betroth you" — he is permitted to marry her relatives, and she is prohibited from marrying his relatives. "I betrothed you," and she says, "You betrothed only my daughter," he is prohibited from marrying the relatives of the older woman, and the older woman is permitted to marry his relatives. He is permitted to marry the relatives of the young girl, and the young girl is permitted to marry his relatives.

T. 4:13 "I have betrothed you, but she says, " You have betrothed only my daughter, " he is prohibited to marry the relatives of the older woman, and the older woman is prohibited to marry his relatives. And he Is permitted to marry the relatives of the younger woman, and the younger woman is permitted to marry his relatives.

M. 3:11 "I have betrothed your daughter," and she says, "You betrothed only me," he is prohibited to marry the relatives of the girl, and the girl is permitted to marry his relatives. He is permitted to marry the relatives of the older woman, but the older woman is prohibited from marrying his relatives."

T. 4:14 "I betrothed your daughter," and she says, " You betrothed only me, " he is prohibited from marrying the relatives of the younger girl, and the younger girl is permitted to marry his relatives. And he is permitted to marry the relatives of the older woman, and the older woman is prohibited from marrying his relatives [M. Qid. 3:10].

The Halakhah's facility at inventing and resolving cases of doubt finds ample instantiation here. The first, M. 3:7-8, comes about by the father's action, the second by the man's and the woman's, M. 3:10-11. The principles that govern in the resolution of doubt apply everywhere in the Halakhah.

II.   CASTES FOR THE PURPOSES OF MARRIAGE

    A.   *THE BASIC PRINCIPLES OF GENEALOGY. THE STATUS OF THE OFFSPRING OF IMPAIRED MARRIAGES 3:12-13*

M. 3:12 In any situation in which there is a valid betrothal and no commission of a transgression, the offspring follows the

status of the male, What is such a situation? It is [in particular] the situation in which a priest girl, a Levite girl, or an Israelite girl was married to a priest, a Levite, or an Israelite. And any situation in which there is a valid betrothal, but there also is the commission of a transgression, the offspring follows the status of the impaired [inferior] party. And what is such a situation? It is a widow married to a high priest, a divorcée or woman who has undergone the rite of removing the shoe married to an ordinary priest, a mamzer girl, or a Netin girl married to an Israelite, an Israelite girl married to a mamzer or a Netin. And in any situation in which a woman has no right to enter betrothal with this man but has the right to enter into betrothal with others, the offspring is a mamzer. What is such a situation? This is a man who had sexual relations with any of those women prohibited to him by the Torah. But any situation in which a woman has no right to enter into betrothal with this man or with any other man — the offspring is in her status. And what is such a situation? It is the offspring of a slave girl or a gentile girl.

T. 4:15 A priest-girl, a Levite-girl, and an Israelite-girl who were married to a proselyte — the offspring is in the status of a proselyte. [And if they married] a freed slave, the offspring is in the status of a freed slave [cf. M. Qid. 3:12].

T. 4:16 A gentile, or a slave who had sexual relations with an Israelite girl, and she produced a son — the offspring is a mamzer.

The basic principle of intra-Israelite genealogy is, the caste-status of the offspring follows that of the undoubted father. But this is forthwith qualified for a situation in which the betrothal is valid but impaired in some aspect; then the offspring follows the caste status of the inferior party. The key is, what is the status of the offspring of a slave girl or a gentile girl? The answer is, the offspring is in the status of the mother.

B. *CASTES AND MARRIAGE BETWEEN CASTES*

M. 4:1 Ten castes came up from Babylonia: (1) priests, (2) Levites, (3) Israelites, (4) impaired priests, (5) converts, and (6) freed slaves, (7) mamzers, (8) Netins, (9) "silenced ones" [shetuqi], and (10) foundlings. Priests, Levites, and Israelites are permitted to marry among one another. Levites, Israelites, impaired priests, converts, and freed slaves are permitted to marry among one another. Converts, freed slaves, mamzers, Netins, "silenced ones," and foundlings are permitted to marry among one another.

Y. 4:1 II:5 *He who converts for the sake of love [of a Jew], whether a man because of a woman, or a woman because of a man, and so too those who converted in order to enter Israelite royal* service, and so too those who converted out of fear of the lions [that is, the Samaritans], and so too the converts in the time of Mordecai and Esther [who converted out of fear] — they do not accept them.

M. 4:2 And what are "silenced ones"? Any who knows the identity of his mother but does not know the identity of his father. And foundlings? Any who was discovered in the market and knows neither his father nor his mother.

M. 4:3 All those who are forbidden from entering into the congregation are permitted to marry one another.

M. 4:4 He who marries a priest girl has to investigate her [genealogy] for four [generations, via the] mothers, who are eight: (1) Her mother, and (2) the mother of her mother, and (3) the mother of the father of her mother, and (4) her mother, and (5) the mother of her father, and (6) her mother, and (7) the mother of the father of her father, and (8) her mother. And in the case of a Levite girl and an Israelite girl, they add on to them yet another [generation for genealogical inquiry].

M. 4:5 They do not carry a genealogical inquiry backward from [proof that one's priestly ancestor has served] at the altar, nor from [proof that one's Levitical ancestor has served] on the platform, and from [proof that one's learned ancestor has served] in the Sanhedrin. [It is taken for granted that at the time of the appointment, a full inquiry was undertaken.] And all those whose fathers are known to have held office as public officials or as charity collectors — they marry them into the priesthood, and it is not necessary to conduct an inquiry.

M. 4:6 The daughter of a male of impaired priestly stock is invalid for marriage into the priesthood for all time. An Israelite who married a woman of impaired priestly stock — his daughter is valid for marriage into the priesthood. A man of impaired priestly stock who married an Israelite girl — his daughter is invalid for marriage into the priesthood.

T. 5:3 The daughter of a father of impaired priestly stock is invalid for marrying into the priesthood for all time [M. Qid. 4:6A, D]. A girl of mixed stock is invalid for marriage into the priesthood. [If] she was married to an Israelite, her daughter is valid for marrying into the priesthood. A female convert and a woman of impaired priestly stock are invalid for marriage into the priesthood. [If] she was married to an Israelite, her daughter is valid for marriage into the priesthood. A girl taken captive is invalid for marriage into the priesthood. [If] she was married to an Israelite, her daughter is valid for marriage into the priesthood. A slave-girl is invalid for marriage into the priesthood. [If] she was married to an Israelite, her daughter is valid for marriage into the priesthood. It turns out that Israelites are a [genealogical] purification-pool for priests, and a slave-girl is a purification-pool for all those who are invalid.

B. 4:6-7 III.7/77A [IF A HIGH PRIEST HAD SEXUAL RELATIONS WITH] A WIDOW, A WIDOW, A WIDOW, HE IS LIABLE ON ONLY A SINGLE COUNT; A DIVORCÉE, A DIVORCÉE, A DIVORCÉE, HE IS LIABLE ON ONLY A SINGLE COUNT. [IF A HIGH PRIEST HAD SEXUAL RELATIONS WITH] A WIDOW, A DIVORCÉE, A WOMAN OF IMPAIRED PRIESTLY STOCK, AND A WHORE, IF IT IS IN RESPECT TO THE SAME WOMAN WHO HAS ENTERED THESE VERY CONDITIONS BY ACTIONS TAKEN IN THAT EXACT ORDER, HE IS LIABLE ON EACH COUNT. IF THE SAME WOMAN FIRST OF ALL COMMITTED AN ACT OF FORNICATION, THEN WAS PROFANED FROM PRIESTLY STOCK, THEN WAS DIVORCED, AND THEN WAS WIDOWED, HE IS LIABLE ON ONLY A SINGLE COUNT.

Israel is divided into ten castes, as specified at M. 4:1. At issue is which castes may intermarry with which others, and this is spelled out. Those "forbidden from entering into the congregation" of Israel are entirely free to intermarry. The critical issue is marriage into the priesthood, M. 4:4-6.

C.   *CASES OF DOUBT-4:8-11*

M. 4:8 He who says, "This son of mine is a mamzer" is not believed. And even if both parties say concerning the foetus in the mother's womb, "It is a mamzer" — they are not believed.

M. 4:9 He who gave the power to his agent to accept tokens of betrothal for his daughter, but then he himself betrothed her — if his came first, his act of betrothal is valid. And if those of his agent came first, his act of betrothal is valid. And if it is not known [which came first], both parties give a writ of divorce. But if they wanted, one of them gives a writ of divorce, and one consummates the marriage. And so: A woman who gave the power to her agent to accept tokens of betrothal in her behalf, and then she herself went and accepted tokens of betrothal in her own behalf — if hers came first, her act of betrothal is valid. And if those of her agent came first, his act of betrothal is valid. And if it is not known [which of them came first], both parties give a writ of divorce. But if they wanted, one of them gives a writ of divorce and one of them consummates the marriage.

M. 4:10 He who went along with his wife overseas, and he and his wife and children came home, and he said, "The woman who went abroad with me, lo, this is she, and these are her children" — he does not have to bring proof concerning the woman or the children. [If he said,] "She died, and these are her children," he does bring proof about the children, But he does not bring proof about the woman.

M. 4:11 [If he said], "I married a woman overseas. Lo, this is she, and these are her children" — he brings proof concerning the woman, but he does not have to bring proof concerning the children. "...She died, and these are her children," he has to bring proof concerning the woman and the children.

T. 5:6 He who went, along with his wife, overseas, and he came along with his wife and children, and said, "The woman who went overseas with me, lo, this is she, and these are her children, " does not have to bring proof concerning her or concerning the children. [If he said], "She died, and these are her children, " he brings proof concerning the children, but he does not have to bring proof concerning the woman

T. 5:7 [For] a woman is believed to say, "These are my children." And [he who says], "A woman whom I married overseas, lo this is she and these are her children, " has to bring proof concerning the woman, but does not have to bring proof concerning the children [M. Qid. 4:11].

M. 4:12 A man should not remain alone with two women, but a woman may remain alone with two men. A man may stay alone with his mother or with his daughter. And he sleeps with them with flesh touching. But if they [the son who is with the mother, the daughter with the father] grew up, this one sleeps in her garment, and that one sleeps in his garment.

T. 5:9 A woman remains alone with two men [M. Qid. 4:12A], even if both of them are Samaritans even if both of them are slaves even if one of them is a Samaritan and one a slave except for a minor, for she is shameless about having sexual relations in his presence.

T. 5:10 As to his sister and his sister-in-law and all those women in a prohibited relationship to him which are listed in the Torah — he should not be alone with them [M. Qid. 4:12A] except before two [witnesses]. But she should not be alone even with a hundred gentiles.

M. 4:13 An unmarried man may not teach scribes. Nor may a woman teach scribes.

M. 4:14 Whoever has business with women should not be alone with women. And a man should not teach his son a trade which he has to practice among women.

T. 5:14 Whoever has business with women should not be alone with women [M. Qid. 4:14D] — for example, goldsmiths, carders, [hand-mill] cleaners, peddlers, wool-dressers, barbers, launderers, and mill-stone chiselers.

Cases of doubt are resolved in accord with familiar principles, applicable everywhere. Once we speak of doubt, we proceed to the matter treated at M. 4:12. It is assumed that men are virtuous, women, profligate, and family-members meticulous in their sexual conduct with one another. That leads to the rules about proper conduct between unmarried men and women in general, and professions that lead to sinful situations.

IV. DOCUMENTARY TRAITS

A. THE MISHNAH AND THE TOSEFTA

The Tosefta's complements present no surprises; they consistently amplify and clarify matters, but I discern no point at which the Tosefta interprets the present category-formation in terms different from the Mishnah's.

B. THE YERUSHALMI AND THE BAVLI

The two Talmuds take over the Halakhah and accomplish their usual task of refinement and harmonization.

C. THE AGGADAH OF INCARNATE SANCTIFICATION

I have insisted on the actuality of the transaction of sanctification. And that has led to the clear judgment that Israel is holy in not a symbolic or merely taxonomic sense but in a physical, material way. Israel is holy, holiness incarnate in the children of Abraham, Isaac, and Jacob bearing those genealogical consequences that we have identified, the status of priesthood transferred through the father's seed, the status of Israel-ness conveyed through the mother's womb. Up to this point, however, I have not attempted to explain the mechanics of "holy seed," the power of genealogy to define a counterpart category to that of nourishment in the sanctification of Israel. To interpret the Halakhic category-formation that focuses upon genealogy, how it is transmitted, how it is preserved, we have to ask, what corpus of doctrine accounts for the conviction that Israel is Israel by reason of ancestry, not only activity. An Aggadic category, *Zekhut* — "the heritage of virtue and its consequent entitlements" thus, unearned grace — corresponds in theology to the category, genealogy, in the Halakhah. *Zekhut* refers to the empowerment of a supernatural character that derives from the virtue of one's ancestry or from one's own virtuous deeds of a very particular order, with the proviso that one has the power to transmit to his or her descendants that supernatural entitlement of grace that his or her own deeds have gained. When it is the virtue of one's ancestors that have endowed the heir with Heavenly favor, it is called *"zekhut Abot,"* the unearned merit deriving from one's forefathers — hence the exact counterpart to the Halakhic category, genealogy (e.g., status as sanctified by reason of parentage, caste-status by reason of one's father's status).

Let us start with the foundation: the source of *zekhut*. What are the deeds that one does, or that one's ancestor has done, to produce *zekhut*? Such remarkable deeds involve actions favored by God but not subject to God's power to compel or command, e.g., love of God, which must be given freely or makes no difference. So too, involved is remarkable abstinence or generosity beyond the expectations of the commandments of the Torah. Whence then the lien on Heaven? It is through deeds of a supererogatory character — to which Heaven responds by deeds of a supererogatory character: acts of grace responding to acts of grace. We deal, then, with supernatural favor to this one, who through deeds done to win the favor of the other or self-abnegation or restraint exhibits the attitude that in Heaven precipitates a counterpart attitude, hence generating *zekhut*, rather than to that one, who does not. So while man cannot coerce Heaven, he can through *zekhut* gain acts of favor from Heaven, and that is by doing what Heaven cannot require: an uncoerced response of divine grace to an attitude and consequent deed of grace. Heaven thus responds to man's attitude in carrying out not his duties but more than his duties.

The character of *zekhut* such as is attained by an individual's actions is best defined by exemplary accounts of the matter, e.g., cases in which ordinary persons are endowed with supernatural power (prayers for rain being answered, for instance), which cannot be attributed to Torah-study. Ordinary folk, not disciples of sages, have access to *zekhut* entirely outside of study of the Torah. In stories not told about rabbis, a single remarkable deed, exemplary for its deep humanity, sufficed to win for an ordinary person the *zekhut* that elicits the same marks of supernatural favor enjoyed by some rabbis on account of their Torah-study. Even though a man was degraded, one action sufficed to win for him that heavenly glory to which rabbis in lives of Torah-study aspired. The mark of the system's integration around *zekhut* lies in its insistence that all Israelites, not only sages, could gain *zekhut* for themselves (and their descendants). A single remarkable deed, exemplary for its deep humanity, sufficed to win for an ordinary person the *zekhut* that elicits supernatural favor enjoyed by some rabbis on account of their Torah-study. The advantages or privileges conferred by *zekhut* may be inherited and also passed on; it stresses "entitlements" because advantages or privileges always, invariably result from receiving *zekhut* from ancestors or acquiring it on one's own; and "virtue" refers to those supererogatory acts that demand a reward because they form matters of choice, the gift of the individual and his or her act of free will, an act that is at the same time (1) uncompelled, e.g., by the obligations imposed by the Torah, but (2) also valued by the Torah one's own volition that also is beyond all requirements of the law.

What about *zekhut Abot*? One's store of *zekhut* may derive from a relationship, that is, from one's forebears. For Israel, in particular, *Zekhut* also derives from the founding saints of Israel, Abraham, Isaac, Jacob, their wives and children, and, by extension, one may acquire *zekhut* via the otherwise-unrequited actions of one's own forebears. God remembers the merit of the ancestors and counts it to the advantage of their heirs, e.g., in the Halakhah, e.g., in the liturgy for praying for rain, at M. Taanit 2:4ff.:

> M. 2:4 For the first [ending] he says, "He who answered Abraham on Mount Moriah will answer you and hear the sound of your cry this day. Blessed are you, O Lord, redeemer of Israel."
> M. 2:5 For the second he says, "He who answered our fathers at the Red Sea will answer you and hear the sound of your cry this day. Blessed are you, O Lord, who remembers forgotten things."
> M. 2:6 For the third he says, "He who answered Joshua at Gilgal will answer you and hear the sound of your cry thus day. Blessed are you, O Lord who hears the sound of the Shofar."
> M. 2:7 For the fourth he says, "He who answered Samuel at Mizpeh will answer you and hear the sound of your cry this day. Blessed are you, O Lord, who hears a cry."
> M. 2:8 For the fifth he says, "He who answered Elijah at Mount Carmel will answer you and hear the sound of your cry this day. Blessed are you, O Lord, who hears prayer."
> M. 2:9 For the sixth he says, "He who answered Jonah in the belly of the fish will answer you and hear the sound of your cry this day. Blessed are you, O Lord, who answers prayer in a time of trouble." For the seventh he says, "He who answered David and Solomon, his son, in Jerusalem, will answer you and hear the sound of your cry this day. Blessed are you, O Lord, who has mercy on the land."

Here is an explicit appeal to the merit acquired by the fathers in behalf of their offspring, the genealogy of sanctification fully exposed. Not only so, but when the sound of the Shofar is heard by God, he is reminded of the readiness of Abraham and Isaac at Moriah to make the supreme sacrifice, and so God's mercies are aroused. *Zekhut* thus extends to the heirs of the saints, and that is in proportion to the actions of the patriarchs:

> IV.6 A. Said R. Judah said Rab, "Whatever Abraham himself did for the ministering angels, the Holy One, blessed be he, himself did for his children." Whatever Abraham did for

B. "'And Abraham ran to the herd' [is matched by] 'And there went forth a wind from the Lord' (Ex. 16:4)."
C. "'And he took butter and milk' [is matched by] 'Behold I will rain bread from heaven for you' (Ex. 17:6)."
D. "'And he stood by them under the tree' [is matched by] 'Behold, I will stand before you there upon the rock' (Ex. 17:6)."
E. "'And Abraham went with them to bring them on the way' [is matched by] 'And the Lord went before them by day' (Ex. 13:21)."
F. "'Let a little water, I pray you, be gotten' [is matched by] 'And you shall hit the rock, and water will come out of it that the people may drink' (Ex. 17:6)."
G. *But this conflicts with what R. Hama bar. Hanina said, for R. Hama bar Hanina said, and so did the household of R. Ishmael teach on Tannaite authority,* "As a reward for three things that Abraham did, his heirs got three things."
H. "As a reward for 'and he took butter and milk,' they got the manna."
I. "As a reward for 'and he stood by them,' they received the pillar of cloud."
J. "As a reward for "let a little water, I pray you, be brought,' they got Miriam's well."

Bavli Baba Mesia 7:1 IV.6/86b

The notion of inheriting the entitlements bequeathed by the patriarchs and matriarchs is spelled out in a specific context. God remembers the deeds of the patriarchs and credits their descendants with the merit thereby earned, so with Abraham and Isaac on Mount Moriah. The merit of the patriarchs forms an inheritance of entitled grace for Israel. *Zekhut* defines the point at which the supererogatory action takes over, and the commandments no longer govern; then God's love for Israel's progenitors encompasses their heirs — by reason of that love. So much for the Aggadic counterpart to the Halakhic category-formation, genealogy. But if the Aggadah supplies an explanation for the concept of holy seed, for the physicalization of sanctification in the process of procreation, only the Halakhah works out the consequences for ordinary everyday life.

V. THE HERMENEUTICS OF QIDDUSHIN

A. **WHAT FUSES THE HALAKHIC DATA INTO A CATEGORY-FORMATION?**

Much of the category-formation encompasses details of the Halakhah generated by the generic hermeneutics, e.g., cases of interstitiality, mixtures, types of causation, and doubt. But some of the Halakhah, as we have seen, takes up issues particular to the category-formation before us, and that is the sector of the Halakhah for which the hermeneutics of the category-formation at hand accounts. Asking how the data fuse to form a category-formation brings us back to the analogical-contrastive analysis outlined at the outset. For what we have to explain is the union of betrothal and rules of genealogy.

THE TABLE (ALTAR) AND THE BED: What we have seen is that from the altar lines of sanctification radiate outward to encompass the table and the bed; these then form a continuous reality, the paired media for the procreation and maintenance of life. But the relationship is not only generic. Particular points of comparison emerge in the very language commonly used for both animals for the altar and women for men. That is, a woman is consecrated to a particular man, just as an animal is consecrated to the altar for the expiation of a particular inadvertent sin that has been carried out by a particular person. A sin-offering consecrated for a particular person and a specific action he has inadvertently performed proves null if it is used for another offering than the designated class, another person, or another sin by the same person. A woman consecrated for a particular man is subject to exactly the same considerations of sanctification (mutatis mutandis). In both cases the relationship is one of consecration, meaning, differentiation from all secular purposes and designated for a sacred function or task. Just as the Temple altar provides the governing comparison for the formation of the laws about the slaughter of animals for meat for the Israelite table, so the Temple altar provides the pertinent analogy for the transaction that links a selected woman to a given man in a relationship of sanctity. What marks the woman as unique is that, when she is consecrated, she makes a choice of this circumstance, not that, so to effect her sanctification she assents in an act of will responding to the act of will of the counterpart to the sacrifier, the proposed groom. Then she is Isaac at Moriah.

DEGREES OF THE POWER OF INTENTIONALITY: THE WOMAN AND THE SLAVE: Let us broaden the discussion by contrasting the power of the woman to effect an act of intentionality in the transaction of betrothal with the impotence of counterparts in her category, slaves and minors, to effect their will in any way. Along with slaves and minors, women form a classification of Israelites deemed not fully capable of independent will, intentionality, entire responsibility, and action and therefore subject not only to God's will but also to the will of another, the husband or father in the case of the woman, the master in the case of the slave, and the parent in the case of the child, thus M. Ber. 3:3: Women, slaves, and minors are exempt from the recitation of the *Shema'* and from the obligation to wear phylacteries, but are obligated to the recitation of the prayer, and to post a *mezuzah* and to recite the blessing over the meal. But they do not form part of the community of holy Israel that is obligated to recite blessings publicly, thus M. Ber. 7:2: Women, slaves or minors who ate together with adult Israelite males may not invite others to bless on their account. While comparable to slaves and minors in forming a classification of persons of lesser powers of intentionality than the Israelite man, the Israelite woman in the aspect of betrothal stands far above the others of her class.

THE WOMAN AND THE MAN: That comparison and contrast carry us to the main one: how does a woman's intentionality compare with a man's? How does she differ, even with the power to reject an act of sanctification to a particular man, from man? The analogical-contrastive process here reaches the heart of matters, and, not surprisingly, we find ourselves crossing from one category-formation to another. We begin with the one at hand and the explicit comparison of man and woman in the obligation to perform religious duties or commandments. Does the Halakhah of the (written) Torah differentiate explicitly? Indeed it does. When Scripture refers to "man," it may cover both man and woman, but special conditions yield the word-choice, so Sifra CXCV:II.1-2: "Every one [Hebrew: man] of you shall revere his mother and his father, and you shall keep my Sabbaths": I know only that a man is subject to the instruction. How do I know that a woman is also involved? Scripture says, "...shall revere" using the plural. Lo, both genders are covered. If so, why does Scripture refer to "man"? It is because a man controls what he needs, while a woman does not control what she needs, since others have dominion over her. Here we find in explicit language exactly the point just now registered. The householder (and his male equivalents within other social structures) is possessed of an autonomous will, like God's and in contest with God's. The woman's autonomy is limited by her father's, then her husband's will. The former pertains willy-nilly, the latter with her consent to accept the dominion of that particular man.

In a number of specific contexts, moreover, a man and woman are differentiated not in capacity to effect an act of intentionality but in the functions that they perform or to which they are obligated, e.g., M. Sot. 3:8: What is the difference between a man and a woman? A man goes around with unbound hair and torn garments, but a woman does not go around with unbound hair and torn garments (Lev. 13:44-5). A man imposes a Nazirite vow on his son, and a woman does not impose a Nazirite vow upon her son (M. Naz.

4:6). A man brings the hair offering for the Nazirite vow of his father, and a woman does not bring a hair offering for the Nazirite vow of her father. The man sells his daughter, and the woman does not sell her daughter Ex. 21:6. The man arranges for a betrothal of his daughter, and the woman does not arrange for the betrothal of her daughter (M. Qid. 2:1). A man who incurs the death penalty is stoned naked, but a woman is not stoned naked. A man is hanged after being put to death, and a woman is not hanged (M. San. 6:3-4). A man is sold to make restitution for having stolen something, but a woman is not sold to make restitution for having stolen something (Ex. 22:2). So women are subject to men, daughters to fathers, then wives to husbands; widows are assumed to return to their fathers' households. But man needs woman to complete his existence. Woman is to man as man is to God in the structure of hierarchical classification that is actualized in the Halakhah.

B. THE ACTIVITY OF THE CATEGORY-FORMATION

Now we understand why the category-formation, Qiddushin, encompasses a systematic account of the laws of acquiring various classifications of possessions, from persons to things to real estate. The problematic of the Halakhah of Qiddushin, the sanctification of a particular woman for a particular man, emerges in the intersection of the language of acquisition with the language of sanctification. A householder buys a cow, in acquiring it, he does not sanctify it. Unless he means to offer it on the altar in Jerusalem, a person who utilizes the same cow, e.g., milks it or uses it for ploughing, does not offend God. The issue of sanctification does not enter the transaction. But a householder acquires a woman thereby consecrates the woman as his wife. Another person who utilizes the same woman, e.g., has sexual relations with her and produces children by her, enormously outrages God (not to mention the husband). The category, sanctification and its opposite, applies. Yet in both instances the result is, acquiring title to, rights over the cow or the woman. Indeed, slaves, movables, and real estate prove analogous to the betrothal of a woman. The transaction by which a householder acquires a wife, slave, movables or real estate forms the genus, the language and categories and action-symbols proving constant.

But when it comes to the woman, an enormous point of difference renders the woman an active participant in the transfer of title. It is the now very familiar one: only when the woman consents does her status as person, not merely as property, change; and the change is called not merely acquisition but sanctification. So the opening exposition of the Halakhah serves to establish the genus — money, writ, usucaption for the slave, money, writ, act of sexual relations, comparable to usucaption, for the woman. These are compared and contrasted and firmly situated in a single classification: things that are acquired by the householder through a common repertoire of procedures of transfer of title from owner to owner.

The speciation commences in the comparison as to obligations of the standing before God of the woman to the man, the respective status of each being differentiated by reason of the non-negotiable obligation of a woman at specific times to home and family; that takes priority. The introduction of the exposition that stresses how men and women are equally liable, e.g., to all negative commandments and most positive ones, concludes in a remarkable manner the presentation of the modes of acquisition of women, slaves, cattle, and the like. What is remarkable is that no counterpart discussion is accorded to slaves. The difference, which is implicit, is that while women remain possessed of an autonomous will, not being subject to the unmediated will of their husbands, slaves are deemed in the law to have no autonomous will whatsoever. So the Halakhic unit that commences with the genus, the acquisition of persons and property, concludes with the distinct species, the woman, with the differentiation of the woman from all other classes of things that are acquired by the householder.

The Halakhah of sanctification of a woman to a particular man ("betrothal") pursues a fairly standard agendum of issues: agency, value, and stipulations. When it comes to agency, the point to note is that a woman may designate her own agent, just as a man does, for the transaction; a slave cannot do the same. As to value, the issue of joining together discrete items to form the requisite value for the transaction — comparable to the issue of connection — makes an appearance; the language that effects the transaction comes under discussion; and similar standard analytical questions — the impact of stipulations and conditions, met and unmet — are pursued. Stipulations not met nullify the exchange; deception has the same result. The situation prevailing at the critical turning is deemed decisive: In the case of any condition which is valid at the moment of betrothal, even though it was annulled afterward, lo, this woman is betrothed. And in the case of any condition which is not valid at the moment of betrothal, even though it was validated afterward, lo, this woman is not betrothed.

Stipulations must be met, conditions satisfied, instructions carried out. Where the woman has agreed to the transaction without deceit and bears no responsibility for an unmet stipulation or condition, the transaction takes effect; she is betrothed. How cases of doubt are sorted out receives attention. None of these discussions presents surprises, and the rules that govern are in no way particular to the topic at hand. Indeed, out of the Halakhic principles at hand one could easily construct a handbook of responsibility in ethical transactions. The premise throughout does not require articulation: the woman must consent to the transaction or it is null. But the fact that the woman can appoint an agent and establish conditions and stipulations as much as the man can bears the implication that the woman is an equal partner in the transaction and must consent to it. (That same point will come before us when we deal with the under-age girl whose father marries her off; when she comes of age, she has the right to refuse the arrangement and simply walk out of the marriage.)

God's stake in the transaction of the sanctification of a woman extends beyond individuals to the castes among which the community of Israel is distributed: priests, Levites, Israelites, and others. A man and a woman belong to a particular classification, and that governs whether or not, to begin with, sanctification is possible, sanctity takes effect in their relationship. In this regard the woman is like the crop of the Land of Israel: she is potentially holy, for reasons already spelled out becoming holy by the matched acts of will of the husband and the betrothed and God. That potentiality then accounts for the specification of genealogically-unacceptable unions. The Written Torah defines the classifications of persons who may not intermarry — gentiles do not enter the picture — within the purview of the Torah. A woman's personal status is affected by prior unions, e.g. a marriage to a man to whom the Torah prohibits her, such as a widow to a high priest, a divorcée or equivalent to an ordinary priest, the mamzer (child of parents legally unable ever to marry, such as a brother and a sister, or a married woman and a man other than her husband) to an ordinary Israelite, and so on. These castes are defined in the Halakhah, exquisitely summarized at M. 4:1's catalogue of ten castes.

Here we see how the metaphor of the altar overspreads the formation of the household's family unit. The effect of an act of betrothal is qualified by the caste status of the parties to the betrothal. Just as blemished beasts are not susceptible of sanctification for the altar, so persons of blemished genealogy cannot enter into consecrated relationships with those of unblemished family. The family that forms the foundation of the household then compares with the offering on the altar. What the Halakhah does is extend to the entire community of Israel the Written Torah's intense interest in the eugenics of the priesthood — thus, once more, the now-familiar pattern, at the critical points, of appealing to the altar for a paradigm of the household.

C. THE CONSISTENCY OF THE CATEGORY-FORMATION

The opening exposition accounts for the coherence of the sub-topics of the category-formation, Qiddushin, and shows how they coalesce. But, as we have seen, the category-formation, Qiddushin, works out its interests in the generic hermeneutics of the Halakhah, not so much in the particular hermeneutics of the present category-formation.

D. THE GENERATIVITY OF THE CATEGORY-FORMATION

How does the category-formation extend its reach to encompass a variety of particulars, not encompassed by definition within the category, the sanctification of a woman by a man for the purposes of procreation? Let us start with an obvious point of generativity, the extension of the Halakhah of betrothal to cover all manner of acquisitions. The act of betrothal forms a particular detail of the larger theory of how a man acquires title to, or possession of, persons or property of various classifications. That is the this-worldly side of the Halakhah; the transcendent part emerges with the result: the sanctification of the relationship between a particular woman and a particular man, so that she is consecrated to him and to no other.[33] The upshot is, just as a farmer acquired a slave or an ox or real estate, so he effected possession of, gained title to, a woman. But while the slave or ox or field could never be called "consecrated" to that particular farmer, so that the language of sanctification never operates in such transactions, the act of acquisition of a woman also transformed the relationship of the woman not only to that man who acquired her but to all other men.

But that is only a detail. Where do we encounter the power of the category-formation to make its own a considerable range of topics? We understand the answer when we step back and identify the truly fundamental exercise of analogy and contrast that has nurtured the laws before us. The paramount analogy is the one not made explicit within the Halakhah at all but that is everywhere implicit: Israel as a whole is like the priesthood, "a kingdom of priests and a holy people." If I had to select the generative analogy at the foundation of all else, that is the one I should choose, and it accounts for the generativity of the entire category-formation at hand. As much as food defines a dimension of sanctification, so too, sex and genealogy, the foundations of the Israelite household, invoke the same consideration and accord with the same governing metaphor, that of the Temple and its altar. Within the walls of the Israelite household is recapitulated the basic conception of valid or invalid marital bonds that, to begin with, Scripture legislates for the priesthood. The Written Torah leaves no doubt that God deems a matter of sanctification that Israel conduct its sexual life in the model of the sanctity of its cultic life. The fundamental premise of the Halakhah is that as God oversees the conduct of Temple priests, so God closely watches the conduct of Israel in all that has to do with maintaining life, food and sex above all. But the metaphor of the Temple and priesthood for the household and family is vastly transcended.

---

[33] No one in the formative age deemed the relationship mutual; a particular man was not consecrated to a particular woman, since the Halakhah presupposes polygamy.

Accordingly, when we turn from the sustenance of life to its creation, we move in a straight path from the table to the bed. Both form essential components in sanctifying Israel, and, as we now see, in both matters the same principle governs, just as a single set of conceptions, having to do with the health of the animal and the disposition of its blood, for example, unify the Israelite table and the altar of the Temple in Jerusalem. So the Israelite table and the Temple altar stand on a single continuum, subject to the same rules (where applicable and appropriate). The same is so when we come to the procreation of life, the process of forming, maintaining, and dismantling a family. These prove to be analogous, where applicable and appropriate, to carrying on the sacrificial process. Just as meat for the Israelite's table comparable to meat for the Lord's altar, so that not only the category, sanctification, is the same, but the conceptions that define sanctity in both settings are coherent, so we find in the case of the Israelite's marital bed. The point of distinction is therefore not to be missed. The difference between the consecrated offering for the altar and the consecrated woman for the marriage canopy, governing the entire process of sanctification of woman to man, lies in what distinguishes the human being, man or woman, from the beast: the freedom of will, the power of intentionality. The man may declare the woman sanctified, but if she objects, the act is null. If of age, she must accept the tokens of betrothal, directly or through her agent. If not of age, when she comes of age, she may reject an act of betrothal, even consummated, taken by others with control over her in her minority, her father if he is alive, her brothers if he is deceased. Then she simply ups and walks out, not requiring even a writ of divorce. No sanctification has ever taken place, the woman not having confirmed what has happened through the exercise of will of others with temporary jurisdiction over her. So the woman consecrated for her husband is like the beast sanctified for the altar, but with the familiar, formidable difference, from which all else in the Halakhah flows, one way or the other.

WITHDRAWN